A History of China

3500

R. M. CROSKEY

W9-CMN-916

R. M. CROSKEY

A History of China

BY

WITOLD RODZINSKI

In Two Volumes
VOLUME I

PERGAMON PRESS
OXFORD · NEW YORK · TORONTO · SYDNEY · PARIS · FRANKFURT

U.K.	Pergamon Press Ltd., Headington Hill Hall, Oxford OX3 0BW, England
U.S.A.	Pergamon Press Inc., Maxwell House, Fairview Park, Elmsford, New York 10523, U.S.A.
CANADA	Pergamon of Canada, Suite 104, 150 Consumers Road, Willowdale, Ontario M2J 1P9, Canada
AUSTRALIA	Pergamon Press (Aust.) Pty. Ltd., P.O. Box 544, Potts Point, N.S.W. 2011, Australia
FRANCE	Pergamon Press SARL, 24 rue des Ecoles, 75240 Paris, Cedex 05, France
FEDERAL REPUBLIC OF GERMANY	Pergamon Press GmbH, 6242 Kronberg/Taunus, Pferdstrasse 1, Federal Republic of Germany

Copyright © 1979 Witold Rodzinski

All Rights Reserved. No part of this publication may be reproduced, stored in a retrieval system or transmitted in any form or by any means: electronic, electrostatic, magnetic tape, mechanical, photocopying, recording or otherwise, without permission in writing from the publisher

First English edition 1979

British Library Cataloguing in Publication Data

Rodzinski, Witold
A history of China.
1. China—History
I. Title
951   DS735   77-30253
ISBN 0-08-021806-7

Printed and bound at William Clowes & Sons Limited Beccles and London

TO JENNY

Without whom this book would never have seen the light of day

Contents

PART IV.   THE PERIOD OF DIVISION

PART V.   THE RESTORATION OF THE EMPIRE; SUI AND T'ANG

List of Maps

List of Illustrations

Preface to the English Edition

Over seven years have passed since the writing of this work was begun. Most of the time has been devoted to the gathering of materials and the preparation of the subsequent volume, intended to cover the years 1919-1949, which will conclude this project. However, interest in and concern with the time span and the problems raised in the present volume have not slackened, and efforts have been made to keep abreast of the vast, new literature on the subject, which has been increasing at a rapid pace in recent years.

The above-mentioned efforts were greatly facilitated by the time spent in 1975 as a Visiting Scholar at the East Asian Institute, Columbia University. Furthermore, a number of American scholars were kind enough to read the English manuscript; this happens to be the original, while the Polish version is a translation thereof done by the author. Professors L. Carrington Goodrich, John W. Meskill (both at Columbia University), Steven I. Levine (then at the East Asian Institute) and Philip A. Kuhn (University of Chicago) devoted much time and effort to reading this lengthy work and conveyed their helpful remarks.

The opportunity to spend the academic year 1976-1977 as a Visiting Fellow at Clare Hall, Cambridge, has been of still greater assistance in continuing research and has made the final preparation of the English edition possible. Professor Denis Twitchett and Dr. Michael Loewe of the Faculty of Oriental Studies gave unstintingly of their time and offered many valuable suggestions. The same applies to two American scholars, present in Cambridge during this period, Professors Derk Bodde (University of Pennsylvania) and Frederic Wakeman, Jr. (University of California, Berkeley), who have been equally generous in their help. Professor Joan Robinson and Dr. Joseph Needham have also shown much interest and offered their advice.

The present version does not differ significantly from the original and from the Polish edition. As full an account as possible was taken of the suggestions made by the scholars mentioned above, as well as of the conclusions of many recent monographic studies, without, however, any large-scale alterations or rewriting. Most of the revisions made pertain to the first half of the work—the pre-Ch'ing period, which is actually rather an extended introduction than a full treatment of the subject. The second half, which constituted the basic scope of study and research, remains virtually unchanged, especially in so far as the question of international relations in East Asia in the 19th and 20th centuries is concerned.

One fundamental problem should be referred to at this stage—the definition of the term "feudalism" as employed in this work. It is used primarily to describe the specific relations of production in a pre-modern, pre-capitalist society, such as that of China up to and including the 19th century. These relations prevailed in what was the dominant and most important economic domain—agriculture, and, while the forms differed at given periods, the main content was the exploitation, by various means and methods, of the primary producers in that society—the peasants. In view of the fact that the struggle of the peasants against exploitation and oppression constitutes one of the principal threads of Chinese history throughout the ages, it would appear advisable that due attention be paid to this question.

Many Western authors use the term "feudalism" only to denote legal and political phenomena and thus, for example, refer to the political organization of the Chou period as feudal—which it undoubtedly was—maintaining that the existence of a centralized monarchy, from Ch'in on, meant the end of feudalism in China. This approach, however, ignores what seems to be truly fundamental in Chinese history, the socio-economic basis on which the monarchy, with all its permutations in changes of dynasties and forms of organization, rested.

The problem of feudalism is only one of many—as pointed out in the Preface to the Polish Edition—which remain to be elucidated more fully in the future. Much work by many scholars will still have to be accomplished in the vast field of Chinese history before truly satisfactory answers can be arrived at and presented in the form of a convincing synthesis. One of the aims of the present work is to point to those questions which seem to the author to be among the most important, while the answers to some of them can be considered only as tentative.

Cambridge, May 1977

Preface to the Polish Edition

A History of China, which figures in the series of one-volume studies devoted to the history of individual states, is the first work pertaining to a country whose civilization and culture were shaped in a different and distinct manner in many respects, as compared to the states influenced by the Mediterranean and European world. It is also the first Polish attempt at a synthesis in compact form of the immense, almost 4000 years, span of Chinese history while paying attention, simultaneously, to the more important aspects of cultural evolution.

In accord with the assumptions of the series in which this book is published, its proportions were determined so that over half of the material pertains to the last three centuries, i.e. to the period which may be considered as the modern one from the point of view of the general world historical process. This criterion, however, corresponds only partially to the process of development of Chinese history, inasmuch as one should rather consider the middle of the 19th century as the proper date for the beginning of Chinese modern history; almost half of the work relates to this period, beginning with the Opium Wars and the Taiping Revolution. In view of the vast scope of Chinese history the establishing of proportions in this fashion is undoubtedly a debatable issue; when one considers the immensity of available material—and there is no other nation which possesses such a copious and uninterrupted flow of testimonies of its past—one could easily devote much more attention to earlier periods. It would seem, however, that while a number of fundamental problems connected with earlier history, whose influence on modern and contemporary times is much greater in the case of China than would appear at first glance, have an undeniable significance—the proportions adopted here are justified, above all, by the fact that they are to serve the purpose of achieving a better understanding of the modern Chinese period and perhaps even of the present day. Such was one of the fundamental aims in the undertaking of this work.

The contemporary period of Chinese history is not covered in this volume, inasmuch as the terminal date was fixed at 1919, on the May Fourth Movement, which indubitably constituted the beginning of an entirely new stage, in many respects, of the Chinese historical process.

The work has arisen as the result of the author's personal interest and study of the history of China for more than thirty-five years, enhanced considerably by a number of stays in China during the years 1953-1967 which perhaps aided in the attempt to grasp the unusual complexity of this country's history and the inexhaustible riches of its ancient culture. During the majority of these stays the cordial assistance of a number of Chinese friends such as, for example, Chi Ch'ao-ting (1904-1963), Shen Chien-tu (1915-1955) and Mme Kung P'eng (1918?-1971) was an encouragement towards further work on the fascinating history of their country. The above also explains partially the decision to devote relatively considerable space in the first half of the book to problems of cultural evolution. It should be clearly noted, however, that the discussion of these problems is simply an attempt to touch upon the immense achievements of the Chinese in this sphere. It is obvious that every one of these aspects, e.g. philosophy or painting, fully deserves a separate treatment, at least as lengthy as the present volume. The choice of the subjects raised is, however, not fortuitous, for the intention was to emphasize those elements which appear to be the most important for the specific nature of the evolution of Chinese civilization and which—in the opinion of the present writer—constitute the most essential contribution of Chinese culture. The selection does not by any means pretend to embrace all the elements; for example, there is not a single word on Chinese music, undoubtedly interesting, which played a specific role in the totality of Chinese culture. This perhaps was the result of purely subjective factors.

The history of China and its culture as presented in this book pertains primarily to the history and achievements of the Chinese nationality—the Han—the main and most important of the many inhabiting the present area of the Chinese People's Republic. This does not mean that other nationalities, and, in particular, those which in certain periods conquered a part or the entire country, did not play an essential role in the shaping of its fate. It was not they, however, who exerted the decisive influence but the Chinese nationality whose cultural superiority also brought about, in many cases, the full assimilation and disappearance from the historical arena of other peoples, although not without absorbing a number of new cultural elements. Thus this work is devoted to the Chinese people, the basic creator of the civilization of the Middle Kingdom.

If the interest mentioned above pertained earlier primarily to contemporary Chinese history and the author's special field remains modern history with particular consideration of the problems of China's contacts with the rest of the world and the issues arising therefrom, particularly in the ideological sphere, the necessity of reaching out to earlier periods became ever more obvious. It is a banality to state that it is impossible to study the modern history of a given country without a proper knowledge of its past, but this applies especially clearly and pertinently to the history of China. There is practically no other country in which the accumulations of the past in all fields did not affect—and to a given degree still affect—the future of the country's fate to such a degree as precisely in the case of China. Herein, too, lies one of the most essential features of its historical evolution.

In the literature of the subject, both Chinese as well as European and American, a number of works exist, quite different in size and scope, in which the author has sought to embrace the totality of Chinese history. The greater part of them was referred to in the preparation of the present book but almost exclusively for the earlier periods preceding the 17th century; all the books in European languages are mentioned in the bibliography. Of the Chinese works attention should be drawn to that of Lü Chen-yü, *Chien-ming Chung-kuo T'ung-shih* ("Outline of Chinese History"). Use was made, however, to a considerable extent of source materials, both for earlier periods and, in particular, for later ones, as well as of monographic studies also mentioned in the bibliography.

In Polish historical writing, however, the history of China was—and unfortunately to a great degree still is—a totally neglected field. It is thus difficult to base oneself on works of Polish authors since for the overwhelming majority of historical and cultural subjects they simply do not exist. The situation is somewhat better in regards to translation from classical Chinese literature. Here Polish sinology can point to works on a high level as, for example, the translation of the famous philosophical work *Chuang tzu,* undertaken by J. Chmielewski, W. Jabłoński and O. Wojtasiewicz. Such a state of affairs is not fortuitous. The growth of interest in Chinese history and culture in Europe was strictly connected with the evolution of the contacts of the European countries with China, beginning in the 16th and 17th centuries, gaining in force in the 19th century and assuming quite clearly a character of penetration and aggression which is described in detail in the present work. It is against this background that there arose a rich, although extremely varied, in respect to value and quality, historical literature pertaining to different periods but mainly, however, to the 19th and 20th centuries. Poland, herself deprived of independence and statehood, did not participate in this process of the "Opening of China"; hence the minute contribution of Polish authors to this field, as well as a lack of an established and universally accepted terminology, a proper Polish transcription of Chinese, not to mention historiographical traditions or proper libraries. Paradoxically, this lack of traditions may have also certain advantages for it signifies, simultaneously, perhaps a lesser addiction to Europocentrism and to a feeling of alleged civilizational superiority which are characteristic of many European and American works, particularly those of the 19th century; it also frees one from the tendency—at times, it is true, unconscious, but in some cases very definitely intentional—to engage in apologies for the conduct and behaviour of "one's own" colonizers in East Asia. In addition, it would seem that it should be easier, for obvious reasons, for a Polish author to feel empathy for the problems of national liberation which to such a significant degree form a part of the political history of China in the 19th and 20th centuries.

Of the works pertaining to Chinese history available to the reader in Polish, attention should be drawn to the following: *The History of China* (edited by Shang Yüeh), translated from the Chinese, which covers the entire span of history up to the eve of the Opium Wars, although treating the first half of the 19th century rather briefly, is still undoubtedly a valuable work, in particular in view of the considerable quantity of factual material. The critical remarks in the introduction written by its Polish editor (W.R.) are still fully valid. The interpretation of a number of essential problems of historical development, especially that of slavery, remains highly controversial, while those parts pertaining to culture still appear to be quite inadequate, after the passage of ten years, since these are much too meagre for the Polish reader. In the field of modern history there is also G. Yefimov's *Outline of Chinese Modern and Contemporary History,* translated from the Russian, whose first 200 pages cover the period from the 17th century to 1919. This work is, however, considerably outdated and includes very many debatable interpretations. The only extant Polish work, J. Lobman's *China Throughout the Ages,* written colourfully and with insight, is due to its very limited size only—in the author's words—"a sketchy outline" intended to present a "first impression" of Chinese history.

The difficulties encountered in the preparation of the present work, generally obvious in themselves, arose, however, not only from the immense chronological span of Chinese history and the unusually rich, though very varied literature, by no means always easily available in Poland, but also—and this may be most important—from the unbelievable complexity of some aspects of the Chinese historical process, many of which are still to be resolved. In the course of the narration attention is drawn to the majority of these problems; more than likely the central problem is periodization itself. Leaving aside the question of the existence of a slavery formation—there are still no proofs or arguments which would support such a hypothesis—it is not fortuitous that the word "medieval" was not used a single time in this work, for its application would have signified an attempt to force the Chinese historical process into the framework of a purely European and by no means worldwide historiographical convention, i.e. it would have simply been a specific expression of Europocentrism. But this problem is simultaneously also the obverse of another more fundamental problem, i.e. the phenomenal duration of the feudal formation in China which, in turn, implied the necessity of employing a periodization traditional in Chinese historiography, based on dynastic periods, while being fully conscious of its inadequacies. Although in the present work certain initial and limited attempts to explain the causes of this phenomenon have been made, they do not pretend in the least to furnish a full answer, especially in view of the fact that the present stage of detailed research on these problems has not yet, in spite of the many efforts of Chinese historians, reached the point which would make such a presentation possible. The above reservation pertains also to other problems of no less interest and importance, such as the causes of the relative stagnation of Chinese civilization in comparison with Europe after having reached its peak achievements in the Sung epoch, or the question of the existence of embryonic forms of capitalism and the possibility of their transformation into a new system without the "Opening of China" in the 19th century undertaken by the foreign powers, as well as the differences in reactions to this "opening" as shown by China and Japan. These are all undoubtedly unusually fascinating and significant problems to which it is certain one will have to return in the future, and which are only some of the vast wealth of similar ones that arise from the complex history of this great country.

The problem of transcription of Chinese names and expressions continues to present certain difficulties which arise from the lack of uniformity of the methods applied in Polish publications. The transcription employed, for example, in the *Large Universal Encyclopedia* is unacceptable for a number of reasons, i.e. because it omits the apostrophe which is indispensable for differentiating a great quantity of similar expressions (e.g. Tang and T'ang). The method employed in a number of Polish sinological works is based, in principle, on the convention of the French transcription; this appears in particular in connection with the letters H and K, e.g. Hia (Hsia) or Kiao (Chiao), etc. In view of the fact, however, that in world literature the English Wade-Giles transcription continues to be dominant and that the number of works pertaining to all aspects of Chinese history and civilization in English, written by both Chinese and non-Chinese authors, exceeds many times works in French, as well as for the purpose of applying a method which makes it possible for the Polish reader to re-create easily this transcription from the one employed in the present work, it was decided to base oneself again, as in the case of the Shang Yüeh *History of China*, on the Wade-Giles system.

(Two paragraphs of details explaining the transcription follow.)

The maps were drawn by the author on the basis of many works, primarily on the Chinese *Atlas of Chinese History* (Shanghai, 1955). The illustrations were selected, above all, to throw light on the sections dealing with cultural evolution.

Warsaw—Małe Ciche, 1970-1972

PART I

Introduction

CHAPTER 1

The Rise of Ancient Chinese Civilization

I. Archaeological Data

In the second millennium B.C. North China witnessed the birth of one of the four oldest civilizations in the world. While the development of Chinese civilization indubitably took place later than that of the others—Egyptian, Mesopotamian or Indian—it is the only one which has continued to persist in a fundamentally uninterrupted fashion from its very beginnings, undergoing many transformations during the span of almost 4000 years of its existence, but simultaneously retaining many features that reach back to early and even to the most remote periods. It is this unique continuity of historical evolution which constitutes one of the most essential traits of the Chinese historical process, endowing it with a quite specific character.

The majority of areas of China including the Yellow River basin, the main cradle of Chinese civilization, have shown signs of habitation by man from the earliest ages on. Probably the most famous of archaeological finds in this respect was the discovery in 1927 of the first remnants of the Peking Man *(Sinanthropus pekinensis)*, whose origin dates back to the beginning or middle of the Pleistocene, thus from 400,000 to 500,000 years ago. The find was made in Chou-k'ou-tien, 30 miles south-west from Peking, and very considerable research was conducted here in the years 1927-1937 by Chinese and Western palaeontologists. The Peking Man was a pre-human hominid with a brain capacity of from 850 to 1200 cm^3 as against the average of 1350 cm^3 for the *Homo sapiens*. He was, however, already a user of very primitive stone and bone implements, a food gatherer and hunter, possessed also of the ability to use fire. According to some sources the Peking Man remnants, which were quite plentiful, showed five features which were common to later races of man in East Asia and not encountered elsewhere. One of these is the shovel-shaped incisor. On the basis of this there is a possibility that the East Asian variety of the *Homo sapiens* could have evolved from the Peking Man into the Mongoloid race. But this problem is still unclear and it is equally possible that a later species could have arisen to replace or absorb the earlier one. There is a distinct and long break of continuity, probably caused by glaciation, and no findings of human remains that could be dated from Mesolithic times. In 1963 and 1964 finds of human remnants were made in Lant'ien (Shensi); these are similar to the Peking Man, but probably older by 100,000 years. This type has been called *Homo erectus lantianensis*.

Although the Paleolithic Age furnishes more data from the upper levels of Chou-k'ou-tien, where remnants of a species undoubtedly already modern man (*Homo sapiens*) dating back 100,000 years were found, the picture of the development of the human species in China becomes clearer only in the Neolithic period, i.e. from perhaps 4000-3000 B.C. Implements from this age have been found in practically all parts of China and there is little doubt that Neolithic man was the direct ancestor of the modern Chinese. The importance of these finds lies, among others, in the fact that it makes it possible to discard now most of the European theories, which were fashionable in the 19th and the first two decades of the 20th centuries, regarding the role of migration and the assigning of the origins of Chinese civilization to assorted other parts of the world (Egypt, Sumer, Central Asia, etc.). It is now a certainty that the development of man in East Asia is indigenous. This fact was undoubtedly also influenced by the geographical environment in which the development took place, i.e. the considerable degree of isolation of China: from the east, the insurmountable expanse of the Pacific; from the west, the great mountain and desert barriers; from the south-west, the equally impassable mountains and jungle. All these factors indubitably contributed to this independent development. This does not mean to say that throughout all of Chinese history, including the earliest period as well, external influences did not exist. Up to the 19th century they did not, however, play a particularly significant or, what is more, decisive role.

This isolation brought it about that Chinese civilization during many centuries and in particular during its formation stage remained, on the whole, unaware of the existence of any other centres that were equal to its level of achievements and it could thus consider itself to be the sole civilization in the world. Herein lay the basic cause for the arising of Sinocentrism, a phenomenon which constitutes one of the specific traits of Chinese civilization, to be discussed in connection with the shaping of the Chinese world outlook. It is worth noting that this state of ignorance was fully reciprocated, especially as far as the Mediterranean world was concerned.

Modern archaeology has established the existence of a large number of cultures whose remnants are to be found in most parts of China but especially in North China, more specifically in the areas of the middle and lower reaches of the Yellow River. It is from this "cradle" of the Huang Ho, which covered only a small part of present-day China, that the process of the expansion of Chinese civilization began. It lasted for hundreds, in fact thousands, of years until it reached its present frontiers, simultaneously influencing a number of adjacent countries in a significant way. Throughout this entire period its main bearer was the Chinese peasant-agriculturalist who adapted himself to the most varied climes and continuously developed his technique of soil cultivation, raising it ultimately to an extremely high level, akin to gardening. All this, however, called for an immense exertion of hard, human toil. Due to these efforts vast terrains, formerly wooded or marshy, were transformed into a soil of unusual fertility. The factor that played the crucial role in its cultivation was not the climate, the soil or the flora, but man himself. Due to this, agriculture in which always a vast majority—up to 90 per cent—of the population was engaged became so clearly

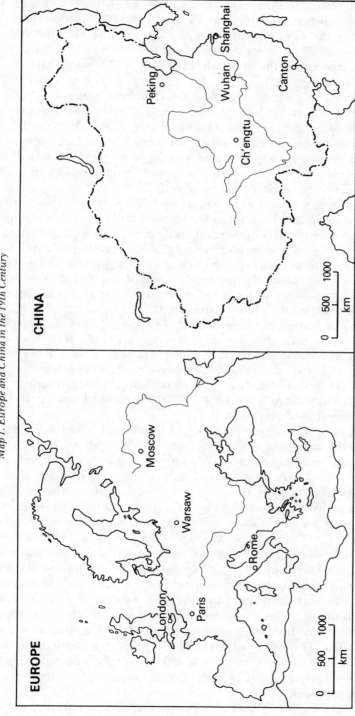

Map 1. Europe and China in the 19th Century

dominant. It determined the fundamental character of the Chinese civilization, making its mark on the development of almost all the domains of Chinese culture. It was also in this process that the Chinese nationality—*Han jen*, the men of Han—evolved, composed undoubtedly of a large number of various ethnic strains, which now constitutes the largest of all the nationalities of People's China. Its history is the basic subject of this book.

Of the cultures mentioned above, two are of special importance—the Yang-shao and Lung-shan. The Yang-shao culture (named after a site in West Honan) has been found mostly in North China but elements of it extend as far as Manchuria and the border of Sinkiang. It shows a more advanced stage in the manufacture of implements and some of these, as well as some of the pottery, are actually prototypes of those still used in the present. The skeletal finds show that the people who created this culture were anthropologically the same as the modern North Chinese.

This culture is especially known for its extremely fine pottery. It was usually painted, with red as the dominant colour. It has been maintained that the painted pottery was intended primarily for ritual purposes and a plainer grey pottery was manufactured for everyday use. The painted pottery had stylized patterns, mostly geometric. The potter's wheel was not yet in use and it was produced by the coiling process. This pottery was the product of a people far advanced in the development of this craft. An interesting note is the presence of a tripod pot which is still utilized in China, thus giving evidence of continuity of this culture with later civilization.

The remnants of Yang-shao sites show that the population was a sedentary and agricultural one, its main crop being millet. There was some domestication of animals, especially pigs and dogs. No trace of metal has been found, however, and the implements are still stone and bone. Equally no trace of writing has been discovered. The Yang-shao can be considered a transitional culture, a Chalcolithic one, from stone to metal. It is usually dated from 3000 to 2000 B.C. and in some parts of China it continued well into the Chou period.

The Lung-shan culture is named after a site in Shantung, 25 miles east of Tsinan. It is noted for its hard, well-made, thin and lustrous black pottery of exceedingly fine quality. The pottery was not painted and the forms are prototypes of those later used. It is also certain that the potter's wheel was already employed. The Lung-shan culture is more advanced than the Yang-shao and can be definitely considered as the earlier predecessor of the first historical Chinese civilization—the Shang. It is the product of a long-settled agricultural population with the same crops and domesticated animals as those of the Shang. Millet remained the main crop but wheat (which probably came from the Near East) was also present. Apart from pigs and dogs, remains of horses, sheep and cattle have also been found. It is also certain that the cultivation of silk dates back from the Neolithic and thus the Lung-shan period. The wheel was also known but there was still no trace of metal found in Lung-shan sites and the tools remained primarily of stone, although many of these were manufactured from shells. The people lived in villages surrounded by thick walls made of pounded earth such as those later used in North China towns. The area in which Lung-shan finds have been made extends from Shantung down to Kiangsu, Anhwei and Chekiang. It dates from the first half of the second millennium on and can be perhaps considered as the intermediate between Yang-shao and the Shang.

In both cases it is difficult to ascertain clearly the ethnic nature of these cultures,

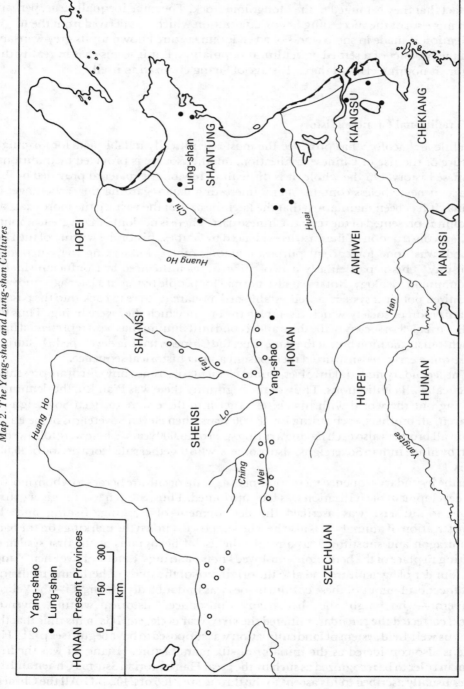

Map 2. The Yang-shao and Lung-shan Cultures

which were in any event only the two most important among many others, apart from the fact that they belonged to the Mongoloid stock. The same is equally true, perhaps even more so, of the succeeding Shang civilization which was derived from them.

Mention is made in some works of a Hsiaot'un culture known for its grey ware and also the product of a settled agricultural population. But it seems that in reality this culture is nothing else but the early stage of Shang civilization itself.

II. Traditional Chinese History

While archaeology has provided the most scientifically reliable data for forming a picture of the rise of Chinese civilization, another source is provided by traditional Chinese history. On the whole, it is difficult to rely on the material provided by this source; it nevertheless contains many interesting data regarding the earliest ages of China. It has been maintained that the later the date of the writing the more exact an account is presented of the remote Chinese past. There is no doubt that a great amount of the reconstruction of the past, as evidenced by Chinese historical writing of the Han period, was done for current purposes, among others, for seeking the sanction of antiquity. This is particularly true of all writings influenced by Confucianism, the predominant ideology. But it was also normal for people living in a later age, under an organized political system, a well-established monarchy, to read back into the past an organization of society which resembled the one in which they were living. Thus the earlier tribal clan society of the third and second millenniums has been represented in an anachronistic fashion but, at the same time, the Chinese, having developed a historical sense quite early, reconstructed their past in a strict historical sequence.

The legendary material involves certain elements of cosmogony which are present in practically all civilizations. Thus, at the beginning there was P'an Ku, the demiurge, carving out the world with his chisel. After him there were thirteen Sovereigns of Heaven, all brothers, each ruling for 18,000 years; then eleven Sovereigns of the Earth, again all brothers also each having a ruling span of 18,000 years. These were followed in turn by nine Human Sovereigns, also brothers, who together ruled for a period of 45,600 years.

In the legendary sequence there come next a group of culture heroes to whom most of the development of civilization was later attributed. Thus, Sui Jen was the giver of fire, while to Fu Hsi was ascribed the development of hunting, fishing and the domestication of animals. It is also he who supposedly noted the markings on the back of a dragon and substituted, as a result, the use of hexograms as the first system of writing in place of the heretofore employed knots on strings. Later we have Shen Nung, the founder of agriculture and also the originator of the study of herbs and medicine. But the most famous of these culture heroes was undoubtedly Huang Ti—the Yellow Emperor—who fought the "barbarians", introduced historical writing, invented brick, corrected the calendar, initiated the sixty-year cycle, etc. It is in his time that the famous well-field system of land cultivation was supposed to have begun (see p. 21). His wife is also considered as the initiator of silk manufacture. Huang Ti was the first human ruler to be recognized as such by the great Han historian Ssu-ma Ch'ien and the dates usually ascribed to his ascent to the throne are 2486 or 2402 B.C. All the Chinese rulers during the later Chou period claimed their descent from Huang Ti.

The mythical empire was then ruled by Huang Ti's progeny, his son Chuan Hsü, his grandson K'u (whom both the rulers of the Shang and the Chou dynasties claimed as their ancestor) and then by the two rulers made most famous by Confucianist writings, Yao and Shun. All these rulers were supposed to have taught their people the arts of civilization, to have established the forms of government and the rules of morality. According to the Confucianists, this was the Golden Age when the government of the world was perfect. Yao and Shun were particularly emphasized as the model rulers and traditional history stressed that they chose as successors not their sons but the ablest of men available. More than likely both Yao and Shun, if they had existed as historical persons, were tribal chiefs and the virtues ascribed to them are a reflection of the level of tribal society at which chiefs were still elected by a tribal meeting.

Shun, himself chosen by Yao, also selected his successor, Yü, who was later extolled as the classic example of devotion to duty. Appointed to regulate the rivers after a disastrous deluge, he worked at this task for thirteen years, never going home once, even when he heard his children cry while passing by his house. But after Yü the descent in the line of rulers was made hereditary and Yü himself was regarded as the founder of the Hsia dynasty, for which two sets of dates exist: the first, 2205-1766 B.C., the traditional one, and the other based on the Bamboo Annals (see p. 44), 1989-1557 B.C.

The problem of the Hsia dynasty is a most interesting one. As presented in traditional Chinese history, it is little more than a list of rulers and their pedigree with an occasional anecdote thrown in. In the first two decades of the 20th century the tendency among modern Chinese scholars was to reject the historicity of the Hsia completely. But the same was done with the Shang dynasty, which, as we shall shortly see, was quite erroneous. This tendency was derived from a hypercritical approach which, in turn, was a reaction against traditional views, dominant for many centuries. It is true that so far there is no satisfactory evidence that such a dynasty as the Hsia did, in fact, exist. No vessels or implements and, what is more important, no writings which could be ascribed to a Hsia period have been identified. But the implements and general level of culture of the Shang period are so advanced that one must presuppose that a previous development did exist and this could well be that which is referred to as the Hsia. It is probable that the Hsia were a tribe or a tribal confederacy in the Shensi and Shansi area and also possible that they were already able to use metal. It is also probable that they had not evolved any form of writing, but this is by no means certain. More than likely both the Yang-shao and the Lung-shan cultures reflect some aspects of the Hsia period. There are, in fact, very few signs of the mythological in the account of the Hsia. Their rulers were mortal men with a normal life span. It has been well said that the very aridity of Hsia history speaks in its favour, inasmuch that if the Chinese had invented this dynasty later on they showed a singular lack of imagination, and this is a quality which has never been ascribed to them. It should also be noted that the ancient Chinese all unanimously accepted the existence of the Hsia, that Confucius and his school definitely regarded the Hsia as historical, and that the Chinese used for a long period the term "all the Hsia" as the name for themselves. But there is no literature which could be ascribed to the Hsia period. It is quite possible that future archaeological finds will provide more data to the solution of this fascinating problem and perhaps make possible a closer identification of the Hsia period with the earlier-known archaeological cultures.

In general, the picture derived of Chinese society before the emergence of the Shang dynasty is one of scattered peasant communities working hard to become masters of the North China Plain, burning and clearing off the brush in the loess area, draining marshes in the northeast and developing their agricultural technique and especially the art of irrigation to a higher level. It is this development of agriculture by the early Chinese tribes which led to a differentiation of them from other tribes in the general area, a differentiation which was, more than likely, based not on ethnic but on cultural standards. There is some dispute between authors as to where the first centre of this development is to be sought; some believe that the middle and lower reaches of the Yellow River are to be regarded as the cradle of early Chinese civilization, while others argue in favour of the loess highlands.

In its organization Chinese society in the pre-Shang period was probably going through a transition from a tribal form to a class society. The problem of this transition is still a very controversial subject among Chinese historians themselves. There has been a tendency to regard this development in a somewhat schematic manner, with the supposition that such a transition necessitates the rise of a slave society. This view, which in effect is a Europocentric one, seems inappropriate in its application to East Asia and its basic fault lies in the assumption that the development of society in the Mediterranean world was a typical one and necessarily followed in other parts of the world. But the experience even of Europe itself, particularly of the Slav and Germanic tribes, shows that this is not so and that the transition from a tribal form of organization to an early form of feudalism can be accomplished without the existence of an intermediary stage of a developed slave society. In fact, the development pattern of the Mediterranean world constituted not a rule but rather an exception from the point of view of history of mankind as a whole. The data available at present, both archaeological and historical, on early Chinese development seem to show that in the case of China the general pattern also resembled that of Slav Europe and not the Mediterranean world and thus no stage of slave society was present.

III. Shang Society

With the formation of the Shang state (between 1750 and 1523, depending on which chronology is used) we emerge into a real historical period where knowledge already exists derived from both contemporary and later sources. But this statement could not have been made even half a century ago; for as late as 1924 the entire second millennium was regarded by many authors as unhistorical until proved otherwise by archaeological discoveries. While the chronology is still unreliable and remains so until 841 B.C., the first definitely fixed date in Chinese history, the materials which archaeology has provided and which corroborate to an amazing degree the accounts existing in Chinese traditional historical writings are sufficient to form a concrete picture of Shang society. We are dealing here with an advanced, bronze civilization, although this is restricted, in fact, to the upper classes. The society is still composed of numerous peasant communities dominated by a series of small city states which, in turn, are ruled by the strongest of these, the Shang.

The political history of the Shang is almost as bare a record of names, deaths and successions of rulers as the history of the Hsia. The dynasty was supposedly found by T'ang, a model of virtue and humanity, who overthrew Chieh, the last vicious ruler of

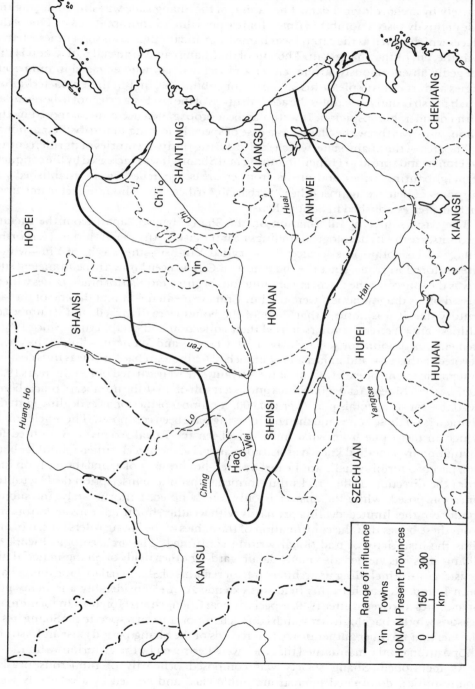

Map 3. Shang 13th Century B.C.

the Hsia. A list of thirty rulers exists derived from traditional history (primarily, but not only, from the work of Ssu-ma Ch'ien) and this has been confirmed almost in its entirety by archaeological data. The capital of the Shang state was shifted during the rule of this dynasty a number of times, for reasons which do not appear clear. One of the places which served as the capital was named Yin and the dynasty is sometimes referred to as the Yin or the Shang-Yin. The rule of the Shang came to an end with Chou Hsin, allegedly an enormously strong, clever and vicious man who engaged in numerous orgies and cruelties to please his favourite concubine Ta Chi. But this characterization much too strikingly resembles the account given of the last Hsia ruler not to be regarded with considerable suspicion. It well may be a propaganda account composed by the Chou, who overthrew the Shang, as a case of special pleading to justify their actions.

The area of the Shang state, which varied during the five centuries of its rule, centred on Honan and spread to Hupei, Shantung and Shansi. It was increased by the conquest of neighbouring tribes and on its frontier areas "marches" were established for purposes of defence against other "barbarian" tribes. The Chou, in fact, came from such an area established in South Shensi.

The basic source of information on the Shang dynasty, apart from the literary accounts, are the archaeological findings near the city of Anyang in Honan. Here in the village of Hsiaot'un was located the so-called Yin-hsü—the wastes of Yin—which already for a long time, since the 2nd century B.C., had been known to be an ancient site. It was the source for the discovery of numerous bronzes and also for oracle bones which, passed off as dragon bones, were used in Chinese medicine. It is at the end of the last century that it was noticed that some of the bones were inscribed, and a number of Chinese and Western scholars started their collection and deciphering. Since 1902 a tremendous amount of research, by both Chinese and Western scholars, has been devoted to this task and in fact a new branch of Chinese archaeology was thus created. Systematic scientific excavations of the Anyang site were carried out in the years 1928-1937 by the Chinese Academia Sinica and as a result of these the number of oracle bones available for study totals now over 100,000. A number of dictionaries dealing with the characters on these bones and their deciphering have been composed. The oracle bones, which in fact came from what must have been the Royal Archives, were used for divination by a method known as scapulimancy, i.e. the object, either a shoulder bone or a part of a tortoise shell, was heated by a red-hot bronze poker and the reply divined from the direction of the cracks thus formed. Most of the inscription deals with the question posed, while the answer is only briefly noted. Unfortunately, the subject matter is rather limited, dealing primarily with weather, hunting, crops and so on. It is from these bones that the confirmation of the names of the Shang rulers is derived and thus the historicity of traditional writing confirmed. The archaeological work on Shang sites has yielded also many data regarding other fields of Shang material and artistic culture including its architecture, for remains of Shang palaces and tombs have been found. Research in this field was extended quite considerably and many new Shang sites uncovered after 1949, especially near Chengchou (Honan). One of the main reasons why archaeological research is of such importance in respect to the Shang lies in the fact that no other authentic written records of the Shang period exist and a strong supposition can be maintained that they were destroyed by the victorious Chou.

As mentioned, Shang society was composed primarily of numerous peasant communities, dominated by a strong noble class and headed by a relatively well-organized monarchy. Thus the class structure of the society is undoubted and its cleavages are sharp and distinct. But it is more than likely that the majority of the peasants were still mainly free members of peasant communes, though owing taxes and labour service to their noble overlords. The degree of their dependence on the ruling class was probably also related to their location, i.e. the distance of their home from the centres of the nobles' power, the walled town. The nobility were the organizers of the tribute system drawn from the peasants and primarily a warrior caste. They fought with the use of the two-horse chariot (three men in each chariot), probably a Shang invention, and were armed with bronze weapons—spears, axes, halberts and knives. Their main sport, in which they engaged with great passion, was hunting. In this they took advantage of the fact that in the climatic conditions of that time—considerably more forested areas and much less population—the quantity and variety of game, including the elephant and rhinoceros, much exceeded that of later ages. The towns must have had a considerable artisan population, as shown by the material culture of the age, with work done in the making of clothes, pottery, metal, bone, ivory, weaving and so on. It is supposed that the artisans were hereditary servants of the nobility and whether their status was that of serfs or slaves is not clear. Whatever the case, there is little doubt that it was agriculture which was the dominant field of production and that in agriculture it was the peasants who were the main source of labour power. Thus even the existence of semi-slaves employed in the crafts or the undoubtedly attested existence of slaves, former prisoners of war, often employed in pasturage, does not really entitle one to make the assumption that the Shang society was a slave society, on the Mediterranean model. It should be rather classified as a proto-feudal or very early stage of feudal society.

The nobility as a warrior caste had, in fact, a monopoly on weapons and chariots and in this lay one of the main sources of power. Their military strength was used for two-fold purposes: to wage war against the neighbours of the Shang and to keep their own population under control. The Shang were an aggressive power conducting many campaigns and foraging to faraway regions in their search for more tribute, cattle, horses, slaves, copper and tin, furs and ivory. Apart from the chariots, which were their main weapon of attack, they also employed infantry, some of it armoured and with shields made of wood and leather. They were able to send out into battle armies of up to 5000 men.

The Shang monarchy was already a relatively well-organized institution with an expanded bureaucracy of officials, titles of their positions being known. The Shang king—*wang*—at the top of the pyramid of the Shang society had considerable personal power and great wealth. He also had an important religious role as the high priest who offered sacrifices to the supreme beings. It would seem, in passing, that even in this earliest historical Chinese society there was no tendency for the rise of a separate priestly caste. It is probable that royal power was stronger in the capital and close-by areas than in the outlying districts where Shang rule was not so firm. The succession of rulers was usually from brother to brother but society was already definitely patriarchal, although signs that a matriarchal system had previously existed were also present. The nobility doubled as priests, especially inasmuch as the conduct of ancestor worship, which was later to become one of the most important components of popular worship, was their privilege and monopoly. This was so, among other reasons, because the peasantry was outside the clan system and in this period had no surnames, thus no pedigree and no ancestors to worship. This religious role of the nobles is perhaps another reason why a separate priestly caste did not arise in China.

While the towns of the Shang revealed a high level of development of material culture with skilled crafts, and also the existence of trade with the use of cowries as currency, the economy, as a whole, was still based on a quite primitive agriculture. This was the main pursuit of the majority of the population and the techniques employed were basically the same as those of the Lung-shan culture. Bronze was too rare and costly to be employed and the implements were mainly made of stone and wood. The hoe, mattock and the foot plough were the main agricultural implements. Some irrigation, but still on a very small scale, was used. Millet, of which there were numerous kinds, was still the main crop. Silk cloth was already made but its use was restricted to the nobility, while the peasants used hemp for their clothing, as indeed they did until the general introduction of cotton in the 12th century A.D.

The Shang engaged in considerable cattle-breeding and herding and, while this was not the main field of production, they did have proportionately more livestock than existed in later periods (this is shown also by the lavish sacrifices of cattle in connection with funerals). This factor was perhaps due to the relatively small population and, later on, land was more and more devoted solely to the raising of food crops instead of pasturage, for in Chinese climatic conditions agriculture is capable of feeding many more people than is livestock breeding.

While the nobles lived in palaces and houses in towns, the peasants in their villages were still, for all practical purposes, living in Neolithic conditions, in semi-subterranean dwellings or, in the loess region, in caves. It is in connection with agriculture that the Shang developed a fairly accurate calendar, dividing the year into 12 or 13 months of 30 or 29 days. The cyclical system was also introduced at this time, six 10-day periods constituting one cycle and six cycles one year. The *kan-chih* system of naming days and years (which consists of the use of the so-called twelve earthly branches and ten heavenly stems, i.e. twenty-two different characters which in a determined order give sixty distinct combinations) also dates from the Shang period.

IV. Shang Culture

The most significant achievement of Chinese civilization in the Shang period was, indubitably, the extensive practice of writing which is attested for the first time in this era. Most of the examples of Shang writing are derived from the oracle bone inscriptions though some also come from bronzes; the bronze inscriptions of the Shang age are usually much shorter than those of later periods and a more primitive script is employed than that on the oracle bones. It is more than probable that the Shang wrote also on wood, bamboo and silk—but all of these are perishable materials and none have survived. Anyhow relatively few remains of ancient times in China are to be found as compared, for instance, with Egypt and West Asia. One of the reasons for this, though not the sole one, lies in the geographic location. Chinese civilization rose not on the dry margin of a desert but on a rich, alluvial plain which was many times flooded and ploughed up. FitzGerald was correct in calling this environment "ahistorical".

The Shang writing as represented by the oracle inscriptions is already a highly developed and sophisticated form. There is no doubt that the language is Chinese, and one author states that this is a striking proof of the correctness of the Chinese feeling of identity with the ancient inhabitants of their land. While the Chinese script is not the oldest in the world (Egyptian hieroglyphics and Near East cuneiform are obviously older), it is the one that has been in use continuously for the longest period of time.

In Shang writing all the principal characteristics of the Chinese script were already present. Apart from pictographs and ideographs the principle of using a key (signific) and a phonetic element for creating new words was already present. It is this principle which has enabled the Chinese to invent new characters almost as easily as for European scientists to have coined new words from Latin and Greek; thus over nine-tenths of the Chinese characters are constructed on this basis. Later on a number of the keys, ultimately set at 214, were selected as radicals in order to classify the characters.

The Shang inscriptions provide over 3000 characters and of these over 1000 have been deciphered. Although the shapes have changed, many of these characters are quite obviously the same as the present ones. The stage of writing reached by the Shang was already of considerable stylization and it leads one to assume that an earlier development of the script must have necessarily taken place with a duration of at least a few hundred years. This could have occurred either during the Hsia or at the very beginning of the Shang. Thus far nothing is known of this earlier stage, but one can hope that future archaeological finds may eventually provide material to illuminate this problem. Due to the character of the Chinese script there is practically no indication of what the spoken language was like in ancient times, but modern sinological research, especially the works of the outstanding Swedish scholar B. Karlgren, has done much to reconstruct ancient Chinese, from the Chou period on, showing that while its basic structure was similar to modern Chinese it was much less homophonous than the modern language.

Chinese writing has a number of shortcomings—its difficulty, its taxing of the memory and the amount of time necessary to master it—but the complexity of the characters gives them a specific vitality and, as has been summed up by Reischauer: "No one who has learned Chinese characters can ever free himself of the notion that somehow the written word has richer substance and more subtle overtones than the spoken word it was originally designed to represent."

From the earliest times the Chinese attached great value to their script; it assumed an almost magical nature for them. The terse, lapidary nature of the writing made for a vividness which had a profound and lasting influence on the Chinese literary language. The script had and has a far greater aesthetic appeal than a phonetic alphabet could ever possess and thus it was intimately connected with the development of Chinese art.

The Chinese script was also of great significance as an element in preserving the cultural unity of China and, for that matter, of those parts of East Asia where it also was later employed. Had it not been for its use it is more than likely that as the language and Chinese civilization developed, the divisions which ensued would have led to a complete separation of the languages (as was the case of the Romance languages in Europe), while the script, which was everywhere comprehensible, because it is not phonetic but algebraic in nature, made possible the maintenance of linguistic unity. Its role was not only confined to this; from the end of the Chou era, an ever greater divergence between the literary language and the colloquial developed. But in spite of this divergence any Chinese who had mastered the characters could avail himself of Chinese literature from practically any period and find it, after some study, comprehensible. This is a thing which no European is able to do with the ancient literature of his own language, assuming that he possesses one.

The Shang was eminently a bronze civilization. The origins of bronze in China have been the subject of debate among Western scholars for many years and very many assorted theories to account for it have been put forth, the majority of them seeking to find a Western origin. But the latest archaeological finds have provided enough material to make it possible to state definitely that bronze in China was an indigenous development. Its beginnings were more than likely placed in the early Shang period, and it is very probable that its use developed independently at this time in different parts of China.

Shang casters in bronze produced primarily ritual vessels of many various types, weapons and equipment for chariots and horses. As mentioned previously, practically the entire production was for the use of the Shang nobility.

It is the ritual vessels which, due to their superb beauty, are of prime interest from the point of view of art. The casting was superior even to that of the European Renaissance and it can be stated that it was never surpassed or equalled anywhere in the world. The technique, as exemplified by the pieces of the late Shang period, was very advanced and the conception and execution of the pieces show a vigour and boldness which deserve the use of that much-abused word—genius. While the art of bronze continued later into the Chou period, most art historians agree that the finest specimens are to be dated from the Shang rather than from the Chou period, although the transition is a gradual one. So many bronzes were produced in the Shang era that they are now to be found in practically all the major museums in the world.

The ritual vessels, of which there were over fifty types, were used to contain food, wine and water and employed for sacrifices in ancestor worship. They were preserved with the greatest of care. This was due not only to their sacral nature but also to the fact that they were of great intrinsic value due to the scarcity of metal. In a way the bronze vessels could also be regarded as a form of accumulation of wealth. Bronze production was also a sign of the level of contacts and trade of the Shang, as it is assumed that there was relatively little copper and tin in the Shang area—though it was mined there also—and that most of the necessary ores were brought in from South China.

Thus the work of unknown Shang craftsmen has given rise to some of the most splendid achievements in the field of art on a world scale. It has been suggested that one of the reasons for the great mastery shown by the Shang bronze casters lay in the fact that they were artists producing at their leisure for their noble patrons and not artisans producing for a market.

The Shang vessels were richly ornamented—perhaps even too much so, as if the artists had a horror of empty space—with patterns of geometric, anthropomorphic and zoomorphic designs. These were, undoubtedly, of religious significance, especially the mythical dragons and the mysterious animal mask, the *t'ao-t'ieh*. The design was mostly *en face* and rarely from the profile and this is undoubtedly a characteristic trait of East Asian art. An interesting analogy with the art of the Indians on the North-west Pacific coast (totems) has been drawn by one author. Both the shape and the decoration of the bronze vessels show that they were based primarily on the copying of earlier vessels made from wood and gourds, even to the point of following the notches that had been made by the knife. But mostly the prototypes, as regards shape, were taken from earlier Chinese pottery. Most of the existing specimens of Shang bronze workmanship date from the late Shang period and data on the preceding eras are still very limited. But just as in the case of the script, the level achieved here presupposes considerable earlier development.

The Shang craftsmen were also fine workers in stone as well as excellent carvers of bone and antlers. They were especially good in what was perhaps the oldest of Chinese art forms, definitely reaching back to the Neolithic, working in jade. This stone was prized by the Chinese from the earliest times for its purity and beauty and extensively used for ritual purposes.

The religion of the Shang was primarily a form of nature and fertility cults. As mentioned, the nobility also observed an already-well-developed cult of ancestor worship, in which the need was felt to satisfy them by offering proper sacrifices. The Shang had no organized pantheon, but a supreme deity—Ti—who was worshipped by the king did exist. This worship of the supreme being was considered the prerogative of the ruler and remained such later on as well. There are no texts dealing with religious observance from the Shang period, for the earliest texts date from the Chou. It is quite possible that when the texts were written down the original meaning of the rites was already then not fully understood and thus the nature of the fertility cult was ignored.

The nature cult included the worship of a number of local divinities, of streams and rivers. Human sacrifices were used rather frequently in the worship of both the gods and ancestors; it is possible that one of the causes of the wars waged by the Shang was to furnish a necessary supply of prisoners for this purpose.

Alongside of various forms of nature worship the belief in spirits of all kinds was particularly widespread; ancestor worship was its special manifestation. These animistic elements, reaching back to the earliest times, survived to the 20th century, especially in popular cults. The appearance later on of more crystallized and more organized forms of religions, such as, for example, the arrival and expansion of Buddhism, did not lead basically to a weakening of these beliefs which, in fact, became intermingled with new elements derived precisely from Buddhism and religious Taoism. However, the strength of these popular cults and, in particular, of ancestor worship, when it ceased to be the monopoly of the upper classes and became the most important of all practices and customs, also gave rise to the noteworthy phenomenon that no new religion ever succeeded in becoming truly dominant. Such a state of affairs was to lead, in turn, to the specifically eclectic and very mundane approach of the vast majority of the population to religious matters.

PART II

China Under the Chou Dynasty

CHAPTER 2

Western Chou

I. The Establishment of the Chou Dynasty

The Chou period was of fundamental importance in the development of Chinese society showing, as it did, greater maturity, except possibly in the field of art. It is in this age that all the features of civilization considered typically "Chinese" fully emerge. The change-over from the Shang to the Chou did not, in reality, involve any essential break in the continuity of growth of Chinese civilization.

The Chou people had been established since probably the 15th century B.C. in the area of Central Shensi, forming something in the nature of a frontier state. It is assumed by some authors that ethnically the population in this area was possibly more closely related to Turkish and Tibetan strains, but that the ruling house itself was undoubtedly of Chinese origin. Whatever the case, the Chou in the fertile Wei and Ching River valleys were an established, sedentary, agricultural population, although constant wars with neighbouring "barbarian" tribes undoubtedly had an influence on the character of their state. In effect, the Chou were just as Chinese as the Shang, but simply less well acquainted with the arts of civilization. In culture, they were under strong Shang influence and, as proven by archaeological finds, also possessed the art of writing, the use of bronze and employed chariots in warfare.

Two generations before the war with the Shang, the Chou moved further east in Central Shensi and established their capital in Hao, very near the famous site of Ch'ang-an (Sian). It is probable that they were a tributary state of the Shang, but one which kept increasing in strength and became a serious rival to the ruling house of Shang.

One of the direct causes of the conflict between the Chou and the Shang was the persecution by Chou Hsin—the last Shang ruler—of Ch'ang, the Duke of Chou, called also the Chief of the West (Ch'ang was referred to later as Wen Wang, the Accomplished King, the title bestowed on him posthumously by his son). The chronology of this period is still a subject for debate and thus at least four dates can be put forth as the year in which the Chou started their war against the Shang—1122, 1111, 1066, 1028. In the accounts of this conflict, Chou Hsin is represented as a monster of depravity and cruelty, as degenerate a ruler as the last of the Hsia. The striking similarity of the two accounts makes both of them doubtful.

When the war commenced, the Chou were ruled by Ch'ang's son, Fa, and it was he who led the great expedition to the east. The strength of his army is uncertain, varying inflated figures being given, and the problem reveals the difficulties encountered in utilizing ancient Chinese sources. They are derived, among others, from the fact that the basic concept for determining a large number of people or objects was the word *wan*, meaning also "ten thousand". Thus, a carefree usage of this word led quite often to exaggerated figures.

The Chou army was composed not only of the forces of the Chou themselves but included a number of allies from other states opposed to Shang rule. The Shang army, on the other hand, included a number of recently taken prisoners of war (or slaves, as some would have it), and during the battles these quickly went over to the side of the Chou, this being perhaps the main cause for the defeat of the Shang.

Chou Hsin fled back to his capital where he burned himself alive in the famous palace tower he had built. The leader of the Chou, later known as Wu Wang (the Martial King), ceremoniously shot three arrows into the dead body, decapitated it and hung the head on the Great White Standard of the Chou. The same fate met Chou Hsin's concubine, supposedly responsible for many of his crimes.

The Chou kings later sought to justify their actions by referring in highly moral tones to the necessity of punishing the depraved Shang rulers, but if one were to search for the motives of this conflict, the main ones probably lie in the search for power and booty on the part of the Chou. After the victory a long process of further conquests and consolidation of the gained territories took place which lasted over twenty years. All the existing accounts of the war are biased as they are derived from narratives used in rites in the Chou ancestral temple.

In establishing their rule the Chou set up garrisons of their own forces in various strategic areas which—in Maspero's words—were like "islands in the sea" ruling over stretches of thinly populated land. The country was divided into a number of fiefs (probably around 120), which included both the land and the people living on it, and given out mostly to members of the Chou royal family and clan—the Ch'i. But some territory was also left to the Shang, including an area which was probably their original home and later became the State of Sung. In the old Shang capital of Yin, Chou Hsin's son, Wu Keng, was left as ruler (Marquis of Yin) under the control of three brothers of Wu Wang. Supposedly this was done so that sacrifices to the Shang ancestors could be continued.

Shortly though, after the death of Wu Wang, a revolt of the conquered Shang and of the three Chou royal brothers took place and a three-year struggle was waged by the *de-facto* ruler, Tan, Duke of Chou, who was then acting as Regent for his nephew, Ch'eng, the 13-year-old successor of Wu Wang. After victory was gained a still greater number of fiefs were established so that fifteen brothers of Wu Wang and over forty clan relatives were among the main fief holders. (Records remain showing who was established where.)

A large part of the Shang population was also resettled by the Chou, while others undoubtedly succeeded in fleeing to the Yangtse and the Huai River area. According to one account some of the Shang fled to Korea and it is their arrival there that marks the

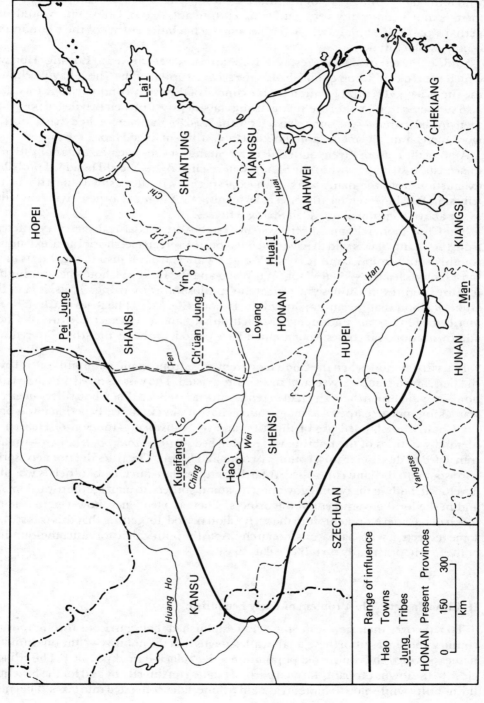

Map 4. Western Chou, 9th Century B.C.

beginning of civilization in that country. It is also possible that it was Shang emigrés who formed the ruling class of the future great state of Ch'u in the Yangtse Valley, for there is much continuity between Shang culture and that of Ch'u. This would also perhaps partially explain why Ch'u became such a bitter enemy of the Chou in the centuries that follow.

Some of the resettled Shang, especially the artisans, were moved to Loyang (Honan), which the Duke of Chou established as the second capital of the Chou, having chosen the site as a good central location for the control of the newly conquered territory. It is also supposed that some of the Shang ruling class, deprived of their privileged position, then turned to trade—the same character being used for the name of the dynasty and the word merchant. The main capital of the Chou still remained Hao.

Among the reasons given for the fall of the Shang are the effeteness of its nobility and the constant struggle within the Shang state itself. To this should be added probably exhaustion from the many wars it waged, especially in the east with neighbouring tribes. Its fall, however, had the effect of widening the range of Chinese civilization due to the above-mentioned spread of Shang refugees.

The Chou monarchy and the fief system it established was basically not very different from the Shang; it was said to have under its control a greater territorial area, extending roughly south from Liaoning to the Yangtse Valley, from Kansu to the sea. Its three most famous leaders—Wen Wang, Wu Wang and the Duke of Chou—became highly idealized figures in Chinese historical and philosophical writing. Thus, it is to the Duke of Chou that the authorship of the famous *Chou li* ("The Rites of Chou") was ascribed. This is an undoubtedly anachronistic and over-exact picture of Chou administration and comes from a much later period, probably the 4th or 3rd century B.C.

In its first period, when the Chou monarchy was strong, it did maintain control over the fiefs, and a complex system of investiture existed. The vassals owed the Chou ruler homage, paid him tribute and had to render military service. The Chou ruler—*wang*—was a king (not an emperor as many sources have it), but in the early period it was only the Chou who claimed use of this title and its equivalent—the Son of Heaven. A hierarchy of titles of the nobility was established—*kung, hou, po, tzu, nan*—usually translated as duke, marquis, count, viscount and baron. The titles did not necessarily correspond to the land controlled. A fairly complex bureaucracy of officials was also developed, both in the central government, among others, to manage the royal domain, and in the local government of the princes. There is a tendency, however, to read too much of later developments into the early Chou period, forgetting that this was still, in some respects, a semi-barbarous monarchy. As to the political history after the founding of the Chou, practically no reliable data exist.

II. Chou Society. The Problem of Early Feudalism

To rule over their new state, the Chou established their garrisons throughout the country and it was from these small walled towns that the nobility—"the one hundred names"—ruled the conquered population—the "black-haired people". The villages close to the towns probably formed parts of estates run directly by and for the benefit of the nobility while more remote areas paid tribute, later converted into taxes. The entire village population was also subject to *corvée*, which assumed in time ever-greater importance in connection with public works, especially with the growth of irrigation and water control.

The system of landholding and relations in production of this period is still a subject for considerable debate among historians. It is possible that the so-called well-field system existed at this time. This supposedly was based on a division of land into nine squares, the drawing of which resembled the Chinese character for the word "well", *ching*, 井, hence the name. The reference to this system comes primarily from Mencius, as well as from the *Tso chuan*. It is possible that the well-field system represented a type of communal ownership and cultivation of land; the eight outward squares were cultivated by the peasants for themselves, while the products of the centre square were handed over to the ruling lord. What does seem to emerge clearly, however, is that the great majority of the tillers of the land, while subject both to *corvée* and tribute, were members of the old village commune, although subject to control and exploitation by the warrior caste of the nobles. They were not slaves, which is not to say that there was no slavery as such in Chou society; it did exist in domestic service and perhaps also in the crafts, although this is by no means certain. There is little doubt that no appreciable amount of slave labour was used in agriculture, which formed the basis of the economy. Hence, it seems incorrect to call this a period of slave society and the Chou should be rather described as a feudal society in its early formative stage, when a complex elaboration of the state organism was only taking place. The culmination of this was the later centralized empire. Thus, the basic relations and characteristics of rural conditions in feudal China were already established under the Chou. In the early Chou period the ownership of land was theoretically vested in the hands of the king. Practically speaking, the land was controlled by the nobility with peasant individual land ownership developing only towards the end of the Chou period, when the complete collapse of the old village commune occurred.

Agriculture in the Western Chou period did not differ appreciably from the Shang but in connection with the destruction of game and the decrease in livestock breeding it became indubitably the most important and fundamental domain in the Chinese economy. There was some change in technique and perhaps more irrigation, nonetheless its basis was still very primitive and the implements employed were primarily stone and wood. Some Chinese authors believe that bronze tools were used in agriculture, but this seems more than doubtful. It must be remembered that iron came into use in China rather late and dates only from the 7th century B.C. or later.

There was also no great change in most aspects of culture. However, in religion, the Chou did bring in their own worship of Heaven, a cult which was closely connected with the ancestral worship of the Chou royal house. As mentioned, the Chou *wang* was regarded as the Son of Heaven, ruling on the strength of a mandate received from Heaven. The Chou were much more adverse to human sacrifices than the Shang. They also had little use for a separate priestly caste as their patriarchal system, in which the head of the family or the ruler carried out priestly functions, made the existence of such a caste redundant. Some of those who were concerned with Shang cults became, under the Chou, scribes or village priests and, it is assumed by some authors, also gave rise later to the class of "scholars" (*shih*) which was to play an important role in the later Chou period. Generally speaking, a fusion of Chou beliefs and customs with those of the Shang took place, and this was true, as we shall see later, in practically all fields of culture.

III. The Struggle with the "Barbarians": Weakening of Royal Power

Throughout the whole Western Chou period, the Chou king and the rulers of the states waged a continuous struggle with semi-nomad tribes in North and North-west China. Some of these, who appeared under various names, were probably the ancestors of the people later referred to as the Hsiung-nu (Huns). According to one theory, the result of this struggle was ultimately to force these tribes to abandon the limited agriculture they practised, and thus turn themselves into pure "warrior nomad" tribes, also moving further to the north. This struggle is a factor which is present throughout most of Chinese history and one of utmost importance. But, in reality, a large part of the area included in the Chou domain was also inhabited by tribes who were simply on a lower level of development than the Chou and with these the struggle was no less fierce. They were referred to by various names—Ti, I, Jung, etc. Ultimately, most of these were either exterminated or, more than likely, assimilated into the general Chinese culture. It is possible that ethnically these tribes did not differ from the Chou Chinese. The same is probably not the case with the tribes in the Yangtse Valley and south of it, most called Man, who bore ethnic affinity with the inhabitants of South-east Asia.

When the Chou royal house was still strong it took the lead in this warfare and thus the domain of the Chou kingdom was extended, for example, to the valley of the Han River. Expeditions and conquests were also made beyond the Yangtse and the reign of Mu Wang (962-908) is especially noted for this. His name is connected with a famous historical romance which embroiders on his expeditions and tells of a trip to the far west to visit Hsi Wang Mu. (Mythologically this personage became later a goddess, the Queen Mother of the West.) As the rule of the Chou king became weaker, more and more of his struggle was carried out by the princes themselves and they rendered less and less aid in the waging of it to the monarch.

In the 9th century B.C. the Chou rulers—the Annals maintain—became indolent and incapable. One of them had a particular reputation for tyranny; this was Li Wang (878-842), a miserly, cruel and arrogant king. Once he boasted to the Duke of Shao "I have suppressed all criticism and the people no longer dare to speak". The Duke replied, "You have gagged the people but to do this is as dangerous as damming up the waters. When the course of water is stopped, it overflows elsewhere. It is the same with the mouths of the people."

The duke's forebodings were soon proven justified. The king was driven out in 841 by a revolt, the first of its kind to be noted in Chinese history. A period of regency then followed known as *Kung Ho* (841-828); according to one version, these words mean "public harmony" and the regency was carried out by two princes, the Dukes of Shao and Chou. According to another account, the rule was exercised by Ho, the Count of Kung. The first version is more likely. From the year 841 the chronology begins to be exact and also records become more and more authentic.

During the 9th century B.C. the rulers of the appanages became stronger, the organization of their states more complex, the officials in them more powerful, whilst cadet branches also increased in influence. All of this was at the expense of the Chou monarchy and investiture started to fall into abeyance. The basic reason for this was that the kingdom was probably too large, and its administration too unwieldy, to be successfully ruled from the centre for a longer period of time. The princes were set on enlarging their own states, waging war against each other for this purpose, and disregarding in this and other respects the rule of the Chou king. A certain exception was the reign of Hsüan Wang (827-781), Li's son, who was partially successful in controlling his vassals and also waged many campaigns against the "barbarian" tribes, though with varying success.

The final crisis of the Western Chou came during the reign of his successor Yu Wang (781-771), a hopelessly weak and ineffectual ruler. Ssu-ma Ch'ien tells the following story. The king had a favourite concubine, Pao Ssu, who never smiled; to make her do so beacons on towers, which served as a signal to the lords to assist against an invasion by barbarians, were lighted. The lords hurried to the king's aid and the concubine laughed with delight at their dismay when they discovered that the alarm was a false one. The trick was repeated several times and when a real attack by the Ch'üan or Dog Jung did ensue, the beacons were lit in vain. The king perished and Hao, the Chou capital, was burned and sacked.

The next Chou monarch, P'ing Wang, moved the capital to Loyang in 770 B.C. The catastrophe shattered what was left of the authority of the Chou kings and henceforth they entered into a period of hopeless decline. The territory of the royal domain decreased constantly, until ultimately the kings were left only with some land around the capital. They became *rois fainéants*. The Chou king still retained his ceremonial functions, as the Supreme Ruler, inasmuch as only the Son of Heaven was considered capable of performing the necessary religious rites. Hence it is the feudal states and not the royal line which became the centre of interest in political history.

CHAPTER 3

Eastern Chou

I. The Further Spread of Chinese Civilization

The Eastern Chou period can be said to extend from the transfer of the capital to Loyang to the ultimate triumph of Ch'in and its establishment of rule over all of China (771-221 B.C.). In Chinese historical writing the period is also subdivided into two— *Ch'un ch'iu* (Spring and Autumn, 722-481) and *Chan kuo* (The Warring States, 403-221 B.C.). Both of these names are titles of famous works, to be dealt with later on. Some Chinese authors prefer to use the term Eastern Chou only for the years 770-403. In general, this is a period of profound changes in all fields, of political and social upheaval, of great and rapid development, of tremendous creativeness. It is especially noted as the classic and most flourishing era of Chinese thought.

If during the Western Chou China was perhaps somewhat behind in its development as compared to West Asia, during the Eastern Chou it more than caught up with the other main centres of civilization. This was the result of a number of basic technical changes in the mode of production. The most important of these changes were the introduction of iron, which dates probably from the 7th century, and the utilization of casting, almost from the outset, thus many centuries earlier than in Europe. Iron was first used for the manufacture of agricultural tools and later on for weapons as well. Its application in agriculture was responsible for a great yield of crops and the iron-tipped animal-drawn plough which was now put into use for the first time has been aptly described as an agricultural revolution. The use of iron tools made the extension of the system of irrigation and water control much more possible and thus during the Eastern Chou period, especially in its later part, a large number of extensive projects of this kind were carried out in various parts of the country. The great irrigation project near Ch'engtu in Szechuan can serve as an illustration of this. Here in the 3rd century B.C. the Min River was regulated successfully and this resulted in reducing a vast area of 3 million *mu* to irrigated cultivation. The engineering work was done so well that the project is still in use today.

The growth of agricultural production also resulted in an increase in population. It was also reflected in a change in the diet of the Chinese, in a decrease in the consumption of meat—which the peasants consumed little of anyhow—as less land was available for pasture.

Economic development was by no means restricted only to agriculture. The crafts became even more specialized; better silk and luxury goods were produced. Painting, both on walls and on silk, was already started. All this created the basis for the future development of the famous artistic crafts and of Chinese art itself. While the social position of the artisans during the earlier part of this period is unclear—they were

24

probably servants of the state or the nobility—by the end of the Eastern Chou the craftsmen became free artisans themselves.

The above-mentioned growth of the economy, which occurred particularly in the *Chan kuo* period, led also to a marked increase in trade, to the utilization of better, new roads, of canals and rivers. A great increase in wealth was accompanied also by the rise in prominence of the merchants who invested their profits mainly in land and played a large role in the collecting of taxes. They were resented and discriminated against by the landowning aristocracy and hence later placed as the lowest category in the classical four-group division of the population: (1) *shih*—nobles, (2) *nung*—farmers, (3) *kung* —artisans and (4) *shang*—merchants.

The rise of the economy led, in turn, to the ever-greater use of money and to a transition in its forms from the earlier use of rolls of silk and ingots of precious metals to copper coinage which first took various shapes and sizes (miniature knives, shovels, etc.) and finally to the copper cash which was to remain in use for over 2000 years. Gold and silver came also into circulation but usually by weight and not in the shape of coins.

The stimulation of economic growth led, as well, to an increase in the number and size of the towns and by the end of the Eastern Chou many large cities were to be found in various parts of China. Thus, for example, Lin-tzu, the capital of Ch'i in Shantung, had supposedly by the 3rd century B.C. seventy thousand households. The towns served both as market-places and as administrative centres, the residence of the aristocracy.

In effect, China during the Eastern Chou was moving quickly in the direction of a money economy and, as Eberhard has it, "an observer to whom the later Chinese history was not known could have predicted the eventual development of a capitalistic society out of the apparent tendencies". But, in fact, in spite of all the advances made in this period, most of China still remained in conditions of natural economy and the self-sufficiency of the villages was still the dominant aspect.

Considerable changes in the social structure of Chou China also took place during this period. Land ceased to be the property of only the great aristocratic clans and now, as these clans disintegrated, it began to be owned by heads of families. These individual families could be either great landowners or small peasant freeholders. Previously the rule of primogeniture had been observed; this was now cast aside and thus a tendency to break up large landholdings introduced. Land now became definitely private property, to be sold and bought. As a result, a large part of the peasantry became free, small landholders. This was due also to migration and the clearing of new land, especially in the south. Some of the peasants still remained on the estates owned by the aristocracy, but the well-field system—if it ever existed—was more than probably already abandoned. Taken as a whole, the period can be considered as a transition to perhaps less oppressive forms of feudal relations, although the free peasants had, in effect, little security of holding and were the object of exploitation by the state (taxes, *corveé*) and by the merchants and the great landowners (usury). It is difficult to tell how many of the free peasants were also tenants and what the proportions were between those who worked their own land and those who worked on the nobles' estates.

Sharp social distinctions between the aristocracy and the peasantry were still fully maintained. In fact, these were so acute as to give rise to suggestions by some Western historians that this cleavage must have resulted from a conquest in earlier times of China and that the nobility were the descendants of a conquering race. This theory is pure speculation without any foundations whatsoever.

During the Eastern Chou, while all political power was still in the hands of the great aristocratic clans, many of them related to the Chou royal family, the former underwent a steady process of disintegration. Thus differences now arose also within the ruling class and by no means all of the clan members were great landowners; some of them had small holdings and some of them no land at all. It is from the landless nobility that the future *shih,* the scribes, teachers, administrators, etc., came. It must be remembered, however, that even in eastern Chou times one cannot draw analogies between the Chinese aristocracy and that of the European medieval age, attractive as this might seem. The Chinese noble was literate, trained in music, poetry, rites, the arts and archery.

The Eastern Chou period saw a considerable expansion of territory in all directions. In the North and North-west new land was brought into cultivation and it is in connection with this that the conflict with the nomads of this area became an ever-greater problem. The first defensive walls against nomadic incursions date from the 5th and 4th centuries B.C. but some were built to serve as a defence against competing Chinese states as well. This is also the era of the first settlings on a large scale of the Yangtse Valley, or rather of the introduction of the Chinese methods of agriculture into this area and also of the beginning of migration to South China. The long and complicated process which led to this increase of the area of Chinese civilization was the result not only of many wars but also of the assimilation of closely related peoples, once considered "barbarians", who, when they adopted the Chinese way of life, became thereby Chinese.

II. The Struggle for Power

At the beginning of the Spring and Autumn period (722-481) political power was already, in fact, in the hands of the rulers of the various states, which were being transformed into separate territorial units. The Chou *wang* after 771 B.C. was increasingly powerless and his role reduced to that of an arbiter in the quarrels of his vassals and to ceremonial functions.

In theory, war was supposed to be conducted only against the "barbarians", and not between the Chou states which shared the same culture and institutions. In reality, most of the warfare was conducted between these states and resulted in the continuous reduction in their number, the smaller one being swallowed up by the greater. By the Spring and Autumn period there were only around 100 left, and of these only fourteen of the largest ones were of importance. These were: Ch'in, Chin, Ch'u, Ch'i, Lu, Wey,* Yen, Ts'ao, Sung, Ch'en, Ts'oi, Cheng, Wu, Yüeh.

Of the states mentioned above the four strongest were Ch'in, Chin, Ch'i, Ch'u and it is among them, primarily, that the struggle for supremacy was waged throughout the entire period, ending ultimately in the victory of Ch'in. One of the principal aims of this conflict was to control the central area of China, mainly Honan province, in which the Chou royal domain and a number of other states were located and which was regarded as the cultural and political centre of the country. It is to this area that the term *Chung kuo*—the Central Country, hence later the Middle Kingdom—was first applied, while the peoples who formed part of the Chou kingdom referred to themselves at this period as the Hua or the Hsia.

* Wey is spelled thus on purpose, though it should be written Wei, to differentiate it from a later successor state to Chin; in Chinese the problem does not arise as the characters are different.

Fig. 1.   Yang-shao urn. (Lee, S. E., *Far Eastern Art.* London, 1964, p. 33.)

Fig. 2.   Lung-shan pot. (Cheng Te-k'un, *Archaeology in China*, vol. I, *Prehistoric China.* Cambridge, 1959, pl. XXX.)

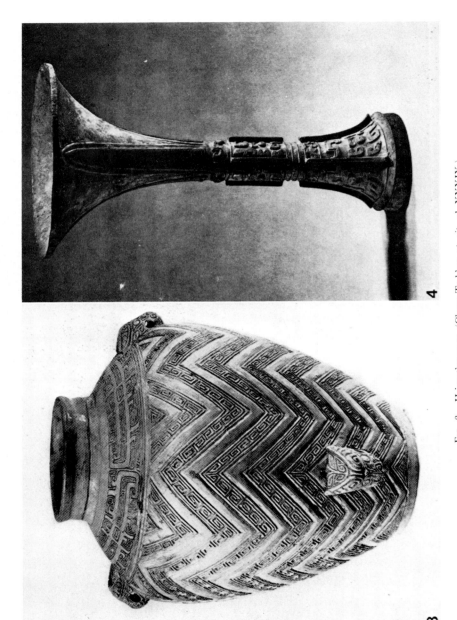

Fig. 3. Hsiao-t'un vase. (Cheng Te-k'un, *op. cit.*, pl. XXXIX.)

Fig. 4. Bronze cup, Shang. (*Hsin Chung-kuo ch'u-tu wen-wu.* Peking, 1972, pl. 47.)

5

6

FIG. 5. Bronze vessel, Shang. (Kümmel, O., *Die Kunst Chinas, Japans und Koreas*. Berlin, 1929.)

FIG. 6. Bronze vessel, Shang. (Lee, S. E., *op. cit.*, p. 34.)

Fig. 7. Bronze cup, Western Chou. (Cheng Te-k'un, *op. cit.*, vol. III, 1963, *Chou China*, pl. 17b.)

Fig. 8. Bronze vessel, Warring States. (Cheng Te-k'un, *op. cit.*, vol. III, *Chou China*, pl. 28.)

FIG. 9.   Bronze inlaid with gold, Warring States. (*Hsin Chung-kuo* . . . , *op. cit.*, pl. 72.)

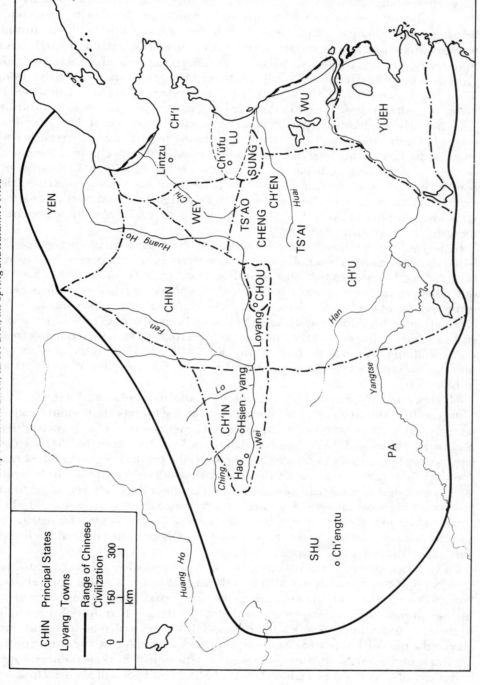

Map 5. Eastern Chou, ca. 600 B.C., the Spring and Autumn Period

In the long run, it was the frontier areas, as exemplified by Ch'in, which developed the greatest strength and played the most significant role in the conflict. The history of the wars and intrigues of both the Spring and Autumn and the Warring States is most intricate and fascinating but can be dealt with here only very briefly. The main aim of the wars, apart from the question of control of Central China, was plunder and increase in territory. In the early period the states were not contiguous but rather separated by great stretches of land inhabited by tribes still considered "barbarian", i.e. those peoples who had not adopted the Chinese way of life. As these were successively conquered and assimilated the borders of the states met and this, in turn, gave rise to further conflicts.

In the Spring and Autumn period, however, warfare was on a fairly limited scale and somewhat chivalrous in nature. It was mainly the nobles and their retainers who engaged in it, chariots were still extensively employed (one chariot accompanied usually by 20-25 foot soldiers) and the armies were of small size. Definite rules of conduct in warfare were on the whole followed and the campaigns at times resembled a form of bloodless military chess. Strategy was on a high level, as shown by the famous work on the art of warfare by Sun Wu (end of 6th century B.C.). All this was to change radically in the Warring States era.

In the 7th century it was the state of Ch'i which played the most prominent role. Due to the absorption of a number of small states the territory of Ch'i soon extended to most of Shantung. It possessed rich agricultural land, had a highly developed production of salt, which was a state monopoly, led also in the use of iron and the development of trade (probably one of the first to use coinage as a means of exchange). Its economic wealth, especially after the reforms undertaken by Kuan Chung (a book of much later origin is still ascribed to him) during the rule of Duke Huan (685-643), made it possible for it to take a leading position in the Chou realm. Kuan Chung's reforms included, amongst others, a lowering of taxes for peasants and artisans and a reorganization of the state's military forces.

Ch'i became in 680 the first leader of the league, an alliance of a number of Chou states formed at this time to serve as common defence against the most important enemy, the state of Ch'u in the Yangtse Valley. The system of Leagues was practised sporadically for over two centuries and it also signified that the political power of the Chou *wang* had been reduced practically to nought, inasmuch as the *pa*, the hegemon of the League, was the actual ruler over most of China, compared by some authors to the Shogun in later Japan. The League held assemblies of the heads of the states, according to strict protocol, and the advantages of holding the leadership were considerable, for a heavy tribute was paid to the hegemon by the smaller states. This was a great burden for them and any attempt to evade payment was usually cruelly punished not only by fines but also by the invasion of the culprit's territory.

Ch'i did not succeed in maintaining its hegemony and, after a short period of Sung leadership, it passed to Chin, which was then ruled by the able Ch'ung Erh, Duke Wen (636-628) whose adventures during his many years of exile were known to every literate Chinese for over 2000 years thanks to the picturesque account of them contained in the *Tso chuan*. In his time a number of social changes took place in Chin: among others, the peasants were freed from the well-field system. A new and strong military organization was established and, with brief interruptions, Chin kept the hegemony for over a century. Its territory included most of Shansi and parts of Shensi, Honan and Hopei; its main rival was Ch'u, but in the west, Ch'in was also becoming a danger to it.

The state of Ch'u was located in the Yangtse Valley and included an area stretching from East Szechuan through Hunan and Kiangsi; later, its area was even larger, reaching the sea. As mentioned, it is supposed that the population here was ethnically not Chinese, but of Man origin, while the ruling class itself was Chinese. During the Spring and Autumn period Ch'u expanded its territory also in two directions: to the west up to the Han Valley and to the east into the Huai River area. The long struggle between Chin and Ch'u with its shifting results had the ultimate effect of bringing ruin to both states.

Three states—Ch'in, Wu and Yüeh—can be considered as being located on the frontiers of Chinese civilization and were regarded by the Chou states as semi-barbarian. The role of these states in this struggle was of utmost importance and final victory rested with one of them.

In the 8th century B.C. when disaster overtook Western Chou, the Ch'in were granted the old lands of the Chou in South and East Shensi, and it is from this area that they steadily increased their strength and territory, among others, in constant warfare with the "barbarian" tribes to the north and west. At one time, in the 7th century, Ch'in also pretended to the hegemony, but its real rise in power is a later phenomenon.

The state of Wu included all of Kiangsu and the northern part of Anhwei. Its population likewise was probably not ethnically Chinese. It fought against Ch'u, mostly as an ally of Chin, and achieved in this a great victory when its armies were led by a refugee from Ch'u, Wu Tzu-hsü. The Wu armies occupied most of Ch'u, including its capital, and there Wu Tzu-hsü had the last Ch'u king's body exhumed and personally gave it 300 lashes, thus taking revenge for the death of his father and brother at the hands of the former king. The victory of Wu, which had spent a century in gathering its strength, was crowned by assuming the hegemony in 482 B.C. But the triumph was short-lived, for Wu had neglected to subdue completely, when it had the chance to do so, its southern neighbour, the state of Yüeh. Yüeh embraced most of Chekiang province and its population was also definitely non-Chinese. The name occurs throughout most of Chinese history for areas in South China and is the same as that used for Vietnam (Yüeh=Viet). It is possible that the original population of Yüeh was of the same stock and that perhaps the present-day Vietnamese migrated from this area to Vietnam.

In 473 B.C. the state of Wu was overthrown by Yüeh. At the moment of triumph, the able minister Fan Li, originally from Ch'u, left the service of the king of Yüeh, fled by boat with his treasure to the most civilized part of China—Ch'i—where he then became one of the richest merchants of China. When later asked why he had done so he answered in verse:

> When the bird is slain, the bow is cast aside.
> When the fleet deer is caught, the hounds are cooked.
> When the enemy has been vanquished, the minister to whom
>   victory is due is dispensed with.

The wars in this period were not only among the states but within them as well. Ever greater conflict ensued of the rulers and the great families of officials and landowners. Thus, in Ch'i the ruling family was overthrown by the T'ien; while in Chin the ruling dynasty succumbed also to the attacks of three great families, who then divided the entire territory of the state among themselves, thus leading to the creation of three new states—from north to south—Chao, Wei and Han. Their rights as new rulers were officially recognized by the Chou *wang* in 403 and they are often referred to as the Three Chin.

The ensuing period of Warring States was an era of perhaps the greatest strife in

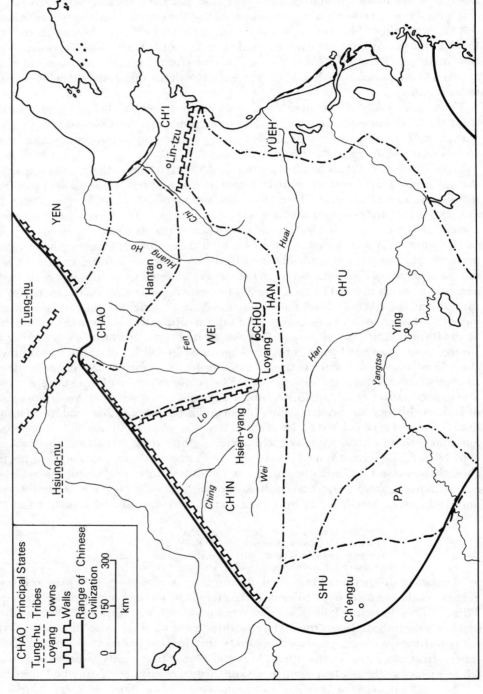

Map 6. Eastern Chou, ca. 300 B.C., the Warring States Period

CHAO Principal States
Tung-hu Tribes
o Loyang Towns
⊔⊓⊔⊓ Walls
Range of Chinese Civilization

0 150 300
km

Chinese history up to, but not including, the 20th century. This was a cruel, brutal struggle, with continuous conquests and aggression in which only the "fittest" could survive. Chinese traditional history refers to the Seven Great Martial States—Ch'i, Ch'u, the Three Chin, Yen and Ch'in. Of these seven, Yen located in North-east China—the area around Peking as well as the Liaotung Peninsula—was rather outside the main picture. During the Warring States era still more of the small states disappeared, annexed by their more powerful neighbours.

Important changes took place in the nature of warfare. Instead of the semi-chivalrous conduct of the Spring and Autumn era, the struggle waged now aimed at the extermination of the enemy; this was especially true of warfare waged by Ch'in. Large masses of infantry were now employed, while the chariots of the earlier era were put aside. The weapons were of iron and since the 5th century a considerable use was made of cavalry (this was probably the influence of the northern nomads) with the concomitant change in clothing (trousers instead of robes). There was a manifold increase in the size of armies and undoubtedly a proportionate, if not still greater, increase in the suffering of the population.

Against the background of constant warfare, confusion and disintegration one important social phenomenon should be noted—the emergence, as a distinct group, of the *shih*, usually coming from impoverished aristocratic and official families. It is this group which gave rise to the wandering scholars going from court to court to serve as advisers and ministers to the princes. Some of these were truly concerned with the development of thought (see Chapter 4) but others were political adventurers and careerists, unscrupulous to the extreme. They put forth schemes of the greatest vileness and basest treachery and were ready to change their masters at a moment's notice if only their advancement could be furthered thereby. Most of them gravitated to the main rival states—Ch'in and Ch'u. Their careers were colourful, their fate uncertain and their end often tragic (see below—the death of Shang Yang). It is undoubted that these men had a great influence on the political development of the Warring States era. The *shih* included also astronomers, astrologers, keepers of the calendar, doctors, warriors, etc., as well as a large and unruly group of sycophants in the various princes' courts.

From the beginning of the 4th century B.C. the rise of Ch'in to power becomes ever more marked. The rulers of this state took full advantage of a geographical location which gave it excellent possibilities for defence, and in this period gained control of two strategic areas of utmost importance—the area west of the Yellow River which made further advance to the east into the North China Plain feasible, as well as the entrance from the north to the Han Valley which was a key to an advance southward into the Yangtse Basin. Towards the end of the 4th century, Ch'in conquered the states of Shu and Pa (most of Szechuan); this was of crucial importance for it provided Ch'in with additional economic resources and strength, while simultaneously outflanking its main rival, Ch'u, whose vast territory at this period also extended from the eastern border of Szechuan to the sea.

Most important, however, in the rise of Ch'in were the internal reforms carried out there which are linked with the name of Kung-sun Yang. He came from Wei, a grandson of its marquis, and is also known by the title and fief granted him later by the Ch'in ruler as the Lord of Shang. He became minister to Duke Hsiao (361-338) and the reforms which he proposed and put into effect are the classical embodiment in practice of the ideas of the Legalist school (see pp. 40-41).

The main reforms were as follows: (a) the elimination of the clan organization and the establishment of an administration on a territorial basis; (b) the introduction of a draconian penal code and the organization of a system of collective responsibility (here is the beginning of the notorious *pao-chia* system), which involved compulsory mutual spying and the denunciation of "traitors" on pain of death; (c) the reorganization of military forces with great emphasis placed on achievements in warfare; titles and rewards to be granted only for merits in this field; (d) the stressing of the development of agriculture, the establishment of peasant ownership and the elimination of the remnants of the well-field system along with the introduction of a land tax as the main source of state income. The policy was accompanied by discrimination towards trade; (e) complete hostility to the arts and letters which were regarded only as a source of troublesome, subversive ideas; (f) implementation of a policy to attract new settlers from other states, both farmers and skilled artisans, to strengthen the state.

As a result of the above reforms which were put into practice Ch'in was set for the final struggle for power as the most ruthless, authoritarian and militarist state in China. The fate of the Lord of Shang himself should be noted in passing. In implementing his reforms he had antagonized the son of Duke Hsiao; when this man came to the throne, Yang's days were numbered. He fled abroad but was handed over to the Ch'in and torn apart by five horses. His whole family was also wiped out. But the reforms remained in effect and from approximately 312 B.C. on Ch'in proceeded to put into action its plan of military conquest, seizing steadily and surely more and more territory, "as a silkworm devours mulberry leaves" in the expressive words of Ssu-ma Ch'ien.

One of the weapons used effectively by the Ch'in was cruelty and terror on a mass scale. While there is an undoubted tendency in Chinese sources to use exaggerated round figures, there is little doubt that the figures relating to tens of thousands of enemy heads cut off by the Ch'in armies are close to the truth. The Ch'in soldiers were paid special bonuses on the basis of the heads which they presented and decapitated all within reach, both killed and wounded. Thus the notorious massacre in 260 B.C. at Ch'ang-ping of the entire Chao army which had previously surrendered—all 400,000 were supposedly buried alive—was in line with Ch'in practice. The Ch'in were the Assyrians of East Asia, although they left no bas-reliefs to boast of their sanguinary achievements. They well deserved the name of "the ferocious beast of Ch'in", as a minister of Ch'u called them.

In spite of what some historians maintain, there is no reason to assume that the unification of China was in this period inevitable, for what could have equally well resulted, in this vast area, was the formation of three separate countries, for example, Ch'in, Ch'i and Ch'u. The unification could have also had a different character and taken another course; as carried out by Ch'in, it was primarily the result of its rapacious aggressiveness, as well as of the failure of the other states to oppose Ch'in effectively. There was, it is true, an attempt to organize a league of six states, the so-called vertical, north to south, alliance against Ch'in. This was an effort undertaken by Su Ch'in and its frustration by his rival, Chang I, is the subject of a famous historical romance. The basic reason for the failure was to be found in the rivalries among the six states and the skill with which Ch'in was able to play on them, proposing always alliances with one of them against another (the horizontal alliances). All the rulers of the states had already, since 325, assumed the title *wang*, while the sad remnant of the royal domain divided into two parts was conquered by Ch'in and the last Chou king was deposed in 256 B.C.

CHAPTER 4

Chou Culture

I. Classical Chinese Philosophy

The Eastern Chou period has been described as the most glorious age of Chinese philosophy which was the greatest cultural achievement of this era. A great variety of philosophical ideas and views arose in this age, thus leading to the use of the name "Hundred Schools". Of these a number were of truly fundamental importance for the shaping of the future development of Chinese civilization.

The question arises as to the reasons for the flourishing of philosophy in this period. The fact that the country was divided into a number of states created a situation in which a lack of uniformity of thought prevailed and no strong orthodoxy in ideas was dominant; thus more individuality, variety and vitality of ideas was possible. Nevertheless, the most important cause probably lay in the character of the age, which was one of great ferment, of crisis and decay, both social and political, of early Chou society, when old values were both breaking down and subject to question. It is the search for answers to the problems posed by this situation that gave rise to the new schools of thought.

This background explains, at least in part, the nature of Chou thought. It is basically social and political, dealing with the problems of society and of man's place in it; thus it is primarily a humanistic philosophy. The principal questions posed and the answers given related to the problem of organizing an ideal society. In this quest, however, all the philosophers took for granted the existing social and political forms—the monarchy, the rule of a landholding upper class—and looked for answers in the field of morals and ethics.

Although undoubtedly tinged with earlier religious beliefs dating both from the early Chou and Shang periods, the schools which developed during the Eastern Chou did not really deal with any problems that could be considered close to religious themes. Social and political questions overshadowed all others and thus there is very little concern in the writings of the "Hundred Schools" with cosmology and metaphysics; if dealt with at all, these subjects are always completely subordinate to the problems of man and society. This phenomenon is also partly due to the fact that the philosophers were simultaneously, or strove to be, statesmen and politicians, as well as thinkers. They were, in fact, the prototypes of the later Chinese phenomenon—the scholar-official.

A parallel has been often drawn between the development of Chinese thought and the simultaneous flourishing of Greek philosophy. The many striking resemblances (although vital differences should not be overlooked) cannot be a coincidence; similar social-political problems were facing both civilizations—the Greek city states as well as the Chinese principalities. A crisis which involved the entire community and its culture pertained to Hellas as well as to the Hsia. In both cases, it has been remarked, the crisis was solved not by a successful implementation of philosophical ideas but by the conquests by semi-barbarian frontier peoples—Macedon and Ch'in.

Both the demands of chronology and the fundamental importance of his views for the future shaping of Chinese philosophy and Chinese civilization necessitate beginning an account of Chinese thought with Confucius. K'ung Ch'iu (Confucius is the Latinized form of K'ung Tzu, Master Kung) was born in 551 B.C. (?) in the state of Lu (Shantung). He came from an impoverished aristocratic family, which claimed descent from the ruling house of Sung and thus from the ancient Shang kings. Lu itself was a state in which early Chou customs and views were conserved to a greater degree than in most other parts of China. There are, in fact, very few reliable data on Confucius' life. The biography in Ssu-ma Ch'ien's work is considered by many authors to be of dubious value. What can be stated is that after holding some official position in his own state he was then forced to exile himself and for some years travelled from court to court of the princely states seeking a post where his views would be accepted and acted upon. In this, his career was basically a failure; but from an early stage on, disciples gathered around him and during the last years of his life he returned home and devoted his time solely to teaching them and numerous other pupils. He died in 479 B.C. (?). How did his disciples see him as a man? According to them, Confucius was dignified, conscientious, thoughtful, affable, calm, high-minded, studious, a lover of antiquity and music, of books and rites. This, however, is but a collection of all the attributes of the *chün tzu*— the superior man, or gentleman as represented in Confucius' teachings. What were his ideas?

According to Confucius himself, the ideas he put forth were not his own; he called himself a transmitter and not a creator. The statement is true, inasmuch as practically all the ideas of his teachings were derived from earlier writings which formed the basis of his study. What he transmitted, however, was the entire heritage of earlier Chou civilization and, in transmitting, he commented upon it in a creative fashion. It was to antiquity that Confucius looked for a model of a perfect society, considering it to have been a Golden Age; its heroes Yao, Shun, the Kings Wen and Wu, the Duke of Chou—all legendary or semi-historical—were regarded by him as paragons of virtue whose example should be followed by contemporary rulers. This harking back to antiquity was based on at least two reasons—Confucius' authentic love for the past, due to his own background, and the enhanced authority which would be thus bestowed on the views he propagated. It should be noted that these views were not systematized by Confucius himself but rather are scattered throughout what remains of his teachings.

As Nature and Heaven move according to a set pattern or a way (*tao*), thus in this ideal society of the Golden Age man also carried out his assigned role in his proper place and observed all the customary rites (*li*) connected with this. As the patriarchal family was the basic social unit, thus also the relations within the family and the acknowledgement of proper authorities was stressed by Confucius as being of fundamental importance. Hence in the famous Five Human Relations—formulated later on the basis of his teachings by Mencius—four of them deal with relations within the family and friends; only the fifth with those between the ruler and subject. The state is but an extension of the family and its ruler is the patriarchal father of his people. It is his virtue and benevolence that can bring contentment to the people and thus assure good government and a perfect society.

This search for good government was motivated primarily by the feudal anarchy of the time in which Confucius lived. Time and time again he saw the only remedy in a return to the past. It is this basically conservative aspect of his views which explain, at least partially, why Confucian ideas could be considered, in a later age, as a fitting ideology for the upper class. But his ideas went further than just harking back to the past. Confucius stressed equally the need for proper education with an emphasis placed on moral and ethical principles. His *chün-tzu* (which originally meant son of a noble) was supposed to be upright (*chih*), righteous (*i*), loyal (*chung*), forgiving and tolerant (*shu*). Above all, however, he had to possess *jen* (altruistic love, humaneness, human heartedness) and follow the principle "what you do not want someone else to do to you, do not do to others". He was also to be a cultured (*wen*) man, as well as a follower of rites (*li*).

It was the possession of the above qualities, and not birth alone, which determined who was a superior man, one whose proper role in society was to rule or assist in ruling. Confucius himself adhered to this principle of ignoring descent, for he accepted as his pupil anyone who wanted to learn, regardless of his origin. It is his role as an educator, the first one as such in Chinese history, which is probably Confucius' most important single contribution to Chinese civilization. The moral and ethical code which he sought to establish was a code for the ruling upper class; this aristocratic approach was characteristic not only for Confucius but for almost all the philosophers of the classical period, regardless of the differences in their views. The people were to be led and ruled; but they were not considered as participants in society and certainly not to be allotted any political role.

There is very little in Confucius' teaching of metaphysical speculation, practically nothing of the supernatural or mystic. As said above, it was primarily a moral and ethical code of behaviour that Confucius propounded. In the next three centuries, his views did not meet with any great renown and, as Chinese thought developed still more in the 4th and 3rd centuries B.C., his ideas were only one trend of thought amongst very many different schools. They were not the object of a cult, nor could they possibly be considered, in their historical setting, to be a form of religious ideology. Confucianism did become at a much later stage a form of state ideology, to which the word religion could be partially applied. One should note, in passing, that, as in so many other cases, a world of difference lies between the views and teachings of Confucius himself and of those who claimed in later years to be his followers. The fate of many original thinkers—that their ideas become completely distorted by future generations, although their name continues to be employed—did not by-pass Confucius either. It should be remarked that the word Confucianism does not exist in Chinese—it is a European invention. In Chinese the word is *ju*, which means simply scholars and was in current use before Confucius' time. Later on, as the Confucians claimed a monopoly on the interpretation and knowledge of the Classics, they came to be regarded as the scholars *par excellence*—hence the name.

Confucius left no writings. On the authority of Mencius it is customary to attribute the editing of the *Ch'un ch'iu* to Confucius. This is a dry-as-dust, laconic chronicle of the state of Lu for the years 722-481 B.C. It is said that in editing it he made a choice of words which subtly denote his approval or condemnation of the conduct and actions of the rulers and other personages. In this he applied the theory ascribed to him of the "rectification of names" (they had to be rectified because they had lost their real, original meaning) and thus gave vent to his reaction against the general looseness of morals in his times.

Some authors maintain that to prove his point Confucius did not hesitate to tamper with historical data. If this be true, he was thus the first, but by no means the last, in Chinese historical writing to do so. Traditionally, Confucius is also credited with having collected both the historical documents which are contained in the *Book of History*, as well as the poems in the *Book of Odes*; this is more than likely not true but, on the other hand, it seems fairly certain that he employed the material contained in these two books as the basis for his teaching.

The only extant source for his views which can be regarded as authentic is the *Lun yü*—the Analects. This work (20 chapters, 497 paragraphs) is a collection of his sayings and anecdotes relating to him, compiled by his disciples or rather their disciples. It constitutes the earliest work of the Confucian school and is of fundamental importance.

In the century following Confucius' death his disciples, among them members of his own family, continued to expound his views, but it is not until the period of Mencius that his teachings found a truly able propagator. Mencius (371?-289?)—Meng K'o—was born in the small state of Tsou, south of Lu, close to Confucius' birthplace. His background both in regard to family and early youth was quite similar to that of Confucius. A great role in his upbringing is always attributed to his famous mother. The hundred years between the death of Confucius and the birth of Mencius saw China plunged into a still greater social and political crisis. This is undoubtedly reflected in Mencius' presentation of the Confucian views he adopted. His career also bore great resemblance to that of Confucius; he spent many years in travels from state to state, seeking posts at the princes' courts and a ruler who would implement his advice and create a perfect government, thus helping to rescue the country from disaster. This was also of no avail and he spent the last years of his life in retirement, writing and teaching his numerous pupils.

In his views on society Mencius did introduce certain new political elements which may be regarded as perhaps less conservative than the views of Confucius. While taking no less an idealist view of the role of Heaven in human affairs than his predecessor, he stressed much more strongly the concept *Vox populi, vox dei*, and developed further the idea of the Mandate of Heaven. Thus, a worthless ruler could and should be removed because by his evil actions he would have lost the mandate; but this was to be done by his ministers or family and not by the people, towards whom Mencius' attitude was as paternalistic as that of Confucius.

The class essence of Confucianism is revealed to an even greater extent in some of Mencius' views, especially in his assertion that society is composed basically of only two strata—those who work with their brawn and those who work with their mind. It is the fate of the former to support and to be ruled by the latter. He did maintain, time and again, the necessity of looking after the welfare of the people, emphasizing the economic aspect of this and stating plainly that therein lay the essential ingredient of good government.

However, the most important contribution of Mencius was his insistence on the basic goodness of man's nature. He used this point for stressing the need for education which was to prevent the loss of the innately good qualities with which a man is born. Mencius emphasized also all the virtues which Confucius had enumerated, laying special stress, however, on the importance of filial piety in human relations. He extolled Confucius and, as the Plato—or St. Paul if one prefers—of Confucianism, he waged vigorous polemics against the enemies of Confucian views, directing his fire primarily against the ideas of Mo Ti and Yang Chu. He assailed the basic component of Mo Ti's doctrine—his theory of Universal Love—as, in reality, a negation of love as such. On the other hand, he attacked Yang Chu's views, probably unfairly, as completely egotistic and selfish and also thereby a denial of any love in human relations. These polemics did undoubtedly contribute to a considerable degree to a victory of Confucian ideas over that of their opponents; Mencius wrote in a splendid and persuasive style, especially as compared to Mo Ti. His writings were also collected and edited by his disciples and later, as the Confucian creed took on its final shape, the book bearing his name—*Meng-tzu*—became a fundamental part of the Confucian canon, one of the Four Books, the basic Confucian Classics, together with the *Lun yü*, the *Ta hsüeh* ("The Great Learning") and the *Chung yung* ("Doctrine of the Mean"). These last two come from the *Li chi* ("The Book of Rites").

In the 3rd century B.C. the most prominent philosopher who is usually represented as a continuator of Confucianism was Hsün Ch'ing (*fl.* 298-238?). It is rather difficult to regard him as a thinker completely in the Confucian tradition, for there are many elements in his views which seem to be derived either from Taoism or, still more often, from the ideas of the Legalists. As a writer and teacher he had very considerable influence in his time and up to the middle of the Han dynasty; this was represented, among others, by the work of his disciples, Han Fei and Li Ssu, both of them stalwarts of the Legalist School (see p. 41). Hsün Ch'ing's views have been described as containing certain materialist elements; this is probably derived from the fact that in his views Heaven no longer played a part in human affairs but was regarded as a natural phenomenon. Thus a case could be made to present Hsün Ch'ing as one of the earliest agnostics, if not atheists, in Chinese philosophy. In his views on society and man he differed sharply from Mencius in respect to the character of human nature, maintaining its initial evilness. According to him this originally bad nature could, and should, be transformed through education. It was this view of man's nature which contributed to the fact that Hsün Ch'ing's followers expounded Legalist views on the necessity for a strong government and severe punishments. The book containing his view, the *Hsün-tzu*, in 32 chapters, is a collection not of sayings like the Analects but of well-written and lucidly argued essays.

One of the most interesting of the Chinese philosophers of the Warring States period, the object of Mencius' polemics, was Yang Chu. His works have not survived except for a debatable fragment in a famous Taoist book, the *Lieh-tzu*, and his views are mostly known from the attacks on him by other writers, especially Mencius. His was a pessimistic and fatalist philosophy strongly opposed to the ideals of the Confucians. He mocked the ancient heroes, whom they made so much of, and was concerned primarily not with the fate of society but with that of the individual. He, or his school, is represented as advocating a hedonist selfishness combined with cynical despair. This well might be a reflection of the ever-growing crisis of the Warring States period. There is no trace of mysticism in his views but he is regarded, at the same time, by some authorities as the precursor of Taoism. It is perhaps quite possible that his real views were not as extreme as represented, in a parody form, by his enemies.

Taoism is the only school of the Eastern Chou period which survived, along with

Confucianism, the greater disaster of Ch'in rule (see pp. 45-50), and whose influence remained, though in vastly changed form, a vital factor in Chinese life for many centuries. The earliest work of the Taoist school is the *Tao te ching* ("The Way and Its Power") ascribed to Lao Tzu. It is highly problematic whether such a man ever existed; the name means simply the Old Master. According to the traditional version, he was supposed to be an older contemporary of Confucius; according to more modern research, he lived, if at all, in the 4th century, from which most authorities date the work. His biography in the history of Ssu-ma Ch'ien is a confused and contradictory account which has been aptly called by Waley "A confession that for the writing of such a biography no materials existed at all". Many legends were formed around the figure of Lao Tzu in Later Taoist writings (among them, his famous trip to the West), the main motive of which was to enhance the prestige of the Taoist creed.

The book itself—a short work of only somewhat over 5000 characters—is perhaps, along with the Analects, the most famous work in classical Chinese literature and the most often translated into Western languages. Its language is vague and difficult and thus the translations differ from each other quite radically, although they can be considered all sound philologically. It is possible that the vagueness of the language was deliberate.

The Taoism of the *Tao te ching* can be considered primarily as a philosophy of protest against the injustices and the disruption and corruption of contemporary society. The solution advocated amounts, in fact, to a withdrawal from society, to a contemplation of Nature; the aim of life should be to attain harmony with the Tao; the Tao here is not the way of Society, as defined in the Confucian creed, but is more probably the First Principle of the Universe or, as Needham puts it, the Order of Nature.

The most fundamental guide to life which is to be found in Lao Tzu's teaching is the principle of *wu wei*, which can be rendered either as "doing nothing", "passive achievements" or most probably as "doing what is natural". The return to primitivism is connected with an out and out opposition to government as such (i.e. to the feudal society of the times) with the concomitant belief that the less active a government is— the better a chance exists for human happiness. In this, Lao Tzu harked to a still more remote past than the Confucian, for his ideal is not the Golden Age of the Sage Kings but the primitive peasant community which existed still earlier. In dealing, as did all the Chou philosophers, with his vision of an ideal government, he paints the following picture of what the Sage would do to create the perfect society:

Given a small country with a few inhabitants, he could bring it about that though there should be among the people contrivancies requiring ten times, a hundred times less labour, they would not use them. He could bring it about that the people would be ready to lay down their lives and lay them down again in defence of their homes, rather than emigrate. There might still be boats and carriages, but no one would go in them; there might still be weapons of war but no one would drill with them. He could bring it about that the people should have no use for any form of writing save knotted ropes, should be contented with their food, pleased with their clothing, satisfied with their homes, should take pleasure in their rustic tasks. The next place might be so near at hand that one could hear the cocks crowing in it, the dogs barking, but the people would grow old and die without ever having been there.

Taoist ideas were developed still further by Chuang Chou (?369-?286). Very little is known about him but there seems to be no doubt that he was a historical person. The book ascribed to him, *Chuang-tzu*, is more than likely in part his work, with additions made to it by his school and, as is the case of so many classical works, with later interpolations. The work is one of great literary skill, witty and wise, containing parables and allegories both picturesque and marvellously effective; it is considered by many as the greatest work in Chinese literature.

On the whole, the basic approach to the problems of life is much the same as in the *Tao te ching*, but in the *Chuang-tzu* there is still less interest in questions relating to the proper ordering of government and society. It is considered by some authorities to be primarily a plea for individual freedom and in this respect shows an egotistic tendency which could well have been derived from the ideas of Yang Chu. There is much in the work which expresses Chuang Chou's emphasis on the relativity of all phenomena, both social and natural, and more elements of the mystic and fantastic than in Lao Tzu. There is, however, much that is controversial regarding the interpretation of this work and some authorities maintain that the mystic element has been stressed too much in most translations into European languages.

The mysticism of Taoism was not a barrier to its serving a useful role in the development of knowledge; for the knowledge which is attacked in the *Chuang-tzu* is the knowledge of the Confucians, pertaining only to society and not to nature. The Taoists' contemplation of nature was not a purely passive one; their interest in it led them to experimentation and thus made them, in a later period, the founders of alchemy, contributing in general much to the development of what was achieved in China in the field of early science. Simultaneously, Taoism became at a certain stage connected with the native popular, magic cults and with the search for immortality as well (this in turn was bound up with the interest in alchemy). It is more than likely this connection which resulted in the ultimate transformation of Taoism from a philosophy into a religious cult, ridden with superstition and the object of disdain to Chinese scholars. This development was partially a reaction against Confucianism, as well as a reflection of popular feeling; it also explains the role which later Taoism played in many peasant uprisings throughout Chinese history, for it became much more a plebeian religion than a creed for the upper classes.

Philosophical Taoism, forming a school which was more complete and coherent than any of the others in the Eastern Chou period, did have a great appeal to the intellectual elite. The withdrawal to a contemplation of nature, which was later often practised by many Chinese scholar-officials, did not imply the necessity of manual labour—for the recluse philosopher would still, most often, have his servants; a country estate could also well serve as a place of refuge. This was not a philosophy for the "common people", especially for peasants struggling to make a bare living. This explains partially why it was possible for members of the Chinese upper class throughout many centuries to be often both Confucianist and Taoist in their belief. They would be Confucianists while holding their official posts and Taoists when retired, whether by their own choice or not.

Taoism's negation of participation in an organized society is perhaps its most revealing feature, for this, in effect, was a rejection of feudalism, and therefore this philosophy could hardly be adapted as the official ideology of the ruling class, as Confucianism ultimately was. One of the indisputably great merits of Taoism, connected with its attitude to nature, lies in the very considerable effect and inspiration it provided for the development of Chinese culture, for its poetry and, especially, painting. It is here that the Taoist ideas have found perhaps their most perfect and beautiful embodiment.

The most serious rival to Confucianism in the 5th and 4th centuries B.C. was the school of Mo Ti—Mohism. The life of Mo Ti was in many respects similar to that of Confucius; he was also a wandering scholar and founder of a school of thought. His philosophy concerned itself, like that of Confucius, primarily with the problems of achieving an ideal society. The views of Mo Ti are contained in the book *Mo-tzu*, a work of 53 chapters, written in rather simple, even pedestrian prose. The approach, which has been called by some a materialist one, is basically a utilitarian evaluation of all social phenomena. Mo Ti's aim and vision were the enrichment of the country, the increase of population, the preservation of order and the assurance of the people's welfare. It is from the standpoint of utilitarianism that he opposed the extravagant rites, so dear to the Confucians, as wasteful. This is also the source of his opposition to the aggressive wars waged by the feudal princes which he castigated as wasteful, unbrotherly and murderous, thus condemning them on both utilitarian and moral grounds. Mo Ti's opposition to war was not a doctrine of pure pacifism, for he was at the same time an advocate of defensive warfare which would serve to make aggressive war impossible. His followers were renowned for their skill in the art of defence, especially fortification, and offered their services to all the states and rulers who needed them.

The principal doctrine in Mo Ti's philosophy was that of Universal Love which, if extended to all people and states on an equal basis, would eliminate the basic sources of social conflict and war. Mo Ti counterposed his concept of Universal Love to the moral virtues stressed by the Confucians and to their accentuation of the importance of family relations. While he also appealed partly to antiquity, going even further back to the legendary Hsia—which gave him complete liberty to interpret the views of the Ancient Sages as he saw fit—Mo Ti sought to justify his doctrines primarily by an appeal to reason. It is for this purpose that his followers, the Later Mohists, delved into logic and dialectics, where their contribution is of prime importance. In some respects this attempt to give the Mohist creed a rational and coherent foundation was successful and Mo Ti's work was continued by the Later Mohists whose views are also interesting for the study of the development of rudimentary science.

Mo Ti also made use of religious sanctions to bolster his doctrine—some authors see a resemblance between his ideas and those of Early Christianity—but in his concept of God and Heaven there is no element of immortality. He neither offered Heaven nor threatened with Hell, as FitzGerald has put it.

Mo Ti's disciples and followers formed a highly organized and strictly disciplined community in which absolute obedience to the leader of the sect prevailed. A succession to Mo Ti was maintained for a long period of time, until Mohism disappeared in the holocaust of the Ch'in reign. The reasons for this are far from clear; perhaps the utopianism, inherent in the views of this school, made it less adaptable to the needs of a feudal monarchy than the much more flexible creed of the Confucians. There was no place in Han society for this creed, especially for its views on war and on frugality, for its intrinsically humanitarian approach to life.

The Warring States period saw a proliferation of philosophical schools; of these perhaps the most important, apart from Taoism and Mohism, was that of the Legalists—the *Fa chia*. This was undoubtedly the most politically minded of all the schools, to the point where some authorities question whether it deserves the title of a philosophical school at all. While the Legalists were undoubtedly influenced in some of their views by the main schools—Confucianism, Mohism and Taoism—they were essentially the exponents of *Realpolitik* and the determined opponents of all other trends of philosophical and social thought. They had a distinct aversion to practically all manifestations of culture. Hence for them history, philosophy, the arts, as well as morality and ethics, were all superfluous and subversive.

The Legalist doctrine was the only one which had been actually put into practice in ancient China, as exemplified by the reforms of Shang Yang in the state of Ch'in (see above, p. 31). Their vision of an ideally organized society was one in which the people, deprived of course of any education, were not to engage in thinking or discussing affairs but obliged to show blind obedience to a powerful ruler. (The Legalists would have had not the slightest trouble in understanding Mussolini's *Credere, Obbedire*.) They regarded human nature as incorrigibly evil and selfish, and from this drew the conclusion that society could be ruled only by means of severe and detailed laws, envisaging cruel and harsh punishments. Their basic aim was to build the strongest possible military state and therefore only two issues were of importance to them—the maintenance of strong military forces and the development of agriculture, intimately bound up with the first. The ruling class was to be—and, in fact, was in the Ch'in state— a military bureaucracy of large landowners, to replace the hereditary clan aristocracy. It was thus the Legalists who provided the theoretical foundation, as well as concrete precepts, for the creation of the ruthless, rapacious absolutism of the Ch'in monarchy.

Shang Yang put these ideas into practice and his views are represented in the book *Shang chün shu* ("Book of Lord Shang"). This, in fact, was not written by him and is a work of the 3rd century B.C. but nevertheless, represents his ideas quite faithfully. The most complete and authentic exposition of the Legalist outlook—a synthesis of their views—is to be found in the *Han-fei-tzu*. This work is mostly from the pen of Han Fei (*ca.* 280-233 B.C.) who was a disciple of Hsün Ch'ing. However, he derived his views not only from the latter but also from Taoism. The ideals of antiquity were rejected by Han Fei with scornful scepticism. His approach to the problems of society was basically machiavellian; he stressed the importance of law and of the power of the ruler, as well as the need for the establishment of a proper system of punishments and rewards—a purely carrot-and-stick proposition.

Another prominent Legalist, known not so much by his works as by the way in which he put Legalist ideas into practice, was Li Ssu, the chief minister of the first Ch'in Emperor, also a disciple of Hsün Tzu. He logically proceeded from the Legalist antipathy towards other philosophical schools to an attempt to eradicate them entirely by the infamous process of the Burning of the Books.

While Legalism triumphed under the Ch'in, it also shared their fate and was disgraced by the excesses of this terroristic regime disappearing, as an organized school, after their downfall. However, many of the Legalist views survived throughout the entire period of Chinese feudalism, among them, the concept of the supremacy of one orthodox doctrine. It seems more than probable that many Legalist practices as revealed, for instance, in the attitude to and treatment of the people, also survived, although they were later camouflaged by a façade of Confucian morality and benevolence.

In the same period a school referred to as the *Ming chia* (School of Names) which has been rendered in English as the Logicians or Dialecticians, was also prominent. Unfortunately, almost no works of this school have survived, except for some fragments, contained mostly in the *Chuang tzu*. The best known representatives of this school were Hui Shih (*ca.* 365-310 B.C.), renowned for his famous Ten Paradoxes, and Kung-sun Lung (*ca.* 320-250 B.C.). Both of them, although differing completely in their approach, attempted to advance the development of logic and of dialectical thinking, to distinguish universal from concrete concepts, primarily by the employment of paradoxical propositions.

It is also in this age that the first early materialist views took their shape, although their sources probably reached back much further into the past. Two principal concepts were formulated; the first of these was the dualist theory regarding negative and positive principles as the primary source of all natural phenomena—the *yin-yang* theory, which later became also part and parcel of the Confucian world outlook. The second theory was that of the Five Elements (Wood, Metal, Fire, Water and Earth), which also was to serve as the key to the explanation of the workings of nature and was later interlocked intimately with human affairs, playing here the role of a supposedly determining factor. Tsou Yen (either *ca.* 350-270 or *ca.* 305-240) is credited with combining both above theories into one coherent scheme, which has been called by some the Naturalist School. Needham considers him the real founder of all Chinese scientific thought.

II. Literature

The Chou period, which saw the continuous development and progress of writing and the formation of basic literary genres, was of fundamental importance for the future. This pertained both to poetry and prose, of which the latter appeared in much greater quantity if not quality. Definite changes in style among the various periods have been established by scholars and by the end of this era one can ascertain that the literary language had already taken a stabilized shape.

In poetry, it is the *Shih ching*—the Classic or Book of Odes—one of the Five Classics of the Confucian Canon, which is the best known and most important work. It has been translated many times into various European languages. This is, in fact, the first anthology of Chinese poetry (305 poems) dating from the 10th to the 7th century B.C. The poems vary in nature from simple love songs and folk motifs to ritual hymns and paeans of a political nature. The majority of them were meant to be sung and were set to music; this, however, was already lost by the time of the Han dynasty.

According to Ssu-ma Ch'ien, the selection was supposedly made by Confucius himself; it is also said that some of the poems had been collected by various rulers because they purportedly reflected the sentiments of the people. Whatever the true origin of this anthology, the contents do provide an excellent picture of the social conditions of the time, and especially a realistic portrayal of peasant life.

This art form played a large role in Chinese cultural life from the very beginning, but there is a long gap before the appearance of any subsequent collection of poetry. The first was the *Ch'u tz'u* ("Elegies of Ch'u"). While the authorship of the Elegies is still a subject for debate, it seems almost undoubted that the *Li sao* ("The Lament") is the work of Ch'ü Yüan (?343-?280 B.C.), the most famous poet of ancient China, as well as the first one to be known by name. Ch'ü Yüan was supposedly a talented noble courtier in the southern state of Ch'u who was compelled by the intrigues of his rivals to quit the court and to go into exile. According to tradition, he committed suicide in despair over his own fate and that of his country, which was the object of constant attacks by Ch'in. The *Li sao*, a poem of 374 lines, is beautifully constructed, employing magnificent imagery, which reflects the distinct, rich culture of the Yangtse Valley, frowned upon by the Confucians of the North. It is undoubtedly autobiographical, though it is rather difficult to disentangle the facts from their legendary settings.

The prose of the Chou period is somewhat difficult to classify; if one were to use the word in an extended meaning, most of it could be called primarily historical, while containing many philosophical ideas as well. All of them show the influence of the philosophical schools of this era, but particularly that of Confucianism. This is, among others, also the result of the editing to which they were subjected in later periods, when Confucianism was already the dominant ideology. None of them survived in a completely original form and the question of their authenticity has given rise to an immense literature of exegesis, mainly Chinese but also Western.

The most important work of the early Chou period is the *Shu ching* ("The Book of History"), a collection of greatly varying historical source material; the speeches, proclamations and declarations of rulers. Much of this material is in the form of direct speech. The *Shu ching* has long been a special object of controversy as to its authenticity; a large part of it, which was for many centuries regarded as acceptable, was later proved to be a forgery of a much later date. Its language is by no means easy, for its lapidary conciseness renders it difficult to translate into European languages. It is also one of the Five Confucian Classics and of inestimable influence on the development of Chinese thought.

In addition to the *Shih ching* and *Shu ching* the Five Classics include the *I ching* ("The Book of Changes"), which is primarily devoted to the systems of divination based on the use of the eight trigrams and sixty-four hexagrams; the *Li chi* ("The Book of Rites"), which dates probably from the 2nd century B.C. and deals mostly with the matter of rites and ceremonies, and the *Ch'un ch'iu* already previously mentioned. A very considerable number of commentaries were composed in later times to the Five Classics and a number of these are considered a component part of the Confucian Canon.

The *Tso chuan* ("The Tso Commentary") is especially closely connected with the Spring and Autumn Annals. Traditionally, it is regarded as a commentary on this work, but in reality it is of completely independent origin. Its authorship was traditionally ascribed to a certain Tso Ch'iu-ming, supposedly a disciple of Confucius. In fact, it dates from a later period, probably the end of the 4th or the beginning of the 3rd century B.C. It covers a somewhat longer chronological period than the *Ch'un ch'iu*— the years 722-468. The *Tso chuan* is actually the main historical source for this era and the most important historical text of the entire Chou period. It is based primarily on the chronicles of the states of Ch'in and Ch'u, since lost, but also includes some less reliable material, more than likely drawn from historical romances which were already in existence during the period of its compilation. Its literary style is vivid and it provides a great wealth of detail, especially when contrasted with the dreary Spring and Autumn Annals. While it occasionally engages in Confucian moralizing, it does provide a fascinating picture of the period though this is, of course, restricted solely to the life of the ruling nobility. It reveals also the great influence of the *Book of History* and the *Book of Odes* which are quoted many times by the personages appearing in it.

Another work which deals with the same period and contains material similar to that found in the *Tso chuan* is the *Kuo yü* ("Conversations from the States"). This is a compilation of selected historical anecdotes and speeches, often given in a condensed form. It is considered much less reliable than the *Tso chuan* because it is supposed to contain even more material derived from historical romances. It is also more stylized and more obviously didactic but, nevertheless, contains many interesting passages.

The *Chan kuo ts'e* ("The Intrigues of the Warring States") comes from the period to which it has given the name. It is still less of a historical work than the two mentioned above and is of rather dubious value as a historical source. It is more a collection of humorous, pungent anecdotes, but its stories of clever, often shamelessly cynical plots and schemes do give a faithful picture of this terrible, brutal period.

Mention should also be made of the "Bamboo Annals", a record of the State of Wei. The history of this work is interesting in itself; it was buried in 295 B.C. in the tomb of a Wei prince and discovered by a robber in the years A.D. 279-281. His pilfering of the tomb resulted in the burning of a part of the Annals which he used as a torch, and disarranging of the others. A number of other works were found in the tomb as well. Later on the text of the Annals was lost once more and the present version is a reconstruction from quotations and the subject of much controversy. It is similar in style to the Spring and Autumn Annals and its terseness thus also limits, to some degree, its usefulness as a historical source.

PART III

The Unification of China and the Establishment of a Centralized Monarchy

CHAPTER 5

The Unification of China

I. The Ch'in Road to Empire

The years 250-221 B.C. saw the final achievement of the long-established aims of the rulers of Ch'in; a temporary abeyance of further aggression was brought about by the successive deaths within a short period of a number of the rulers, but this came to an end with the accession to the throne of Duke Cheng (246 B.C.).

It is in this period that Lü Pu-wei, a rich merchant, also rose to power, becoming the chief minister of Ch'in, the first commoner and only merchant to achieve such prominence. (An interesting philosophical compendium, the *Lü-shih ch'un ch'iu*, was compiled under his patronage.) Tradition made Lü Pu-wei the real father of Duke Cheng, the result of a wily scheme. While Lü Pu-wei was in power, Ch'in did not launch any further wars against the other states; the end of his influence came in 237 B.C., when he was exiled and then committed suicide two years later. He was succeeded by a group of Legalist ministers, the most important of whom was Li Ssu, a student of Hsün Ch'ing. He was the real creator of the policies of Ch'in; an unscrupulous and simultaneously brilliant man, he was also allegedly responsible for the death of his classmate and fellow student—Han Fei.

Under the Legalist ministers the campaigns against the other states were begun once more. The Ch'in prepared themselves for warfare very thoroughly, exerting constant pressure on their enemies and utilizing their superiority in the waging of war, which lay, among others, in their use of cavalry. The complete ruthlessness which had become characteristic of the Ch'in in the previous century remained their dominant trait; considerable use was also made of their favourite policy of mass terror. The results were quickly forthcoming. Thus, in 249 the small, pathetic remnant of Chou was destroyed, the other states met their fate in turn—in 230 Han, 228 Chao, 225 Wei, 223 Ch'u, 222 Yen and 221 Ch'i. Ch'in was now the undisputed master of all of China. It is not accidental

45

Map 7. The Ch'in Empire

that the name for the country in most European and Asiatic languages is derived from the name Ch'in.

The victory of Ch'in was the result not only of its military and political superiority but also of the inability of its opponents to combine for common defensive action against the Ch'in. The Ch'in rulers had always played on the division among the other states with great skill. The famous Chinese parable of the quarreling mussel and the oyster-catcher and the fisherman who caught them both has been applied quite correctly to the history of this period.

The conquest of the entire country posed the very great problems of how the new state was to be organized. The decision, logically enough, was made not to follow the old Chou pattern of distributing fiefs to the family of the ruler and to his followers, but to apply the administrative system, which had already been in existence in Ch'in, to the entire country. Thus thirty-six commanderies (*chün*) (with the conquest of the South this number was later raised to forty-two) were established, these being divided in turn into districts (*hsien*). Each commandery was to be ruled by a military governor as well as a civilian one, while a third official was established as supervisor. This system of three rival officials had the aim of preventing any local official from becoming too strong. An elaborate bureaucratic system of non-hereditary officials was established, headed by the Emperor himself as an autocratic ruler, and thus the pattern was formed of a centralized, absolute, feudal monarchy which was to last China for over 2000 years. Cheng, the King of Ch'in, now declared himself the First Emperor of the Ch'in —Shih Huang-ti; in this title he combined the words *huang* and *ti* used for the legendary rulers of China. He was to be the First Emperor and his successors for 10,000 generations were to continue the rule of the House of Ch'in.

It was not only the administrative system of Ch'in that was extended to all China but the other features of its social organization as well. Thus the principle of private land ownership was also now spread to the entire country, eliminating the remnants both of ownership of the clan aristocracy as well as the holdings of the village commune. The class which benefited from this was primarily composed of the Ch'in new military bureaucracy.

The entire country was disarmed in order to strengthen and safeguard the newly established government. The arms collected were melted down and the metal used to cast bells and huge statues. Some 120,000 families of the old hereditary aristocracy were allegedly deported from the conquered states to Shensi and settled around the Ch'in capital of Hsien-yang (to the north-west of Sian). This was a great blow to the old aristocracy, depriving it of the main basis of its strength, its land.

A whole series of measures of unification and standardization were also undertaken. Weights and measures as well as coinage were standardized—the cash being made universal at this time. The length of axles of carts and carriages was also set. (The problem arose from the ruts formed on country roads in the loess lands and the need for increased efficiency of transport.) A great road-building programme, with principal trunk roads running from the capital to the main areas of the empire, was launched, both for military purposes and to facilitate the transportation of food to the capital. The policy of standardization also affected the written scripts which up to this time had developed differently in the various parts of the country. The undertaking of this reform is ascribed to Li Ssu himself, and it is at this time that the so-called "small seal" type of script was introduced.

Shih Huang launched a vast building programme, especially in his capital, Hsien-yang; here a huge palace was constructed (completed in 212 B.C.) which was supposed to measure 2500 feet east to west and 500 feet south to north. Its main audience hall was allegedly able to contain 10,000 people. The Emperor also was credited with having 270 other residences, all located within a radius of 60 miles from the capital. During his lifetime the construction of a vast mausoleum was begun. It was in the vicinity of this mausoleum that the fascinating discovery of numerous life-sized statues of Ch'in warriors was made in 1975. In all these projects an immense quantity of forced labour— Ssu-ma Ch'ien gives the figure of 700,000—was employed.

Perhaps the most famous, or rather infamous, measure of the reign, which was also bound up with the consolidation of power, was the persecution of all the philosophical schools and their representatives, disapproved of by the Legalists. In 213 Li Ssu presented a memorial in which he asserted that the scholars were "studying the past only to defame the present and stir up the people" and proposed that:

> All the historic chronicles of the states, excepting that of Ch'in, be burned; all men who possess the *Shu*, the *Shih* and the works of the Hundred Schools must take them all to the magistrates to be burned. Those who dare to discuss and comment on the *Shu* and the *Shih* shall be put to death; those who praise ancient institutions to decry the present regime shall be exterminated with all the members of their families... The only books to be permitted are those pertaining to medicine, divination, agriculture and forestry.

The proposal was approved by the Emperor and carried into effect. It should be noted that copies of all the proscribed books were kept in the Imperial Library and that some selected scholars were allowed to possess them. But the Imperial Library was completely destroyed during the downfall of the Ch'in.

The result of the above policy was an immeasurable loss to the culture of ancient China as the majority of the works were lost forever. The persecution of the scholars led to the death of at least 460 who were executed in the capital, perhaps being buried alive. All the later Confucian historians condemned Shih Huang with particular vehemence for this barbarous act. Actually the works of the Confucian school survived much better than most of the others, perhaps because the Confucians possessed the greatest number of scholars who remembered the texts and were thus able to reconstruct them later after the downfall of the Ch'in. The destruction of the books was rendered easier by the fact that they were written mostly on slips of wood and thus were bulky and difficult to conceal.

The new Ch'in empire concentrated not only on internal consolidation but on territorial expansion as well. In the North-west, a series of campaigns were launched against the nomadic tribes of the Hsiung-nu (perhaps the sames as the Huns of European experience) who had recently organized themselves into a tribal confederation. The result was to drive the Hsiung-nu out of the area south of the great bend of the Yellow River—the semi-desert of the Ordos. This was accomplished by Meng T'ien, one of the ablest of the Ch'in generals, with an army of supposedly 300,000. In the area thus conquered new towns were built and forty-four districts or *hsien* established and colonized. It is in connection with these campaigns that another famous undertaking was launched—the construction of the Great Wall. This was, in fact, primarily the joining up and extension of walls already in existence. Its ultimate result was the creation of a wall reaching from Kansu to the sea, a length of 1400 miles. The wall, called by some the greatest feat of engineering in ancient China, was built both by the army of Meng T'ien and masses of forced and convict labour; there was never a lack of convicts in the Ch'in empire—they were sent up to the wall by the tens of thousands and perished there in numbers almost as large. The Great Wall did partially serve as a barrier against nomad invasion, but it also played another role—as pointed out by Lattimore—that of separating the Chinese agricultural population from the nomadic tribes, thus preventing them from escaping to a different type of life. The Wall which exists at present follows the line of the Ch'in period only in some areas and dates mostly from the Ming Period.

The main direction of territorial expansion was, however, not the north-west but the south. It is here that a Ch'in army of purportedly 500,000 launched an attack against the state of Nan-yüeh (inhabited by a non-Chinese people, more than probably related to the Vietnamese). The result of the campaigns, which lasted from 221 to 214, was the conquest of Fukien, Kwantung and Kwangsi as well as the north of present-day Vietnam. This conquest involved very heavy losses for the Ch'in troops both as a result of the resistance which they encountered and the diseases to which they succumbed. A policy of mass colonization of the newly conquered areas, now organized into four new commanderies, was also begun and supposedly over half a million men were sent down to the south.

In the achievement of all that has been mentioned above, the terroristic methods of government, which had been employed still earlier in Ch'in itself, were now even more marked when applied to all of China. The wars and the building programme of the First Emperor ruined the economy and the burden of taxes and forced labour to be borne by the peasantry increased manifold—according to Ssu-ma Ch'ien twenty to thirty times. This soon gave rise to ever-greater disaffection in the entire country and to a profound crisis which was marked even before the end of Shih Huang's reign. The benefits of unification, primarily the ending of warfare among the states, where now much outweighed by the effects of the oppression and terror of Ch'in rule.

Shih Huang died in 210, during one of the many trips that he had taken around his empire. He was 50 years of age and had been a king for twenty-five years and an emperor for twelve. A conspiracy was formed by Li Ssu, Chao Kao (the chief eunuch) and the Emperor's younger son, Hu-hai, to conceal the ruler's death. As the cortege travelled to the capital, a cart of rancid salt fish accompanied the imperial carriage to disguise the smell of the decomposing corpse. The Emperor in his last will had ordered his heir and eldest son, Fu-su, to proceed to the capital to prepare his burial; for his opposition to Shih Huang's policy towards the scholars, Fu-su had been exiled earlier to the North-west and assigned to Meng Tien's army. The conspirators now forged a new will and sent a letter purportedly from the Emperor, ordering Fu-su and Meng T'ien to commit suicide. The Emperor's son complied at once, the general, the best of the Ch'in military, only later on while in prison. Thus the throne was assumed by Hu-hai as Erh-shih Huang-ti—the Second Emperor—but the real power was in the hands of the eunuch.

Shih Huang was buried in his fantastically elaborate and ornate mausoleum; many of his concubines also followed him to his grave. The workers who placed his coffin and treasures therein were buried alive to preserve the secret of the entrance.

The personality of Shih Huang is the subject of much controversy. Some European historians are pleased to depict him as a very great man; thus Grousset presents him as the Chinese Caesar, one of the greatest geniuses in world history, while Granet also sings his praises. There is little evidence to substantiate this. He was an industrious man—supposedly he worked his way through 120 pounds of documents a day—but more than likely of average ability and it was his ministers, particularly Li Ssu, who were the real masters of the country and creators of Ch'in policy. Shih Huang was not only cruel but also credulous, constantly engaged in a search for an elixir of immortality, and in this became the dupe of many charlatans. He was undoubtedly a megalomaniac, as indicated, among others, by his title, as well as by his palaces. His dynasty of 10,000 generations lasted merely four years after his death. This was by no means only because his successors were less able, but because the empire he had built was so thoroughly oppressive and hateful to the entire people.

Nonetheless, in spite of the short span, the significance of the Ch'in empire was very great, inasmuch as in introducing the centralized absolute monarchy it had carried out a tremendous social upheaval. In some ways the Ch'in had realized the dream of many generations of earlier Chinese thinkers, of unifying all the area "within the four seas"; however, the reality turned out to be quite different from what was envisaged in the dream. The dynasty fell, but the despotic monarchy remained as the longest-lasting political institution in world history.

II. The Fall of the Ch'in

The short rule of Erh-shih was even more oppressive and cruel than that of his father. Following the policy advocated by Chao Kao, members of the royal family were persecuted, many of the imperial princes killed and the same fate met many of the most faithful officials of the Ch'in. Li Ssu also soon fell victim to the intrigues of his eunuch rival and was executed in 208. An atmosphere of total terror prevailed at the Ch'in court in which not a single man felt safe.

In 209 B.C. the first rebellion against Ch'in rule took place which can be regarded simultaneously as the first of the great peasant uprisings that form one of the dominant motifs of Chinese history. In Anhwei, a detachment of 900 recruits was delayed by a storm from reaching an appointed place. Knowing that a death penalty awaited them for such a delay, they rebelled. Led by Ch'en Sheng and Wu Kuang, both peasants, they successfully spread the revolt to a large part of China and were joined by many thousands of peasants, as well as by members of the old aristocracy. In a short time the armies of the insurgents numbered well over 100,000 and even threatened the Ch'in capital itself. The movement was, however, disorganized, its aims unclear and bitter rivalries ensued among its various leaders. Within six months its armies were shattered by the Ch'in general Chang Han. The defeat of the initial insurgents did not improve the position of the Ch'in, for revolts were simultaneously launched by other individuals from various social classes against Ch'in rule, and in a short time all of East and Central China was up in arms. A situation of complete chaos was created in which all the former states, which had been liquidated by Ch'in, were also temporarily restored.

The rule of the Ch'in was further undermined by the dominance of the eunuch Chao Kao. In 207 B.C. he forced Erh-shih to commit suicide and replaced him on the throne by Tzu-ying, the son of Fu-su. He made of him, however, not an emperor, but the King of Ch'in—a reflection of the fact that the empire had already disintegrated. Very shortly, Tzu-ying killed the eunuch and after only 46 days on the throne he himself surrendered to Liu Pang, one of the principal leaders of the anti-Ch'in rebellion.

The insurgent forces were led by various adventurers, two of whom were truly outstanding. One was Liu Pang, a peasant from Kiangsu, who had been a petty official in his youth. Persistent, shrewd, prudent, an excellent judge of men, Liu Pang was a superb politician. He became an opponent of the Ch'in because while conveying a group of convicts some of them escaped. Fearing punishment—death, of course, under the draconian but self-defeating laws of the Ch'in—he freed the remainder and became an outlaw with a part of the liberated convicts. Later on, already at the head of a thousand men, he captured P'ei, the main city of his native district, and thus became one of the main rebel leaders.

The other was Hsiang Yü, who came from an old aristocratic family of the state of Ch'u. Very tall and strong, a poet and a polished gentleman, extraordinarily brave, arrogant and cruel, Hsiang Yü was in politics no match for the peasant Liu Pang. He rose to become the supreme commander of the army of the restored state of Ch'u, the main force of the rebels.

In 207 B.C. the insurgent armies struggled successfully against the Ch'in. Hsiang Yü defeated the main Ch'in army under Chang Han; after surrender, the entire force joined him, only to be treacherously massacred later on. In the meantime, Liu Pang and his forces invaded Ch'in and entered the capital, where he accepted the surrender of Tzu-ying. Liu Pang maintained strict discipline in his army and pursued a policy of great moderation towards the Ch'in population. He abolished the severe laws of the Ch'in and was therefore greeted with enthusiasm by the people. He then retired from the capital without either looting it or massacring the inhabitants. Later, the much stronger forces of Hsiang Yü also entered Ch'in, for the control of this key strategic area was of vital importance. When, however, Hsiang Yü came to Hsien-yang, he killed Tzu-ying and most of the Ch'in royal family, looted all the treasures of the Ch'in and burned all the palaces. It was at this time that the first confrontation of the main contenders for power, Liu Pang and Hsiang Yü, took place; due to his much weaker position (he had allegedly only 100,000 soldiers against the 400,000 of his opponent), Liu Pang compromised and accepted the title of the King of Han (which meant a rule over the Han River area, as well as over Pa and Shu, i.e. Eastern and Central Szechuan), although he should have received, according to a previous agreement, control over the entire state of Ch'in. Hsiang Yü departed with his forces to the East, to rule over most of China, as by far the strongest of all the newly established princes.

The compromise was of short duration and then there ensued a struggle for the mastery of all China between these two contenders which lasted for almost five years. It is known in Chinese history as the struggle between Han and Ch'u and it ended in the defeat and suicide of Hsiang Yü. This occurred in spite of the fact Hsiang Yü was by far the better general and Liu Pang was often defeated by him. The latter was much the abler politician and gained considerable support by his policy towards the peasants (granting them land) and towards his own army (freedom from taxes). The story of the conflict of these two rivals is one of the most dramatic in all of Chinese history and is superbly recounted by Ssu-ma Ch'ien.

After his victory over Hsiang Yü in 202 B.C. Liu Pang's generals offered him the title Emperor. As etiquette—of which he knew little at the time—required, he refused three times and then accepted, thus laying the foundation of the Han dynasty, which was to last for 400 years. The date customarily given for the beginning of the dynasty is 206 B.C., the year in which Liu Pang became the King of Han, whence the name of the dynasty.

The result of the devastating series of rebellions and wars was thus not the restoration of the situation which had existed before the conquest of China by Ch'in but the continuation of a unified, absolute monarchy, although it differed considerably from the Ch'in in its form, as we shall see later. Of the many reasons for this, the principal one perhaps was that the old states had been destroyed by Ch'in too thoroughly to make an effective restoration possible. The social changes which had taken place during this period, especially the practical disappearance of the old hereditary aristocracy wiped out in these struggles, also affected the character of the new monarchy. It is thus, in many respects, a quite new alignment of social forces which is to be found engaged in the process of the building of the Han monarchy.

CHAPTER 6

Western Han

I. The Establishment of the Han Dynasty

At the end of the war between Han and Ch'u the condition of China was deplorable indeed. Remnants of the armies were still scattered throughout the country, the cities had been looted and plundered, the dams and granaries damaged; total chaos reigned. The population had suffered great losses and agricultural production was disastrously low. Thus, the main problem which faced the new ruler, Emperor Kao, as Liu Pang was now called (though he is more often referred to by his posthumous temple name of Kao-tsu), was the restoration of order and the economy.

One of his first measures was a far-reaching demobilization of his army accompanied by a resettlement of the soldiers on the land. Depending on where they settled, the soldiers were freed from taxes for six or twelve years. Owners of the land who had abandoned it during the wars were now encouraged to return, while all persons who had been forced to sell themselves into slavery were set free.

A well-known illustration of the conditions which prevailed is the story that the Emperor could not find four horses of the same colour to draw his carriage; a horse then cost the fantastic sum of 300 pounds of gold, while 120 pounds of rice was worth a pound of gold. Although the later military campaigns were something of a handicap, the subsequent period did see a great recovery of the economy. In this, the lenient policy towards the peasantry was of prime importance; in 197 B.C. the land tax had been set at one-fifteenth of the harvest, much lower than during the Ch'in (it was later lowered still further to one-thirtieth). The poll tax was likewise set at the relatively low figure of 120 cash, later reduced to 40. There was also considerably less demand on the peasantry for forced labour in the early years of Han rule.

Thus, in the first sixty to seventy years of the Han monarchy agricultural production increased rapidly, the fallow lands were put under cultivation and considerable progress was made on the road forward to that intensiveness of agriculture which was to become its most significant characteristic. This growth of the agrarian economy also led to a steady rise in the population, which by the end of the 1st century B.C. already reached a figure of from 50 to 60 million. It was unevenly distributed, with the main concentration in the North and North-west, whereas Central and especially South China were at this time still rather sparsely inhabited. A very important role in this development of agriculture was played by improved technique, the most significant of which was the much greater use of iron implements, resulting from enlarged iron production—or possibly bringing this increase in iron production into being. Bronze was still used throughout some of the Han period for weapons, but later on its main employment was for coinage. A very considerable expansion of irrigation and of the

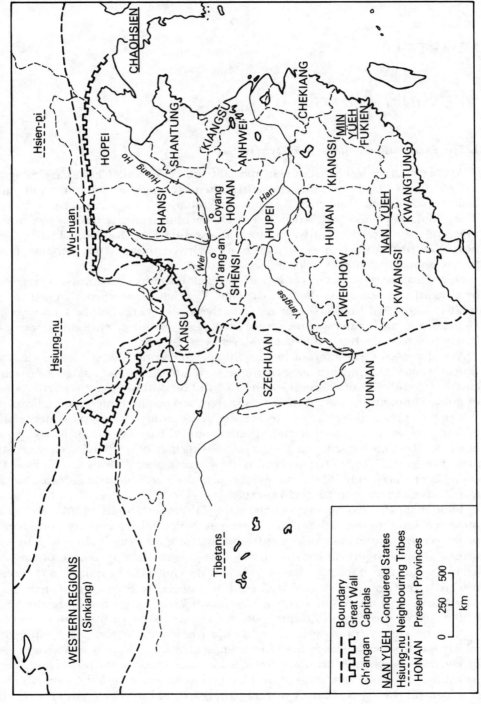

Map 8. The Han Empire, ca. 100 B.C.

CHAOHSIEN

Hsien-pi

HOPEI

Huang Ho

SHANTUNG

KIANGSU

ANHWEI

CHEKIANG

MIN YÜEH

FUKIEN

KIANGSI

Han

Loyang

HONAN

HUNAN

KWANGTUNG

Wu-huan

SHANSI

Wei

Ch'ang-an

SHENSI

HUPEI

KWEICHOW

NAN YÜEH

Yangtse

KWANGSI

Hsiung-nu

KANSU

SZECHUAN

YUNNAN

Tibetans

WESTERN REGIONS
(Sinkiang)

Boundary
Great Wall
Ch'angan   Capitals

NAN YÜEH   Conquered States
Hsiung-nu   Neighbouring Tribes
HONAN   Present Provinces

0   250   500
km

canal network also took place.

The Han period witnessed much development in the crafts, especially in textiles which were both the major domestic industry of the peasantry and a major state manufacture; Han textiles were already noted for their very high quality. Mining and salt production also increased. All of this development naturally led to a growth of domestic and, later, foreign trade and the increase in the size and significance of the towns. Definite progress was made in the direction of a money economy but the extent to which this was true should not be exaggerated for the greater part of the country was still tied to the practically self-sufficient natural economy of the small village community.

In establishing his rule Kao-tsu maintained most of the basic features of the Ch'in administration, while alleviating much of the Ch'in severity. His political cunning led him to depart from Ch'in practice, however, in one very important respect. Being convinced that the Ch'in had fallen due to a lack of faithful supporters, he distributed fiefs to his principal generals and followers with the titles of king (*wang*) and marquis (*hou*). Thus, the country was, in fact, divided into two areas, of which one remained under the direct rule of the central government and the other under the sway of the kings, though these were never allowed to become truly independent of the central authority. Very soon Kao-tsu deprived most of his closest generals, to whom he owed his victory, of both their kingdoms and their lives. Later he followed a policy of granting kingdoms only to the members of his own clan, the Liu. This cynical policy was perhaps due also to the fact that he did not want to be reminded of his own past by those who had once been his equals; although, on the other hand, some of those who had joined him at the very beginning of his career, his co-villagers, did preserve their high positions to the very end.

Kao-tsu ultimately made Ch'ang-an his capital; although he would have preferred to remain in his native East, he appreciated the strategic value of Shensi from which "one could hold the Empire by the throat", as one of his advisers had put it. The kingdoms created by him did prove to be a source of danger to the central government, in spite of the fact that the rulers were always under a considerable amount of control and vigilance by the central government. The most important struggle in this connection occurred, however, much later, when in 154 B.C. a revolt of seven of the kings against the Empire took place. This was successfully put down and the same policy of curtailing the power of the kings continued steadily. The most astute method applied was the setting aside of the heretofore existing rule of primogeniture (127 B.C.). The imperial councillor Chu-fu Yen thus formulated this method: "The princes all have sons by the dozens—they should be allowed, as an imperial favour, to divide their territory among all the sons, and all of these should be able to receive a title as well." The result was most favourable and the problem was solved, by this and other means.

II. The Nature of Han Society and State

The elimination of the old hereditary aristocracy during the period of the Ch'in and the wars which followed, as well as of the Ch'in aristocracy during these wars, led to significant changes in the class structure. A new class of landowners arose, most of these being not of noble descent but coming from the ranks of the followers of Kao-tsu. From the beginning of the Han certain basic features of Chinese feudalism were already present which, in fact, remain unchanged up to 1949. The most important of these was the existence of a class of large landowners, possessing great landed estates which they farmed either by the use of hired labour or by employing tenant farmers. A probable correlation exists in this respect; the absentee landowner would be more likely to let his land out to tenant farmers, while an active landowner would have more tendency to employ hired labour. The great bulk of the rural population, and thereby of the population of the country as a whole, was composed of small peasant landholders. The level of life of the peasantry remained throughout the Han period close to a marginal existence. The peasants were the object of constant exploitation, not only by the landlords and usurers but also by the state. They were subject to forced labour and the *corvee* system (usually one month a year); the latter meant employment on a large scale on public works of all kinds, the most important being the maintenance of the canal and irrigation system, flood control and transport of staples. They were also the primary source of manpower for the army and had to be available for military service from the age of 23 to 50. The peasantry was also the financial backbone of the state; it was the land tax paid by them which constituted the main source of the government's income.

Slavery in the Han period, though there was some increase in the earlier years, never played a role of any significance in the economy. It has been estimated that the number of slaves never exceeded 1 per cent of the population (this by the best authority on the subject, Wilbur). Slaves were primarily employed in domestic service although a number of them, difficult to determine, were also used in the crafts and in mining. There is no evidence to show that slavery was ever employed to any appreciable degree in agriculture. Two basic reasons may account, among others, for the fact that slavery did not develop in the Han period as well, in contrast to its rapid development in the Mediterranean area in the same era. Due to the availability of considerable quantities of cheap peasant labour, both for agriculture and *corvée*, slavery was economically unnecessary. Secondly, the intensive nature of Chinese agriculture, already marked in this period, rendered the use of slave labour in this, the most important domain of the economy, impracticable.

The class of landowners has been characterized by some Western and Chinese historians as the gentry, this term being the closest rendition of the Chinese *shen-shih*. When applied to China the word has a somewhat different meaning than its European sense; the Chinese gentry had a two-fold nature—it was not only a class of landowners but also the same social group from which the government bureaucracy was recruited. It was, thus, a ruling class both economically and politically, remaining basically a closed caste with differences within itself, depending on the political and economic strength of the given family. While considerable changes in the composition of the gentry did take place over the centuries, it is nevertheless this class which ruled the country for the entire period of Chinese feudalism. The gentry families, usually quite large in size, were often divided, with one branch residing in the capital and holding down official positions while another would remain in the countryside to oversee the family's landed estates. This made for considerable flexibility and enabled the families to survive for many generations, regardless of the fluctuations of political fate.

The Han monarchy was, in theory, as absolutist as the Ch'in, with a completely untrammelled rule by the Son of Heaven, isolated in his splendid palaces. In practice, the rule was usually exercised to a considerable degree by the chief ministers but this, in turn, depended largely on the personality of the ruler. He could, and sometimes did, rule by himself in a completely despotic fashion. The Han quickly expanded their government bureaucracy to elaborate proportions. By the 1st century B.C. there were around 130,000 officials, though this was, perhaps, not too great a figure when compared with the size of the population. In the early Han period the officials were chosen on the basis of recommendation, with education being an indispensable prerequisite. The selection by means of the examination system came into being in the 2nd century B.C. The main part of the bureaucracy was in the capital and dealt with the problems of the imperial government itself. This, in the Han era, was still largely personal and somewhat elementary in form, although the basic structure, later developed further under the T'ang, was already present. Thus the three highest official posts as well as the nine ministries already existed. While the central government had the decisive voice in all fields, the provincial governments, a replica of the central government on a smaller scale, were allowed considerable freedom in administering their own areas; this was partly due to the difficulties of communication in this immense country. One result of this was that a crisis of the central government did not necessarily signify an automatic crisis in the provinces. Reischauer put it thus: "So long as tax and *corvée* labour schedules were met and all subversive activities were avoided, the people were usually free to administer their own village affairs and carry out their own customary justice as they saw fit. The government thus was a relatively small, highly centralized body that floated on a sea of isolated peasant communities."

During the Han period the control of the government became, to an ever-increasing degree, the object of struggle between various cliques of gentry families. The issue at stake was particularly the power to appoint officials. Another factor of importance was the role of the empresses, especially when ruling as dowagers and regents for a minor emperor. In such circumstances the relatives of the empress would tend to become a powerful clique and a rival to the imperial family itself. One further factor was the increasing role played by the eunuchs; this is a most interesting problem, inasmuch as the eunuchs, mostly of plebeian origin, are invariably presented in traditional Chinese history as the greatest evil. It should be noted, however, that such accounts were always written by their main enemies, the scholar-officials. It seems clear that often the eunuchs were used as an instrument by the Emperor in his struggle against the cliques of officials and that their rise to power was the result of this. In the later period of the Han dynasty the emperors often became only puppets in the hands of rival cliques, either of officials or eunuchs, to be made and removed by these.

III. Early Han Confucianism

For establishing his government Kao-tsu felt the need of experienced administrators; it was impossible for him to turn to the Legalists, inasmuch as they had been thoroughly discredited by their association with the Ch'in, and thus, in spite of his own great contempt for scholars, he was forced to turn to the Confucianists for assistance. The problem is well illustrated by his famous talk with his chamberlain, Lu Chia, who had already performed valuable services for him in bringing the kingdom of Nan-yüeh, which had become independent after the fall of the Ch'in, to acknowledge itself as a vassal of the Han.

Lu Chia constantly quoted the "Odes and the Annals" (*Shih ching* and *Shu ching*) to the Emperor, who ended by becoming exasperated, "I conquered the empire on horseback", he cried, "what is the good of these Annals and Odes?" Lu Chia replied, "That is true, but it is *not* on horseback that you will be able to govern it. The emperors T'ang and Wu got it by violence, but governed it following the people's will. War and peace are two aspects of an eternal art...if the Ch'in, having become masters of the empire, had ruled it in humanity and righteousness, if they had imitated the ancient sages, you would not have got it." The Emperor changed colour, and said, "Show me then what it was that lost the empire for the Ch'in, and how it was I got it, and what it was that won or lost kingdoms of old." So Lu Chia wrote a book dealing generally with the cause of the rise and fall of states, in 12 chapters, which he read one after the other to the Emperor, who never failed to praise them.

It was also to another Confucianist, Shu-sun T'ung, that Kao-tsu turned to establish a new imperial ritual for his court. The man did the job so well that, after the new ceremonies had been completed, the Emperor said, "Now I finally understand what imperial majesty is."

The Confucianism of the early Han had, by this time, relatively little in common with the ethical teachings of Confucius and Mencius. It was rather a synthesis of the remnants of the classical philosophical schools and the *yin-yang* and Five Elements theories, with the latter being quite prominent. It did carry over to a new age and society some of the customs of ancient China and, in time, the ethical ideas were stressed to a greater degree but were to serve a different purpose than that for which they had been intended.

The triumph of Confucianism in the Han era was a long process. The edict against Confucian literature was repealed in 191 B.C. and as much of this literature as possible was reconstructed. The Confucianists succeeded in occupying the top positions in the bureaucracy and in gaining control of the education of the ruling class. Thus when an Imperial University was established in 124 B.C. (it had fifty students at the beginning but already around 3000 a century later) its curriculum was based on the study of the Confucian Canon and its graduates assumed official posts. Knowledge of the Confucian classics became an indispensable element for admission into bureaucracy. In this drawn-out process Confucianism became increasingly not only the sole orthodox ideology but it was also well on its way to becoming a state cult.

The Confucian ideas regarding government can be seen in the following speech of one of their most prominent representatives, Tung Chung-shu (179-104 B.C.), made to Emperor Wu shortly after his accession to the throne:

A ruler must start by rectifying himself; from this he can proceed to rectify his court, his officials, his people and his country. When everything is perfectly regulated, when evil disappears, then the *yin* and the *yang* will be in perfect equilibrium; the wind and the rain will come at a proper time and all beings will live and multiply in peace. The apogee of perfection of government will be achieved.

Here is another example from a speech of an equally prominent Confucianist of this same period, Kung-sun Hung (d. 121 B.C.):

When the people prosper they will not revolt; when they are treated reasonably, they do not transgress; when treated politely, they are also polite. When the people are loved they will also love; when they are shown affection, they will obey. When spoken to softly, they will be easily managed. If treated benevolently, the people will unite in its heart with the ruler...and thus harmony will be achieved.

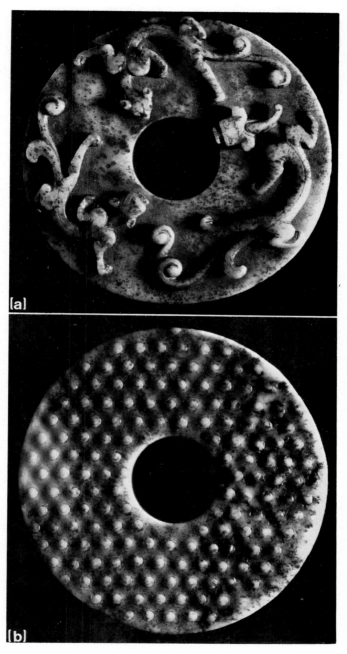

Fig. 10(a&b).   Jade disk, Eastern Chou or Han. (Author's collection.)

Fig. 11.   Silk brocade, Western Han. (*Ch'ang-sha Ma-wang-tui i-hao Han mu fa-chüeh chien-pao.*
Ch'angsha, 1972, pl. 4/1.)

Fig. 12.   Lacquer dishes, Western Han. (*Ch'ang-sha Ma-wang-tui . . .* , *op. cit.*, pl. 8/3.)

Fig. 13. Silk flag (fragment), Western Han. (*Ch'ang-sha Ma-wang-tui* . . . , *op. cit.*, p. 2.)

Fig. 14. Incense burner. Bronze inlaid with gold, Western Han. (*Hsin Chung-kuo* . . . , *op. cit.*, pl. 98.)

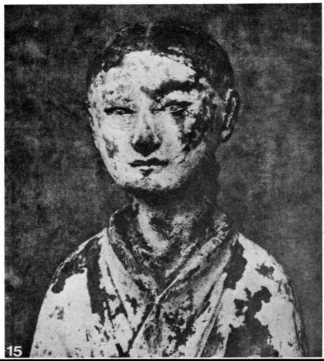

Fig. 15.   Ceramic figure, Eastern Han (?). (*Wei-ta-ti i-shu chuan-tung-tu*. Shanghai, 1955, vol. I, pl. 2/IX.)

Fig. 16.   Bronze horse, Eastern Han. (*Hsin Chung-kuo* . . . , *op. cit.*, pl. 110.)

The above ideas, in a set of similar variants, were repeated innumerable times by the Confucian officials and they reflected their concept of the paternalistic role of a properly ordered government. The aim was clear—to act so as to reduce tensions and social contradictions between the ruled and the rulers. It is difficult to ascertain, at present, to what degree the Confucianists of this period were fully aware of this aim. However, the inculcation of these conceptions for many centuries had an essential influence on the shaping of the consciousness of all strata of Chinese society. To what extent these ideas were truly put into effect is a separate problem. Nonetheless, their significance for the evolution of political thought in the Han era, and in later periods as well, remains indubitable.

IV. Political Development

The founder, Kao-tsu, died in 195 B.C. at the age of 52 from a neglected arrow wound; his contempt was not only for the scholars but for doctors as well. While it was his son Hui (194-188 B.C.) who assumed the throne as his successor, real power was in the hands of the Empress Dowager Lü, an indomitable, unbelievably cruel and despotic woman. After Hui's death from dissipation, the Empress continued to rule, through the use of puppet child emperors until her death in 179 B.C. She placed members of her own family and clan in all the principal positions of the government. After her death, however, the Lius organized a *coup d'état*, regained power and exterminated the entire Lü clan. A son of Kao-tsu who became the Emperor Wen (179-157 B.C.) was placed on the throne. He was a very rare figure in Chinese or any other annals—an able, modest and frugal ruler. He did not build any new palaces and his main concern was the welfare of the people. He paid particular attention to further development of agriculture—"The root of the country's prosperity". China was at peace during his reign and it is from this period that the saying comes: "When men do not cultivate the land, the Empire suffers from hunger; when women do not spin—the Empire suffers from cold." Considerable reserves of food were accumulated in the state granaries in line with the proverb which also originated at this time: "Pearls and jade, gold and silver do not feed one when one is hungry, do not warm one when one is cold."

As a reflection of the stability of the country a further mitigation of the severe punishments employed in Ch'in and previous times took place. The Ch'in practice of exterminating entire families of the convicted individual was abolished (although, in fact, it was to be used again in the future), while the varying punishments by mutilations were replaced by flogging.

The best known of all the Han emperors of the middle period, among others, due to the length of his reign, was Emperor Wu (140-87). Wu-ti was an ambitious, ruthless, violent and credulous man—dabbling in all possible magical practices—who ruled as a complete despot. His reign witnessed also the most important territorial expansion of the Chinese empire since the time of the Ch'in.

V. The Expansion of the Han Empire

The most important political problem which faced the Chinese state during the Han period was its relations with the nomad neighbours to the North and North-west. This, as will be recalled, was not a recent development and the Ch'in dynasty had made an attempt to deal with this problem by its campaigns against the Hsiung-nu. The Hsiung-nu had recovered swiftly from the blows which had been dealt them by the First Emperor, and during the war between Liu Pang and Hsiang Yü had recaptured the territory they had lost in the Ordos region. Under the rule of Mao Tun (or Mei Tei), the son of T'ou Man who had founded the Hsiung-nu empire, the problem of relations between China and the Hsiung-nu became more acute. Mao Tun was extremely ruthless—he had killed his own father and all the chiefs who had opposed him—as well as an able leader. In his time the empire of the Hsiung-nu, in reality a federation of tribes of different ethnic origins, extended over an immense area from the Pamir Mountains to Liaotung.

The Hsiung-nu raided North China incessantly and during one of their expeditions Mao Tun succeeded in 201 B.C. in surrounding Emperor Kao-tsu and his entire army in the town of P'ing-ch'eng (the present Tat'ung, N. Shensi). It was only by agreeing to humiliating terms that the Chinese were able to arrive at a peace treaty. In effect, in the guise of presents the Han sent tribute to the Hsiung-nu for a long period of time, as well as consenting to marriages between the Chinese imperial house and the Hsiung-nu rulers. Large quantities of grain, silk and other luxury articles were thus sent to the North which undoubtedly had an effect on the Hsiung-nu way of life but not to the degree of changing their basic habits; the plundering raids affecting all the Chinese provinces of the North and North-west did not cease.

During the reign of Wu-ti a plan was devised to crush the Hsiung-nu and to drive them north of the Gobi Desert. In 133 B.C. an attempt was made to capture the Shan-yü—the ruler of the Hsiung-nu; this failed and subsequently, from 129 B.C. on, one campaign after another was launched by the Chinese against the Hsiung-nu. Large armies of from 50,000 to 100,000 men were hurled against them, and while the Chinese suffered tremendous losses they ultimately succeeded in breaking the main strength of the Hsiung-nu and forcing them not only out of the Ordos area but to the north of the Gobi as well. The success was also due to the employment of new tactics by the Chinese—much greater mobility and the use of light cavalry. This, in reality, was the adoption of the Hsiung-nu methods of warfare. The great master of this new type of warfare was Huo Ch'ü-ping, the best-known Chinese general of this period. In 121 B.C. he penetrated deeply into the territory of the Hsiung-nu and in 119 B.C. succeeded in conquering the area known as the Kansu Corridor which was a vital link to the West, enabling further expansion in this direction. The success of this and further campaigns resulted in a considerable weakening of the Hsiung-nu empire and the surrender of a number of their tribes to Chinese rule; some of these were resettled in areas south of the Great Wall. But it was only after 58 B.C. that the Hsiung-nu empire disintegrated completely, primarily due to the internal division. One part of the Hsiung-nu began its long trek westward which was ultimately to bring it to Europe, while the remainder of this people ceased to be a serious threat to the Chinese for the next three to four centuries.

It is in connection with the Hsiung-nu campaigns and the government sponsored export trade that the further extension westward of the Great Wall was made, now reaching all the way to Tun-huang—a site famous later on in the history of Chinese archaeology and art. It should be added that the weakening of the Hsiung-nu was due not only to the military victories of the Chinese army but also to the constant employment of a policy of intrigue, spying and diversion with the aim of bringing about disunity and disorder within the nomad tribes. This policy was based on the concept, constantly applied by the Chinese dynasties, of getting "barbarians" to fight "barbarians".

The victories were gained at the cost of immense losses of life and great expenditure. Vast quantities of gold were distributed in rewards to the soldiers, while the expenses of supplying the armies in these remote areas were huge. The economic consequences of the campaigns against the Hsiung-nu, as well as of the other wars waged in Wu-ti's time, were disastrous for the country's development.

There was by no means unanimity in the Chinese court as to the policies to be followed towards the Hsiung-nu; some of the officials were throughout strongly opposed to these ventures. One of them, Chu-fu Yen, expressed this viewpoint thus:

> "No matter how large a country is, if it loves war—it shall perish. If it makes war imprudently—it will be in danger . . . for arms are evil instruments. The experience of many generations has proved that one can never hope to be able to govern the Hsiung-nu. To invade, to pillage and then to fly away—such is their life. Heaven made them thus."

In his struggle against the Hsiung-nu Wu-ti wished to avail himself also of political means, and sought allies among the neighbours of the Hsiung-nu for joint action against them. It is for this purpose that a Chinese official, Chang Ch'ien, was sent out in 138 B.C. on a mission to the Yüeh-chih (probably an Indo-European-speaking people) who had been earlier defeated and driven to the west from Kansu by the Hsiung-nu. Chang Ch'ien set out west with a hundred followers but was shortly captured by the Hsiung-nu and remained their prisoner for ten years. He later succeeded in escaping with his Hsiung-nu wife; instead of fleeing back to China he continued on his mission, and proceeded westwards to look for the Yüeh-chih. When he gained the Ili area he found the Wu-sun people living there (their linguistic and ethnic origin is quite unclear; some authors consider them Indo-European, others Mongolo-Turkish). The Yüeh-chih had been forced by them to move still further westward. They were, in fact, at this period engaged in the process of conquering Bactria (the Ta-hsia of the Chinese) and thus putting an end to one of the last of the Hellenistic kingdoms in Central Asia. Crossing over some of the most difficult terrain in the world, Chang Ch'ien finally found the Yüeh-chih, only to discover that they were not in the slightest interested in returning to the east to fight against the Hsiung-nu (a century and a half later the Yüeh-chih, under the name of Kushans, were to rule a vast empire including most of Northwest India). Chang Ch'ien returned by a different route, south of the T'ien Shan, but was again captured by the Hsiung-nu. Once more he managed to escape and after thirteen years since his departure he returned to China with his wife and one follower.

Chang Ch'ien's report on his epic travels was of the greatest importance in stimulating the Chinese government to extend its rule westward. Earlier, the geographical knowledge of Central Asia possessed by the Chinese amounted to practically nothing. The expansion which ensued gave access to the two principal caravan routes through Central Asia, one running to the north and the other to the south of the T'ien Shan. Usage of this famous Silk Route undoubtedly stimulated

China's trade with the West but the hopes of great profits to which it gave rise were not realized and, in fact, the balance of trade was not, ultimately, in China's favour.

Chang Ch'ien had also reported that while in Bactria he had seen products which could have originated only in Szechuan and was informed that they had come from India. This, therefore, implied that routes must be in existence linking Szechuan and India and thus gave rise to the idea of searching for these which, it was assumed, passed through Yunnan and Burma. In spite of all efforts these routes were never found, but the search for them was a contributing factor in stimulating Chinese expansion to the South and South-west.

In 115 B.C. Chang Ch'ien was sent off once more, this time on a mission to the Wu-sun, with the similar aim of seeking allies for the Chinese against the Hsiung-nu. This mission failed as well, but the expedition, in which members of his party simultaneously penetrated other parts of Central Asia, led to a further extension of Chinese knowledge regarding these regions.*

The above missions were subsequently followed by new campaigns in 104 and 102 B.C. by Chinese armies led by Li Kuang-li and resulted in the conquest of all the small oasis states—36 is the number usually given—of the Tarim Basin. One of the motives for these campaigns was not only the hope for greater trade but the desire to acquire a superior type of horse from Ferghana (Ta-yüan), the Chinese breed being considered much inferior. The horses were needed especially for the wars against the Hsiung-nu, and while in various periods the Chinese did attempt to meet this problem by raising horses in North China it would seem that they were never able to raise a sufficient number. The results of the expansion of Han rule to the Western Regions did bring about an increase of trade as well as significant contacts with countries still further to the West. A number of new products, especially grapes and alfalfa, were introduced into China at this time. The cultural influences on China which resulted from this meeting with the West were also of very great importance and will be dealt with later.

The reign of Wu-ti also saw the launching of major campaigns in other directions, particularly to the south. While the wars against the Hsiung-nu were undoubtedly much more costly, both in manpower and money, the campaigns in the south were more important in their ultimate results. Here, the areas which had been conquered by the Ch'in dynasty had broken away from Chinese rule after its fall and a number of independent states had been established. The most important of these, ruled by a former Ch'in general, was the great state of Nan-yüeh which included present Kwangtung and Kwangsi provinces as well as North Vietnam. Having previously acquired knowledge of the connection of Nan-yüeh with Central China through the river system, the Han launched a campaign of conquest in 119 B.C. which led to a speedy overrunning of the entire territory of Nan-yüeh and its attachment, permanent as far as Kwangtung and Kwangsi are concerned, to the Chinese empire. From this time onward an ever-increasing migration of Chinese to the south and the assimilation of the native population continued and thus, within a few centuries, the area became Chinese-

---

* The Chinese referred to all the territory both north and south of the T'ien Shan, as well as to the lands to the west of the Pamirs, simply as the Western Regions. We shall use this term instead of the anachronistic Chinese Turkestan (the Turks did not inhabit this area until the 6th century A.D.) or the even more inappropriate term Sinkiang, which dates from the 18th century.

speaking. Somewhat earlier, the two once independent states in Chekiang and Fukien were also conquered so that, in effect, practically the entire southern seaboard was now included in the Han Empire. In this area a policy of wholesale deportation of the native population to the north of the Yangtse was pursued, which was replaced by Chinese colonization. The provinces of Yunnan and Kweichow were also partially subjected to Chinese rule, the local states being forced to recognize themselves as vassals of the Han. This conquest, however, did not prove to be permanent.

In the North-east, Wu-ti, wishing also to outflank the Hsiung-nu, extended Chinese rule to North Korea, which was penetrated in 109 B.C. Large colonies of Chinese settlers were also established here and one of these, Lo-lang (on the site of the present P'yongyang), became a prosperous and large city. It lasted to 313 A.D. as an important centre for the spreading of Chinese culture, and has been the source of numerous fascinating archaeological discoveries, which provide an excellent picture of the art and life of Han times. It is also from these colonies in North Korea that Chinese culture spread not only to the rest of Korea itself but also, undoubtedly, to Japan.

Thus during the reign of Wu-ti Chinese territory was extended to borders which in some ways are analogous to the present frontiers of China. The price for this expansion, however, was economic ruin and the dissipation of all the reserves which had been stored up in the early Han period. The drain on human and material resources was immense, resulting in a financial and social crisis which had fatal consequences for the future of the country. In dealing with this growing crisis a large number of measures were undertaken which are of considerable interest, because they likewise are often to be met with in future periods of Chinese history.

One of the most important aspects of the financial crisis was the problem of coinage. While in earlier Han times coinage was not a state monopoly, it became so during Wu-ti's reign. Inasmuch, however, as the government continuously depreciated the value of the currency, false coinage became endemic. All attempts to suppress this private coinage were a failure, in spite of the draconian methods employed—the death penalty and mass arrests. The problem was ultimately solved only by the government again issuing coins possessing a high intrinsic value.

Various methods were evolved to raise the needed revenue. Thus, titles were sold on a large scale. Perhaps the most famous device was the one employed by Wu-ti, who forced the feudal lords to purchase, when presenting themselves at court to pay homage, strips of the hide of a rare white stag, found only in the Imperial hunting preserves, for which they had to pay the price of 400,000 cash. The Han monarchy had, in general, continued the policy of its predecessors in discriminating against the merchants. This reflected, basically, the aversion of the landowning class to commerce which, while often expressed in moralistic terms, was, in reality, derived from the fact that the merchants were considered as rivals, both economically and politically. The same attitude applied also to the owners of private manufactures, often merchants as well. This policy was followed by Wu-ti and when the financial crisis of his regime grew sharper, the merchants were subjected to particularly harsh treatment; in 119 B.C. they were forced to declare all their capital and pay to the state treasury a 10 per cent tax.

Most of the above measures were of a stop-gap nature. Of still greater importance was the introduction in 119 B.C. of the state monopoly for the production and manufacture of salt and iron. It was now placed under the management of imperial commissioners and became the source of a very considerable revenue to the state. All infractions of these monopolies were also punished with great severity—the usual penalty being amputation of the left foot.

A very interesting discussion on the advantages and disadvantages of these monopolies was held in 81 B.C. Although many of the officials were opposed to the measures, the monopolies continued in force. The government evolved as well a policy of "equalization", i.e. the purchasing and transport of grain on a large scale, in competition with the merchants, with the principal aim of controlling the price level. This also was of considerable financial advantage. All the above measures, however, were unable to accomplish more than a temporary easing of the situation, inasmuch as they did not grapple with the fundamental sources of the economic and social crisis. One of the statements in this discussion illustrates superbly the essence of class contradictions of Han society; it can be also applied fully to later periods.

> Those who live in high halls and spreading mansions, broad chambers and deep rooms, know nothing of the discomforts of one-room huts and narrow hovels, of roofs that leak and floors that sweat.
>
> Those with a hundred team of horses tethered in their stables and wealth heaped in their storehouses, who hoard up the old and stow away the new, do not know the anxiety of facing days that have a beginning but no end, of weighing goods by the pennyworth....
>
> Those who recline on soft couches or felt mats, with servants and attendants crowding about them, know nothing of the hardships of a cartpuller or the boathauler, straining up the hills, dragging against the current ....
>
> Those who sit in the place of authority and lean on their writing desks, examine criminal charges brought before them and scribble their decisions, know nothing of the terror of cangues and bonds, the pain of whips and rods.

CHAPTER 7

The Crisis of the Western Han Dynasty

I. The Essence of the Social Crisis

All the financial and economic difficulties which had arisen by the end of the reign of Emperor Wu were sharpened still further by perhaps the most important phenomenon of all, the social crisis. The main aspect of this was the constant growth of large landed estates at the expense of the small peasants. The peasantry was to an ever greater degree falling into debt and into the hands of usurers; in these circumstances the peasants were forced to sell their land, and often themselves and their families. Thus they were transformed from small independent landholders into tenants, farm labourers or slaves. This process increased in rapidity during the 1st century B.C. The problem was intimately interconnected with the financial crisis, inasmuch as the owners of great estates managed to avoid paying their proper share of taxes, and when the number of small peasants who formed the bulk of the taxpayers decreased, this, in turn, affected adversely the government's revenue.

The situation was further exacerbated by a continuous growth of population; the census figure for A.D. 2 is over 50 million people. While, on the whole, the early Chinese censuses cannot be considered completely reliable—they were not based on a *per caput* calculation of the population but on the number of households and were undertaken for fiscal purposes, thus many attempts at evasion were made and much inexactitude resulted—the above figure can be considered approximately correct. The result of this population increase, which was very unevenly distributed, was still greater pressure on the land and a reduction, therefore, in the size of the small peasant holdings. This, in turn, made the situation of the peasants still more difficult and the food supply of the country, as a whole, became more and more critical. Some of the economic measures undertaken during the reign of Emperor Wu, especially the "equalization" granary and transport system, alleviated the critical situation to a certain degree, but in the last half of the 1st century B.C. conditions became still more acute.

The factor of land concentration and its concomitant, impoverishment of the peasantry, was imminent in the nature of Chinese feudal society itself and is of crucial significance for understanding its development. It is basically cyclical in character, recurring at intervals which can almost be plotted, and leading most often to a great social crisis, customarily ending in a peasant rebellion and the downfall of the reigning dynasty. The Confucians' stress on the need of a paternalistic concern for the welfare of the people and the need for proper attention to agriculture was not merely empty moralizing but also an awareness of these problems, although they were not able to advance any feasible solution, inasmuch as they were themselves basically members and representatives of the landowning classes.

II. The Decline of Western Han Rule

The years following Wu-ti's reign witnessed a further decline in the power and prestige of the Han dynasty. At the court the struggle between cliques of officials and eunuchs, who now were playing a greater role, also increased. An ever greater political role was played as well by families related to the empresses; this was especially true after 33 B.C., when the Wang clan, the relatives of the Empress Dowager, the widow of Emperor Yüan, rose to power in a way which was quite similar to the eminence of the Lu clan at the beginning of the Han period. The most prominent member of the Wangs was the Empress' nephew, Wang Mang; a very able, studious and scholarly, temperate and frugal, as well as ambitious and astute man, he had already reached the top posts in the government by the age of 28. His personality was especially marked by contrast with the drunken and degenerate Emperor Ch'eng (32-7 B.C.) and even more so with the next Emperor Ai (6-1 B.C.), a still more dissolute and incapable ruler. Although during the reign of this last emperor the Wang family was removed from power, Wang Mang steadily built up for himself a group of supporters, primarily within the top bureaucracy.

Wang Mang posed, probably sincerely, as an ardent Confucianist and a believer in the return to antiquity, to the model government of the Ancient Sages. He advocated and did much to encourage the study of the Confucian Classics and based himself on these in the formulation of his policies. He was particularly fond of the *Chou li*, as well as of the so-called "Ancient Text" of the *Shu Ching*.* In later years he was often unjustly accused of having falsified both of these for the purpose of furthering his own political aims. Wang Mang's advocacy of the study of the Confucian Canon was successful in gaining the support of a considerable number of Confucian scholars.

By A.D. 1 Wang Mang was the Regent and the *de facto* ruler of the empire. In A.D. 9 he dethroned the baby ruler (not killing him, however) and declared himself the First Emperor of the Hsin Dynasty ("New", but perhaps also derived from his earlier title, the Marquis of Hsin). Thus, the 200-year rule of the Liu family had seemingly come to an end. All the members of the very numerous Liu clan (they were quite prolific, especially in view of the fact that polygamy prevailed throughout all of feudalism, up to the 20th century, but limited almost exclusively to the upper classes) were deprived of their aristocratic titles.

III. The Reign of Wang Mang

The short period of Wang Mang's rule over the Chinese empire (A.D. 9-23) is one of the most dramatic and interesting periods in Chinese history, especially due to the reforms which the Emperor tried to implement in order to attempt to solve the ever-

---

* The "Ancient Text" (*ku-wen*) was supposedly discovered around the middle of the 2nd century B.C. in the wall of Confucius' house and a commentary written to it by one of his descendants, K'ung An-kuo. The name derives from the fact that it was written in older characters, pre-dating the Ch'in period. It was a longer text than the so-called "New Text" (*chin-wen*), i.e. the text written down from memory in the early Han period in newer characters. A famous controversy regarding the validity of this "Ancient Text" lasted for many centuries. The original version probably disappeared during the fall of the Han, to reappear at the beginning of the 4th century. This later version was proved to be a forgery in the 16th century after having been regarded for over a millennium as a fundamental component of the Confucian Canon.

growing social and economic crisis. All the later orthodox Confucian historians invariably condemn him as a "usurper", thus everything written about him is the work of his enemies and, therefore, necessarily biased.

The most important reforms were proclaimed already in A.D. 9—these included a plan for the "nationalization" of all agrarian land (the land to be considered as the Emperor's), the prohibition of the free sale and purchase of land, the confiscation of large estates and the division of land among the peasants. The aim was to provide every peasant with his own plot of land. In line with his archaizing tendencies, Wang Mang announced his desire to restore the ancient well-field system. Private slave ownership was to be limited and further trade in slaves prohibited.

The government monopolies of salt and iron were strengthened and others introduced (wine and other products). Government control was also extended to lakes and woods, which had been considered as commons, and taxes were to be paid for the use of these. Provision was made for the granting by the government of credit to the peasants at a rate of 3 per cent a month, much less than that demanded by the usurers. The government's monopoly on coinage was also reasserted and severe measures against counterfeiters undertaken. Simultaneously, Wang Mang pursued a policy of depreciation of the currency and of a compulsory calling in of gold, which resulted in the amassing of a vast amount of this metal, supposedly five million ounces.

All the above measures were to serve a two-fold purpose: to alleviate the conditions of the peasants and to provide new, additional sources of revenue to the government. They met with such intensive opposition on the part of the rich landowners and were sabotaged to such a degree by the bureaucracy that within three years Wang Mang was forced to repeal the main measures, those pertaining to the land and to the slaves. It is possible that the reforms could have succeeded had the Emperor had at his disposal a subservient and honest officialdom. This was not the case, although he attempted to purge the bureaucracy; thus officials found guilty of corruption had four-fifths of their wealth confiscated. There was little likelihood, however, that the officials could or would carry out reforms which were directed against the interests of their own families and class. In effect, neither the government nor the peasantry was any better off, inasmuch as most of the revenue found its way into the pockets of the officials. Thus the discontent of the population was only still further increased.

The great majority of Wang Mang's measures, with the exception of the land reform schemes, were not really innovations. Most of them had been used in earlier times, especially during the reign of Emperor Wu. It is a nonsensical anachronism to regard Wang Mang as "the first socialist" in China, as has sometimes been done. It is equally inappropriate to consider his reforms as backward and reactionary. In reality, they were a remarkable attempt to solve the current problems and contradictions within the framework of the feudal society. They failed not only due to the reasons mentioned above but, basically, because they were undertaken within this framework.

The rule of Wang Mang was further complicated by his entanglement in a war against the Hsiung-nu; he had supposedly provoked this conflict himself, perhaps for the classical purpose of turning attention away from the domestic situation. Whatever the truth of the matter, the conflict with the Hsiung-nu began in A.D. 10; Wang Mang sought to raise an army of 300,000, which was to accomplish a final conquest of all the Hsiung-nu territories. The plans failed completely and resulted instead in constant Hsiung-nu raids on North China. By A.D. 16 the Hsiung-nu had succeeded in cutting the road leading to Central Asia, which resulted in the loss of all the Chinese possessions in the Western Regions, always a bone of contention between the Hsiung-nu and the Chinese. Further armies against the Hsiung-nu, composed largely of convicts and slaves, were organized in A.D. 19.

A series of natural disasters also took place, giving rise to famine conditions on a mass scale—the most critical of these was the catastrophic flooding of the Yellow River which changed its course in A.D. 11. As a result, peasant discontent increased markedly, taking the form of local uprisings from A.D. 14 on. The army established against the Hsiung-nu largely disintegrated—200,000 soldiers deserted and began pillaging the countryside. The first peasant rebellions were still relatively restricted in their activity, for the insurgents only plundered the countryside in search of food and refrained from attacking the towns and officials.

By A.D. 18 the situation changed considerably and the peasant movement assumed a different character. This was due among others to the emergence of the Red Eyebrows, a secret society, probably Taoist in origin, which turned the movement into a vast peasant uprising. It originated in Shantung, a province famous for activities of this type, and quickly spread its influence to the area between the famous sacred Mount T'ai and the Huai River, the same area in which Liu Pang had started his career. Its principal leader was Fang Ch'ung and in a short time the Red Eyebrows started on a campaign of attacking the towns and killing government officials. This was one of the largest peasant rebellions in Chinese history, the first one on a really great scale, but by no means the last. This phenomenon of peasant revolt is definitely a cyclical feature of Chinese development and one of its most outstanding characteristics.

Wang Mang sent his armies against the Red Eyebrows but they met with complete failure, among others due to the reason that their behaviour was so outrageous that the people preferred the Red Eyebrows to them. Shortly, the Red Eyebrows became masters of all East China.

In this situation the extremely numerous Liu clan also embarked on a campaign against Wang Mang. Members of the clan succeeded in gaining control of other, basically peasant, units—the Green Forest Army, for example, and marched to the north against Wang Mang. There was much competition among the Lius as to who should be the future emperor. The ablest leader among them was Liu Hsiu, a large landowner from East Honan, but it was another, Liu Hsüan, who was declared emperor.

As a result of a two-way struggle, both against the Red Eyebrows and the supporters of the Lius, the armies of Wang Mang suffered a series of defeats, the most crushing of which was inflicted upon them by the Liu army. By A.D. 23 Wang Mang was deserted by most of his supporters and the Liu army approached Ch'ang-an. At this moment a revolt also broke out in the capital itself and, with a few of his remaining faithful followers, Wang Mang took refuge in a tower on an island on an artificial lake; he was still dressed in his full imperial regalia believing that destiny would rescue him. The tower was taken and Wang Mang, still seated on his throne, was killed and beheaded.

The death of Wang Mang did not by any means put an end to the conflict. The occupation of Ch'ang-an by the Liu army soon led the people to regret the dead "usurper". A general struggle for power of all against all now ensued. The Red Eyebrows also marched to the west in A.D. 24 and took Ch'ang-an for themselves, driving out Liu Hsüan, while most of his supporters joined them. Later on they were forced to abandon Ch'ang-an, due to famine, and to retreat to the east. Most of their armies were defeated piecemeal by Liu Hsiu, who incorporated the survivors into his own forces. Liu Hsiu, enjoying the support of the landowners, then began a long campaign for consolidating his power. He declared himself emperor in A.D. 25 (Liu Hsüan died in the same year) and then successfully eliminated, step by step, all his rivals to the throne. In re-establishing the Han dynasty he transferred the capital to Loyang, in his native province, *inter alia* for the reason that Ch'ang-an had been completely destroyed. The name Eastern Han is derived from this transfer of the capital.

The Red Eyebrows movement demonstrated in many ways the ever-present limitations of the peasant rebellions in China. The insurgents could bring about the downfall of a ruling dynasty but they had no idea whatsoever of what it could be replaced by, except another new dynasty. Thus, after they captured Ch'ang-an, the Red Eyebrows themselves found another Liu in their ranks whom they made an emperor. In other cases, it was the leaders of the peasant movement who declared themselves as the new emperors. Usually, it was primarily the representatives of the upper classes who benefited from the peasant rebellions and who were able to set themselves up in power with the help of peasant armies; such was also the case of the restoration of the Han.

CHAPTER 8

Eastern Han

I. The Restoration of the Centralized Monarchy

After his accession to the throne in A.D. 25 Liu Hsiu—known in history as Emperor Kuang Wu (25-57)—conducted a struggle of over ten years for the stabilization of his power. This involved also the waging of campaigns against independent rulers in Shantung and Szechuan. The already somewhat conventional pattern for the establishment of a new dynasty was followed by Kuang Wu. The disasters of the prolonged wars had resulted in a great loss of life and the ruin of the economy; they also brought about the disappearance of a large part of the older Han aristocracy and thus the reduction in a number of great landowners. This, in turn, made a temporary solution of the social problem feasible, inasmuch as enough land was now available for distribution to the peasantry. At the beginning of the Eastern Han period the imperial clan, which always tended to become the largest landowner in the country, was still small and its political role was restricted by the Emperor, i.e. by depriving the Liu princes in 37 of their titles of king (137 were affected by this).

The tax burden on the peasantry was considerably lightened, the land tax being lowered from one-tenth to one-thirtieth. A number of those who had sold themselves into slavery or had become government slaves as a result of alleged crimes were freed. Large amounts of state land were distributed to the peasants and the great armies of the war period were demobilized. A reduction in the size of the bureaucracy was also undertaken and the number of petty officials—"the scourge of the people"—was reduced by nine-tenths in around 400 districts.

The result of all the above measures was a restoration of political stability and, after a period of seventy to eighty years, the economy also recovered completely, reaching once more the level of the middle of the 1st century B.C. It should be noted, however, that the land-owning class was, from the outset of the Eastern Han, in a stronger position than it had been after the fall of the Ch'in. The growth of great estates began from the first years of the Eastern Han period and the marked increase in the employment of tenant farmers was the source of enrichment to the landowners, inasmuch as they received at least half of the tenants' crops as rent, while simultaneously paying only the newly lowered taxes of one-thirtieth. It is already in this period that the great estates took on the character of completely self-sufficient domains, transformed into strongholds, with their own retainers and armed forces.

The general upturn of the economy which lasted for the first century of the Eastern Han dynasty followed, in general, the previous pattern, for there is no clear indication of any fundamental changes or innovations in methods of production. There was, however, a shift in the importance of particular areas since the North-west (Shensi), having been ruined extensively during the wars, was now of much lesser economic importance, while the northern part of the Great Chinese Plain (Honan, Hopei and Shantung) became during this period the principal economic area. The renewed growth of trade and of money economy led once more to the rise of the towns, while the new capital Loyang assumed great importance.

The administration of the new Han Empire followed, on the whole, the basic lines of its predecessor. The officials were still recruited mostly on the basis of recommendation and came almost entirely from the landowner class; one of the main sources for recruitment continued to be the Imperial University where the number of students steadily increased, reaching the figure of 30,000 in A.D.46. The prestige of the Confucian scholar-official was also consciously enhanced by Emperor Kuang Wu of whom it is said that, after conquering the empire with the sword, he surrounded himself by scholars and not by generals, having pensioned off the latter as soon as possible.

II. Political Development

The reigns of the next two Emperors, Ming (57-75) and Chang (75-88), continued the development of Kuang Wu's times along much the same general lines. The reign of Emperor Ming is noteworthy primarily for the introduction of Buddhism (see p. 101), which was favoured by the Emperor himself; for this he was subsequently severely condemned by orthodox Confucian historians. The coming of Buddhism was the result of the extension of Chinese rule to the Western Regions which were Buddhist already in this period and also constituted a link between China and India. In 67 the first Buddhist texts were translated into Chinese, the beginning of a vast literature.

The essence of the later political history of the Eastern Han dynasty is the struggle for power among various cliques—officials, families of consorts and eunuchs with extremely complicated relations and alliances ensuing between these three competing groups. At times, it was the Emperor himself who used the eunuchs to fight against the families of consorts who were monopolizing power; the eunuchs, having direct access to the Emperor, were logical tools for this purpose. They were able to take full advantage of this position and thus become a great political power themselves. This was reflected also in the right which they acquired to possess titles (from 126 on) and to adopt sons. Their main interest, apart from political power, was the enrichment of themselves and their families and, as the control over the administration fell more and more into their hands, the sale of offices became one of the prime sources of their wealth. After the first three rulers of the dynasty, all the subsequent emperors who mounted the throne were minors and, in effect, most of them were playthings in the hands of the eunuchs.

In the second century of the Eastern Han rule the conflict for power grew steadily sharper. The consort families were just as greedy of wealth and power as the eunuchs. Thus, for example, the Liang family which controlled the government in the middle of the 2nd century had provided the dynasty with three empresses and six royal concubines, while members of the family included seven marquises, three marshals, fifty-seven ministers and generals. This powerful family met its end at the hands of Emperor Huan (146-167) and the eunuchs, the entire Liang clan being massacred in 159. In the last decades of the Eastern Han the struggle became still fiercer. The officials formed a special Association to fight against the domination of the eunuchs but failed to gain sufficient support of the military for this purpose. The Association, which was formed in 168, represented practically all the scholar-officials of the Empire and enjoyed also the support of the students of the Imperial Academy. The eunuchs succeeded in crushing the Association, representing it to the Emperor as a threat to the throne, and killing over a hundred of its leading members who were later to be regarded as Confucian Martyrs. A reign of terror followed the initial repression and anyone in the Empire distinguished by his bravery, knowledge or virtue was noted down by the eunuchs as being suspected of belonging to the Association. In subsequent years the ruling eunuch clique put to death over 10,000 innocent people.

III. Eastern Han Territorial Expansion

After the initial period of restoration of domestic stability the rulers of the Eastern Han dynasty proceeded to regain the positions of their predecessors and to recover the territory which had been lost to China during the reign of Wang Mang. In effect, the success attained in this respect was as great as that of the Western Han but it proved to be of short duration.

The Chinese emperors still regained the Hsiung-nu as their main enemy. The position of the Hsiung-nu had been considerably weakened by a series of famines, especially in A.D.45, which had reduced their flocks by one-half. They had also become less nomadic in their habits and more dependent on trade with China. The Hsiung-nu were now subject to constant attacks by their eastern neighbours, the Hsien-pi and the Wu-huan, both descendants of the Tung-hu (scholars differ as to the ethnic origin of these tribes; some consider them to be proto-Mongols, others regard them as proto-Tungus). These tribes were still pure nomads and became allies of the Chinese in their struggle against the Hsiung-nu, the Chinese being always interested in having other "barbarian" attack the Hsiung-nu and more than willing to pay tribute to the Hsien-pi and the Wu-huan for this purpose.

In 48 the Hsiung-nu tribes became divided into two groups, northern and southern. The northern group was of greater importance, especially as it has considerable influence on the situation in the Western Regions. The southern Hsiung-nu submitted to Chinese rule and many of them were settled in North China where they were to act as frontier guards for the Chinese Empire—the analogy with Rome is striking. In this way the Hsiung-nu problem became much less pressing than it had been in earlier times.

The above developments rendered the renewal of Chinese power in the Western Regions much more feasible. The reconquest of Central Asia was linked up primarily with the name of Pan Ch'ao (32-102), the brother of the famous historian Pan Ku, and the most illustrious general of the period. He began his mission in 73 and by the use of great ingenuity, guile and bravery he was instrumental in recovering the Chinese positions in the Western Regions to the point where by 91 all kingdoms of the Tarim Basin had once more declared themselves vassals of China. It should be noted, in passing, that the great majority of these oasis states were still Indo-European by language at this period. On the whole, these states welcomed Chinese aid against the northern Hsiung-nu; only after having tasted Chinese rule did they find it equally oppressive and commenced to revolt against it. Pan Ch'ao pursued a policy of expansion which entailed the smallest cost possible to the Chinese government by employing the forces of the Western Region states as allies in his offensives for conquest of other areas. This was but the application of the now already traditional Chinese policy of using "barbarians" to fight "barbarians". The policy of expansion was a continuous subject of debate at the court, inasmuch as some of the officials opposed it as being too costly and unnecessary. Pan Ch'ao had been regarded by some Chinese authors not only as a great administrator and conqueror but also as "a great diplomat". This is a rather curious usage of the term since one of his most renowned feats was the accomplishment of the murder of a Hsiung-nu ambassador and his whole suite at the court of one of the Western Region states.

The primary result of the Chinese reconquest of the Western Regions, and probably one of its main purposes, was to place the control of the "Silk Route" once more in Chinese hands. This control was now strengthened by the settling of Chinese merchants in this area. The main item of export was still silk, both raw and cloth, along with Chinese handicrafts. The Chinese imported glass, jade, precious stones, ivory, fine wool and linen as well as horses.

In 90 Pan Ch'ao succeeded in defeating an incursion of a Kushan army 70,000 strong and these were so impressed by his victory that they paid tribute to him for a period of time. In 91 he was named the Protector General of the Western Regions and in 97 he undertook an expedition across the Pamir mountains, reaching the shores of the Caspian Sea. This marked the furthest advance westward of the Chinese. It is at this time that he sent one of his officials, Kan Ying, on a mission to establish contact with the Roman Empire. The mission failed due to the obstacles created by the Parthians, who were by no means anxious to be deprived of their role as middlemen in the trade between China and the West. Pan Ch'ao retired in 102, and in the subsequent decades a slow but steady loss of the Chinese positions in the Western Regions ensued which was due, primarily, to the general decline of the power of the Eastern Han.

In the South, Chinese rule in North Vietnam was challenged by a revolution of the Vietnamese in 42 led by an able woman, Cheng Ch'ai (Trung Trac), and her sister. This was put down by the Han general Ma Yüan in the next year; a policy of sinification was hence pursued and, since the area remained under Chinese rule for centuries, this had a profound influence on the cultural development of Vietnam.

A protracted and difficult struggle was also waged against the nomad Ch'iang (ethnically Tibetan) tribes who raided the more fertile upper reaches of the Yellow River. Some of these tribesmen, who were conscripted in 107 for service in the Western Regions, rebelled against Han rule and were joined in this by Chinese colonists as well. This conflict, which extended to the Kansu and Ch'inghai area, lasted for over ten years.

The territorial expansion of the Eastern Han led to the establishment of still more contacts with the rest of the world. The Chinese of this period were perhaps aware of the existence of the Roman Empire (Ta Ch'in), while in 166 the Annals note the arrival of an alleged mission from Marcus Aurelius to China; it is more than probable that this was, in fact, a group of Syrian merchants which arrived in South China by way of Southeast Asia and passed itself off as an embassy. These contacts had especially great influence on the development of Chinese culture.

IV. The Crisis of the Eastern Han

By the middle of the 2nd century social and economic conditions had again deteriorated to a level similar to that of the end of the Western Han period. An identical, cyclical development took place: the concentration of land ownership resulting in the decrease of small independent holders and the increase of the tax burden on the remaining small peasants. To escape these burdens the peasants tended now either to flee to sparsely settled lands in the South or to become tenants on the great estates. A series of peasant uprisings can be noted from 126 on, all of which were suppressed. The central government was weakened not only due to this crisis and to the above-mentioned conflict of cliques at the court, but its general position was also undermined by the growth in strength of the great landowning families which tended to monopolize all power in the provinces. Thus a process of gradual but steady decentralization ensued and the later division of the Empire was but a final crowning of this development.

As has often been pointed out, there is an obvious and far-reaching resemblance between the fall of the Eastern Han dynasty and the decline of the Roman Empire. Similar, though not identical, conditions produced similar results. The consequences, however, in the case of China were much less far-reaching, for the continuity of Chinese civilization and culture was preserved to an infinitely greater degree during this period than was the case in Europe.

The most immediate cause of the collapse of the Eastern Han, which was itself the result of the social crisis and a reflection of the weakness of the monarchy, was the great peasant insurrection of the Yellow Turbans. This was yet again a secret society, basically Taoist in nature. Its leader, Chang Chüeh, was a faith healer and the founder of the *T'ai P'ing Tao* ("The Road of Universal Peace") sect; within a few years Chang Chüeh and his closest adherents spread their activity to the area between the Yellow River and the Yangtse and succeeded in gaining tens of thousands of followers amongst the peasantry. These were organized into thirty-six units of various sizes each under its own leader. The ideology of the sect was a mixture of Taoist ideas with elements of folk religion; this gained for it the support of the peasants as it could be counterposed to official Confucianism—the creed of the landowners. The place of the Yellow Turbans movement in Chinese history is of considerable importance; it has been stated that it remained a vivid memory for the peasants of North China up to the end of the 19th century, not excluding the followers of the I Ho T'uan.

The Yellow Turbans set their plans for revolt against the Han government which was to be begun by a rising in the capital in February 184. These intentions were foiled by an informer and over a thousand suspected Yellow Turban sympathizers in the capital were killed. It was too late, however, to call off the uprising in the provinces; this was launched in March and a great initial success was obtained. The Yellow Turbans marched in great force on Loyang, while the officials were everywhere fleeing for their lives. In spite of the bitterness of the conflicts between the cliques at the court, most of the landlords realized the danger of the peasant uprising and joined forces in attacking the Yellow Turbans. Chang Chüeh died in August and the leadership of the movement was carried on, in turn, by his two brothers. By November, however, the main armies of the Yellow Turbans were crushed and then a savage campaign of repression was launched. Many thousands of suspects were massacred in almost every district of North and East China. This repression did not put an end to the movement for new peasant forces were organized, the Black Mountain Army, which also enlisted hundreds of thousands of followers. But this too was, in turn, defeated. In effect, it took the landowners twenty years to bring about the complete suppression of this peasant rebellion, which also embraced Szechuan, where a similar sect, the Five Bushels movement, was active for many years.

V. The Fall of the Eastern Han

In the process of the struggle against the Yellow Turbans the central government lost what little was left of its power and significance. Practically all the fighting against the peasants was carried out by provincial generals who in the process became classical cases of warlords, lusting for power. These generals came mostly from rich landowning families and the armies which they commanded were private and professional.

In 189 two of these provincial armies moved on Loyang and served to support a *coup d'état* against eunuch rule in the court. There had been a long series of previous attempts to overthrow the power of the eunuch clique, but all of these had been foiled by the excellent espionage system which the eunuchs had at their disposal. This time the conspiracy of some courtiers, backed by armed force, was successful and a massacre of all the eunuchs in Loyang was carried out, with over 2000 killed.

A period of complete anarchy now ensued the main feature of which was the struggle between the provincial generals for power, the possession of the person of the Emperor and then, ultimately, for the Empire itself. In 190 one of the provincial generals, Tung Cho, whose troops had moved into Loyang in the previous year, dethroned the reigning Emperor and placed his brother Hsien on the throne as his unhappy puppet. Although Hsien nominally ruled until 220, the Eastern Han dynasty had, in fact, ceased to exist. There now ensured a dark and evil period of constant war and violence, of dismemberment of the empire, the first phase of which bears the name of *San Kuo*—the Three Kingdoms.

CHAPTER 9

Han Culture

I. General Remarks

It is customary to refer to the Han era as imperial and thus to contrast it with the classical Chou period. This is true not only in the political sense; the creation and consolidation of the Empire led to a considerable flourishing of culture in many fields. In comparison with the Chou, the Han period is much better known, since a greater quantity of written as well as archaeological sources exists. In these four centuries culture became much more widespread, embracing a larger ruling upper class, and undoubtedly also filtered down to the population as a whole. The higher cultural level of the upper class was also bound up with the growth of the governmental bureaucracy and with the increase of available education.

The Han era, perhaps due to its political nature, was not a period of philosophical searching but that of a systematization, on the whole rather eclectic, of ideas that had originated earlier. It was also a time for gathering up the fragments and records of the past, a period in which time was already ripe to attempt a representation of a comprehensive picture of the past; it was thus primarily a time for historical writing. The growth of Confucian orthodoxy, a steady but sure process, which led to the domination of Confucianism by the Eastern Han period, did not create a climate which would have been conducive to the development of novel ideas, departing from the set pattern.

During the Han probably the most important aspect of all is the formation of a truly national culture based on a common script and literature which was able to survive all the future political vicissitudes. It is not fortuitous that the Chinese to this day call themselves *Han jen*—the men of Han.

II. Historical Writing

No people have been more interested in history than the Chinese; it has been for them the principal source of information on human society—their philosophy, as formed in Chou times, has made the problem of this society of primary importance—and thus history was also to serve as a model for the present. All this was true of the Han period but it should also be remarked that this age was already unable to grasp a completely true picture of its own past, for it saw this past in terms of the present and thus extended the institutions existing in its day into the past. This anachronistic view was by no means a deliberate attempt to falsify history, but simply a misinterpretation, probably inevitable if one considers the level of knowledge of this period. In general, as has been noted by critical Chinese historians from the 18th century on, the Han writers' reconstruction of the past was such that the farther away a given period in ancient history—the greater the precision in its largely imaginary reconstruction. Nonetheless, historical writing was the true glory of the Han era and its greatest achievement.

The most important historical work of the period was the *Shih chi* ("Records of the Historian") by Ssu-ma Ch'ien. Both the work and the man deserved a more detailed account. Ssu-ma Ch'ien (145 B.C.?-90 B.C.?) came from an aristocratic family in Ch'in which claimed descent from a long line of former scribes. His father, Ssu-ma T'an, occupied the post of Grand Astrologer, being simultaneously in charge of the archives (the institution of scribes who were both annals writers and archive keepers dates at least from the 8th century B.C.). It was he who conceived the idea of writing a comprehensive history of China from its beginnings to the present.

After having finished his education at the age of 20, Ssu-ma Ch'ien started on a great series of travels during which he visited almost all parts of the Han empire while, at the same time, gathering material for this work. Upon his father's death in 110 B.C. he took over his post and continued the project; there is little doubt that most of the *Shih chi* is his work. Its writing was based not only on his extensive and prodigious research—he probably read every book then extant on the subject—but also on materials taken from the Imperial Archives and Library to which he had access. Much use was made by him of the latter, especially in the part of his work which deals with the Han period. Simultaneously, as a high official in the imperial court, he had been an eyewitness to many important events and, what is still more vital, acquired an understanding of the mechanism of politics. His intellectual daring in undertaking such a great project is obvious, especially if one considers that the work was not so much a history of China only but of all the knowable world, from the Chinese point of view.

In 99 Ssu-ma Ch'ien suffered a great personal tragedy. In supporting the cause of his friend, General Li Ling (also famous in Chinese literature), who had been forced to surrender to the Hsiung-nu, he gained the displeasure of Emperor Wu and was sentenced to undergo the penalty of castration. He could have avoided this penalty by paying a heavy fine, but his family was poor and all his friends deserted him. He underwent the penalty instead of committing suicide, as would have been customary. Thus he sacrificed—but only temporarily—his honour and reputation for the sake of continuing work on his great project—a decision for which the world has been grateful. Later he reflected on his decision in a moving letter to a friend, Jen An. His view of Wu-ti was not unaffected by this; there is much veiled satire in parts of his work, but no chapter on the Emperor himself exists—it was either never written or later suppressed.

Ssu-ma Ch'ien's own modest description of the *Shih chi* is pertinent: "My narrative consists of no more than the systematization of material that has been handed down to us; there is, therefore, no creation—only a faithful representation."

It is much more than that. It is one of the prime sources of ancient Chinese history, as well as one of the most famous and valuable works in Chinese literature. It is true that Ssu-ma Ch'ien incorporated in his work all available ancient material by reproducing it very often *in toto*; thus for the earlier periods he used materials from the *Shu ching*, for the period of struggle between Liu Pang and Hsiang Yü he employed practically the entire book by Lu Chia, which is since lost. Such a method was by no means considered to be plagiarism but rather, in the Chinese view, a mark of respect for preceding authorities. His own original writing is mainly on the Han period and this too is undoubtedly the most valuable part of his work.

The *Shih chi* is composed of 130 chapters and contains, according to the author himself, 526,500 characters in the original version (the Chinese 1972 edition is in ten volumes, 3322 pages).* It has come down to the present almost intact, fate having been kinder to it than to many ancient Greek or Roman historians, Livy for example. Its organization is both of interest and importance. The first twelve chapters contain the basic Annals of the emperors from the mythical period to Wu-ti (*ca.* 100 B.C.). The subsequent ten chapters contain chronological tables of various ruling houses of the Chou period, the Han imperial clan and high officials. Then come eight essays on rituals, music, the calendar, astronomy, astrology, imperial rites, rivers and canals and weights and measures. The next thirty chapters deal with the history of princely houses, mostly Chou but also some of the Han. The last seventy chapters are devoted to biographies of various individuals, as well as to essays on geography and neighbouring peoples, e.g. the Hsiung-nu and Nan-yüeh.

The *Shih chi* is thus a veritable encyclopaedia, a mine of information on all aspects of Han civilization while being, primarily, a political history. Ssu-ma Ch'ien appreciated the influence of many factors on history but in his view history is, above all, the outcome of man's will and action. His aim in writing was to strive for objectivity but this did not imply a lack of his own viewpoint. On the contrary, he makes his views quite clear, sometimes very strongly so; however, his comments, often in a moral and didactic form, are always distinguished from the historical material he presents. His style has been regarded by many generations of Chinese (Japanese, Koreans and Vietnamese as well) as brilliant. He excels in apt characterizations and in dramatic episodes which are enlivened by the use of much direct speech.

The form in which he organized his work enabled Ssu-ma Ch'ien to give a flowing account of events without too many digressions; simultaneously, however, it causes material pertaining to a given person or event to be scattered throughout the various chapters. This makes for a many-sided view but does cause certain obvious difficulties.

The form of the *Shih chi* was of crucial importance because it became the pattern for all future Chinese historians. The standards of historical writing which were set by Ssu-ma Ch'ien were high indeed and unequalled in the West until modern times.

The next great work which is almost as famous as the *Shih chi* is the *Han shu* ("The History of the Early Han"). This was conceived by Pan Piao (3-54) as a continuation of the *Shih chi*. He gathered material for this purpose but the work was, in fact, written by his son Pan Ku (32-92)—the elder brother of the General Pan Ch'ao. He changed the project so as to cover the entire period of the Western Han. Thus the *Han shu* became the prototype of all the future dynastic histories which take the span of one dynasty as its subject. Pan Ku was jailed in 92—for alleged involvement with the Tou clan which had been then thrown out of power—and died in prison without completing the work. This was accomplished by his sister Pan Chao (d. *ca.* 116), probably the most famous woman writer in Chinese history, also a poetess and essayist. Thus the completion of the *Han shu* took a period of almost eighty years.

---

* The French translation by Chavannes includes the first 47 chapters. The English translation by B. Watson doubles some of the earlier chapters and includes 51 from the later part. The 1967 reprint of Chavannes provides a complete list of translations from the *Shih chi* into European languages.

In writing the *Han shu* Pan Ku used the *Shih chi* almost verbatim for the first period of Han rule and thus practically half of the book is based on it.* The *Han shu* is also a voluminous work of 100 chapters. It is patterned on the *Shih chi* with the exception that Pan Ku eliminated the section on the princely houses—which was of little importance for the Han period—but provided more essays on law, the Five Elements, geography and literature. Its style is considered not to be as brilliant as the *Shih chi*, though concise and fluent, easier to read, but seldom as interesting as the *Shih chi*. Pan Ku was less passionately *engagé* in writing history than Ssu-ma Ch'ien and also more a conservative and orthodox Confucianist. This difference can also be seen in the criticism of Ssu-ma Ch'ien which has been undertaken by Pan Piao; he considered that the latter did not attach proper value to ancient texts and that had he been a better Confucianist, his work would then have been close to perfection.

The *Han shu* was regarded, however, as too bulky and difficult, so an epitome of it was prepared by Hs'ün Yüeh (148-209), called the *Han chi* (Han Records), in thirty chapters. Luckily, the epitome did not replace the original, which is still extant in an almost perfect condition.

In the Eastern Han period official historians were already appointed at the court for the purpose of collecting records and materials pertaining to all the government's activities. This led later to the establishment by the T'ang of a Bureau of Historiography. Thus both the material basis and the organization were created which made possible the writing of the series of dynastic histories, this being considered in fact a governmental function. The custom established was that each new dynasty held itself responsible for issuing the history of its predecessor. The result was the production of twenty-four standard dynastic histories; twenty-five if one adds a new Yüan history issued in 1921. The 1747 edition of these histories is contained in 219 large volumes. Thus an unparalleled historical record for a period of over 2000 years, voluminous and authoritative, exists which is much more reliable and extensive than that possessed by any other people for such a long span of time. It should be noted, in passing, that other forms of historical writings apart from the official also existed throughout this entire period.

The form given to Chinese historiography by the *Shih chi* and the *Han shu* differs in many ways from the patterns established by European historical writing. Many factors account for this; the Greek and Roman historians were influenced by the epic and the drama, forms which were practically non-existent in Ancient China. Their works were also meant to be recited, while the Chinese were only to be read. The innate qualities of the Chinese language also played a role; its terseness and conciseness show their effect in the style of Chinese historical writing.

III. Philosophy

Although the Han period was primarily an age of great historical writing a considerable number of philosophical works also appeared. They contained, however, relatively few novel ideas as it is primarily the systematization and synthetization of

---

* In connection with this a controversy over the authenticity of the present version of the *Shih chi* exists; whether it has not been recopied from the *Han shu*. This was voiced by the noted 18th-century historian Ts'ui Shu (1740-1816).

previous beliefs which was the concern of Han philosophers. Mention has already been made of the political aspect of Han Confucianism, its transformation in this era into an orthodox state ideology. From a philosophical point of view the dominant Confucian school tended to incorporate into its system a number of beliefs such as the *yin-yang* system and the Five Elements Theory, which had previously represented independent tendencies. These views, as well as numerous others, such as those on divination based on the *I Ching*, etc., were used for the creation of a new cosmology which was now to be a component part of the Confucian creed.

Simultaneously, Taoist thought also continued to develop, represented, among others, by such works as the *Huai-nan tzu*. This book, the work of various authors, was compiled at the court of Liu An, the prince of Huai-nan (d. 122 B.C.); many different views are represented here, but basically it is a Taoist attempt at presenting a new cosmology. It should be remembered, however, that it was in the Han period that Taoism began its transformation from the philosophy of Lao Tzu and Chuang Tzu to a popular religion with the elements of magic and varied superstitions being predominant.

Within the Confucian school, although it was being elevated into an orthodox doctrine, a conflict of trends continued between a basically rationalist approach and one in which elements of irrational mysticism, speculation and superstition played an even-greater role. The most interesting and original of the Han philosophers, a representative of the first tendency, was Wang Ch'ung (27-97), referred to by Needham as "the most atheistic and agnostic of the Confucian rationalists". Wang Ch'ung came from a poor family and gained much of his knowledge from books borrowed from book sellers. His independent mind accounted for the fact that he never became more than a petty official and, in reality, he remained a teacher most of his life. His great work *Lun heng* ("Critical Essays" or "Discourses Weighed in the Balance") consists of eighty-five essays on various subjects. In it Wang Ch'ung following his basic motive, expressed in his own words as "hatred of fiction and falsehood", attacked from a sceptic and rationalist point of view many of the great mass of current superstitious ideas. In particular, he criticized the idea of linking man's fate with Heaven and maintained that since both man and Heaven were natural bodies no interconnection—in both directions—was possible between them. He likewise attacked views on the immortality of the soul, as well as numerous other beliefs in the supernatural.

Wang Ch'ung considered the senses and the intellect as the sole basis of all knowledge. He strongly opposed the harking back to antiquity so cherished by most Confucianists. Nonetheless, he was a man of his times in the sense that he also adhered to the *yin-yang* and Five Elements Theories as the basis for the explanation of natural phenomena. Moreover, he was a firm believer in a very far-reaching form of predestination. Wang Ch'ung's views could have served as a basis for an early development of a scientific outlook had he had followers. Such views as his, however, were strongly opposed by the orthodox Confucianists for they implied an undermining of their entire ideological and political position. Wang Ch'ung wrote in a brilliant style, using a simple distinctive language which was quite close to the colloquial. He was also renowned for his great wit.

IV. Literature

The Han period witnessed the concentration of considerable effort aimed at the reconstruction of the lost works of the classic era. It was the Confucianists who took the lead in this and their work here helped to establish their dominant position, inasmuch as to a great extent the concepts of scholarship and Confucianism became synonymous.

The greater part of the Confucian Canon was restored but in the process a series of interesting problems arose, i.e. the question of the differences between the so-called Ancient and New Texts (see p. 66). It should be noted, in passing, that the differences between the adherents of the Ancient and New Texts did not pertain only to matters of exegesis and textual criticism but were compounded by considerable differences in philosophical approach. Broadly speaking, the New Text school, represented by Tung Chung-shu, favoured the newly emerging, eclectic Confucianism, while the Ancient Text school desired a return to the original ethical and rationalist approach of the founder.

In their work of reconstruction of the texts the Han scholars attained a high level of literary criticism which was many centuries ahead of Europe. Many of the works of this period, e.g. Mao Ch'ang's edition of the *Shih ching*, became later the accepted standard version. Important work was also done by Liu Hsiang (79-8 B.C.) and his son Liu Hsin (46 B.C.-A.D. 23) who edited the *Chan-kuo ts'e* as well as the *Tso chuan* and also compiled a famous general bibliography of all extant Chinese literature. In their work the Han scholars were very careful and scrupulous transmitters of texts and it was in their time that the tradition of clearly separating commentaries on the texts from the body of the text itself was established. Their work was of basic importance and assured the continuity of the Chinese literary tradition.

Pioneering work was also done in the field of lexicography; the best-known example of this was the first dictionary, the work of Hsü Shen (d. A.D. 120), whose *Shuowen* contained over 10,000 characters and was arranged on the principle of grouping the characters according to their radicals; 540 were used in the *Shuo wen*—reduced in the 17th century to the 214 radicals still employed. The *Shuo wen* was, until the period of modern scholarship, of primary importance for etymological research.

In Han literature a new prose style developed which was noted for its simplicity and which was relatively close to the vernacular. This is considered to be one of the great periods of Chinese prose, renowned for its power and subtlety of expression. In reality, there were at least two styles; the narrative, as exemplified by historical writing which was simple and direct, and the more elaborate rhetorical style with matching patterns.

In poetry the works of Ch'ü Yüan still exerted considerable influence, especially on court poetry. This, however, took on an exuberant language which became more and more artificial and grandiloquent. Thus, this was a poetry almost exclusively by and for scholars. Mention should be made of one of the most eminent poets, Ssu-ma Hsiang-ju (179-147 B.C.), whose works are marked by an unusually rich language. On the other hand, the *yüeh-fu*, mostly folk songs collected by the Imperial Court, were somewhat similar to the odes of the *Shih ching* in being natural and simple, as well as in providing a good picture of the social conditions of the time.

V. Technology

The four centuries of the Han saw a considerable improvement in the technique of production in many fields. This was particularly true of agriculture; here drought-resistant rice was introduced, inter-tillage employed, rotation of early and late crops begun, as well as use made of hillside slopes for the planting of fruit, vegetables and bamboo. An important invention, both for agriculture and transport, was the introduction of the breast collar for draught animals.

In astronomy, observations advanced and thus sun spots were already observed in 28 B.C. (in Europe only in Galileo's time). The calendar was further perfected but perhaps the most interesting was the invention in A.D. 132 of the first seismograph by Chang Heng, who was also a famous astronomer.

Generally speaking, Chinese technology of the Han period was already not only abreast, but also in many respects ahead, of the other centres of civilization in the world. Over the entire period of time from the Han to the modern age the flow of ideas was more from the East to the West than from the West to the East. Two of the greatest Chinese inventions date from this era. There is no doubt that the traditional Chinese claim to have invented paper by the 1st century A.D. is true, as this has been confirmed by archaeological discoveries, those of A. Stein in Central Asia. It is not fortuitous that this discovery was made in a country where the written word was so highly regarded. It has been, however, remarked that this invention was made perhaps too early, i.e. too long a period lapsed between it and the invention of printing. As a result, due to the perishability of paper very few manuscripts have survived from the intermediary period. It took over a thousand years for this great invention to make its way to Europe. This demonstrates clearly the degree of isolation of the separate centres of civilization in Europe and Asia which did not undergo any essential changes until the 13th and 14th centuries. It is not possible to grasp the specific nature of many aspects of Chinese civilization without bearing this factor in mind. One should not, nevertheless, go to extremes and absolutize the role of this isolation which, although it had such great significance, was never completely hermetic in any period.

By the 2nd century A.D. the Chinese were already manufacturing pottery of a porcellaneous material which could be called proto-porcelain. From this it was only a relatively short period for them to take the next step to porcelain. One should note, in passing, the considerable hygienic benefits of this invention as compared with other types of utensil.

VI. Art

The creation of a unified empire was also reflected in the art forms; under the new conditions art was no longer purely religious in nature nor was it restricted solely to the princely houses, as was the case in the Chou period. It became much more widespread and the formation of a large and powerful class of scholar-officials who considered themselves, and in many cases actually were, cultivated gentlemen was partially responsible for this. The gentry had actually a double function in the development of Chinese art; they were, on the one hand, patrons, numerous and often liberal, while on the other hand, as will be seen later, they were themselves participants and creators of many of the art forms.

Most of what has come to us of Han art is derived from the provinces; even so, it is on a very high level. Logically, however, it can be assumed that the art of the capital must have been on a still much higher level. Unfortunately, the fate of Ch'ang-an and Loyang was such as we have seen, and nothing is left of imperial art and the collections of the emperors. It is an open question whether future archaeological discoveries will have much to add in this respect; however, the recent finds of Chinese archaeologists in the years 1968-1972, such as the discovery in Manch'eng (Hopei) of the magnificent tomb of Prince Liu Sheng (*ca.* 100 B.C.) and the unusually interesting grave of the wife of Marquis Tai (190-140 B.C.) in Mawangtui (near Ch'angsha, Hunan), provide extremely rich and valuable material.

Some interesting advance was made in sculpture where work in the round was done on both animal and human subject matter. This is known primarily from tomb statuary in which some of the best-known examples are the statues at the tomb of Huo Ch'ü-ping. Some very fine examples of lions and chimeras also exist. This tradition of Chinese stone sculpture reaching back to the Shang was to be almost completely overshadowed in the near future by Buddhist religious sculpture.

It is debatable whether the bas-reliefs in stone are to be regarded as sculpture; whatever the case, some of them, especially those from the famous Wu family tomb in Shantung which dates from the 2nd century A.D., are justly famous. A very delicate chiselling technique has been employed here, like painting on stone. The topics are of great interest as they are mostly, though not only, secular, with hunting, battle and historical scenes predominating. They throw an invaluable light on Chinese history. While it is possible that this art form was derived from contacts with West Asia, the style here is already thoroughly Chinese.

The style of the above bas-reliefs, as well as most other Han art objects, contains many novel features. One of these is the great use of animal motifs for ornamentation and here too it is possible that this is the result of the contacts established with Central Asia, where the so-called Scythian style was present. However, the Chinese added to the animals employed in this style—the tiger, deer, etc.—their own cherished mythical creations—the phoenix and the dragon.

Most of the features of Han style can be found also on silk fabrics. Han silk demonstrated an extremely high technical level and its quality was superb. The fabrics were plain or polychrome, often decorated in both the animal style as well as geometrical patterns. A large number of finds of Han silk have been made as a result of archaeological work, e.g. that of P. Pelliot and A. Stein in Central Asia, of P. Kozlov in Mongolia and recently of Chinese archaeologists.

In the decorative arts the Han period also shows much variety and vitality. This is especially true of a domain which was begun in *Chan Kuo* or Han times—lacquer. It was previously thought that lacquer originated in a much later period but the famous archaeological finds in Lo-lang (P'yong-yang) provided over 200 specimens of exquisite craftsmanship, most of it coming from West Szechuan. Some magnificent specimens of Han jewellery have also been discovered at the same sites. The recently discovered (1972) Mawangtui tomb contains some superb lacquer ware probably locally produced.

Older art forms were also continued in the Han period. Bronze was still employed for the manufacture of sacrificial vessels and ceremonial weapons as well as for a new purpose—mirrors. The technique remained very high but the great vitality and imagination of the Shang and early Chou years is definitely missing. The mirrors, however, have been regarded as masterpieces of bronze workmanship. The use of inlays, both gold and silver, became characteristic of the bronze products of the Han period. Jade carving continued as well and its extension was made possible by the use of new sources of the raw material, the mines in Khotan in the Western Regions.

One of the greatest, if not the greatest, of Chinese art forms, painting, has its roots very definitely in the Han period. There is no doubt that painting on silk was already practised in this time on a large scale; this is confirmed by literary accounts of the imperial collections which were completely destroyed at the fall of the Eastern Han. This is the primary reason why, unfortunately, almost nothing has survived of early Chinese painting and it must be judged on the basis of frescoes, a few of which have been discovered, and of painting done on other substances such as lacquer and tiles. It is true that in 1949 a fascinating discovery was made in Ch'angsha of a painting on silk dating probably from the Warring States period. The beautiful painted silk flag from Mawangtui and the Liaoning fresco are of equal interest. This makes the loss of practically all Han painting all the more regrettable.

Nothing has also survived of Han architecture; only clay models from tombs give some inkling of it. Here again, as in the case of painting, literary records are the principal source. Judging from these, Han architecture must have been magnificent and the technique complex. The pillars were inlaid with jade, the walls and cornices decorated with precious stones, the woodwork carved, painted and gilded, the stairs carved from marble. But the Han craftsmen built in wood, and thus all the superb palaces of the Han emperors followed the same fate as that of their predecessors, the Ch'in—sooner or later they went up in smoke, and the smoke carried away with it the work of countless generations of vastly skilled Chinese artisans.

PART IV

The Period of Division

CHAPTER 10

The Three Kingdoms and the Chin Dynasty

I. The Three Kingdoms

The fall of the Eastern Han marked the beginning of an evil era, a 400-year period of the division of China, later further deepened by the invasion from the north of nomad barbarian tribes and the establishment by them of states in North China. The centralized, absolute monarchy collapsed in this process and a distinct retrogression in the political and economic life of the country ensued. The degree of destruction, especially of the cities, and the loss of population was immense. In spite of all this, however, the crisis of the Chinese Empire did not produce such far-reaching results as the simultaneous fall of the Roman Empire. As mentioned, no general collapse of the Chinese civilization took place and its basic continuity was preserved. It is in this period that Chinese civilization showed its extraordinary integrative and absorptive capacity in its success in assimilating the nomadic invaders. Thus, while Chinese society, as shaped in the Han period, received tremendous blows in this period, it emerged from it basically unchanged. It is true that a number of transformations did take place and that the composition of the ruling class was undoubtedly altered in some respects; nevertheless, the basic alignment of social forces which later gave rise to the restoration of the unified empire in the Sui-T'ang period remained the same. Whether this development was a blessing or not from the point of view of the country's future is more than problematic.

Shortly after setting up the child Emperor Hsien as his puppet, Tung Cho, now the object of attack by other generals, left Loyang and headed for the strategic area of Ch'ang-an in Shensi. Upon his departure the splendid capital of the Eastern Han was pillaged and burned and much of its population perished. A period of vicious and involved struggles between the contending generals now followed, each aiming at

Map 9. The Three Kingdoms, ca. A.D. 230

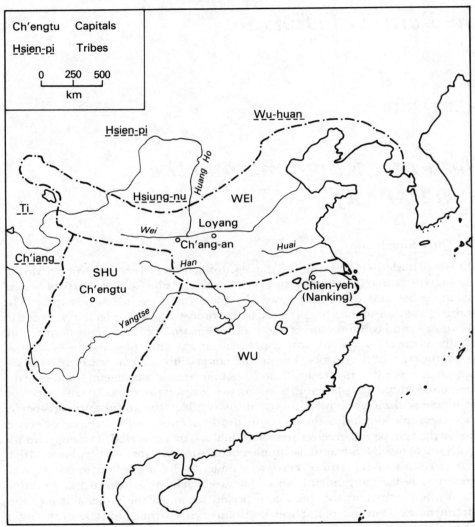

acquiring as much territory as possible. The contenders also strove to gain control of the person of the Emperor, wishing to utilize this for the exercise of supreme power. Ultimately, the result of this struggle was the establishment of three separate states: Wei, Shu and Wu, each a rival for power over all of China and each claiming to be legitimate ruler of the Empire. In Chinese traditional history it is only the state of Shu which has been granted the title of Empire and this is only due to the fact that its ruler was a descendant of the Han. This choice disregards the final episode in Han history whereby the last emperor abdicated in favour of the future ruler of Wei. The other states are regarded simply as kingdoms. In effect, one could equally well speak of three empires, for each of these states set up an identical imperial administration. It is customary, though, to use the term Three Kingdoms; the Chinese word *kuo* can be translated as empire, kingdom or state, depending on the circumstances.

The formation at this period of three separate states in China was made possible largely due to the level of economic development which had already been reached. Each of the areas which composed the Three Kingdoms was already economically sufficient for the maintenance of a separate state. In effect, the formation of the Three Kingdoms reflected also the rivalry of the key economic areas in China and thus of basic inner forces within China itself. This development also throws an interesting light on the specific nature of Chinese feudal society; its intensive agriculture entailed a need of a system of irrigation which made state control and supervision necessary. The aims of the state in carrying out these functions were, among others, to ensure the obtaining of necessary food supplies for its army.

Strangely enough, the Three Kingdoms are probably one of the best-known periods of history to the Chinese themselves. This is solely the result of literature; the famous Ming novel "The Romance of the Three Kingdoms", a curious mixture of legend and history, is the cause for this phenomenon (see p. 213). Thus the main personages of this era, their actions and sayings are known to almost every Chinese. In the novel, however, and in the many plays derived from it, the period becomes transformed to a certain degree into one of romance and chivalry. In truth, it was an epoch of treachery and violence, a transition from relative stability to complete anarchy and chaos.

The strongest of the Three Kingdoms which was ultimately to overcome its rivals was Wei. It controlled most of North China, the lands north of the Yangtse, including the Yellow River Valley, the original cradle of Chinese civilization and in this period still its main agricultural area. It had the largest population—one estimate basing itself on the 140 census gives this as around 29 million. The founder of Wei was Ts'ao Ts'ao, a ruthless, cunning, cruel and brutal man, a leading contender in the struggle of the generals, whose initial rise to power was the result of his warfare against the Yellow Turbans. Ts'ao Ts'ao succeeded in gaining control in 198 of Emperor Hsien and had himself proclaimed the Saviour of the Empire with the aim of establishing control of the entire country and ultimately ascending to the throne himself. In 208 Ts'ao Ts'ao led an immense army to the south in order to conquer the rest of China. This attempt failed, inasmuch as in a famous battle in the same year his entire fleet, which had been assembled for the purpose of crossing the Yangtse, was burned down by fireships and a great part of his army destroyed.

Death deprived Ts'ao Ts'ao of the possibility of fulfilling his ambition in becoming Emperor. It was his son and successor, Ts'ao Pei, who realized these plans by dethroning in 221 the last Han Emperor and proclaiming himself in his place. The

Ts'ao family, however, soon lost most of its power in struggles against the great families of Wei. The most prominent of these was the Ssu-ma clan which succeeded in gaining control of the state and ultimately in seizing the throne as well.

The Wei government paid considerable attention to the rebuilding of the shattered economy, especially agriculture, of this area. The main method employed was the establishment of agricultural colonies, both military and civil, under state control; the system of military colonies had been already extensively used during the Western Han period in frontier districts. The Wei also undertook a large number of extensive waterwork projects. As a result of these measures agricultural production did increase which enabled the Wei to accumulate the reserves necessary for military campaigns against its rivals. In the Chinese warfare of this era this was a most crucial factor and Wei preferred to starve out enemy forces rather than to meet them in direct combat.

The second of the Three Kingdoms was Shu or Han-Shu (221-263), established by Liu Pei, a descendant of one of the earlier emperors. The nucleus of the state was Shu, West Szechuan, where Liu Pei began to rule in 214. After gaining control of the Han River valley he declared himself also the King of Han in 219 and later, in 221, after the dethroning of the last Emperor, he declared himself Emperor in competition to the Wei. Liu Pei, as well as his two devoted friends Kuan Yü (who later became curiously transformed by the 16th century into the God of War) and Chang Fei, were made especially famous by "The Romance of the Three Kingdoms". Perhaps more important, and certainly more interesting, was Chu-ko Liang (181-234), Liu Pei's adviser and later chief minister; he was renowned for his political acumen, clever strategy and fertile inventiveness. It was actually he who put Liu Pei in power. It was also Chu-ko Liang who was responsible for the expansion of Shu—the conquest of native tribes in Yunnan, Kweichow and South Szechuan, for a sensible system of administration and for the establishment of good relations with the neighbouring Tibetan tribes to the west. The population of Shu was considerably less than that of Wei—the estimate on the basis of figures of 140 is 7.5 million. It possessed, however, a large Chinese peasant population settled on the fertile and well-irrigated Ch'engtu plain. Its strategic position was also advantageous as it could be attacked only from two directions, both difficult, the north-east and the Yangtse River.

Liu Pei died in 222, leaving the throne to his completely incapable son. Chu-ko Liang remained as chief minister and while he lived the state continued to prosper. However, after his death, in 234, during a campaign against Wu, the political fortunes of Shu declined. It fell victim to an expedition sent against it by Wei and in 263 Liu Pei's indolent son surrendered his capital, Ch'engtu, without the slightest resistance. It should be noted, in passing, that this was only one of the many times—at least seven—when Szechuan was independent from the rest of China. In the words of Liang Ch'i-ch'ao, "Whenever there were disturbances in China, Szechuan was held by an independent ruler and it was always the last to lose its independence." The reasons for this lay, amongst others, in its advantageous strategic position and great riches; it was always a most tempting prize for all adventurers.

The last of the Three Kingdoms—Wu (221-280)—included the provinces on the middle and lower reaches of the Yangtse as well as Fukien, Kwangtung, Kwangsi and North Vietnam. Its population, estimated on the same basis as above, was over 11 million, relatively very sparse considering the vast area of this kingdom. Wu also contained a high proportion of non-Chinese tribes which were undoubtedly more backward in their general social and economic development. The establishment of Wu and the setting up of an imperial court in its capital, the present Nanking, was of great significance for the development of the economy of this area, inasmuch as it provided a great market which served to stimulate both agriculture and trade. It is in this period that the transformation of the Yangtse Valley area, which was to lead to its becoming the principal economic area of all China, really began. The state was established by Sun Ch'üan who declared himself emperor in 229.

The Three Kingdoms, aptly called condotierre states by Eberhard, all claimed to be legitimate heirs of the Han Empire but all of them were, in reality, only very pale imitations of their predecessor. They were weak internally and this was primarily due to the conflict of the central government with the great landowning families, a phenomenon which was already true of the Eastern Han period. The constant wars between the Three Kingdoms led to an almost total ruin of the economy, to a great loss in population and especially to an immense destruction of the towns. This retrogression was best exemplified by the return to the use of barter due to the extraordinary scarcity of currency and by a return to natural economy; all this against the background of the very considerable advances which had been made earlier towards the direction of the development of a money economy. All three states made use of military colonization for the purpose of restoring agricultural production; the social crisis was, however, only deepened during this period. The peasantry, ruined by the incessant warfare of which it bore all the main burdens, fled in vast numbers from the land. A great number of the peasants were forced to become tenants of the great landowner families; others sought to escape by migration to the south, while still others reverted to a classical pattern in Chinese history and became outlaws. A series of peasant uprisings also dates from this period.

II. Western Chin

In 265 the last emperor of Wei of the Ts'ao family was removed from the throne by his general Ssu-ma Yen who established a new dynasty, the Chin, with himself as its first emperor (Wu-ti, 265-289). The history of this new dynasty is extraordinarily dismal, although Chinese Annals provide many other dreary examples. After his ascent to the throne Ssu-ma Yen devoted himself primarily to the pleasures of his huge harem (supposedly close to 10,000 women) and neglected the government completely. His one well-known act was to distribute appanages to his fifteen sons and the consequences of this were disastrous.

Having already conquered Shu, Chin now prepared for a campaign against the state of Wu. This was rendered easier by the internal conflicts in Wu and thus when the Chin army, purportedly 250,000 strong, crossed the Yangtse in 280 it gained an easy and almost bloodless victory. A temporary unification of all China was thus achieved but this lasted only to 304, when the great irruption of the nomad tribes into North China commenced. The newly united country was in very bad condition due, primarily, to the effects of the wars of the preceding period. The loss of population was especially significant and it probably surpassed that of the years dividing the Western and Eastern Han dynasty. The census in 280 gave a figure of only over 16 million as against that of over 56 million derived from the census in 156. From these figures some authors have drawn the conclusion that three-fifths of the population had lost their lives. This does not seem likely for, although the population loss must have been immense, the disparity is probably due to a greater degree to social changes. Both censuses were taken on the basis of households and the figures of 280 signify that a vast number of independent peasant households had simply ceased to exist, inasmuch as the previously free smallholders had in the meantime been forced to become tenants of the great landowners.

The new Chin government sought to demobilize its army in the customary fashion and to settle the soldiers on the land; on the whole, these measures failed to achieve their aim, inasmuch as a considerable number of the soldiers escaped to outlying areas, including those occupied by nomad tribes, in order to get away from the government tax collectors and the great landowners. This led to a further weakening of the central government while, simultaneously, the Ssu-ma princes were allowed to maintain their own armed forces in their appanages.

After the death of Wu-ti in 289 an unceasing struggle for power among the many Chin princes ensued, a terrible chronicle of intrigues and murders in which a particularly unsavoury role was played by the ferocious Empress Chia. The high point of this conflict was the so-called Rebellion of the Eight Princes which ravaged the country from 291 to 306. One of the results of this internecine struggle was a weakening of the Chin which made the future aggression of the nomad tribes much more feasible. The administration both of the central government and of the princely domains was corrupt; in the provinces it was largely in the hands of the great families. Taxes and other burdens on the population increased markedly even in comparison with the Three Kingdoms.

III. The Nomad Tribes in North China

A considerable number of the nomad tribes which were to rule over North China for the next period of over 300 years were to be found already within the borders of the Empire, having been settled there earlier by the Chinese rulers. Thus a situation somewhat similar to the entry of the Germanic tribes into the Roman Empire existed. It was the combination of these tribes within China, which still adhered basically to their own forms of social and political organization, with their kinsmen living outside of the Empire, which was to prove fatal to Chinese rule in the North. It should be pointed out, in passing, that there was no great slave population in North China which could possibly join the nomads in their action of bringing down the Chinese governmental machine.

The Chinese Annals of this period refer to the nomad tribes under the general term of the Five Hu—the Five Barbarian Peoples. They included the Ti and the Ch'iang, both of Tibetan stock, who were to be found in Kansu, Shensi and Ch'inghai. These were shepherds and not horse breeders, who fought primarily as infantry. Their infiltration into these areas was very extensive and some sources maintain that they formed in many parts of these provinces almost half of the population. Next came the Huns (formerly referred to as the Hsiung-nu) and the Chieh, supposedly of Turkic origin, who were located mostly in Shansi. Then came the Hsien-pi tribes, who have been described as either proto-Mongol or Tungus in origin and were located mostly in Hopei and Liaotung. The most important role among the Hsien-pi was to be played by the Mu-jung clan. The tribe which was ultimately to be of the greatest importance and the principal ruler in later times of North China, the Toba (T'opa), which was either of Turkic or Tungus origin, was still located north of the Great Wall in this period.

The nomad tribesmen were employed by the Chin princes as auxiliary troops in the wars which they waged against each other. Their great military advantage lay in the fact that they were excellent mounted archers, quite invincible in the conditions of the North China Plain. Some authors stress that the 4th century saw the beginning of a millennium of the military supremacy of the nomad mounted archer which was not to end before the introduction of firearms; this idea, while attractive, is nevertheless somewhat exaggerated.

While the nomads were being treated as allies and as defenders of North China against their fellow nomads north of the Great Wall they were, at the same time, the object of considerable oppression and exploitation by the Chin rulers and the Chinese great landowners; this led to a great increase of tension and hatred among them for Chinese rule.

The first group of nomad tribes to take up the struggle against Chinese rule in North China were the Huns, perhaps for the reason that theirs had been the longest contact with the Chinese and they had thereby acquired the best knowledge of the true weaknesses of the Chinese government. In 304 the leaders of the Hun tribes in the Fen Valley in Shansi declared Liu Yüan their king. He had spent some time as a hostage in Loyang and adopted the title of Han, claiming descent from the imperial family whose name he bore. The claim was based on the fact that Han princesses had been given in marriage to the Hun rulers. Starting with only 20,000 cavalry, then increased later to 50,000, he succeeded in extending his rule over a large part of North China. By 308 he proclaimed himself emperor and established his capital in P'ing-ch'eng (Tat'ung, Shansi). While his armies spread destruction to other parts of the North, the Fen Valley—the nucleus of his state—was well administered and an oasis of peace for the Chinese population as well. His son and successor, Liu Ts'ung, captured and destroyed the Chin capital of Loyang, while in 316 Ch'ang-an was taken by the Han general Shih Lo—an illiterate former slave whose career is symbolic of the period. Equally appalling scenes of carnage and destruction took place here. According to Chinese Annals only a hundred families were left alive in Ch'ang-an and only 2 per cent of the population of the Wei Valley area survived the Hun invasion. Thus, the rule of the Western Chin dynasty and of Chinese government came, for all practical purposes, to an end. There now ensued in North China, until then the most advanced region in every respect, a period of complete chaos and anarchy, lasting in fact from 304 to 439, during which a great number of ephemeral states were established, most of them by the conquering nomad tribes. It has been stated that these states resembled soap bubbles, distending to great size, some of them extending their rule over all of North China only to collapse, without any obvious reason, and to disappear with astonishing rapidity.

It is worth noting that these nomad conquests of North China occurred in more or less the same period as their incursion into Europe and thus a great simultaneous expansion of these peoples took place which was unparalleled until the 13th century, when the Mongols were to repeat much the same process. The basic causes for this phenomenon are still unclear though many hypotheses have been advanced, the most likely of which is a rapid growth of population which completely exceeded the possibilities of nomad economy.

Fundamentally, the rule of the nomad tribes entailed primarily destruction for the areas they occupied, especially in the first period of their invasion. This, however, affected not only the Chinese population but also the nomads themselves; the wars which they conducted against each other with unmitigated savagery led to a constant depletion of their strength and thus to their ultimate defeat and disappearance.

The main cause, however, why nomad rule over North China during this period was to prove ephemeral was the ability, already mentioned earlier, of the Chinese population to assimilate these conquering tribes. Of the many reasons which contributed to this result the most important, undoubtedly, was the great difference in the size of the population. In spite of all the losses that it suffered and the migration to the South, the Chinese peasant population vastly outnumbered the relatively small number of the nomad tribes. It is this factor which also posed a basic question to the nomads when they began their rule over a thickly populated agricultural area—how to remain nomadic, i.e. not to abandon their original way of life under such conditions. To put the question somewhat differently, what should be done with the Chinese peasants? There were only three alternatives: (1) to drive them away, (2) to exterminate them and change the country into pastureland, as was advocated by Shih Lo who genuinely hated all the Chinese, and (3) simply to become a ruling caste governing and exploiting this vast peasant community. In fact, they opted for the third alternative, but not having any of the skills or experience necessary for administering this type of community they were forced to rely on the assistance of the Chinese gentry officials to run the country for them.

The state founded by Liu Yüan, first called the Han and then known as the Earlier Chao, lasted until 329 when it was replaced by Later Chao, with Shih Lo as the first ruler, which lasted till 352. This, in turn, succumbed to defeat at the hands of other nomad tribes. The unceasing rivalry and mutual destruction of the nomad states was undoubtedly one of the principal reasons why Chinese rule could be maintained at all in the south of the country.

IV. Eastern Chin

After the fall of Ch'ang-an one of the surviving Chin princes was able to establish in 317 a new Chin government to the south of the Yangtse. Its capital was Chien-yeh (Nanking) and thus Chinese rule was still maintained over a vast part of the country. This government is referred to as the Eastern Chin dynasty which lasted till 419 and subsequently was followed by four more Chinese dynasties, all ruling approximately the same area until the unification of China by the Sui in 589.

The Eastern Chin government was to a considerable degree established and run by those of the great families which had managed to escape from the North with their followers and as much of their wealth as possible. In this fact rested also one of the main features of the political history of the Eastern Chin, inasmuch as an almost unceasing conflict was waged between these newcomers and the Chinese landlords in this area who had settled here in earlier times. In addition, the Ssu-ma clan, although it had been much reduced in size, had learned absolutely nothing from its previous experiences; it was just as greedy and cruel as it had been before, just as prone to intrigues and a vicious struggle for power.

The new dynasty in the South made relatively few attempts to recover the lands that had been lost in North China, although at times such opportunities were presented by the struggles between the rival nomad states. Exceptions to this were the campaigns led by Tsu T'i in the years 313-321, largely on his own initiative, which had a considerable degree of success. The lack of support by the government, however, for this "forward policy" led to the loss of the territory that had been regained.

The economy of the Eastern Chin area was much less affected by warfare than North China and some progress was made during the 4th century. This was primarily due to the large-scale migration from the North which resulted in a marked increase in land under cultivation. Social conditions, however, steadily deteriorated under Eastern Chin rule and this was reflected by a number of peasant uprisings. The largest and most interesting of these took place in East Chekiang and was led by Sun En. Its main base was an island off the coast from which successful attacks were made on the mainland; in official Chinese history, Sun En figures as a pirate. In 399 the population of eight prefectures rose to join Sun En's forces, killing all the officials it could lay its hands on. A long struggle against the imperial forces followed which lasted to 403. During its course Sun En was even able to sail up the Yangtse with a great fleet of 1000 junks and a force of supposedly 100,000 men; ultimately, however, the rising was defeated by the imperial forces under General Liu Yü—a man of peasant origin—the same who was to overthrow the Eastern Chin later on. The areas affected by the rising were reconquered and, as the Annals say, the pacification carried out was such that "the people bitterly regretted the rule of the rebels".

V. North China Under Nomad Rule

In the kaleidoscopic changes of governments in North China it was the turn of the Tibetans, after the downfall of the Huns—primarily due to mutual destruction—to gain mastery over the entire area. This was the achievement of the Fu family which established the state of Earlier Ch'in, of which Shensi was the nucleus (351-394). During the rule of Fu Chien the most serious attempt ever to be undertaken by the nomads to conquer the rest of China took place. In 383 a vast army, purportedly 600,000 infantry and 370,000 cavalry (the figures are obviously inflated), was mobilized and marched down to the Yangtse. When he was told of the difficulties which faced him, especially in view of the fact that cavalry, the great main weapon of the nomads, was unsuitable to the conditions of the Yangtse Valley, Fu Chien disregarded all the warnings; his saying is famous, "My army is so huge that if all the men in it throw their whips in to the Yangtse this will suffice to cover it." At the crucial battle of the Fei River in the same year his army was completely crushed by a much smaller Chin force. This was due to many factors—very bad generalship, treachery within his own camp, and, above all, the fact that the army contained a very large number of extremely unwilling Chinese conscripts. It was these who, during what was intended to be a tactical retreat, panicked and fled. The slaughter which followed was supposedly so great that over half of the army perished in the rout.

The result was a speedy collapse of the Earlier Ch'in state in the North; its place was taken by a large number of successor states which fought, as customary, between themselves for the hegemony over North China. Thus, in 386 there were seven separate states; in 400—nine; in 415—seven; in 425—five. Then the rise to power of the Toba resulted once more in the unification of the North into one empire. By the end of this period, however, the nomad population of North China was very considerably reduced—a great number of the nomads had lost their lives in the constant wars. Much of the ruling class had intermarried with the Chinese gentry and were rapidly merging with the Chinese landowners, while more and more of the tribesmen abandoned their nomad way of life, settled down to a sedentary, agricultural existence and underwent an equally rapid sinification. Many of the tribes simply disappeared from the scene, having left behind them havoc and devastation.

CHAPTER 11

Northern and Southern Dynasties

I. The Rise to Power of the Toba

In the Period of Division it was only the Toba of all the nomad tribes which had invaded China who succeeded in creating a state that was something more than an ephemeral image. The question of the ethnic origin of the Toba is still, as has been mentioned, unclear but whatever the descent of the ruling group they were, in fact, a federation of tribes of different origins; it has been stated that they were composed of 119 different tribes, or parts of tribes. As they increased in strength and influence many various remnants of other nomad peoples came under their rule.

The Toba had founded a state, Tai, in North China in the middle of the 4th century but their real rise to power commenced only after the fall of Fu Chien's empire. In 386 their ruler declared himself King and, in 398, Emperor of Wei (Northern Wei). From the very outset the Toba rulers had listened to and accepted the advice of the numerous Chinese officials who had joined them; the main content of this was that they should adopt Chinese methods of administration for the purpose of ruling over the Chinese population of North China. Thus they did not break up the territory which they conquered but built a unified state with a Chinese administration while, simultaneously, they sought to maintain in existence their own distinct tribal organization. They adhered to these policies during the period in which their rule extended itself over more and more of the North China Plain. The majority of their campaigns was directed against the Yen state of the Hsien-pi Mu-jung clan which they succeeded in overcoming and annexing, due primarily to the inner divisions and incessant conflicts of the Mu-jung princes.

The collaboration of the Chinese officials, i.e. of the Chinese landowning gentry, with the Toba should be examined more closely. There is no doubt that the establishment of a more permanent nomad state in North China would have been quite impossible without the co-operation of the Chinese upper class as it was only this group which could provide the necessary knowledge and personnel for the running of a state based on the exploitation of an agricultural economy and population. Hence, when a modern Chinese author praises the Toba for "drawing on the rich experiences in the administration of China" he fails to appreciate the irony of the situation, that the nomad barbarians could succeed in exploiting the Chinese peasant masses only because the Chinese great landowners were willing to help them to do so for the sake of their own class interests. This type of collaboration was by no means restricted to the Wei period; we shall meet with this phenomenon time and again, whenever the nomad people conquer either the North or all of China, up to and including the Manchu period.

By 439 the Toba had gained complete success; they had extended their rule to all of

Map 10. Period of Division, ca. 500

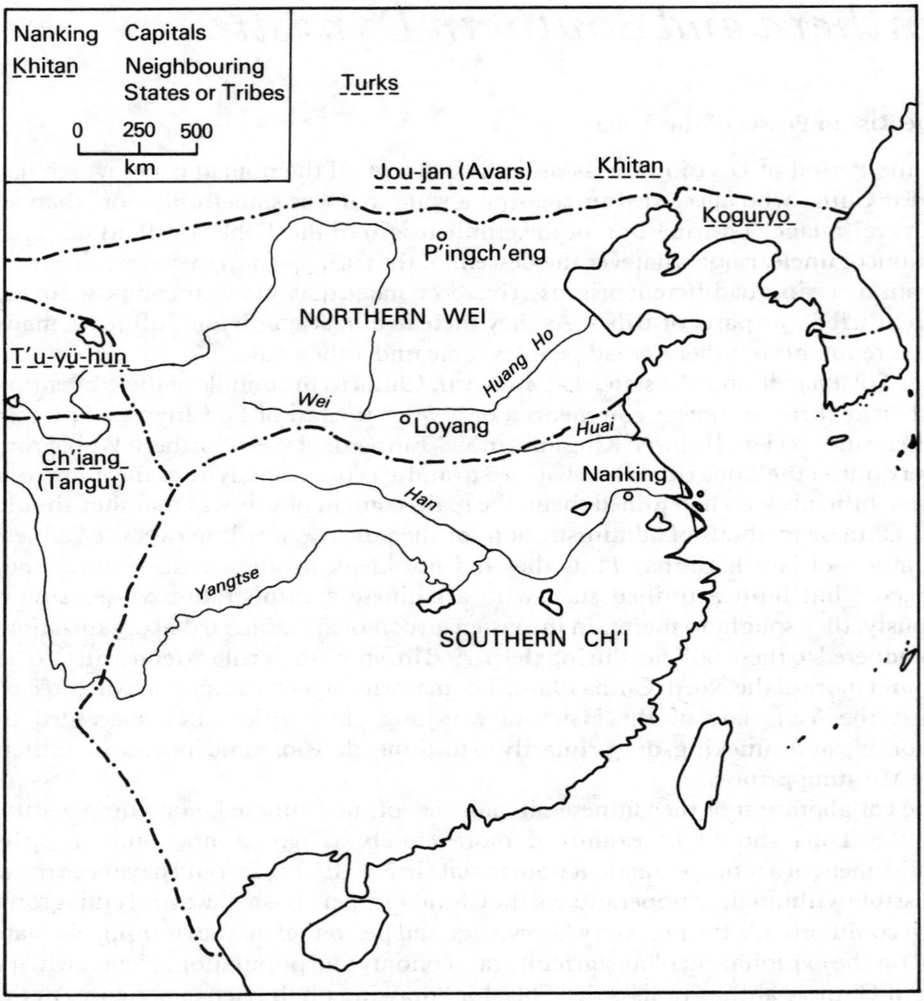

North China and built a powerful empire. They were now to continue their warfare in two directions; it should be noted, in passing, that, although they were quicker in assuming a Chinese way of life, they were just as aggressive as any other of the nomad peoples. The first direction was a continuous campaign to the South for almost a century with the basic aim of bringing all of China under their sway. In these campaigns the Toba made considerable use of their Chinese subjects as infantry and the devastation which they inflicted on various parts of Central China was as terrible as that by any of their predecessors. The last of the campaigns against the South undertaken on a truly large scale took place in 507.

The second direction was a constant struggle of the Toba against the neighbouring nomad tribes to the north. These were the Jou-jan or Avars who now threatened the Wei Empire in exactly the same way as the Hsiung-nu had threatened the Han. The main campaigns waged against the Avars lasted from 409 to 449, during which time the Toba succeeded in reducing this danger to themselves and seriously weakening the power of the Avars. In connection with the threat of the Avars the Wei repaired the Great Wall and extended it considerably to the west. This throws an interesting light on the transformations which the Toba had undergone and on the degree to which they were already following the normal course of policy in the interest of a Chinese agricultural state defending itself against nomad incursions. In the 6th century the Avars were eliminated as an important factor by the rise of the Turkic tribes, their former dependents, who defeated them and created their own great empire instead. There are two conflicting versions as to the final end of the Avars; one maintains that they were completely wiped out by the Turks, after their remnants had been handed over to them by the Wei. The second belief is that they fled westward, reaching the Danube by 565. This latter version has been challenged for a long period of time—in fact since Gibbon—it is claimed that the Avars, so famous in European history, were in reality another Turkic tribe which had simply made use of the famous name.

As a means of consolidating their rule and improving the economy the Wei government also concerned itself with the land problem. In 485 the so-called land-equalization system, based on a proposal made by a Chinese official, was introduced which provided for a distribution of state land to the peasants. Agricultural land was given for life tenure, while land to be used for orchards, especially mulberry trees, was granted in perpetuity. These measures are assumed to have succeeded in the raising of the level of agricultural production. Nevertheless, it must be stated that this whole problem is quite obscure. Some authors maintain that this policy was applied to practically all the land; it seems much more probable that it was applied only to the land which had been abandoned during the preceding period. Other authors incline to the belief that this legislation was of a purely declarative, utopian character and that it was never really enforced. The only facts which can be ascertained with any degree of assurance is that the formation of great landed estates, owned both by the Toba aristocracy and the Chinese great landowners, went on apace and that this concentration of land ownership in the north of China was quite similar to the processes which were taking place in the South. In both cases it would seem that in this age a major part of the peasant population had ceased to be small holders and had become tenant farmers.

The Toba simultaneously faced a practically insoluble problem, how to maintain a nomad existence while being settled in an agricultural country. As long as they were still a basically horse-using people they had need of extensive areas of pasturage for their mounts (50 *mu* per horse) and this always raised the question of whether the land should be employed for agriculture or for pasture, at the expense of the Chinese peasants. It would seem that the problem was temporarily solved by a compromise.

As a result of their collaboration with the Chinese great landowners and their establishment of a Chinese type of administration, the Toba rulers underwent a very rapid process of sinification. A good example of this was the removal of the Wei capital from P'ing-ch'eng in North Shansi to Loyang in 493, a move which was advantageous to the Chinese but disadvantageous to those of the Toba who still pursued a nomad way of life. During this period, 480-496, a whole series of measures aimed at speeding up the process of sinification was undertaken; Chinese was adopted as the official language of the court; the Toba nobility were to assume Chinese names and were encouraged to intermarry with Chinese great families; the name of the dynasty was changed to Yüan and the use of the Toba language, dress and customs was prohibited. All of these measures were greatly resented by that part of the Toba nobility and people who still retained the nomad way of life of their ancestors. This, in turn, gave rise to many conflicts between them and the sinified rulers. Actually, from the beginning of the 6th century the Wei state can be considered as a basically Chinese entity and it is quite certain that the Wei Emperor regarded himself as a purely Chinese ruler. As time went on the role played by the Chinese officials and landowners in the Wei empire became more and more dominant.

In its administration the Wei government did not differ appreciably from other Chinese feudal regimes, although some authors, especially modern Chinese, maintain that it was more oppressive. It was, however, undoubtedly noted for its high taxes, extensive use of *corvée* labour and especially for the heavy demands it made on the peasantry for military service. In order to assure an efficient exploitation of the peasant population the Wei rulers established the so-called Three Leaders system, in which the respective leaders of the hamlet, village and district were responsible for the collection of taxes, *corvée* labour and military service. (Five families, theoretically, made up one hamlet; five hamlets—one village; five villages—one district.)

The Wei emperors were, on the whole, favourably disposed to Buddhism; under their rule it reached its period of greatest expansion and even for a time became the official state religion (see Chapter 12). It is possible that the Toba rulers considered this support of Buddhism politically advantageous as a counterweight to the Confucianist Chinese gentry. However, as the strength of the Chinese great families increased, Confucianism also rose once more in importance and soon returned, after the establishment of the capital in Loyang, to its former position of a dominant ideology.

II. The Fall of the Toba Empire

By 520 the rule of the Wei had been considerably weakened both by the opposition to its policies of that part of the Toba people who had still retained their nomad way of life and by increasing peasant unrest. A two-year-long revolt of troops (523-525) seriously undermined the strength of the government; it was further weakened by a large-scale peasant uprising in Hopei which lasted until 528. The result of these events and of the customary internecine struggle between the Toba princes was the breakup of

the empire into two parts—Eastern Wei (534-550) and Western Wei (534-557). In both
these states the Toba rulers became, in reality, mere figure-heads and all power was
concentrated in the hands of Chinese generals and officials. Shortly, the Wei rulers were
removed from power by their major-domos in both of these states; thus Eastern Wei was
transformed into the state of Northern Ch'i (550-577) and Western Wei into Northern
Chou (557-581).

In both Northern Ch'i and Northern Chou the process of sinification had made such
progress that both of these states should be regarded as Chinese. In its administrative
aspects the system of the Wei empire was continued by both the states. The greater part
of the nomad tribesmen had settled on the land and merged with the Chinese peasants.
In fact, the Toba as a people now disappear from history, totally assimilated by the
Chinese population. "The great Chinese ocean which salts every river flowing into it"
had done its work here extremely well. Thus the long reign of the nomad tribes over
North China had resulted not in the barbarization of the country and of the Chinese, as
was the case of the Germanic invasions in Europe, but in the assimilation and the
disappearance of the conquerors. This was due, among others, also to the fact that
Chinese culture during the Han period had penetrated quite deeply into the peasant
masses. They were its repository and they were responsible for maintaining and
preserving the Chinese national identity of the country. As mentioned, both the fact of
their great numerical superiority, which was an advantage, as well as the lack of any
large slave population of foreign origin went a long way to account for this. All of this
explains why North China emerged from this unhappy age as a land still essentially
Chinese.

The political history of the two successor states to the Wei Empire—presented by the
Annals as the story of the ruling houses, which is unfortunately true of most traditional
Chinese history—is a sordid and depressing account of involved intrigues, innumer-
able murders and scheming plots. The rulers of Northern Ch'i were perhaps among the
most fantastically degenerate monsters in the long line of "bad rulers" in China. In 577
Northern Chou succeeded in conquering Northern Ch'i and thus uniting the North
once more. Its rulers, however, were to meet the fate of so many other dynasties in
Chinese history. The rise of the Yang family to power sealed their fate. In 580 the
imperial clan of the Northern Chou, the Yü-wen, was massacred by General Yang
Chien, the future founder of the Sui dynasty, who then succeeded in conquering South
China and thus in bringing about the end of the Period of Division.

III. The Southern Dynasties

In the South, after the fall of Eastern Chin, four further dynasties occupied the throne
in Nanking, which remained the capital throughout most of this period. These were the
Liu Sung (420-479), the Southern Ch'i (479-502), the Liang (502-557) and the Ch'en
(557-589). As can be seen all of these dynasties were of relatively short duration. They
were all established by generals and the throne was quickly lost by their successors to
new pretenders to power. In this situation of general instability and weakness of the
central government the country was, in effect, ruled by the great families of landowner-
officials, whose hold was particularly strong in the provinces. This class constituted a
small oligarchy of great magnates, a closed elite which kept all the positions of power in

its own hands. During this period the principles of the bureaucratic system, as had been shaped during the Han, were in abeyance and the formal establishment of the so-called Nine Rank System of higher officials (which was initiated by Ts'ao Ts'ao in 220) facilitated the oligarchy's monopoly of all political power.

The economic base of the ruling class lay primarily in the great increase in size of its landed estates and the transformation of a large part of the peasant population, of the former small freeholders, into tenant farmers on these estates. Some authors maintain that the growth of what could be called a manorial system was the most important characteristic of this age. This process was probably aided by the undoubted upswing **and further development of the economy of the South. It was, due above all, to the huge** migration from the North which provided the necessary labour power in this sparsely populated area; it was accompanied also by the steady assimilation of the non-Chinese population in the South and its absorption into the Chinese system of economy. Some sources estimate that as a result of these processes the population of the South increased five-fold in the 280-464 period. These extremely important changes affected not only the Yangtse Valley area but also Szechuan, Fukien and Kwangtung. Economic growth, as well as the increase in the number and size of large estates, was particularly marked in South Kiangsu and Chekiang, while other parts of the South progressed more slowly. The overall result of this economic development was a return once more to a money economy in the South after the setback of the Three Kingdoms.

While wars were a constant phenomenon in this period—between the South and the North as well as domestic struggles—it should be remembered that simultaneously there were always very large areas in this vast land which did live in comparative peace and thus economic development was made possible. One result of these processes which was of vital significance was the increase in the relative gravity of the South; this constituted a definite shift from the North to the Yangtse area. The latter became henceforth the most important economic and political area of the country as a whole.

It is truly not worth while to delve into the details of the political history of these Southern Dynasties, for here the sordidness is much the same as that of the North. The Liu Sung dynasty was perhaps one of the most repellent of all in Chinese history, aptly described by one historian as a series of drunken, licentious and murderous rulers. The first ruler of the Southern Ch'i started his reign by killing off the entire Liu family; his line did not differ appreciably from his predecessors. The founder of the Liang, though later famed, after his conversion, as the great patron of Buddhism in China, also commenced his reign by killing off all the survivors of the Ch'i ruling family, of which he himself was a member. The true importance of this period is to be found not in its political history, therefore, but in the very vital transformation of Chinese society—in the great colonization of the South, as well as in the developments of Chinese culture which are bound up with the rise of Buddhism.

CHAPTER 12

Culture During the Period of Division

I. Buddhism in China

According to tradition, the entry of Buddhism into China dates back to the 1st century A.D. although the exact period of its penetration is, in fact, unknown. In the early era, however, it had very little significance for it was an alien religion propagated by foreign monks, restricted in its followers mostly to colonies of Central Asian merchants. The scope of its activities was limited to the area of the capital where it was regarded as something of a bizarre curiosity. It was the extensive contacts which had been established during the Han period with Central Asia that had been responsible for the influx of Buddhist ideas; they followed the trade routes and the creed itself was in this time primarily an urban religion. The missionaries who propagated Buddhism came not only from the thriving Buddhist communities of Central Asia but also from India itself. In this era Buddhism was still a flourishing and active religion in India as well, capable of undertaking missionary work on a large scale. It is only after the downfall of the Eastern Han that, in the ensuing turmoil and confusion, Buddhism began to gain rapidly in influence. This process took place almost unobserved, i.e. because—in Maspero's view—Buddhism was regarded for a long time simply as a peculiar variety of Taoism.

The penetration of Buddhism into China was a factor of utmost importance for it affected all spheres of Chinese life. Until the middle of the 19th century, when the impact of the West began to be felt, no foreign influence had ever been as significant as that of Buddhism. The effects of Buddhism have been compared by some authors to those of Christianity in Europe; this seems somewhat exaggerated, although some aspects of the analogy are worth considering. There is, for instance, the amazing outward resemblance to the meretricious pomp and pageantry of Roman Catholic worship which so shocked the Jesuit missionaries. Its other-worldliness was perhaps even more far-reaching than that of the Christian creed and, on the whole, it might seem in certain respects to be an even more pessimistic doctrine. Its influence in China was paramount for centuries and it penetrated to all classes of Chinese society.

It is a strange phenomenon that a foreign religion which contrasted in so many ways to Confucian ideology was able to succeed to the degree to which Buddhism did. Its advocacy of celibacy, monasticism (which always tended to create an *imperium in imperio*), asceticism, mendicancy, the doctrine of personal salvation—all of this ran contrary to current Chinese ideas and customs and this in basic matters affecting the life of the individual and the community. There seems little doubt that the success of Buddhism was primarily due to the fact that the immense crisis of the Chinese state and society from the beginning of the 3rd century made resistance to Buddhism by

Confucianism much more difficult. This crisis had shaken to its foundations the ever-present belief that China was the only truly civilized society in the world. An interesting analogy could be made with the situation in China in the 19th and 20th centuries. It also seems clear that the calamities of this era made the appeal of an other-worldly creed much more attractive.

It is not fortuitous that Buddhism first gained strength in North China—in the kingdoms established by the nomad barbarians—many of which are now remembered primarily for the development of Buddhist schools and art in their area and period—for it is here that Chinese traditional society was shattered to the greatest degree. The protection given to Buddhism by the rulers of North China was due also to the fact that many of the Confucian gentry had fled to the South, and in their need for scholars to aid in running the administration the rulers often turned for assistance to the Buddhist monks. An immense expansion of Buddhist influence in North China took place in the 4th and 5th centuries. By 405 supposedly nine-tenths of the population in the North was already Buddhist; the creed was first taken up by the ruling class and subsequently by the peasantry. By 500 most of China was already considered to be Buddhist. The figures usually given for the beginning of the 6th century are 30,000 temples and a community of 2 million monks and nuns.

The rise of Buddhism did not automatically signify the disappearance and elimination of either Taoism or Confucianism; the Chinese did not, at this or any other time, absolutize their religious beliefs and it was possible to be simultaneously an adherent of all three creeds. Nor did Buddhism demand a complete and total rejection of beliefs differing from it for, as an example, it tolerated the continuation of ancestor worship.

The protection given to Buddhism by Chinese rulers (first in the North but then also in the South as is shown by the famous example of Emperor Wu of the Liang) was probably due also to their appreciation of its social role: its encouragement of passivity towards one's present existence and its emphasis on hopes based on the possibility of a better life in the reincarnation. The benevolent attitude and protection of the Buddhist religion was not a constant phenomenon, for a number of persecutions did take place, as for example the one in Northern Wei in 444. These, however, were usually the result of the intrigues of the Taoist or Confucian rivals of the Buddhists and were always of short duration and limited effect. It should be stressed that religious persecution in China never resembled that of Europe; it did not signify the burning at the stake, the torture and massacre of believers in different creeds. It meant, at most, a destruction of monasteries and the turning of the monks and nuns back to normal secular life. A non-absolutist character of religious beliefs was matched by a non-absolutist attitude of the state towards religion, although the state did watch the Buddhist establishment carefully to see whether it did not become too great a secular power.

Buddhism recovered quickly from the persecution of 444 and the later Toba rulers, mostly fervent Buddhists, transformed it into an official state religion and heaped immense wealth on the church. The great growth of Buddhist monasticism referred to above was not only the result of religious belief but was also a reflection of the social crisis—it was a form of escape from heavy obligations, from military service and the *corvée*. An ever-greater number of peasants became tenants on the lands of the Buddhist church because they found it to be a less oppressive landowner. It was undoubtedly also this protection of the rulers which accounted for the remarkable fact that the spread of

Buddhism was one of the rare instances in which religion was propagated not by force, not by the sword, but by peaceful means.

In spite of its immense strength in the 5th and 6th centuries (which, as we shall see later, was still maintained in the 7th and 8th centuries under the Sui and early T'ang) Buddhism never developed into a great political power as did the Christian churches in Europe. This was perhaps due to the looseness of the organization of the Buddhist church, to the presence of different sects within it and also to the non-absolutist nature of the religion itself, as well as the continued and tolerated existence of rival creeds.

Buddhism was already divided into many different schools and sects before its arrival and expansion in China. The main form which was propagated in China was, broadly speaking, the Mahayana. This creed was quite different in many respects from the original ethical teachings of Gautama; it was, in fact, practically a new religion, well provided with an entire, immense pantheon of god-like Buddhas and Bodhisattvas. Herein lay its basis for popular appeal, while simultaneously it had a highly developed metaphysical philosophy. As a creed, Mahayana Buddhism was open to foreign ideas and cults and was ready to compromise with both Taoism and Confucianism, even to the extent of appropriating a number of their ideas; in this, to a great degree, rested the reasons for its success in China. As the influence of Buddhism grew, the Mahayana creed became more and more Chinese in its form and ideas, so that ultimately it bore very little resemblance to the original Indian creed. This is particularly true of the Buddhist sects which originated in China, even if they furnished themselves with completely legendary pedigrees regarding their purported Indian origin.

The introduction of Buddhism signified also the penetration into China of Indian influence on a vast scale, the acquainting of China with Indian achievements and ideas in the fields of philosophy, literature, mathematics, astronomy and especially art and architecture. All of this was of crucial importance for the future development of Chinese culture. It should be noted, however, that this was a meeting of two mature civilizations and thus the effect was quite different from, for example, the influx and influence of Chinese civilization on Korea or Japan. It was this appeal of complex philosophical ideas, of a rich literature, of an ornate ritual and ceremony combined with the attractiveness of an escapist monastic life and a doctrine of personal salvation which accounted for the success of Buddhism.

Of the many schools and sects of Buddhism at least three deserve a brief mention. The most important, and usually regarded as the main form of Chinese Buddhism, was the Pure Land (*Ching tu*) sect which involved the worship of the Amitabha (Amida) Buddha and of such Bodhisattvas as Kuan Yin. This became, for all practical purposes, a new form of popular religion which primarily stressed faith and repetition of sacred names in order to ensure a future entry into Amitabha's Western Paradise, "A place of complete beauty with jewelled trees, lofty palaces and lotus ponds enlivened by heavenly musicians and dancers".

A more philosophical sect was the *T'ien-t'ai* (named after a mountain in Chekiang, the location of a monastery where the founder of the sect resided) which was formed towards the end of the 6th century. The sect stressed a scholastic study of the vast Buddhist canon and the observance of rituals but placed its main emphasis on moderation. It had considerable appeal to Chinese scholars and many learned monks were associated with it. It is maintained that the ideas of this sect reflected, to a certain extent, the effects of Confucianism.

The most far-reaching in its departure from orthodox Buddhist religious practice and ideas and simultaneously the most completely Chinese of the important Buddhist sects was Ch'an (Zen in Japanese) which, originating in the 6th century, became influential from the 9th century on. This was a subjective, irrational (or perhaps anti-rational), iconoclastic creed which placed the main emphasis on the necessity of gaining inward enlightenment through meditation, combining this with a thoroughly negative attitude to rituals, observances and canonical literature. It is in Ch'an that the influence of Taoism comes out most strongly and obviously; there is much resemblance between its ideas and the Taoist stress on simplicity, austerity and quietism. The sect had considerable importance in various periods, affecting Chinese thought from the Sung to the Ming, but perhaps its greatest significance lay in its influence on Chinese art; here it was to serve as the source of inspiration for some of the most magnificent paintings ever to be produced in China. It has been deservedly called by Goodrich "probably the finest flowering of Indian culture in China".

It should be mentioned, in passing, that the worship of the Maitreya Buddha, the future Buddha to come, which in the early stage was part and parcel of the orthodox Buddhist creed, was later to take on certain revolutionary implications, to which its messianistic essence lends itself well, and became the ideological basis for the activity of secret societies which often organized and led the struggle of the peasants. Such was, for example, the White Lotus Society, about whose activity we shall hear more in the future. It is first mentioned in 386 but it is unclear what the connection is between the first organization and the future society bearing the same name.

Originally the propagation of Buddhism was the work of foreign missionaries of many nationalities both from Central Asia and India; the Chinese were only officially allowed to become monks in the 4th century. This gave rise to the great and difficult problem of translating the immense Buddhist literature into Chinese, starting from around A.D. 150. Many ingenious ways of solving this problem were evolved; thus, for example, an Indian monk would recite a sutra which would then be translated by an interpreter and then, in turn, the translation would be set into proper Chinese. The Chinese language was also enriched by a completely new terminology which was devised for this purpose (6000 to 7000 words). The difficulties of translation are perhaps best illustrated by the apt saying of Kumarajiva (344-413), one of the most famous of the Buddhist missionaries, who maintained that: "Translating Sanskrit into Chinese is like feeding a man with rice chewed by another; it is not merely tasteless; it is nauseating as well."

The above observation, however, did not stop him from translating ninety-eight Buddhist scriptures, of which fifty-two are still extant. As a result of the work of both foreign and Chinese translators a tremendous corpus of Buddhist literature was rendered into Chinese; thus, in 517, Emperor Wu of the Liang was able to have published the entire Tripitaka (the Buddhist Canon) and future editions of this followed. It should be noted, in passing, that many of the early Buddhist sutras are now known only in their Chinese version.

The spread of Buddhism in China also gave rise to a great number of pilgrimages of Chinese to India in the search of original Buddhist writings as well as images and also for the purpose of visiting places which had been made holy by their association with Gautama. One hundred and eighty-six names of Chinese pilgrims are known for the period 259-790; there were undoubtedly many more of these brave men who faced the great hazards of this long journey over some of the most difficult terrain in the world and often paid for it with their lives. One of the most famous of these was Fa-hsien. He left China in 399 and, after travelling through the states of Central Asia and present-day Afghanistan, he reached India where he subsequently studied at the main Buddhist centres, collected books and images and travelled widely. Later on he visited Ceylon and finally took ship for China; his route took him to Java, and after many perilous adventures he succeeded in reaching Shantung in 414 with his entire precious collection intact. He spent the rest of his life translating the vast material he had brought with him; he also wrote an account of his travels which is invaluable both for the history and geography of this period.

II. Taoism

While in this period it is undoubtedly the rise of Buddhism which is the most important phenomenon in the ideological sphere, a number of significant developments took place in other fields, especially in Taoism, some of these under the influence and as a result of the spread of Buddhism.

The triumph of Confucianism during the Han period did not bring about an extinction of Taoism; the ideas of philosophical Taoism were still current between the 3rd and 6th centuries. One of the perhaps best-known groups of Taoists were the famous Seven Sages of the Bamboo Grove (second half of the 3rd century) who were noted for their supposed eccentric behaviour. The accounts of their activities must be taken with a grain of salt, inasmuch as practically all the material relating to them comes from inimical sources. It is probable that the actions of these very talented men, the most prominent was Hsi K'ang (232-262), were, in fact, a form of protest against the stifling pressure of Confucian conformism and hypocrisy. Their ideas might not seem so strange if one were to bear in mind the intellectual and moral chaos of the Three Kingdoms.

[margin note: 7 Sages]

At the same time a new trend developed in philosophical Taoism, referred to by some authorities as Neo-Taoism, in which some of the above group also participated. Apart from its rather obstruse metaphysical speculation, the main line of thought of the Neo-Taoists was an attempt to synthesize Confucianism and Taoism, i.e. to adapt Taoism to the Confucian milieu. Some authors (Hou Wei-lu, for example) consider that in this the Neo-Taoists practically emasculated the teachings of Lao Tzu and Chuang Tzu, especially depriving them of their anti-feudal essence. The Neo-Taoists were noted for their commentaries to the Taoist classics. Thus, Wang Pi (226-249), whom Fung Yu-lan called "one of the most precocious geniuses in the history of Chinese thought", devoted a large commentary to the *Tao te ching* while Kuo Hsiang (d. 312) and Hsiang Hsiu *(ca.* 221-*ca.* 300) wrote on the *Chuang-tzu* and the *I ching*.

The sceptical rationalist trend in Chinese thought which had been so ably represented earlier by Wang Ch'ung was echoed by Pao Ching-yen (end 3rd century—beginning 4th century) and it was also continued in the opposition of some of the scholars to the rise of Buddhism. Of these the most noted was Fan Chen (450-515), a scholar-official who debated against the Buddhists and wrote a famous essay "On the Destructibility of the Soul" in which he derided Buddhist ideas on the transmigration and independent existence of the soul.

The future development of Taoism did not, however, lie in the direction of a further evolution of philosophical ideas. As a result of a complex process the nature of Taoism changed quite radically; a merger with popular, nature cults took place with the result that Taoism became transformed more and more into a popular religion. Thus, the elements of magic and a large number of superstitions became dominant in the Taoist creed, while the search for immortality, particularly through the use of alchemical practices, became one of its principal aims. At least two names deserve to be noted here: Ko Hung (253-333)—the greatest alchemist in Chinese history and considered by some the real founder of religious Taoism—and K'uo Ch'ien-chih (d. 432), responsible for regulating the ceremonies and observances, as well as for formulating the theology of the new Taoist church. It is doubtful whether the name of Taoism should be applied to this new creed; it is done so primarily because the advocates of the new creed still claimed to be the followers of the founders of philosophical Taoism. In reality, there is practically nothing in common between philosophical and religious Taoism. The creed was despised by the Confucian scholar-officials for its superstitious nature. In spite of its dabbling in the occult, the religious Taoists, due to their experimentation, were of importance in the development of Chinese proto-science and were especially closely connected with the development of Chinese medicine and its vast pharmacopoeia.

Stimulated by the rise of Buddhism, religious Taoism borrowed freely from its rival and created a pantheon, canon and lithurgy of its own, all based on the Buddhist model. The Taoist ideas also influenced the development of Buddhism itself, but there is no doubt that in this process of mutual influence and borrowing it was Buddhism that was the greater giver. The result of this was that the lines which divided these two popular religions grew considerably dimmer as time went on; this accounted partially for the ease with which the Chinese availed themselves of the practices of both the churches.

In organizing their church the Taoists, while modelling themselves on the Buddhists, also constructed an appropriate legendary history to account for its origin. The Taoist church, which was perhaps even more divided into sects than the Buddhists, was also never able to become a strong political power. Nevertheless, its influence among the peasants was considerable, while its rivalry with Buddhism was a constant factor in the political history of this and later periods.

III. Buddhist Art

The influence of Buddhism on the development of Chinese art is perhaps the most significant aspect of its rise in China. The worshipping of images, propagated and encouraged by Mahayana Buddhism, led to the formation of new art forms in China, particularly in sculpture, which differed radically from what had existed earlier in this field. While Chinese Buddhist sculpture is not the greatest field of Chinese art, its scope is impressive and some of the objects produced are truly "treasures of loveliness". One cannot deny that, taken as a whole, it is a great contribution to Chinese art.

In the early period Buddhist sculpture derived practically its entire iconography from foreign sources. The main points of origin were the states of Central Asia which up to the Islamic invasion had been, as mentioned, thriving Buddhist communities. It is more than probable that most of the sculptors in this period were also not Chinese. But

Fig. 17. Bodhisattvas, Northern Wei. (*Mai-chi-shan shih-k'u.* Peking, 1954, pl. 94.)

Fig. 18. Statue of Buddha in Yun-kang, *ca.* 480. (Kümmel, O., *op. cit.*, pl. II.)

Fig. 19.   Buddha, gilded bronze, Northern Wei. *Wei-ta-ti* . . . , *op. cit.*, vol. I, pl. 3/XI.)

Fig. 20.   Bas-relief, T'ang, *ca.* 649. (Kümmel, O., *op. cit.*, p. 52.)

FIG. 21.   Artist unknown, "Girl with a Tray". Style of T'ang period. (Author's collection.)

FIG. 22.   Painted ceramic figure, T'ang. (Prodan, M., *The Art of the T'ang Potter*. London, 1960, pl. 27.)

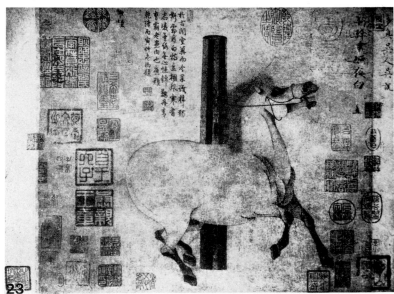

FIG. 23. Han Kan, "Tethered Horse", T'ang. (Cohn, W., *Chinese Painting*. New York, 1950, pl. 24.)

FIG. 24. Li Chen, "The Indian Monk Pu-k'ung", T'ang. (Cohn, W., *op. cit.*, pl. 23.)

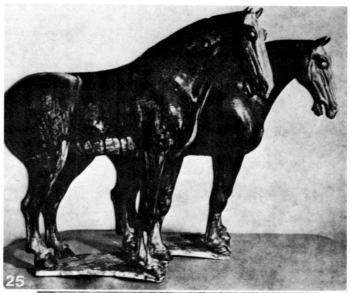

Fig. 25. Painted ceramic figures, T'ang. (Prodan, M., *op. cit.*, pl. 72.)

Fig. 26. Kuan T'ung, "Landscape", Five Dynasties. (Sickman, L. and Soper, A., *The Art and Architecture of China*. Harmondsworth, 1956, pl. 84b.)

Fig. 27.   Tung Yüan, "Landscape", Southern T'ang. (Cohn, W., *op. cit.*, pl. 42.)

Fig. 28.   Kuo Hsi, "Winter Landscape", Northern Sung. (Cohn, W., *op. cit.*, pl. 51.)

just as the Buddhist religion itself became sinified, thus also Buddhist sculpture became more and more Chinese in its style and execution and the various foreign influences—Hellenistic, Central Asian, Indian, etc.—merged and melted into what was to become a purely Chinese art form which during its apogee in the 6th century was noted for its striking beauty, austerity and sincerity. In this period it was also undoubtedly the dominant art form in China and made a great impact on Korea and, through Korea, on Japan.

Buddhist sculpture, like that of pre-Renaissance Europe, was the work of anonymous craftsmen, of guilds of sculptors who travelled from temple to temple with their copybooks and carried out their work on commission. They worked in stone, clay, wood and bronze; the bronze was gilded while all the other materials were painted. It should be remembered that the vast majority of this work has been lost; the bronzes suffered particularly, having been melted down, while the work done in other materials also suffered destruction. What is left, however, is happily enough to provide an appreciation of this art; this is especially true of the work in stone which, while it has been extensively vandalized by foreign art collectors, had the best chance for survival.

The two most famous complexes of Buddhist sculpture are the cave temples of Yün-kang and Lung-men. Yün-kang (near T'a-tung—the old P'ing-ch'eng, North Shansi) is a group of twenty enormous caves, along with many smaller ones, most of them filled with sculpture. The main work was done here in the years 460-494 but some of it dates also from a later period, 500-535. Much of the sculpture is monumental in size and concept. The style, especially of the early period, still shows very strong foreign influence. The sculptures of Yün-kang have been justly considered to be one of the great wonders of the Eastern World.

The sculptures of Lung-men (10 miles south of Loyang) were made after the removal of the Wei capital to Loyang and thus date from the first half of the 6th century. This is also a great complex of cave temples; the sculpture here is, however, considered to be almost purely Chinese in style and it is probable that most of the sculptors who worked here were Chinese. The grey limestone of Lung-men was much better adapted to sculpture than the coarse sandstone of Yün-kang and some of the work is of truly gigantic proportions.

In regarding Buddhist sculpture one is struck by the fact that importance is attached primarily to the rendition of the face of the statue, while much less attention was paid to the body. Almost all the sculpture has also an entire frontal aspect, the back of the statues being almost a flat slab.

Numerous other centres of Buddhist religious art existed, since temples were very numerous, particularly in North China. Mention should be made of yet another, the famous temple complex of Tun-huang (West Kansu). This is noted not so much for its sculpture, which was in clay due to the lack of proper stone here, as for its mural painting—almost the only source of Buddhist religious painting of this period, inasmuch as most of it elsewhere has perished, especially the works on silk. Tun-huang was, however, a remote provincial centre and thus it can be assumed that Buddhist painting was on a considerably higher level, probably rivalling sculpture in its complexity and achievements. Sculpture and painting were the two main fields of Buddhist influence on Chinese art; its effect was also felt, although to a lesser degree, in architecture.

IV. Painting, Literature

While the vast political crisis of the Period of Division had undoubted negative effects on cultural development and losses in this domain were immense as a result of incessant warfare, further growth did take place in practically all fields.

The two extremely closely interrelated Chinese arts—calligraphy and painting—made considerable strides during these four centuries, developing on the basis of old Chinese traditions which were quite distinct from the influences brought in by Buddhism. Unfortunately, practically nothing has survived of the works by the masters of this age, although their names are well known and some of them are held to have been great creators. In calligraphy, Wang Hsi-chih (321-379) was considered to be the greatest master. His writing, regarded as unsurpassable in its beauty, was described:

> Light as floating clouds
> Vigorous as a startled dragon.

Among the painters the most famous was Ku K'ai-chih (*ca.* 344-406), who was connected with the Chin court. The well-known scroll, "Admonishment of the Instructress to Court Ladies", in the British Museum is ascribed to him, though its authenticity has been the subject of much debate. Even if it were to be a later copy, it shows already great mastery in the portrayal of figures, while the fragments of landscape are still quite primitive, especially in the view of future achievements in this field. Another famous painter, Chang Seng-yu, was active at the court of the Emperor Wu of the Liang. He was renowned as a painter of frescoes, many of them dealing with Buddhist religious subjects. The first formulation of canons of painting also dates from this era; this was the work of Hsieh Ho *(fl. ca.* 500). His famous Six Principles on which painting should be based formed, in effect, the foundation on which was to be erected, in the future, a huge edifice of art criticism. Thus, continuity in this, perhaps the most significant field of Chinese art, was maintained despite all the vicissitudes of the age.

Literature continued to flourish in the courts of the Southern Dynasties and the previous traditions of Chinese poetry were followed. Poetry, however, in this period became more and more elaborate in its construction, its language highly artificial and full of allusions and thus unintelligible to all except the small coteries of literate aristocrats. Standing apart from this type of poetry was the work of the greatest poet of the period and one of the greatest of Chinese writers—T'ao Yüan-ming (T'ao Ch'ien, 375-427). His work was noteworthy for its simplicity and great beauty; he was a Taoist in his beliefs, an official who retired from his post to enjoy the world of nature in his small countryside estate. In a wonderful prose poem he described his joy upon his return to his home in the country. T'ao Yüan-ming was also the author of the famed allegorical tale "The Peach Blossom Fountain" as well as the creator of much poetry.

The first beginnings of literary criticism also date from this period; the most noted is the large treatise of Liu Hsieh (*ca.* 465-520), "The Literary Mind and the Carving of Dragons", in which various forms of literary work are analysed and discussed.

The broader contacts of the Chinese in this age led to the development of at least one science—geography. Thus it is in this period that Chinese cartography began; one of the earliest maps of China was drawn up by P'ei Hsiu (224-271) who employed a rectangular grid system. The first local gazetteers, which afterwards developed into a vast literature, saw the light of day in this era. They dealt with local topography and history and constitute an invaluable source material.

Three inventions, all of which were of great importance to the future, can also be placed in this period. These are the wheelbarrow, the water mill and the use of tea. The latter was first discovered and used in the south of China and later by the 8th century spread throughout the entire country. It not only affected the habits of the people but also influenced the later development of the manufacture of porcelain tea ware.

PART V

The Restoration of the Empire; Sui and T'ang

CHAPTER 13

Sui Unification

I. The Establishment of the Sui Empire

Upon establishing himself as the ruler of North China, having deposed the Emperor of the Northern Chou and murdered the ruling family, Yang Chien declared himself, in 581, Emperor of the Sui and proceeded on his vast design of reuniting the entire country. In 587 the small state of Later Liang was annexed and in 589 the campaign for the conquest of South China was launched. The social crisis in the South as well as the debauched character of the last Ch'en Emperor made matters easier for the Sui. The invasion was preceded by the issuance of a manifesto, 300,000 copies of which were distributed in the South, in which all the Ch'en Emperor's "evil doings" were detailed. The Sui army, supposedly over 500,000 strong, had an easy victory and the Ch'en Emperor was brought back a prisoner to Ch'ang-an. In contrast to his treatment of the Yü-wen family, the lives of the Ch'en were spared, they were pensioned off, but to make sure that they would be unable to plot a return to power they were exiled to distant provinces. Thus Yang Chien, referred to in history as Wen-ti (581-604), now became the Emperor of all China.

Some authors draw the obvious analogy between the Sui and the Ch'in based on the fact that both the dynasties had a very short duration and also stressing that both of them tried to do too much in too short a period of time, thus causing a crisis which brought about their downfall. This is partially true but the circumstances in which they came to power were rather different. The social crisis in China at the end of the Northern and Southern Dynasties Period was probably even greater than that at the end of Chou. Sui reunification did, in fact, signify the final victory of the Chinese landowners over their former nomad rulers but the problems which faced the Sui rulers were very considerable. Among these was the fact that the four centuries of division had caused marked differences in the development of the North and the South and this not only in social and economic conditions but in culture and even in language as well. These problems were exacerbated in the first period by the tendency of the Sui to treat the South as a conquered country.

The main political problem which faced the new Sui Emperor was the formation, or perhaps rather the re-creation, of a strong centralized government. A number of reforms were carried out with this aim in mind. The bureaucracy was reorganized, redundant officials were dismissed and a strict system of supervision of officialdom was enforced. The army was also re-shaped and demobilized to a great degree; an attempt was made to confiscate and destroy all the arms held privately in the entire country. The penal code was considerably simplified.

Wen-ti also undertook a series of measures which were aimed at bringing about the restoration of the country's economy, and especially the development of agriculture. In this the Sui made use of the old Northern Wei system of land equalization and great quantities of state-owned or ownerless wasteland were distributed to the peasants in return for which both taxes and *corvée* labour were then demanded. The heavy *corvée* burden of the Northern Dynasties Period was, however, reduced, as was the term of required military service. The Sui built a large number of granaries, four of them close to their new capital Ta-hsing ch'eng (known as Ch'ang-an under the T'ang), two more later on near Loyang; these were of huge size and thus the necessary food reserves could be and were accumulated. It is also during Wen-ti's reign that the great programme of canal building was initiated: a canal running parallel to the shallow Wei River, 300 *li* in length, was constructed. This expansion of the canal system was continued up to the 8th century but, in fact, the most intensive period of building took place during the reign of Wen-ti's successor.

The policies mentioned above bore fruit rapidly; speedy reconstruction of the economy took place, giving rise to considerable prosperity and great wealth for the Sui Emperor. Millions of piculs of grain found their way into the new granaries; tens of millions of rolls of silk cloth into the imperial storehouses. The population also increased, though the figures given by many authors showing a jump from 25 to 30 million in 586 to 46 million in 606 are obviously unreliable. It seems more probable that the efficiency of the government had increased markedly and thus the census figures of the later date were more accurate. Wen-ti made full use of the economic development for consolidating the new dynasty. His personality was also undoubtedly a factor; like most of his class (he came from a prominent noble family) he was as much a soldier as an administrator. He has been described as tyrannical, crafty, distrustful and miserly.

The growing domestic strength of the Sui government was reflected in the relations of China with the neighbouring peoples and country. The main problem here was the great power of the newly formed Turkish Empire. Luckily for the Sui, this empire was weakened in 581 by a division into two parts, Eastern and Western. The government of Wen-ti followed the usual Chinese policy towards its nomadic northern neighbours, already hallowed by tradition, and played the two Turkish states off against each other. In this it met with considerable success; the policy was implemented by P'ei Chu, one of the main diplomatic agents of the Sui who was also very active in the restoration of Chinese trade with the states of Central Asia. The general result of all this was the re-establishment by the Sui of Chinese influence in the Western Regions which had, for all practical purposes, been lost since the time of the Han.

A policy of expansion was also undertaken in other directions and, for example, Chinese sovereignty over North Vietnam was reaffirmed in 605. Thus, the beginning of a re-emergence of an Imperial China now took place after a lapse of almost four centuries. The court of the Sui in Ch'ang-an was once more visited by envoys and missions from the neighbouring states and countries, including also Japan, now approaching unity and nationhood.

Upon coming to power Wen-ti followed a policy of favouring both Buddhism and Taoism, undoubtedly for the purpose of gaining support. Later on he became a fervent Buddhist and supported the Buddhist church as a means for facilitating the unification of the North and the South. He simultaneously became hostile to the Confucianists and caused all their schools—with the exception of the Palace School which trained future officials—to be closed. This gained him the hatred of future Confucian historians.

II. The Reign of Yang-ti

In 604 Wen-ti fell victim to palace intrigues; it is more than likely that he was murdered on the orders of Kuang, the crown prince and former viceroy of the South, who feared for his succession. Kuang ascended the throne and is known in history as Emperor Yang (604-618). The personality of Yang-ti has been the cause of considerable controversy. Numerous authors, especially Western, have sought to exonerate him by claiming him to be a victim of orthodox Confucian historians, who supposedly made of him a stereotype "bad, last ruler"; they maintain simultaneously that the vast projects which he undertook were historically necessary. In view of the magnitude of the suffering which the Chinese people had to bear during his rule, such apologia seem to be, to say the least, out of place. Yang-ti was undoubtedly talented but his pathological megalomania seems to be quite obvious from his actions.

One of the first deeds of his reign was the rebuilding of Loyang as the second capital. Various reasons have been adduced for this; among them, the existence of greater facilities for supplying food to the new capital and the providing of a market for the great landowners of Central and South China. This move brought in its train the construction of new palaces in Loyang; they were built on a grandiose scale and much luxurious ornamentation was employed. The chronicles state that two million men were mobilized to work on this project, a vast number of whom died, especially in transporting the necessary material, such as rare timber from South China. Simultaneously, Yang-ti ordered the building of what was, for all practical purposes, an additional third capital, the city of Chiang-tu (the present Yangchow), on the north bank of the Yangtse, which had been his seat of administration as Viceroy of the South, and of which he was deeply enamoured. Yang-ti also ordered in 607-608 a rebuilding and extension of the Great Wall; 1.2 million men were impressed for this purpose and half of them are supposed to have died.

The greatest of Yang-ti's vast construction projects, however, was the further extension of the canal network with Loyang as its centre. The project was only partially planned as an overall scheme; primarily, use was made of the rivers, and the canals were meant to connect them. Thus, the Yellow River was linked with the Huai by means of the Pien and the Ssu Rivers; subsequently, the Huai was connected with the Yangtse and further—by canals—with Hangchow. A part of this system was to form the

Grand Canal of the future. The project, as undertaken in Yang-ti's time, made communication by boat possible all the way from Loyang down to Hangchow.

It seems likely that the two principal aims of this project were to facilitate the transport of tax grain to feed the capital and to render easier the movement of troops. Yang-ti was accused by the Confucian historians of constructing the canals primarily for his own pleasure. He provided the argument used against him by his famous first boat trip from Loyang to Yangchow, in which he was accompanied by his entire court. The Emperor himself led a cortége 200 *li* long, sailing in his fabulous Dragon Boat, which was four storeys (45 feet) high and 200 feet long. Along the route forty palaces were specially built for him and food had to be provided from an area extending 500 *li* on both sides of the canal to feed this horde of imperial locusts.

All the men from the age of 15 to 50 were impressed from nearby areas into service for work on the canals. The punishment for evasion was decapitation. Every family had to provide as well a child, old man or woman to serve as menials. According to the chronicles, 5,430,000 people were mobilized. A special police force of 50,000 was employed to control this labour force and punishment for failing to work with sufficient vigour was by means of **flogging** and the use of neck weights. It is true that with the primitive technique which was available in China (this is called eotechnics by Needham, who also uses the graphic phrase "a million men with teaspoons") a mass mobilization of the labour force was always necessary for the undertaking of any large-scale projects, especially such as canals or other waterworks connected with flood control. This does not, however, necessitate such apologia as have been mentioned above.

The vast schemes of Yang-ti within the country caused immense losses to the people and were a great drain on the wealth which had been accumulated during his father's reign. Moreover, they were accompanied by no less ambitious designs in foreign policy. The conquest of the state of the T'u-yü-hun tribes (in Kansu and Ch'inghai) who were considered a threat to the lines of communication into Central Asia was accomplished successfully and resulted in the further strengthening of Sui rule in the Western Regions. Yang-ti made a special trip to the North-west to celebrate these triumphs and receive tribute from rulers of the Western Regions.

The Sui armies also conducted in 605 an expedition against the state of Champa in South Vietnam. In 610 the first Chinese expedition against Taiwan took place. It was, however, Yang-ti's aggression against Korea which proved to be instrumental in bringing about his downfall as well as that of the Sui dynasty. The cause for the campaign against Korea was the failure of the King of Koguryo (the Northern Korean Kingdom, which covered an area including also the part of South Manchuria east of the Liao River) to acknowledge Chinese sovereignty and to pay tribute, while the Sui wished to reduce Korea to the position it was in during the Han era. It is also possible that Yang-ti feared an alliance between the Eastern Turks and Koguryo. He decided on war in 610 and the mobilization of Chinese forces was begun in 611. This was supposed to be the greatest army in Chinese history before the 20th century and, if the sources are to be believed, it numbered 1,130,000 men organized in 24 divisions. When marching to the North-east, division after division, the army stretched for a thousand *li*; 50,000 baggage carts and 200 great war junks were also built and immense supplies of food shipped to the North-east. Hundreds of thousands of men were impressed into service as porters and so on. In 612 the main Chinese force crossed into Korea and attacked the capital P'yongyang. All the Chinese attacks were beaten off due to the brilliant and extremely brave Korean defence. As a result, of the over 300,000 Chinese troops who had crossed the Yalu only 2700 returned.

This first campaign already placed a great strain on the resources of the Sui government and the first signs of rebellion against Yang-ti's rule were already visible. The Emperor, however, continued his war and launched a second campaign in 613 which also brought him no success. It was cut short by a rebellion in China—an attack on Loyang by Yang Hsüan-kan, a member of the imperial family. Yang-ti returned quickly from Korea to deal with this and the rebellion was crushed by his generals. After it was ended, over 30,000 people were executed, most of them innocent of any participation in the revolt.

The third campaign against Korea was launched in 614. Now the Sui generals faced the problem of mass desertion which was dealt with by the cruellest possible means. The Koreans, however, were also exhausted by the war and thus when the Chinese army approached P'yongyang once more, the Korean king sued for peace. Yang-ti was glad to retreat and later summoned the Korean king to Loyang to pay tribute. The latter wisely refused. In retribution, the chronicles state, the furious emperor had the Korean ambassador cooked and served up as a meal for his generals. The *métier* of an ambassador is not always the easiest.

It is well known that Yang-ti was a very literate and well-educated man, as well as an able poet and a patron of literature. On his orders an anthology on various subjects was compiled which contained 17,000 chapters. Later on he ordered the imperial library of Ch'ang-an and Loyang to be collated and this gave rise to another anthology in 37,000 chapters (both, unfortunately, were lost).

The great crisis of the Sui empire brought about by the failure of the expedition against Korea was still further deepened by the humiliating experience of 615. In this year the Eastern Turks invaded China and were successful in surrounding Yang-ti and his entire army in North Shansi. They were finally bought off by the payment of vast tribute. By now misery had spread throughout all of China, the government was bankrupt, "the people swarmed like bees", i.e. peasant uprisings had begun everywhere. They were particularly noted in Shantung and the other parts of North and North-east China which had been most affected by the Korean campaign. Within a short period of time over eighty rebel groups were in the field, some of them from 10,000 to over 100,000 men in strength. Later on, a number of these groups merged and two main armies were active; one sought to take Loyang and another campaigned in Hopei. In step with the peasant uprisings the great landowners and officials also began to desert the Sui and to seek their own fortune in this chaotic situation. In 616 Yang-ti fled south to Yangchow, apparently having lost hope of saving his dynasty. He supposedly spent the last period of his life in his favourite pursuits of drinking and dissipation, completely indifferent to his own fate. He was strangled in 618 by conspirators from among his own court officials.

During the next five years China once more dissolved into complete chaos and anarchy. At one moment there were three rival emperors, while many governors had set themselves up as kings of independent states. Thus the situation was similar to that which preceded the establishment of the Eastern Han dynasty. If, however, it was rural distress and the peasant uprisings which had begun the downfall of the Sui, as usual, it was not the peasants who benefited from the outcome of the struggle for power but the aristocratic Li family from Shensi which was to establish the new T'ang dynasty.

CHAPTER 14

Early T'ang

I. The Establishment of the T'ang Dynasty

The period of the T'ang dynasty is one of the most significant in Chinese history. It is an era which is considered by many historians to be perhaps the most glorious of all, especially in respect to cultural development. There is no doubt that in this age China was the largest, most populous, best governed, and more than probably the most civilized country in the entire world. The T'ang era also marks the beginning of a millennium in which China's status on a world scale remained practically unchanged.

In the turmoil which resulted from the downfall of the Sui the Li family from Shensi made a successful bid for power. While claiming origin from the princes of the former state of Western Liang and ultimately descent from Li Kuang, the famous general of Han times, the family had been, in fact, quite recently ennobled by the rulers of Northern Chou. Like the Sui royal family, with which it was closely linked by marriage, it had considerable Turkish and Hsien-pi blood, the result of many intermarriages with the ruling families of the Northern Dynasties. During the crisis of the Sui, Li Yüan was the military governor of T'aiyüan in Shansi and well connected with many of the great families in the North-west. In 617, when it was obvious that the Sui were finished, Li Yüan marched on Ch'ang-an with an army of 200,000 which included many Turkish auxiliaries. In the subsequent year Li Yüan proclaimed himself Emperor of the T'ang (Kao-tsu, 618-626). In the ensuing years the T'ang extended their rule over all of China, defeating their many rivals for imperial power by all means available, from bribes and intrigues to constant warfare. In this process an invaluable factor was the assistance which they received from the Eastern Turkish state, then the extremely powerful neighbour of China and always their ally. The Turks had a sizeable military force and—in the usually exaggerated terms of Chinese sources—the Turkish Khan was said to have one million archers at his beck and call. The assistance of the Turks was obviously not gratuitous—it was paid for by "presents", i.e. a heavy tribute.

The new T'ang emperor had no sooner firmly established the new regime than his ambitious and talented son, Li Shih-min, carried out a coup against him. In 626 he killed the heir apparent and another of his brothers, who were supposedly plotting against him (their entire families were also slain to "avoid future revenge"), and brought about his father's "voluntary" abdication. Li Shih-min reigned from 627 to 649; he is known by his posthumous name of T'ai-tsung (all the T'ang emperors are referred to by their posthumous names). He is, undoubtedly, one of the best-known Chinese emperors and glorified as such by orthodox Chinese historical writing. Many Western authors also consider him as the ablest of all the emperors; he was undoubtedly a very gifted individual, as good a general as he was a statesman, and this seems to be

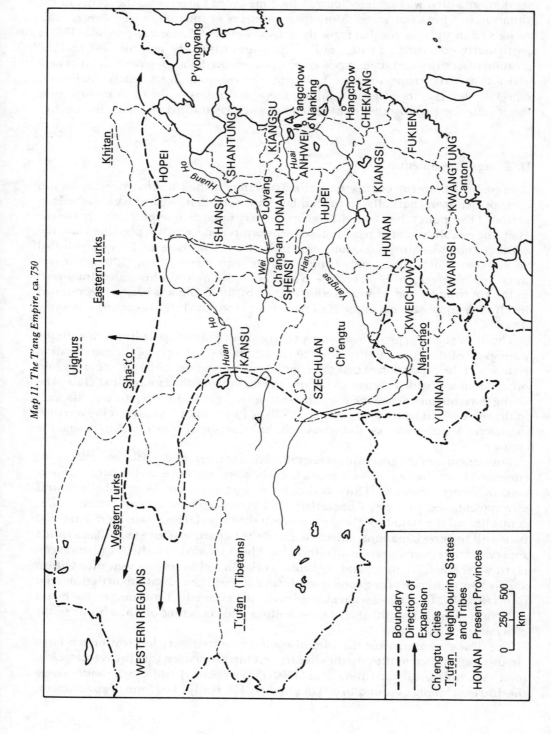

Map 11. The T'ang Empire, ca. 750

borne out by his policies. His reign was, in fact, the zenith of the T'ang dynasty and the reputation which was achieved during his time lasted longer than the reality of the situation in China warranted. More than a century of internal peace followed Tai-tsung's reign and it is this that made the consolidation of T'ang rule possible. This is particularly noteworthy in view of the difficulties which the reunification and the creation of a centralized state in new conditions involved; the long period of previous division and the many interests favouring the continuation of such conditions, especially the provincial great families, the actual rulers of the country—all these factors militated against the establishment of a new centralized absolutist monarchy.

II. T'ang Government

In evolving the forms of a new centralized government the T'ang based themselves on their predecessors, partially on the Sui but, in reality, they reached back to the Han period. Their policy, however, differed in one very important respect from that of the Han: the establishment of semi-independent princedoms was not permitted and the entire country was ruled as one state and empire. For this purpose the T'ang established an elaborate bureaucracy and centralized state machinery which, although it was modelled largely on the Han, became in due time much more sophisticated. Inasmuch as the government and administration created by the T'ang was basically continued by all their successors up to the 20th century, it is worthwhile to examine it in some detail.

The T'ang bureaucracy was not only enlarged but it also ceased ultimately to be the monopoly of the great families. Due to the steady development of the examination system and the expansion of education which was connected with this, the entry into officialdom was widened so as to include the majority of the landowning class. The T'ang government has been characterized as highly organized and reasonably efficient, in the sense that it was able to carry out its basic functions, i.e. to collect the revenue, to undertake public works, to preserve the existing social system and to defend the country.

The structure of the government resembled that of a pyramid: all the basic decisions emanated from the capital—Ch'ang-an. At the apex was the emperor, whose power was, in theory, absolute. Three bodies formed what should be called the central government: the Imperial Chancellery (it received reports, ratified nominations, controlled all the actions of the government); the Imperial Secretariat (prepared and issued all the proclamations, edicts, etc.); and the Department for State Affairs which supervised the six main executive ministries. They included: (1) officials, (2) finances, (3) rites, (4) army, (5) justice and (6) public works. In addition, there were nine Offices and five Bureaus controlling special administrative fields and the affairs of the Imperial Court. Another feature, which remained permanent from the T'ang on, was the Board of Censors which had the duty of controlling and reporting on the actions of the officials.

The T'ang reconstructed the administration of the country by creating ten large circuits (later raised to fifteen); the country was further divided into prefectures, *chou* (over 350), and these in turn into around 1500 counties (*hsien*), while at the bottom were the districts (*hsiang*), around 16,000 in number. The really basic form of government, the only level with which the great majority of the population had any contact, was the county under the rule of a magistrate. This was also the lowest level at which the central bureaucracy functioned.

The examination system was initiated in a partial form during the Han but had been in abeyance during practically all of the Period of Division. Under the Sui and T'ang it was taken up again and developed still further, reaching its full scope by the 8th century and becoming an important, although not the major, form for the recruiting of officials to the government bureaucracy. It should be noted, however, that the descendants of high officials had the right of entry into the register of officials without taking examinations. The examination subjects were expanded as time progressed and they were based primarily on the Confucian classics, the mastery of which was essential for passing. Many Western authors stress that the examination system and the bureaucracy which it helped to produce gave rise to something that can be called a civil service which, in their view, may be considered one of the greatest achievements of Chinese civilization. It is a fact that from the T'ang period on an ever-increasing proportion of officials was recruited from successful candidates at the examinations, that most of the political leaders for the next thirteen centuries did pass the examinations and were thus chosen on grounds of intellectual talent. It is also true that this system was less aristocratic than the recommendation on the basis of family standing which was used during the Period of Division. In its later development, however, during the Ming and Ch'ing periods, the examination system became a stifling straitjacket both on the educational system and on the intellectual life of the country, imposing on its participants a rigid orthodox Confucian ideology. It did successfully channel most of the people possessing intellectual ability into government posts, thus making them a component part of the state apparatus. The system was inevitably, due to its very nature, conservative, perpetuating outworn ideas and practices. Moreover, it should be pointed out—and this is perhaps most important—that despite the many legends to the effect that a talented peasant's son could hope to pass the examinations and thus make a brilliant career as a high government official—the intricacies of the subject matter which presupposed many years of study, in fact, restricted the entrance into officialdom to the landlord class. Thus, as Goodrich observed, "Only the sons of the well-to-do could find the time and expense for the examinations; the long line of civil servants sprang from the leisured families living on rents from the land."

The enlargement of education on both a local and central level was closely bound up with the development of the examination system. The main educational centre was the Imperial University in Ch'ang-an which by the 8th century numbered over 2000 students, some of these coming from neighbouring countries. In principle, admittance was restricted to those who were to be trained as future officials. It is to a large degree in connection with this development of both the examination system and education that Confucianism re-established its position as the dominant political ideology, no matter that Buddhism remained the most sophisticated philosophy, and Taoism the personal religious creed of all the later T'ang emperors. As mentioned, both the education and the examinations were based on Confucian canonical literature. Having adapted itself already as a system of political precepts and ruling-class ethics and morality in Han times, Confucianism had suffered centuries of eclipse, but now demonstrated once more its value and was appreciated in this respect by the T'ang rulers, especially by T'ai-tsung himself. The further flourishing of Buddhism, and of Taoism, did not basically affect this growing political role of the Confucian ideology.

In the establishment of the new government the T'ang emperors also paid attention to the legal code and procedures. While based on those of the preceding dynasties, the T'ang legal code was simplified in comparison with these and was supposedly less severe in its penal provisions, particularly when contrasted with some of the draconian measures which had been introduced by the Sui.

III. Economic and Social Policies

The T'ang rulers, and particularly T'ai-tsung himself, were attentive to the lessons of history and took note of what had been the main cause of the downfall of the Sui—peasant rebellion. They realized that the consolidation of their rule made necessary a proper settlement of all agrarian problems. For this reason, among others, the T'ang government at the outset of its rule also reverted to the policy of land equalization, which had been initiated by the Wei and continued by the Sui, and applied it on an even larger scale. Thus provisions were made for the distribution to the peasants of abandoned land, which had again increased very considerably during the chaos following the downfall of the Sui. In less populated villages 100 *mu* of land was granted to every adult male, 80 to be returned to the state after death and 20 to be retained by the family. In more heavily populated areas the figure varied from 40 to 80 *mu*. In return for the land the peasant was obliged to pay annual taxes—2 piculs of grain, 20 feet of silk cloth and render 20 days of *corvée* labour (less than under the Sui). He could undertake more *corvée* work and thus reduce the grain and silk tax, or buy himself out of the *corvée* by increasing the silk tax (3 feet per day of *corvée*). There are insufficient data, unfortunately, to ascertain to what extent these policies were carried out throughout T'ang China and to observe the process of change in their implementation. It seems certain that after some time the land granted was never returned to the state but became the permanent property of the peasants.

The basis for this policy was not only the need to ease the social tensions but also the desire to assure a steady revenue for the government and, simultaneously, to maintain in existence for this purpose a free, tax-paying, *corvée*-rendering peasantry who would also be registered and available for conscription into the army. The taxes were intended to be reasonable, on the basis of T'ai-tsung's saying: "It is dangerous to burden the people with excessive labour services . . . an Emperor who collects too heavy taxes is like a man eating his own flesh; when the flesh is all eaten up—the man dies."

The above policy did result in a great increase of agricultural production inasmuch as vast amounts of fallow land were brought under cultivation. The T'ang government's revenue receipts were proportionately large and made it much richer than the Han had ever been. This was also partially due to the fact that new agricultural areas, particularly the Yangtse Valley, were now producing on a large scale for the first time, while agrarian techniques had improved markedly. This financial stability of the government lasted for over a century and was, so to speak, the other side of the medal of the political stability of the same period.

The implementation of the land-equalization programme made the carrying out of an accurate census and registration of land necessary. These were carried out fairly systematically and provide very interesting although debatable data.

The T'ang policy towards the peasantry outlined above did not by any means imply that any direct action was taken against the landowners; the estates in the hands of the great landowning families were not affected by any government measure, since anyone holding any official status was given the right to hold large landed properties, and was unaffected by the limits on privately held lands. Huge estates were also owned by the Buddhist monasteries. As time progressed, the customary cycle of an increase in the size of the great estates at the expense of the small peasant holders, and accompanying dispossession and impoverishment of them, was to recommence, as we shall see, in the middle and late T'ang periods. In the early T'ang period it seems probable that a new class of landowners was taking shape which was largely composed of the older great families who remained influential as servants of the dynasty and of new landowning families whose fortunes were closely bound up with their official careers under the T'ang. The relative weakness of the great families, which resulted from the wars that followed the downfall of the Sui, was undoubtedly an advantage to the T'ang rulers. It is also more than probable that they were able to play on the sectional differences between the various regional groups among them.

An additional and equally important reason for the conciliatory policies, which the early T'ang rulers pursued in dealing with the peasants, lay in the fact that the latter were in this period the bulwark of the defence system. Many of the peasants in areas of strategic importance were also obliged to serve in militia units for a specified period of time—usually one month in five. There were approximately 630 militia units, each of them theoretically composed of 1000 men. This system prevailed until almost the middle of the 8th century when it disintegrated, for a number of reasons, and was replaced by a standing army.

The vast masses of a tax-paying, *corvée*-rendering and militia-serving peasantry supported by their endeavours the T'ang ruling class—a feudal aristocracy of considerable size and wealth. Thus not only the imperial family and higher nobility paid no taxes but practically all the higher officials as well. They were all supported by the state out of taxes. The great wealth and leisure of this upper class made of it a liberal patron of the arts; simultaneously, the aristocrats sought for new luxuries and this served as a stimulant for the development of handicrafts and of domestic and foreign trade.

In its economic policy the T'ang government revived the examples of the Han in the maintenance of the state monopolies, such as salt and coinage. It also levied taxes on a number of items of general consumption as, for example, wine and, later on, tea. All of these were an important source of additional revenue. The government was also the owner of a large number of manufactories; these, however, produced not for the market but for the use of the government itself. Generally speaking, the earlier tendencies of discrimination against the merchants were continued under the early T'ang. From the late 8th century, however, these restrictions rapidly collapsed. In particular, the officials of the later T'ang bureaucracy utilized their posts for their own economic advantage and against the interests of the merchants; one is almost tempted to remark that the origins of later-day "bureaucratic capitalism" may be found already in T'ang times.

The general success in restoring agricultural production and the rise of prosperity resulting from it also brought in its train a further development of the crafts. Marked progress was made in the development of the manufacture of silk, paper and porcelain, some of which was on quite a large scale. Craft guilds were already formed in the T'ang towns. All this led, in turn, to an increase in domestic trade which was stimulated also by improved communications, including a new postal system on the main trunk roads which emanated from the capital. Foreign trade as well grew to heretofore unseen proportions but during the T'ang period it was to a large degree in the hands of foreigners. There were numerous colonies of foreign merchants not only in the capital itself but also in Yangchow, in Canton and in other ports on the south coast.

The cities and towns grew in size and importance; first of all Ch'ang-an, which was well laid out in checkerboard fashion and occupied a much larger area than the present city of Sian on the same location. By the 8th century its population was estimated at over one million. The same growth was true of other cities such as Loyang and Canton, while a number of the provincial capitals also had populations of over 100,000. It must be noted, however, that this urban development had little resemblance to that of Europe; the Chinese towns did not witness a rise in strength and influence of a burgher class. This was probably primarily due to the above-mentioned general policy towards merchants, as well as to the fact that most of the towns were under the direct control of the government, serving as centres of provincial administration.

The first century of T'ang rule, a Golden Age, was in a way reflected by Ch'ang-an—the largest and most civilized city in the world during this era. Its location, however, while advantageous from a strategic point of view, was inconvenient economically as the surrounding area's productivity was declining and the transport of grain to it presented a considerable problem. This is, in fact, the last period in which the capital was located in the North-west. In some respects Ch'ang-an, with its vast population, assumed more and more the character of a parasitical organism living off the rest of the country. What was perhaps most noteworthy, however, was the cosmopolitan character of the T'ang capital. Here people from all parts of Asia mixed freely—it was a melting pot which reflected the T'ang policy of tolerance and welcome to foreigners, both derived, perhaps, from a feeling of complete stability and confidence. This was the least xenophobic period in Chinese history.

IV. The Expansion of the Empire

From the very outset the T'ang rulers embarked on a policy of enlarging their possessions and ultimately succeeded in creating for a period of time an empire which was even larger territorially than the Han at its apogee.

The greatest rival and handicap to the expansion of the Chinese Empire were the Eastern Turks, the same who as allies had been partly responsible for putting the Li family into power. Due to the nature of nomad feudalism the structure of the states of the northern nomads was always unstable and impermanent and broken up with relative ease by the rise to power of new tribes which would lead, in turn, to the formation of new confederations and empires in the steppes. The Chinese continued their age-old practice of playing on the divisions between the tribes with the constant aim of weakening them to the utmost. The main prize at stake was still the control of the Western Regions, i.e. the states of the Tarim Basin as well as of the trade routes to the west, running to the north and south of the T'ien Shan.

In the first years of T'ang rule the Eastern Turks were a truly formidable power and a great rival of the Chinese. In 624 they undertook an invasion of North-west China which brought them practically to the gates of Ch'ang-an. This attack was beaten off successfully by Li Shih-min. Later on, taking advantage of the rebellion of a number of the tribes, including the Uighurs, against the rule of the Eastern Turks, T'ai-tsung waged in 627-628 a war which led to the overthrow of the Eastern Turkish Empire and the incorporation of considerable territory into the Chinese Empire (the Ordos region and most of East Mongolia), as well as the settlement within China of a large number of Turkish tribesmen, some sources giving a figure of almost 1,000,000.

The struggle was then continued by China against the Western Turks with the principal aim of breaking their control over the states of Central Asia. This was partially accomplished by the war in 639-640 and by 648 T'ang control of the Western Regions was firmly established. In the achievement of these victories the alliance with the Uighur tribes proved invaluable; they were to continue to play an extremely vital role in Chinese history for the next two centuries.

The control of the trade routes leading through Central Asia led to a great expansion of foreign trade but, in general, its character remained similar to that of the Han period. Silk continued to constitute the main item of Chinese export while numerous luxury goods were imported. Some authors maintain that the balance of trade was decidedly unfavourable to China and that it ultimately became one of the factors which led to the deterioration of the Chinese economy by the middle of the 8th century.

The establishment of T'ang power in the Western Regions also led to the extension of Chinese sovereignty still farther to the west. Up to the middle of the 8th century the area west of the Pamirs—Tashkent, Bukhara, Samarkand, Ferghana and much of Afghanistan—were all considered to be within the Chinese sphere of influence although Chinese influence was challenged by the Western Turks (Turgesh) and by the Islamic conquests of the late 7th and early 8th centuries. The degree of Chinese control too was very low. In spite of the tendency, however, of some of the Chinese authors to gloss over this matter, even indirect Chinese rule was by no means welcome to the peoples subjected to it. The Turkish tribes, in particular, waged from 683 on an unceasing series of wars aimed at ridding themselves of the Chinese yoke and ultimately succeeded in throwing it off.

The early T'ang period also witnessed the establishment of very close contacts with Tibet which had become a unified kingdom in the first half of the 7th century under the rule of the famous Srong-btsan sGam-po (617-650). A T'ang princess, Wen-chang, became one of his wives and this led to the introduction of Chinese culture into Tibet; her entourage included many Chinese artisans. In the second half of the 7th century the Tibetans became a considerable military force and a strong rival of the Chinese for the control of Central Asia. On the whole, the Chinese in this period succeeded in beating back the Tibetan attacks in this region but the situation was changed drastically in the course of the next century.

The plans of Yang-ti for the conquest of Korea were also continued by T'ai-tsung in three campaigns, 644-646. These met with equally little success due to the brave resistance of the Koreans but did not entail such disastrous results for the T'ang as they had for the Sui. During the reign of his successor, Kao-tsung, the Chinese armies joined in 660 with the forces of Silla (the kingdom in South-east Korea) to destroy the kingdom of Paekche (South-west Korea). Later on, in 668, the Chinese and Silla both attacked and succeeded in conquering the North Korean kingdom of Koguryo, the previous main object of Sui and T'ang attacks. The effect of these victories, however, was shortlived. Violent resistance followed, as a result of which Chinese troops were forced to withdraw and Silla succeeded ultimately in 678 in unifying the entire country. While Korea recognized Chinese suzerainty, it was, in fact, an independent country and not the Chinese colony which the T'ang rulers had wanted to create. Nevertheless, the influence of China, especially of Chinese culture and writing, was immense. T'ang institutions were copied on a vast scale and the whole Korean government was organized on Chinese lines. This sinification of Korea was closely bound up with the earlier acceptance at the end of the 4th century of Buddhism from China which now was to play a still greater role. Buddhism was also of equal significance as a means of transmitting Chinese culture to Japan.

Up to the T'ang period Chinese cultural influence on Japan was introduced largely indirectly through the intermediary of Korea. During the first two centuries of T'ang rule, however, especially during the 8th century, direct contact between Japan and China developed on an ever-increasing scale and resulted in an almost wholesale borrowing of all elements of Chinese culture which affected practically all aspects of Japanese life. It has been said that numerous T'ang customs can still be found even in present-day Japan and it is well known that examples of T'ang art and architecture are easier to find in Japan than in China itself. The Japanese, for instance, built their new capital Nara as a smaller copy of Ch'ang-an. In the 8th century numerous missions from Japan visited China, taking back with them vast quantities of books, art objects and, what is more important perhaps, a direct knowledge of the Chinese way of life. Some of the Japanese accounts of these missions constitute also an invaluable source material for Chinese history.

Apart from the countries already mentioned the T'ang empire established much closer relations than had existed heretofore with other parts of Asia. Thus extensive contacts were maintained with various parts of India, especially the North, with Ceylon and with the countries of South-east Asia. The development of foreign trade also led to more contacts with Persia and the rising power of the Arab world. It was the Arabs and the Persians who took the lead in this expansion of trade, employing mostly the southern sea routes, and thus the Arab merchant colony in Canton became rich and powerful.

Contact was also established by the T'ang with the Byzantine Empire. There are records of four missions sent from Fu-lin (this was the Chinese name for Byzantium) between the years 643 and 719. The primary aim of the Byzantine rulers was to seek an alliance with the Chinese against the growing danger of Arab expansion. The T'ang, however, did not act on these proposals and did nothing to check the spread of Arab conquests. They rejected also the appeals for aid of the Persian rulers, when the latter faced the direct threat of Arab invasion. Ultimately, this policy was to cost the T'ang their rule over Central Asia.

The greatly increased scope of relations with other parts of the world was undoubtedly of considerable advantage in the development of Chinese culture, in the acquisition of new elements from other lands. It should be pointed out, however, that in this period China was, in fact, more advanced technically than the rest of the world and that in this exchange China was more the giver than the taker. Nothing that China acquired could equal the importance of paper and porcelain—the two great Chinese inventions which were transmitted in this period to the rest of the world.

One of the results of these contacts was the introduction into China of a further number of foreign religions. Basically, all of these were connected with the foreign communities, mostly of merchants, who were then settled in China; none of them succeeded in penetrating or influencing Chinese life in the way which Buddhism had earlier on. Zoroastrianism was connected with the colonies of Persian merchants and later on with Persian refugees from the Arab conquest. Manichaeism was brought in by the Syrian merchants and while the Manichaean priests engaged in much missionary activity, their main success was not with the Chinese but with the Uighurs who were converted in their entirety to this dourly dualistic but most interesting faith. This resulted, however, in the fact that the fate of Manichaeism was bound up with the political fortunes of the Uighurs; as long as these were a great power the religion was permitted to expand in China as well. The Nestorian form of Christianity was also introduced by Syrian and Persian merchants; it too benefited from the T'ang policy of toleration and gained as well some support both from the Chinese rulers and from certain high Chinese dignitaries. A famous account of the history of the Nestorian Church in China was inscribed in Syriac and Chinese on a beautiful stele erected in Ch'ang-an in 781 and rediscovered in the 17th century.

The same period also saw the introduction into China of Islam which was brought in by Arab merchants. The future growth, however, of the very large Moslem community in China (especially in Yunnan, Kansu and Sinkiang) undoubtedly dates from a much later period and is not directly connected with the first coming of Islam. The Mohammedan traditional accounts of the history of their religion in China are unfortunately completely unreliable.

The policy adopted by T'ai-tsung towards all these religions was one of complete toleration; they were allowed to build their temples and spread their creeds. It was perhaps the feeling of stability, as well as a conviction of the inherent superiority of the Chinese way of life which accounted for this policy. But the whole tenor of T'ang thought was syncretist and non-exclusive. T'ai-tsung himself was a Confucianist in politics, but also patronized Buddhists and Taoists. Whatever the motives, this policy of toleration was continued as long as the prosperity of the T'ang Empire was more or less maintained. It was to come to an end only in the middle of the 9th century.

V. The First Century of T'ang Rule

The policies established at the outset of the T'ang era were followed, in general, during the long reign of T'ai-tsung's successor, Kao-tsung (650-683). The stability of the government was not appreciably affected by the struggle for power in the court itself. In these conflicts the most prominent role was played by the Empress Wu who was, in truth, the real ruler of the country throughout most of Kao-tsung's reign after 656. An energetic and able, totally ruthless and unscrupulous woman, she continued to rule after his death. At the very beginning she made use of two of her sons as puppet emperors; the first of these, Chung-tsung (684; 705-710) was after a few months set aside, imprisoned and replaced for a few years by another son, Jui-tsung (684-690; 710-712). Soon thereafter he was also cast aside and the Empress declared herself to be the supreme ruler (calling herself Huang-ti, Emperor) in 690, establishing a new dynasty, the Chou, which lasted until 705 when she was finally forced at the age of 82 to resign from the throne. Chung-tsung, who had been released from prison earlier, was restored to the throne and the T'ang dynasty thus reconstituted.

In her rule Empress Wu based herself not only on the support of her family, which was the usual practice, but she seemingly also had the backing of a large part of the newly expanded bureaucracy. The examination system was still further developed during her years of power. She has been compared, on the whole correctly, both to the Empress Lü of the Han and to Tz'u-hsi of the Ch'ing. An ardent Buddhist, she gave great support to the Buddhist church and as a result of this Buddhism reached the apogee of its economic and political might during her reign. The Buddhist monasteries were the repositories for much capital, the owners of vast quantities of metal (primarily copper, mostly in the form of statues) and were thus able to control the money market. They were probably also the greatest single group of landowners in the entire country. On the whole, the Buddhists were able to maintain this dominant position for the next century and a half.

Chung-tsung, himself a nonenity, was poisoned in 710 by his own Empress Wei who undoubtedly hoped to assume as much power as the Empress Wu had previously exercised. She was, however, killed with her entire clan as the result of a palace coup led by Li Lung-chi, the son of Jui-tsung, who put his father on the throne. In 712 Jui-tsung resigned in favour of his son who was to become the famous Emperor Hsüan-tsung (712-756). His long and eventful reign marks, in fact, a turning-point in the development of China and in the fate of the T'ang dynasty which brought to the surface all the slow processes of change which had been transforming Chinese society during the first century of T'ang rule.

CHAPTER 15

The Decay and Fall of the T'ang Dynasty

I. Changes in the Middle T'ang Period

From the beginning of the 8th century, throughout the entire reign of Hsüan-tsung the economic and social principles on which the T'ang government had been based underwent a process of slow but steady decay. The most important manifestation of this was the breakdown of the land equalization system and the concomitant growth of great landed estates. One of the major factors responsible for this was the steady increase of the peasant population which caused it to press on what remained basically the same amount of land, thus leading to a diminution in the size of the peasant holdings and to their lessened viability. As time went on, the peasants were unable to meet their taxes, fell more and more into debt and were forced to sell the land to the benefit of the great landowners. The oppressive action of usually corrupt officials who demanded taxes regardless of circumstances added to the growing agrarian crisis. Thus, fewer and fewer free peasants remained, while simultaneously the demand of the government for revenue did not decrease but increased. According to the census of 754 only 7.6 million out of a total population of 52.8 million paid any taxes at all. The deterioration of the Empire's position on the frontiers also gave rise to the government's policy of recruiting large numbers of peasants for long-term military duty in these areas and this, in turn, led to a further worsening of their situation.

The breakdown of the land equalization system also signified, in fact, the end of the militia system which was closely bound up with it, and its replacement early in Hsüan-tsung's reign (722) by a mercenary regular army. By 740 this army was composed already of 490,000 men, almost all of them stationed on the frontiers. This, in turn, only increased the government's need for revenue. The employment of *corvée* labour was also progressively giving way to the use of hired labour for public works, especially for grain transport, and this as well called for increased government expenditures. In the fiscal reforms of 780 the land equalization system was totally disregarded; in reality it had already ceased to function for many previous decades.

Against this background the process of growth of the great estates continued steadily. By the middle of the 8th century the great estates, including those of the Buddhist establishment, already held much of the best land. After this date they steadily assumed a dominant place in the agricultural economy. Many of the former free peasants had been by now transformed into either tenant farmers or farm labourers on these estates. Absentee landlordism existed and the manorial estates were generally hereditary, handed down from generation to generation, although often reduced in size by the absence of primogeniture. An interesting visual example of such an estate is Wang

Ch'uan, the property of the famous poet and painter Wang Wei, who depicted it on a very famous hand scroll. The process of the establishment of the manorial estates had in fact commenced already during the Eastern Han period but it is in the middle T'ang that this type of feudal relations in the Chinese countryside began to take a new form, which reached its mature shape under the Sung. While the composition of the landowning class was to undergo some changes in the future the relations which were established during this period were fundamentally to continue to exist without any essential change up to the middle of the 20th century. The landowning families had acquired, as well, a practical monopoly of all the important posts of the central bureaucracy which they then, in turn, employed for increasing their wealth and landed property. In spite of conflicts between sectional interests and within the class itself, it was, on the whole, a homogeneous body which was able to maintain and preserve its position for many centuries despite the numerous, vast and desperate revolts of the peasantry.

In order to meet its financial needs, which were sharpened by the crisis that followed the An Lu-shan rebellion and resulted largely from the breakdown of the land equalization system, the T'ang government instituted in the 760s new tax methods. These included a land tax which was now fixed on the basis of the amount of land held by each household and not as previously on a *per caput* basis. This was accompanied by a general tax on property. In 780, however, an entirely new system was introduced, the so-called Double Tax (double because collected bi-annually), which combined the previous taxes with the important new proviso that the taxes were to be assessed in money, although still mostly paid in kind. The new taxes were to be paid theoretically by all the landowners, including the holders of large estates; thus, in the first years a lightening of the tax burden on the peasantry did take place. This situation, however, changed rapidly. Forty years of constant deflation meant that the peasants had to pay far more in kind to meet their tax assessments. The great landowners by means of their control of the government machinery managed to evade taxes on a vast scale and shifted the burden onto the peasants whose condition continued to deteriorate. The disappearance of small peasant holdings continued throughout the 9th and 10th centuries, and more and more peasants became tenants or labourers on large estates.

By the middle of the 8th century the position of the T'ang empire had also weakened to a considerable degree. The Tibetans had renewed their attacks on the Chinese North-west and on Central Asia, but of much greater significance for Chinese rule in this area was the crushing defeat of the Chinese in 751 inflicted by an Arab army in the battle of Atlach (on the Talass River in North Kirghizia). This has been correctly called one of the most important battles in world history, for it ultimately determined the fate of Central Asia for many centuries to come. Chinese rule tumbled like a house of cards and the Chinese power never again intervened in these regions until the 18th-century invasion by the alien Manchus. The area, once one of the mainstays of Buddhism, was now rapidly converted to Islam.

In the North-east a new threat to China appeared in the form of the Khitan tribes (of Hsien-pi origin) advancing south from their original homeland in Manchuria. Simultaneously, in the South-west the tribes of Yunnan, now newly unified into the kingdom of Nan-chao, not only successfully repelled all Chinese attempts to master this area, but in 751 inflicted a severe defeat on the T'ang armies and later were to attack

China as well. Nan-chao managed to keep itself free from Chinese rule until the conquest of the country by the Mongols in the 13th century.

The wars mentioned above were a great strain on the human and financial resources of the T'ang government. It is against this background that it undertook measures which constituted a radical departure from its principles of centralized rule and were ultimately to prove fatal to the very existence of the T'ang dynasty. A number of special military governors were established in the frontier areas (ten at the outset) to meet the external danger. In time the military governors became more of a threat to the central government than a defence against the enemy; they became "a tail too big to wag".

The reign of Hsüan-tsung is a very complex and contradictory period. While all the processes described above were taking place, the Empire seemed—at least outwardly— to be more prosperous and stable than ever before. The increase of population was steady; 705—37 million; 726—41.4 million; 740—48 million; 754—52.8 million; of this, 75 per cent was still north of the Yangtse. The wealth of the country was obvious and undoubted. Complete peace reigned internally and "one could undertake a voyage within the empire for a distance of 10,000 *li* without being armed". Thus, it seemed that the T'ang had reached a new pinnacle of glory. This is especially true if the period were to be regarded from the point of view of the arts, for it was precisely in this era that the greatest flourishing of T'ang culture took place; the most famous poets and painters of the epoch were active at the court of Hsüan-tsung whose reputation as a great patron of the arts was truly deserved. The famous rebellion of An Lu-shan was to show, however, how deeply the rot had set in under this splendid exterior.

The personality of Hsüan-tsung himself in some ways exemplified this period. The munificent patron of the arts underwent a strange metamorphosis from an able and sensible young ruler to a superstitious and decadent tyrant in his later years. In fact, it was not he who ruled during the latter period from about 740 but his Chancellor Li Lin-fu (in office 736-752), who established himself an unchallenged master of the Empire. It was Li Lin-fu who brought about the famous meeting of Hsüan-tsung with Yang Kuei-fei. This alleged beauty was the wife of Hsüan-tsung's son. Enamoured of her, the Emperor took her from his son and then gave him another wife in her place. She became the most powerful person in the Empire, her relatives sharing in her rise. After Li Lin-fu's death, one of her cousins replaced him as virtual dictator. Her role and fate were known to almost every Chinese as they are the subject of innumerable tales and plays; she is also the heroine of a famous poem by Po Chü-i.

II. The An Lu-shan Rebellion

An Lu-shan, the courtier and favourite of Hsüan-tsung and Yang Kuei-fei, was of mixed Turkish and Sogdian origin and had been originally the slave of a Chinese officer. He made his career first in the army but then primarily at court. Sly, ribald, fantastically obese, he ingratiated himself with the Emperor and held the post of the military governor of three districts in the North-east where he was supposed to defend the Empire against the threat of a Khitan invasion. He was Li Lin-fu's ally; after Li's death he felt his position threatened. Although An Lu-shan was suspected by many of conspiring against the government, he retained the Emperor's confidence throughout. In 755 his plans were ready; he marched with an army of 150,000, which included many nomad tribesmen, from his headquarters in Peking to conquer the Empire. The incapacity of the T'ang government was demonstrated immediately; no effective military resistance was offered and An Lu-shan soon became the master of the T'ang eastern capital, Loyang, where in 756 he declared himself Emperor of a new dynasty, the Yen. He then sent his principal general Shih Ssu-ming (also of Turkish origin) to attack Ch'ang-an. Hsüan-tsung fled towards Szechuan with a part of his court. On the way the escorting troops rebelled, killed the Chancellor, who was Yang Kuei-fei's cousin, and demanded her death as well. The Emperor allowed her to be strangled by one of his eunuchs and having thus pacified his troops proceeded on his trip to Ch'engtu. Simultaneously, his son decided to stay behind to organize resistance against the forces of An Lu-shan who had already succeeded in taking Ch'ang-an. He declared himself Emperor (Su-tsung 756-762) and proceeded to the North-west where he managed to obtain the aid of the powerful Uighurs. For these the situation was most favourable; if they succeeded in aiding to restore T'ang rule they would be exceedingly well rewarded—if the T'ang restoration were to prove impossible, then China would be open for them to plunder and perhaps even to rule. Their hopes were not in vain, for they later received a tribute of 20,000 rolls of silk annually and lorded it over Ch'ang-an for many years to come.

In a long and costly campaign the T'ang succeeded in crushing the rebellion by 763. An Lu-shan himself had been killed earlier, in 757, by his own son. The son was, in turn, slain by Shih Ssu-ming who was then commander of all the rebel armies. Shih Ssu-ming, whose military ability was undoubted, suffered an identical fate and was subsequently murdered by his own son. Although ultimately defeated, the An Lu-shan rebellion revealed fully all the inherent weaknesses of the T'ang government. In effect, it broke its power, and while the dynasty lasted almost another century and a half it never recovered fully, in spite of the attempts made by some of the subsequent T'ang rulers, as for example Emperor Hsien-tsung (806-820), to restore a strong, centralized monarchy.

The losses of manpower and wealth which resulted from the rebellion were immense. The next census in 766 gave the figure of the population as only 16.9 million, while the figures in 754 were 52.8 million. It is impossible, however, to believe, as some authors would have it, that 36 million people perished, especially in view of the fact that large parts of the country were not affected by the fighting. It is more likely that these figures reveal a far-reaching disorganization of the government and its inability to have a proper census carried out. The T'ang government never recovered full control, particularly in the northern provinces, and censuses of the following period continued to show a much lower population than that of 754; the areas under the rule of the more independent military governors failed to follow the instructions of the central government also in this respect as they did in so many others.

While so much of North and North-west China had been ravaged by the rebellion, all of the Yangtse Valley and the areas to the south of it had remained basically undisturbed. These areas were now of ever greater importance economically and constituted the real grain basket of China. The centre of gravity had by now definitely shifted to the South from the North-west and North, which had previously been much more important. In this period the population of the southern provinces, e.g. Kwangtung, increased rapidly. The Cantonese still call themselves *T'ang jen*—men of T'ang.

III. Later T'ang

The T'ang dynasty remained on the throne for over a full century before a great peasant rebellion finally sent it tumbling to its doom. During this period relative prosperity and peace still prevailed, as it had done for a longer period in the southern part of the country. This has caused one author to remark that there had been few eras in world history when a civilized area has existed in peace for such a long time. The remark is, unfortunately, true enough and a very bitter comment on the history of the human race.

Although they were formally ensconced on the throne of their ancestors the T'ang emperors ruled only indirectly over much of the country. Real power became concentrated increasingly in the hands of the military governors; their number rose to fifty and in some regions the posts became hereditary. These satraps included even some of the former lieutenants of An Lu-shan, especially in Hopei and Honan. The increased strength of the military governors resulted also in part from the worsening situation of the Empire in relation to its neighbours. The Tibetan tribes were especially aggressive in this period; in 763 they conquered most of Kansu and even managed to take and devastate Ch'ang-an. It was only the rivalry between them and the Uighurs— ably exploited by Kuo Tzu-i, the general and statesman primarily responsible for restoring the T'ang to their throne—which made the position of the T'ang at all tenable. The Tibetan incursions covered wide areas, not only North-west China, but Central Asia as well. The power of the Uighurs was broken ultimately by the rise of a new nomad federation, the Kirghiz, who inflicted a severe defeat on the Uighurs (832) and replaced them as the main force on the steppes. Simultaneously, the Tibetan kingdom disintegrated as a result of the dying out of the royal line (843) and both these events gave the Chinese a certain breathing spell in the West and North-west.

The impotent central government was headed by a succession of weak emperors, most of whom were puppets in the hands of the eunuchs who now more and more played the same role as they had during the last period of Eastern Han rule. The emperors were also credulous victims of the Taoist alchemists and three of them died from taking an elixir of immortality. The court became a scene of bitter factional strife among rival groups of officials and various groups of eunuchs, and the eunuchs and the officials, while simultaneously the military governors engaged in periodic rebellions against the central government, as in the years 781-784.

The financial position of the government was as bad as its political situation; this was primarily due to the steady development of the agrarian crisis but also partially due to the fact that the military governors retained most of the revenue of the areas under their control for themselves. One attempted solution was to embark on a policy of special taxation of the merchant community; the only result of this was considerable damage to trade. There is little doubt that the economic motive was one of the major factors in the undertaking of actions against Buddhism and other religions, although it is true that the Emperor in whose reign these persecutions took place, Wu-tsung (841-846), was also a very fervent Taoist. The first persecution was directed against the Manichaeans, now deprived of their protection by the Uighurs. In 843 all their temples were destroyed, their books burned, some of their priestesses slain, the religion proscribed and all their property confiscated. In 845 it was the turn of the Buddhists, the Zoroastrians and the Nestorians, the main attack being against the Buddhists—4600 temples and monasteries, 40,000 smaller shrines were ordered to be destroyed; 260,000 monks and nuns were secularized; 150,000 temple slaves turned over to the state; all statues melted down and the metal confiscated and, what was most important, all the vast amount of land in the hands of the Buddhist establishment was taken over by the government. The figures given for the land—"several tens of millions *ch'ing*"—are obviously exaggerated, as this would amount to more than the entire arable land in China; this means simply that the amount was very great indeed.

Two years later the new Emperor Hsüan-tsung (847-859), himself a Buddhist, repealed his predecessor's edict. The Buddhist church revived and recovered much of its previous strength but it never fully regained its position, wealth and prestige. Any possibility that it had of becoming a state church in the future was thus eliminated. This was not necessarily a negative phenomenon if one considers the behaviour of all religions when they become possessed of total political power. While Buddhism was to recover, and this was due perhaps to the fact that it had really become acclimatized in China, Zoroastrianism and Nestorianism disappeared without trace. Islam seems not to have been affected, perhaps because it had still less significance, especially in the capital itself, than these two creeds. The elimination of the foreign cults did not mean, however, that the Chinese government was not continuously aware of them; this is illustrated by the fascinating conversation of an Arab merchant with the Chinese Emperor I-tsung (860-873), during which the Emperor showed the merchant Chinese paintings portraying the main personalities of a number of Western religions. The foreign merchant communities also continued to exist in China, as is shown by the fact that their prosperous settlement in Canton was wiped out only in 879 during the course of a peasant rebellion. At this time 120,000 Moslems, Zoroastrians, Christians and Jews were supposed to have been slain together with the Chinese population of the city.

IV. The Huang Ch'ao Rebellion and the End of T'ang Rule

From the middle of the 9th century the social crisis deepened rapidly and the number of local peasant uprisings increased. The army also became less and less reliable; this was exemplified by a rebellion in 869 of troops stationed in Kweichow who marched back of their own will to their native province of Kiangsu and were put down with great difficulty.

The year 874 marked the beginning of one of the greatest peasant rebellions in Chinese history. It was started in South Hopei under the leadership of Wang Hsien-chih and Huang Ch'ao. The latter came from a merchant family, was himself a dealer or smuggler in salt; he had failed in the examinations and had been unable to obtain an official post. Huang Ch'ao published a declaration in which he attacked the T'ang government for its heavy taxation, its cruel laws and the corruption of its officials. His personal aim, later on, was to replace the T'ang dynasty by one to be founded by himself. Nevertheless, most of his followers were poor peasants.

At the outset of the rebellion the government resolved to arm the population against the insurgents. The result of this was only to increase markedly the strength of the latter. The provincial armies were of suspect loyalty and avoided battle, and in a short time the rebellion had affected much of East China. Wang Hsien-chih died in battle in 878 and Huang Ch'ao then became the supreme leader of the insurgents. His army was repeatedly defeated by the T'ang and undertook a long southward march through Chekiang, Fukien and down to Canton. At this stage Huang Ch'ao offered to end the rebellion under the condition that he be made governor of Canton. His offer was rejected by the T'ang government and Huang Ch'ao's army then took and sacked the city. The southern climate, however, almost destroyed the insurgent army, many of whom died of malaria. The remnants marched north again back to the Yangtse valley. During this period Huang Ch'ao's depleted army could easily have been destroyed, but the military governors were not too anxious to undertake this, partly because the continuation of the war was to their advantage; "it enriches us", as one of them frankly put it. As a result, Huang Ch'ao with newly enlarged forces was able to conquer Loyang in November 880 and a month later he dispersed without difficulty a starving T'ang army and took Ch'ang-an. Here, all the high officials and members of the imperial family who had been captured were massacred. Huang Ch'ao proclaimed himself Emperor of a new dynasty—the Ch'i.

The successes of Huang Ch'ao and his peasant army proved, however, to be illusory. While the campaigns they waged had covered an immense part of the country they had never done more than pillage and move on. They never occupied territory and no stable government had been formed in the areas overrun. The army found itself isolated in Ch'ang-an where Huang Ch'ao's regime proved totally incompetent, alienating every section of the population. It managed, nevertheless, to hold its position here for two years, while becoming the object of ever stronger attacks by the T'ang government and the military governors. In the face of the danger posed by Huang Ch'ao the court and the military governors managed to unite their forces, inasmuch as the interests of both parties were equally threatened by the peasant rebellion. It was not, however, in reality the forces of the Chinese feudal rulers which brought about the defeat of the insurgents. The Emperor Hsi-tsung (874-888) had fled earlier to Szechuan, just as Hsüan-tsung had done in his time; he now turned for help to Li K'o-yung, the leader of the Sha-t'o, a small Turkish tribe. The Sha-t'o had settled somewhat earlier in Shansi and had the deserved reputation of being the bravest of the brave of the Turks. Li K'o-yung, a young, 28-year-old, very able general, called "The One-Eyed Dragon", organized a corps of his tribesmen, at first 10,000, later increased to 40,000. He dressed them all in black; they became known as Li's Black Crows, and a terror to all Chinese, rebel and otherwise. It was Li K'o-yung who forced Huang Ch'ao out of Ch'ang-an and pursued the remnants of his army to Shantung, Huang Ch'ao's native province. Here, in the Mount T'ai area, Huang Ch'ao met his death. There are three versions of this: (1) he was killed by the Sha-t'o, (2) he committed suicide, (3) he was killed with his entire family by his own nephew who hoped to get a reward.

Although the rebellion was crushed and had failed in its aim of destroying the T'ang dynasty, the end of the T'ang, in reality, was its result, for now all semblance of central authority had been destroyed and its erstwhile defenders were shortly to terminate its rule. In the course of the war the campaigns of the insurgents had covered great areas of South and Central China. The social disruption of life and property was far greater than that which had accompanied the An Lu-shan rebellion—there are no data, however, to ascertain the exact scope.

The Emperor returned to Ch'ang-an, a deserted city where grass grew in the streets and hares and foxes gambolled. He and his successors were but unhappy playthings in the hands of the generals Li K'o-yung and Chu Wen—the principal rivals for power.

Chu Wen had been formerly one of Huang Ch'ao's generals who had deserted him and gone over to the T'ang. The T'ang emperor gave him a new given name—Ch'uan-chung, which meant "completely faithful", a most ironic choice. The next T'ang ruler, Chao-tsung (889-904), fell ultimately into the hands of Chu Wen. He was subsequently murdered by him and the entire imperial family was practically wiped out. His successor suffered the same fate. Chu Wen then declared himself emperor of a new dynasty, the Liang. After his enthronement he held a banquet which was attended by all the surviving high dignitaries of the T'ang. He thanked them for making his elevation to the throne possible, for it was due, as he said, to their baseness, treachery and cowardice that the T'ang dynasty had met its doom.

CHAPTER 16

T'ang Literature and Art

1. Literature

In the T'ang era the development of China into a powerful, united country was also accompanied by a greater flourishing of culture than had ever taken place in the Middle Kingdom. This pertained to practically all fields, but was particularly true of literature and painting.

In the history of Chinese literature it is for its poetry that the T'ang age is especially famous. It has been often described as the most glorious, the golden era of Chinese poetry unparalleled before or since. The output of the T'ang poets was truly prodigious; the 1707 edition of complete T'ang poetry includes 48,900 poems by 2,200 writers and is contained in 30 very large volumes.

The present writer does not feel competent to discuss the problems of the complex nature of Chinese poetry, its rules of tone and rhyme, its characteristic brevity or its penchant for allusions. It should be remarked that translation of Chinese poetry into European languages poses particularly difficult problems and that only a relatively small part of this great heritage of Chinese culture has been made available, although some of it has been rendered superbly. A number of translations, nonetheless, as, for example, Waley's, are truly masterful.

It has been often stated that T'ang poetry gives in many ways a better picture of the era than any other form of literature due to the richness of its content. This is probably so, notwithstanding the fact that the poems were practically in all cases by members of only one stratum of Chinese society. As scholar-officials, they saw life primarily through Confucian spectacles, but in many cases, however, these did not distort their vision and they were able to convey all that surrounded them. Their scale of values was broad and emphasized primarily the more civilized pursuits of man; they refrained from glorifying war.

By common consensus of Chinese writers on the subject, two names are always placed in the forefront as the greatest of the T'ang and therefore of Chinese poets, Li Po and Tu Fu.

Li Po (or Li T'ai-po, 701-762) is often considered the most versatile of all the Chinese poets. His mastery of the language was complete; he employed a great variety of forms and style and dealt with many different subjects. He developed the art of literary allusion to the highest possible level. He was undoubtedly a born poetical genius and the flow of magnificent, purely lyrical verse never ceased throughout his life. As a youth he studied Taoist practices and spent a considerable time wandering around the country, settling as a hermit for a period. With his friends of a similar disposition he formed a famous group known as the Six Recluses of the Bamboo Stream who spent their time in versifying and drinking wine. In his travels he met Tu Fu in 738 and they formed a lifelong friendship. Li Po spent some time in the Emperor's court in Ch'ang-an but his independent nature did not permit him to become a proper obsequious courtier; he was soon in disgrace and resumed his wanderings. Legend has him drowning in the Yangtse; having drunk too much of his beloved wine, wishing to embrace a reflection of the moon in the water, he leaned out too far from the boat.

Tu Fu (712-770) was recognized from his early youth for his brilliant talent. He failed, however, in making the usual career and did not obtain an official post until he was 40. His life was a difficult one with much suffering and hardships, especially during the years of the An Lu-shan rebellion. His outlook on life was far more sober than that of Li Po and his poetry is considered more profound and emotionally rich. Tu Fu had a deep understanding and awareness of the human suffering that surrounded him. His works also cover an immense range with the employment of new forms.

Of the great T'ang poets of the same period mention should be made of at least one more—Wang Wei (701-761) who has been called by Waley the most classical of Chinese poets. He represented a type by no means rare in Chinese history—the all-round genius—as he was equally famous as a painter, calligrapher and musician. Thus later on he was considered the ideal by the scholar-officials with their artistic aspirations. Wang Wei wrote in a seemingly plain but, in fact, highly developed style; his verse is considered more reflective and personal than that of Li Po.

While T'ang poetry reached its full splendour already by the 8th century the development of literature in the later part of the T'ang period is also noteworthy, in both poetry and prose. Taken as a whole, the T'ang era can be considered as the foundation for all future development of Chinese literature.

The most famous poet of the latter period was Po Chü-i (772-846), regarded as a disciple of Tu Fu. His career adhered much more closely to the standard pattern, inasmuch as he spent his entire life as an official, on the whole successfully, rising by the end to high posts in the bureaucracy. His early poetry includes many political satires, but probably his best-known work, the one which made him famous, is "The Everlasting Remorse" which dealt with the fate of Yang Kuei-fei. This was written as imitation of popular narrative ballads and is also one of the longest of Chinese poems. Thereafter most of his verse is very personal and deals with subjects common to the fate of all men; when read together the poems can be regarded as his very moving autobiography. Po Chü-i was renowned for the verbal simplicity of his work and wrote in a language close in the vernacular. The story is often told of him that he would read his verse to an old country woman and would not be satisfied with it until she understood it all.

Han Yü (768-824), although known also as a poet, was much more famous as an essayist. He was a thoroughgoing fundamentalist Confucianist and a bitter opponent of Buddhism. Although he had little influence in his own time, he was regarded as one of the principal thinkers responsible for the restoration of Confucianism, as a precursor and patron saint of the Neo-Confucianists. Han Yü was also credited with the introduction of a new style of writing which was based on the older classical literature of the Warring States and Western Han period, as opposed to the more artificial style which had developed during the Period of Division. His style is said to be original, pure and vigorous. He is perhaps best known for his philippics against Buddhism. The most famous of these is his attack on the worshipping of Buddhist relics, written on the occasion of the bringing of Buddha's supposed finger bone to Ch'ang-an in 819. He was exiled to Kwangtung for this pronouncement. His opposition to Buddhism actually followed two trends of thought; he criticized its superstitious nature, but perhaps even more its foreign origin, and he voiced a growing trend towards xenophobia. The following words represent his views concisely:

"We have our society, our civilization, our government, our custom and habits. These all conform to our principles and everything with us is rational and logical. Thanks to this we live in peace . . . live properly, say the Sages, and if you do so there is nothing to fear—Heaven, man or conscience. What need have we then of barbarian religions?"

A younger contemporary of Han Yü, Liu Tsung-yüan (773-819), was almost equally famous as a great essayist and known for his efforts to create a new literary style. His works include the famous parable *The Snake Catchers,* an ironical depiction of the ravaging of the peasants by the tax-collectors. Liu Tsung-yüan was probably more in line with the sceptical tradition and a self-professed "Legalist". He was a supporter of the short-lived reform movement of 805 against eunuch rule and other abuses which took place at the beginning of the 9th century. As a result he spent the rest of his life in exile.

The T'ang period also saw the appearance of a new form of literary creation—the short story. This originated already in the 6th century but the best examples date from the middle of the 8th century and provide a vivid picture of T'ang society.

It is in the middle of the 8th century that the Hanlin was founded. This was, in effect, the oldest academy of letters in the world and existed until the end of the Empire in the 20th century. Already during its initial stage it gathered the best scholars of the country and it was charged with the responsibility for all the court's literary work, the writing of edicts and proclamations.

The Buddhist establishment which was still flourishing in this era was also the source of great literary activity in very many fields. Only one very interesting example of this will be given—that of the famous Chinese pilgrim Hsüan-tsang. In 629 he followed the path of many of his predecessors to India by way of Central Asia to visit the holy places of Buddhism and to gather new Buddhist texts. After 16 years of studying he returned with 675 books. Hsüan-tsang then spent the next 20 years on translating his treasures; his energy was prodigious and he is credited with rendering, with his associates, over 1300 works into Chinese. His perhaps most interesting and valuable work, however, is the account of his travels, *Hsi-yü Chi* ("Records of Travels in the Western Countries"), which is noted for its accuracy. His travels became later the subject for many novels and plays and is one of the best-known works in Chinese literature.

Intimately bound up with literary development is printing, one of the greatest of Chinese inventions. While the printing of books on a large scale dates only from the 10th century, the process must have originated much earlier, somewhere at the end of the 6th or the beginning of the 7th century. It developed logically from the knowledge of seals and rubbings. The form adopted, that of carving an entire page of text on a wooden block, resulted more than likely from the vast number and variety of Chinese characters; the use of individual types for each character was a later development which still preceded its invention in Europe. The earliest-known example of printing is a Japanese text dating from 764. In Chinese, it is a copy of the Buddhist Diamond Sutra dated 868, which was found in Tun-huang. This is also illustrated with wood-cuts. It has been well stated that it is not an accident that both paper and printing were Chinese inventions inasmuch as they were products of a civilization which was literary *par excellence*. It seems redundant to stress the value of this contribution to world culture.

II. T'ang Historiography

It is in the T'ang period that Chinese historical writing assumed an organizational form which was of crucial importance for its future development. This was connected with the establishment of the History Office which was first set up for the purpose of writing the history of the five preceding dynasties and for the preparation and collection of materials for the elaboration of T'ang history as well. It is from this time on that historical writing becomes, in principle, a governmental function and this, in turn, determined to a large degree the nature of all future work in this field.

The basic purpose of government-sponsored historical writing was to record the past, not only for the sake of the past as such (although the greatest interest of the Chinese in their history, as already mentioned, is an ever-present factor) but also for the purpose of drawing lessons from the past to serve current action. This idea is aptly represented by the title which the Sung Emperor Shen-tsung later on bestowed on the great work of Ssu-ma Kuang—"The Comprehensive Mirror to Aid in Governing" (see p. 175). Following the Confucian tradition the aim of the historian was not to create but to transmit the records of the past. It is both this and its governmental function which account for the strongly conservative nature of traditional Chinese historiography.

This approach, as well as the methods used, resulted in the fact that the historical works contained relatively little analysis or synthesis of the material presented. Basically, they served both a political and a didactic purpose. Their subject-matter was exclusively political. They recorded the exercise of power, especially by the Emperor and his court. Their "dynastic" character implied a necessity to praise the present rulers and to castigate their predecessors; it involved also the use of standard, stereotyped formulas such as the classical "bad last ruler" and "Mandate of Heaven" concepts. The dominant scheme of writing history, as that of particular dynasties, resulted also in its division into somewhat artificial time periods which made an overall view or perspective very difficult to achieve. Balázs aptly remarked that the traditional histories were "written primarily by bureaucrats for bureaucrats" and this also influenced their character.

As standardized in the T'ang period, the work of the court historians was composed of the following elements. A Diary of Activity and Repose of the Emperor was kept on a daily basis. During the T'ang the tradition was still maintained that the Emperor did not have the right to look into the text, although both T'ai-tsung and Hsüan-tsung broke the rule; this proved too much for the Sung emperors and this valuable tradition was then dispensed with. The material from the Diary together with other reports from the ministries was combined to compose the Daily Records. These, in turn, served as the basis for the writing of the Veritable Records of each reign which constituted, in fact, a current history of the dynasty. At times they were used to write a full history of the reigning dynasty, a National History. It is these National Histories and Veritable Records which were employed by the succeeding dynasty for the writing of the Standard History of its predecessor.

The material employed in the above work was derived primarily from official documentation and most of it was in the form of direct, although often abbreviated, quotations from these sources. Thus a vast material documentation was provided which was then compiled by what too often was a scissors and paste method. The organization of the Standard Histories followed the pattern set by Ssu-ma Ch'ien and Pan Ku, i.e. a composite form of annals, biographies and monographic studies. It should be pointed out, however, that apart from the Standard Histories, a great variety of other types of historical writing was also practised. Likewise, not all the historical works of this and subsequent periods were the work of the official state historians.

The Chinese historians prided themselves on their objectivity but as regards the History Office it is quite clear that here the pressure of political considerations, apart from the political views of the historians themselves, would be a factor which would lead to a considerable departure from this principle. The practices of official historical writing were the object of very incisive criticism by Liu Chih-chi (662-721) in his *Shih-t'ung* ("Generalities on History"). Liu was a man of independent ideas with a lifelong enthusiasm for historical studies and considerable talent and insight. His work is the first in the world on the writing of history and constitutes at the same time a theoretical manual on the subject. It was influenced by and is similar in pattern to the famous work literature by Liu Hsieh (see p. 108). In it the author classified historical works, treated technical problems but, above all, dealt with the basic question of a historian's *métier*—the problem of "honest writing". Liu Chih-chi adopted a critical approach to historical sources and was later known for his "scandalous boldness" in daring to question the veracity not only of some of the materials of the Classics, but even of Confucius himself. In this, he continued perhaps the sceptical tradition of Wang Ch'ung. It does not mean, however, that he questioned the Confucian tradition fundamentally. In reality, very few, if any, Chinese historians or other scholars ever succeeded in breaking the bonds of this tradition until the 19th century.

Another form of historical writing which developed in the T'ang period was that of institutional political history. This was represented by the works of Tu Yu (735-812), especially his famous *T'ung-tien* ("Comprehensive Statutes"), an encyclopaedic compendium of 200 chapters. In this work Tu Yu broke away from the chronological pattern of the Standard Histories and, desirous of studying a number of problems in their historical development, he arranged his data according to subject-matter. Thus, he deals with: (1) political economy, (2) examinations, (3) officials, (4) rites, (5) music, (6) army, (7) law, (8) geography of the empire and (9) geography of frontier regions. Tu Yu's work became a model for many future encyclopaedias of a similar nature.

III. Sculpture

Buddhist sculpture reached its final pinnacle of development in the early T'ang period and subsequently lost much of its original vigour. Unfortunately, even less T'ang sculpture than that of the earlier dynasties has survived. There are two reasons for this: firstly, the T'ang sculptors used less stone and preferred other materials such as bronze, clay and wood—all of which were, of course, more perishable; secondly, the great persecution of Buddhism in 845, as well as ever-recurrent temple fires, brought about the loss of practically all sculpture in the perishable materials. Thus, once more one is forced to look to Korea and Japan in order to obtain an idea of what these works must have been like.

A monumental Buddha from Lung-men provides a very fine example of early T'ang stone sculpture. It has been stated that as Buddhism itself became more and more Chinese, thus also the style in sculpture changed and underwent a process of softening and humanization. Buddhist sculpture never recovered fully from the ravages of the persecution in 845, and later on became rather a secondary art concerned with the ornamentation of the temples.

Some authorities are inclined to consider Buddhist sculpture as a basically foreign art form. The traditional Chinese sculpture was restricted to two forms. One of these, in stone, was represented primarily by tomb figures and dates back to the Han. It was still continued in T'ang in its monumental, heavy and solid shape. Possible exceptions to this are the bas-relief horses on the tomb of Tai-t'sung. Generally the level of sculpture was much lower than that of painting—perhaps the use of the brush in writing naturally turned men with an artistic talent to painting.

There exists another form of sculpture for which the T'ang period is justly famous—the pottery figurines. This is a curious phenomenon, inasmuch as these beautiful, lively and graceful figures which include a vast variety of subjects, from the renowned horses to dancing girls, were never intended to be seen by human beings as they were placed in tombs to serve as replicas of what had surrounded the deceased during his sojourn on earth. This function is perhaps also the reason for the high dègree of realism; the figures were to revive once more with their owner in another world. The pottery figures show a great variety of social and racial human types and constitute a wonderful picture of the T'ang age. This art form was the work of anonymous craftsmen and this was true also, in most cases, of most of the other objects of T'ang pottery and sculpture. The general level of ceramics was already very high, and while the pottery of the Sung period is more renowned, all the groundwork had already been laid in the T'ang period.

IV. Architecture

Both the Sui and the T'ang dynasties are considered to be an age of the greatest flourishing of Chinese architecture, a time when the Imperial Court supported building on a vast scale for both secular and religious purposes. It is generally stated that palaces and temples were basically interchangeable in their structure. It is in this period that architecture attained a classical simplicity and balance, partially due perhaps to the availability of great talents and the immense wealth devoted to construction. The scale of building was truly great, especially of Buddhist temples, and in this respect one should go back even earlier, to the reign of Emperor Wu of the Liang. In this field, however, both the nature of the materials employed—primarily wood—and the religious persecution, especially the one of 845, resulted in the fact that practically nothing has survived with the exception of one small wooden temple in North Shansi. Only a few pagodas of stone and brick remain of T'ang architecture in China. Here once more one must look at Japan where twenty-two structures from the period when T'ang influences were the strongest are still extant and these give some idea of how magnificent this architecture must have been in its heyday.

V. Painting

It is in the T'ang era that all the basic foundations were laid down for the future development of this greatest of the Chinese arts; the traditions of this period dominated Chinese painting for the rest of its future growth. It is already at this time that one of the social aspects of this art form is marked; it is not so much the work of professional artists but rather of amateurs, of scholar-officials, a mode of self-expression. Thus painting is done for pleasure and not as a means of gaining a livelihood. There was no compulsion for an artist to seek recognition, nor to strive for the attainment of a proper social status, inasmuch as he already possessed the latter.

It is probable that the greatest amount of work in this period was devoted to religious subjects, especially Buddhist. Not a single work of the great T'ang masters in the genre has survived. It is true that a considerable quantity of Buddhist painting dating from this period still exists, but most of it comes from the small provincial town of Tun-huang right at the edge of the Empire. The famous caves, already mentioned, were richly decorated; almost 480 out of 1000 shrines have survived in perfect conditions. These contain a great variety of paintings and it has been calculated that if they were put together their length would amount to 50 *li*. While they are undoubtedly interesting, especially in that they provide many data on the social life of the times, this is not the work of great artists but the production of craftsmen, although of good quality.

It was not in the religious subjects, Buddhist or Taoist, but in figure painting and, above all, landscape that the Chinese genius in painting revealed itself fully. It is possible to maintain that landscape painting is perhaps the greatest contribution of China to world art. Sickman has remarked that the Chinese painters "lavished upon the world of hills and streams and trees all the keen analysis and penetration that the best artists of Europe have brought to their study of the appearance and character of humanity". In this the influence of both Taoism and Ch'an Buddhism are obvious and of the greatest significance. In the hands of the brilliant T'ang masters this genre had already evolved as a vehicle which could express emotions on a par with poetry.

Figure painting, which drew on the achievements of the earlier period, developed considerably during the T'ang. The most famous names include that of Yen Li-pen *(fl.* 640-670), a court painter of both T'ai-tsung and Kao-tsung. The famous scroll "Portraits of the Emperors" has been attributed to him. Other noted painters in this field were Chang Hsüan *(fl.* 713-742?) and Chou Fang *(fl.* 780-810), both remembered for their paintings of the graceful, plump, roundfaced ladies of the T'ang court. It is, however, more than likely that in the case of these three artists what we have today are only copies of their work. Han Kan (?720-780) is equally well known but not for his human beings as much as for his famous horses; he was the first of a long line of painters of this subject. There is, in fact, only one T'ang painter, Li Chen (*ca.* 800), of whom it can be said with any amount of certitude that his original paintings are still extant. These are the portraits of Buddhist patriarchs which were taken to Japan in the 9th century and are still preserved in Tokyo. They are a fine representation of early Chinese portraiture.

The ravages of time, wars and persecutions affected, in particular, the work of the man considered the greatest master of the T'ang period and the most famous of all Chinese painters. Not a single genuine work of Wu Tao-tzu (*ca.* 700-760) has survived and knowledge about him and his painting is based primarily on literary accounts. He was said to have possessed great natural genius and boundless energy; his name is known to all educated Chinese. He was credited with having painted over 300 frescoes in Ch'ang-an and Loyang, mostly on Buddhist subjects, the field to which so much great effort was devoted and lost. By the 11th century only a handful of his originals were said to have survived. It is perhaps possible to derive some idea of his broad realistic and sculpturesque style from stone engravings which are said to be modelled on his paintings; these supposedly reveal his superb mastery of brushwork and line.

The situation is unfortunately no better in regards to the existence of original works by two masters who are considered the founders of the two basic styles of Chinese landscape painting. Li Ssu-hsün (651-716) is regarded as the originator of painting in a minute, finely drawn style employing colours on silk with a dominance of blue and green. This style continued throughout the history of Chinese painting and some of the Ming artists (e.g. Ch'iu Ying) were its last able representatives. This was also, however, a style which was adapted with relative ease by skilled craftsmen and thus innumerable scrolls which do not possess any particular artistic value were produced in this manner.

The second of these masters was Wang Wei, already mentioned as a poet. While painting also in the style of Li Ssu-hsün, he is credited as well with inaugurating monochrome painting in ink. It is probable, however, that both these masters, in fact, did not initiate but continued tendencies already existing. Wang Wei's famous painting of his estate Wang Ch'uan, perhaps one of the first of the hand scroll type, has been the subject of countless copies and paraphrases. A copy of it engraved on stone also exists. Wang Wei was reputed to be the founder of the so-called Southern School of Chinese painting. This division, however, of Chinese painters into a Northern and a Southern School (which had nothing to do with geography but was an analogy to a division which took place in Ch'an Buddhism) was an arbitrary invention of Ming art critics for the purpose of buttressing their own ideas of aesthetic values. It is of no real value whatsoever and has unfortunately been repeated uncritically by many writers on the history of Chinese painting. It would seem much more advisable to regard a particular Chinese painting on its merits than on its supposed affiliation to these two schools. The work of the artists of the next historical period, the Sung, will show how truly well the groundwork for this great art was established by the T'ang masters.

PART VI

The Sung Dynasties and the Northern Invasions

CHAPTER 17

The Five Dynasties and Northern Sung

I. The Five Dynasties and the Ten Kingdoms

The fall of the T'ang was followed by an epoch known in Chinese history as the Five Dynasties and Ten Kingdoms; this was an era in which the centralized, unified state underwent complete disintegration, an age of total chaos and turmoil, even more confusing than that which followed the fall of the Eastern Han. This was undoubtedly one of the darkest periods in Chinese annals, especially in Northern China, an era of great suffering and privation for the people as a result of continued warfare, inhuman laws, countless taxes and other burdens. What is perhaps most significant, however, is that this time the period of division was much shorter and covered a relatively brief span of fifty-four years. Many factors accounted for this but it is more than likely that the greater awareness of the Chinese of their political and cultural unity—a heritage from the T'ang era—was the most important.

The Five Dynasties are referred to by this name only due to the fact that the Chinese historians later sought to establish a seeming continuity of imperial rule and thus they endowed these brief regimes with the attributes of empire. In reality, these dynasties controlled only a part of North and Central China, while the rest of the country was divided into a series of independent states, which varied as to their area and length of duration, known as the Ten Kingdoms. The latter usually lasted much longer than the Northern dynasties and the conditions in these states were also much better in practically all respects. There was relatively very little warfare in these areas and thus the economy and prosperity of the Ten Kingdoms was basically unaffected, while a continuity of culture was simultaneously preserved. On the whole, the government of the Ten Kingdoms was also infinitely superior to regimes in the North.

The governments in the North were, in effect, ephemeral military dictatorships in which alien groups, especially the Sha-t'o Turks, played a large role, and which

Map 12. The Five Dynasties and Ten Kingdoms, ca. 955

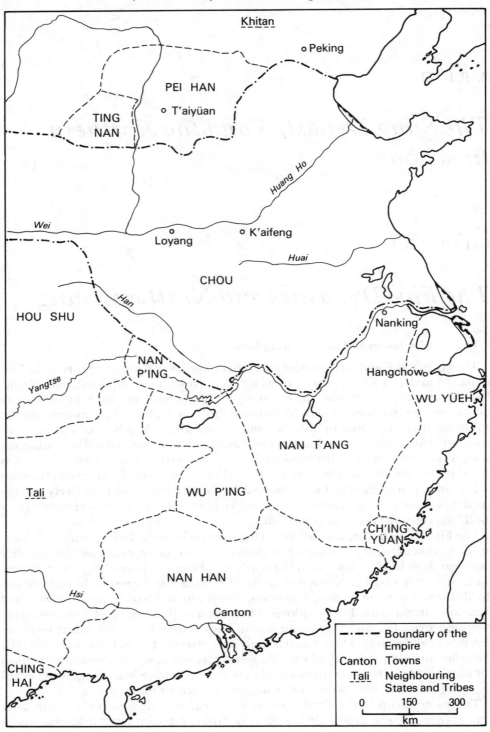

continued all the varied, vicious practices of rule by the military which had developed during the Late T'ang era. None of them was able to consolidate its rule and all of them in turn fell a victim to usurpation. In the area of the "Empire" civil war of a complicated nature was practically endemic and as a result the economy was in a ruinous state. In fifty-four years thirteen emperors from eight different families sat on the Dragon Throne; of these over half were of Turkish origin. This period witnessed also the final and complete ruin of the North-west—the origin cradle of Chinese civilization and the shift of the political centre of the country to the Central Plain, as marked by the ultimate transfer of the capital to K'aifeng.

The Later Liang had been, as mentioned earlier, established by Chu Wen. The main political feature of its rule was the rivalry with the family of the Sha-t'o leader, Li K'o-yung, and after his death in 908 with his son Li Ts'un-hsü, the king of Chin (Shansi). Chu Wen, the man who had massacred all the last T'ang princes, was murdered by his own son in 912. The latter was, in turn, killed by his brother. The Liang state became an easy prey to the attacks of Chin; when the armies of Li Ts'un-hsü advanced most of the Liang generals went over to his side. The third and last ruler of the Liang committed suicide and Li Ts'un-hsü now established himself in 923 as Emperor of the Later T'ang.

While the ruling family of Later T'ang and a part of its army were Sha-t'o Turks, these formed, in fact, a very small group, perhaps at most 100,000, and thus, in effect, it was the Chinese great landowning families who provided most of the bureaucrats, and controlled local society during this dynasty as well as throughout the Five Dynasties period. It was during the Later T'ang (923-936) that the only period occurred when peace in the North was maintained for any length of time—seven years (926-933). This was during the reign of the second of the T'ang rulers.

The Later T'ang were overthrown by a rebellion of one of its generals, Shih Ching-t'ang, also a Sha-t'o, who had formed an alliance for this purpose with the Khitan; the latter were now becoming more and more of a power in the north of China and an ever greater menace to Chinese rule. For their assistance the Khitan received from the new Chin Emperor—this is what Shih called his dynasty (936-947)—sixteen districts in North Shansi and North Hopei (including the area where Peking is situated) as well as 300,000 rolls of silk. This made them the rulers for the first time of purely Chinese territory.

The Khitan had originally lived in the area of Western Liaoning and Eastern Inner Mongolia where they pursued a semi-nomadic existence. It is asserted that they were the descendants of the Hsien-pi and spoke a language related to Mongolian. In 907 the eight Khitan tribes formed a strong confederation which was already able to send into battle a force of supposedly 300,000 horsemen. The real rise to power of the Khitan was connected with the activity of Apaochi (this is the Chinese version of his name) of the ruling Yeh-lü clan. After a period of severe struggle against other chieftains he established himself as the monarch of the Khitan realm, undoubtedly influenced in this by the model of China. In 916 Apaochi declared himself Emperor of the Khitan and concentrated his efforts on strengthening his state, being helped in this by his Chinese adviser, Han Yen-hui.

The principal key to the success of the Khitan was their great military superiority which was based on their superb cavalry and an effective organization of their army on a decimal system. Within the army the elite bodyguard was of special importance; in time this expanded to a number of 50,000 to 70,000 horsemen. After the death of Apaochi in 926 the throne was assumed by his son Te-kuang with the help of his remarkably shrewd and ruthless mother. The Khitan continued to expand their rule to the South; in 926 they destroyed the powerful sedentary state of P'ohai in Manchuria (this had been established by some of the Tungus and Koreans in 710) and were now ready to commence incursions on a larger scale against China proper. In 937 the Khitan adopted the name of Liao for their state and dynasty and their intentions of seeking to become rulers of all China were thus ever more evident.

Although the Khitan had been responsible for placing the Chin dynasty on the throne the relations between them and the Chinese soon deteriorated, ultimately leading to the first great Khitan attack in 944 and then to a full-scale invasion in 946. The success of the Khitan armies was complete—they captured the capital, K'aifeng, and took the Chin emperor prisoner. It is more than probable that they contemplated the establishment of their rule over the entire area of the Chin empire, but the resistance of the Chinese population was much too troublesome for them and in the following year they retreated back to the North. They behaved in the customary fashion of the northern nomad tribes, murdering and pillaging on a mass scale, so that the area for hundreds of *li* around K'aifeng was turned into a desert.

The next of the Five Dynasties, the Later Han, was established by Liu Chih-yüan (also a Sha-t'o) partly as the result of the Chinese resistance and rebellions against the Khitan. This proved to be the shortest of all the dynasties—lasting barely four years, 947-950. Its second ruler was overthrown by his own army which raised General Kuo Wei, a Chinese, to the imperial throne. Claiming descent from the ancient rulers of China he named his dynasty Chou. He and his successor were the only rulers during the Five Dynasties period with any positive administrative aims, and showed some concern for the situation of the peasantry and the condition of the economy. In the case of Kuo Wei he explained this by the fact that he himself had been born in poverty and knew well the sufferings of the people. The Chou rulers lowered taxes and sought to encourage agricultural production. They also planned to regain the territory in the North which had been lost to the Khitan. During an expedition against the Khitan the second Chou emperor died, leaving only a minor to succeed him on the throne. It is against this setting that the coup which led to the establishment of the Sung took place.

During the time when the "Empire" was the scene of the struggles for power described above, the states in the south of China continued to develop in relative peace. Among the most important was Southern T'ang (937-975) which superseded the state of Wu (902-937) existing in the same area—Anhwei, Kiangsu, Kiangsi. In this state agriculture flourished and labour power was plentiful thanks to the great number of refugees who fled there from the strife-torn North. It was a prosperous, cultured and well-ruled state. In Southern T'ang, as well as in the other southern kingdoms, a considerable increase in the cultivation of wasteland took place and irrigation works were constructed and expanded on a large scale. Domestic and foreign trade, especially in tea and silk, also developed to a marked degree.

The other states included also Ch'u, which embraced Hunan; Southern Han, which included Kwangtung and Kwangsi; Min, which corresponded to Fukien; Wu-Yüeh covering the area of Chekiang and a part of Kiangsu, and Shu, which included most of Szechuan. The names of these states reveal clearly a conscious archaizing, in that they refer back to states which had existed in these areas during the times of the Chou.

Map 13. Northern Sung, ca. 1100

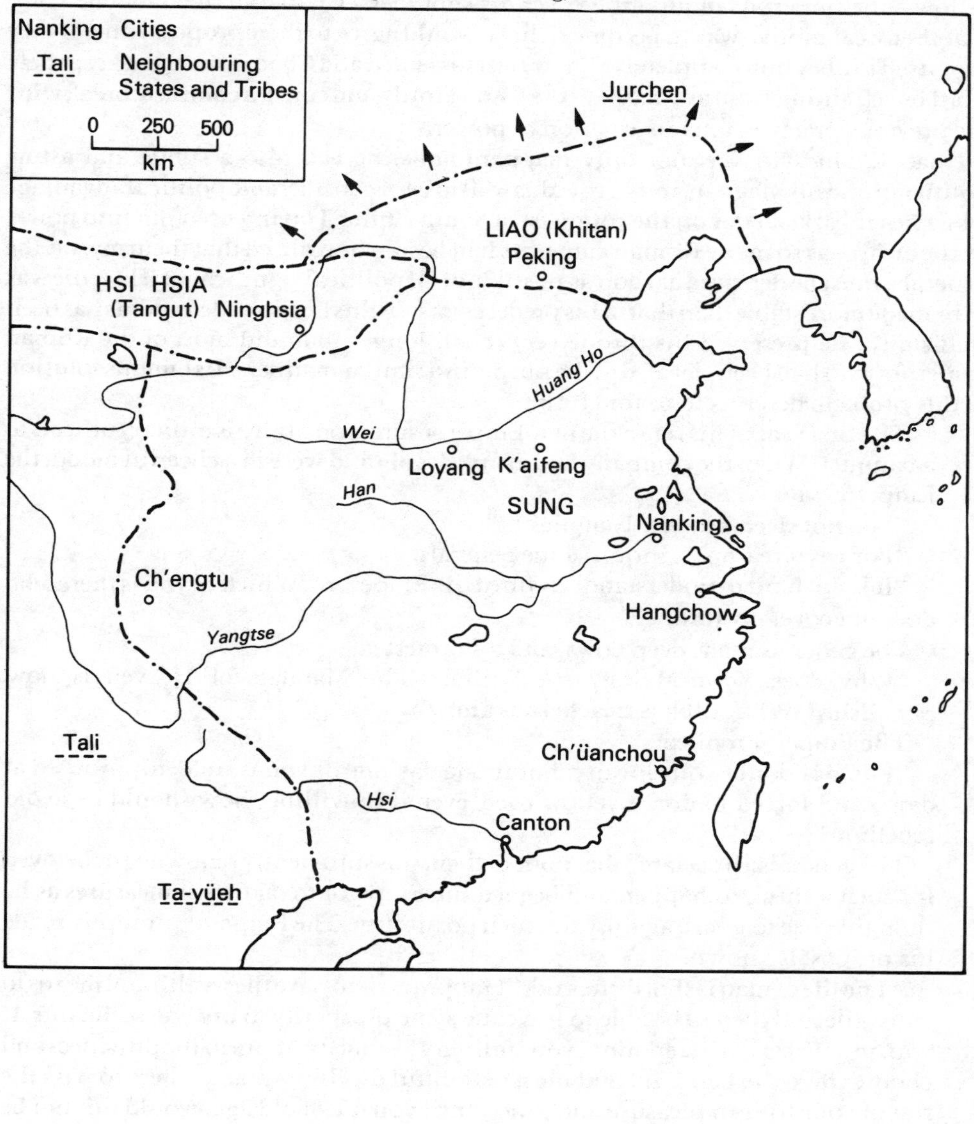

| Nanking | Cities |
| Tali | Neighbouring States and Tribes |

0   250   500
km

Jurchen

LIAO (Khitan)
Peking

HSI HSIA
(Tangut) Ninghsia

Huang Ho

Wei
Loyang K'aifeng

Han
SUNG

Nanking

Ch'engtu

Hangchow

Yangtse

Tali

Ch'üanchou

Hsi
Canton

Ta-yüeh

II. The Establishment of the Sung Dynasty

One of the leading generals of the Chou army and the commander of the Imperial Guard was Chao K'uang-yin. When the second Chou emperor died, the officers of the army plotted to place Chao as their own nominee on the imperial throne. The scene of this action is one of the best known in Chinese history. The officers entered Chao's tent with their sabres drawn and communicated to him their desire. One of them threw a yellow—the imperial colour—robe over his shoulders. Chao told them that he knew that their real motive was to become rich; he would agree to their proposal only if they promised to obey him completely. The officers assented and Chao made them keep their word by refraining from any harm to the Chou family and court, a complete break with the previous practices after usurpation of power.

Chao K'uang-yin was not only magnanimous, he was also a subtle and astute politician and his magnanimity proved as well to be of considerable political advantage when he embarked later on the conquest of South China. Having been put into power by the army—as so many Roman emperors had been—he realized that the army, i.e. the generals, must be deprived as soon as possible of all political significance if his rule was to be made more stable than that of his predecessors. In this he succeeded and, as has been well stated, he preserved his throne very much longer than did most of the Roman emperors who had been elevated to the purple in a similar manner. His famous solution of this problem deserves to be told fully:

The first year of his reign the new Emperor summoned all his military officers to a banquet. When the company had drunk deeply and were in a cheerful mood, the Emperor said:

"I do not sleep peacefully at night."

"For what reason?", inquired the generals.

"It is not hard to understand", replied the Emperor. "Which of you is there who does not covet my throne?"

The generals made deep bows, and all protested:

"Why does Your Majesty speak thus? The Mandate of Heaven is now established. Who still has treacherous aims?"

The Emperor replied:

"I do not doubt your loyalty, but if one day one of you is suddenly aroused at dawn and forced to don a yellow robe, even if unwilling, how should he avoid rebellion?"

The generals all declared that none of them was sufficiently renowned or beloved for such a thing to happen and begged the Emperor to take such measures as he thought wise to guard against any such possibility. The Emperor promptly made his proposals known:

"The life of man is short", he said. "Happiness is to have the wealth and means to enjoy life and then to be able to leave the same prosperity to one's descendants. If you, my officers, will renounce your military authority, retire to the provinces and choose there the best land and most delightful dwelling-places, there to pass the rest of your lives in pleasure and peace until you die of old age, would this not be better than to live a life of peril and uncertainty? So that no shadow of suspicion shall remain between prince and ministers, we will ally your families with marriages, thus, ruler and subject linked in friendship and amity, we will enjoy tranquility."

The generals immediately vowed to follow the Emperor's wishes, and the next day, pretending imaginary maladies, all offered their resignations. The Emperor accepted their offer. All were given titles of honour and richly endowed with wealth and land.

By means of this political master-stroke T'ai-tsu (K'uang-yin's posthumous title) put an end to over two centuries of the ruinous rule by the military in China. This was followed up by a reorganization of the army which was converted into a purely mercenary force and placed under strict control of the central government. The posts of military governors were then abolished. In the army itself the Imperial Guard became of particular importance, and as time progressed it composed almost half of the armed forces and was stationed primarily in central areas close to the capital. A policy of changing army commanders very often was also adhered to.

Simultaneously, drawing on the experiences of the downfall of the T'ang, the civil administration was also thoroughly reorganized by T'ai-tsu. The restoration of the examination system took place and as Sung rule was consolidated this system became the main source of recruitment for the government bureaucracy. By 1065 the examinations had reached their full form; they were held every three years on three levels—in the prefecture, the capital and the palace. Those who had managed to pass all three levels and obtain the top degree, *chin shih,* had in fact, a practical monopoly on obtaining the top official posts. As in the earlier periods these successful candidates came primarily from landlord families, but the possibilities of a great career in the government bureaucracy constituted also an added inducement to loyalty towards the central government. In time, the growth of the Sung civilian bureaucracy became excessive, its efficiency declined, while the costs of its maintenance reached exorbitant heights. This emphasis on the civilian character of the administration did, however, especially in the early Sung period, bring about a decisive dominance of the civilian element as against the military in Chinese political life. It is perhaps in this period that the famous saying was coined:

> Nails are not to be made out of good iron,
> Nor soldiers out of good men.

The re-establishment of a strong centralized monarchy was linked up by T'ai-tsu with a policy of subduing all the independent states in the South. In this he followed the strategy of "First the South and then the North", and thus refrained in the initial period from attempts to regain the territory that had been lost to the Khitan. The conquest of the South was accomplished, on the whole, with relative ease and without too much use of force. This was partly due to the fact that the population probably desired a unified country, as the traditions of this were already quite strong and were associated with the idea of peace, prosperity and perhaps even glory—all the heritage of the best years of the T'ang. The feeling of cultural unity was also stronger than earlier, and this was surely helped by the algebraic nature of the Chinese written language which constituted a great unifying factor.

T'ai-tsu's well-known policy of magnanimity was also followed during the absorption of the South and applied to the rulers of the former states. This undoubtedly facilitated the process of the conquest considerably. The annexation of the South was completed by his brother and successor, T'ai-tsung (976-997). This succession from brother to brother resulted from the last will of their mother. Affirming that the Sung had gained the throne only due to the fact that the last of the Chou had been a minor, she insisted earlier on her deathbed that the succession of brothers be established. Her sound advice was dutifully followed, but only once; for T'ai-tsung then deprived his older brother's sons of their foreseen right to inherit, and left the throne to his own son.

In his reign, as a sequel to the conquest of the last independent Chinese state, Northern Han in Shansi (this had been established by a relative of the Later Han dynasty and was always supported by the Khitan), T'ai-tsung attempted to wage war in 979 against the Khitan but his forces were heavily defeated. Once again, in 986, the Chinese launched a series of campaigns against the Khitan, but met with an equal lack of success. Thereafter no more efforts were made to regain the territory held by the Khitan. Some modern Chinese historians castigate this policy and state that it was derived from the supposedly faulty strategy of "First the South, then the North", which thus gave the Khitan the possibility of strengthening their state.

Regardless of whether the above carping criticism is correct or not, the Liao did, in fact, become a great power. In its heyday—the 11th century—the power of the Khitan extended from the Gulf of P'ohai to the T'ien Shan range in Central Asia. In this state, however, the Khitan themselves constituted a minority. According to one estimate the population of the Liao state in this period numbered around 4 million: 750,000 Khitan, 650,000 P'ohai and 2.6 million Chinese. In administering their empire the Khitan ruling class used the Chinese system of administration for the areas of North China, including the use of examinations, to which only the Chinese were admitted; simultaneously they sought to preserve the tribal basis of administration for the areas not populated by the Chinese. In effect, the Khitan came more and more under the influence of Chinese culture in all fields. Although they had devised two forms for writing their own language (one based on Uighur and the other on Chinese), the process of sinification made rapid progress in spite of conscious attempts on the part of the Liao government to avoid this. The result was the progressive loss of military prowess, reflecting also the gradual abandonment of the nomad way of life. The Liao during the last century of their rule are considered by many authors to be practically as much a Chinese dynasty and state as the Sung.

The Sung dynasty, as established by its first two and ablest emperors, differed in some important respects from both the T'ang and the Han. It was even more an absolute monarchy than its predecessors and the individual role of the emperor was undoubtedly of greater importance. The estimates made of the character of the Sung rulers who followed the first two emperors differ considerably. Some authors consider them as mediocrities, amiable perhaps for their appreciation and patronage of the arts; others think that they were maligned by Confucian (and perhaps not only Confucian) Chinese historians and were, in reality, tolerant and humane rulers, the most enlightened sovereigns ever to sit on the Chinese throne, but perhaps too civilized to face up to the danger of nomad invasion. However, there is little disagreement, on the whole, as to the conclusion that the Sung period was the most brilliant era in the cultural and intellectual development of China and perhaps the true apogee of traditional Chinese civilization. The political stability achieved by the Sung monarchy was also considerable; there was no real challenge either to imperial rule or to the rule of the great landowner families who provided the vast majority of the governing bureaucratic caste.

The Sung empire differed in one further important respect from the T'ang and the

Han. Its territory was restricted primarily to areas inhabited by the Chinese. The Vietnamese had regained their independence in 939 and were never again, except for a few years in the 15th century, to fall under the direct rule of the Chinese. The rise of the Khitan ended also the possibility of direct Chinese interference in the affairs of Korea. Furthermore, there was no possibility for the Sung to spread their power or influence either towards Central Asia or to the areas to the north of the Great Wall, due to the existence of both the Liao and the Hsi Hsia states. It is difficult to determine to what degree this was the result of conscious policy-making or of the fact that the Sung were quite unable to break through the ring of the encircling, well-organized states. The inability, however, to launch on a policy of territorial expansion, regardless of its causes, did not by any means affect adversely, as will be seen below, the further growth of prosperity of the country.

III. Sung Relations with the Liao and Hsi Hsia

After having failed in their attempts to regain the territory which had been lost to the Khitan, the Sung rulers were soon faced with further aggression on the part of the latter. A new invasion of the Khitan was ended by a peace treaty concluded in 1004 by the Emperor Ch'ien-tsung (998-1022). This left the territorial *status quo* unchanged but provided for the payment of an annual tribute by the Sung to the Liao which at first amounted to 100,000 ounces of silver and 200,000 rolls of silk. The conclusion of this treaty—considered both humiliating and overly conciliatory by most modern Chinese historians—did secure, in effect, several decades of peace in the relations between the Sung and the Khitan. Inasmuch as the monetary value of the tribute amounted to something less than 2 per cent of the annual budget, some of the Sung leaders undoubtedly thought that this Danegeld was a cheap price for the peace thus gained.

The Liao, however, were not the only troublesome neighbour of the Sung Empire. Towards the end of the 10th century the primarily pastoral Tangut tribes in the North-west under the leadership of the Toba clan (related to the former rulers of Wei but by this time completely Tibetanized) established their own state, called by the Chinese Hsi (Western) Hsia. The name recalls not the first semi-legendary dynasty but the state which existed in this area in the 5th century A.D. Western Hsia became a strong, warlike power and its rule extended over most of Kansu and a part of Shensi with its capital in Ninghsia. The population was mostly Tangut (i.e. Tibetan) and partially Chinese. The development of culture in the Hsia state was quite rapid. They devised their own script (based on the Chinese by way of Khitan, very difficult to decipher) in which considerable remains of literature are still extant. While Buddhism became the official religion of the Hsia, they adopted at the same time Chinese methods of administration and thus Confucianism also gained ground, especially through the highly developed system of education. The degree and speed of sinification was such that by the 12th century the Hsia were probably almost as civilized as the Sung. In the earlier period, however, conflict between the Sung and the Hsia was waged on a large scale, perhaps primarily because the Hsia had cut the Sung off almost from the routes leading to Central Asia. The warfare which had been waged intermittently between 1034 and 1044 was ended by a treaty in which the Sung Empire agreed to pay to the Hsia an annual tribute of 72,000 ounces of silver, 153,000 rolls of silk and 30,000 *chin* of tea. Further military campaigns of the Sung against the Hsia launched in the same century ended disastrously for the Sung.

The Hsia were also a power which was feared by the Liao; an attack on them by the Khitan in 1048 met with crushing defeat. In the curious triangle of relations among the Hsia, the Sung and the Liao, trade as well as other contacts developed considerably. Politically, the Liao did draw one advantage; by threatening the Sung with the possibility of joining together with the Hsia in a war against them, the Khitan succeeded in 1041 in obtaining an increase in the tribute paid to them to the level of 22,000 ounces of silver and 300,000 rolls of silk.

IV. Economic and Social Development

Although its territory was smaller than that of any other previously unified empire, the Sung, especially during the first century after the establishment of the dynasty, saw a constant and steady growth of its economy and prosperity.

The customary attention paid in the initial period to the development of agriculture and the problems of irrigation connected with this brought about the results of a steady increase in agricultural production. From the very outset, however, the social problem was prominent and became gradually more and more acute. The main element herein, a still more rapid growth in great landed estates, became a marked characteristic of the Sung period. This element was inherited from the T'ang era, when the agrarian crisis had been one of the primary causes of the downfall of the T'ang. The alleviation of this problem during the first decades of Sung rule had been rather limited in scope.

While during the Sung a considerable quantity of virgin land, especially in the South, was now placed under cultivation, it rapidly came into the hands either of the great landowners or of the state. This led, in turn, to a further impoverishment of the small free peasants, to a loss of their land to the benefit of the great estates and to a transformation of the peasant holders into tenant farmers or agricultural labourers. Thus, according to some Chinese authors, by the end of the 10th century over one-third of the peasant population were already tenant farmers and by the beginning of the 11th century the figure had risen to over one-half. By the second half of the 11th century the situation of the last years of the T'ang had been reached once more; a major part of the arable land was probably already in the hands of great landowners. The rent paid by the tenant was exorbitant and amounted to from 50 to 70 per cent of the crops. The sources for this period, including the writings of the most prominent Sung scholars, provide a wealth of material relating to this problem and give a vivid picture of the critical position of the peasantry.

Notwithstanding the social problems mentioned above agricultural production did increase and the development of the Sung economy in industry and trade was considerable. This can be seen, for example, in the increased production of metal. Thus, by the 11th century 13 times more silver, 8 times more copper and 14 times more iron was produced than at the beginning of the 9th century. The great expansion of trade meant also not only a rise of great commercial centres such as K'aifeng, Ch'engtu, Lin-an (Hangchow), but also that of very numerous new small towns which served as busy trade centres. This considerable economic development brought about also a return once more to a money economy, but on a much greater scale than had ever been achieved during the best T'ang period. One of the manifestations of this was the introduction of paper money (there was even a variety of a perfumed mixture of silk and paper) the use of which became more and more widespread as the shortage of currency became more marked and posed an ever greater problem.

The scale and scope of the growth of the economy was matched also by an increase in the population: 1083—90 million, 1124—100 million, and thus by the 12th century the Sung Empire, in a smaller area, had reached a population level of almost double that of the T'ang. These developments did not prevent considerable financial problems from arising for the Sung government. While during the first decades the central government, partially due to improved conditions of financial control which had been instituted, became fabulously wealthy, the situation changed drastically and led, from the middle of the 11th century on, to the presence of continuous deficits verging on government bankruptcy. The two principal reasons for this were the cost of the army and of the bureaucracy. In spite of the tribute paid to the Liao and Hsi Hsia, the Sung government increased the size of its army immensely without, it should be added, any improvement in its efficiency and effectiveness. In 975 the armed forces numbered 378,000; in 1017—912,000; in 1045—1,259,000. By this last date the expenditures for the army consumed 80 per cent of the government's annual budget. Some authors maintain that this huge army was, however, also a way for solving the problems arising from both urban and rural impoverishment and mass unemployment.

Although the taxes on the land became less important as the economy developed, their main burden rested more and more on the small peasant holders, inasmuch as the great landowners were always successful in their schemes for avoiding taxation. The lowest scale of the land tax was fixed for a quantity of land which was in excess of that possessed by many peasants and this made it an even harder burden to bear. The growing impoverishment of the peasants mentioned above, as well as the changes in their status, marked the beginning of a new cyclical social crisis which was, in fact, inherent in the Chinese feudal system of relations of production in agriculture. It is, in particular, against this background that the increased political strife within the ruling class itself and the reform programme of Wang An-shih should be considered.

V. The Reforms of Wang An-shih

By the middle of the 11th century Chinese officialdom was becoming ever more strongly engaged in fierce political controversy and divided as a result of this into political factions. On the whole, two basic opposing groups took shape. The first one was a conservative faction, thoroughly opposed to any changes whatsoever in the forms of the government or the policies that had been heretofore pursued. This group represented a majority of the higher officials, who came from the great landowning families. It was led by many outstanding scholars, such as Ou-yang Hsiu and Ssu-ma Kuang (see pp. 176, 175), and included in its ranks also all the Neo-Confucian philosophers. The second was a reform group, represented primarily by Wang An-shih himself; it sought new ways and means for solving the problems which were being posed by the growing social crisis so as to strengthen both the government and the country. Of these two groups the conservatives were in much the stronger position; they had all of tradition behind them, as well as the inevitably growing inertia of a bureaucratic form of government, inherently unfavourable to any change or progress. They had one additional advantage from a long-range point of view. They wrote the history, of this and later periods as well, and were thus able to present the views and actions of their opponents in the worst possible light, making it difficult to ascertain at present the real truth of the matter. But this, at least, was a form of political warfare with words and brush, not with death sentences and the executioner's sword, and thus an improvement over earlier periods of Chinese history.

The conflict between these two parties grew ever sharper as the social crisis increased and became, simultaneously, more obviously a struggle for power, for control over the empire. In the conditions of the Sung absolute monarchy the key to the struggle was to gain the confidence of the Emperor; Wang An-shih succeeded in accomplishing this when the new ruler, the 20-year-old Shen-tsung, came to the throne in 1068; the first ten years of the latter's reign had been described as, in fact, the reign of Wang An-shih.

Wang An-shih (1021-1086) was—and in some ways still is—the centre of a great controversy, both in respect to the essence and effects of his policies and in regard to his personality as well. He came from Kiangsi of a poor family of small landowners. He was undoubtedly a man of a very original case of mind, described as frugal, sincere and serenely confident of his own righteousness—thus arrogant and obstinate in the eyes of his opponents. He was surely far-sighted in the sense that he was completely aware of the social crisis, as the result of his many travels which revealed to him the rottenness of official life and the discrimination practised against the people. There is also no doubt whatsoever regarding his passionate concern for the welfare of the people. Wang An-shih was an excellent writer and polemicist, a scholar with his own ideas on the interpretation of the Confucian Classics, as well as a notable poet.

Soon after Wang An-shih was made Chancellor in 1068 a Permanent Commission for Reforms was established. Teams of inquiry were shortly thereafter sent out by the Commission into the provinces to investigate the existing conditions. It was on this basis that quite soon the famous programme of reform was introduced and implemented. Its fundamental aim was to improve the conditions of the peasants and to raise agricultural production and thereby, simultaneously, strengthen the government's financial position as well as the country's defensive potential.

The main economic reforms were the following: (a) the granting of government loans to peasants on the security of future crops at a much lower interest rate (2 per cent a month) than that customarily demanded by the landlord usurers; (b) the introduction of changes into the *corvée* system making it possible for the peasants to purchase their way out of *corvée* labour by monetary payments, accompanied by taxes on all those who were not subject to the *corvée*; (c) the fixing of prices on the sale of land in order to limit profits on such transactions; (d) a planned new registration of all land ownership, aimed primarily at the unearthing of tax evasion—the opposition to this measure by the great landowners was so violent that it could only be carried out partially; (e) the establishment of government pawnshops and grain markets which constituted another blow at the economic position of the landowners; (f) the provision for the sale of grain tribute locally, instead of the traditional shipment of it to the capital, aimed at lowering the costs and at fighting speculation on grain shortages. In all these economic reforms a principle of equitable taxation was to be applied, i.e. the assessment of both the rich and poor on a property basis.

In addition to the economic measures Wang An-shih's programme introduced also

Fig. 29.   The T'ien-ning-ssu Pagoda, Peking, Liao. (Sickman, L. and Soper, A., *op. cit.*, pl. 173A.)

Fig. 30.   Kuan Yu (?), "Bamboos", Northern Sund. (Author's collection.)

FIG. 31.   Li Lung-mien, "Five Horses from Khotan", Northern Sung. (Cohn, W., *op. cit.*, pl. 66.)

FIG. 32.   The Lung-hsing-ssu Library, Chengting, Hopei, Liao. (Sickman, L. and Soper, A., *op. cit.*, pl. 168.)

Fig. 33.   Ma Yüan, "Wandering Minstrels", Southern Sung. (*Wei-ta-ti* . . . , *op. cit.*, vol. II, pl. 7/IV.)

Fig. 34.   Hsia Kuei, "A Thousand Miles of the Yangtse", Southern Sung. (Cohn, W., *op. cit.*, pl. 95.)

Fig. 35(a&b). Ch'ien Hsüan, "A Travelling Village Family", Southern Sung. (Author's collection.)

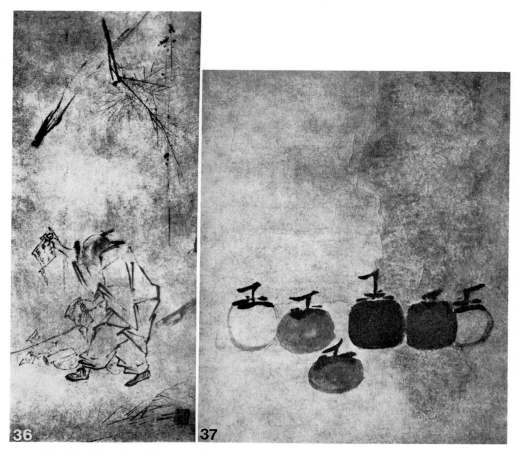

FIG. 36.   Liang K'ai, "Hui-neng, the Sixth Ch'an Patriarch", Southern Sung. (Cohn, W., *op. cit.*, pl. 104.)

FIG. 37. Mu Ch'i, "Six Persimmons", Southern Sung. (Lee, S. E., *op. cit.*, p. 360.)

Fig. 38.   Statue of a Lohan, painted ceramic. (Sickman, L. and Soper, A., *op. cit.*, pl. 83.)

Fig. 39.   Chang Kan-li, "A Village Estate", Southern Sung. (Author's collection.)

political provisions of which the principal one was the establishment of a system of collective responsibility in the countryside—the *pao-chia*—which was to serve as a means of policing the rural areas as well as to serve as the basis for future recruiting of a militia. It was intended to replace eventually the largely useless and vastly expensive standing army by a reintroduction of the militia system. Wang An-shih also introduced important changes into the examination system, replacing poetry with more practical subjects such as history, geography, economics, law and medicine. In what could be considered an ideological justification and buttressing of his policies, Wang An-shih prepared his own commentary on the "Rites of Chou" (the favourite utopia of all reformers from Wang Mang on to the Taiping and perhaps later), while his followers wrote new commentaries on the "Book of History" and the "Book of Odes"; the employment of these commentaries became obligatory in the examination system. The number of government schools was also increased for the purpose of rivalling the influence of the private academies, then one of the principal centres of education.

Taken as a whole, the ideas expressed in Wang An-shih's reforms were not new; a number of them are especially reminiscent of the programme of Wang Mang. Although they were not intended either to transform or to undermine the existing feudal system they did, however, affect adversely the interests of the great landowners and aroused their bitter opposition. The entire bureaucracy was sharply divided into two factions. While Wang An-shih continued, with a short interruption, as Chancellor only to 1076, the reforms remained basically in force until the death of Emperor Shen-tsung in 1086. The career of Wang An-shih himself, however, ended when he ceased to be Chancellor. After the death of Shen-tsung the conservatives came back into power under the regency of the Empress Kao and all the New Laws, as the reforms had been called, were immediately abolished. The reformers did, however, return later to power, when Ts'ai Ching became Chancellor in 1094, but in this period the fundamental sense of the reforms had been perverted and they had lost their essential meaning; they were used primarily for the furthering of private ambitions, for vicious political feuding and served as a basis for growing taxation leading to an ever more corrupt regime.

What was the effect of the reforms? They did not produce the disasters which their opponents had prophesied, but they were also probably none too successful, although some temporary gains were undoubtedly made. They were not implemented in the way that Wang An-shih had envisaged and the main reason for this lay in the lack of an enthusiastic, intelligent and unselfish officialdom. Reforms of this type could not be carried out by a bureaucracy coming from landlord families as they were directed partly against their own interests. Thus the officials sabotaged the reforms at will and although Wang An-shih recruited a large number of new officials, they soon became corrupt and were no better than the old ones. In a way the problem was similar to that faced by Wang Mang. But then how could a programme of reform adversely affecting the interests of a ruling class be carried out with its participation and without basic changes in the political structure? It has also been said that one of the main reasons for the failure lay in the fact that the peasants gave the programme no support, inasmuch as they resented some of the features of the reform, especially the police control of the *pao-chia* system. But then, Wang An-shih was not a revolutionary, interested in arousing and leading a peasant war against the landlords.

The fact that the Sung government had failed to find any solution to the problems which faced it was borne out by the events of the first quarter of the 12th century.

social crisis increased in its intensity and peasant unrest was transformed, for the first time during the Sung period, into large-scale uprisings. An example of this was the rising in Chekiang led by Fang La, which was also connected with the activity of a religious sect, possibly of Manichaean origin. The movement spread throughout a large part of the province and was suppressed with great slaughter in 1121.

Thus the Sung Empire, its court more and more incompetent and corrupt, with the baneful influence of the eunuchs again raising its head during the reign of Hui-tsung (1101-1125), was in an extremely weak position to face a new external danger, the threat of a new invasion by the northern nomads—this time the Jurchen.

CHAPTER 18

Southern Sung

I. The Jurchen Menace

The Sung Empire, already seriously weakened, was soon to face a new threat from the north due to the emergence of a new nomad people bent on the conquest of the rich, agricultural south. These were the Jurchen who were of the Tungusic origin and whose original home lay in North and East Manchuria. They had been for a period of time the subjects of the Khitan; at the beginning of the 12th century they increased markedly in strength and the Jurchen tribal federation under the leadership of Akuta (the Chinese form of his name) succeeded in throwing off the domination of the Liao (1114). In 1115 Akuta declared himself emperor of the Chin (called Alchuk in Jurchen, which was the name of a river; the Chinese translation of the meaning of the word—gold—was *chin*). He then launched his armies on a series of campaigns against the Liao. The success of the Chin was amazingly rapid and the main Liao armies were swiftly and shatteringly defeated. By 1124 the entire state of the Khitan was in the hands of the Jurchen; they had made good their boast that iron (*liao*) rusts, but gold (*chin*) never does.

Only a small part of the Khitan managed to save themselves from the general débâcle. Yeh-lü Ta-shih, a member of the ruling family, led the remnants of the Khitan westward and ultimately succeeded in making his way to Eastern Turkestan. In this area he was able to establish himself with the help of the Uighur tribes who had been subjects of the Khitan and to set up the state of Western Liao (called Kara Kitai by the Mongols). Later on, the state was considerably enlarged by the conquest of neighbouring Turkish peoples. The Khitan here became converted to Nestorianism and Western Liao has been considered a "thorn in the side of the Moslems" in Central Asia. It was a prosperous, highly developed and cultured state of considerable interest for the history of this period and it lasted till 1219, when it was swept away by the Mongol avalanche. It is perhaps more likely that the word "Cathay" in Western European languages as well as the word "Kitai" in Russian are derived from the name of this state rather than from the Khitan of Liao as is traditionally assumed.

The Sung rulers did not by any means consider the rise of the Jurchen to be a threat to themselves. They hoped to use once more the age-worn policy of fighting "barbarians" with the help of "barbarians" and thus made advances to the Chin, proposing an alliance against the Liao. In return for the recovery of the Chinese territory which had been lost to the Khitan the Sung offered to pay the same tribute to the Jurchen as they had to the Liao. The Sung army took the field in 1122 against the Liao, but it proved to be as inept as it had been in the past and suffered a number of humiliating defeats.

There was little trust between these newly found "allies" and the problem of dividing the territory of the fallen Liao state was the cause of much conflict, devious manoeuvres

Map 14. Southern Sung, ca. 1180

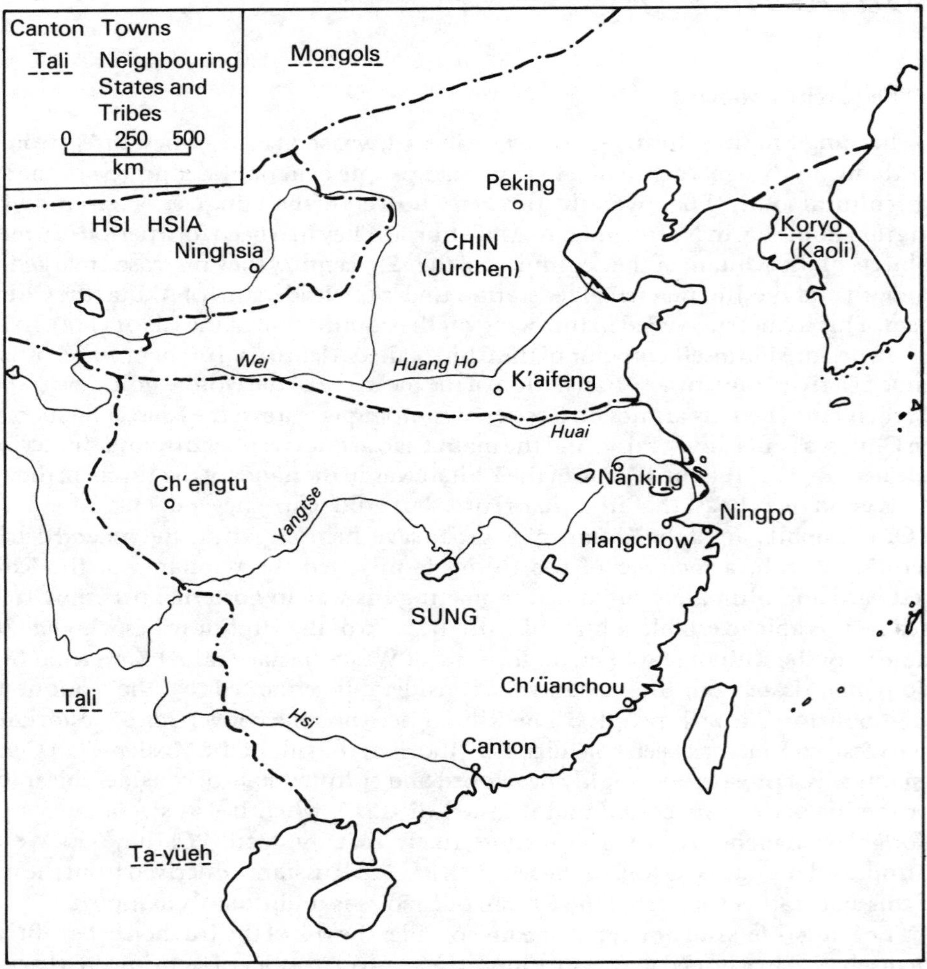

Canton	Towns
Tali	Neighbouring States and Tribes

0   250   500
km

<u>Mongols</u>

HSI HSIA

Ninghsia

Peking

<u>CHIN</u>
(Jurchen)

<u>Koryo</u>
(Kaoli)

Wei

Huang Ho

K'aifeng

Huai

Ch'engtu

Yangtse

Nanking

Ningpo

Hangchow

SUNG

<u>Tali</u>

Hsi

Ch'üanchou

Canton

<u>Ta-yüeh</u>

and treachery on both sides. Their confidence in their strength having increased considerably after the easy victories over the Liao, the Chin did not wait long before commencing attacks against the Sung. In 1126 the first large-scale invasion of the Sung Empire began and the Jurchen cavalry advanced straight on towards the Sung capital of K'aifeng. The Chinese were badly prepared for defence and when K'aifeng itself was besieged the Sung government quickly agreed to the demanded ransom—5 million ounces of gold, 50 million ounces of silver and 1 million rolls of silk—in order to bring about a retreat of the Chin. After having received about half of this ransom, the Chin armies made their way back to the north, devastating the entire countryside in their path, only to return a few months later to attack once more, according to some authors using as a pretext a particularly inane and treacherous violation of the truce by the Sung. In this offensive they now succeeded in capturing K'aifeng.

The defence of the Sung Empire against the Chin invasion was seriously complicated by very far-reaching divergences within the Sung ruling group over the policies to be pursued; whether to wage an active war or to attempt to buy off the Jurchen, as had previously been done with the Khitan. The result of this was a constant shifting and changing of policy, the replacement of leading personalities in the government which ultimately brought about such a state of confusion that any real defence against the Chin was made extremely difficult, if not impossible.

After having occupied K'aifeng for four months the Chin retreated once more to the north taking with them as captives two Sung emperors, i.e. Hui-tsung, who had a year earlier resigned in favour of his son (Ch'in-tsung, 1126-1127), and the latter, as well as practically the entire imperial family, over 3000 courtiers and the vast bulk of the Sung imperial treasures. The captives were sent to Kirin and the overwhelming majority of them never returned to the south. Another of Hui-tsung's sons had managed to escape the fate of the imperial family; it was he (Kao-tsung, 1127-1162) who ascended the throne in Nanking in 1127 and it is with him that the line of the Southern Sung—as against the first period, thereafter referred to as the Northern Sung—begins. He ultimately established his capital in Lin-an (Hangchow) in 1135.

The wars waged by the Chin against the Sung continued, in effect, for the next fourteen years. The Jurchen cavalry always proved superior to the Sung armies, and thus in 1128 the Chin were able to cross the Yangtse, take Lin-an and then ride down to capture Ningpo. The terrain south of the Yangtse was, however, very difficult for them and the resistance of the Chinese population in this area was also quite considerable. Thus, ultimately, the border between the two states was established further to the north, in the area of the Huai River. Earlier, however, the Chin had set up a certain Liu Yü as emperor of a puppet state of Ch'i (mainly in Honan), but this creation turned out to be of relatively little use to them and it was done away with in 1137.

In the years preceding 1141 the Chinese armies achieved a number of successes against the Chin thanks to the support given them by the population of Central and North China; there was a distinct possibility that a determined war effort could have either eliminated or considerably reduced the area of Chin rule in North China. The policy of the dominant clique in the Sung government which was supported by the Emperor favoured, however, a policy of seeking an agreement and peace with the Chin at the price of territorial concessions. The main representative of this tendency was Ch'in Kuei, whose mysterious escape from Chin captivity had given rise to the theory that he was a Chin agent. He became once more Chancellor in 1138, and his theory that "the

South is for the men of the South and the North is for the men of the North" meant, in effect, that the areas held by the Chin should be left to them. It was he who was responsible for recalling the Sung armies at the moment of their greatest successes and also for the imprisonment and subsequent murder in prison of the ablest and most successful Sung general, Yüeh Fei, an ardent advocate of continuing the war against the Chin (he died in 1142 at the age of 39, together with his son). It is not surprising that Ch'in Kuei is regarded in all Chinese histories as the arch-type of a traitor, while Yüeh Fei, on the other hand, is portrayed as a great national hero.

In 1141 a final treaty was signed by the Sung and the Chin in which the Sung Empire declared itself to be a vassal of the Chin and agreed to pay an annual tribute of 250,000 ounces of silver and 250,000 rolls of silk. The border between the two states was established on the Huai River and ran to the west through Honan and Shensi where it followed the Wei River. This peace treaty is regarded by most modern Chinese historians as an act of capitulation and treason. In reality, the group responsible for this policy was composed mostly of great landowners from South China who were little concerned with the problem of regaining the North and who followed this line of conduct consistently until the end of Sung rule.

While a number of further conflicts did take place between the Chin and the Southern Sung—an unsuccessful Chin invasion in 1161; an expedition of the Sung to the north in 1163, also a failure; a further Sung attempt to organize a northern expedition in 1208, forestalled by a Chin offensive—the situation was basically stabilized after the 1141 treaty until the first decade of the 13th century, when the rise of the Mongols introduced a completely new factor into Ching—Sung relations.

The rule of the Chin in North China differed in some important respects from that of the Liao. For one thing, the area of the Chin state was more extensive and the Chinese population under their rule more numerous than under the Liao. On the whole, the rule of the Chin was much harsher for the Chinese than that of the Liao. A very considerable amount of land was confiscated from the peasants by the Jurchen rulers and a particularly oppressive system of control over the population was instituted. An important role was played in this by special colonies established for this purpose among the Chinese population. These Jurchen colonists were the mainstay of Chin military power; the great majority of them also became great landowners with the Chinese peasants as their tenants. These colonists seemed to have been especially oppressive and an object of hatred for the Chinese. According to one Chinese source, most of them were massacred after the fall of the Chin state.

The Chin rulers, especially in the first period, neglected the economy and failed to maintain the irrigation system properly. As a result, agricultural production fell and the population of the Chin state also decreased markedly. In addition to high tax burdens the peasants suffered also from large-scale recruiting for the army as the relatively small number of Jurchen tribesmen was insufficient for the military needs of the Chin state.

The Chin, however, just like their predecessors, were forced to adopt Chinese administrative methods for ruling the agricultural parts of their state. This was an inevitable phenomenon and its implication was the employment of more and more Chinese as officials in the administration, inasmuch as these were the only people possessing the necessary capabilities. In effect, the peasants of North China were suffering from a double oppression—that of the Chin rulers and the Chinese bureaucracy and great landowners.

The Chin state, like the Liao, had five capitals, the main one being in Yenching (Peking) from 1153 on. The country was divided into nineteen small provinces, prefectures and districts, basically on the model of the T'ang administration. The Jurchen developed their own script (in fact, two scripts, one based on Chinese and another based on Khitan) and made an even more conscious attempt than the Khitan to avoid losing their identity as people. Edicts were issued prohibiting the adoption of Chinese names, clothing, customs, etc. In one of them, dating from 1187, it was said: "Our ways were simple and straightforward—let us seek to preserve them!" Nevertheless, the process of sinification also made rapid progress among the Chin ruling class and practically the entire Jurchen people can be considered to constitute this class, in view of the fact that the great majority of them had become landowners. The very fact of the issuing of the above-mentioned edicts shows that the process of sinification had probably begun quite rapidly as soon as Chin rule had been stabilized in the newly conquered territories. This process seems to be inevitable whenever a nomad people settles down as a ruling class to exploit a conquered agricultural population; it is not limited to China or Asia, as the case of the Bulgars in Europe shows. Many Chinese historians view this as a surrender to the superiority of Chinese culture; while this is undoubtedly partially true, the fact that the nomad conquerors were always a very small minority in relation to the Chinese population is also a factor which should be constantly borne in mind.

II. The Development of the Southern Sung

Although the territorial size of the Southern Sung empire was only two-thirds that of its predecessor, the country rapidly became much wealthier. The century and a half between the coming of the Chin and the final fall of the Southern Sung under the onslaught of the Mongols was a period of constant, rapid and many-sided development which included some important changes in the structure of Chinese society.

Agriculture in this period developed to a marked degree and the use of new strains of rice (introduced from South Vietnam) made possible an increase in its production due to double annual cropping. The growing of tea expanded greatly, while more and more cotton was planted and its cultivation was spread further to the north (Anhwei and Kiangsu) than had been the case earlier. The Sung government paid very considerable attention to the expansion of waterworks. According to Needham, 491 major projects were undertaken in the Sung period as against 91 for the T'ang. This concern for the improvement of agriculture on the part of the government was based probably on the problems arising from the growth of population, further stimulated by the influx of refugees from the Chin-occupied North, which made the assurance of adequate food supplies imperative. A corollary, however, to the growth of agricultural production was a still further increase in the size and number of great estates, and thus no solution was found to the basic social problems of agriculture which had already proved so troublesome during the Northern Sung.

The Southern Sung period is especially noted for its development of trade, both domestic and foreign. It has been called by some authors (Reischauer, for instance) a "commercial revolution" and this is primarily due to the fact that the role of merchants and private trade increased to such a marked degree. This process was reflected, among others, in a change in the sources of government revenue; its income from taxes on commerce became more important than the income from the land tax, the heretofore fundamental basis of government finance. The increase, however, in production and wealth did not prevent the emergence of acute financial problems. The increase of trade resulted in a shortage of copper currency, and although this was supplemented by a greater use of gold and silver (although, oddly enough, never in the shape of coins) the solution of the problem was sought in a still greater use of paper money. This, however, in turn gave rise to new problems for the Sung government could not resist the temptation of over-issuing paper money and, thus, the phenomenon of a rapid and then galloping inflation became a plague during the last period of Sung rule.

China's trade contacts with foreign countries increased in the Southern Sung era on a vast scale. Porcelain now headed the list of Chinese exports, followed by silk and handicrafts products. Chinese books and paintings were also exported to those countries (Japan, Korea) where Chinese culture had spread earlier. A new feature of this period was that the trade with Japan, Korea and South-east Asia came now into the hands of Chinese merchants, successfully competing in South-east Asia with the Arabs and the Persians who had previously monopolized most of the foreign trade. The latter held on, however, to their dominant positions in the trade between China and India and countries further to the west. One of the results of this development was that China now emerged as a seafaring country on a large scale and the importance of the southern and eastern coastal provinces was thereby correspondingly enhanced. The foreign trade of this period constituted also a very considerable source of revenue for the Sung government which kept it under strict control and supervision.

The flourishing of the economy was reflected in the further growth of the cities and towns. This was especially true of the picturesquely situated Southern Sung capital—Lin-an. Its population rose to over one million and even in the period when it had succumbed to Mongol rule it was described breathlessly by Marco Polo as "The finest and noblest city in the world".

The economic development of the Southern Sung reached a level in which more than likely all the necessary preconditions for a future development of capitalism were already present. The political and social structure of the country, however, definitely did not favour such a course, inasmuch as the rising merchant class was no match, under Chinese conditions, for the strong absolute monarchy. What is perhaps more important, the real ruling class of the country—the great bureaucratic-landowning families, who lived on a lavish scale in splendid palaces in the capital and increased their wealth by speculation in land and money—always staunchly opposed any line of development which was not to their direct benefit and interest and conducted steadily a policy of discrimination and limitation against the merchants. The result of this was that much, if not most, of merchant capital was not reinvested in further trade or industry but put into land. This was so because land provided better security and also because it made possible the passage of the merchants into the gentry class. The very fact that such a high level of economic development had already been reached was perhaps another important factor; there was, in effect, no really strong stimulus present which would lead to a seeking of new roads for the creation and accumulation of further wealth. The ever-present existence of an overabundance of extremely cheap labour was also a factor which militated—then as well as later on—against any considerable development or incentive to seek more modern methods of manufacture.

The prosperity and wealth of the Southern Sung were also reflected in a splendid flourishing of culture. It is sufficient to repeat at this time that many authors regard this era as the apogee of traditional Chinese civilization. This is true in the sense that this period was the highwater mark in the development of Chinese feudal society and that most of the fundamental features of the 700 years during which this social order was still to last in China were derived from the Sung times, while in the future originality in practically all fields, political as well as cultural, was to diminish constantly.

III. The Rise of the Mongols

The sufferings and turmoil which the Chinese people had undergone as a result of the Khitan and Jurchen invasions were to pale in comparison with what the future had in store for them. The Mongol invasion and conquest of China has been called by one author an unmitigated curse. This is completely true and it pertains not only to the Chinese, but also to all the other people who had the misfortune to find themselves in the path of these savage, pitiless nomad horsemen.

The original home of the Mongol tribes, i.e. those who were to be the leading force in the creation of the Mongol empire, was in the area of the Kerulen and Onon Rivers (the North and North-east of the present Mongolian People's Republic). Their economy was restricted almost entirely to livestock breeding with agriculture completely absent; thus the Mongols were pure nomads as against both the Khitan and Jurchen who had long led a semi-nomadic existence. They were divided into patriarchal clans and these, in turn, were linked up into tribes which waged constant war against each other for the possession of pasturage and herds. The first half of the 12th century saw the beginning of a new federation of tribes, and the first mention of the Mongols under this name in Chinese sources dates from 1147, when a treaty had been signed by the Chin with the Mongols after conflicts which had ended with the defeat of the Jurchen.

The real rise of the Mongols to power and influence is inevitably connected with the name of Chingghis Khan. He was born in 1162 as Temujin, the son of Yesukai, a leader of a federation of some of the Mongol tribes. He succeeded his father at the age of 13 and after a long and difficult struggle he managed to assert his authority over a majority of the tribes, having successfully waged war against all his rivals. In 1206 he was proclaimed by the Kurultai—the meeting of the Mongolian notables—held on the banks of the Kerulen, as Chingghis Khan—the supreme leader. From this moment on until his death in 1227 he waged unceasing war against all his neighbours, sowing death and destruction wherever he and his horsemen rode.

The key to the success of Mongol aggression lay not only in the fact that, like other pure nomads, they were superb horsemen and excellent archers, but also in the fact that they represented a stage which was the climax of a long period of development of the nomad technique of warfare and military organization. They employed a decimal system in the structure of their army which was similar to that of the Khitan and the tactics which they used did not differ basically from those of the Khitan and the Jurchen. There is perhaps only one innovation which could be claimed for the Mongols; as consistent practitioners of genocide they used terror, i.e. massacres on an immense scale of all those who dared to oppose them, as one of the basic weapons in their arsenal, which was more important than their famous bows, their resilient armour or their fleet, untiring horses. Chingghis also organized an elite bodyguard, composed primarily of the sons of tribal chiefs; this too, however, was not an original idea. In time, it grew to a force of around 10,000 men and became the chief source from which future generals of the Mongol army and governors of the conquered provinces were later to be drawn.

Many various reasons have been advanced to explain the motivation lying behind the Mongol expansion—among these, for example, the factor of the basic economic instability of a purely nomad society due, perhaps, to periodic over-population or climatic changes. Most of these explanations seem to appear to be much too elaborate and overly sophisticated. The truth was probably much simpler—the greed for plunder and power figured most prominently as the main motives in the aggression of the nomads, especially when rich agricultural terrains, easy to conquer, were close to hand. What is noteworthy is that the expansion was accomplished by a people which was never numerous; the estimates on the Mongol population at the beginning of the 13th century range from a maximum of 2.5 million to as low as one million. The explanation of this phenomenon lies in the fact that in their later, great campaigns against Europe, West Asia and China, the Mongol army was composed largely of other, non-Mongolian peoples, who had joined them, *nolens volens*, especially the various Turkish tribes of Central Asia. It is true, however, that in the military sphere the Mongols did show considerable adaptability and a willingness to acquire and employ techniques which had been earlier unknown to them, particularly in siege warfare, and used for this purpose specialists from many of the various peoples they had conquered.

Of the three states which existed at that time in the present area of China, Western Hsia was the first to fall victim to the armies of Chingghis Khan; it was invaded in 1208, although still not conquered permanently. A further campaign against the Hsia was waged in 1209, but the main attention of the Mongols was now diverted to the Chin Empire. From 1211 to 1215 war was waged almost constantly against the Jurchen, which ended in the fall of Yenching (with the customary massacre of most of the population) and the establishment of Mongol rule over all of North China down to the Yellow River. The Chin Emperor had already, during the struggle, transferred his capital in 1214 to K'aifeng.

The continuation of a long and bitter feud with another Mongol tribe, the Naiman, led subsequently to the conquest of Western Liao (which had been subjected to Naiman rule only a few years earlier) and brought the empire of Chingghis Khan to the borders of the Moslem state of Khorezm in Central Asia. Chingghis Khan, feeling sure that the overcoming of the Chin was only a question of time, left China and proceeded westwards. A five-year war (1219-1224), initially against Khorezm, but then extended to vast areas of Persia and Northern India, lies outside the scope of our subject matter, but mention should be made at least of the tremendous destruction to the flourishing civilization of these countries and of the cities of Bukhara, Samarkand, Herat, Merv, Nishapur and many others, as well as of the millions of inhabitants slaughtered in cold blood. The great victories of the Mongols in this period strengthened them considerably and made possible their future aggression against China, West Asia and Europe.

The last campaign to be conducted by Chingghis Khan himself in China was against the Hsia, who had revolted in 1224 and joined the Chin in their resistance to Mongol rule. Chingghis now waged a war of complete extermination against this people and state which resulted in its utter and total destruction. According to some sources only from 1 to 2 per cent of the population survived. Chingghis Khan died at the age of 66 during this campaign. In order to assure the succession to his son Ogodei his death was kept a secret, and as his funeral cortège proceeded on its slow and long route to Northern Mongolia all those who encountered it were killed.

Much pompous nonsense has been written about Chingghis, extolling his alleged greatness. His own words give the best key to his personality. He once asked his generals as to what, according to them, constituted true happiness. None of them answered to his satisfaction. He then told them: "Happiness lies in conquering one's enemies, in driving them in front of oneself, in taking their property, in savouring their despair, in outraging their wives and daughters." This autoportrait requires no comments.

Chingghis Khan, while dividing his lands between his sons, nominated Ogodei as his principal successor, and his last words dealt with the ways to be employed for the final conquest of the Chin Empire. After a two-year period, during which rule was exercised by Chingghis's younger son, Tule, Ogodei was placed on the Mongol throne in 1229, and undertook the campaign against what was left of the Chin state. The major part of the Chin, as well as many Chinese, took shelter in the capital K'aifeng, which was soon to be besieged; there were supposedly 7 million people within its walls, and multitudes died of starvation and disease. After the usual fearful slaughter accompanying the siege, K'aifeng was forced to surrender in 1233. Ogodei was ready to give the orders for carrying out the customary massacre of the remaining, still very considerable, population in fulfilment of the rule ascribed to Chingghis Khan that any city from which a single arrow or stone was cast at the Mongols should be wiped out completely. He was persuaded to desist from this by his adviser, Yeh-lü Ch'u-ts'ai. This remarkable man, a very tall, magnificently bearded Khitan prince, and a completely sinicized, able scholar, who had been captured by the Mongols at the fall of Yenching, had already saved the lives of millions of Chinese in North China. Having become adviser to Chingghis Khan—the Mongols needed people who were well acquainted with the country and its languages—he opposed the plan of many of the Mongol leaders who wished to exterminate the entire Chinese population and turn the whole country into a vast pastureland for their herds. Playing on Mongol cupidity and repeating Lu Chia's adage (see p. 58) he explained to Chingghis Khan:

> "Now that you have conquered everywhere under Heaven and all the riches of the four seas, you can have everything you want, but you have not yet organized it. You should set up taxation on land and merchants, and should make profits on wine, salt, iron, and the produce of the mountains and marshes. In this way in a single year you will obtain 500,000 ounces of silver, 80,000 rolls of silk and 400,000 piculs of grain. How can you say that the Chinese people are no use to you?"

Chingghis agreed, and thus the beginnings were laid once more for the administration of North China by Chinese officials. Now, at the fall of K'aifeng, Yeh-lü Ch'u-ts'ai again appealed to Mongol greed and said to Ogodei:

> "It is now ten years that you are fighting to build an empire. What need have you of a city without inhabitants? . . . All the skilled artisans and all the capable officials of the Chin have taken refuge here in K'aifeng. If you massacre them—you will be deprived of their assistance."

The actions of this outstanding man are certainly more noteworthy than those of his savage and superstitious masters. He died shortly after the end of Ogodei's reign. Ogodei's widow suspected that he had amassed great riches in the service of the Mongols and wanted to confiscate them; it was found, however, that his property consisted only of a zither...and books.

The Sung rulers had, to their misfortune, a great aptitude for repeating their own previous mistakes. Their alliance with the Jurchen against the Khitan had had disastrous consequences for them. Now once again they sought an alliance with the new barbarians against their old enemy, with the Mongols against the Chin. They thus deprived themselves of a buffer state and this time the results were total ruin and downfall. In 1233, following this inane and suicidal policy, they joined with the Mongols in closing in for the kill of the Chin state, in the vain hope of recovering thereby some of the territory which had previously been lost to the Chin. Sung forces participated alongside of the Mongols in the siege of Ts'ai-chou, the last Chin stronghold. This ended in 1234 with the inevitable victory of the "allies", the suicide of the last Emperor of the Chin and the liquidation of the Chin state. Some of the Jurchen later received the permission of the Mongols to return to their original homeland. These were to become the ancestors of the Manchus, who retained a distinct remembrance of the fate of their forefathers; they amply repaid the Chinese. After the fall of the Chin, Sung forces advanced to take possession of K'aifeng and Loyang; according to one source in doing so they broke their previous arrangement with the Mongols. Whatever the circumstances, they were chased out ignominiously and a further Mongol assault against the Sung Empire was already clearly foretold at this time.

IV. The Mongol Conquest of the Sung Empire

There was no doubt whatsoever that the Mongols would not be able to resist the temptation of conquering the Sung Empire with its great wealth and immense resources. This conquest, however, was to be a long-drawn-out process, lasting forty-five years counting from the fall of the Chin. A number of reasons account for this; the diversion of the attention of the Mongols to their vast campaigns in Europe and West Asia (these are outside of our scope) together with the periodic unsettlement of Mongol leadership (especially during the years 1241-1251) and the very considerable degree of resistance of the Chinese to the incursion of this terrible enemy. It has been correctly stated that the long duration of the Mongol war and the subsequent Mongol rule made an ineradicable impression on the minds of the Chinese, in a way similar to the effects of the Mongol yoke on the minds of the Russians. It should also be noted that the Mongol campaigns waged against the Sung were much longer and more difficult than their campaigns in West Asia and Europe, although China was much closer to their base of operations. Needham maintains that in dealing with the Sung the Mongols were up against the best technically and subtlest fighters of all their opponents.

The first campaigns against the Sung Empire were launched in 1235. A huge force divided into five armies advanced on China in three directions: into Szechuan, the Han Valley and towards the Huai Basin. The successes gained by the Mongols, however, proved to be temporary and practically all the territory was later retaken by Chinese forces. It was not until 1251, after the enthronement of Mangu (1251-1259) as the Great Khan, that the next campaign against China was begun. This was undertaken primarily by Kubilai, Mangu's younger brother. The strategy employed aimed at surrounding the Sung realm from all sides; thus in 1253 Kubilai conquered both Tibet and the Kingdom of Tali (in Yunnan, it had taken the place of the former Kingdom of Nan-chao), as well as having become the master of most of Szechuan.

In 1257 the campaign was continued and three great Mongol armies rode into China to attack the positions of the Sung in Szechuan, Hunan and the Yangtse Valley. Mangu himself joined the campaign in Szechuan and died there in 1259 during the siege of a town not far from Chungking (according to one account from dysentery, according to another version from wounds sustained). Mangu's death gave rise to a long and bitter struggle for succession between Kubilai and another brother, Arik-böge. Kubilai had himself proclaimed Emperor in 1260 by the Mongol princes while still in China, but then hurried on to Mongolia where the civil war against his brother, which ended in Kubilai's victory, lasted until 1264. It is against this background that a truce had been reached in 1260 between the Mongols and the Sung; this was, however, to be only a brief respite of which very little use, if any, was made by the Sung government.

In 1264 Kubilai transferred his capital from Karakorum to Yenching (to be called Tatu—the great city, in Chinese and Khanbaligh—the city of the Khan, in Turkish). Kubilai had his capital rebuilt on a vast scale and it was here, in 1271, that he proclaimed himself Emperor of the Yüan dynasty, thus clearly setting forth his claim to rule all China.

The year 1268 marked the beginning of the last great eleven-year-long campaign against the Sung. The advance of the Mongols was held up considerably by the truly heroic five-year defence of the twin cities of Hsiangyang and Fanch'eng, on the opposite banks of the Han River, which constituted a key defence point for the area of the Upper Yangtse Valley (1268-1273). The Sung government, again torn by a struggle between factions wishing to surrender or to continue the war against the Mongols, left the cities, in effect, to their own fate. Once Hsiangyang had fallen, thanks primarily to the skill of Moslem engineers from Central Asia, the chief Mongol general, Bayan, proceeded, in 1274, with an immense army, which included a number of Chinese generals who had gone over to the Mongols, on a march to the east down both sides of the Yangtse. As was usual in the annals of the Mongol campaigns, this one too was marked by hideous massacres, the best known being that of the city of Ch'angchou in Kiangsu where vast numbers of people are said to have been butchered in 1275. In the next year the Mongol armies swarmed down to capture the Sung capital of Lin-an, where no resistance was offered, and took the young Sung Emperor prisoner, as well as most of the imperial family. At this stage the great majority of the Sung ruling class was willing to give up the struggle and surrender completely to the Mongols in order to save their lives and property. The Mongols made this possible and, in fact, they left the estates of the Chinese great landowners mostly untouched. These proved to be willing collaborators with the Mongols throughout the entire reign of the Yüan dynasty.

A group of loyal officials escaped, however, to the South taking with them two very young Sung princes, brothers of the captured Emperor. In Foochow one of these was declared the Sung Emperor, but the Mongols continued their advance to the South against the remnants of the Sung armed forces; they were aided in this by the Chinese generals who had joined them. They succeeded shortly in defeating one of the few Sung armies which still resisted them, commanded by Wen T'ien-hsiang. After his capture he refused to follow the example of other high Chinese officials, to desert his former Sung masters; he paid with his life later on for his decision.

The new Sung Emperor died in 1278 at the age of 11 and two Sung officials, Lu Hsiu-fu and Chang Shih-chieh, proceeded with what was left of the Sung fleet and the last Sung prince to Kwangtung; here they proclaimed the boy Emperor. In 1279 the Mongol armies and fleet (these were actually Sung ships that had gone over to the Mongols) under the command of a Chinese general closed in on the last of the Sung forces. In a disastrous naval battle the Sung were completely defeated. To avoid the dishonour of surrender Lu Hsiu-fu took the last Emperor of the Sung—he was 9 years old—into his arms and jumped into the sea. His action was followed by the suicide of hundreds of others. Later on, a storm smashed the rest of the Sung fleet and caused the death of its commander, Chang Shih-chieh. With this—all resistance ended. The Sung dynasty had fallen. For the first time in its history—but unfortunately not the last—all of China was under the yoke of foreign conquerors.

CHAPTER 19

Sung Culture

I. The Place of Sung Culture

The Period of Division between the T'ang and the Sung—the Five Dynasties and Ten Kingdoms—had not interrupted, as we have seen, the continuity of development of Chinese civilization to any appreciable degree. Although the civil wars and the Khitan incursions into North China caused much damage, the more peaceful South witnessed a further growth of Chinese culture in all fields. When the Sung had achieved the unification of the Empire the conditions for further development were improved still further. While it might be assumed at first glance that the social turmoil and the dangers from the North which faced both the Sung dynasties would create an atmosphere which would not be particularly conducive to a flourishing of the arts—just the opposite. happens to be true. In effect, the entire Sung period is one of the highest level in the development of culture in most of its aspects and the contrast with contemporary Europe is particularly striking, as this was an era in which European culture was at perhaps one of its lowest points.

II. Painting—Northern Sung

There is little doubt that of the many fields in which Sung culture progressed, painting was the most significant domain, the one in which the greatest contributions were made. The Sung era is the greatest age of Chinese painting, never to be surpassed in the future. In the opinion of many Chinese authors painting is the greatest of their fine arts and this view is undoubtedly based largely on the immense achievements of the Sung masters.

Sung painting was the chosen form of expression of this epoch, reflecting the picture of those times probably even better than literature or history. It constituted perhaps the quintessence of all the skills demonstrated unceasingly—for over 2000 years—in the masterly work of the Chinese craftsmen, utilizing and basing itself on their unusual subtlety, love of beauty and profound artistic feeling.

While Sung painting proceeded from and was based on T'ang traditions which were continued during the Five Dynasties Period, it nevertheless formed its own inimitable traits and also advanced further the development of two fields—landscape and bird and flower painting—which had previously been only in an initial stage and were now raised to great prominence.

A digression seems indicated here for the purpose of pointing out at least a few of the specific traits of Chinese painting. These are derived, among others, from the materials employed—the brush, Chinese ink, water colours, silk and paper. In using these it is basically impossible to correct the work done (by erasure or overpainting) and thus it is vital to employ a perfect and sure technique. This also implies the necessity of a light, rapid and firm brush stroke to prevent the spreading of ink. Largely as a result of the techniques employed, Chinese painting almost never uses models and is thus never a portraiture—regardless of the object depicted—but is based primarily on the painter's memory image of the subject to be portrayed. This, in turn, leads to a retention of only the salient features of the subject and is perhaps the most characteristic trait of this art. Thus, Chinese pictures are basically abstractions although, simultaneously, they are based on an extremely keen, careful observation and study of the subject matter. The aim is not so much to capture the immediate reality of the subject as to grasp its true essence.

Chinese painting employs a different concept of perspective from that developed in Europe during the 15th and 16th centuries. There is no fixed vanishing point, no one-point perspective from which the spectator is expected to regard a picture. Rather he is free to use his imagination and to change his position in order to view the various parts of the painting. This applies primarily to landscapes; nowhere is it more true than in the hand scroll—the long panoramic vistas which constitute the greatest achievement of this art form. The hand scroll is the only type of painting in the world where true progress in time is attained as the spectator follows the gradual unfolding, section by section, of the view which resembles very much a *leitmotif* in music.

The identity of materials and techniques employed cause Chinese painting and calligraphy to be regarded as really twin arts. While it is difficult for Europeans to appreciate this fully, the same mastery of the brush in writing the complex and beautiful characters produces, in the view of the Chinese, who are aware of all the difficulties involved in achieving this mastery, a form of art equal to that of painting. In later periods, but starting with the Sung, it was often customary to combine both forms; for example, a landscape would also have an appropriate calligraphic text inscribed on it, usually, although not necessarily, dealing with the subject depicted. The closeness of the two forms is nowhere as apparent as in what is perhaps the most abstract form of Chinese painting—the bamboo—done primarily in monochrome black ink, whose origins lie in the Sung period. Wen Tung (*fl.* 1050-1089) is considered to be its first eminent representative.

It is the mastery of the brush—the writing tool—which determines the fact that painting was an art practised primarily by the educated and thus, logically, it developed in time into the favourite art of the scholar-official while its subject matter became intimately bound up with literary themes and the employment of symbolism which was understandable fully only to those educated in Chinese literature. Thus, for example, the innumerable pine trees to be found in Chinese landscape painting are said to be a symbol of the steadfastness of the Chinese scholar.

A certain noticeable repetitiousness of motifs in Chinese painting, particularly in landscapes, is derived both from the usage of memory images and, perhaps even more, from the specific Chinese concept of originality; in the latter stress is placed primarily on freshness and intensity of technique rather than on composition. This phenomenon is also bound up with the honoured established practice of copying old masters, either by tracing or free hand, to learn their technique. It has been well said that for a Chinese artist to paint in the manner of an old master was considered no more a plagiarism than for a musician to play the work of a famous composer.

The tradition of learning from the old—and in spite of the great losses of art works a tremendous amount of the old did survive to be studied and copied—led in time to such an accumulation of existing established patterns as to produce a stultifying effect on the style of individual artists. This, however, is mostly a later phenomenon and did not affect the Sung painters to any appreciable degree. Although they based themselves very faithfully on the work of their predecessors, this was still an era of great creativeness and invention.

As the favourite art form of the scholar-officials, Chinese painting became also the subject of a great amount of study. An immense amount of data from literary sources exists on Chinese painting and, in fact, especially for the early period, there is much more of this than surviving examples of the art itself. This is especially true in relation to the T'ang, but it applies partially also to the Northern Sung, where the number of authentic originals which survived is probably quite small. The literary sources are thus invaluable for tracing the development of the art.

Undoubtedly the greatest achievement of Sung painting—during both the Northern and Southern dynasties— was the landscape. It can be maintained that the Chinese landscapes produced during this period are unrivalled in quality in the history of world art and certainly unsurpassed in beauty and subtlety. The development of this genre during the Sung reflected the fact that art more and more ceased to play the role of only a decorative function; it is also now that it became a secular form of art, thus departing from the dominance of religious, mainly Buddhist, subject matter. The inspiration was probably to a great extent Taoist; this, of course, in the philosophical sense, in the adaptation of the Taoist approach to nature, and not in the religious connotation. It has been stated that the attitude to nature reflected by Chinese landscape painting is possible only as a product of a long-lasting civilization, of many centuries of continuous culture.

In the Sung era, more so than in the earlier periods, painting ceased to be the product of craftsmen and became more and more the art of known masters. Of the great multitude of eminent painters of the 300 years which cover the span of the two Sung dynasties only a mere handful can be mentioned here. The criteria of choice are somewhat arbitrary: those who can perhaps be considered most representative, and whose works can be shown by illustration.

The earliest of the great landscape painters of the early Northern Sung were Li Ch'eng (*fl.* 940-967), Kuan T'ung (*ca.* 950) and Fan K'uan (*fl.* 990-1030). Whether the pictures attributed to them are authentic is debatable, but they do show the style of these masters which was of fundamental importance and influence on future development. A painter from an even earlier period, who was active still in the Southern T'ang, Tung Yüan (*fl.* 947-970), is probably of no lesser importance.

Of the landscapists in the later Northern Sung period the most outstanding were Kuo Hsi (*ca.* 1020-1090), famous for his panoramic hand scrolls and his writing on art theory, as well as Mi Fu (1051-1107), considered later on as the ideal type of the Chinese scholar-official artist due to his many-sided talent. He was a writer (including a work on painting), poet, eminent calligrapher and, in Waley's words, "a great connoisseur of antiquities, a passionate collector of painting and calligraphy". His style showed great originality and was a long step forward in a direction of a purely impressionist technique.

The T'ang traditions of figure painting were also continued in the Sung period. Of the many practitioners, perhaps the most famous was Li Lung-mien (1049-1106), a brilliant scholar and a high official. He is considered by some authorities as, in fact, the last great artist in this field, in the sense that the T'ang figure painting tradition was never really equalled in the later period. His scroll of horses and grooms is particularly well known.

In the field of painting of birds and flowers the Sung artists attained results which rival their great achievements in landscapes; they found in this usually small and very delicate form a new major source of artistic expression. The Chinese bird and flower painting has, in fact, very little in common with European still-life, being a much more intimate attempt to seek identity with the object depicted. Its beginnings date from the Five Dynasties period and one of its greatest early exponents was Huang Ch'üan (d. 965), who painted in the kingdom of Shu. By the end of the Northern Sung the form had reached a certain perfection in drawing and composition, in a realism based on keen observation, as can be seen in the many exquisite album leaves of this period devoted to these subjects.

An outstanding practitioner of the above form was the Emperor Hui-tsung (born 1082; ruled 1101-1125). He was very much of a failure as a ruler but quite gifted as a painter. Hui-tsung was not only noted for his own work, but is perhaps even more famous as a munificent patron of the arts, probably the most enthusiastic of all the highly cultured Northern Sung rulers, all of whom supported the development of the arts. He also expanded considerably the imperial collection of paintings. According to the still extant catalogue, which was compiled towards the end of his reign, the collection contained 6396 pictures, the work of 231 artists, most of them from the Sung period. This was the greatest collection ever assembled up to this time, but it was by no means the only one as there were a number of private ones as well. It should be mentioned, in passing, that the Sung era was noted not only for its interest in painting, but also for its general appreciation of antiquities and archaeology. It is in this period that the first collections and study of ancient bronzes, inscriptions and other art objects began to be made; many very valuable studies and catalogues, some of them excellently illustrated, were compiled and published.

In addition, Hui-tsung was known for his organization of the Imperial Academy of Painting. While court support for painters was not a new idea it took on in his time a more organized form with a number of titles and marks of honour for eminent painters including the famous Golden Girdle. Whether this form of state patronage had beneficial effects on the development of painting should remain an open question. The fact is, nevertheless, that a large number of the most famous painters of this period was associated with Hui-tsung's Academy in K'aifeng.

III. Painting—Southern Sung

The taking of K'aifeng by the Chin in 1127 was an unmitigated disaster in the history of Chinese art as well. The entire magnificent imperial collection was looted and most of it, undoubtedly, destroyed and lost. The fate of many artists was probably not better than that of Hui-tsung himself—they also were captured and exiled to the wilds of Northern Manchuria.

However, as the rule of the Southern Sung stabilized, and the Imperial Court established itself in Lin-an, the thread of former activity was picked up again. The Academy was reconstituted and some of the artists active in K'aifeng found their way there. The marvellously scenic setting of Hangchow was in itself a stimulus to painting and it was subsequently depicted so many times as to verge finally dangerously close to becoming a cliché.

Basically, painting in the Southern Sung continued to develop further along previous lines in all fields. However—although this generalization might be overstated—it showed a tendency of expressing an even greater detachment from the world than the art of its predecessor. No echo of the Chin encroachments or of the growing danger of Mongol invasion can be noted in the products of the Sung artists.

The great achievements of landscape paintings were continued by many artists. The two most famous were Ma Yüan and Hsia Kuei. Ma Yüan (*ca.* 1190-1224) came from a long line of well-known painters who had been connected with the Southern Sung Academy. His pictures, as well as those of Hsia Kuei, are softer in mood than those of the Northern Sung, but they are endowed with a dramatic intensity and excel in giving expression to an appearance of limitless space. Hsia Kuei (*fl.* 1180-1230) is especially known for his great panorama scrolls of which the most famous is the landscape of the Yangtse. It has been said that in Southern Sung landscape painting pictorial suggestion has been carried as far as possible while still retaining contact with reality. In fact, for capturing of a mood, it is unexcelled anywhere and anytime.

In figure painting mention should be made, at least, of Li T'ang (1049-*ca.*1130) whose buffaloes, skilled in his hands, became unfortunately the subject of only too many inferior pictures during future generations. Extremely fine work in the painting of birds and flowers was done by Ch'ien Hsüan (1235-1290) whose archaizing style did not exclude an astounding realism.

The most significant work done in the Southern Sung period was perhaps that of the painters who were outside the main current and who, in particular, were unconnected with the Academy—the Ch'an Buddhist painters. Under the influence of their philosophical views—which as we remember were perhaps really Taoist in origin— where the idea of achieving oneness with the world implied an intensive cultivation of nature and where the stress on intuitiveness placed emphasis on terseness, brevity and intensity—Ch'an painting produced some of the most remarkable works in the entire history of Chinese painting. The technique of monochrome ink was ideally suited for expressing their aims and it is in this mode that the works of two of the greatest of these artists—Liang K'ai and Mu Ch'i—were done. Liang K'ai (*ca.* 1200) was first an academy painter and later on retired to a Ch'an monastery near Hangchow. He changed his style of painting completely and his famous pictures of Li Po and of the Ch'an patriarch date from this period. Mu Ch'i (1181-1239) was probably a Ch'an monk most of his adult life and the abbot of a monastery also close to Hangchow. In the work of both of these artists the Ch'an ideal of spontaneity, simplicity and instant inspiration was superbly realized. While the style was to be continued in the future—and for that matter into the 20th century—the work of this period has been seldom, if ever, equalled.

It is sometimes maintained in histories dealing with Chinese art that the end of the Sung era also marked the end of truly great painting in China. This is not really so, inasmuch as great work was done not only in the Yüan period—which, in effect, was culturally simply a continuation of the Sung—but also in the later Ming and even in the

Ch'ing period. What is, however, true perhaps is that the very excellence of the work produced by the Sung artists constituted a handicap for future generations, inasmuch as it created a pattern of such overpowering influence as very few artists in the future could resist, and hence it led to the stultifying effects of an overzealous studying of the past mentioned previously.

IV. Other Art Forms

While the great period of Buddhist religious sculpture lay already in the past, good work was still done in the Sung era, but not as much in the medium of stone, where the work was rather derivative, as in clay and wood. A distinct tradition developed here which was to continue up to the 14th century. The work is marked by a high degree of realism and very successful portraiture (especially in the figures of Lohans), while the figures of Buddhist deities became more and more human in their appearance—simultaneously less Indian and more Chinese. This art was basically the work of travelling craftsmen and with time it tended to become stereotyped. Taken as a whole, this period up to the 14th century is the last in which Buddhist religious art still possesses some merit. The continuing decay of the Buddhist church was subsequently also reflected in the fall of its arts. In the future one must look for achievements in Chinese sculpture rather in the lesser forms of work in jade, ivory and wood.

The greatest achievement in the minor arts of the Sung period are undoubtedly to be found in ceramics. While they based themselves on the forms and techniques which were already highly developed during the T'ang, the Sung potters raised their craft to the level of utmost possible perfection. The shapes of the great variety of ware produced were more delicate than the earlier pieces. The glazes became still finer, especially the crackle effect which could now be controlled at the will of the potter. The famous beautiful green celadons, pure white and incised brown ware were produced in various kilns throughout the country; many of them were for the use of the court and an ever-greater quantity was earmarked for export. The beginnings of the blue and white ware, further to be developed in the Ming period, also date from this era. For a long time already the porcelain of the Sung period has been considered, in both China and Europe, as the best ever produced and collected as objects of rare beauty and value.

V. Historical Writing; Literature

The Sung era witnessed a considerable expansion of education and literacy, a flourishing of great scholarship and an immense intellectual effort whose aim was primarily a synthesis of the vast material furnished by the past. As a result a number of outstanding works were produced, especially in the field of history. This general development was bound up also with the results of the further growth and general use of printing. Thus, for example, wood blocks for the Classics were cut during the years 932-951 and they were printed in 130 volumes. A great number of various works were also similarly made available to the reading public. While movable types were already in use in 1045, they did not replace the wood block system of printing in this period. The printing of the Sung period is deservedly noted for its superb technical level.

The most renowned historian of the Sung era was Ssu-ma Kuang (1019-1096), an eminent scholar who was also one of the leaders of the conservative faction. When he was removed from office in 1070 he was allowed to retire on a sinecure to Loyang and permitted to take with him his entire library; thus he was able to devote all his time to the completion, with the help of three associates, of his immense *Tzu-chih t'ung-chien* ("The Comprehensive Mirror to Aid in Governing"). This was undoubtedly the most ambitious work undertaken in the field of Chinese history since the time of the *Shih chi* of Ssu-ma Ch'ien and is regarded as one of the greatest achievements of traditional Chinese historiography. It constituted a break with the practices employed in the standard dynastic histories, inasmuch as a great continuity of narrative and a vast span of history was dealt with.

The *T'ung-chien* is arranged in a form of annals in chronological order and covers the period from 403 B.C. to A.D. 959. Ssu-ma Kuang wished to continue the narration of Chinese history from where the *Tso chuan* —of which he was enamoured—left off to the beginning of the Sung dynasty. The form of his work is also partially modelled on the *Tso chuan*. He commenced his work first by preparing a detailed chronology of the entire period and obtained the support of the Emperor for his project. Subsequently, a long draft, several times longer than the final work, was prepared and this was ultimately edited by him to its present shape; the work itself consists of 294 chapters plus an outline of 30 chapters and an appendix of 30 more chapters which is devoted to comments on the variations of facts as presented by the sources. (The 1958 Chinese edition is in ten volumes, over 9,800 pages.) This examination of divergences in the sources is one of Ssu-ma Kuang's most valuable contributions. In general, his work is noted for its accuracy and comprehensiveness, as well as for the sound criteria which he employed in appraising his material. It was based on practically all the material available to him at this time. In the future the work was continued by other authors to include the Sung and Yuan periods as well.

It is from the *T'ung-chien* that an equally famous condensation, the *T'ung-chien kang-mu* ("Outlines and Details of the Comprehensive Mirror"), was made. It was planned by Chu Hsi and carried out by his disciples; it is more of a moralistic, didactic work than the original, but it constituted the standard history of China up to 1912 and had a tremendous influence. It was translated in the 18th century by the French Jesuit scholar de Mailla (see page 232) and was one of the principal works to be used by European authors (e.g. Gibbon) for a long time to come. H. Cordier's *Histoire générale de la Chine* is based primarily on this.

Another reworking of the Comprehensive Mirror was made by Yüan Shu (1131-1205). He arranged the material according to major incidents, somewhat more in the style of European historical writing. These three works constituted the main introduction to history for Chinese students up to the 20th century.

A work of almost equal magnitude to that of Ssu-ma Kuang was the *T'ung chih* ("General Treatise") by Cheng Ch'iao (1104-1162 or 1108-1166) which covered the period from 2800 B.C. to A.D. 600. He based himself on the concept of Ssu-ma Ch'ien but it has been stated that, in effect, he strung together material from the annals and biographies contained in the Standard Histories. His work included also fifteen monographs of an encyclopaedic character on various subjects including philology, phonetics, families and clans, etc.

The Sung period was also renowned for its encyclopaedic compendia. These played a very useful role on preserving much material which would have been otherwise lost. The two most famous of these were the *T'ai-p'ing yü-lan* ("Imperial Encyclopaedia of the T'ai P'ing reign period") edited by Li Fang (925-996). It was a huge work in 1000 chapters, based on over 800 authorities (1812 edition, 32 large volumes). The second was the *T'ai-p'ing kuang-chi* ("Miscellaneous Records"), a work of 500 chapters devoted to biographical and other information from literary sources, also edited by Li Fang.

The great economic development of the Sung era also resulted in considerable interest in technology and the sciences. It is from this period as well that much literature dealing with natural sciences, biology and botany is to be found. It is in the time of the Sung that two of the most famous Chinese inventions originated—gunpowder and the compass.

In literature, although the T'ang traditions of poetry were continued, the age is perhaps more noted for prose writing. To an even greater degree than earlier most of the writers were simultaneously officials and most statesmen were noted men of letters; this was a close approach to the Confucian ideal of the universal man—one who would be a scholar, poet and artist, and perhaps also a philosopher and statesman. To a considerable degree the three most famous writers of this period come very near to this picture. Ou-yang Hsiu (1007-1072) was a famous historian who together with Sung Ch'i (998-1061) wrote a New History of the T'ang Dynasty to supersede one which had been composed earlier and was thought to be inadequate (in fact, both are listed in the series of Standard Histories). He was also a high official throughout much of his life, probably the principal intellectual leader of the conservative opposition to Wang An-shih, whose patron he had been earlier on, and the author of numerous political essays. Ou-yang Hsiu was also a poet and employed at times the vernacular in his verse.

As noted earlier, Wang An-shih was himself an excellent writer. The style of his prose—and his subjects were usually closely bound up with his political activities—is considered lucid and succinct. He was also one of the best, although little known, poets of the Sung period. The greatest perhaps of these three was Su Shih (1036-1101, better known by his literary name, Su Tung-p'o). He likewise spent most of his life as an official. His many-sided talents included calligraphy and painting—he was especially noted for his rendering of bamboo. Su Tung-p'o was a brilliant essayist on current and historical topics and has a reputation for clear, flowing language as well as great imagination. He was a man of vast erudition and the author of a considerable quantity of verse. His writings had much influence on the future development of Chinese literature.

VI. Philosophy

A large number of authors consider that the achievements of the Sung era in the field of philosophy equal, or even surpass, the results reached in the arts. This evaluation is a subjective one—as most of such evaluations necessarily are—and it depends on the criteria employed. In the sense of historical importance it is undoubtedly true that the school of Neo-Confucianism, evolved in the Sung period, was of crucial importance for the development—or perhaps better, the lack of development—in the future of Chinese thought, inasmuch as it became the dominant force in this realm up to the 20th century. In this respect it is true that the Sung Neo-Confucian philosophers are second in importance in the history of Chinese philosophy, giving place only to those of the classical Chou period.

In general, Sung philosophy implied a return to Chinese sources and ideas after the long period in which the influence of Buddhist thought had been dominant in this field. In a way it was an archaistic and almost nationalist reaction against the above phenomenon. The great spread of education and the development of the examination system, based on the study of the Classics—the Confucian Canon—made this resurgence of Confucianism both possible and easy. The problem lay in adapting this philosophy to the current needs as the major form of ideology, while simultaneously answering and dealing satisfactorily with the problems which had been raised by Buddhism and largely ignored by earlier Confucianism, primarily those of metaphysics. This challenge of Buddhism (and partially also of Taoism) was met by the reconstruction out of older elements of Chinese thought (including the Five Elements and the *yin-yang* theory) of a cosmology which could rival that of Buddhism. Some modern Chinese authors maintain that this was accomplished, among others, largely by plagiarizing Buddhist ideas. In fact, however, the Sung philosophers had been under great influence of Buddhist and Taoist ideas and this was necessarily reflected in their work. Neo-Confucianism has been often referred to, therefore, as a synthesis of Confucianism, Buddhism and Taoism with Confucianism as its dominant element. If one were, however, to accept this view, then it is necessary to make the reservation that in this synthesis the Taoist search for immortality, as well as Buddhist mysticism and other-worldliness were both, on the whole, successfully ignored or by-passed and the largely agnostic character of earlier Confucianism was maintained.

Of the six most famous Sung philosophers, five were active in the 11th century and most of them, logically enough, were to be found in the ranks of the opponents of Wang An-shih. They included Chou Tun-i (1017-1073), whose study of the Classic of Changes led to his development of the concept of the Supreme Ultimate which became of basic importance in the Neo-Confucian metaphysics. The influence of Taoist thought in his work is very marked. His contemporary Shao Yung (1011-1077) has been called the intellectual counsellor of the group opposed to Wang An-shih. He also dealt with problems of cosmology, but his approach was perhaps even more complex than that of Chou Tun-i and he evolved a numerological theory as the basis for his views. He also developed a concept of the Perfect Sage, able to grasp the ultimate meanings of reality. His ideas were equally influenced by Taoism. Other elements of Neo-Confucian thought were contributed by the two brothers Ch'eng Hao (1031-1085) and Ch'eng I (1032-1107). They were both, especially the younger, voluminous writers and strong opponents of Wang An-shih. They formed what is known as the Loyang school and developed a concept of *li* (Reason or Principle) as an element ever present in all the manifestations of the universe. Their uncle, Chang Tsai (1020-1077), emphasized in his turn the importance of matter as the primary element in the universe.

The most famous and important of the Sung philosophers was a man of a later generation—Chu Hsi (1130-1200). He spent most of his life as an official although he never gained top posts. His contribution to historical writing has already been mentioned, but much more important was his role as the greatest commentator on the Confucian Classics since the period of the Han. His work in this field became in due time regarded as the standard interpretation of this heritage. Herein lies one of the main problems in dealing with Neo-Confucianism and the work of Chu Hsi in this field. He claimed to be only an interpreter and not an innovator—much as Confucius had said of himself. In effect, however, in ignoring the historical background in which Confucian ideas were formed and in tacking on to Confucianism the whole ballast of Buddhist-influenced metaphysics, Chu Hsi changed the nature of Confucianism considerably. Some authors maintain that this was an inevitable modernization or adaption to new conditions.

Undoubtedly, Chu Hsi's greatest achievement was the synthesis of the work of his predecessors, mentioned above, in which he elaborated a complex but systematized metaphysical cosmology, employing practically all the concepts which had been evolved by them—as well as the older Chinese ideas of the Five Elements and *yin-yang*—combining all this into a logically sound entity, based on an objective, idealist conception of the world. He has been often compared, for his great talent in synthesis, to St. Thomas Aquinas.

Some authors maintain, however, and this seems to be correct, that the metaphysical aspect of Neo-Confucianism was not as important as its social and political views which were also systematized by Chu Hsi. Here, following the traditional concern of Confucianism with the problems of human society, a return to the questions raised by Mencius concerning human nature occurred. Chu Hsi supported the views of Mencius regarding the so-called inherent goodness of human nature, but this was strictly bound up with the emphasizing of the paternalistic aspects of Confucian teachings, whose ultimate effects are those of strengthening and preserving the existing social order. The emphasis on the values and importance of the Five Relations and other similar concepts were all directed, in the final analysis, towards creating an intellectual climate in which the rule of the gentry bureaucracy would not only remain unchallenged, but would be acknowledged as morally and intellectually acceptable.

Chu Hsi's reconstruction and systematization of Confucian ideas was thought to be, not surprisingly, too far-reaching by his contemporaries. The majority of the scholars of his period regarded his views and those of his school (called the School of the Tao ("way") as Neo-Confucianism is known in Chinese) as heretical. Chu Hsi and his followers were even subjected to a certain amount of persecution. It is only after his death that his views were to become recognized and transformed into an official doctrine which is referred to at times as Chu Hsi-ism. In a relatively short time his views became the basis for a rigid orthodoxy—the only possible accepted world outlook, as well as the sole valid commentary on the Classics.

In this new role Neo-Confucianism was transformed into a straightjacket on the further intellectual development of China—and by no means only in the field of philosophy—giving rise merely to empty and shallow scholasticism. In maintaining this position—in reality until the 20th century—Neo-Confucianism contributed to the fossilization and petrification of Chinese culture and civilization which was then, in turn, partially responsible for the unhappy fate of the country when faced with the intrusion of the Western world. Perhaps even earlier, during the Manchu invasion, the course of history could have been different if the society which faced that invasion had not been so intellectually stultified by Neo-Confucianism as Ming society had been by the 17th century. However, the rigidity of Chinese culture after the Sung, in the creation of which Neo-Confucianism played an essential, though by no means the only, role, is a very complex problem which up to now has not really been sufficiently examined or satisfactorily elucidated.

The stability, although partially superficial, of Chinese feudal society, to which the contribution to Neo-Confucianism was undoubtedly of great importance, was the result of a large number of factors. The effectiveness of social and political organization was such as to obviate the necessity for searching methods and ways of improvement, reform or progress; the rule of the gentry officials was basically unchallenged—except by the invasions of the northern nomads with whom they were, in reality, able to compromise. The high level of culture, wealth and economic development of the country—which surpassed that of the rest of the world during the Sung period—led to a strengthening of the feeling of the superiority of China in respect to all other countries, to a further stimulation of the complex of the "Middle Kingdom", of regarding China as the only truly civilized part of the world and thus, ultimately, to the complacency which was to prove fatal. The price which China was to pay in the future for its greatness and flourishing in this era was immense indeed; perhaps quite incommensurate with the brilliant achievements of Sung civilization.

PART VII

Mongol Rule and the Ming Restoration

CHAPTER 20

The Yüan Dynasty

I. Mongol Rule in China

The defeat of the last supporters of the Sung signified the extension of Mongol rule to the entire country although already for decades considerable parts of China had been under Mongol sway. This was the greatest victory up to that time of the northern nomads over their southern agricultural neighbours and it meant the subjection of the latter to the most despotic and ruthless regime they had probably ever been under, aggravated by the additional factor of a consciously pursued policy of national oppression and discrimination. This policy was derived to a large degree from the mutual hatred and distrust of the Mongols and the Chinese which lasted throughout the Yüan period.

The Mongols based themselves on Chinese forms of administration, inasmuch as these were the only ones which could be employed to rule the country and to exploit its agricultural economy; in this they continued the practices of the Sung and the T'ang, while introducing some very important variations. After the conquest of Southern Sung the population of the country was divided into four groups. The first of these was composed of the Mongols themselves—they were to remain a privileged elite which was to maintain its military strength, while their garrisons were placed in key points throughout the entire country. Most of the top posts in the administration were also reserved for the Mongols. The second group consisted of various Central Asian peoples, mostly Turkish, who were allies of the Mongols, such as, for example, the Uighurs, whose influence on the Mongols was very considerable (the Mongols, for instance, derived their alphabet from the Uighurs). The position of this group was almost as favourable as that of the Mongols and it is from them that the Mongols also drew much of the personnel for their bureaucracy in China. This aid was invaluable as these people were already much more civilized and experienced than the Mongols themselves. The third group was composed of the Chinese of North China which had been conquered earlier and included some of the remnants of the Khitan and the Jurchen; it was permitted a much smaller political role. Finally, the fourth group—

Map 15. Mongol Rule. Kubilai's Empire

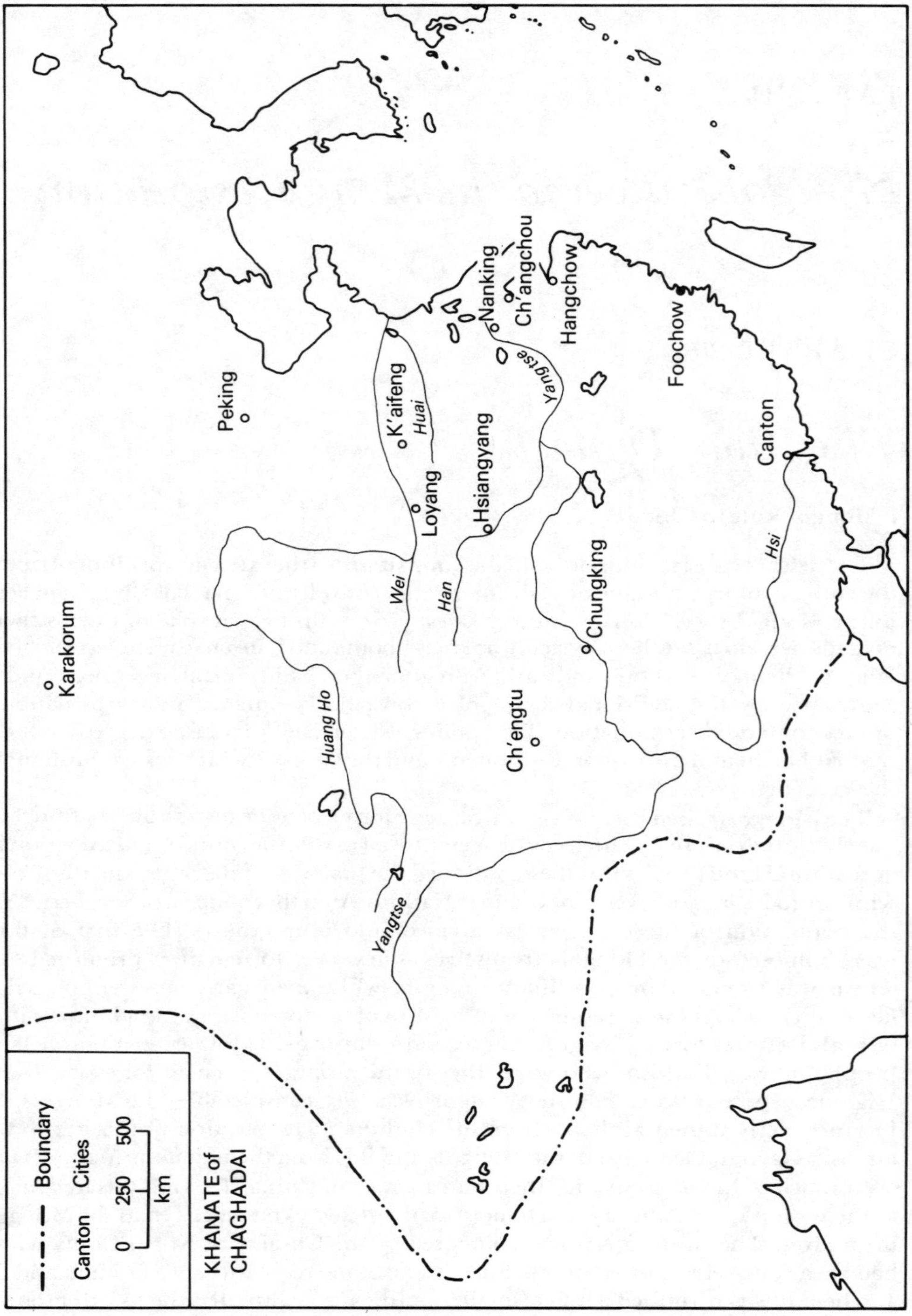

Karakorum

Peking

K'aifeng
Loyang
Huai
Wei
Han
Huang Ho
Yangtse

Hsiangyang

Nanking
Ch'angchou
Hangchow
Yangtse

Foochow

Canton

Chungking

Ch'engtu

Hsi

KHANATE of
CHAGHADAI

Boundary
Canton Cities

0   250   500
km

the Chinese of the South—was trusted the least of all by the Mongols, deprived of all participation in the government, forbidden to possess arms, to hold meetings and so forth.

In these circumstances the Chinese landlord families were for the first time in Chinese history deprived of their customary official posts, i.e. of their hold on the government. In effect, however, a large part of them, especially in Central and South China, continued to collaborate with the conquerors, who left them mostly undisturbed in the possession of their landed estates. It has often been said that many of this class refused to collaborate, and withdrew to their estates to engage in literary and artistic pursuits. It is doubtful, however, whether this withdrawal was in all cases voluntary; it seems rather that the Mongols did not follow the pattern of the previous nomad conquerors and did not wish to avail themselves of the services of all the Chinese officials. It should be noted, in passing, that a number of prominent scholars, and especially artists, did refuse to work for the Mongols, rejecting, for example, invitations to the court of Kubilai.

The reasons why the Mongols felt able to dispense with the "assistance" of the Chinese gentry lay perhaps in the fact that this was the first total conquest of the country. Simultaneously, the gulf, in practically all respects, in regards to culture and customs was even greater between the Mongols and the Chinese than in the preceding cases when both the Khitan and the Jurchen had become sinicized with great rapidity. Perhaps even more significant in this respect was the fact that China constituted only one part of the great Mongol empire—although it was the richest and most important—and was soon, in effect, to be transformed into an independent realm within the empire; thus the Mongols were able to draw on the human resources of the other parts of their empire for the purpose of maintaining their rule in China. It is true that in 1315 the examination system was restored and thus the influx of Chinese into the bureaucracy was continued on an increased scale, but the policy of reserving the top posts for the Mongols and their Central Asian clients was preserved. However, most of the lower posts, and especially the clerical ones, were all in the hands of the Chinese.

The employment of large numbers of foreigners was connected also with the Mongol policy in religious matters. From the outset the dominant tendency of the Mongol government was one, for political reasons, of far-reaching tolerance of all "tolerable" religions. The Mongols themselves had been originally Shamanists and tended in time to become primarily Buddhists, especially when they came under the influence of probably the crudest and most debased form of this religion—Tibetan Lamaism— which in time became the dominant religion of all Mongol tribes. This was perhaps due to the large element of Shamanism in the Tibetan religion which made it easier for the Mongols to understand and accept. The Chinese accounts of this period are full of stories concerning the outrageous behaviour of the lamas when they had become a power, due to the protection shown them by the Mongol rulers.

During the Yüan period Christianity reappeared once more in China in both its Nestorian and Catholic forms. There were numerous Nestorian converts among the Mongol aristocracy and the Nestorian church enjoyed considerable prosperity. The missions of the Franciscans were also active, though their converts were to be found primarily among the Mongols and Turks and not the Chinese; the highwater mark of their work was the establishment in 1307 of an archbishopric in Peking. Both these cults, however, were swept away together with the Mongols when the rule of the latter came to an end as being too closely associated with them.

The fate of Islam, which also spread very considerably during the Yüan period, was to be different. The propagation of this fate was the result of the employment by the Mongols of large numbers of Central Asians, the great majority of whom were already Moslems at this time. It is due to their influence that the spread of Islam in the north-west and south-west of China (Kansu, Yunnan) was on such a scale that these communities were able to maintain themselves even after their Mongol patrons had been ejected from China.

The only major religious cult which was not to prosper under Mongol rule was Taoism which had had a great revival under the Chin. The Mongol rulers, Kubilai in particular, as lavish patrons of the Buddhist church, took the Buddhist side in this controversy. As a result a burning of the Taoist Canon took place (excluding, however, the philosophical works such as the *Tao te ching*), the Taoist church was driven underground where it later was to play an important part in political activity against Mongol rule. The Buddhist church, on the other hand, became a great political power, undoubtedly used by the Mongols as a counterweight to Confucianism; it also increased markedly in wealth, becoming once more one of the great landowners in the country.

After the death in1294 at the age of 80 of Kubilai, the conqueror of the Southern Sung and the founder of the Yüan dynasty, the throne was to be occupied throughout the rest of the Mongol rule by a number of nonentities. His grandson reigned till 1307 and later on six emperors were to follow each other rapidly on the throne. The last Mongol emperor ruled from 1333 to 1368. The Mongol ruling class showed a partic-ularly strong propensity for murderous intrigues and vicious inner struggles for power which proved to be a very important factor in bringing about their downfall. This was shown even during the reign of Kubilai, the strongest of all the Mongol emperors in China, who had on his hands a powerful rebellion of two Mongol princes, Khaidu in Central Asia and Nayan in Manchuria.

II. The Social and Economic Consequences of Mongol Rule

The Mongols ruled China as a conquered country and the consequences of this approach were to be seen not only in the political sphere, but in social and economic development as well. Taken as a whole, the Mongol domination was not only a handicap to the further growth of the country's economy but also, in fact, the cause of regression.

At the outset the Mongol invaders had confiscated great quantities of land from the Chinese owners, particularly in North China, some of which was turned into pasturage. They also distributed much state and private land to the members of the Mongol aristocracy, as well as endowing Buddhist temples on a lavish scale. This policy, connected with still heavier taxes, signified ruin for many of the free peasants, their falling into debt (with usury rates up to 100 per cent annually) and ultimately the loss of their land. Thus the number of great estates increased even still more than in the Sung period and correspondingly the number of tenant farmers grew as well. A still further result of these developments was a great second wave of peasant migration to the South, this time from the Yangtse Valley to Fukien, Kwangtung and Kwangsi.

The Mongol rulers, perhaps due to their nomad origin, were ignorant of the need to conserve properly the system of waterworks in North China and this neglect, following that of the Chin period, was the cause of many breakdowns of the dikes, among others on the Yellow River, which then resulted in great destruction to life and property and, in turn, brought about a still further impoverishment of the peasants. The census data for 1290 put the population at 58.8 million; this should be compared with the figure for 1125 which was over 100 million. Assuming even considerable inexactitude in the way this census was held, the difference in the figures shows how great the loss of life must have been, resulting from the wars of the 13th century and especially from the Mongol conquest itself.

The position of the artisans in Yüan times was not much better than that of the peasants. Following the custom which had been employed by them while conquering Central and West Asia, the Mongols in China also converted a large part of the craftsmen into their dependants, working only for the government, and thus stifled free development of the crafts to a considerable degree. The artisans who remained free were the object of very heavy taxation.

The incorporation of China into the huge Mongol Empire with its open and safe trade routes reaching to Baghdad and Kiev led to a considerable development of foreign trade. This was, however, of no marked benefit to China, inasmuch as almost the entire trade was in the hands of foreign merchants, particularly Moslems from Central Asia (who also acted very often as tax-farmers for the government), and the profits from foreign trade were taken out of China proper. This led to a drain on metallic currency and further complicated a worsening economic situation. This was, in turn, further aggravated as a result of the Mongol policy of continuing the Sung practice of employing paper money on a still greater scale, which inevitably led to inflation and ultimately to a far-reaching depreciation of the currency. All these developments took place against the background of the immense corruption and graft of the Mongol administration, as exemplified by the career of Ahmed Fanakati, one of Kubilai's ministers, who was notorious for his extortions and the vast fortune he derived from them. He was disgraced only posthumously after having been assassinated by a Chinese.

Kubilai had established his capital in Peking and this, as the centre of the entire Mongol Empire, he expanded hugely. While Peking was laid out on a grand scale (partly following the present outline of the city, since the Ming built on Yüan foundations) this magnificence, which reflected the Mongol love of barbaric splendour was, in fact, as Eberhard puts it, the obverse side of the continuous impoverishment of China as a whole. The new capital required vast food supplies from the south and for this purpose the Grand Canal was extended to reach close to Peking and a great fleet was also organized for carrying grain to the north. Immense quantities of forced labour were employed for the projects connected with the building of the capital and the extension of the canal.

III. The Mongol Campaigns in East Asia; China and the World

While the building of the Mongol Empire in West and Central Asia, as well as in East Europe, is outside of our scope, some attention should be paid to the campaigns conducted by the Mongols in East Asia, where China was actually employed as the main base. The Mongol greed for plunder, power and conquest remained quite unsatiated up to the end of the 13th century. This led, in effect, to a great number of expeditions against practically all the countries which neighboured with China. Thus a series of attempts to subdue Indo-china (both present Vietnam and Cambodia) as well as Burma took place. These invasions were usually successful during the first stage of attack; the Mongols, however, were never able to consolidate their foothold in South-east Asia. This was due basically to two reasons; the undaunted and brave resistance of the population of this area—particularly true of the Vietnamese who waged an extremely effective guerrilla warfare against the Mongol invaders—and the unfavourable climatic conditions which proved fatal to the nomads from the steppes. Mongol cavalry was also of very little use in jungle conditions and was even more powerless against the sea, as proved by the campaigns against Japan.

The first expedition against Japan was launched by the power- and prestige-mad Kubilai in 1274. It was composed of 300 large ships and 400-500 smaller craft, with over 15,000 Mongol and Chinese and 8,000 Korean troops, while the seamen were all Korean and Chinese. It met with complete disaster due to Japanese resistance and to violent storms. After the fall of the Southern Sung Kubilai employed the shipbuilding capacity of South China, as well as of his vassal Korea (which had been invaded by the Mongols in 1231 and conquered completely by 1258) to create armadas, Korean and Chinese, for a new invasion of the islands. The expeditionary force was manned by 100,000 Chinese troops from the South (ironically, these were units which had deserted the Sung) and 40,000 from the North, composed of Mongols, North Chinese and Koreans. Neither the Chinese nor the Koreans were particularly eager to fight for their Mongol masters. After the initial landing had been made and successfully resisted by the Japanese, the famous typhoons—*Kamikaze,* The Divine Wind—wrecked the major part of the ships, in August 1281, leaving a part of the army stranded. Most of the survivors were killed by the Japanese, with the exception of some Chinese and Koreans, saved for their skill as shipbuilders. A new expedition was prepared by Kubilai to take revenge for his earlier defeats but it was never to sail. Both the victory as well as the memory of the Mongol invasion was to play an important role in future relations between Japan and China.

Due to the fact that China formed a part of the vast Mongol Empire and to the great increased trade contacts mentioned previously, relations between Europe and China were on a greater scale than ever before and, for that matter, more significant than any future contacts up to the 19th century. Of the large number of merchants and missionaries, many of whom have left accounts of their travels to the lands of the Great Khan of the Mongols, none is so well known as the Venetian merchant, Marco Polo. His long stay in China, his service as an official under Kubilai and his many travels throughout parts of the Mongol realm, including much of China, which he relates in his book *Description of the World*—the product of his stay in a Genoese jail as a prisoner of war—gave Europe the best and most detailed account of the Middle Kingdom, not to be superseded until the work of the Jesuit missionaries of the 17th century. In spite of some inaccuracies Marco Polo's account is still invaluable as one of the best sources on the Mongol period. The book itself has been the object of a considerable amount of modern research the result of which has done much to emphasize its general reliability.*

* From the Polish point of view an earlier mission of the Franciscan monk Giovanni de Plano Carpini is of

The contacts were two-sided, as undoubtedly many Chinese at this time were also in Europe, especially in the parts of the Mongol realm as, for example, the so-called Chinese quarters in Moscow and Novgorod bear witness. However, the relations of China with West Asia, with Persia and the Arabs were much more intensive than those with Europe and here the interpenetration of mutual influences was on a great scale. It is through these contacts with West Asia that the great Chinese inventions—printing, paper and powder—started on their way to the West. Nonetheless, taken as a whole, the increased contacts with other parts of the world during the Yüan had remarkably little effects on the future development of Chinese civilization. Probably one reason for this lay in the sweeping away of all things foreign, connected with the memory of Mongol rule, which took place when Chinese political power was restored and a great emphasis placed on the return to things Chinese. Another factor lay in the previously mentioned inherent feeling regarding the superiority of their civilization which was held by the Chinese already during the Sung—and not without a considerable degree of justification; this feeling was not only undiminished but it was, in effect, greatly enhanced as a result of the barbarous rule of the Mongols.

IV. The Downfall of the Yüan Dynasty

A number of factors were responsible for the relative rapidity of the decline and fall of Mongol rule in China. The degeneration of the Mongol ruling class which was shown, among others, by their constant inner struggles was of considerable importance. Equally vital was the fact that within one generation the Mongols living in China had already lost most of their vaunted military prowess—the sole basis of their "right to rule"—and the Mongol armies, the terror of the entire civilized world, had become largely useless as a force for maintaining the dynasty in power. The Mongol Empire had also, as was to be expected, disintegrated into a number of separate states where the Mongols, while remaining a ruling class, had lost much of their national identity and of the feeling of Mongol unity. This undoubtedly also led to a weakening of the position of the Mongols in China as well; the Mongol rulers in the other states, often rivals, for that matter, of the power in Peking, were of no help in maintaining Mongol rule in China, inasmuch as they were much too concerned by far with their own interests.

In contrast to the previous conquerors from the north, the Mongols during their period of domination over China had undergone the process of sinicization to a much lesser degree. A number of reasons account for this apart from the previously mentioned great differences which separated initially the Mongols from the Chinese in culture and customs. The conscious effort of the Mongols to retain their identity as a distinct ruling caste were more successful than those of their predecessors also due to the fact that there were more Mongols in China than there had been Khitan or Jurchen. The figure usually given is one million, although this must have included in fact many non-Mongols. The pure nomad origin of the Mongols was undoubtedly also a factor. The most important reason of all, however, was probably the relatively short duration of their rule—less than a century, counting from the downfall of the Southern Sung. It is

interest inasmuch as he took with him as interpreter Benedict, a Polish monk from Wrocław, more than likely the first Pole who had ever gone to East Asia. Plano Carpini left Europe in 1245, reaching the court of Guyuk, the Great Khan, in 1246, and returned through Kiev and Poland in the next year. He left an interesting account of his mission, which itself was a failure.

quite possible that the process of sinification would have made further progress if they had succeeded in maintaining their power. But then the failure to assimilate was perhaps one of the basic causes for the inability of the Mongols to preserve their rule.

The great hostility of the Chinese to Mongol rule is revealed by practically all the works of the Chinese historians, both earlier and modern. Not without considerable justification they dwell on the damaging effects of Mongol domination on the development of China, on the immense sufferings which the Chinese people had to endure as a result of the Mongol invasion and rule. There is little attempt to conceal a feeling of profound contempt as well for the low level of Mongol culture and customs, with a stress laid on the vices said to be characteristic of the Mongols—their drunkenness, dirtiness, as well as their unspeakable cruelty. All of this was true enough—but perhaps at the bottom of this Chinese attitude lay also the problem of the inability of the Chinese to answer the fundamental crucial question—how did it come about that a great, much more populous and civilized nation had ever fallen under the yoke of such barbarians, even if it were for only a relatively short period of time?

The most important factor, however, which was instrumental in bringing about the downfall of the Mongols was the active struggle of the Chinese peasants. While the Chinese gentry continued, as a whole, their collaboration with the Mongols, it was the peasantry, bearing what became an unsupportable burden of two-fold oppression—by the Chinese landlords and the additional exploitation by the Mongol regime—who constituted the fundamental force seeking to change the existing situation. The steadily deepening agrarian crisis, along with the constantly deteriorating economic conditions—with famine on an immense scale, even by Chinese standards—all these created additional stimuli to the beginning of a series of peasant risings. The peasants had simply nothing at all to lose any more. The first risings took place in the 1320s. They were put down, however, but not so much by the Mongols themselves as by armed units raised by the Chinese landlords who in this way helped to maintain the Mongol regime.

A crucial role in the organization of the peasant insurrections was played by the secret societies whose activity was by no means restricted only to this era, although this is undoubtedly one of the most important and interesting periods in their appearance on the arena of Chinese history. Two of these societies were of special importance. The first was the White Lotus which was formed in the first half of the 12th century, although some authorities believe that it was linked with the sect of the same name which originated in the beginning of the 4th century as an offshoot of the T'ien-t'ai Buddhist cult. Its Buddhist character was maintained, but this was of an unorthodox nature with the main stress placed on messianic teachings regarding the coming of the last Buddha—Maitreya. The sect also propagated ideas of mutual aid and co-operation, as well as care for the needs of the population. The second society was the White Cloud, more than likely of Manichaean origin, which was already active during the end of the Northern Sung, when its followers became leaders of a peasant rising in Chekiang.

It would appear that at the beginning of the 14th century both of these societies had united, and using the name of White Lotus began to engage in revolutionary activities against the Mongols, as a result of which the existence of the organization was prohibited by the government in 1308 and 1322. Some authors believe that the White Lotus was the main force responsible for the successful overthrow of the Yüan dynasty. This is probably true, if taken in the sense that the White Lotus was the force which organized the peasants for the struggle against the Mongols. The sect certainly did carry out this role in the formation of the Red Turban movement.

In 1351 the dykes on the Yellow River broke and the government impressed a force of 150,000 peasants and 20,000 soldiers for repair work. The members of the White Lotus utilized the chance of the great concentration of manpower to organize a revolt. The success of their propaganda was considerable and the movement—which took the name of the Red Turbans from their distinctive head-dress—spread rapidly. The Red Turbans were soon the masters of a large part of Honan with an army of over 100,000 strong. The revolt soon extended to neighbouring provinces—Hupei, Shantung and Anhwei. In the latter, the most successful leader to emerge in 1352 was Kuo Tzu-hsing.

The Mongols had no effective means for coping with the rebellion except to renew the old legislation against the Chinese, such as the prohibition of possessing arms. Even somewhat earlier, when Chinese discontent was obviously increasing, the only proposal that the Mongol minister Bayan was said to have made was one that all the Chinese bearing the surnames of Chang, Wang, Li, Liu and Chao should be massacred. These are the five most common surnames of all and, according to some estimates, almost half of the Chinese population bear them. Even the Mongols, however, were unable at this stage to implement this ingenious proposal.

As the Red Turban movement grew in size and influence, its leaders, who were mostly of peasant origin, as was the great mass of its followers, favoured the restoration of the Sung dynasty and put forth in 1355 Han Lin-erh, who came from a family very prominent in the White Lotus sect, as the supposed descendant of Hui-tsung, placing him on the throne. In fact, however, the movement at this stage was probably more social than national, with the peasants struggling just as much against the Chinese gentry as against the Mongol government.

One very important factor which militated against the success of the Red Turbans was the constant struggle for power between its various leaders which had the ultimate result of weakening the movement and, in fact, prolonging Mongol rule. This phenomenon was characteristic of many peasant rebellions and was to be repeated also during one of the greatest—the Taiping in the 19th century. Nevertheless, the northern group of the Red Turban armies was capable of launching in the years 1357-1359 a series of raids into North China, coming at one point quite close to Peking. A number of cities were captured but the methods of warfare, rather close to brigandage, were similar to that of some earlier peasant risings, Huang Ch'ao's, for example, and thus no real attempt was made to consolidate the territory that had been won. The Chinese gentry, frightened by the social aims of the peasant armies, joined the Mongol government in the struggle against them and by 1363 all the Red Turban forces in North China had been defeated.

In the meantime, in the Yangtse Valley area, a new peasant leader appeared who was destined to accomplish the total overthrow of the Yüan. This was Chu Yüan-chang—the future founder of the Ming dynasty—who has been often compared, correctly, to Liu Pang of the Han. He was born in 1328 in Anhwei, in the Huai River area, north-west of Nanking, the son of poor tenant peasants. When he was 17 his entire family died from famine and the plague, and the orphan became a Buddhist monk in order to gain his livelihood. He spent at least three years as a mendicant monk and it is more than likely that at this time he became a member of the White Lotus, though later on, after he had become an Emperor, he himself denied this strongly. This denial is not particularly surprising in view of the fact that at that time he proscribed the existence of this revolutionary organization.

In 1353 Chu Yüan-chang joined the force of Kuo Tzu-hsing and here, due to his talents and bravery, he rose rapidly to a leading position, his famous ugliness not being a handicap. On the death of Kuo Tzu-hsing in 1355, he took over command of all his forces and also managed to recruit a number of his own co-villagers who became his most trusted assistants.

Shortly thereafter Chu Yüan-chang's forces were joined by some members of the gentry whose influence on him was to prove of great importance for his future. They advised him to desist from the policy which was followed by other peasant leaders of struggling against the Chinese landlords, to take Liu Pang as a model, and thus to attract Chinese of all classes to his side and thereby to clear the path for the overthrow of the Mongol dynasty and to aim for the throne himself. Chu Yüan-chang followed this advice faithfully; this differentiated him fundamentally from the other Red Turban leaders and helped to make his future success much easier. He concentrated on strengthening his own forces and succeeded in taking Nanking in 1356. This gave him partial control of the richest economic area—the lower Yangtse Valley—which became the base of his operations. As a result of his policies the Chinese gentry, which now saw the Mongol cause as lost, joined him *en masse* together with their own armed forces. Chu Yüan-chang concentrated also on establishing an efficient administration in the areas under his control, as well as on encouraging the development of agricultural production in order to ensure adequate supplies for his army. This became a disciplined force in stark contrast to other peasant armies; it was forbidden to take food from the peasants and the soldiers themselves even tilled the land. In the years 1363-1367 Chu Yüan-chang devoted his attention to waging a series of struggles against other contenders for power and succeeded in extending his rule first to most of Anhwei, Honan, Hupei and Kiangsi and then later to Kiangsu and Chekiang. It was these successes which made it possible for him to become also the master of the South—of Fukien, Kwangtung and Kwangsi.

In 1367 Chu Yüan-chang felt strong enough and ready to start on a final campaign against the Mongols; he sent his best general, Hsü Ta, with an army of 250,000 on an expedition to the north. This undertaking was greatly facilitated by the fact that in the years 1363-1365 the Mongols had engaged once more—in spite of the dangers facing them from the Chinese—in bitter struggles among themselves. The Northern Expedition of Hsü Ta was an easy triumph; he took Tatu (Peking) in 1368. The Mongols offered practically no resistance and the last Yüan emperor fled back to his original homeland. The rest of the Mongol garrisons in other parts of China were also defeated, with some of the Mongols remaining to serve the new Chinese rulers. The Mongol yoke on China had been broken. In the same year Chu Yüan-chang declared himself the first Emperor of the Ming ("Brilliant") dynasty in his capital of Nanking.

V. Chinese Culture During the Yüan Period

"The Mongols were merely policemen." This apt phrase of Arthur Waley succinctly disposes of the problem whether Mongol rule during its ninety years had any real influence on the development of Chinese culture. It had practically none and certainly the Mongols had no contribution of their own to make. This section is placed here primarily for chronological convenience and not because political history had influenced the development of culture to any significant degree. Chinese culture continued to develop on the basis of its previous achievements and continuity with the Sung era was for all purposes uninterrupted. Some authors maintain that the additional leisure time acquired by the Chinese scholars—as a result of not obtaining all the customary official posts—led to a greater emphasis on literary pursuits and thus to the development of the drama for which this period is noted. This thesis does not seem, however, particularly convincing, inasmuch as the Chinese scholar-officials were never overworked to begin with.

Chinese drama differs markedly from the European theatre in that it is a mixed form which includes music, singing, acrobatics and therefore it is often called, more correctly, Chinese opera. Its sources lie, in effect, in scenic performances of the 10th and 11th centuries; no librettos, however, have survived but only titles of the plays. It is solely from the Yüan period that both the texts of the drama and the names of the authors have been preserved. The subject matter varied considerably but a very great amount is drawn from Chinese history.Of the many drama writers of this era the two most famous were Kuan Han-cheng (*ca.*1234-1300), a prolific author whom Chinese writers consider to have been brilliant, and Wang Shih-fu (*fl.* end 13th-beginning 14th century), the author of the famous love story "The Western Chamber" which was based on a short story from the T'ang era. Some writers consider this to be more of a novel than a drama but this does not affect its literary merit in any way. Chinese drama continued to develop also in the Ming period when a number of other famous plays were written. It is also in that period that the novel, which will be dealt with later, became an established form of literature, although some authors see its beginnings still in the Yüan period.

The traditions of Sung scholarship were continued in the Yüan era although the patronage of the court was not a factor of any significance. The most important work which dealt with political and social history was that of Ma Tuan-lin (*ca.* 1250-1325), the *Wen-hsien t'ung-k'ao* ("General Study of Literary Remains") which was based on the *T'ung tien* of Tu Yu but considerably enlarged and supplemented down to 1254.

It was in painting that the most marked further creativeness of Chinese culture during the Yüan period was revealed. This is not only, however, a continuation of patterns established during the Sung era but also a development in its own right, although most painters did look back to the masters of the Northern Sung as a source of inspiration. In these years painting in some ways became still closer to calligraphy and the custom of inscribing poems or other texts in beautiful script on the pictures became still more widespread. More and more of the painting was that which was to become predominant in the future—the *wen jen hua*—the art of the scholars.

One of the most noted artists was Chao Meng-fu (1254-1322), a very versatile painter with landscapes, figures and bamboo to his credit. He was probably most famous for his pictures of horses—these done more than likely for his Mongol clients. In spite of the fact that he was a descendant of the Sung imperial family, he was one of the few famous artists who actively collaborated with the Yüan court. He was also considered the greatest calligrapher of the period.

In the history of Chinese painting Five Masters of landscape painting in the Yüan era are usually referred to. These include Kao K'o-kung (1248-1310), who painted in a markedly impressionist style, taking Mi Fu as his model. Wu Chen (1280-1354), a Taoist recluse, was both a landscapist and a painter of bamboo who was perhaps more famous for the latter, although his painting of pines is considered a classic. Wang Meng (1310-1385) and Huang Kung-wang (1269-1354), the first noted for his archaizing tendencies and the second for paintings which resembled "essays in constructional design", are considered as especially important in setting the trends for the future development of scholars' painting. Probably the most interesting, however, of all the Yüan artists was Ni Tsan (1301-1374). First a wealthy collector and aesthete, he later rid himself of most of his property and became a wanderer around the country; he is regarded as the classical type of an amateur painter who worked solely for his pleasure and disposed of his pictures as his fancy moved him. In his paintings Ni Tsan advanced the tendency inherent in Chinese painting towards simplicity to probably its ultimate possible limits. His quite unmistakable style has been called shadowy and it is said of him that he treasured ink like gold for so sparing was he in its use. His influence on future painters was profound but few could ever hope to equal his mastery.

Further significant work was done in the field of bamboo painting where Li K'an (1245-1324) followed in the footsteps of the great Northern Sung master, Wen T'ung (d. 1079), the most significant founder of this form of art. Other painters such as Wang Chen-p'eng (*fl.* 1310-1330) or Ch'en Lin (*fl.* 1280-1310) also adhered to patterns from previous periods in their art. Among the subjects which were developed during the Yüan period the most important perhaps was the depicting of plum blossoms which was to become a great favourite in the future.

Some authorities consider the Yüan era as the last great age of Chinese painting during which this art was still creative, capable of producing new ideas and showing true inspiration. This is undoubtedly partially so, in the sense that the influence of past traditions during the Ming and Ch'ing periods became definitely too restrictive on the artist, but simultaneously, as will be seen later, the list of talented painters was by no means closed with the end of the 14th century.

CHAPTER 21

Ming Restoration

I. The Establishment of the Ming Dynasty

The Chinese Empire, which was now restored as a result of the vast peasant uprisings, was greater in area than any of its immediate predecessors; it included new territory in the south-west (Yunnan and Kweichow) which had been conquered by the Mongols, as well as territory in the north-east, Liaotung. In contrast, however, to the Han and the T'ang there was no extension of the empire to Central Asia; perhaps because these territories had ceased to be as important as they had been formerly for the development of Chinese foreign trade.

The rebirth of Chinese state power as effected by the Ming signified a return to Chinese ways, but not so much to those of the Sung as of the T'ang, which was regarded as a much more fitting symbol of Chinese greatness. As a whole, the Ming era was one of reversion to Chinese sources, of restoring Chinese culture, with perhaps even some overtones of nationalism as a reaction to Mongol rule. This going back to the past was, however, by no means completely devoid of a number of new and interesting elements, although there was undoubtedly less inventiveness, in all respects, in this period than there had been in some of the earlier eras.

The founder of the Ming dynasty, Chu Yüan-chang, remained on the throne for thirty years after the establishment of the dynasty (died in 1398) and left a strong personal impression on the formation of the Ming state. He was a man of undoubted ability and intelligence, a frugal and hard-working ruler, but as time went on he developed more and more into a despotic autocrat.* He became suspicious of his surroundings to the point of paranoia and his reign witnessed a number of alleged plots which were put down with unusual cruelty. The large number of victims included Hung-wu's closest former followers to whose aid he owed his throne. The Emperor had men executed even on the suspicion of making puns regarding his person and he also instituted the custom of beatings to be inflicted on high officials as a form of punishment for purported misdemeanours.

In his domestic policies Hung-wu followed the traditional pattern of a new dynasty in easing social tensions and improving the conditions of the economy by paying attention to the needs of the peasants. In his case his own origin may have contributed to this. A considerable resettlement of peasants was undertaken which was connected with the special efforts to bring fallow land under cultivation. A great amount of work was also done in improving the irrigation system which had been neglected

---

*He is usually referred to as Hung-wu—this is the reign title and henceforth it became customary to refer to the Chinese emperors by the title of their reign and not by either their posthumous or personal name. Strictly speaking, one should say "the Hung-wu emperor", but this is already too pedantic.

Map 16. The Ming Empire, ca. 1600

during the Mongol rule; thus over 40,000 projects were completed by 1395. The efforts of the government were crowned by success in that a considerable increase in agricultural production did result, as well as an increase in population during the first decades of Ming rule. An improvement also took place in the position of the artisans who already at the beginning of the Ming dynasty were freed from the restrictions of the Yüan period and this process was to continue later on—their compulsory work for the government being replaced by taxation at the beginning of the 16th century. Towards the merchants, however, the Ming dynasty followed from the beginning the traditional policy of restriction and discrimination.

Hung-wu continued to maintain his capital in Nanking, the true centre of his power. He expanded the city greatly and its walls which were built in his time were 20 miles in length, the largest in the world. This was characteristic of the Ming, as their place in Chinese history is perhaps primarily that of builders on an immense scale—of towns, fortifications and walls; of bridges, temples and shrines. In fact, most of the traditional Chinese architecture which survives today is of Ming origin.

It is during Hung-wu's reign that the basic shape of the system of the Ming government was established. Its administration followed largely the pattern of the T'ang with six ministries (officials, revenue, rites, war, justice, works) in charge of most of the current affairs. The administrative division of the country was almost identical with that to be continued throughout the Ch'ing period and into the 20th century. The Ming empire was divided into fifteen provinces which all correspond to the present ones with the exception that Hunan and Hupei were combined into one—Nanking—while Hopei was called the metropolitan province (Ching-shih to be called Chinli, under the Ch'ing) and was larger in area. At the bottom of the ladder of the administrative structure were the districts—*hsien*—around 1170, and the rule that the magistrate must originate from another area was introduced in Ming times. Three elements were present in the administration—a separate civil and military organization as well as the supervisory—the censorate. The specific trait of the Ming monarchy was a still greater centralization of all political and military power in the hands of the Emperor. Thus, the heads of the ministries were all directly responsible to the Emperor and the previously existing office of Chancellor was abolished by Hung-wu in 1380 after the alleged plot of the Chancellor Hu Wei-yung. There is no doubt that the Mongol example of despotic rule influenced the character of the Ming monarchy; herein is to be found one more negative aspect of their domination in China—a heritage which they left behind after they themselves had been swept out of the country. In this respect the Chinese experience is by no means unique.

To assure the stability of his regime Hung-wu hastened to proscribe the existence of the secret societies of which, as previously mentioned, he had more than likely himself been a member. There was, however, one policy which went against the general tendency of creating a strong, absolutist government. As he grew older and still more distrustful of his officials, Hung-wu began to rely solely on the members of his own family and to create feudal appanages with the title of *wang* for his sons and grandsons. While this policy did not weaken the power of the central government to the degree which it had during the Han, it was probably partially responsible for the struggle for power which ensued after Hung-wu's death.

Following an attempt, for a period of time, to recruit officials through the recommendation system, Hung-wu restored in 1382 the examination system, which was to remain in force until the fall of the Empire in the 20th century. In Ming times the preparation for the taking of examinations, which were conducted on the same three-level basis as during the Sung, became a more and more costly affair. Thus, to prepare for the highest degree—*chin shih*—the cost was estimated at 600 ounces of silver. Hence even more than earlier the possibility of taking and passing the examinations and the subsequent entrance into the bureaucracy was restricted, in effect, only to the rich. In this period the subject matter of the examinations was even more completely limited to the Confucian Classics and the interpretation of them by Chu Hsi was regarded as the only acceptable and orthodox one. All this made in the long run for intellectual inflexibility and the examination system became, in fact, a handicap and a straitjacket for the development of any creative and independent thought. The prescribed form of the literary essay (the so-called eight-legged, introduced in 1487) also stifled all inventiveness.

In foreign policy the primary problem during Hung-wu's reign remained that of the Mongols. During the first years of his rule the final expulsion of the Mongol garrisons from all parts of China occurred and was completed by 1382. This was followed by expeditions into Mongolia itself, with the aim of smashing their forces permanently. Here, however, the success of the Chinese was only partial, as the Mongols, once they had returned to their native homeland, were never really beaten completely. The campaigns against the Mongols called for the stationing of large armies in North China and led also to the policy of establishing military colonies in this area. Such colonies were set up also in the South (Yunnan) and this led in turn to the partial sinification of regions where the population up to this time had been predominantly non-Chinese.

From the beginning of the Ming period a new menace arose to threaten China—that of Japanese piracy. This was derived partially from the unsettled political situation in Japan and it developed into a constant phenomenon which was to last for almost two centuries. In the years 1369-1372 three missions were sent by Hung-wu to the Japanese court in an attempt to bring about a cessation of the raids. These efforts were unsuccessful, among others, because the Japanese were still confident, after their great victory over the Mongols, that their position was impregnable. Thus the Ming government was forced to expand considerably the defence system of the south-east coastal provinces (Fukien, Chekiang) and this resulted in some success in curbing the effects of the raids. Piracy notwithstanding, trade relations between China and Japan developed very considerably in the 15th and 16th centuries. At least eleven large Japanese missions came over to China during the years 1433-1549, primarily for trade purposes. In the Chinese government there were considerable differences regarding policies to be followed in respect to the threat of Japanese piracy. This was primarily due to the fact that the great landlord families from areas further away from the coast were much less interested in the problem, as well as in the trade with Japan, and were thus opposed to defensive measures, proposing instead a complete cessation of relations with the Island Kingdom.

The restored Chinese monarchy once more regarded itself as the Middle Kingdom—the only true centre of civilization in the world. This basic assumption affected the relations of China with all its neighbouring states, as well as its entire foreign policy. Thus, relations could be conceived of only as those between a superior and inferior—suzerain and vassal, even if suzerainty was often only of a very formal and superficial character. This formed the basis of the tribute system which was characteristic of Ming foreign relations; this system, however, was often, in effect, only an outward form for very considerable foreign trade. In many cases foreign merchants, especially those from Central Asia, presented themselves as the bearers of fictitious tribute from imaginary states solely for the purpose of conducting trade.

After the death of Hung-wu the plans which he had laid for the succession went astray. His 16-year-old grandson Hui-ti (1399-1402) ascended the throne but he was soon engaged in a bitter conflict with his own uncles. The most powerful of these, the Prince of Yen, who was in control of the armies of North China, quickly challenged his nephew's right to the throne. A bitter and devastating civil war ensued, which ravaged much of North and Central China, and culminated in 1402 by the taking of Nanking by the Yen forces. The young Emperor vanished during the burning of his palace. He was presumed to have died, although some sources maintain that at the moment when the enemy troops entered the capital he was given by a faithful official a box which had supposedly been left for him by Hung-wu in the case of such an emergency. It contained a monk's robe, diploma and scissors. Cutting off his hair and disguised as a Buddhist monk he escaped from the city with a group of his most faithful followers to spend many years wandering throughout the country from monastery to monastery. In 1440, his identity was supposedly discovered, as a result of a poem he had written, and he was brought back to the capital where he peacefully lived out the last year of his life.

Whatever the real fate of Hui-ti was, his uncle proclaimed himself Emperor—he is known as Yung-lo from his reign title (1403-1424)—and inaugurated his rule by a vast massacre, together with their families, of all the many loyal ministers and followers of his predecessor. Yung-lo is famed as the second and last "strong ruler" of the Ming dynasty and it was during his reign that Ming absolutism took on its ultimate shape with an even greater degree of resemblance to the Yüan type of rule and with an imitation of the Mongols' unrestrained luxury and "magnificence". Yung-lo is perhaps best known for his decision (1416) to move the capital from Nanking to Peking (1421) and to rebuild the latter into a great, monumental capital. The basic outlines of the Peking of 1949 were still very much those as created in his time. When one views the Imperial City—for example, from the top of Prospect Hill which is just to the north of it —one cannot refrain from being impressed by the great vista and the perfect symmetry of the series of palaces and dwellings which follow each other on the North-South axis, with their yellow-gold tiles shimmering in the sun. While admiring the view, however, the thought must arise of the immense costs which were involved, with materials brought in from thousands of miles away, and of the labour of the countless tens of thousands of peasants impressed to create this magnificence for the sole use of their despotic masters.

The removal of the capital to Peking has been considered by some authors (Fitz-Gerald, for example) as fatal in its consequences for the future of the Ming dynasty inasmuch as it involved the state to a much greater degree in the conflict with the northern nomads and thus led to its ultimate fall. This seems to be a rather superficial view, since the causes for the decay and collapse of the dynasty lay in reasons which were much more basic, as will be seen later, than simply the location of the capital. What this transfer did involve was the economic problem of feeding the new capital i.e., the necessity of transporting food from the south. At this period this was rendered more difficult inasmuch as sea transport was imperilled by Japanese and Chinese pirates. As a result much work was done in repairing and extending the Grand Canal so as to serve as the main route for grain transport.

Yung-lo did, in fact, use his new capital as a base for campaigns against the Mongols. After their expulsion from China the Mongols had divided into two main groupings, Eastern and Western, the Eastern Mongols employing for a time the name of Tatars and the Western being called Oirats. Thus the unity which had made them such a dangerous power in the 13th century was now a thing of the past. The Chinese availed themselves of this split in their traditional fashion, playing off both sides against each other. In spite of the division, however, the Mongols still constituted a threat to North China and Yung-lo himself led five expeditions against them, all on a considerable scale, dying during the last one (1410, 1414, 1422, 1423, 1424). As a whole, success was obtained, although only in a sense that the danger of a possible reconquest of China was eliminated—for the Mongols had never quite given up the idea of restoring their lost fortunes—but the Mongol problem remained to plague the Ming rulers during this as well as the following century. The Mongol raids were a constant phenomenon, but they were also accompanied by yearly trade missions which did considerable business in exchanging horses and furs for Chinese products, especially tea. There remained also a problem for Chinese historians—a rather distasteful question and one quite difficult to explain—why could not the nomads, so much weaker numerically, be mastered by the power of the great Chinese Empire, even in the strongest, first period of a restored Chinese dynasty?

During Yung-lo's reign the Chinese attempted once more the conquest of Vietnam and gained some successes in their aggression which proved, however, to be temporary. By 1431 the Ming had to resign from exercising direct rule over Vietnam, while the Vietnamese agreed to recognize Chinese suzerainty.

Undoubtedly the most interesting phenomenon of the Yung-lo period was the unprecedented maritime activity of the Chinese. Between the years 1405 and 1433 China sent out seven great maritime expeditions which covered not only the area already well known to Chinese sailors, the Malay Archipelago, but also crossed the Indian Ocean to reach India, Ceylon and to travel still further to the west, to the Persian Gulf, Aden and the east coast of Africa. These expeditions constitute a fascinating puzzle inasmuch as the basic motives for sending them or for their sudden complete cessation are quite clear. All of them were under the command of Cheng Ho, a Moslem eunuch; an account of the travels is still extant.

During the first trip sixty-three treasure ships took part, many of considerable size; the large ones were 440 feet in length and 180 feet wide, the medium ones 370 feet long and 150 feet wide. A large number of smaller vessels were also included. A total of 27,876 men set sail on this expedition, including the seamen, soldiers, merchants and so forth. The following motives for organizing this enterprise seem to be the most likely: one aim was to seek allies against the new danger of Mongol aggression as this was the period of the great conquests of Tamerlane, who, in fact, readied a vast force of over 200,000 men to attack China in December 1404 but died shortly after starting on his campaign. Another purpose was the desire to demonstrate the power of the new government in China and gain appropriate prestige. Finally, the wish to expand still further Chinese trade with other parts of Asia also played a role. In this era there were already sizeable Chinese communities in some parts of South-east Asia, which were to become still more important in the future. These were composed mostly of merchants and thus constituted a good base for the expansion of commercial relations between China and the countries in which they had settled (Malaya, Sumatra, Java and the Philippines).

The maritime expeditions resulted in a considerable increase of Chinese geographical knowledge and also did bring about a growth of trade and the enhancement of prestige. As a side product, numerous curiosities were brought back such as ostriches, zebras and giraffes. More important is the fact that these expeditions demonstrated the very high contemporary level of Chinese navigation and shipbuilding. All this effort, however, was basically wasted as after 1433 the Ming government suddenly ceased practically all activity in this field and no further expeditions were organized. The main reason, probably, was that the economic development of China herself was not on a level which could sustain sufficient interest in the further expansion of foreign trade. The expeditions were quite costly and were criticized for this, especially by those officials who opposed the projects, particularly because they were headed by their rivals, the eunuchs. The officials, coming as always from great gentry families, were not interested themselves in the expansion of trade. The danger of Tamerlane's invasion had disappeared, while the Japanese pirates remained a constant menace to the safety of the great fleet. Thus, in spite of this very promising start, China failed to develop into a major sea power. The consequences of this were far-reaching indeed and even ultimately fatal as in the final analysis it meant ceding the seas to the rising power of the Europeans. The results of this for China later on were the worst possible.

II. The Further Development of Ming Rule

While during the first half-century Ming rule had considerable achievements to its credit in restoring Chinese government, a slow but steady process of decay of the feudal absolutist system had started even during this period. One of the main characteristic traits of this process was the increase in the struggle for power at the top level of the government between various cliques of office-holders. In this the rise of the eunuchs was perhaps most important. In spite of the warnings of Hung-wu himself that the eunuchs should never be permitted to hold any political positions whatsoever and should be restricted to their functions in the imperial harem, they had begun already in the Yung-lo period to become a significant political factor. One of the main reasons for this development is that the Emperor saw in them a most useful foil against the cliques of officials and regarded them as completely reliable servants of the throne. From servants the eunuchs, in time, became the masters of both the emperors and the empire. Already in 1420 a special palace school for the education of eunuchs was established and henceforth eunuchs acquired the necessary capabilities to engage in government affairs. Some authors maintain, although this seems doubtful, that the eunuchs usually came from and were connected with small gentry families who were rivals to the great gentry families which provided the majority of high officials. Whatever their origin and connections—and it seems more probable that they were mostly of plebeian origin—the eunuchs proved to be an unmitigated disaster for the Ming dynasty. They utilized their advantageous situation as being the closest to the seat of power to become the main controlling force of the government. Their basic aim was power and wealth and by often gaining control of the emperors, even changing them if necessary, they ruled the country with complete despotism for their own benefit. Totally corrupt, they utilized this control for selling offices to the highest bidder and exacting simultaneously continuous contributions from the officials. At the same time they carried out the functions of a secret police, keeping confidential files on all the important officials which were accessible, in theory, only to the emperor. Their number increased steadily; while in the middle of the Ming they were estimated at 10,000, there were supposedly around 100,000 of them towards the end of the Ming dynasty. They had also achieved almost complete control of a large number of the key central government departments, not excluding the armed forces.

One of the earliest examples of the great power of the eunuchs was the case of Wang Chen. He had become the main personality in the government during the reign of Ying-tsung (1436-1449, 1457-1464) and his egomania and ineptitude were responsible for great disasters. The Mongols were again on the warpath under the able leadership of Esen, chief of the Oirats, and proceeded to invade North China on a large scale. Wang Chen led the army together with the young Emperor against the Mongol invaders and his utter incapacity as a general resulted in the surrounding, in 1449, of the entire Chinese army 30 miles north-west of Peking, where it was then cut to pieces by the Mongols. Wang Chen himself perished and the Emperor was taken prisoner. This battle marked, in fact, the end of Ming military superiority *vis-à-vis* the Mongols. The Emperor's brother, Ching-ti, took the throne and the Mongols were prevented from succeeding in capturing Peking only by a stout defence well organized by General Yü Chien. As a result the Mongols gave back the Emperor to the Chinese in 1450. They were still not strong enough to make proper use of their victories. The returned Emperor lived quietly in retirement in Peking but was later restored to the throne by a coup in 1457. His first deed was to kill off the supporters of his brother, including Yü Chien.

The second half of the 15th century witnessed the further growth in the struggle of cliques and the rise to power of the eunuchs. It is in these years that one of the greediest and mightiest of them all, Liu Chin, reached the pinnacle of influence. It should be remembered that Chinese eunuchs were as active in favouring the interests of their families and relatives as any other Chinese officials, and that they also were able to adopt sons. Their nepotism was perhaps more obvious but by no means unique. When Liu Chin fell from office in 1510 the fortune he had amassed was estimated at over 251 million ounces of silver, not counting an immense quantity of jewellery, art works and so on. The vast scale of corruption and extortion of the eunuchs became in time one of the major factors in bringing about the downfall of the Ming dynasty. The uneventful political history of 16th-century China, especially the long reign of Chia-ching (1521-1566), showed the slowly growing symptoms of an inner crisis with the first peasant revolts which were to be a harbinger of the future.

III. Economic and Social Background

While the political history of the Ming period presents, on the whole, a rather dreary and dismal aspect this should not lead one to ignore the quite significant development of the country which progressed in many fields in spite of the political situation. This is particularly true of the further growth of the economy. Some authors go even so far as to maintain that the Ming era saw an agricultural revolution in the Chinese countryside.

This was due to the use of new irrigation methods and to the further improvement of rice thanks to a new strain brought in from South Vietnam (Champa) which made the achieving of two rice harvests a year possible. New crops such as Indian corn, the sweet potato and peanuts were also introduced. Crop rotation was now also employed on a larger scale, fertilizers and composts used—all this resulted in a considerable increase of agricultural production. The population also grew in size, reaching a figure of around 100 million or more towards the end of the Ming period. All of this, however, was of little benefit to the majority of the rural population, inasmuch as one of the main characteristics of the Ming period was a still further concentration of land ownership, and thus the position of the peasants not only did not improve but deteriorated still further.

The main centre of economic development, to an even greater degree than earlier, was the Yangtse Valley. A marked advance of urbanization took place in this area— Nanking was a great city with a population of over one million (Peking itself was smaller with around 660,000) and it was only the largest among other important cities. This growth of the cities and towns was, primarily, connected with the development of both industry and trade. Thus, Soochow now became the main centre of the silk textile industry and Sungkiang the prime producer of cotton cloth—cotton as a crop having increased markedly during the Ming period. The greatest growth, perhaps, was that of Ching-te-chen (Kiangsi), the large porcelain manufacturing centre where over 3,000 kilns, both state and privately owned, were in operation. Vast quantities of porcelain were exported, but the majority produced were articles for everyday use. A number of cities and ports on the south-east coast also increased in size and importance.

Even to a greater degree than during the Sung period the industrial development mentioned above and the growth of commerce connected with it, both domestic and foreign, gave rise to the situation in which elements which could lead to a path of capitalist development were already present in China. They remained, however, only in this embryonic stage without being able to make any significant advance. While the previously mentioned factors—the policy of the absolutist monarchy and the rule of the great landlord families—still constituted the principal handicaps, it should also be borne in mind that in most of the country the natural economy of the villages, combining self-sufficient agriculture and handicrafts, was still predominant and that the development of certain more advanced areas in China was probably not significant enough to have a basic influence on this vast country as a whole.

The government administration as established by the first Ming ruler, while it was quite elaborate and minutely detailed, did not imply as great a bureaucratic machine as it might appear. The reason for this lay in the fact that the government was assisted in the running of the country by the gentry, which itself undertook many of the functions of local government. Even more clearly than in earlier periods, the landlord families, always of considerable size, from whom the great majority of officials were drawn, became the complete masters and rulers of the countryside and of the peasants, taking all the possible political and economic advantages evolving from this situation. They actively aided the representatives of the central government, especially the magistrate on the *hsien* level, supervised public works, controlled education and organized the local militia. They saw to it particularly that most of the burdens
government, both taxes and labour, would be shunted off onto the

reaching dominance of the landed gentry in the Ming epoch that led to the great and rapid sharpening of the social crisis in the Chinese countryside.

While in the early Ming period taxes of every sort and kind proliferated, an attempt was made in the 16th century to simplify the system for the double purpose of obtaining more revenue and facilitating collection. This was the so-called "single-whip" (a pun on the identically sounding real name, "combined into one") system which was put into effect gradually throughout the whole country. The tax was now collected in silver which was also easier to transport. The new form of taxation did not, however, improve the financial position of the government for long, as the rich were up to their usual swindling, falsifying of land registers, etc., and again shifted the burden onto the peasants, for whom the tax thus really became a whip. The use of silver for tax purposes reflected also its much greater use as currency which was the result of general economic development. In this era increasing amounts of silver were coming into China, largely from Latin America, and this led later on to the use of the Spanish Carolus peso (later the famous Mexican dollar) as a common form of currency.

IV. The Ming Empire and the World

In the 16th century China continued to be plagued by troubles from two of its neighbours—the Mongols and the Japanese. The Mongols continued their inveterate habits of combining trade with the areas south of the Great Wall with plundering raids. Whenever a stronger leader appeared who would prove able to unite a number of the tribes, the danger to China automatically increased. Thus in 1550 Mongol cavalry was once more raiding right up to the walls of Peking itself. The Ming rebuilt the Great Wall extensively, but just as earlier it could constitute only a handicap and not a real obstacle to the marauders.

The menace of Japanese piracy was perhaps even greater. The attacks of the Japanese became especially intensive from the middle decades of the 16th century on, when the Japanese fleets not only raided the coast of Fukien and Chekiang but also sailed up the Yangtse to loot and burn the towns. Piracy was, in fact, a well-organized enterprise in which the Japanese nobles invested and participated. But what is characteristic of this period was the collaboration of the Chinese in this "profession". According to one Chinese source as much as 90 per cent of the pirates were really Chinese who were preying on their own land. The Ming government at first attempted to deal with the problem by prohibiting all trade with Japan but this proved quite ineffective. Ultimately they switched to a policy of organizing strong forces in the coastal provinces; this proved finally successful and by 1565 the threat of Japanese raids was radically reduced.

The struggle against the Mongols and the Japanese—the two "unseizable" enemies—was the cause of vast expense and a wastage of resources for the Ming government and it undoubtedly constituted one of the major factors in weakening the position of the dynasty, although the main roots of its decay lay, as will be seen, in domestic problems.

The most significant factor, however, of the 16th century was the coming of the Europeans to China. While China under the Ming was by no means as static a country as it is sometimes represented, its rate of change and development was much slower than

Fig. 40.   Kao K'o-kung, "Landscape after Rain", Yüan. (Cohn, W., *op. cit.*, pl. 139.)

Fig. 41.   Wu Chen, "Landscape with Two Pines", Yüan. (Cohn, W., *op. cit.*, pl. 151.)

Fig. 46.   Wen Cheng-ming, "The Chen Shang Workshop", Ming. (*Hua-yüan t'o-ying*. Shanghai, 1955, vol. II, pl. 12.)

Fig. 47.   Blue and white porcelain, Chia-ching period (1522–1567), Ming. (Author's collection.)

Fig. 48.   T'ang Yin, "A Carousal in the Grove", Ming. (Author's collection.)

Fig. 49.   Gate-tower, Ming tombs, Peking. (Author's photo.)

FIG. 50.   Ch'iu Ying, "The Painter at Work", Ming. (Author's collection.)

that of Europe in the same period. While at the beginning of the Ming era China was still ahead of Europe in most fields, the picture was to change considerably by the end of the Ming period. It is against this background that the arrival of the Europeans should be considered, with all its significant portents for the future of China and its relations with the world.

Up to the arrival of the Europeans the Chinese policy towards the foreign merchants, as exemplified by the treatment of the Arabs and the Persians, had been, on the whole, liberal, and large prosperous foreign trading communities had existed for centuries. All this was now due to change radically as a result of the action of the Portuguese and other Europeans who followed in their tracks. The Europeans came to China in a double capacity of pirates and merchants, the fine line between these two professions being very difficult to draw in the 16th century. Their violent and arrogant behaviour, and the plunders and massacres which they committed, caused them to be regarded by the Chinese as enemies who were as dangerous as the Japanese, thus, as foreign devils. The Portuguese especially, although the other Europeans were not any different, acted on the assumption that, in FitzGerald's words, "Because a man had a peculiar religion he was at liberty to plunder and massacre all those who held a different faith." Their deeds in China demonstrated that they adhered to this idea fully.

It was the Portuguese who were the first to arrive; a ship commanded by Rafael Perestrello reached Canton in 1516 after the first direct trip made from Europe to China. He was well received but the situation changed when in the next year four Portuguese ships under the command of Fernão de Andrade arrived at Canton. The Portuguese wanted to send an embassy to the Chinese court and Thomé Pirès was dispatched to Peking. The Chinese were, however, already aware of the Portuguese conquest of Malacca and of their depredations there; this, as well as the misbehaviour of the Portuguese in Canton, caused the mission to be driven away, while Pirès was imprisoned. A further attempt was made by the Portuguese in 1522 by Affonso de Mello Coutinho which also suffered defeat. In spite of these initial setbacks the Portuguese succeeded, probably by bribing local officials, in establishing themselves in Ningpo (Chekiang) and in Ch'üanchou (Fukien), where considerable trade with the Chinese was developed. In both cases, however, the unspeakably brutal behaviour of the Portuguese caused a revulsion of Chinese feeling against the newcomers. In 1545 the Portuguese colony in Ningpo was completely wiped out after three years of existence and later, in 1549, the same fate met the settlement in Ch'üanchou. Somewhat later, the Portuguese did succeed finally in gaining, in 1557, a permanent foothold near Canton by establishing themselves in Macao. The Chinese did not drive them out of this colony but later cut off the little peninsula by a special wall. Macao developed into a prosperous settlement and the centre for Portuguese trade not only with China but with all of East Asia.

The behaviour of other Europeans followed much the same pattern as that of the Portuguese. Their great competitors, the Dutch, also raided the shores of China and then established themselves temporarily on Taiwan in 1624, where they remained until they were expelled from the island by Koxinga in 1661 (see p. 222). The Spaniards after their conquest of the Philippines perpetrated two massacres on a large scale of the Chinese merchants who were resident there (1603, 1639). The English came for the first time in 1637 when three ships under the command of John Weddell landed at Canton. Their stay here was also marked by violence and combat with the Chinese and ended in their withdrawal. The Chinese attitude towards relations with the Europeans was shaped largely by these experiences of the 16th and early 17th centuries and, as a consequence, this led to the adoption of the policy of restricting trade and contact with them to a minimum (in fact, later only to Canton) and thus making the further entry of European merchants into China practically impossible.

It was not only, however, the European pirate-merchants who were reaching the shores of China in this period. East Asia became also the field for considerable, energetic missionary action, conducted primarily by the Roman Catholics. Among the Catholic missionaries it was undoubtedly the Jesuits who were the most prominent and successful. As regards China they conceived the idea, at a relatively early stage of their activity, that the best policy would be not so much to proselytize among the masses of the people, but to concentrate their efforts on the ruling class, and thus achieve the conversion of the entire country by this method of working from above.

The most eminent and best known of the Jesuit missionaries was the Italian, Matteo Ricci (1552-1610). He came to China in 1583 and joined the Jesuit mission which had been established in Macao; here he devoted considerable time to the study of Chinese which, as a brilliant linguist, he mastered completely. Ultimately, he succeeded in reaching Peking in 1601, received permission to remain and stayed there until his death in 1610. Ricci exemplified exceedingly well the Jesuit policy of compromise with the Chinese way of life as far as possible. He adopted, for example, the Chinese robes of a scholar. Well trained in European science, he succeeded in impressing the Emperor and a number of courtiers by his knowledge of astronomy, mathematics and geography. He presented the Emperor with a map of the world which he had drawn. Ricci had also some success in converting a number of high officials and in his proselytizing he laid the groundwork for the Jesuit policy of a "broad" approach to Chinese customs. Thus, the ancestors cult was not considered by them as pagan religious worship but as a civil observance which could be tolerated. The most prominent of his converts was Hsü Kuang-ch'i (1562-1633), a future minister and the author of a very valuable work on Chinese agriculture. He helped Ricci considerably in translating a number of works dealing with mathematics, hydraulics, astronomy and geography and was thus the first Chinese to translate from European languages. The Jesuits also introduced into China the methods for manufacturing modern European artillery in which the Ming were very much interested in view of the growing struggle against the Manchus. On his deathbed Ricci proclaimed to his colleagues: "I leave before you an open door." This prophecy, however, did not prove to be true, although the fall of the Ming affected the fate of the Jesuit mission only marginally. As could be expected, they continued their activity under the new rulers of China as well.

CHAPTER 22

Late Ming

I. The Crisis of Ming Rule

All the elements which testified to the decay of the Ming government manifested themselves in a still more acute form during the last two decades of the 16th and the first two decades of the 17th century. This period corresponds to the reign of Wan-li (1573-1620), a completely ineffectual ruler. While at the beginning of his reign some attempts were made at reform, these were soon abandoned and the situation both at the court and in the country became steadily more hopeless. Unlimited corruption, a complete disregard of the existing conditions, the violent struggle for power between cliques—all increased in intensity.

The domestic situation of the Ming dynasty was still further complicated by events which occurred close to the Chinese borders. In 1592 the Japanese invasion of Korea was launched. This was the work of Toyotomi Hideyoshi, the military dictator and *de facto* ruler of Japan who had shortly before completed the unification of Japan. His grandiose plans now called for a conquest of the world—and to him the world was China, Korea being only a gateway to the principal goal. These plans reflected, on the one hand, Hideyoshi's indisputable megalomania and, on the other hand, the fact that after the civil wars in Japan he had at his disposal a considerable and partly redundant army. The Japanese had tried to persuade the Koreans either to join them as allies or to offer free passage for Japanese troops; the Korean king refused this request and the grand invasion was launched in April 1592. A Japanese army of well over 160,000 landed in Pusan and was shortly able to take the capital, Seoul. The Korean government was weak, its generals ineffective and its armies, unused to warfare, could not offer strong resistance to the Japanese, especially as the latter employed firearms which were unknown to the Koreans. Only on the sea did the superior Korean navy manage to hold its own against the Japanese aggressors.

Shortly thereafter, the Japanese armies continued their attack and began to approach the Yalu River, the frontier between Korea and the Ming empire. The Korean king, who had fled earlier from his capital to the area bordering the Yalu, appealed unceasingly for help from his suzerain, the Chinese Emperor, but the Ming acted on this only when practically all of Korea had been occupied. The Chinese armies then slowly moved into Korea; the first units were badly defeated but after new, very sizeable reinforcements entered the country they succeeded, by the middle of 1593, through hard and long struggles, in forcing the Japanese to evacuate most of the country and to take refuge in Pusan at the southern tip of the peninsula. A vital factor in this success was the guerrilla warfare waged by the Korean peasants on a very large scale.

In 1597, however, after complicated negotiations with the Chinese had failed,

Hideyoshi resolved on recommencing his invasion and a second force of 100,000 men was dispatched. This army, with the remaining Japanese forces in Korea, made up a total of almost as large as the first invading force. Most of the Chinese forces had been withdrawn in the meantime and thus once more the Japanese were able to march up and capture Seoul. The Ming government was again compelled to send in its armies and succeeded in driving the Japanese down to the south. These efforts were facilitated by new victories of the Korean fleet against the Japanese which, as before, imperilled their line of communications with the home islands. Of considerable interest here was the use in these battles of the so-called "turtle ships" of the Korean navy, probably the first armoured naval vessels in world history.

The death of Hideyoshi in 1598 changed the situation radically and brought about the retreat of the remaining Japanese forces. The effects of this protracted and sanguinary war were very far-reaching. For Korea it was a disaster from which she never really recovered, inasmuch as the devastations and depredations of the Japanese soldiery were on a vast scale. For the Ming government the results were also extremely serious as the campaigns were quite costly and constituted a heavy drain on its already very shaky finances. The Chinese had also used their armed forces here at the expense of weakening later their position against the Manchus and thus facilitated the rise of the latter.

At the Ming court intrigues and plots rose to a new height. Wan-li's successor fell victim to the eunuchs; he was reputed to be poisoned by the renowned red pills administered to him by one of the top eunuchs. It would seem that he had been indiscreet enough to express his opinion that their power was excessive. During the reign of his half-witted son—whose only interest was in carpentry—the real power of the country was exercised by Wei Chung-hsien, perhaps one of the most notorious in the long line of influential eunuchs during the Ming era. The terror and corruption of his rule was more than even the usually quite subservient Chinese officials could endure. A large number of them grouped themselves in opposition to the existing conditions with the basic aim of eliminating eunuch rule and restoring Confucian principles of government. The group was known as the Tung-lin, from the name of an academy where they first met. Wei Chung-hsien and his minions met this challenge to his authority by a large-scale persecution in 1625-1626 of the Tung-lin members which ended with the execution of a considerable number of the most prominent officials. At the same time the eunuchs interfered, with fatal results, in the military campaigns which were waged in the North-east against the Manchus, among others, killing Hsiung T'ing-pi, one of the few able generals whom the Ming possessed at this time.

When the new Emperor came to the throne in 1627 (Ch'ung-cheng—1627-1644) Wei Chung-hsien fell from power and paid for his crimes. The situation had already gone too far, however, for the Emperor, in spite of his undoubted abilities, to be able to master it. The government was bankrupt and the revenue which came in was completely inadequate for the purpose of meeting current needs; these were greatly increased by the much higher military expenditures which resulted from the struggle against the Manchus. In 1639, they amounted to 20 million taels while the whole budget at the beginning of the Ming period had been only 2 million.

The main source of the crisis lay, however, in social problems—in the disaffection of the Chinese peasants with the ruinous oppression which was constantly increasing during the last period of Ming rule. This found its expression in one of the longest and largest peasant rebellions in Chinese history. We have already seen that peasant insurrections are by no means a rare phenomenon in Chinese annals; they constituted, in fact, under feudal conditions, the only possible and available form of ultimate protest against inhuman degradation and misery.

A terrible famine in North Shensi sparked off the great peasant rebellion which lasted until 1644 and became the primary cause of the downfall of the Ming dynasty. In scale it can probably be compared only to the Taiping movement of the 19th century and perhaps also to the struggle waged in the 20th century by the peasant armies led by the Chinese Communists. As was customary in the case of the Chinese peasant rebellion, the movement was largely spontaneous, deficient in organization and programme and more in the form of elemental protest. While the insurrection spread over large parts of North and Central China, its development was amazingly uneven. At one time great armies would advance in all directions only to be suddenly totally defeated and dispersed.

An attempt was made to coordinate the actions of the various insurgent armies by holding a meeting of their leaders, in 1635, for the purposes of establishing a common strategy. Shortly thereafter, however, the peasant armies again suffered a series of heavy defeats. It is with the rise of Li Tzu-ch'eng to the position of the most important leader of the peasant rebellion, which can be dated from 1640, that the movement assumed a new character and advanced to great victories. Li Tzu-ch'eng himself (born 1606) was a peasant from Shensi and had participated in the uprising from its very beginnings. The story of the last years of the great peasant rebellion is intertwined completely with the Manchu problem which must be dealt with in detail at this point.

II. The Rise of the Manchus

The Manchu tribes inhabited the central, north and north-east parts of Manchuria and belonged to the Tungus-speaking group of people. They were, in fact, closely related to, if not the direct descendants of, the Jurchen who had ruled North China as the Chin dynasty. In their Manchurian habitat the Jurchen were primarily hunters and fishermen but also practised some agriculture, which they learned from their Chinese neighbours. They were never full nomads like the Mongols, although they were also partially herdsmen and excellent horsemen and archers. Under the early Ming all of Manchuria was under Chinese sway and the Chinese ruled this area by the application of their usual divide and rule policy, setting the Jurchen tribes against each other, while considering all of them as vassals of the Chinese Empire.

One part of Manchuria, the Liaotung peninsula (which then formed a part of Shantung province) was predominantly Chinese in population and agriculture in the Chinese mode was the main form of the economy. Liaotung had, for that matter, been a part of the Chinese civilized area ever since the time of the Han, if not earlier. It possessed a crucial strategic importance as the control of it opened the way to North China. It therefore later became one of the main arenas of struggle between the Manchus and the Chinese.

The rise of the Manchus was closely bound up with the activity of Nurhachi (1559-1626), a member of the Aisin Gioro clan and the chief of one of the Jurchen tribes. He has been often compared to Chingghis Khan for his success in uniting the Jurchen tribes into a formidable force and state which was able to undertake the conquest of China. The process of this unification was a prolonged series of wars, negotiations and plots which covered a period of thirty years. In accomplishing this Nurhachi drew considerably on Chinese statecraft with which he was well acquainted. As one of the more prominent Jurchen tribal chiefs he had been in Peking, in 1590, as the head of a group of a hundred Jurchen chiefs bearing tribute. He knew the Chinese language and literature and had received in 1595 the high title of Dragon and Tiger General from the Chinese court. While striving to accomplish the unification of the Jurchen, always against Chinese opposition, plots and counter measures, he continued to trade on a large scale. The principal export of the Jurchen were horses and ginseng, the root so prized by the Chinese for its supposed regenerative qualities.

One of Nurhachi's most significant innovations, although it was partly based on the Chinese example, i.e., on the Ming organization of military commanderies in Manchuria, was the establishment of the Banner organization. This was primarily for military purposes but the Banners had also an administrative significance and the institution cut across previously existing tribal divisions. Militarily, the Banners were an extremely effective form of organization. The most important role in the Banner system was always played by Nurhachi's own tribe and especially by his own clan. At the outset four Banners were established and later the number was increased to eight. Each Banner was distinguished by a flag of a different colour; the original four Banners had the colours yellow, white, blue and red—the next four were yellow, white, blue, all bordered with red, and red bordered with white.

Some authors consider the adoption of the Banner system as the crucial point in the changeover from an early feudal tribal society to one organized on feudal-bureaucratic lines. This shift probably corresponded to the social transformations which were going on within Manchu society. It seems, however, that the later adoption, practically *in toto,* of the Chinese monarchical organization of the state, which took place before the conquest of China proper, was of even greater importance. As the Manchus grew stronger and the area of their rule expanded, the Banner system was enlarged by the creation of eight Mongol Banners (after the subjugation of most of Inner Mongolia) and of eight Chinese Banners (after the conquest of Liaotung). By 1644 there were 278 Manchu, 120 Mongol and 165 Chinese companies in the Banners; assuming 300 men a company, this meant that the total armed forces at the disposal of the Manchu rulers when the conquest of China commenced amounted to only around 169,000.

The organization of the state by the Manchus on Chinese lines in the areas under their rule was of utmost significance. This was connected with their conquest of Liaotung, which made them the masters of a very considerable Chinese population. It is estimated that there were 3 million Chinese in this area as against probably a total of only 300,000 Manchus. Already in 1616 Nurhachi declared the establishment of the Late Chin state, which was a direct reference to the ancestors of the Manchus of the 12th and 13th centuries and thus a renewal of their claims. The administration of this state was set up on the Chinese model with the help of numerous Chinese officials who were ready and willing to serve their new masters. This assistance was of crucial importance in the success of the Manchus. Thus, Fan Wen-ch'ang (1597-1666), who surrendered to the Manchus in 1618, was instrumental in establishing the central government. Later on, in 1644, he presented a memorandum to Dorgon urging him to seize the opportunity to conquer the Chinese Empire but to spare the common people and to avoid the previous destruction. With another Chinese collaborator, Ning Wan-wo (d. 1665) who had joined the Manchus in 1630, Fan Wen-ch'ang had already in 1632 drawn up a plan for his masters for the conquest of China.

In 1618, after having compiled the curious document known as the Seven Great Complaints, which was his declaration of war against the Ming, Nurhachi attacked the Chinese positions in Central Manchuria and captured the town of Fushun. This was followed by the first surrender of Chinese generals and officials to the Manchus on a large scale. It served as an important example for the future and revealed simultaneously the well-planned political strategy of the Manchus who aimed at attracting as many Chinese to their side as possible. In 1619 Nurhachi succeeded in defeating a vast Ming army, four times the size of his forces, which had been dispatched against him. This victory made possible the later conquest of Shenyang (Mukden) and Liaoyang in 1621. Shortly thereafter the Manchus began to attack the Chinese territory to the west of the Liao River.

Thus, the Manchus, in contrast to the Mongols, Jurchen and Khitan, were in the process of establishing a state organization on Chinese lines even before they had succeeded in conquering China itself. It is this formation of a strong frontier state which enabled them later on to accomplish this conquest and which was also one of the main factors in their success of becoming both the most important and the longest lasting of all the nomad conquerors of China. Their rule was to survive for over two and a half centuries although, in effect, they more than likely would have been overthrown, as we shall see later, by the Taiping revolution in the 1850s had it not been for the aid which the Western powers then gave them. It should be noted also that, just as in earlier circumstances, the Manchu invasion of China was made feasible by the inner weakness and decay of the Chinese Empire itself.

In spite of the total incompetence of the Ming court, the Manchus had a difficult time in their campaigns in Liaohsi, but the disintegration of the Ming government under the blows of the peasant rebellion ultimately facilitated their further advance. Nurhachi himself met with his first defeat in attempting to take the Ming fortress of Ningyüan and died shortly thereafter in 1626. He was succeeded by his eighth son, Abahai (1592-1643), an able general and political leader. It was he who prescribed in 1635 the use of the word Manchu (its etymological meaning is still unclear), instead of Jurchen, inasmuch as the later word had a connotation of Chinese suzerainty. It was also Abahai who declared, in 1636, the establishment of the Ch'ing ("Pure") dynasty in place of the Late Chin. This was a direct challenge to the Ming, implying a claim to the creation of a new dynasty entitled to rule all China. Abahai also strengthened his authority as Emperor at the expense of the principal members of the imperial clan.

Abahai's primary concern, however, was the launching of further military expeditions to increase the power and to extend the territory of the Manchu state. Two expeditions against Korea (1627, 1638) were successful in converting the vassal of the Ming into an obedient servant of the Ch'ing, while simultaneouly covering the left flank of the Manchus. Perhaps even more important was the penetration of Inner Mongolia and the subjection to Manchu rule of the Mongol tribes here, which actually culminated in a type of a Manchu-Mongol alliance with fatal effects for the Chinese. During the same time the entire Amur region was also brought under complete Manchu control. Their new sway over Inner Mongolia made it now much easier for the Manchus to launch a series of devastating raids into North China, right up to the walls of Peking itself (1629). These were conducted in the true northern nomad fashion, with plunder and massacres, as well as the taking away of tens of thousands of the Chinese population to serve as slaves to the Manchus. The victories of the Manchus in these years also brought about an increase in the surrender to them of a large number of Ming generals together with their troops; these were to play a very important role in the later campaigns of the Ch'ing. In the years 1636-1643 the Manchus crossed the Great Wall at will to conduct their depredations to the south of it. The direct entrance from the north-east was blocked, however, by the great strong fortress of Shanhaikuan on the coast where the Great Wall comes down to the sea. Abahai did not live to see the triumph of his people—he died in 1643, succeeded on the throne by his 6-year-old son Fu-lin, while his brother Dorgon (1621-1650), the fourteenth son of Nurhachi, became the principal regent.

III. The Fall of the Ming Dynasty

In 1640, after having been heavily defeated by government forces, Li Tzu-ch'eng retired to his native Shensi. Here, he regrouped his remaining forces and recommenced the campaign against the Ming but with a more elaborate social and political programme. He advanced the slogan of land equalization to attract peasant support while, at the same time, he called for the overthrow of the Ming dynasty. In these latter aspirations the influence of some of the gentry who had joined him can be seen. In the next year his armies, snowballing once more in size, marched into Honan where they succeeded in capturing Loyang. The Prince of Fu, one of the richest (possessing 2 million *mu* of land) and most hated of the Ming princes, was taken prisoner here and killed. While Li Tzu-ch'eng was active in North China, another peasant leader, with an unenviable reputation for extreme cruelty and countless massacres, Chang Hsien-chung (1606-1646), became master of most of Szechuan. There was no co-ordination between these two leaders inasmuch as they both saw each other as potential rivals for the setting up of a new dynasty in the event that the fall of the Ming would be accomplished.

By the beginning of 1644, Li Tzu-ch'eng's forces were strong enough for him to launch a vast campaign for the final overthrow of the Ming government. In January of that year he declared the establishment of the Shun dynasty and from his base in Shensi began to march to the north-east towards Peking. Most of the strongpoints on the way to the capital, including the principal city of Shansi, T'aiyüan, surrendered without a fight. On March 18 Li Tzu-ch'eng's troops entered the imperial capital where the defence was negligent, while the gates were opened by some of the eunuchs. Ch'ung-cheng, betrayed by most of his officials, ultimately refused to seek safety by flight to the south and on the next day hanged himself in a pavilion on Prospect Hill, situated a few hundred yards north of the imperial palace. Around 200 of his closest entourage and family followed his example and also committed suicide. Most of the top Ming officials were imprisoned by Li's men.

The Ming government had, in fact, come to an end in the capital but there were still numerous Ming armies in other parts of China. Of these the most important was the army stationed in Shanhaikuan for defence against the Manchus. This was commanded by Wu San-kuei (1612-1678), who came from a landlord family originating in Liaotung. He was thus well acquainted with the Manchu policy of attracting Chinese officials to their side and of leaving the interests of the Chinese landlords untouched. Very much depended on the nature of his decision, inasmuch as the Manchus at this moment were closely following the events in China, only too anxious to avail themselves of the opportunity created for them by the fall of Peking.

Negotiations between Li Tzu-ch'eng and Wu San-kuei ensued, in which Li sought to persuade Wu to join him in a common action against the Manchus. He failed in this, not due to the usual legend that Wu's favourite concubine had been captured by Li's forces, but due to the fact that Wu San-kuei, a man of inordinate ambitions, was himself anxious for the throne and unwilling to ally himself with an army of peasant rebels. Thus, ultimately, Li Tzu-ch'eng led an army of 200,000 men against Wu San-kuei, while the latter turned to the Manchu regent, Prince Dorgon, offering his services and requesting Manchu aid. As a sign of subservience to the Manchus he submitted to having his head partly shaved and to wearing a queue. In Chinese history Wu is usually regarded as the arch-symbol of the Chinese traitor but—as will be seen—he was only the most prominent one in this period.

When Li Tzu-ch'eng's army was engaged in a battle with the troops of Wu San-kuei, the Manchu cavalry, which had been watching the struggle from the sidelines waiting for its outcome, joined at the crucial moment to crush and defeat the peasant troops. Li fled with the remnants of his forces to Peking. Here, on April 29, he had himself enthroned as the Emperor of the Shun Dynasty and on the same day withdrew from the capital and headed for Shensi, where he hoped to establish himself. Shortly thereafter the Manchus entered the city and Dorgon proclaimed the young Manchu ruler Fu-lin as the Chinese emperor and heir to the Ming. Simultaneously, the Manchus presented themselves as the avengers of the fallen Ming emperor and announced their aim of suppressing the peasant rebellion. This appeal to the class prejudices of the Chinese gentry-officials was well calculated and produced the sought-for effects. The majority of the Chinese ruling class did, in fact, recognize the new Manchu rule, and Ming officials and generals surrendered to them *en masse*, "licking the boots of the new masters", as the Chinese modern historians express it. What is most important is that they joined the Manchus in the organization of armed forces to put down the remaining peasant armies. It is undoubtedly this action on the part of the Chinese landlord gentry that—seeing the great disproportion of forces between the Chinese and Manchus—made the Manchu take-over of power possible.

Thus, the Manchus became established as rulers of North China and a joint Manchu-Chinese army, under the command of Wu San-kuei, proceeded to Shensi to wage war against Li Tzu-ch'eng. In this Wu was successful and Li was finally forced to retreat from Shensi to Hupei where he met his death in April 1645 (some accounts maintain, however, that he escaped and became a Buddhist monk). The remaining forces of his army, which were still sizeable, either 300,000 or 500,000—probably far fewer—later joined up with Ming loyalists in Central China who were continuing the struggle against Manchu aggression. It took the Manchus, however, over twenty years to reduce the forces of the followers of the fallen dynasty. The great peasant rebellion had now been basically crushed thanks to the joint action of the northern nomad invaders and the Chinese landlords. The price paid for this "victory" was the imposition once more of foreign rule on China which, this time, was to last until 1912.

CHAPTER 23

Ming Culture

I. General

In its culture, just as in politics, the Ming was a conscious effort of turning back to the past, to Chinese sources, an attempt to revive native intellectual and artistic traditions. In this the Ming referred back to the T'ang but, as had been said by Waley, the result was a T'ang without verve and without grandeur. Nevertheless, the almost three centuries of the Ming dynasty cannot be dismissed out of hand, for its achievements in many fields of culture were considerable.

In the field of philosophy the Chu Hsi interpretation of the Classics, as well as his philosophical views, maintained their dominance until the end of the 15th century, having in the meantime been turned into a rigid and orthodox creed. It should be noted, however, that already in the times of the Southern Sung a second trend of thought was present within Neo-Confucianism which, in distinction from the views of Chu Hsi, held forth ideas which should be classified as subjective idealism. The main representative of this tendency was Lu Chiu-yüan (1139-1193), and it was largely on the basis of his thoughts that the most noted philosopher of the Ming period, Wang Yang-ming (1472-1529), advanced his own ideas. He evolved a quite highly developed and even more than usual speculative philosophy in which most attention was paid to the problems of the essence of human nature. Here, undoubtedly under the influence of Buddhist ideas, Wang Yang-ming stressed the importance of meditation and intuitive knowledge. His views became a considerable vogue and were widely spread throughout the country. Some authors maintain that Wang's philosophy, in fact, overshadowed the Chu Hsi orthodoxy throughout the rest of the Ming period. Its effects were later on (see p. 235) regarded to have been, on the whole, very negative, but its influence, especially in Japan, was considerable.

The Ming period, as one devoted to the rescuing of things from the past rather than to creating, was an age of encyclopaedias and monographic studies. Of these the most famous was the *Yung-lo ta-tien* encyclopaedia which was ordered by the Emperor in 1403 and finished in 1408. This was an immense work compiled by 2180 scholars and when finished consisted of 11,095 volumes in 22,877 chapters. It dealt with history, ethics, science, industry, art, geography and religion—in fact, with all human knowledge available in China at the beginning of the 15th century. In its compilation many ancient and rare works were incorporated *in toto*. It was too expensive to print and two additional copies were later made; but the encylopaedia met a tragic fate similar to that of so many other objects of Chinese culture. Two of the copies were lost in 1644, while the third, preserved in the Hanlin Academy in Peking, was destroyed, almost in its entirety, when the Academy burned down during the siege of the legations in 1900. Thus only 368 volumes are now known to be extant.

A number of other encyclopaedic works were also composed but perhaps the most interesting single work was the great herbal—*Materia Medica*—finished in 1578 by Li Shih-chen after twenty-six years of intensive work. In it the author also gave 8160 prescriptions. Important work was also done in the field of philological studies.

II. Literature

It is probably in the field of *belles-lettres* that the greatest of the achievements of the Ming period can be found. It has been said that while poetry was the glory of the T'ang, drama of the Yüan, the novel is the glory of the Ming. This new form of literature developed from the century-old material used by the story-tellers, and their librettos, as well as plays derived from their themes, provided the basic material of most of the novels. Primarily because the novels were written in the vernacular, though not only for this reason, the scholars scoffed at this form, considering it to be frivolous, licentious and subversive, while reading it on the sly. This is one reason why so little is known about the authors of even the most famous novels, for a number of them did their best to hide their authorship. Nevertheless, the novels acquired an immense popularity and the heroes of the best-loved novels were better known than the most illustrious figures of history to the Chinese, while most of their ideas regarding Chinese history were derived from the novels.

The novel had been regarded by many authors as the most vital development in Chinese literature of the last 600 years, but this fact was acknowledged in China only after the Cultural Revolution of the early 1920s, when the novel finally received the recognition which was its due. Lu Hsün himself contributed to this, being one of the earliest serious researchers of this subject. Perhaps the outstanding feature of the Ming novel is its high degree of realism and the considerable amount of social criticism it contains. In these works historical themes play a significant, great role and this is true of the two great novels with which we shall deal below.

The *Shui-hu chuan* (translated into English as "Water Margin" or "All Men are Brothers") is a great picaresque epic dealing with the fate of 108 heroes, rebels against contemporary society. They are led by Sung Chiang, a historical character of the Northern Sung period. The book is noted for the excellent characterization of all its individuals, for many vivid, dramatic scenes. It was actually a revolutionary book for, while dealing with the Sung, it was nothing but a thinly veiled criticism of Ming conditions, a form of literary protest. It was supposed to have been written by Shih Nai-an (*ca.* 1296-1370), of whom practically nothing is known, but different versions of it were composed down to the 17th century.

The *San-kuo chih yen-i* ("The Romance of the Three Kingdoms") is perhaps the best known of all Chinese works of literature. Its author was supposed to be Lo Kuan-chung (? 1330-1400). Here too the matter is complicated by the existence of various versions. It is a weighty work of 120 chapters and in dealing with the era of the Three Kingdoms it changed this vicious period of feudal strife almost into a romantic age, a dramatic and colourful pageant. In this work the characters are clearly divided into heroes and villains and thus Liu Pei is presented as loving the people and assisted by loyal friends,

Kuan Yü and Chang Fei. As has been well remarked, the compact of eternal loyalty which these friends took in the Peach Orchard was known to every Chinese. But undoubtedly the most interesting is the presentation of Chu-ko Liang, the great political strategist of the period. His immense intelligence, skill and cleverness are illustrated time and time again. Ts'ao Ts'ao is cast, appropriately enough, in the role of the main villain. It is difficult to overstress the immense and lasting influence of this work.

The *Hsi-yu chi* ("Pilgrimage to the West"; or "Monkey") is only partially historical inasmuch that, while it deals with the famous Buddhist pilgrim Hsüan-tsang, it is really based in early Buddhist legends regarding him and contains a great amount of the fantastic and the supernatural. It was written by Wu Ch'eng-en (*ca.* 1500-1582), a scholar and official who successfully hid his authorship during his lifetime. The true hero of this novel, however, is not the pilgrim but one of his voyage companions, the monkey, Sun Wu-kung. In his numerous, fantastic adventures the monkey is presented as actually an intensely human being and has become one of the most popular characters in Chinese literature. The book is written with great imagination and humour containing a mixture of folklore, allegory, religion and history, as well as much social criticism and sharp satire.

Quite different from the above three is the great, realistic novel *Chin P'ing Mei* (in English the work is usually referred to as "The Golden Lotus"). While it is partially connected by subject matter with the "Water Margin" (some of the same heroes appear in both), it is a story dealing with the life of a rich apothecary, an indubitable rake and profligate. It is perhaps the first work in which women are presented as completely real individuals and not stock figures. The book gives an excellent picture of Ming society, for while it pretends to take place in the Northern Sung period, there is little doubt that it deals with the contemporary scene. There have been innumerable suppositions as to who was its real author, but no definite conclusion has ever been reached. It was written probably somewhere at the end of the 16th century. Inasmuch as it contains some rather frankly described erotic scenes, it was subject often to official Chinese censorship which, it might be mentioned in passing, was in existence already from the period of the Northern Sung. Ironically, one of the great writers of that period, Ou-yang Hsiu, was responsible for drafting the regulations.

The above four novels are considered the greatest to be produced in the Ming period. But it was not only the novel in which Ming literature was noted; drama was further developed and perhaps the most famous play of the period was "The Peony Pavilion" by T'ang Hsien-tsu (*ca.* 1550-1617), which was regarded as an attack on the falseness of contemporary morality.

III. Painting

In painting there is, in fact, no clear break between the Yüan and the Ming periods. Generally speaking, the Ming era is one of great connoisseurship in which magnificent collections of paintings were formed, an era in which art criticism was highly developed. It is probably due to the Ming collectors that many of the scrolls of previous eras have been preserved for posterity. But in painting itself this was not an age noted for great creativeness, though the fashion in Europe earlier in the 20th century to scoff sarcastically at Ming painting and shrug it off as completely sterile and derivative was quite exaggerated and based on insufficient knowledge. Well over 1000 Ming painters are known to have been active during this era and the production was enormous. One author has characterized this art as showing growing baroque tendencies in its display of colour and ornamentation; while this is true one cannot forget that a number of great painters also existed, especially in the first century of Ming rule. On the other hand, the already-mentioned effect of many centuries of tradition did, undoubtedly, weigh heavily on their brushes.

It is customary to refer to two schools—the first of these was Che (named after the province of Chekiang) which reached its peak at the end of the 15th century. The most famous painter of this school was Tai Chin, active in the first half of the 15th century. In general, this school followed the style and traditions of the Southern Sung Academy. The second school, Wu (named after the ancient state which included Kiangsu), represented what was later referred to as the *wen jen hua*—the painting of the scholars. For them this art, while treated seriously, was performed not on a professional but on an amateur basis, as a free expression of an urge to create. The painters of this school also, in fact, based themselves primarily on the styles of the old masters. The reputed founder of this trend was Shen Chou (1427-1509). He painted in a great variety of styles and was a prolific artist, with many of his works surviving to the present. By some authorities he has been considered the leading painter of the Ming period. A younger associate of his, Wen Cheng-ming (1470-1567?), was probably the next most distinguished representative of this school. While basing himself on the Yüan masters, his works display a great variety of styles and are less conventional than that of most Ming painters. It has been well said that he was able, at times, to liberate himself from the main tendency of the age, to crowd pictures with a superabundance of details. He was also an exquisite calligrapher.

The next two painters to be considered do not really fit in the above-mentioned schools. T'ang Yin (1470-1523) led an unorthodox personal life which placed him outside of the caste of scholar-officials. He was an excellent landscape artist and also a fine painter of figures, flowers and birds. His pictures, genuine ones being quite rare, are noted for their realism.

Ch'iu Ying (1522-1560) was neither a scholar nor a poet and perhaps the closest to a professional painter, living by and for his art. He was renowned for his large, wonderfully detailed and superbly coloured scrolls, mostly on time-honoured historical scenes. Ch'iu Ying was, undoubtedly, the last great painter in the famous "blue and green" tradition. Unfortunately, copies and forgeries by skilled craftsmen of his works are legion.

The above four painters are considered by Chinese and European art critics to be the Four Great Masters of the Ming when it still displayed creative vitality. The later Ming period became more and more conservative; old outworn themes were constantly being repeated and no independent ideas were forthcoming.

It is in this later period that the *wen jen hua* school reached its apogee and found its theorists, of whom the best known was Tung Ch'i-ch'ang (1555-1636). According to them, poetry, painting and calligraphy were to be regarded as the highest forms of expression of the human spirit and to achieve this aim one should seek to present the inward reality of an object and not its outward likeness. This, in turn, led to an intense study of painting techniques which ultimately resulted in the production of painting manuals, such as the famous "Mustard Seed Garden Book", in which ways of painting particular objects were described and classified. It was also Tung and his colleagues who devised the system of classifying all earlier Chinese painters into the already-mentioned Northern and Southern schools (see p. 142), a completely arbitrary division set up to suit their own theories. The triumph of the *wen jen hua* has been described as resulting, in effect, in a dilution of painting with literature and it is a fact that very few great works can be ascribed to the followers of this school. This is true of Tung himself, who spent a considerable part of his life as a high official, while at the same time establishing a reputation as the greatest art expert of his day. His expertise helped to establish his own vast collection of pictures which, it should be mentioned in passing, was later mostly lost, for Tung and his relatives were a thoroughly hated, oppressive *nouveau riche* gentry family and their property was burned down in a riot. The influence, however, of Tung Ch'i-ch'ang and his theories was considerable and the extreme formalism and conservatism of his ideas had, undoubtedly, a negative effect on the future of Chinese painting.

IV. Ceramics, Architecture

The Ming period is also noted for further development in ceramics. The famous Ching-te-chen (Kiangsi) imperial potteries were established in 1369 and shortly became the ceramic metropolis of China. While other potteries also existed, the major part of Ming ware extant today is, undoubtedly, the product of these works. Opinions differ considerably as to the artistic value of Ming porcelain; while some believe that it was the Sung era in which the finest ware was produced, others maintain that in the Ming period the highest achievement of the potter's art was reached.

The Ching-te-chen potteries produced a beautiful translucent white ware which, from early Ming on, was painted in various colours. The most famous probably is the combination of blue on white, but a red colour derived from copper was also used, as well as enamel colours of various hues. All this was a departure from the austerity of Sung monochromes, but in its best products the Ming ware showed a fine freshness of design. From the beginning of the period the usage of placing reign marks was employed but, unfortunately, these cannot be trusted for the purpose of ascertaining from which period a given piece of porcelain comes. For here, as in painting, the manufacture of superb copies was also practised, especially in the Ch'ing period, so that it is, in fact, extremely difficult to tell an original vase from a later imitation.

From the 15th century on ever-greater quantities of Chinese porcelain were exported to various parts of the world; their very great influence on the manufacturing of porcelain in Europe is well known. But it is more than probable that the increase in export also led progressively to a lowering of the quality of the ware produced, especially of that earmarked for export.

In a number of works dealing with Chinese art it is customary to treat the subject of Chinese architecture in connection with the Ming period. There is a certain logic in this inasmuch as the work done in this era, and especially the building of Peking during Yung-lo's reign, provides a vast amount of illustrative material. Peking, as conceived by Yung-lo's architects, is, in some ways, a copy of Ch'ang-an, and the style is not really original but a modification of that used during the Southern Sung. It had been considered to be the epitome of traditional Chinese architecture. Its outstanding traits are undoubtedly an attachment to monumentalism and the apt use of symmetry, especially as seen in the use of the north-south axis which runs through the Imperial City. It is remarkable for its lavish use of colour and ornamentation, for its splendid marble staircases and balustrades. One author quotes two views regarding Peking—in one it is called "a superb essay in coordinated town-planning" and in the other "an extended village of dirty streets and crumbling walls". To the above author, who had never been in Peking, these statements seem to be contradictory and he inclines rather to the first. In fact, both are equally true—for if one considers Peking only as the complex of the buildings of the Imperial City it is superbly planned, while many of the other parts of the city are, or were, in fact nothing but an overgrown, squalid village.

Perhaps the most noteworthy fact regarding Chinese architecture was its consistent use of wood as the primary material, even as this material became scarcer and others were equally available. This is more than likely derived from its very conservative nature and has resulted in, on the one hand, a standardization of construction methods and, on the other, in little variety in style. It should be noted that in Chinese architecture there is really no basic difference between secular and religious buildings, between state palaces and private homes. There was a major difference of size, splendour and elaborateness of ornamentation, but the general scheme remains almost always the same. One might add that in all periods up to 90 per cent of the population, especially in the countryside, lived in hovels.

The Ming period changed little in this domain, but while the Ming at least built with a certain zeal and their archaizing tendencies are not too glaring, the architecture of the next epoch, the Ch'ing, is already completely stereotyped and often executed without a trace of taste or artistic feeling.

PART VIII

China Under Manchu Rule

CHAPTER 24

Early Ch'ing

I. The Establishment of Ch'ing Rule

The entry of the Manchus into Peking in June 1644 marks the beginning of the long rule over China of the Ch'ing dynasty which lasted to 1912. Nevertheless, many decades of complicated struggles were to ensue before the rule of the Ch'ing was extended to all of China and stabilized. Generally speaking, on the advice of their Chinese collaborators, the Ch'ing took over the traditional Chinese system of administration as it had existed under the Ming with but few changes. The basic difference lay in the fact that the Manchus established themselves as a ruling master race which was to control the administration and exploit the country for its own benefit. The Ch'ing made a distinct effort to keep the Manchus' identity separate, so as not to submerge themselves in the Chinese sea and to repeat the mistake of their ancestors, the Chin. In this they were, in truth, successful for two centuries, keeping their rule more or less intact until the advent of the Taiping Revolution.

To maintain their control over China the Manchus preserved their organization of the Eight Banners and garrisons of Bannermen were stationed later on in all strategic centres of the country where they lived in separate residential areas. As a ruling "Herrenvolk", the Manchus were not allowed to engage in trade, or any other labour for that matter, being paid pensions by the government, i.e. fed by the conquered Chinese. This inevitably led to a degeneration of the Manchus as a military force, but the results were to become evident only towards the end of the 18th century.

In running the administration the Ch'ing followed a policy of dividing all the principal posts between Manchus and Chinese for the purpose of strict control. This has been called by some authors a diarchy, which implies a participation in the rule of the country by the Chinese landlord officials. This is basically true, in that the Chinese gentry did collaborate with the new dynasty on an ever-increasing scale and it is this which made Ch'ing rule feasible. The diarchy was not, however, an equal partnership, for the dominance of the Manchus was undoubted. One of the main ways in which the Ch'ing rulers achieved this collaboration was by leaving intact the economic position of the gentry. Although in the initial period much land had been confiscated by the Manchus for their own use, the estates of the Chinese landowners were, in principle, left untouched; thus their "rice bowls" were unbroken. What is more, the gentry played a vital role in helping to supervise the *pao-chia* system of collective responsibility for controlling the peasantry.

After the taking of Peking the great bulk of the country was still in Chinese hands, either in those of the peasant insurgents or under the control of Ming officials. The Ch'ing, though they represented themselves as the avengers of the fallen Ming emperor, had not the slightest desire to relinquish what they had gained and launched themselves on a systematic conquest of the rest of the country. In this they played on the class prejudices of the Chinese gentry, as mentioned earlier, with great skill and thus concentrated first on defeating completely the armies of Li Tzu-ch'eng, sending against them also the troops of their Chinese collaborators under Wu San-kuei. These campaigns were soon crowned by success and thus the Manchus who, at the same time, extended their rule to most of North China, were able to proceed to their next task, to attack the remaining centres of Ming rule in Central and South China.

The Ming princes and their adherents had, after the fall of Peking, re-established their rule with Nanking, always the second capital of the Empire, as their main centre. This is sometimes referred to in Chinese historical writing as the Southern Ming period (1644-1662). But the Ming had learned absolutely nothing from the disaster that had overtaken them. Of the various contenders for the throne in Nanking, the most inadequate of all, Chu Yu-sung, the Prince of Fu (son of the one killed by Li's army), known for his drunkenness and dissipation, was selected to be the new Emperor by a coterie of former Ming officials. Among these the main role was played by Ma Shih-ying and his hanger-on Juan Ta-ch'eng. Both of these worthies had been associated with the worst period of eunuch rule and were notorious for their corruption. Ma Shih-ying dominated the Nanking court during its entire existence and all the vices that had prevailed earlier—extortion, bribery, sale of offices, intrigues and so on—flourished once more. A continuous struggle against opponents of their rule was also waged by these two. Militarily, the position of the Nanking government was not necessarily an unfavourable one; they were still in control of the greater and richer part of China. Four Ming armies were stationed in the area north of the Yangtse under four Guardian Generals but these, instead of preparing to resist the Manchus, were more concerned with waging struggles against each other and pillaging the countryside. The population considered them a great menace and certainly did not support them. Only one scholar-general, Shih K'o-fa, showed any ability or determination to resist the Ch'ing, and he had been forced out of Nanking by the Ma-Juan clique.

The Nanking government sought also to negotiate with the Manchus and thus an embassy was sent to Peking which proposed that the Manchus retire from North China, in return for which they would receive all the territory north of the Great Wall and an annual subsidy of 100,000 taels. Dorgon replied to this with the counter-proposal that the Nanking regime acknowledge the suzerainty of the Ch'ing dynasty and if it did so, it could remain as a vassal kingdom in the south of China. Neither side, obviously, took the negotiations seriously; the Ming embassy's prime function was to spy out the situation in North China, while the Manchus were preparing their troops for a march to the south. Dorgon sought to win over to his side Shih K'o-fa (the fascinating correspondence between them still exists), counting on the fact that he, like most Chinese officials, was more interested in fighting against the peasants than against the Manchus. He failed in this and the Ch'ing troops started their assault on the south by an attack on the great city of Yangchow, on the north bank of the Yangtse, which was defended by Shih K'o-fa. After a brave defence of eight days, the city was stormed and then subjected to a terrible ten-day massacre in which the majority of the population perished. Shih K'o-fa, when captured, refused to follow the example of so many of his colleagues in going over to the Ch'ing and was executed. The Ch'ing armies, led by Hung Ch'eng-ch'ou, one of the most important of the Chinese collaborators, then proceeded, in June 1645, to Nanking. The inept Nanking regime disintegrated; the Emperor fled, shortly to be turned over by one of his own generals to the Ch'ing who sent him to Peking where he died (naturally?) the next year. Ma Shih-ying escaped to Chekiang where he died shortly thereafter, while most of the Emperor's followers surrendered to the Manchus. Although they all considered themselves good Confucianists, loyalty, one of the cardinal Confucian virtues, had very little meaning to them.

After their victory in Nanking the Ch'ing continued their expansion southward, conquering all of Kiangsu and then Chekiang. Two more Ming princes sought to re-establish Ming rule; Chu I-hai, the Prince of Lu, set himself up as regent in Shaohsing (Chekiang). He had little resources and spent the rest of his life scurrying from coastal town to island in the south. The second, Chu Yü-chien, the Prince of T'ang, was proclaimed emperor in Foochow in August 1645. Although attempts were made to establish some coordination between these two regimes, little success was attained. The Foochow government's main supporter was Cheng Chih-lung, a former pirate, then an extremely wealthy merchant and Ming official. The usual conflict of cliques plagued this Ming court in the form of a struggle for power between military and civilian officials. The civilians won and Cheng, as leader of the military, resolved to surrender to the Manchus and by his action (leaving unguarded vital mountain passes) made possible their further advance from Chekiang into Fukien. The Prince of T'ang fled and tried to join up with Ming adherents in Hunan; these were, in fact, the remnants of Li Tzu-ch'eng's troops which had joined up with Ming generals to fight against the Manchus. He failed in this attempt, was captured and executed in 1646. His younger brother escaped to Canton where he headed, for only two months, another shadow-like Ming government which ended when the city was captured by Ch'ing troops, again led by a Chinese general, and he committed suicide.

The last of the Ming princes who sought to restore the empire of his ancestors was Chu Yu-lang, the Prince of Kuei. He first established himself in Kwangtung but shortly in 1647 he was forced to flee to Kwangsi. For the next twelve years he wandered back and forth in South-west China, depending on the see-saw nature of the warfare. The main military forces of this last Ming ruler were, in reality, the remnants of the peasant armies of Chang Hsien-chung, led by li Ting-kuo and Sun K'o-wang, while some Ming loyalist officials also joined his cause. A long stubborn guerrilla warfare was conducted by these forces over the entire area of the South-west, including Szechuan and Hunan. Whatever chances this Ming government might have had to push back the Ch'ing armies, and revolt against the Manchus in the North-west and South made these look bright for a time, were ruined by the continuous dissensions and struggles within its own ranks. Thus, in 1657, the armies of Li Ting-kuo and Sun K'o-wang began a struggle between themselves which ended with the latter going over to the Ch'ing. In 1659 the Prince of Kuei, being steadily pursued by Ch'ing armies led by Wu San-kuei, sought refuge in Burma; here he was kept a prisoner by the Burmese for three years and the attempts of his only remaining faithful follower, Li Ting-kuo, to rescue him were of no avail. Wu San-kuei succeeded in forcing the Burmese to surrender the prince and his family into his hands, took them to the capital of Yunnan, where in 1662 the Prince of Kuei and his son were strangled with a bowstring. Li Ting-kuo died of grief upon hearing the news.

An interesting sidelight on the last of the Ming was the activity of the Jesuits at his court. His mother, wife and son were all converted to Christianity. In 1650 letters were sent to the Pope and the Jesuit general, requesting aid for the Ming cause. These were taken to Europe by a Polish Jesuit, Michael Boym. He reached Venice in 1652 but it was only in 1655 that an answer was finally given by Pope Alexander VII and only in 1659 that Boym returned to China; by then there was nothing left of the Ming court. Boym died in the same year and the letters remained undelivered. The Jesuits had also helped the Southern Ming in the acquiring of European artillery which made the defence of some of their towns (Kueilin, for example) more feasible. But as soon as Ch'ing rule was established we find the Jesuits active once more in Peking.

One more centre of resistance to the advance of the Ch'ing was on the southern coast and was connected with the activity of the famous Cheng Ch'eng-kung, the Koxinga of European literature. He was the son of Cheng Chih-lung, but while his father had gone over to the Manchus, he continued to keep up the struggle against them with the aid of a considerable fleet from the main southern Chinese ports. His base was mostly Amoy and from this island he raided both Fukien and Chekiang during the years 1647-1658, at times succeeding in bringing large areas under his rule. His strength increased to the point where his forces were able to sail up the Yangtse and in 1659 he sought to take Nanking but failed in the attempt. The Ch'ing government replied to this great threat to their rule by a policy of forceable evacuation inland of the population of the sea coasts, all the way from Shantung down to Kwangtung. By leaving a strip of 30-50 *li* uninhabited it was hoped to deprive Koxinga of support from the population. This policy was much more disastrous to the people and the economy of these provinces than it was to him. In 1661 Koxinga sailed with a fleet of 900 ships and 25,000 troops to Taiwan which was in Dutch hands; he succeeded in forcing the Dutch to evacuate and Taiwan thus became the base for anti-Ch'ing campaigns to be continued by the Cheng family until 1683. Koxinga himself died in 1622. His father and brothers, though they had gone over to the Ch'ing side, were executed by the Manchus in 1661 in reprisal for his activities. The Cheng family on Taiwan engaged in numerous internecine struggles, thus weakening its position. In 1683 a Chinese admiral serving the Ch'ing, Shih Lang, sailed against Taiwan, having first occupied the Pescadores with the aid of Dutch ships and troops. Taiwan surrendered and thus the last territory from which struggle had been waged was now in Manchu hands.

The conquest of Central and South China was to a considerable degree the work of Chinese generals and troops which had gone over to the Ch'ing. This was but one manifestation of a general trend in which Chinese officials and landowners surrendered *en masse* and were ready to serve their new masters. Soon after the establishment of the Ch'ing government in Peking, the scholar gentry streamed into the capital in search of posts in the new administration. In the newly conquered South, it was also the Chinese collaborators of the Manchus who were the actual rulers of the territory, establishing themselves as almost semi-independent feudal princes in their satrapies. The principal one was, logically enough, Wu San-kuei under whose direct sway were the provinces of Yunnan and Kweichow, but whose rule and influence extended, in fact, to the entire South-west, inasmuch as the majority of the officials in this area were appointed by him and not by Peking.

This strange state of affairs existed until 1673 when the Ch'ing government decided to deprive these strong potentates of the base of their power, the armies under their control, by calling upon them to disband their forces. The motivation was supposedly an economic one and it is true that the cost of these armies was a great drain on Ch'ing finances. The main aim was obviously political. Wu San-kuei replied to these moves by an open rebellion and succeeded in enlisting the support of the rulers of Kwangtung, Kwangsi and Fukien. In Chinese historical writing this was known as the famous Rebellion of the Three Feudatories. The rule of the Manchus was very seriously threatened by this revolt, inasmuch as real stabilization of their government had not yet been achieved and there was great resistance to their rule in many parts of China, even in the North which had been the most easily subdued. Wu San-kuei, who shortly proclaimed the establishment of a new dynasty, the Chou, with himself as Emperor, as well as the restoration of Ming customs, failed to take full advantage of the situation and to march quickly to the north towards Peking. The Ch'ing were given sufficient time to muster their main forces to the north of the Yangtse and were helped by the usual dissension in the ranks of the Chinese. They succeeded in either defeating or bringing about the defection of the other Chinese princes in the South and were able to concentrate their forces against Wu San-kuei. The suppression of the rebellion was a long and difficult process; much of the struggle was waged in Hunan where Wu San-kuei died in 1678. The Manchus then succeeded in pressing forward to the original base of the rebellion, Yunnan, which they conquered in 1681, exterminating the entire Wu family. Henceforth, Ch'ing rule was not to be seriously threatened by any internal revolt for well over 100 years.

The boy emperor, Shun-chih, who was placed on the Dragon Throne in 1644, played a rather insignificant role in the establishment of Manchu power. While the death of the regent Dorgon in 1651 relieved him of the presence of this powerful personality and made his own rule possible, it also gave rise to the customary struggle of factions for power in the Ch'ing court. Shun-chih relied to a great degree on the help of eunuchs and supposedly preferred Chinese officials. His early death in 1661 led to another period of regency, as he was succeeded by his 8-year-old son, K'ang-hsi.*

When the rebellion of the Three Feudatories began, K'ang-hsi succeeded in ridding himself of his regents and began his long and eventful reign, which lasted until 1722. The very length itself of this reign was a significant factor for the stabilization of Ch'ing power, as were also his undoubted abilities and skilful policies. He had been one of the advocates of challenging the power of the Southern Chinese princes and had proved to be correct in this. The victory over the Wu San-kuei rebellion was a very important contributing factor in the further consolidation of Manchu rule. The establishment and stabilization of Manchu rule in China remains a trying and difficult problem for

---

* K'ang-hsi is the reign title and not the personal name of the Emperor, which was Hsüan-yeh, nor his temple name, Sheng-tsu, by which he is sometimes referred to in Chinese historical writing. We shall use throughout for the Ch'ing emperors, as we had for the Ming, only their reign titles.

modern Chinese historians. They are usually at a loss to explain this phenomenon, just as they find the earlier periods of nomad rule hard to accept. In the case of the Ch'ing this alien rule was still more humiliating and its effects ultimately disastrous for the fate of the Chinese people.

In this process of consolidation K'ang-hsi's personal role was considerable; there is little doubt regarding his ability and intelligence. From early in his reign he pursued a systematic and clever policy of cultivating the Chinese gentry-officials in order to convert them into loyal supporters of the Ch'ing dynasty, assuming the role of a great patron of Chinese culture (see Chapter 26). In carrying out this role his own sound knowledge and probably sincere interest in the Chinese Classics was undoubtedly a major asset. The political aspect of this support for the Chinese cultural tradition should also be borne in mind inasmuch as the Ch'ing supported everything that was the most conservative and orthodox in this tradition, ultimately becoming even greater Confucianists than the Chinese themselves. Needless to say it was the already scholastic forms of Neo-Confucianism which were favoured by K'ang-hsi; he himself was purportedly the author of a Hortatory Edict, a collection of moral maxims which became throughout the entire Ch'ing period a form of obligatory creed to be inculcated in the entire population of China. (It was later read out to the people twice a month.)

The above policies met, on the whole, with success and the collaboration of the Chinese gentry with the Ch'ing regime became during the K'ang-hsi period a general and normal phenomenon. There were numerous honourable exceptions to this but largely from the generation which had been still brought up under the Ming dynasty, while further opposition to Manchu rule, which did continue, took on a quite different shape, as will be shown later.

The long reign of K'ang-hsi also saw the economic rehabilitation of the country: the rise of agricultural production and the increase in land under cultivation. This was the result of maintaining internal peace, lasting to the end of the 18th century—a *Pax Manchurica*. The period also witnessed a steady growth of population, but the spectacular increase in this respect dates from the latter part of the 18th century. The Manchus had reduced taxes during the first period of their rule and the social crisis in the countryside which had led to the downfall of the Ming was somewhat abated. The general upswing of the economy did not affect its essential character and no basic changes occurred in the sense that the policies of the state and of the landowners were still such as to hamper any greater degree of industrial development.

The Ch'ing empire during the K'ang-hsi period undertook a number of campaigns which resulted in a considerable expansion of the territory under Manchu rule. The major part of these was concerned with extending Ch'ing control over areas inhabited by the Mongol tribes. The general policy of the Ch'ing towards the Mongols was that of divide and rule, of playing on the inner divisions of the Mongols, especially that between the Western Mongols (the Eleuths, Ölöd or Kalmuks) and the Eastern Mongols (Khalkha). It was the Manchu practice, which they had already applied to the Inner Mongolian tribes, to assign territories to the Mongol nomads and to confirm their chiefs as a means of exerting Ch'ing authority over them.

The first great campaigns of the Ch'ing against the Mongols were connected with the activities of Galdan (1644-1697), the Khan of the Dzungars, one of the tribes of the Eleuths. In the 1670s and 1680s Galdan had become not only master of all the Western Mongol tribes but also the ruler of the Mohammedan (Uighur) areas of Turkestan, south of the T'ien Shan. He embarked on a policy of restoring the power of the Mongols and to achieve this aim wished to extend his rule also to the east, over the Khalkha in Outer Mongolia. His campaign against them was launched in 1688—an army of 30,000 advancing to the east—and a large part of the Khalkha fled to the south seeking protection and aid from the Ch'ing. In 1690 Galdan again penetrated into Outer Mongolia but this time the Ch'ing were only too eager to avail themselves of the opportunity and their army succeeded in defeating him. As a result of this, all the Khalkha princes paid homage in 1691 to K'ang-hsi and henceforth remained faithful vassals of the Ch'ing for the rest of the dynasty's rule. Galdan regrouped his forces after his first defeat and again penetrated into Outer Mongolia in 1696. K'ang-hsi himself led an army of 80,000 against the Dzungars; the campaign ended with a crushing defeat of Galdan in a battle near Urga (Ulan Bator), where the victory of the Ch'ing was due primarily to their great superiority in firearms. It has been aptly stated that this victory marked the end of nomad power, the millennium in which the mounted nomad archer was superior to all other military forces. The Dzungar Khan fled with the last remnants of his forces (1000 men, 3000 women) and wandered in the Altai Mountains until, deserted by practically all his followers, Galdan—Chingghis Khan *manqué*—committed suicide in 1697. A second great expedition in the same year also led by K'ang-hsi was rendered unnecessary by Galdan's death. The result of the Ch'ing victories in this campaign was the extension of their rule to all of Outer Mongolia as well as to the area of Hami (easternmost part of Dzungaria).

The struggle of the Ch'ing with the Western Mongols continued, in fact, throughout most of the 18th century. The subsequent campaigns were waged against the new Khan of the Dzungars, Tsewang Araptan (1643-1727), nephew and successor to Galdan and heir to his plans as well. This conflict was also closely bound up with the problem of Tibet.

Since the beginning of the 15th century and the establishment of the Yellow Sect of Tibetan Lamaism—as a rival to the older Red Sect—the influence of Lamaism in the Mongol lands had vastly increased. The great majority of the Mongol tribes had become followers of the Yellow Church and was also intimately connected with the political struggles for supremacy in Tibet. Thus one of the Eleuth tribes, the Khoshotes, had been active in Tibetan affairs, in fact, exercising political rule in Tibet from the 1650s until 1717. In this last year the Dzungars, in turn, intervened into Tibetan politics; an army of 6000 Dzungars was sent there by Tsewang Araptan which succeeded in conquering Lhasa and eliminating the rule of the Khoshotes.

The Ch'ing court paid very close attention to events in Tibet, among others, due to the fact that the control of Tibet and of the top positions in the Yellow Church was of crucial importance also for the control of their followers, the Mongol tribes. Thus, in 1720, two Ch'ing armies, which included Mongol troops, marched into Tibet where they succeeded in driving out the Dzungars. Ch'ing garrisons were then left in Lhasa, a new Dalai Lama, subservient to the Ch'ing, was installed to replace the Dalai Lama of the Dzungars and Ch'ing control was established over the Yellow Church. In 1727 a Ch'ing imperial resident was installed in Lhasa. Henceforth Tibet remained under Ch'ing suzerainty until the end of the dynasty.

The expulsion of the Dzungars from Tibet did not end the conflict of the Ch'ing against them; it was continued with varying results throughout the rest of K'ang-hsi's reign. One might note, in passing, that the Dzungars were simultaneously faced with the danger of penetration into the areas under their control by the Russians during the reign of Peter I whom they successfully fought off.

The Russian expansion eastward through Siberia brought them also into closer contact with the Ch'ing empire, especially in the area of the Amur River Valley (in Chinese—Heilungkiang—Black Dragon River). Here the first Russian explorers, mostly Cossacks, sailed down the Amur in the 1650s and the first conflicts between them and the Manchus ensued. The Russians were defeated, but in the 1660s new forces of Cossacks appeared; a fort was built by them in 1669 in Albazin (east of where the Argun flows into the Amur). This fort was considered a thorn in their side by the Manchus; when the Wu San-kuei rebellion had been suppressed, the Ch'ing launched their troops against this Russian position. Albazin was taken and destroyed in 1685 but in the next year it was again occupied and rebuilt by the Russians and, in turn, again besieged by the Manchus. This conflict was suspended in 1687, when news was received that a Russian mission had been sent to commence negotiations with the Ch'ing. This mission, headed by Golovin, did, in fact, reach Lake Baikal in that year, but due to the campaign of the Manchus against Galdan the negotiations were delayed and began only in 1689; they resulted ultimately in the signing of the Treaty of Nerchinsk (September 7, 1689). The Manchus were interested in arriving at an agreement with the Russians for a number of reasons, among others, to avoid the possibility of Russian assistance, especially arms, being given to Galdan. The treaty was negotiated with the help of two Jesuit priests who acted as interpreters (Gerbillon and Pereira) for the Manchus and a Pole, A. Białobłocki, for the Russians. It was written down in five languages—Manchu, Chinese, Mongol, Russian and Latin, the copy in Latin being the one signed. According to the conditions of the treaty the Albazin fort was destroyed, and the boundaries were established to run along the Gorbitsa and Argun Rivers reaching the Hsing-an range; the north shore of the Amur was thus recognized as Ch'ing territory and this was changed only later on by the Treaty of Tientsin (1860).

The Nerchinsk Treaty was the first ever to be signed by China with a European power. It did not, however, settle either the problems of the border between Mongolia and Russia, nor the question of trade. This was accomplished only in the reign of K'ang-hsi's successor by the Treaty of Kiakhta (1727). According to it, the border between Russia and Mongolia was established (practically the same as the present border between the Soviet Union and the Mongolian People's Republic). Permission was granted for 200 Russian merchants to travel to Peking every three years and for a Russian Orthodox Church with four priests attached to it to be built in Peking (its congregation was composed mostly of Russians taken prisoner in the earlier conflicts). The trade was later shifted from Peking to Kiakhta, and while the treaty was revised in 1768 and 1792 the results achieved governed relations between China and Russia until the period of the Second Opium War.

The question of succession to the throne became an object of bitter struggle, intrigues and conspiracies among the K'ang-hsi's numerous sons (almost twenty of his sons reached adulthood). The victor was his fourth son who reigned as Yung-cheng (1723-1736). The circumstances under which he reached the throne are still unclear; it is probable that the will of the old Emperor was falsified and there is no doubt that Yung-cheng got into power with the help of the chief of the Peking gendarmes. He has also been accused by his enemies of hastening his father's death. The first years of his reign were devoted to the strengthening of his position and continuing his conflict with his brothers. Out of a total number of fifteen, five died in prison, at least two of them killed there; two others remained in prison until Yung-cheng's death. Later on, the Emperor also rid himself of those who had helped him to rise to the throne. He was careful to suppress any documents relating to his coming to power and has been charged with falsifying the historical records of his predecessor's reign.

The despotism of the imperial government increased still more during the Yung-cheng period. An elaborate system of secret surveillance was built up and the Emperor's spies swarmed everywhere, reporting on all the deeds of the higher officials. It has been stated, however, that corruption of the government, an endemic disease by no means restricted to the Ch'ing period, was somewhat checked by Yung-cheng and that he also contributed to an improvement of the financial position of the Ch'ing government. One of his important innovations was the establishment of the Grand Council, a small body of officials which, in time, became the most important governmental institution, assisting the Emperor in the carrying out of his personal rule and replacing the Grand Secretariat in most of the essential functions. It was established initially to deal primarily with military affairs but later on its scope included all matters of political importance.

The wars against the Western Mongols were continued intermittently during Yung-cheng's reign but no success was achieved. In fact, the Ch'ing forces suffered in 1731 a severe defeat which was a setback to their plans for their domination over Dzungaria for over twenty years. It is in this period, however, that the Khoshotes were completely subdued with a great loss of life and the area they inhabited, Kokonor (Ch'inghai), was annexed to the empire. In the south-west of China a policy was initiated of subjecting the areas inhabited by the Miao tribes to direct control by the local Ch'ing government. This was to be done by the abolishing of the power of the Miao chiefs and resulted in an almost incessant series of Miao rebellions throughout the century. The primary cause of these revolts lay in the fact that the Ch'ing officials and Chinese landowners were constantly depriving the Miao of their best agricultural land in the lowlands and steadily driving them into the hills.

Yung-cheng drew one conclusion from his own coming to power: the age-old practice of naming an heir-apparent during the life of the Emperor was changed by him and his successor was named by a secret will. This was to be his fourth son, Ch'ien-lung (1736-1796), who was to sit on the Dragon Throne for the longest period noted in Chinese history, in effect, sixty-three years.

II. The Ch'ing Empire in the 18th Century: the Beginnings of Decline

Just as the reign of K'ang-hsi, that of Ch'ien-lung is also often referred to by many authors as a splendid reign of a great emperor. There is, in reality, even less truth in this in respect to Ch'ien-lung than to K'ang-hsi. It is true that in this reign the ultimate extension of Ch'ing power was achieved and the borders of the Empire were established which lasted to 1912. Nevertheless, it is also this period when, under the facade of splendour and expansion, the process of decay and corruption, which was inherent in the nature of the Ch'ing government and society, made steady and ever more rapid progress. This was particularly revealed during the last two decades of Ch'ien-lung's reign, when effective power was in the hands of his favourite, the chief minister, Ho-shen. An extremely clever courtier, Ho-shen achieved dominance over his master and the Emperor's confidence in him was unassailable. His power became so great that he could make or break any official in the entire country; he used his influence to put his henchmen into the key posts of the government. He himself was in control of two boards—Revenue and Civil Offices—and, at one time, held twenty different posts concurrently. Ho-shen's greed knew no bounds and he exacted untold wealth from his position, with the entire governmental apparatus serving him for this purpose. His fortune by the end of his career was estimated at 900 million taels, about 1350 million dollars (see p. 246, footnote). If this were true, it would have amounted to four-sevenths of the entire revenue of the government during the two decades of his power. Under his sway the corruption of the Ch'ing government reached fantastic proportions.

Ch'ien-lung, modelling himself on his grandfather K'ang-hsi, also liked to pose as a great patron of Chinese culture, especially of literature and painting. But his cultivation of the arts was likewise connected with a virulent literary inquisition, the main purpose of which was the persecution of all writers, living and dead, who could be suspected of being anti-dynastic and the elimination of all such works (see Chapter 26). He built up a vast collection of art, especially paintings, many of which still survive, inscribed by his verses and marked by his seal. He was credited also with having composed over 42,000 poems; this, if it were true—and obviously it was not, for the majority were written for him and all were edited by some of his ministers, for whom this was perhaps the most grievous task—would have made him the most prolific writer in the history of Chinese literature.

Inasmuch as K'ang-hsi's reign had lasted sixty years, Ch'ien-lung, not wishing to reign longer than his predecessor—it would have been unseemly—retired in 1796 in favour of his son, Chia-ch'ing. This was pure hypocrisy, for Ch'ien-lung remained as a Super Emperor, "advising" the new Emperor, while Ho-shen remained the chief minister until Ch'ien-lung's death in 1799.

Towards the end of Ch'ien-lung's reign the oppressive nature of the Ch'ing regime as well as the social and economic changes of the 18th century resulted in the emergence of a critical situation and the revival of an active struggle against the Manchus.

Among the many component factors of the economic and social crisis probably the most important is to be found in the rapid increase of population which exceeded considerably the growth of agricultural production and the increase of the area under cultivation. Assuming the population at the beginning of the Ch'ing dynasty to have been around 100 million (the estimates vary from 60 to 150 million), it rose to 143 million in 1741, 243 million in 1778, probably around 300 million by the end of the century, 374 million in 1814 and over 400 million by 1838. There are, unfortunately, no truly reliable data on land under cultivation and estimates differ considerably; one source gives the figure of 549 million *mu* for 1661, 724 million for 1725, 781 million for 1766 and 772 million for the year 1851. Thus, the growth of population was obviously much more rapid than the increase in the arable land area, a factor not compensated for by the increase in agricultural production due to improved methods. The problem was further complicated by the absence of any large-scale emigration or inner colonization and still more by the fact that there was no industrialization capable of absorbing surplus rural population. The inevitable process of concentration of land ownership further deepened the crisis, although this became even more marked in the 19th century.

After the initial period of consolidation of Manchu rule, activity against the Ch'ing dynasty did not cease but changed its forms and went underground, to be continued by the secret societies which have played such a significant role in Chinese history. The three main societies were the following: the White Lotus, an unorthodox Buddhist sect which, as mentioned, had been active against the Mongols and of vital significance in bringing about their downfall. Its main sphere of influence embraced the provinces of North and North-west China. The Ko Lao Hui (Brothers and Elders) was active in Hunan, Chekiang and the Yangtse basin. Like the White Lotus, its main support came from the peasantry but included also artisans and vagabonds. The third society was the T'ien Ti (Heaven and Earth or Triad), whose influence was strongest in the Southern provinces and also among the Chinese immigrants in South-east Asia. All three of the societies were strongly anti-Ch'ing and the object of constant and severe persecution by the Manchu authorities.

The White Lotus Society had attempted a revolt against the Manchus in 1774 which was speedily put down. The movement, whose leader was Liu Sung, nevertheless continued its activities; Liu Sung was arrested and exiled but his followers, led by Liu Chi-hsieh, laid their plans for an uprising in 1792. The plans were divulged and a fierce persecution was launched by the Ch'ing in 1793, especially in West Hupei, with mass arrests and killings. This, in reality, only hastened the rising which was launched in 1795 under the slogan "The officials have forced the people to rise". The rebellion had a distinct anti-dynastic character but was also social in nature, the bulk of the insurgents being peasants, struggling against the gentry. The centre of the movement was the city of Hsiangyang in North-west Hupei; from this area the movement spread rapidly and extended to large parts of Hupei, Honan, Shensi and Szechuan. The struggle lasted for over nine years (1795-1804) and was extremely bitter in character. It was during this insurrection that the increasing worthlessness of the Manchu Banners as a military force was revealed, with the exception of Manchu units from Kirin and Heilungkiang. The Ch'ing generals who fought against the White Lotus were a thoroughly corrupt lot, appropriating most of the funds assigned for the war for their own benefit, as well as that of Ho-shen. The figures for the cost of this "war" range from 100 to 200 million taels (the tael, sometimes referred to as "liang", was 1 oz of silver; but see p. 246, footnote).

The White Lotus Rebellion was finally suppressed by the application of the so-called *chien-pi, ch'ing-yeh* (strengthen the walls and clear the countryside) policy. This was, in effect, a scorched-earth policy meant to deprive the insurgents of food and recruits. A concomitant of it was the fact that the starving peasants were thus forced to join the Ch'ing army to fight against the White Lotus. It was, in fact, these peasant militia units formed by the Ch'ing, numbering 300,000 men by the end of the rebellion, who, struggling against their brother peasants in the White Lotus, won the war. Ultimately, the areas involved in the rising were "pacified" with the help of ruthless suppression and mass executions; several hundred thousand Chinese peasants thus lost their lives. The Ch'ing government credited its Manchu generals with this great victory and showered titles and monetary awards on them—although they had already stolen quite enough—while the militia was soon disarmed. Even the above strategic policy was probably not the work of the Ch'ing generals, having been suggested to them by a Chinese official.

Ch'ien-lung was fond of boasting of the military prowess of the Manchus and of the glory which his reign had seen in the achievement of Ten Great Military Victories. This was quite bombastic for, in truth, some of these were quite insignificant campaigns.

The most important was the continuation of the Ch'ing campaigns against the Eleuths. In the 1750s the Dzungars were considerably weakened by internecine struggle in the course of which one of their chiefs, Amursana, went over to the side of the Ch'ing with 5000 of his men. The Manchus now saw their opportunity to achieve a final solution of the Dzungar problem and to conquer Ili; their armies advanced in 1755 and met with complete success as most of the Eleuths surrendered without a struggle. The achievement proved to be only a very temporary one, inasmuch as Amursana, wishing to become the new ruler of all the Eleuth tribes, started a rebellion against the Ch'ing and gained the support of almost the entire Eleuth people. The next two years saw constant fighting which ended with the death of Amursana and a complete Ch'ing victory. It resulted in the practical disappearance of the Eleuths as a people; out of a population of over 600,000 (200,000 families) 30 per cent were killed by the Manchu armies, 40 per cent died of smallpox and 20 per cent escaped to Siberia. This little-known case of genocide gave the Ch'ing the rule over the entire Ili area, which was in later years used as a favourite place of exile. It was partially repopulated when the Torguts fled back from the Volga in 1771 and put themselves under Ch'ing rule.

The defeat of the Dzungars by the Ch'ing made possible the conquest also of the Uighur population in Eastern Turkestan (south of the T'ien Shan) undertaken in 1758 by the Manchus with their usual cruelty. The result of these two campaigns was to extend the area of the Ch'ing empire by the addition of the vast territory which now comprises Sinkiang province (this was organized in the latter half of the 19th century, after the suppression of further revolts in this area).

Among Ch'ien-lung's so-called great military victories were two campaigns waged against the Chin-ch'uan tribesmen in the wild and almost inaccessible region of West Szechuan. These tribes, ethnically Tibetan, divided into two groups, the Ta Chin-ch'uan and the Hsiao Chin-ch'uan (these are actually the names of rivers "Great and Small Gold" and not the real appellation of the tribes), had succeeded in maintaining their independence from Chinese rule for centuries in their remote mountain villages, capped by thousands of stone towers. The first campaign launched against them by the Ch'ing was in the year 1748-1749. After numerous victories against Ch'ing troops the tribesmen were finally forced to submit to Manchu rule. Nevertheless, in 1772 the tribes rebelled against Ch'ing oppression and a long war, lasting over three years, was waged by the Manchus against them. A few thousand highlanders were able to keep the best of the Ch'ing generals at bay and it was ultimately only the use of European artillery which made their defeat possible. The two campaigns against them were extremely costly, over 70 million taels, from two to three times the cost of the campaign against Ili and Eastern Turkestan. Undoubtedly, much of this sum found its way once more into the pockets of the Manchu generals.

The rebellions of the Chin-ch'uan tribes were by no means the only ones of their kind. During the 18th century the Miao tribes, mostly in Kweichow and Hunan, rose against Ch'ing rule at least four times (1735, 1736, 1741, 1795), as did the Mohammedan population (referred to by modern Chinese authors as the Hui) in Kansu (1781, 1784). All this shows that the non-Chinese nationalities found Manchu rule just as oppressive as did the Chinese themselves. It has been stated that the Manchus were successful, however, in setting the various nationalities against each other, especially the Chinese and the Hui.

In 1790 the Gurkhas of Nepal launched a series of raids into Tibet which they continued in the subsequent year, plundering a considerable number of the principal lamaseries. The Ch'ing replied to this challenge to their rule over Tibet by sending in an army led by Fu-k'ang-an, one of their ablest, as well as most corrupt, generals. In an astounding campaign the Ch'ing succeeded in driving the Gurkhas across the passes of the Himalayas, defeating them time and again. The last battle was waged close to the Gurkha capital of Khatmandu, ending in yet another Manchu victory. The Gurkhas sued for peace, agreed to offer tribute every five years (they continued to do so until 1908). The main result of these campaigns was to make Ch'ing suzerainty over Tibet still firmer. It should be noted, however, that it was the English who benefited from this defeat of the Gurkhas more than the Manchus as it made their later campaigns against Nepal much easier. As a matter of fact, the Gurkhas had appealed for military aid to the East India Company; this was refused because the English did not wish to jeopardize their Canton trade. They offered to mediate instead, but this was of no avail as by that time the war was over.

The wars of the Ch'ien-lung period included also campaigns against the Burmese (1767-1769) which, though they did not bring any new laurels to the Ch'ing generals, did ultimately have some effect on Burma's declaring herself a vassal of the Ch'ing in 1788. During this same period, the Ch'ing intervened also in Vietnam where a change of dynasties was taking place. Subsequently, the Ch'ing recognized the new rulers who in 1789 also declared their country to be a vassal of the Ch'ing.

As can be seen the military campaigns of the Ch'ien-lung period not only served the purpose of territorial aggrandizement but were also a prime source of corruption. The Manchu generals purposely prolonged many of these campaigns to increase their gains, sending in false reports of victories to the ageing Emperor and slaughtering untold thousands of innocent people to back up these claims. The vast areas annexed in the West were of little economic value but perhaps the Ch'ing, who were well aware of European expansion in Asia, saw them also as possible buffer areas against the advance of the Europeans or, to put it another way, wished to extend their rule to these areas before the Europeans could do so.

By the end of Ch'ien-lung's reign it was apparent that one of the main results of Manchu despotic absolutism was to keep the development of China at a snail's pace during the period in which changes in Europe were so dynamic; the gap between the progress of China and of Europe became ever greater with every decade and every year of the 18th century. The reactionary nature of Ch'ing rule, the rule of a self-chosen, self-perpetuating and almost immobile ruling caste resulted in ever-greater intellectual and cultural stagnation, all of which rendered China almost helpless to meet the challenge of the West in the 19th century. It is possible, though not necessarily probable, that a native Chinese dynasty would perhaps have been in a better position to meet this challenge, as the admittedly quite different example of Japan might suggest.

One should note, in passing, that it is this China under K'ang-hsi and Ch'ien-lung which was regarded by 18th-century Europe as a model civilization, blessed with an enlightened and benevolent monarchy. Whence this picture? It was primarily due to the work of the Jesuits who were the main transmitters of things Chinese to Europe until their own dissolution, i.e. from the beginning of the 17th century until the last decades of the 18th. Perhaps the despotism of the Ch'ing appealed to the Jesuit mind and the high hopes which they had for converting China, through the conversion of the rulers themselves, although based on wishful thinking, also undoubtedly coloured the picture they sent back. In effect, the result of the work of the Jesuits had much greater influence on the development of European philosophical thought of the 18th century than it had on the fate of China.

However, it is also true that the Jesuits—and some of them were truly enamoured of Chinese classical culture—were the first to make available to Europe much of the Chinese classical tradition, as well as to acquaint Europeans with Chinese history. The works of Couplet and du Halde were of capital importance in this respect and formed the principle source for ideas regarding China to be found in the writings of Leibniz, Voltaire and Gibbon. The famous *Lettres édifiantes et curieuses* (34 vols., 1702-1776) on China, culled from the materials sent by the Jesuit missionaries, were of no less significance. The work of Gaubil and especially the 13-volume *Histoire générale de la Chine* of de Mailla (Paris, 1777-1785), basically a translation of Chu Hsi's condensation of the "Comprehensive Mirror", but continued up to the 18th century, formed the basis for much future European historical writing on China. The most outstanding Jesuit work, however, was the *"Mémoires concernant l'histoire . . . des chinois"* (17 vols., Paris, 1776-1814) which summed up their scholarly achievements.

The missionary activities of the Jesuits, conducted with varying success up to the end of the 18th century, did not, however, bring about the results that Ricci had expected. There were many causes for this: the transition from a policy of toleration during the K'ang-hsi period to persecutions during Yung-cheng's rule, the sharp conflicts and rivalries of the Catholic missionaries themselves (Franciscans and Dominicans versus the Jesuits) and—probably most important of all—the foreignness and unsuitability of the ideology they propounded, incriminated as well ever more from the 16th century on by the behaviour of its alleged believers, the European colonizers in East Asia.

CHAPTER 25

Culture in the Early and Middle Ch'ing Periods

I. Intellectual Development

An important further development of intellectual thought took place in the Late Ming and Early Ch'ing periods which, while still within the general framework of the Confucian tradition, did serve as a basis for the anti-Manchu reform movement as well as for the beginnings of revolutionary activities in the late 19th century. This development represented a revolt against Neo-Confucian scholasticism and was stimulated by the traumatic experience of the fall of the Ming which led the best minds of the period to pose a number of basic questions regarding the state of Chinese society. Simultaneously, the most prominent thinkers of this early period were noted for their opposition to Manchu rule and were the honourable exception to the collaboration of a vast number of Chinese scholar-officials with the Ch'ing. Three individuals are of the greatest importance here: Huang Tsung-hsi, Ku Yen-wu and Wang Fu-chih. They were all dissenters and had relatively little influence during their lifetime, but were to have much more in the future. It is they who made a real contribution to the development of Chinese thought.

Huang Tsung-hsi (1610-1695) was one of the foremost scholars of the early Ch'ing period; he possessed broad knowledge of the Classics, philosophy and literature but was especially noted as an historian. Huang was the son of a prominent Ming official, a member of the reforming Tung-lin group who died as a victim of eunuch persecution. He himself was an active member of the Fu-she; this was a nation-wide association of scholars (over 2000 members) which as a political force of great significance continued the traditions of the Tung-lin in a struggle against the corruption of the court, seeking to reform the Ming government and thus to save it from collapse. After the Manchus had taken Peking Huang Tsung-hsi joined the Ming loyalists in the South and fought against the Manchus until 1649. The hopelessness of the Ming cause led him subsequently to retire and to devote the rest of his life to learning. Although he was regarded as the greatest specialist on Ming history, he refused all the offers made by K'ang-hsi to work for the Ch'ing dynasty; characteristically, however, he participated in the writing of the *Ming shih* ("Ming History") through his student Wan Ssu-t'ung, feeling that in this way, by representing the truth, he would still serve the Ming without committing an act of personal betrayal.

Huang Tsung-hsi was the author of many works on history and philosophy. The most important, perhaps, was a short work called *Ming-i tai-fang lu* ("A Plan for a Prince") which was basically an analysis of the political and economic weakness of the

Ming dynasty, the most systematic and concrete criticism of Chinese imperial institutions yet made, but still from a Confucian point of view. In this work Huang showed himself hostile to the absolute monarchy, which he believed was a degenerate version of the earlier form of monarchical rule. Here he based himself on the typical old Chinese idea of a regression from the Golden Age of Antiquity, the eternal refrain of Confucian philosophical and historical thought. The monarchy and its officials should all, according to him, serve for the benefit of the people and not for their own interests as they were, in fact, doing. A system of general law was thought to be necessary to assure such a functioning of the government. Huang was also an advocate of land reform to make easier the life of the peasants who were the object of extortionate tax oppression by the state. He also favoured—and this was a novelty—the ending of discrimination against trade and the merchants, as well as against crafts.

Huang Tsung-hsi's historical writing—he was considered the founder of the East Chekiang School—was noted for its striving for more objective standards and for stressing the value of studying recent and contemporary history, instead of concentrating attention solely on ancient history. His largest and probably most important work was the *Ming-ju hsüeh-an* ("The History of Ming Scholarship and Philosophy", 1676); it has been called the first great history of Chinese intellectual thought, notable for its critical and systematic exposition. In it Huang traced the negative influence of Sung Neo-Confucianism as it related to the decay of the Ming. He also started a "History of Thought of the Sung and Yüan Periods", which was completed by his followers. Huang's ideas, especially those opposing the absolute monarchy, were taken up by the reform movement at the end of the 19th century, particularly by Liang Ch'i-ch'ao and T'an Ssu-t'ung, and were also of considerable influence in this respect.

The work of the East Chekiang School was continued also by Huang's pupil, Wan Ssu-t'ung (1638-1702). His early life was that of a poor scholar during which he became the greatest expert on the Ming period. Later, with Huang's blessings, he participated in the writing of the *Ming shih* sponsored by the Ch'ing; he was in fact the editor-in-chief, although he refused an official position. He worked in a private capacity also because he believed that private historical writing was superior to the official. Wan spent thirteen years on this project and was the real author of the "Draft Ming History". Another member of this school, Ch'üan Tsu-wang (1705-1755), was the best historian of his generation. He was a descendant of a Ming loyalist family and was enamoured of the history of the Southern Ming. Ch'üan was an unsuccessful official and his main work on the Ming loyalists was finally published long after his death, although in an expurgated version in fear of Ch'ing persecution. Both these men, just as Huang Tsung-hsi, were outsiders and thus had little influence on official historiography; they do represent, however, a valuable tradition.

The same is also true of perhaps the most original of the Ch'ing historians, the last scholar of the East Chekiang School, and its most liberal and speculative exponent—Chang Hsüeh-ch'eng (1738-1801). He was an unsuccessful, poor scholar all his life with a great talent and an overwhelming love for history. Most of his works are lost but two collections of essays are still extant which contain numerous reflections on the theory of history and its methodology. Starting with a broad conception of history, in regard to scope and material (thus the Classics should be considered basically as historical documents and not as sacred texts), Chang opposed the traditional forms of Chinese historical writing, both the Annals and the Standard Dynastic Histories, favouring instead the form of general history. He stressed also the need to use local histories as an important source of material. Chang saw the necessity of connecting history with the present and thus favoured dealing with recent and current problems as against the general tendency to dwell mainly on ancient times. In his view history had also a didactic and moral purpose; lessons from the past were to be employed to reform the present and to foresee the future. In this, Chang was a thorough Confucianist. In his concept, an historian must have a true understanding of the meaning of events and, while striving for impartiality, he must also be *engagé*. He must not reduce his task to compiling or textual criticism but must seek a synthesis in which inspiration and knowledge should be united. Chang, unfortunately, had little chance to put his own ideas into practice. He was almost unknown and rediscovered only in the 20th century; he has been interestingly compared with Vico by Demiéville.

Ku Yen-wu (1613-1682) was one of the most prominent scholars of the early Ch'ing. In his early youth he was also a member of the reforming Fu-she society. After the Manchu invasion he fought against them in South China and, refusing to collaborate, he spent the rest of his life as a wandering scholar in North China. He remained a Ming loyalist until his death and it is even possible that he was engaged in activities aimed at the overthrowing of Ch'ing rule. Six times he paid his respects to the tombs of the Ming Emperors.

The fall of the Ming called for an explanation and Ku Yen-wu sought to discover its basic causes. According to him it was fundamentally the empty, scholastic philosophizing of the Sung Neo-Confucians which was responsible for the failure of the scholar-officials to face realities and explained the ease with which they were ready to surrender and collaborate with the Ch'ing. He was thus critical of the Chu Hsi School and even more of the Wang Yang-ming doctrine, considering that its subjectivity and scorn of book learning had been debilitating to the Ming intelligentsia. He accused Wang Yang-ming of views which were, in effect, Ch'an Buddhist in origin, and of "pure-talk" (i.e. 3rd-century Taoist sophistry). He derided the effects of scholasticism, considering that its prime example—the eight-legged essay—had done more harm than the infamous Book Burning. All this criticism, from a Confucian position, led him to desire to revitalize classical scholarship while, simultaneously, placing also emphasis on practical activity. He himself was interested in agriculture, irrigation, labour-saving machinery and mining.

Ku Yen-wu put these ideas into practice himself and was noted for his great scholarship, especially in the field of historical phonetics. He was the author of a famous work "Five Books on Phonetics", devoted to the reconstruction of the ancient pronunciation of classical texts. Equally important were his two large works on historical geography which had an interesting emphasis on military and defensive aspects. As an ardent collector of ancient inscriptions he also left behind works on epigraphy.

In the above works Ku evolved methods which lay at the basis of the Han School of Learning of the Ch'ing period. Its aim was the "search for evidence" *(k'ao-cheng)*, the use of all available sources, the evidence of which should be subjected to a creative and critical analysis by means of the inductive method. This led to the establishment of the most fruitful movement in scholarship up to the 20th century, to exact methods of research in the historical sciences. However, this achievement pertained only to the humanities. As a result, Ku is regarded as the leading exponent and principal founder of the so-called Han School (called "Han" because it went back to the Han commentaries on the Classics which it regarded as more reliable than the Sung inasmuch as they were older and therefore closer to the sources). This school attacked the views of the Sung Neo-Confucianists and sought to prove that their cosmology was based on spurious texts of a late date and hence their conclusions were, therefore, often erroneous. It should be noted, in passing, that later on the Han School itself became restricted to a narrow and purely antiquarian approach to knowledge and was noted for its avoidance of synthesis; this was undoubtedly partly due to the political conditions of Ch'ing rule.

The best-known work of Ku Yen-wu was his *Jih-chih lu* ("Notes on Daily Learning"), a collection of significant essays on government, economics, literature, history and philology—the product of thirty years of vast reading and profound thought. It is in these essays that Ku's political ideas are expressed: his opposition to autocracy and his support of decentralization with the aim of giving more power to local governments. He also favoured land reforms, as well as the reintroduction of history into the examination system. Ku Yen-wu's works were a fine example of great intellectual capacity, while his ideas still remained within the framework of Confucian thought.

The third of the outstanding thinkers of the Early Ch'ing period was Wang Fu-chih (1619-1692). He was a member of a prominent scholar family and had fought against the Manchus when they invaded his native province Hunan. He then joined the court of the Ming Prince of Kuei and finally, disgusted by the factional struggle which went on there, he retired from active life. He spent the next forty years studying and writing and it has been said that "his passion for learning was exceeded only by his industry". Wang refused to have any dealings with the Manchus; he considered them to be barbarians and challenged the legitimacy of their rule.

Wang Fu-chih was an able philosopher who was bitterly opposed to the views of Wang Yang-ming; he considered himself a follower of the philosopher Chang Tsai. In fact, however, he developed his ideas in line with the sceptical trend in Confucian thought and went quite far in the direction of a materialistic outlook. He was also a profound student and writer on Buddhism and Taoism. His two best-known works, however, are reflections on history: "On Reading the Comprehensive Mirror" and "On Sung History". It is in these also that he expressed his political views. According to Wang, the state should be for the people and not for the rulers, and the criterion for judging the best form of government is whether it is of the greatest service to the people. He showed as well a critical awareness of the corruption and other failings of a bureaucratic system of government. Wang was a strong defender of Chinese culture and thus an opponent of alien rule over China at any period of its history. He placed great patriotic emphasis in his view of the past, stressing the role of Yüeh Fei as a hero and that of Ch'in Kuei as a traitor. His pronounced anti-barbarian views were undoubtedly intimately connected with his attitude towards the Ch'ing. He also drew the conclusion that China was best able to defend herself when the provinces were strong and the powers of the autocratic central government limited. Simultaneously, he was aware of the fact that China was not necessarily the only existing civilization.

Still more interesting were Wang Fu-chih's ideas on historical evolution. He saw this process as progressing from stage to stage of social development, in far-reaching dependence on the interplay of historical forces and circumstances in which the role of the individual was somewhat limited. However, although Wang was formally a Confucianist, he was one of the very few in the history of Chinese thought —Wang Ch'ung comes to mind—who did not harken back to the Golden Age of the Great Sages for he saw the ancient period in its true light, as a dark and crude epoch. Wang's writings were the only form in which it was possible for him to express his convictions in the conditions of Ch'ing rule. The great majority of them were not published in his own time and only saw the light of day two centuries later. The reason was fear of the Ch'ing inquisition, in spite of the veiled style which he employed. At the end of the 19th century his ideas were rediscovered by the leaders of the anti-Ch'ing reform movement and became popular and of considerable influence.

In the attack on the premises of Sung Neo-Confucian thought an important contribution was also made by the Yen-Li school. This represented the views of two scholars of the early Ch'ing period—Yen Yüang and Li Kung.

Yen Yüan (1635-1704) was a classical scholar, teacher and practitioner of medicine. He had been led by his own personal experiences into doubting the validity of Neo-Confucianism and he came to the conclusion that the views of the Sung philosophers were based on a misinterpretation and discrepancies in reading the Classics; they were greatly tainted by the influence of Buddhist ideas and were thus misleading and heterodox. Yen set himself the aim of studying the Classics to discover the true teaching of the Sages. He came to the conclusion that the Sages had stressed primarily practical activity, whereas the speculative, metaphysical philosophy of the Neo-Confucianists had resulted only in bookishness, in contemplation and abstract morality, in creating a "world of words". Education on this basis was thus worthless because it was mentally stultifying. Yen Yüan, who was probably the most radical critic of Neo-Confucianist philosophy, attacked its metaphysical dualist conception of man's nature (as composed of both a physical element and a heavenly implanted principle), putting forth instead a materialistic concept of a purely physical nature. To the "world of words" he counterposed a "world of action" and put his own ideas into practice by means of his teaching methods. His ideas were then propagated by his main follower, Li Kung (1659-1733), who was also an eminent scholar. He refused to take office under the Ch'ing and thus remained a teacher all his life.

The ideas of these scholars, as well as of the other previously mentioned thinkers of the Early Ch'ing period, were developed most fully by the man regarded as the greatest of the relatively few really able philosophers of the Ch'ing period—Tai Chen (1724-1777). He was a renowned scholar, also considerably interested in science and mathematics. He never became an official and did much work devoted to textual criticism, employing the methods of the Han School, especially in the fields of etymology and phonology. Tai Chen sought to discredit Neo-Confucianism on philosophical grounds. His views have been described, it would seem correctly, as materialistic monism. He followed Yen Yüan's criticism of Neo-Confucianist dualism and stressed the purely physical aspect of man's nature. Simultaneously, he emphasized the recognizability, by means of study, of the principles of governing nature which he considered to be inherently orderly patterns. In connection with this he opposed the tendency towards introspection, meditation and the seeking of sudden englightenment—all of these contained in the Neo-Confucian teachings—amongst others, for the reason that these showed the effect of Buddhist influence.

The struggle of these individuals is important in the history of Chinese thought; but it does not mean that they were successful in overcoming the influence of Neo-Confucian philosophy, which was strongly supported by the Ch'ing rulers as the obligatory, orthodox ideology. It should be noted, moreover, that even this sceptical, materialist trend also dealt with the same identical topics and problems and also used the same Classic texts as did the Neo-Confucianists, while seeking only to give new answers and interpretations without challenging the fundamental premises of Confucianism as such. This state of affairs was to remain in existence until the last decade of the 19th and the first years of the 20th centuries. It should also be noted that in spite of the activity of the Jesuits there is still no evidence of any significant repercussion of the contacts with Europe.

II. Ch'ing Patronage of Culture

The lavish patronage of Chinese Confucian culture by both K'ang-hsi and Ch'ien-lung has been a subject which has given rise to a certain amount of confusion. It seems, however, that the aim of the Manchu rulers in this field is relatively clear. They strove to achieve three results; firstly, to lessen the opposition and thus to bring about the submissiveness of the scholar-official caste (this is particularly true of the K'ang-hsi era); secondly, to impose ideological conformity by inculcating the most orthodox versions of Confucian thought; and thirdly, to show that, in spite of their alien origin, the Ch'ing rulers were capable of demonstrating a proper appreciation of Chinese culture. It should be admitted that, taken as a whole, the Ch'ing succeeded in achieving these aims.

Of the many famous works produced during K'ang-hsi's reign mention should be made of the following. The *Ming shih* was the chief historical achievement of the period; this project was begun in 1679 when K'ang-hsi issued his invitation to 185 of the most renowned scholars to participate in an examination for the post of compilers of the history. It should be noted that 152 accepted the invitation. Much discussion ensued on how the Ming history was to be written, but ultimately it followed the pattern of the previous standard histories and no new departure was undertaken. The other works included the famous K'ang-hsi dictionary, published in 1716, which contained 49,000 characters; a large administrative geography; a great compendium on painting and calligraphy, as well as an immense phrase dictionary. But perhaps the best known of the scholarly productions was the *Ku-chin t'u-shu chi-ch'eng* ("Synthesis of Books and Illustrations of Ancient and Modern Times"), a huge work of 10,000 chapters and 100 million characters. Sixty-four sets of it were printed in the first edition in 1728, using up a quarter-million hand-cut copper type characters. A later 1888 edition is in 1700 volumes. The word encyclopaedia might be misleading, as the work consists mainly of extracts from older books.

In the Ch'ien-lung period a large number of works of a similar nature were also produced and mention must be made, at least, of the most famous, usually referred to as the Imperial Manuscript Library *(Ssu-k'u ch'üan-shu,* "Complete Library in Four Branches"). This was the result of a twenty-year-long project started in 1772 in which 15,000 copyists were employed. An enormous quantity of rare books were collected from the Imperial Library, the Ming Encyclopaedia and from private book collectors; 10,230 of these were reviewed, while 3450 were copied into the Library. Simultaneously, a great Imperial Catalogue was compiled which still constitutes the most complete reference work in the field of Chinese bibliography. The Manuscript Library was too immense to be printed and therefore four handwritten sets of 36,000 volumes each were first made; three further sets were copied later on. Of the seven sets, three were later destroyed. It should be noted, however, that the occasion for the compilation of the Manuscript Library was simultaneously utilized for what has been referred to as the literary inquisition of Ch'ien-lung. The review of all extant literature made it possible to destroy thousands of works, together with their printing blocks, which were found to be offensive to the Ch'ing dynasty. In the works which were allowed to exist, all references to the Manchus and earlier nomads which could be thought pejorative were expunged, as well as any ideas considered to be subversive. An index of banned books was also established. The persecution was by no means only a literary one; just as in the times of K'ang-hsi, a number of authors were executed and their families also punished. Thus the patronage of the arts of the two so-called great Ch'ing emperors had a curious nature, to say the least. The effects were to make only the most orthodox views prevail and to stifle any possibility of creative, independent thought.

III. Painting

The Early and Middle Ch'ing periods are the last time in which it is worthwhile to refer once again to the history of Chinese painting. This was an age of great collectors and of these, as mentioned, the greatest was Ch'ien-lung himself. Over 8000 scrolls were assembled by him which in later times constituted the bulk of the collection in the famous National Palace Museum of Peking. After the fall of the Ch'ing dynasty, however, some of the paintings from this collection were stolen by former Ch'ing officials and the same fate met a considerable number of paintings in 1947, when they were shipped to Taiwan by the Kuomintang.

In the style of painting there is, in effect, no break of continuity between the Ming and the Early Ch'ing period. There is still, however, less creativeness and more and more eclecticism; this is the last expression of the great tradition of this art. Nevertheless, some very able artists are still to be found in the second half of the 17th and the first half of the 18th centuries, most of them scholar-officials. The following artists are the best known out of the many hundreds of the painters of this age. Wang Shih-min (1592-1680) came from a rich gentry family and was an official until 1636, when he retired and devoted the rest of his life to painting. He had been the pupil of Tung Ch'i-ch'ang and was much influenced by Tung's aesthetic ideas. He studied and copied the Yüan masters, using for this purpose his own great collection of paintings, and continued the high level of technical proficiency of the Ming painters. Wang Chien (1598-1677), who also came from a rich gentry family and was likewise the owner of a large collection of great paintings, was closely associated with the above. He also loved to imitate the Yüan masters and both of them were primarily landscape painters. In the younger generation there were two noted painters. One was Wang Hui (1632-1717), who came from a family of famous painters and for twenty years was the favourite pupil of Wang Shih-min. By copying vast quantities of Yüan paintings he acquired a wide range of styles and has been called the "epitome of an eclectic artist". According to himself, his supposed aim was to bring together "the brush stroke of the Yüan, the delicacy of composition of the Sung and the vitality of the T'ang". The second was Wang Yüan-ch'i (1642-1715), the grandson of Shih-min, himself a high court official and court painter to K'ang-hsi. He was also one of the compilers of the already-mentioned vast compendium on painting and calligraphy. He has been called "a painter's painter" and experimented with the effects of colour.

These Four Wangs (all of them from two towns in Kiangsu) together with Wu Li and Yün Shou-p'ing are known as the Six Great Masters of the Ch'ing. With one exception they were all followers of the Literary Men's Painting and all of them can be considered as the last, epigonic representatives of the Ming tradition. Wu Li (1632-1718) was a pupil of Wang Shih-min and a close friend of Wang Hui. He was primarily a painter of landscapes. Although he later became a Jesuit missionary there is no sign of any influence of European painting in his works. Yün Shou-p'ing (1633-1690) was the only one in this group who was not a scholar-official. He was the last of the great flower painters and the story goes that he had decided to concentrate on this genre because he felt that he could not compete in landscape painting with his friend, Wang Hui.

Mention must be made at least of two more painters who were completely outside of the above tradition and who represented rather the significant trend, often referred to as the individualist. Both of them were Buddhist monks. Chu Ta (better known as Pa-ta Shan-jen, 1626-1710?) painted in the style of the great Ch'an Buddhist artists. He was supposedly a Ming prince who had retired to a monastery after the Manchu invasion. His paintings dealt mostly with unusual birds and flowers. While his style is deceptively effortless and simple, his birds are remarkable for their moodiness and expressiveness. Tao-chi (Shih-t'ao, 1630-1707) has been considered by some authors as perhaps the most gifted Ch'ing artist. He was a rebel against tradition who insisted on the need for individuality which he gave vent to in his notes on painting. But this was a voice crying in a wilderness of moribund, sterile conformity which spread more and more under the deadweight influence of Ch'ing rule which, with its penchant for everything hidebound and conservative, contributed substantially—and this was not accidental—to stifling and practically killing off the greatest of the Chinese art forms.

The European influence which dated from the Ch'ien-lung period on had curiously little effect. The work of two Jesuit painters, J. Castiglione (1688-1766) and J. D. Attiret (1702-1768), produced a rather bizarre blend of the two approaches and techniques. There was no sign of any synthesis of the two traditions; whether such a thing will some day come about it is difficult to say. It is idle to speculate on what the future has in store for Chinese painting, although it is hard to believe that this great tradition which was responsible for the production of so many masterpieces will not one day stimulate and lead to a renewed flourishing of a splendid art based on the vast riches of its glorious past.

IV. Ceramics

It is obvious that the Chinese craftsmen did not suddenly lose their great skill with the advent of Manchu rule and that the marvellous workmanship which they displayed, the result of many centuries of tradition, was therefore continued. However, the Ch'ing was a period of extremely limited inventiveness and inspiration in all fields and one in which a shallow archaism prevailed. But this was perhaps least evident in ceramics, inasmuch as this was the youngest and therefore the last of the great Chinese arts to flower. The early Ch'ing era (1680-1750) saw probably the greatest further development in the manufacture of Chinese porcelain. This was especially due to the great expansion of the famous Ching-te-chen works which were rebuilt in the 1680s. This Kiangsi city now had over 3,000 kilns and more than 100,000 workers employed in the manufacture of porcelain. A high level of technical proficiency was achieved and very skilled imitations of older ware were also produced. The Ching-te-chen potteries worked primarily for the Imperial court, although a considerable part of their production was also earmarked for export. Just as in the earlier periods, there were many other centres of ceramic production, of which perhaps one of the most interesting was Tehua in Fukien specializing in porcelain figures.

Ch'ing porcelain was noted for its decoration and the great varieties of colours employed; this is especially true of enamelled ware which is best known under its French classification of *famille verte, noire et rose*. But simultaneously a number of new monochrome glazes were introduced, such as the splendid *sang de boeuf*, which were perhaps the best achievements of the period. In comparison with Ming ware the products of the Ch'ing period, while showing great technical skill, have probably less originality and vitality, although some authors do consider the K'ang-hsi period as the true golden age of Chinese porcelain.

All throughout the 18th century vast quantities of Chinese porcelain were exported to Europe and while this had some influence on the designs employed on the Chinese ware it was of much greater significance for the development of European ceramics. The scope of this export and the prevalence of Chinese porcelain in European collections have made this Chinese art form undoubtedly the best known in the West and thus the subject of a great amount of specialized research and study. After the 18th century, however, although the flood of Chinese ware to Europe did not cease by any means and the quantity produced in China did not decrease, there is little noteworthy in this field, inasmuch as the 19th-century products are already nothing but pure imitations either of the early Ch'ing or of the Ming eras. It would seem that the generally stultifying effect of Ch'ing rule caught up with this field as well.

V. Literature

In the general aridity and petrification of Chinese culture, which was its fate in the 18th century, two novels stand out as the exception to this state of affairs. The first of these is the *Ju-lin wai-shih* ("The Unofficial History of the Literati"; or "The Scholars"), the work of Wu Ching-tzu (1701-1754). Wu came from a prominent scholar family, but himself was an unsuccessful and impoverished writer throughout his entire life. His work is the first novel of social satire, perhaps the strongest of its kind ever to be written. In it he showed up the hypocrisy of contemporary officialdom and attacked the examination system, as well as a great number of current superstitions. The novel is actually a grouping together of a number of episodes which contain excellent characterizations.

It is also in the 18th century that the *Hung-lou meng* ("The Dream of the Red Chamber"), the great Ch'ing novel, according to some the greatest of all Chinese novels, was written. It was the work of Ts'ao Chan (1715-1763) who wrote the first 80 chapters but did not complete the work before his death. The next 40 chapters are from the pen of Kai E. The part written by Ts'ao Chan is largely autobiographical and reflects the fate of his own family, a prominent, rich Chinese gentry clan whose fortune was established by their collaboration with the Manchus from an early date. It is the life of this aristocratic family and the slow process of its decay which constitute the basic subject of the novel and give it considerable sociological significance. The main theme of the novel, however, deals with the tragic love story of two of its main adolescent characters. There is also a vast assemblage of other personages, all of whom are vividly portrayed.

CHAPTER 26

China in the First Decades of the 19th Century

I. Manchu Rule in the First Half of the 19th Century

The decay and decline of Ch'ing rule steadily increased during the first decades of the 19th century. While it is true that the reign of Chia-ch'ing (1796-1820) began by the Emperor accomplishing the overthrow of Ch'ien-lung's favourite, Ho-shen (he permitted him to commit suicide and confiscated his entire fantastic fortune, see p. 228), no real attempt was made to grapple with the corruption which was eroding the whole government administration. The worthlessness of the Manchu Banners had already been proved during the White Lotus rebellion, which had been finally suppressed at such great cost in 1803-1804. This did not, however, put an end to popular discontent and the activities of the secret societies continued on a large scale.

This time it was the T'ien Li (Heavenly Reason) society, probably an offshoot of the White Lotus, which was the principal organizing force of a new armed insurrection against Manchu rule. Its activities had begun by 1811 and the attempted assassination of the Emperor in 1812 is sometimes connected with this society, although the matter is not quite clear. The T'ien Li planned a general uprising for October 1813 to cover the area of Hopei, Honan, Shantung and Shansi, the main feature of which was to be the capture of Peking itself. A betrayal of the plans caused the rising to be launched eight days earlier than had been initially foreseen and this led to a lack of coordination between the various insurgent groups. Nevertheless, the Imperial Palace itself was invaded, although the small force which had accomplished this was quickly exterminated. The rising spread to a considerable part of Shantung, Hopei and Honan and the dispatch of many troops was necessary before it could be successfully suppressed with the customary slaughter of many thousands of the participants.

The crisis of Ch'ing rule deepened still further in the years of Chia-ch'ing's successor, Tao-kuang (1821-1851), which saw both the first open aggression of the Western powers against China—the First Opium War—as well as the beginning of the great peasant revolution, the Taiping Movement. All the factors which went into the making of this crisis and were already present at the end of the Ch'ien-lung period became still more prominent now; in particular, the constant increase of the population, as contrasted with the very limited increase of food production, led to a distinct further impoverishment of the peasantry. The situation was further aggravated by the worsening of the government's financial position and this, in turn, was rendered still more serious by such expensive ventures as, for example, the putting down of the Uighur uprising in Eastern Turkestan—the war against Jehangir, 1826-1827. One of the most important elements, however, in the financial crisis of the Ch'ing government arose from the changes which had taken place in its trade relations with the West and in this the opium problem was of cardinal importance.

II. China and the Western Powers

In the second half of the 18th century and the first decades of the 19th century a further considerable development of trade between China and the main capitalist countries took place. The initiative in this development was always primarily that of the Western powers, inasmuch as this trade was of relatively limited importance to China in view of the almost completely self-sufficient nature of its economy. The often-quoted words which Ch'ien-lung addressed to King George III in answer to the Macartney mission's attempts to increase trade and contacts with China are a good illustration of this condition and of the Chinese state of mind:

> We possess all things. I set no value on objects strange or ingenious, and have no use for your country's manufactures...our Empire possesses all things in prolific abundance and lacks no product within its own borders. There was therefore no need to import the manufactures of outside barbarians in exchange for our own produce. But as the tea, silk and porcelain which the Empire produces are absolute necessities to European nations and to yourselves, we have permitted, as a signal mark of favour, that foreign merchants should be established at Canton, so that your wants might be supplied and your country thus participate in our beneficence.

The Western powers, particularly England, were, on the other hand, interested not only in the acquiring of goods from China, especially the tea, silk and porcelain mentioned by Ch'ien-lung, but also in the opening up of China as a potentially great market for European manufactures. Simultaneously, the Europeans at this stage were always faced with the problem of what to sell to China, in view of the limited demand then extant for European goods. In this whole process the leading position of Great Britain evolved logically from the fact that it was the most highly developed capitalist country of the period and the one which possessed the greatest colonial empire in Asia.

The policy of the Ch'ing government towards trade and contacts with the West stemmed not only from the relatively marginal importance of foreign trade to the Chinese economy, but also from a number of political reasons; these included both the growing internal crisis of the Ch'ing regime, as well as the previous experiences of China with the Europeans dating back to the 16th and 17th centuries. The latter were reinforced by the further spread of European influence and rule in Asia, in particular by the British conquest of India. It is against this background that the Ch'ing government embarked on a conscious policy of the isolation of China from the rest of the world and on a concurrent restriction of commerce, which was conducted on the basis that could be summed up in the words—take it or leave it. These policies were put into effect from the beginning of the 18th century and were made still clearer when in 1757 trade with the West was restricted solely to Canton. (Trade with Russia, it will be remembered, was limited to Kiakhta.) The effects of this policy of isolation were mixed; on the one hand, it undoubtedly served the purpose of protecting China for a certain period of time from the penetration of the European powers but, on the other hand, it resulted in accentuating still more the gap between the rapid development of European civilization and the stagnation of Chinese civilization. Therefore, the ultimate outcome was undoubtedly negative, inasmuch as China was thereby rendered less prepared to face the dangers of the contacts with the West when they did come about on a full scale.

In the Canton trade the institution of greatest importance was the Cohong *(kung-hang)*, a limited guild of merchants, maximum thirteen, which had a practical monopoly on foreign trade. The Cohong was established in 1720 and, with the exception of a short period (1771-1782) when it was temporarily dissolved, it constituted the sole basis for the conduct of the Canton trade. While it had not been initially sponsored by the government, it later became, in fact, a government-supervised and imposed monopoly. It was also the source of an infinite amount of corruption of all the government officials who had any contact with it and with foreign trade. The Cohong monopoly was also accompanied by far-going restrictions on foreign merchants who were thus not only unable to deal with anyone else, but also prohibited from engaging in commerce anywhere else than in Canton. Simultaneously, the foreign merchants were subject to a rather vexatious set of regulations pertaining to their mode of life while in Canton, and a number of the financial aspects of the conduct of the trade, such as customs payments and so forth, were quite irregular and arbitrary in nature. It was also somewhat difficult to foresee the size of bribes which it was necessary to offer to the Chinese officials. One might ask the question—and this was sometimes posed by the Chinese during this period—why, in view of the above, were the European merchants so anxious to continue the China trade under such irksome conditions? The answer is not really difficult—it was primarily due to the very considerable profits which this trade brought them, stemming from a constantly growing demand in Europe for Chinese products.

By far the greatest share of the China trade was in the hands of England. Until its dissolution in 1834 the main British presence in the trade with China was the East India Company, whose political and economic position in India was very closely bound up with the development of commerce with China. Initially one of the main items exported to China and one of the few goods which could be successfully placed on the Chinese market was Indian raw cotton. Up to the end of the 18th century, however, the balance of trade was always very much in China's favour and this gave rise to the necessity of large payments of silver in exchange for the tea and silk exported from China. English trade developed more and more on a pattern of a triangle; English manufactures, particularly textiles, were sent to India; Indian products were then exported to China and, finally, Chinese tea and silk would be imported to England. The crucial problem, however, was what to find to sell to China to avoid the constant necessity of payment in silver. This problem was truly complicated in view of the lack of interest in goods from the West due to the self-sufficiency of the Chinese economy. This point cannot be stressed too strongly as it affected not only this period but the entire relations of the European powers and China during the 19th century. The best account of this is by Robert Hart, whose expertise was really considerable. He wrote: "The Chinese have the best food in the world, rice; the best drink, tea; and the best clothing, cotton, silk and fur. They do not need to buy a penny's worth elsewhere; while their empire is in itself so great, and they themselves so numerous, that sales to each other make up an enormous and sufficient trade and export to foreign countries is unnecessary."

This problem was ultimately solved during the first thirty years of the 19th century by the development of the opium trade by the British on a vast scale.

III. The Opium Question

Opium had been known in China as a medicine since the 8th century. It had probably been introduced into the country by the Arab merchants. The habit of smoking it (initially it was mixed with tobacco) was brought in by the Dutch in the 17th century during their occupation of Taiwan. The custom of smoking opium by itself developed probably in the early 18th century but the prevalence of the habit and its becoming first a social problem and then a plague dates only from the end of that century. The basic causes for this phenomenon have as yet not been thoroughly examined but there seems little doubt that the spread of opium was a reflection of the general demoralization of Chinese society under Ch'ing rule. It is characteristic that the greatest usage of opium was to be found among the personnel of the Ch'ing administration and especially among the Manchu Bannermen; in this period the habit was still primarily restricted to the population of the towns. Starting from the main ports, especially Canton, opium smoking spread inland and by the beginning of the 19th century it had extended widely over the entire country. By 1840 it was estimated that there were at least two million people addicted to the usage of this terrible, ruinous drug.

It is difficult, indeed, to overstate the political and social effects of the opium question. Peffer puts it very succinctly: "In the whole history of East-West relations nothing was so culpable, so squalid, and so nearly unforgettable as the opium evil forced on China." In this spread of opium the importation of the drug into China by the British was a vital factor. It should be stated that all the other countries which traded with China were also involved in this commerce. But the role and share of England was predominant and of cardinal importance. The growth of the opium trade, which was the largest commerce of the time in any single commodity, can be illustrated by the following figures (number of chests annually):

1720s		200-300
1767		1000
1790		4000
1811-1821	yearly average	4494
1821-1828	,, ,,	9708
1828-1835	,, ,,	18,710
1835-1836	trade year	30,000
1838-1839	,, ,,	40,000

The average weight of a chest of opium was 133 lb.

The profits on this "most infamous and atrocious trade" (Gladstone's words) were immense. Already in 1836 the opium sold in China by the British brought in 18 million dollars, one million more than the value of the tea and the silk exported from China.*

*The dollars referred to are the Chinese yuans or the Mexican silver dollars and it is this currency which will be employed throughout the book unless a note is made to the contrary. The dollar was worth at this period 0.72 tael, the Chinese unit of monetary account; thus, one tael=$1.38. Simultaneously, £1=three taels or one tael=6s. 8d. The tael, as mentioned, was the equivalent of one liang, i.e. an ounce of silver, but this weight varied according to locality from 525 to 585 grains and thus there were up to eighty different taels in use.

The tea constituted three-fifths while silk one-fifth of the entire export. What is of undoubtedly greatest significance here is that the ultimate solution of the English deficit in the balance of payments in the China trade had thus been found in the importation of opium. The profits, however, were still in reality much more considerable, inasmuch as the bulk of the opium imported into China was produced by the East India Company in India. Here this production had been the Company's monopoly since 1797 and its cultivation had been made compulsory for its peasant tenants. The gap between the price of a chest of opium in India and its price on the Canton market was very great. Thus the profits which accrued to the Indian government, after the dissolution of the East India Company, from the sale of opium to China amounted to £1,200,000 in 1836, which was one-tenth of its entire revenue. These profits rose still more, to almost £4 million in the 1850s, amounting to one-seventh of the revenue.

Simultaneously, it must be noted that the British government drew considerable profit from the taxes on tea, which was now being bought entirely by the profits from the opium trade. In the 1830s an average of 30 million pounds of tea was imported and the taxes on it amounted already to £3.3 million, one-tenth of the total revenues of the British government. These figures provided the necessary background for understanding the real motivation of British policy in this period and of the essential setting of the First Opium War. The East India Company, which prohibited the sale of opium in India itself, did not officially participate in the trade. The opium, marked with the company's seal, was sold to private English merchants who sailed to China under the Company's licence and who participated in the so-called country trade between India and China which handled three-quarters of the total British exports to China and constituted the economic foundation for the rise of the British foreign merchant community in China. This trade extended, in fact, also to most of the coastal commerce in South-east Asia where the British merchants were successful in eliminating the competition of the heretofore large-scale Chinese trade. Thus, three factors were present, all vitally interested in the continuation and further expansion of the lucrative opium trade: the British government in India, the government of the United Kingdom, and the English private merchants in Canton.

The policy of the Ch'ing government in regard to the opium problem was, during the earlier stages, both vacillating and inconsistent. The first prohibitions of the trade date from 1729 and they were to be repeated later, especially in 1796 and 1800. Thus from the beginning of the 19th century the trade, from the Chinese point of view, was completely illegal and it developed as a smuggling, contraband commerce. The principal smugglers were the foreign merchants, while initially the local smuggling, i.e. from ship to coast, was mostly conducted by the Chinese (but not the Cohong); after 1820, in view of sharper Chinese control, this was also mostly in the hands of the foreign merchants themselves who employed heavily armed vessels for this purpose. The main base of the smugglers was not Canton itself but Lintin (Lingting) Island in the Pearl River estuary; here, special permanently moored receiving ships were employed from which the opium was then sent inland. The smuggling was made possible by the inability of the Ch'ing government to enforce its own prohibitions and by the connivance of corrupt officials for whom the bribes from the opium merchants were an important source of income. Thus the opium trade became, in turn, a further source for the demoralization and decay of the entire Ch'ing government apparatus, inasmuch as the corruption connected with it reached up to the very highest echelons of the imperial bureaucracy.

The economic and social consequences of the opium trade ultimately brought about a new reformulation of Ch'ing government policies. One of the main problems was that not only did the previous situation, in which a favourable balance of trade and the inflow of silver into China existed, cease to prevail as a result of the importation of opium but, what is still more important, a drain of silver from China now resulted. This outflow amounted to from 2 to 3 million taels annually in the period 1821-1830, rising to 10 million taels annually in the years 1831-1833. One source gives the following figures for the period 1829-1840: import of silver—7 million dollars; export of silver— 56 million. The repercussions of this phenomenon on the domestic and economic situation were very serious and far-reaching, inasmuch as they involved a rise in the price of silver in relation to the everyday monetary unit, the copper cash. Thus, if generally speaking one tael of silver in 1800 was worth 1000 cash, by 1838 the price had gone up to at least 1500; this, of course, varied greatly depending on the given locality. Inasmuch as taxes were paid primarily in silver this meant, in turn, a further impoverishment of the peasants and thus led to an aggravation of the social crisis which was already sufficiently acute. It was this factor, as well as the fatal effect of the spread of the opium habit in the Ch'ing army, which led to a re-examination of the entire problem by the Ch'ing government beginning with 1836.

IV. British Policy Towards China

The removal of restrictions which existed on the expansion of trade in China had been one of the basic aims of British foreign policy from the end of the 18th century. Already in 1793 the British government had sent a sizeable mission headed by Lord Macartney (1737-1806; a previous British ambassador in Russia) to China, the expenses of which (around £78,000) were covered, characteristically enough, by the East India Company. Its aims, as outlined in the memorial presented by Macartney to the Ch'ing government, were the following: (1) an opening of other ports besides Canton for English trade (Tientsin, Ningpo, Chusan Island): (2) the establishment of trading facilities in Peking: (3) the cession of an island near Canton or Chusan for this purpose; (4) the regulation of customs payments. In the conduct of the mission itself there was also an implicit desire to establish direct contact with the Ch'ing government. While the mission, which was regarded as a customary tribute-bearing one, was courteously received by Ch'ien-lung in Jehol—even the usual stumbling-block, the Chinese demand that foreign envoys perform the kotow (the three kneelings and nine prostrations) to the Emperor was overcome—all the demands of the British were rejected and thus the mission itself was, in fact, a failure. Very interesting accounts of the mission itself are still extant (as, for example, Macartney's Journal), as well as the answer of Ch'ien-lung which rebutted in detail all the English requests. The mission was bound to fail in view of the fundamental differences in outlook between China and England on foreign relations and the Ch'ing policy in respect to contacts with European powers.

The next British attempt at negotiations was the sending in 1816 of a mission headed by Lord Amherst (1773-1857, later Governor-general of India, 1823-1828). Although the mission did receive permission to proceed from Tientsin to Peking, a comedy of errors then ensued, involving both the question of the kotow and schemes of face-saving officials. The result was that the scheduled meeting between the British envoy and Chia-ch'ing never took place and the mission was ordered to depart from China. Thus its failure was even more resounding than that of its predecessor. It is not improbable that the war which the British had been waging against Nepal in the years 1814-1816, whom the Ch'ing considered as a vassal state after having defeated the Gurkhas in 1792, had a certain bearing on the outcome of this mission.

Fig. 51. Artist unknown, "Tribute from the State of San Fu Chi", Ming (?). (Author's collection.)

Fig. 52.   The White Dagoba, Peking. (Author's photo.)

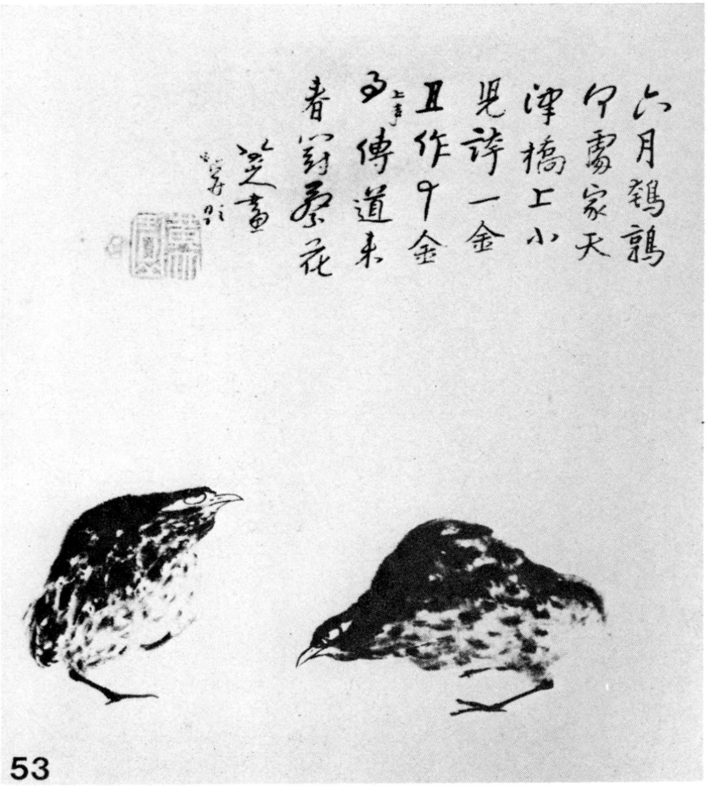

六月鶴鶉
夕畫家天
津橋上小
兒詩一金
且作9金
多傳道来
青谿原花
逸畫

53

FIG. 53. Chu Ta, "Birds", Ch'ing. (*Hua-yüan . . . , op. cit.*, vol. III, pl. 8/6.)

FIG. 54. Wang Yün-ho, "A Hermit's Hut", Ch'ing (?). (Author's collection.)

FIG. 55. Tilling the soil, Szechuan. (Author's photo.)

PART IX

China During the Opium Wars and the Taiping Revolution

CHAPTER 27

The First Opium War

I. The Immediate Background

The end of the monopoly of the East India Company on trade with China, which was actually restricted only to tea, and which had been demanded by the English private merchant community in Canton for a long time, also gave rise to a new situation in the Canton trade system, where the representative of the Company had been the main spokesman and contact between the Chinese authorities and the British merchants. Now the government was brought directly into the problem; in 1834 Lord Napier was nominated the Chief Superintendent of Trade and sent to China in the official capacity of a representative of the British government. His instructions were, amongst others, to seek direct contact with the higher Ch'ing officials in Canton. Napier's behaviour was that of a bull in a china shop and involved the breaking of all the hitherto-established practices and adhered-to precedents, while including also an attempt to use force for the desired communication with Li K'un, the Governor-general of Liangkwang (Kwangtung and Kwangsi). The efforts, which led even to a temporary cessation of trade, were a complete failure. Napier himself fell ill, retired to Macao, and died shortly thereafter. His policy and conduct were conveniently repudiated by the British government and his next two successors as superintendent followed a "policy of quiescence", i.e. of agreeing to the existing *status quo*, a position which was very much to the taste of the Ch'ing officials, inasmuch as they were not in the slightest degree interested in its change.

The situation was altered when this post was taken over by Captain Charles Elliot (1801-1875), a representative of the "forward policy" adhered to by most British merchants in Canton, to the effect that force would be necessary in order to establish the type of relations—"the opening of China"—which they desired and which was also successfully propagated by British manufacturers, enticed by the prospects of a vast Chinese market. This more aggressive position of the English now coincided with the moment when the Ch'ing government, due to the growth of the opium trade and its consequences, was finally determined to tackle the opium question in deadly earnest.

In the years 1836-1838 the debate initiated by the Emperor on the policies to be followed in regards to the opium question involved practically all the top Ch'ing officials. Three basic views were represented: one group put forth proposals in favour of the legalization of the opium trade, maintaining that this would lead to an increase of customs receipts and to a decrease in the drain of silver. The second group held diametrically opposite views and favoured the total suppression of both the illicit trade and the usage of opium. In between these two groups there was undoubtedly a large number of officials who favoured the maintenance of the *status quo* inasmuch as their profits from bribes received in connection with opium smuggling provided them with a very lucrative source of income, while their concern for the state and the welfare of the country was non-existent.

The principal representative of the group favouring decisive measures, aimed at the suppression of all the aspects of the opium traffic, was the Governor-general of Hukwang (Hunan and Hupei), Lin Tse-hsü (1785-1850). Lin was an exceptional figure on the Chinese political arena of this period—a rare phenomenon of a steadfast and incorruptible official who took his Confucian ethics seriously. Already early in his career as an official his just and humane conduct earned him the name, given to him by the people, of "Clear as the Sky". In the provinces under his rule he put into effect a well-thought-out programme for eradicating the opium evil, in which he had considerable success. His memorials to the throne advocating the total suppression of the traffic in China and the elimination of the contraband trade impressed the Emperor greatly; Lin was called to Peking where he had nineteen audiences with the ruler, in which he succeeded completely in convincing the weak and vacillating Tao-Kuang of the correctness of his policy. As a result, he received at the end of 1838 an appointment to serve as an Imperial Commissioner with full powers, to proceed to Canton in order to examine the situation there, and to put a definite end to the opium trade. The events which led to the outbreak of the First Opium War are inextricably intertwined with the carrying out of this mission by Lin.

Lin Tse-hsü arrived in Canton on March 10, 1839. After a week devoted to making enquiries on the spot he informed, on March 18, the Cohong merchants who were responsible for the conduct of the foreign traders that the opium trade must cease completely. In effect, greatly increased Chinese control had already reduced the opium trade in the Canton area to extremely limited proportions. Lin then, addressing himself to the foreign merchants, demanded that they turn over to the Chinese government all the illicit stocks of opium in their possession and sign a bond promising not to import the drug any more. Thus he thereby tackled the very root of the problem—the foreign importers.

The initial negotiations resulted only in the offer by the merchants, who were led by Elliot from March 24 on, to surrender a derisory quantity of 1037 chests, while English ships which carried over 20,000 chests scurried out of the waters close to Canton. Ultimately, Lin ordered the foreign factories to be surrounded by Chinese troops and had all the Chinese servants of the foreign merchants recalled; the merchant colony (around 350 men) was forced to undergo truly terrible privation, having to cook, wash and sweep by themselves. This "inhuman and barbaric" treatment proved effective.

Most of the merchants signed pledges never to revert to the opium trade, which almost all of them later broke. On March 28 Elliot agreed, in the name of the British government, to turn over all the opium held by the English merchants, i.e. 20,282 chests (actually 20,291), which were worth, according to various estimates, from £2.4 to 3 million ($9 to 10 million). It took almost two months to gather all the opium stocks involved and then, after having earlier composed in properly archaic language "an Address to the Spirit of the Sea", as he tells us in his diary, in which he explained to the Spirit what he intended to do, Lin ordered a public destruction, watched by both Chinese and foreigners, of the entire quantity of opium, with the exception of eight chests sent to Peking as a sample. It was not burned, as is often wrongly stated, for fear that the remnants might be collected; it was mixed with lime, salt and water and sluiced off into the sea. June 3—the date when the 22-day-long destruction of the opium began—is a noteworthy landmark in Chinese history.

With the surrender of the opium all the restrictions on the foreign merchants and on trade were removed by Lin Tse-hsü. The British, however, led by Elliot, all left Canton and now refused to give the bond that they would not engage in the future in dealing with opium. What direct trade now remained was largely in the hands of the Americans who gladly availed themselves of the opportunity to make an additional profit by handling British goods. Simultaneously, the British resumed their smuggling on a large scale, especially to the other parts of the coastline where control was not as strict as in Kwangtung, under the eyes of Lin Tse-hsü. Elliot's policy, in fact, was based on waiting for the arrival of sufficient military forces—he had requested them in April—and further instructions from London. Some authors consider that his decision to surrender the opium was basically motivated precisely by the desire to furnish a pretext for military action against China. In reality, the confiscation of the opium and the detention of the merchants was later used as a *casus belli*. In this period Lin himself also attempted to use diplomatic means and addressed a letter to Queen Victoria (which more than likely never reached her), seeking to persuade the British ruler of the evil nature of the trade in which her countrymen were engaged.

The already-strained situation in the Canton area was further aggravated by the murder on July 7 of a local villager, Lin Wei-hsi, by a group of drunken English sailors. Elliot sought to disentangle himself from this problem and to hush up the whole affair by offering judicious bribes to the family of the deceased and by ordering a quick trial of the sailors involved; the punishment imposed was farcical and the sailors were then immediately set free. The Chinese, however, demanded that since the murder had been committed on Chinese soil, the murderers should be handed over for trial by a Chinese court. This the British refused to consider. As a reprisal Lin Tse-hsü ordered a boycott of the British ships in order to deprive them of supplies of food and water from the mainland. Elliot responded by an armed demonstration against Chinese ships in September, but the real conflict started only after the arrival of additional British reinforcements. On November 3 two British ships of war in the Pearl River estuary, which were there to prevent the sailing up to Canton of some English merchant vessels whose captains were willing to sign the required anti-opium bond and to recommence trade, attacked a fleet of twenty-nine Chinese war junks near Ch'uan-pi, sinking four of them. The First Opium War had thus begun. In January Tao-kuang ordered the stoppage of all trade with Great Britain and commanded Lin Tse-hsü to prepare the defence of the Canton area against British attack.

II. The Course of the War

Although the first military action had been taken in November 1839, it was only in April 1840 that the issue of war against China was debated in the House of Commons. There was considerable opposition to this entanglement and perhaps the sharpest comment on it was that of Gladstone who proclaimed that: "A war more unjust in its origin, a war more calculated to cover this country with permanent disgrace, I do not know and have not read of. The British flag is hoisted to protect an infamous traffic." However, the Melbourne government in which Palmerston was Foreign Secretary managed to avoid a vote of censure on its policy towards China by a small margin (271 to 262 votes). Formally, no declaration of war was passed, only an Order in Council was issued to the Admiralty to proceed with the sending of further reinforcements to China for the prosecution of the war. The history of the war and its military campaigns can be divided into three phases: (1) from the initial British attack in November 1839 to the first truce of January 1841, (2) from January 1841 to the second truce in May 1841, (3) the last phase of the war from August 1841, ending with the Nanking Treaty in August 1842.

After the arrival in June 1840 of an expeditionary force from India which included 20 warships (540 guns), 32 other vessels and over 4000 men and was commanded by Admiral Sir George Elliot, a cousin of the other Elliot, the British decided to blockade Canton and to send the main force up to the North. Simultaneously, they sought to force the Ch'ing government to begin direct negotiations which would end in the acceptance of the British conditions. The main aims of the English at this stage were: a demand for compensation for the confiscated opium, an indemnity for the cost of the war, the breaking down of all barriers for a further development of trade, the establishment of relations on an "equal" basis, and the obtaining of an island base which would make future action against China easier. A letter from Palmerston conveying these demands, containing also a perfidious attack on Lin Tse-hsü, was prepared for delivery to the Ch'ing authorities and attempts were made to have it reach Peking. It had proved impossible to send the letter from Canton and when the fleet sailed north it was sought to have the letter delivered to the court through the local authorities in Amoy and then Ningpo. This also ended in failure. The expeditionary force then sailed further up the coast and on July 5, 1840 took the town of Tinghai on Chusan Island in Hangchow Bay which was subsequently used as a British base. By August 10 the fleet reached the port of Taku at the mouth of the Pei River, east of Tientsin. This advance of the British to a point so relatively close to Peking caused considerable panic in the Ch'ing government and one of the highest Manchu officials was now empowered to begin negotiations with the British. This was Ch'i-shan (d. 1854), who was in charge of the defence of the Tientsin area. The main concern of the Ch'ing was now to get the British to leave the area of North China as soon as possible. In his negotiations with the British Ch'i-shan was at least successful in this point by persuading them to return to Canton where the negotiations were supposed to be continued. In September 1840 the British agreed to leave and Ch'i-shan was now named as Imperial Commissioner to replace Lin Tse-hsü.

The appointment of Ch'i-shan and the beginning of negotiations with the British signified, in fact, the victory of that faction at the court which favoured appeasement, or rather, to be more precise, capitulation; this group had been in favour of maintaining the *status quo* in regards to the entire opium question. It was composed mainly of Manchus and was led by Mu-chang-a (1782-1856), the chief Grand Councillor, whose role in the subsequent events was of utmost importance and whose influence on the Emperor and the entire administration was enormous. In the actions of this faction it began to be soon apparent that their main concern was not with the security or the interests of China as a country, but solely with the safety and maintenance of the Ch'ing regime. This tendency became quite obviously paramount during the later stages of the Opium War and was based, among others, on the undoubtedly well-founded fear and distrust of the high Manchu dignitaries of the Chinese population, whose evident opposition to foreign aggression could, and later, in effect, did assume simultaneously an anti-Ch'ing aspect.

One of the first aims of this faction was to bring about the disgrace of two leading Chinese officials, Lin-Tse-hsü, and his main partner in the anti-opium campaign, Teng T'ing-chen (1776-1846), the Governor-general of Liangkwang. In this scheme the faction achieved complete success. Lin and Teng were made the scapegoats for the inability of the Ch'ing government to defend itself against British aggression. Lin Tse-hsü was dismissed from office in September 1840 and later, in 1842, he was exiled to Ili, where Teng had preceded him even earlier. While both of them were pardoned and restored to high posts a few years after the end of the Opium War, this move had the effect of removing from the scene the two main protagonists of determined action against the British. It should also be noted, in passing, that during his stay in Canton, Lin Tse-shü had become fully aware of the fact that the abysmal ignorance of the Chinese in regard to the outside world was a factor which militated against the possiblity of an effective defence in view of the obvious great technical superiority of the West. This was particularly true in the military sphere, for here the disparity between the antiquated weapons of the Manchu army, in effect 200 years behind the times, and those of the West was especially striking. Thus, Lin showed much interest in things Western and caused everything that was available pertaining to European geography and sciences to be translated into Chinese. In this respect he was a pioneer, but one whose actions were not to be followed or acted upon consistently in China for a considerable period of time, inasmuch as the arrogance of the Manchu dignitaries and the complacency of the Chinese scholar-officials—with their Middle Kingdom complex of cultural superiority *vis-à-vis* the Western barbarians—were only very slightly ruffled by the experiences of defeat in the First Opium War.

The negotiations in Canton conducted by Ch'i-shan and Elliot dragged on until January 1841. The British demands were much the same as those mentioned above and to force their acceptance the British launched in January an attack on the forts on Ch'uan-pi Island which guarded the entrance to Canton. These were all taken with a considerable loss of life to the Chinese garrison. This advance of the British on Canton now resulted in the acceptance by Ch'i-shan of the British terms and the signing on January 20 of the so-called Ch'uan-pi Convention. Its terms included: (1) the cession of Hong Kong to the British, (2) the payment of $6,000,000 indemnity, (3) recognition of equality in direct official negotiations between China and Great Britain, (4) full resumption of trade. On the strength of this convention the British immediately occupied Hong Kong. However, the convention was soon to be disowned by both the Ch'ing and the British government. When Tao-kuang finally discovered what the terms of the Convention were—for Ch'i-shan's reporting of it was, to put it mildly, circuitous and cautious—he repudiated him completely. Ch'i-shan was sent back to Peking in chains and his immense fortune of £10 million (30 million taels—11,000 ounces of gold, 17 million ounces of silver, 427,000 acres of land, etc.) was confiscated. (Ch'i-shan was noted as one of the most corrupt officials in a thoroughly rotten regime and one of the richest men in China.) The British government was also dissatisfied with the terms, for the opposite reasons; they did not go far enough, especially the indemnity was considered too small and other vital issues had been unsettled. Thus Elliot was dismissed, to be replaced by Colonel Sir Henry Pottinger as the main British representative.

Tao-kuang, infuriated by Ch'i-shan's open capitulation, now ordered Ch'ing troops commanded by I-shan, another corrupt and inept imperial clansman, to defend Canton and attack the British. In this the Manchus were completely unsuccessful inasmuch as in February the British troops, numbering only 2400, took the main forts on Humen-chai (the Bogue), where they also captured 380 Western guns which Lin Tse-hsü had earlier obtained from foreign merchants. In March they destroyed more of the fortifications close to Canton. Fighting started again on May 21, when all the Chinese defences outside of Canton were broken by the British forces and this led to the signing of a new truce on May 27, 1841. Its main point was that the Ch'ing authorities agreed to ransom the city by paying immediately $6,000,000 and to withdraw their forces from it. The British troops then also evacuated the immediate neighbourhood of Canton, which, for that matter, was somewhat unsafe due to a number of attacks that had been launched by local villagers who had themselves spontaneously set up militia units, perhaps 15,000 strong. It is characteristic that these units were soon disbanded by the Manchus. As on so many occasions the terms were not reported truthfully to Peking; the ransom was disguised as the settling of debts owed by the Chinese merchants to the British.

The arrival in August of Pottinger, the new British representative, marked the beginning of the last stage of the war which lasted exactly one year. Considering that Chinese resistance in Kwangtung had been effectively smashed by the events of May and wishing to exert the necessary pressure on the Ch'ing government, the British now sent an expedition of 26 ships and 3500 troops to conduct military operations in Central China. On August 27 they captured Amoy and in October attacked and seized a number of towns in Chekiang, including Ningpo. Having thus established control over most of East Chekiang, the British awaited further reinforcements from India. The resistance of the Ch'ing forces was completely ineffective. This was due not only to the technical inferiority of the Ch'ing army, but also to the low level of training and efficiency of the Manchu officers. If the Manchu Banners were worthless as a fighting force, this was even more true of the Green Standard Army, composed of Chinese, which was really rather a constabulary and not a true military force at all. In this "army", Ch'ing corruption was particularly rife and many of the units existed only on paper. It should be noted, in passing that the British possessions in India played a crucial role in the campaigns against China, inasmuch as they were the main base for these, as well as the source of a part of the military forces, for it is unfortunately true that Indian sepoys were used in this war, as they were also to be employed in subsequent British aggressions against China.

In the early spring of 1842 the British reinforcements from India arrived: 20 warships, 23 other vessels and over 10,000 troops. The attempts of the Ch'ing government to weaken the British positions in East Chekiang had failed completely, although they had involved quite sizeable forces. A new British offensive was now launched and after a sharp battle the town of Chapu fell on May 18, while Shanghai was taken on June 19 without any struggle. The defence of some points, however, was extremely strong. The Chinese and the Manchu garrisons at times fought to the last man, the latter often committing suicide with their entire families. But the technical superiority of the English equipment was overwhelming. The Ch'ing were no more able to resist the British army than the guns of the British navy. The British fleet and troops now slowly advanced up the great artery—or rather the jugular vein—of China, the Yangtse. On July 21 the British captured Chinkiang in Kiangsu, situated 40 miles east of Nanking on the south bank of the Yangste and a vital strategic point where the Grand Canal intersects the Yangtse. Thus the food supply for Peking from the Yangtse basin was now effectively threatened. The British followed up this success by inching their way towards Nanking, the English opium ships following the flag immediately behind the naval force. By August 10 the British ships were on the Yangtse outside of the city, their guns trained on its walls, and the threat of an attack and capture of this metropolis now faced the Ch'ing government.

III. The Conclusion of the War and the Nanking Treaty

The news of the British advance up the Yangtse had broken whatever desire still existed at the court in Peking to continue resistance. After the loss of Chinkiang, Tao-kuang empowered the new Ch'ing Imperial Commissioner, Ch'i-ying (d. 1858), an Imperial Clansman, to arrange for peace negotiations with the British. The fears of the possible political repercussions of further defeats for the fate of the Ch'ing regime was now uppermost in the minds of the Peking rulers. The talks were begun in Nanking on August 14 and led to the conclusion, under the shadow of British naval guns, of the famous Nanking Treaty on August 26, 1842. They can hardly be described as negotiations inasmuch as the British, quite aware of their military superiority, openly threatened the Ch'ing negotiators with an attack on Nanking. The terms were dictated by the British and the Ch'ing negotiators "were only permitted to polish the translations and to reword some small items. They were not permitted to revise or alter the contents, nor were there many negotiations except exchanges of acrimonious expressions." The treaty thus negotiated was then signed on board H.M.S. *Cornwallis.**

The Nanking Treaty, as the first of the series of unequal treaties which were to sanction the transformation of China into a semi-colony, deserves special attention. Palmerston referred to it, oddly enough, as an event "which will form an epoch in the progress of the civilization of the human race". The Treaty consisted of thirteen articles. the first starting as follows: "There shall henceforward be Peace and Friendship between ... (England and China). "After this semantically curious outset the remaining articles are more down-to-earth. The main provisions were: (1) China to pay $21 million—$6 million as compensation for the confiscated opium, † $3 million to cover the debts of the Canton merchants to the British, $12 million as an indemnity to the British for the expenses of waging the war (Art. 4-7). (2) Five ports to be opened to British trade—Canton, Amoy, Foochow, Ningpo and Shanghai, with the right of residence for

*At first this would seem to be an ironic coincidence but, of course, the ship was not named after the Cornwallis who surrendered at Yorktown but after his brother, the admiral. Still, it gives food for thought.
†In passing, it should be noted that later on the British government successfully swindled the English merchants out of almost half of this sum.

British merchants and consuls (Art. 2). (3) Cession of Hong Kong to Great Britain (Art. 3). (4) Abolition of the Cohong (Art. 5) and the establishment of a customs tariff (Art. 10). (5) A new mode of correspondence between British and Chinese officials on an equal basis.

The provision regarding the customs tariff proved to be of special importance, inasmuch as this was later interpreted to mean that any changes in the tariff rate required also the consent of the British. This signified a complete loss by China of tariff autonomy and constituted one of the principal weapons employed by England for the economic penetration of the entire Chinese market. What is especially characteristic, however, is the fact that the main issue of the war—the opium question—was not even mentioned in the treaty. The Chinese sought to have the British restrict opium growing in India, and its export as well, but met with the reply that if the English did not sell the drug others would. The British then suggested, but unofficially, that they would prefer to see the trade legalized (which it ultimately was after the Second Opium War) but did not insist on this. From their point of view it made, in effect, very little difference for the trade, still completely illicit, continued to expand even more with complete impunity in the 1840s and 1850s now that the Chinese efforts to stop it—and these failed only because the Chinese were not strong enough—had been smashed by the use of armed force. This flourishing trade made use of newly acquired Hong Kong as its main base.

The Nanking Treaty was further supplemented in the subsequent year by the Treaty of the Bogue (Humenchai), signed on October 8, 1843. This contained also one very vital provision, the so-called "most-favoured-nation" principle, which meant that any new privileges to be granted in the future by China in a treaty with another power would also automatically accrue to Great Britain. It also dealt with the tariff problem, and the rate of customs, both import and export, was established at the average low rate of 5 per cent; the Chinese were unable later on to change this until 1928. The "most-favoured-nation" concept had been described by Dennett as "a device by which every nation thereafter could secure for itself any privilege which had been extorted by some other power from China by force, or tricked from her by fraud, without having to assume the moral responsibility for the method by which the concession has been obtained".

From the vantage-point of well over a century later it is much easier to grasp the great importance of the Nanking Treaty in the development of the history of modern China. It marked the beginning of a century of humiliation and degradation for the vast country, leaving an indelible impression on its proud people. By opening up China, it ultimately led to the transformation of Chinese society in almost all respects. It was also a greater traumatic shock than all the previous experiences of this kind, even more than the Manchu conquest. All the previous invasions were ultimately mastered by the Chinese feudal civilization—in this case this could not be and was not accomplished. The resolve to wipe out the disgrace of surrender to foreign aggression occupied the best minds of the country for many decades; the search for means and measures to accomplish this is the basic essence both of Chinese modern intellectual history and of the country's political development. It is impossible to understand the rise of the Chinese reform movement of the 1890s and equally of the Chinese revolutionary movement which started in the same period without bearing this vital factor in mind.

It should be noted again, however, that as far as the ruling group in China was concerned, especially the Manchu aristocracy, the repercussions of the defeat in the

First Opium War were still, in fact, very limited. The Ch'ing government had surrendered to the force of British arms and its main aim in doing so was now to preserve the rule of the Manchu dynasty at—as we shall see later on—any price. It was rather the Chinese population itself, especially in those provinces which were directly affected by the British invasion, such as Kwangtung, which was to take the lead in struggling against the presence of the foreign aggressors.

IV. Other Powers in China

While it was Great Britain which, as the leading capitalist power, took the initiative in breaking down the isolation of the Ch'ing Empire and through her aggression began the process of opening up the entire country to the penetration of foreign influence, both economic and political, the other Western countries were only too eager to share the spoils and to take advantage of the opportunity thus created. The first to line up in the queue were the Americans.

American trade with China was, logically enough, much later in developing than that of the European powers. The first American vessel, the *Empress of China*, arrived in Canton on August 20, 1784. From this late beginning, however, commerce with China continued to grow in size quite rapidly and to increase in importance, taking second place, although far behind England. In the period 1821-1841 the annual average value of the trade was $10 million. The American merchants were also faced with the same problem as the English—they were unable to find sufficient goods which the Chinese market could take and were thus also forced to pay for Chinese products with large quantities of silver. In order to avoid this silver drain the American merchants followed the example of the English and began to engage in opium smuggling; thus all the American firms, with one sole exception, participated in this "trade". However, inasmuch as the British had practically a monopoly on Indian opium, the Americans could import opium only from Turkey and their share of the opium brought to China amounted to only 3 per cent of the total. Hence they were much readier than the English to agree to the demands of Lin Tse-hsü that they give a bond to refrain from this trade in the future.

While giving vent to proper expressions of moral indignation over the actions of the British in China (Cushing's words were typical—"A base cupidity and violence and high-handed infraction of all law, human and divine, which have characterized the operations of the British, individually and collectively, in the seas of China") and maintaining a very profitable neutrality during the Opium War, as soon as the Nanking Treaty was signed, the Americans scurried to take the fullest advantage possible of the British accomplishment. The very same Caleb Cushing (1800-1879; a Massachusetts lawyer and politician) took the lead in suggesting that a special mission be sent to China for the purpose of negotiating a treaty. The aim purportedly was to act as a counterpoise to the English and "thus save the Chinese from that which would be extremely inconvenient for them, viz., the condition of being an exclusive monopoly in the hands of England". This noble motive met with full understanding and support; the sending of the mission, to be headed by Cushing himself, was then decided upon. A most curious document was prepared, a letter from President Tyler to the Emperor of China, drawn up in the style customarily used by the Great White Father in his correspondence with American Indian chiefs. Its essence was a demand for the same conditions as those which.had been obtained by the British. The mission set off in July 1843 and Cushing was equipped not only with the above-mentioned epistle and a collection of American "scientific objects", including a pair of six-shooters, but also with a fancy general's uniform designed to impress the Chinese officials by its splendour.

The mission arrived in Macao on February 24, 1844, accompanied by four naval vessels, which were perhaps a more convincing argument than the President's letter. Although the American merchants in Canton had no trouble whatsoever in their trade with China, Cushing proceeded upon his task. The Ch'ing officials agreed to negotiate after Cushing had ceased to insist on a personal delivery of the President's letter to the Emperor in Peking. The talks were conducted on the Ch'ing side once more by Ch'i-ying who saw as his main task the prevention of Cushing's possible trip to Peking. The negotiations took place in the village of Wanghsia (older spelling, Wanghia) north of Macao and here, on July 3, 1844, the first treaty between the United States and China was signed. On the basis of the most-favoured-nation clause which the treaty contained (Art. 2) the Americans obtained all the privileges of the Nanking settlement, obviously without territory or indemnity. There were, however, two very important differences. The Wanghsia Treaty provided for consular jurisdiction over American citizens in China (Arts. 21 and 25) and this point, which was much more specifically outlined than its mention in the Treaty of the Bogue, thus became the fundamental legal basis for the principle of extraterritoriality which, lasting *de jure* till 1942, was to play such an important role in the establishment of foreign-run communities in China itself and to facilitate, to a very considerable extent, the future penetration of the entire country by all the foreign powers. Secondly, the Treaty now provided for a review of its conditions after a period of twelve years (Art. 24). This was later used during the Second Opium War as one of the pretexts by England and France to force a new treaty upon China. Once more, as in the case of the tariff problem, the Ch'ing negotiators had no idea of the future implications of what they were signing away in this treaty. These principles, however, of the Wanghsia Treaty were to remain "a persistent barrier to China's attempts to recover full control of her own affairs".

The example of Great Britain and America was now followed by France, whose economic interests in East Asia were as yet negligible. The French mission was headed by Th. de Lagrené; its treaty was negotiated and signed on October 24, 1844 in Whampoa (Huangpu, the principal port of Canton). Ch'i-ying again represented the Ch'ing government. The treaty was based almost in its entirety on the one which had been signed by the Americans but there was, however, one additional provision which proved to be later on of considerable importance. The French gained the right to build Catholic churches in the five Treaty Ports (Art. 22). This was later on extended by them to signify a right of protection of the activities of the Catholic missions in all China, in line with the view of the French government which saw itself as the self-appointed protector of Catholicism in East Asia. Thus already during de Lagrené's stay in China (he remained there until January 1846) he persuaded the Ch'ing government to issue two edicts pertaining to the toleration of the activities of Christian missions (December 1844, December 1845), although these were still to be restricted to the five Treaty Ports. The Ch'ing also agreed to a restoration of the property of the Catholic Church which had been confiscated during the actions against it in the first half of the 18th century (edict of February 1846).

The Ch'ing government was not particularly reluctant to conclude these two treaties with America and France inasmuch as it thought that it had nothing much to lose thereby and that it might, on the other hand, decrease the monopoly position of England and perhaps even stimulate a rivalry between England, America and France, thus making more feasible the "management of the outer barbarians" (the phrase is Ch'i-ying's and it is in this way that relations with the foreign powers were referred to for the next two decades). Simultaneously, the Ch'ing government was afraid that the other foreign powers might also possibly use force to obtain their demands.

CHAPTER 28

The Taiping Revolution

I. The Background of the Taiping Movement

Modern Chinese history can be said to begin with both the First Opium War and the Taiping Revolution; both of these events were a reflection of the profound crisis of Chinese society which resulted from the effects of external aggression on the one hand and internal strains on the other hand. Both of these factors were interpenetrating and their mutual reaction produced constantly deepening consequences. The Taiping movement was the most significant outward manifestation of this state of affairs, of the social crisis within the Ch'ing Empire and of the influence of European ideas.

It is necessary to revert once more to the essence of the crisis of feudalism in China. Its main feature lay in the agrarian problem, referred to so often already, in which the concentration of land rendered the position of the peasantry ever more difficult. This problem became particularly acute in the 1830s and 1840s, the two decades preceding the outbreak of the Taiping Revolution. In particular, the number of peasants who had lost their land or had been forced to desert it had increased considerably; the position of the tenants and rural labourers was no easier. All this was still further accentuated by the continued growth of population which had reached, more than likely, the 400 million mark by 1833. This was accompanied by a strange phenomenon, still unexplained, of a drop in the area of registered cultivated land (1812—791 million *mu*; 1851—772 million *mu*). Thus, the already existing disproportion between the increase of population and the inadequate basis of land under cultivation was aggravated.

The political aspects of the crisis have all been referred to before: the decay, corruption and inefficiency of the Ch'ing government. To this should be added its ever more obvious military weakness. All these factors were brought out much more into the open by the First Opium War, while the Ch'ing government itself was still further discredited by its inability to defend the country against foreign aggression and by its policy of saving itself at the expense of the country. The prestige of the Manchu dynasty had been seriously undermined; it was now not only the object of hatred but also, and this is always worse, of contempt. The Ch'ing were obviously ripe to lose the Mandate of Heaven, which they had anyhow only usurped by conquest. The presence on the throne from February 1850 of Hsien-feng, the 20-year-old, weak and incompetent new ruler, was an additional disadvantage to the Manchus. The economic consequences of the Opium War were a further factor in deepening the crisis in the country, inasmuch as the Ch'ing government shifted the burden of the indemnity on to the population in the form of increased taxes. The deteriorating economic condition resulting from this was revealed, among others, by the further rise in the price of silver (by 1845, one tael was

Map. 17.   T'ai P'ing T'ien Kuo

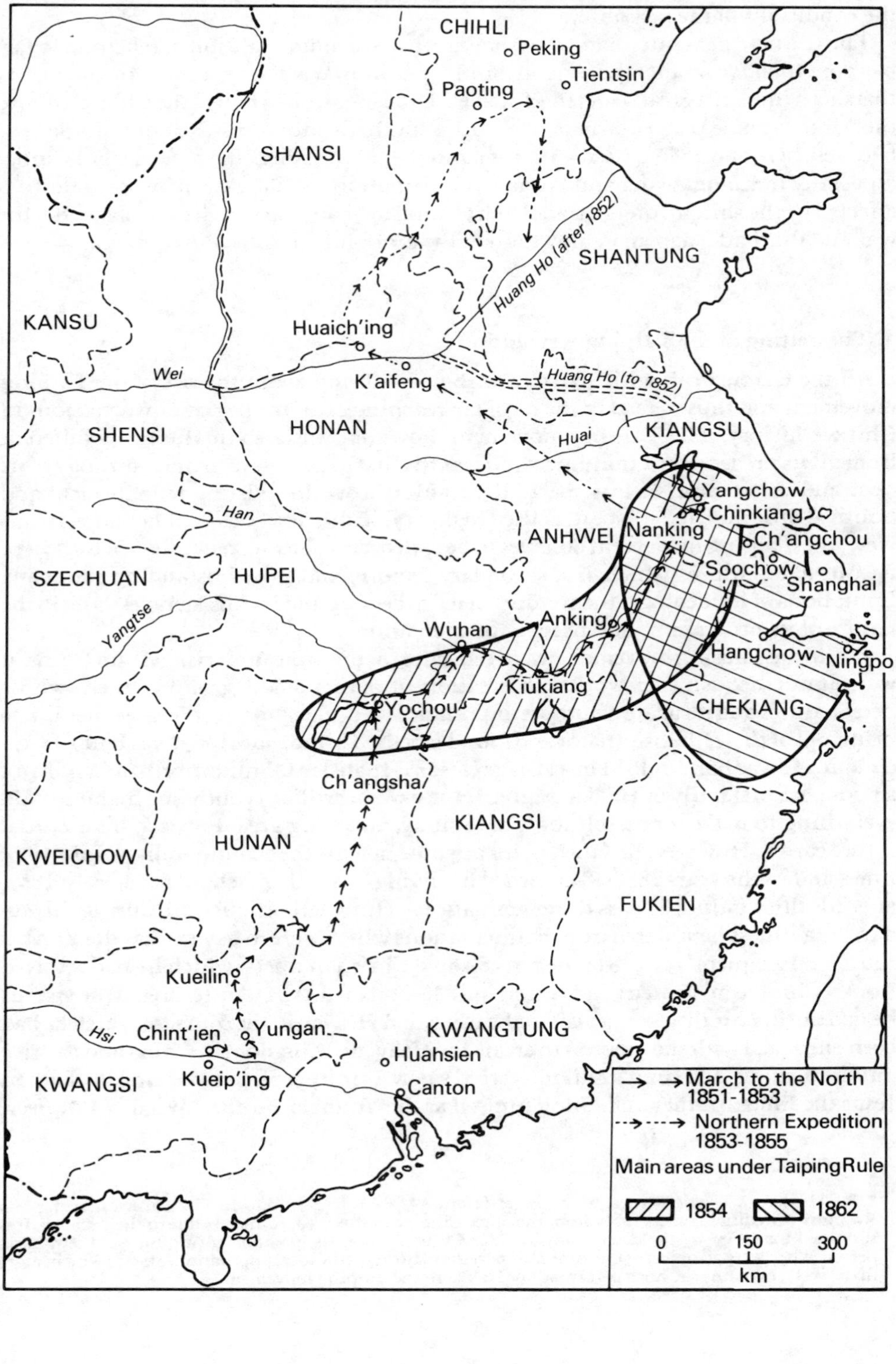

CHIHLI

Peking
Tientsin
Paoting

SHANSI

Huang Ho (after 1852)

SHANTUNG

KANSU

Huaich'ing

Wei

K'aifeng

Huang Ho (to 1852)

SHENSI

HONAN

Huai

KIANGSU

Han

ANHWEI

Nanking

Yangchow
Chinkiang
Ch'angchou
Soochow
Shanghai

SZECHUAN

HUPEI

Yangtse

Wuhan

Anking

Kiukiang

Hangchow   Ningpo

CHEKIANG

Yochou

Ch'angsha

KIANGSI

HUNAN

KWEICHOW

FUKIEN

Kueilin

Hsi   Chint'ien   Yungan

KWANGTUNG

Huahsien

KWANGSI   Kueip'ing   Canton

→ →March to the North
1851–1853

- - -→ Northern Expedition
1853–1855

Main areas under Taiping Rule

▨ 1854   ◩ 1862

0   150   300

km

worth already from 2000 to 2300 cash) which, in turn, led to a still greater worsening of the conditions of the peasantry.

The Chinese peasantry had, as we have seen, a splendid tradition of rebellion to fall back on. In the years after the conclusion of the Opium War the secret societies increased their activities on a great scale; the Triad with its slogan of "Abolish the Ch'ing, restore the Ming" being particularly active in the southern provinces. Not one single year between 1841 and 1850 passed without a number of uprisings in some parts of China, especially in Liangkwang and Hunan. The situation in Liangkwang was in addition affected by the shift in foreign trade from Canton to Shanghai which took place after the war and this had led to an aggravation of the economic situation in this area.

II. The Setting of the Taiping Revolution

All the factors dealt with above contributed to bring about the rise of the Taiping movement and thus to lead to the most far-reaching of all the peasant insurrections in Chinese history. The Taiping movement, however, was also qualitatively different from all its predecessors, inasmuch as it was the first to possess a distinct ideology of its own and to attempt, at least partially, to overthrow the existing feudal social and political order and to replace it, at least in theory, with a new society. Therefore, in our view, the Taiping movement deserves to be called a revolution, regardless of the fact of its ultimate failure, which is a secondary feature, and notwithstanding the many limitations of its ideology, the conduct of its leadership and inconsistencies, both in the nature of its programme and in its implementation.

While the Taiping movement was a reflection of the profound crisis within China, it was simultaneously the work and creation of a very small group of men, whose personalities and ideas are of utmost importance for understanding the movement. The principal of these, the originator and founder of the Taiping ideology, was Hung Hsiu-ch'üan. He was born in 1814 in a village close to Huahsien (35 miles north of Canton) of a poor peasant family of Hakka origin. *Hung was a brilliant youth and his family did everything to make it possible for him to study, attaching great hopes to his eventual future career. However, he failed in his attempts to pass the examinations a number of times and in the years 1830-1843 earned his living as a village school teacher. In 1837, after his third failure to pass the examinations, Hung fell seriously ill; during this 40-day-long illness he suffered from hallucinations which were to have a vital effect on his future. Subsequently, in 1843, he reread some Christian tracts, which he had received from a Chinese missionary in Canton in 1836, and on this basis interpreted the visions he had during his illness as a visit to the Christian Heaven in the course of which he had been entrusted with the mission to create the Heavenly Kingdom in China and to drive out the demons. In Hung's religious creed a new Trinity emerged—of God the Father, Jesus the Elder Brother and Hung himself as the Younger Brother. What is, however,

---

*The Hakka—K'o chia, "guest, or stranger families", are a large group in Fukien, Kwangtung and Kwangsi who differ considerably from the other Chinese in this area, primarily due to their dialect. It is supposed that they are the descendants of later Chinese colonists, perhaps during the Southern Sung period. They were an object of discrimination by the majority of the local population, a factor which, more than likely, explains the high percentage of Hakka in the Taiping movement.

both characteristic and important is the fact that Hung, who was an educated man, well read in the Confucian Classics, combined the elements of Christianity gathered from his reading of the tracts with ideas derived from Chinese classical writings, in particular, from the many utopian trends it contained. In 1843 Hung Hsiu-ch'üan began to preach the new creed in his village, first converting his whole family, of whom the most important was to be his cousin, Hung Jen-kan (1822-1864). He also converted Feng Yün-shan (1822-1852), a fellow school teacher, perhaps a schoolmate, and close friend. Feng was also a Hakka and had likewise, in spite of his abilities, failed to pass the examinations. There is no basis whatsoever to doubt the complete sincerity of both Hung Hsiu-ch'üan and Feng Yün-shan in the views which they held and propagated. Their iconoclastic activities in their native village aroused much hostility and both Hung and Feng were forced to depart for Kwangsi, where Hung had relatives. After a stay there, Hung went back to Huahsien, where he devoted his time primarily to writing and developing further his ideas. The tracts which he composed at this time, while primarily religious, were imbued with significant egalitarian ideas of which the principal one was that all men were brothers under a Supreme Deity. These ideas were potentially anti-feudal and revolutionary; they could be and subsequently were understood and felt to be such by his peasant followers.

During this same period Feng Yün-shan remained in the Kueip'ing region of Kwangsi where he continued to preach the religion of Hung Hsiu-ch'üan, becoming in fact the main prophet and organizer of the new sect. It is he who organized the *Pai Shang-ti Hui* ("The God Worshippers Society") the first grouping of what was to be the core of the Taiping movement. Within a few years Feng had succeeded in gaining over 2000 converts, most of whom were poor peasants but they included also a number of charcoal burners and miners. The majority of them were of Hakka origin, but other Chinese as well as some Miao (or Chuang) were among the members. The base for the movement became Tzuchingshan (Thistle Mount) 50 *li* to the north of Kueip'ing, an easily defensible area.

By 1847 the new sect had increased in influence and succeeded in gaining still more members. It had also created its own armed force—it should be mentioned, in passing, that in the disturbed conditions of Kwangsi a great number of various types of militia units were formed, mainly, but not only by landlords—which it used primarily for self-defence. The iconoclastic activity of the God Worshippers led, however, to a number of conflicts, inasmuch as both the landlords and the Ch'ing authorities began to regard this sect as a potentially dangerous and subversive organization. Thus, Feng Yün-shan was arrested twice, liberated the first time, and on the second occasion rescued by means of bribes offered to the officials with money gathered by the converts from their own meagre possessions. During the same time Hung Hsiu-ch'üan had also spent some time in Canton, where he received further instructions in Protestant Christianity from an American Baptist missionary, I. J. Roberts.

The God Worshippers Society in the years 1847-1849 took on more and more the character of a political movement. Many of the members of the secret societies, especially the Triad, sought to join the Society but both Hung and Feng demanded that all who joined it accept fully their religious views, which was in most cases too difficult for the Triad members. There was also a political difference of considerable importance; the Triad were basically anti-dynastic and favoured a restoration of the Ming. Hung Hsiu-ch'üan's ideas went already further at this stage; he did not favour a

Ming restoration but the replacement of the Ch'ing by a completely new government and dynasty. Thus, as a result, only relatively few of the Triad members joined the God Worshippers in this period, although throughout the entire early stage of the Taiping movement the Triads were of considerable assistance to its progress by their own continuous anti-Ch'ing activities.

After his release from imprisonment Feng Yün-shan went to Kwangtung to join Hung Hsiu-ch'üan and they were both to return to Kwangsi in 1849. In the meantime, during the absence of the original two leaders of the movement, new prominent personalities arose within the God Worshippers community, which was bereft of any direction. The two most important were Yang Hsiu-ch'ing (?1817-1856) and Hsiao Ch'ao-kuei (d. 1852); both of these now claimed an important religious role—Yang declared himself to be the Voice of God, and Hsiao, the Voice of Jesus; both of them claimed to have visions in which they received appropriate instructions from Heaven itself. While, as mentioned above, there is no doubt of the sincerity of Hung Hsiu-ch'üan and Feng Yün-shan, there are considerable grounds for doubting the genuineness of the activities of both Yang and Hsiao. Whatever the case, the effect was that Yang now rose to become the most prominent leader of the God Worshippers, succeeding later on into putting Feng, the original propagator and organizer of the sect, almost completely into the shade. Yang Hsiu-ch'ing was a Hakka from Kwangsi who had been a charcoal burner and also worked in transport; Hsiao Ch'ao-kuei was a poor peasant from Kwangsi and a very close friend and associate of Yang.

Two more future leaders also joined the sect during this period. These were Shih Ta-k'ai (1821 or 1831-1863) and Wei Ch'ang-hui (d. 1859); Shih was also a Hakka who came from a rich peasant family in Kwangsi, while Wei was of gentry origin, a member of the Chuang nationality in Kwangsi who had been a pawnshop owner. These four, in addition to Hung and Feng, formed the historic main leadership of the Taiping movement. It was in its way a special type of brotherhood for, in spite of the egalitarian tendencies of the movement, the six leaders were from the very beginning well above the rank and file members. Of certain importance in the early period was also one Hung Ta-ch'üan (d. 1852). This person has been the cause of much confusion in the historical writing on the Taipings, since some of the first authors dealing with the Taipings considered him to have been the main leader of the movement itself. He was, in fact, a peasant from Hunan, also a frustrated scholar with a good knowledge of military matters, and a leader of one of the Triad societies.

By 1849, against the background of the growth of the sect and its increasing conflict with Ch'ing authorities as well as the maturing of their ideas, the leadership now began to prepare their plans for an open rebellion against the Ch'ing with the aim of realizing the fundamental goals of the movement—to establish a new government and society in accord with their own vision. The periodization of the Taiping movement, considered broadly, is as follows. It consists of two basic periods: the first is that of the spread and victorious advance of the movement in the years 1850-1856. This can be subdivided into (a) the years 1850-1853 which include the march to the North and the taking of Nanking and (b) 1853-1856, the continuation of campaigns against the Ch'ing to the moment of crisis within the Taiping leadership in the autumn of 1856. The second period is the decay and fall of the movement from the autumn of 1856 until July 1864. This, in turn, can be subdivided into (a) 1856-1861, the defence against the first attempts to encircle the Taiping state and (b) 1861-1864, the final surrounding and defeat of the Taiping movement.

III. The Period of Victory

(1) The First Stage: July 1850-March 1853

In accord with their plans the leaders began, in July 1850, to gather the entire membership of the God Worshippers Society in the areas close to Chint'ien village near Thistle Mount in order to complete their preparations for the launching of the revolution. The entire force thus assembled numbered probably between 20,000 and 30,000 men, women and children and thus only around 5000 men of military age. Most of those gathered in Chint'ien were Hakka but also included other Chinese as well as Chuang. The great majority of them, as has been pointed out, were poor peasants, although some charcoal burners and miners were also among the members of the sect. The gathering of the God Worshippers did in due time attract the attention of the Ch'ing authorities and government troops were sent to attack them, only to meet with a number of painful defeats. After more than six months of these local struggles the leadership declared on January 11, 1851 the establishment of the T'ai P'ing T'ien Kuo—The Heavenly Kingdom of Great Peace.* In the term itself one can see the curious symbiosis of Christian and Confucian ideas; the Heavenly Kingdom is obviously Christian in origin, while the Great Peace is equally Confucian. What the name implied was the application of religious and utopian ideas to the creation of a new society in which all men would be brothers. It was thus basically a reflection of the age-old peasant dream of a society in which there would be no rich and no poor, in which justice and equality would prevail for all. In this sense the Taipings could and did make full use of the revolutionary potential of early Christianity, especially if expounded in a fundamentalist fashion. Simultaneously, the Chinese sources for the utopia were of long standing and thus more readily acceptable. They are to be found, among others, in one of the canonical works, "The Book of Rites", especially in the magnificent passage on *Ta T'ung*, "the Great Togetherness", that splendid vision of Paradise Lost.

The fundamental aim, however, of the movement was to abolish the rule of the alien Ch'ing dynasty and, as the movement progressed, this anti-Manchu aspect became more and more apparent both in theory and in practice. Simultaneously, as the Taipings considered themselves the possessors of the sole valid ideology they became automatically the staunch opponents of Confucianism and thereby also of the scholar-officials, the main exponents of Confucianism. Their opposition to the gentry, however, had also a social and political aspect; socially, inasmuch as the gentry were landlords—politically, inasmuch as they were supporters of the Manchus. It need hardly be added that the religious intolerance of the Taipings was likewise directed against Buddhism and Taoism, its potential rivals in this field. The element of religious fanaticism of the early Taipings, i.e. of the original God Worshippers, was an undoubted and very strong factor which goes far to explain their great militancy and

---

*Depending on the context the words T'ai P'ing, which derive from Classical Chinese literature, can be translated either (as is most customary) "Great Peace", or with equal justification as "Great Equality" or "Great Prosperity". In this work we have preferred to use the more customary translation of "Great Peace", although in some respects the other two meanings of the term are perhaps more appropriate as a reflection of the Taiping programme. We use the word Taiping without the correct apostrophes because this is already sanctioned by custom.

their initial successes. They considered themselves, and truly were, a group of the Chosen People. In the organization of the movement at this stage the egalitarian spirit was also reflected in the establishment of a Sacred (i.e. common) Treasury to which all members turned in all their possessions and into which all supplies captured by the Taiping forces were deposited. The members of the movement were then to be cared for, as regards to their everyday needs of food and clothing, by the treasury and this was, in fact, carried out throughout the entire first period. This element of primitive communism was undoubtedly advantageous for a large number of reasons to the Taipings and a source of attraction to the poor. It should be noted, however, that from the very beginning the egalitarianism of this institution was limited by the fact that the leaders got more than their share.

The Taiping armed force was organized as a highly disciplined unit and the model for its establishment was drawn almost in its entirety from that outlined in the *Chou li*; the same book was later to serve as the model for the organization of the government in Nanking. The efficiency of this organization combined with the religious fervour of the Taipings made of its army a formidable, highly motivated force. At this time the command of the troops was also divided between the principal leaders of the movement.

The local Ch'ing officials were completely unable to cope with the Taipings and a special Imperial Commissioner who also proved to be a failure was sent down to Kwangsi. The Taipings then moved all their adherents to the town of Yungan (now Mengshan) in North Kwangsi, where they stayed from September 25, 1851 to April 6, 1852. While the Taipings remained in the town the Ch'ing brought up their troops and completely encircled it. In the meantime a further organization of the Taiping state was undertaken. Hung Hsiu-ch'üan had already declared himself in March 1851 to be the T'ien Wang—the Heavenly King of the Taiping state. He chose not to use the word emperor both for religious reasons, inasmuch as the word was employed in the Taiping rendering of God, as well as for political motives, to avoid undue rivalry of his fellow leaders. To keep them now content they were also granted the title of Wang on December 17, 1851. Thus Yang Hsiu-ch'ing became the Eastern Wang, and simultaneously was the commander-in-chief of the army; Hsiao Ch'iao-kuei was made Western Wang and deputy commander; Feng Yün-shan was the Southern Wang and the general commanding the advance guard; Wei Ch'ang-hui was the Northern Wang and the general commanding the rearguard, while Shih Ta-k'ai was made assistant king.* The last four Wangs, however, were all to be under the orders of the Eastern King, for Yang was already at this stage the most powerful man in the leadership, the main organizer and strategist of the movement. Hung Hsiu-ch'üan was relegated, or relegated himself, more and more to the role of the founding father of the sect. Each of the Wangs was also permitted to establish his own court and to have his own assistant officials and followers. All this was ultimately to have dire consequences for the movement; it was also the first sign of a process of demoralization of the leadership—and this even before it had achieved its great successes—the main component of which was the separation of the leadership from the rank and file of the movement.

*The word Wang can be translated either as king or prince. It was customary in European historical writing to refer to the six leaders as kings, simultaneously to refer to later Taiping leaders who were to receive the same title as princes. This seems to be an unnecessary confusion and we shall translate the word consistently as king for the entire Taiping period.

In April the Taipings, who numbered now probably 40,000, resolved to break the siege of Yungan. They succeeded in this completely, defeated the Ch'ing troops and marched north to besiege Kueilin, the capital of Kwangsi. It is during this period that Hung Ta-ch'üan was captured and later cruelly executed in Peking; the Triad still continued its co-operation with the Taipings. An entire month (April 18-May 19, 1852) was spent by the Taipings in a vain effort to take Kueilin. The main reason for their failure was the lack of proper equipment; they had very few firearms and practically no artillery and it was only their indomitable courage that kept them storming the strong walls of the city, in which the Ch'ing troops took shelter, not daring to meet the Taipings in the open field. Having lost many of their fighters here, the Taipings gave up the siege and decided to march into Hunan. It is at this stage that they ceased to be a local Kwangsi rising and became a general insurrection on a national scale. During the march into Hunan, the Taipings lost perhaps the ablest and certainly the most modest of their leaders, the fervent preacher of the Taiping gospel, Feng Yün-shan, who died from an artillery shell. This event strengthened still further the power of Yang Hsiu-ch'ing, which no one was now in a position to challenge.

Campaigning through South Hunan, where they were joined by thousands more of poor peasants, the Taipings, rushing like a mountain torrent through the vast province, reached its capital, Ch'angsha, by the autumn of 1852. Here once more they sought to take a large city and failed again for the same reasons as in the case of Kueilin. The siege lasted from September 11 to November 30. It was during this period that an appropriate jade seal was discovered, conveniently enough, which was regarded as a sign of the Heavenly King's power. Hung Hsiu-ch'üan was now also saluted with the words *Wan sui* (May he live ten thousand years) which were customarily reserved only for the Emperor.

After their failure at Ch'angsha, where the second of their original leaders, Hsiao Ch'ao-kuei, the close friend of Yang Hsiu-ch'ing, was killed, the Taipings marched to the north where, due to the fright of the Ch'ing generals, they succeeded in capturing the town of Yochou in North-east Hunan (December 13) without any resistance. Here they found a vast store of munitions which dated back still from the time of Wu San-kuei. With the help of these new arms and many more fresh recruits, the Taipings crossed into Hupei and, continuing their march forward with amazing rapidity, they captured Wuchang, the capital of Hupei, which they then held from January 12 to February 9.* Then in February, already a vast host of around half a million men, women and children, the Taipings turned to the east; their fleet of over 10,000 junks sailed down the Yangtse, while their armies marched down on both sides of the Great River. No force whatsoever was capable of stopping this huge avalanche which moved forward at a speed averaging 12 miles a day; the Ch'ing troops fled for their lives. On February 18 the Taipings captured Kiukiang, a key point in North Kiangsi, then on February 24 the important city of Anking in Anhwei. By March 8, already well over one million strong, although their effective fighting forces could not have been more than around 150,000, the Taipings were at the gates of Nanking, the capital of the founder of the Ming dynasty. After a sharp struggle with the Manchu garrison, they captured this extremely vital position on March 19. Keeping up their fantastic speed, they swept further to the

---

*In actual fact, the Taipings captured also the two cities lying north of the Yangtse opposite Wuchang, i.e. Hanyang and Hankow. The three cities together are called Wuhan.

east to take Chinkiang, at the intersection of the Grand Canal, on March 30, and Yangchow on the north bank the next day. In this campaign the most striking feature of the Taiping army was its great mobility and mastery of manoeuvring which more than compensated for the inadequacy of arms.

In their march up from the South the Taipings had waged a truly plebeian struggle; they killed most of the Ch'ing officials who fell into their hands, exterminated all the Manchus, regardless of rank and sex, often drove off and sometimes killed landlords, burned the yamens and the land registers. They were therefore welcomed by the poor peasants wherever they came. But simultaneously, the Taipings failed to set up any administration in most of the territory through which they had passed and the major part of it was quickly regained by the Ch'ing officials and local gentry. After having taken Nanking the Taiping leaders, acting on the decision which they had more than likely made much earlier, proceeded to establish themselves here and turned this city into the capital of the Taiping state, changing its name to T'ienching—Heavenly Capital. This was done at the same time when, in fact, the main forces of the Ch'ing government were still unbroken and thus the Manchus were given a chance to recover from the shock of their great initial defeats.

In settling down in the Nanking area a considerable part of the momentum of the Taiping drive was lost. Thus the decision was truly a fateful one in many respects. Nanking proved to be the Capua of the Taipings; the tendency to demoralization, which had shown itself even at an early stage of the movement, was now given much greater possibility of flourishing. Both the Heavenly King and the Eastern King delighted in a show of splendour and luxury, had magnificent palaces built for themselves in which they housed sizeable harems. A considerable part of the top leadership joined them in this pursuit of temporal delight. The common treasury was used by them now for these purposes.

Of the original core of the God Worshippers perhaps only 10,000 still survived in the great mass of almost 2 million new members of the movement. These were now called the "elder brothers" and almost all of them occupied high positions in the government and army in the new capital. In this way they were also influenced to a greater or lesser degree by the rapidly spreading demoralization, which seems to have affected all the earlier peasant movements in Chinese history as well. Their confidence enhanced by their early victories, the Taiping leaders also disregarded the question of seeking allies for their movement and this was revealed, in particular, in their attitude towards the secret societies which had aided them in their progress from the South. A full acceptance of the Taiping creed was now demanded in an even more determined manner than heretofore.

While the Ch'ing forces had been completely unable to oppose the advance of the Taiping army, they had followed it along the whole route from Kwangsi and now, together with other units from the North, they drew near to Nanking. Within a very short period of time two large camps of Ch'ing troops were set up close to the Taiping capital—the Great Camp of Kiangnan (south of the river) near the Ming mausoleum and the Great Camp of Kiangpei (north of the river). Both of these Camps were to harass Nanking to a quite considerable degree, although they were to be smashed and scattered a number of times, only to be rebuilt again.

(2) The Second Stage: March 1853-September 1856

After their establishment in Nanking the Taipings, in spite of having lost much of the territory they had passed through, were still a considerable power both in the size of their army and in their revolutionary potential. The area which they held extended from Yochou to Chinkiang and from 50 to 100 miles inland on both sides of the Yangtse; this included some of the richest lands of the entire country. In this period also the Taipings had still complete control of the Yangtse and this was of great importance, inasmuch as it made it possible to provide sufficient food supplies both for the capital and for the armies, the bulk of which were stationed around the capital due to the presence of the Ch'ing camps north and south of the river.

The momentum had been partially lost but the Taipings had not relinquished, by any means, their ultimate aim, which was the complete overthrow of Manchu rule. They were still capable of serious military effort and also of a certain amount of significant strategic thought. The main plan conceived now was that of a great pincers movement in which two expeditions were to be launched, one to the north and one to the west, which, if successful, would have resulted in the conquest of North China and of the entire Upper Yangtse valley. The two armies were to conclude their campaigns by meeting in the Wuhan area.

The Northern Expedition is the most famous, perhaps because it was more dramatic and fateful. It was launched in May 1853 and was led by Lin Feng-hsiang and Li K'ai-fang; both of them were Kwangsi men of Chuang nationality and Lin was one of the ablest Taiping generals. The army, however, was a small force of perhaps 30,000 men, whose basic aim was the conquest of Peking. It is unclear why the Taiping leadership did not send a greater force for this purpose. The army marched north-west through Anhwei and then entered Honan; on the whole, it avoided capturing cities but it did make an attempt to take the capital of Honan, K'aifeng. It failed in this and lost much of its manpower. After crossing the Yellow River, which in itself had posed a very difficult problem, the northern expeditionary force then spent almost two months (July 7-September 1) on an unsuccessful siege of the town of Huaich'ing in north-west Honan; in this unexplainable action it lost both valuable time and men. This more than likely proved to be the turning-point of the expedition.

Although reduced now to less than 20,000 men, the army marched forward into Shansi and then, by October, it entered Chihli and came close to Paoting, south-west of Peking. A panic ensued in the capital and the court prepared to flee, while the population showed it was ready to welcome the Taipings. However, the Ch'ing had obtained enough time to gather all forces possible, in much greater numbers than the advancing Taiping troops. For some reason, instead of marching on Peking, the Taipings continued eastward and reached the outskirts of Tientsin by October 30. They were unable to take the city, primarily due to their lack of sufficient artillery. The severe North China winter set in and the Taipings, all southerners unused to the northern climate and insufficiently clothed, now dug in for the winter to await reinforcements, undergoing untold sufferings and privation. The Ch'ing sent large units of cavalry against them—these could be employed in the North China Plain—under the command of their principal general, the Khorchin Mongol Prince, Senggerinchin (Seng-ko-lin-ch'in in Chinese).

In January 1854 the Taiping leaders sent reinforcements, a force of 30,000 to 40,000, to join the Northern Expedition; they were both too few and too late. This force reached north-west Shantung in April but it was unable to join the remnants of the expedition and it was itself surrounded and smashed in May. The original force had by now been divided into two parts, one under Lin Feng-hsiang and the other under Li K'ai-fang. After a prolonged heroic defence under conditions of complete encirclement which lasted for an entire year, both of these units were exterminated in March and May 1855. Lin and later Li were captured and executed and only a few soldiers of the entire army survived, some of whom managed to join the Nien rebels. The Northern Expedition had faced a number of problems which it had been unable to solve. Relatively little contact was made with the local population; the southerners did not know the northern dialect nor were they acquainted with local conditions and thus were unable to obtain the considerable support of the peasants which had been received during the march from Kwangsi to the Yangtse. Likewise, very little effort had been made to link up with the peasant rebel units which were in the field, such as the Nien, primarily due to the fact that the Northern Expedition did not pass through those areas in which they were the strongest.

The Nien were a peasant movement led by secret societies and active in Shantung, Honan and Anhwei. They were primarily anti-dynastic in their actions—although without a definite aim of overthrowing the Ch'ing—and while their social programme seems to have been rather limited, they did succeed in gaining control of considerable parts of the three provinces mentioned above. There was little co-ordination, however, between the various Nien units which preserved their autonomy. The Nien employed large numbers of cavalry and with these were able to conduct a highly mobile warfare, using their fortified villages as a base. The connection with the Taiping movement was always very loose and this lack of co-ordination later affected the fate of both the Nien and the Taipings. Nevertheless, the Nien constituted a considerable force, estimated at around 100,000 in 1853 and rising to from 200,000 to 300,000 by 1855. It should be mentioned that throughout the entire period of the existence of the Taiping state there were numerous uprisings against the Ch'ing in various parts of the country. However, there was little attempt made by the Taipings to utilize these movements and to establish proper co-operation with them; nonetheless, these movements were of an assistance to the Taipings inasmuch as they engaged considerable Ch'ing forces at various periods of time.

The defeat of the Northern Expedition had very serious consequences for the Taipings as it provided the Ch'ing government with its first real chance to rally itself, although, as will be seen later, it was not the Manchus who were able to gain an ultimate victory over the Taipings but another force—the Chinese gentry.

The Western Expedition was launched also in May 1853, a few weeks after the Northern. It marched from the main Taiping positions in Anhwei into Kiangsi and Hupei and its principal aim was to regain the control of Wuhan, which had been lost, and to achieve and consolidate a mastery of the Upper Yangtse area. There were three especially crucial key points in this area the maintenance of which was vital for the existence of the Taiping state, as well as for the control of the Yangtse. These were Wuhan, Kiukiang and Anking; this is why the battles over these three cities provide to a great degree the clue to the nature of the campaigns. While the Western Expedition did finally succeed, in June 1854, in accomplishing the second conquest of Wuhan, it was able to hold on to this position only for half a year, losing it in October to the forces of the

Hunan army of Tseng Kuo-fan (1811-1872). The Hunan army had successfully beaten off Taiping attacks in Hunan, especially on Ch'angsha, and also in 1854 had started to defeat the Taiping fleet which until then had been the master of the Yangtse.

We now come to the problem of the main forces opposing the Taipings; these were not really either the Manchu Banners or the even more worthless Green Standard Army, but new units which were now organized, with the reluctant consent of the Ch'ing regime, by the Chinese gentry. The prototype of these units was the Hunan army (often referred to in the literature of that period as the "Hunan Braves" or the Hsiang Army) which was organized by Tseng Kuo-fan. Tseng was a landowner from Hunan, a successful high official in the Ch'ing administration, and, although he was only one out of forty-three men who were ultimately appointed to organize and lead such local units, he was undoubtedly the most important of them all and his example and influence were extremely extensive. Tseng began to organize his army already in November 1852, but he soon transformed it, so that it did not become as much a local gentry-led defence corps (as similar ones which had already existed earlier against the Taipings and peasant revolts) as a provincial army whose activities later on were by no means restricted only to its native territory.

Although it was to be defeated many times by the Taipings—and once almost annihilated totally—the Hunan army became the main anti-Taiping force during the entire course of the war. Tseng Kuo-fan based himself in the first place on the support of the Hunan gentry; it is they who financed it and officered it, while the soldiers were drawn mostly from well-to-do peasants from remoter and more backward mountain areas. The Hunan army was highly paid, much better than any other of the Ch'ing forces. Tseng built up this force as solely his own personal army; the officers and soldiers were to be loyal in the first place to him and not to the Ch'ing government. He paid them himself out of the contributions from the gentry, out of funds he controlled which were derived from the *likin* (local transit custom taxes) in the areas under his administration, as well as out of sums received from the central govenment. The creation of an army of this type—apart from its role during the Taiping revolution—was to have very far-reaching consequences for the fate of China itself during the entire subsequent century.

Many writers portray Tseng Kuo-fan, and those like him, as acting in the defence of the Confucian tradition and creed against the iconoclastic ideas and activities of the Taipings. This is an erroneous, one-sided and distorted view. While there is no doubt that the Confucian sensibilities of Tseng and his colleagues were offended by the Taiping form of Christianity—which in itself was a reflection of the xenophobic aspect of the Middle Kingdom complex of cultural superiority—this was by no means the sole or the principal issue at stake. It is true that in the Chinese conditions of that time the foreign origin of Taiping Christianity did provide Tseng with an excellent weapon. What is much more important, however, is the fact that the Taipings, especially at the early stage of the movement, had unleashed an agrarian revolution, even if limited in scope, against all Chinese landlords which was also combined with their policy of expropriation of the rich. Thus, it was in the defence of their land rents, of their property, and at times of their own skins—not of the overthrown tablets in the Confucian temples—that the Chinese gentry organized its armed forces against the Taiping Revolution, allying itself for this purpose with the Ch'ing regime and later also with the foreign powers.

From what we have seen of their behaviour, particularly during the Manchu conquest, one can safely assume that had their land and property been left untouched, they might have easily reconciled themselves to the rule of the Taipings, ideology and religion notwithstanding, and perhaps would have even been eager to join the new government, inasmuch as in their hearts the anti-Manchu programme of the Taipings could have found some response. But anti-Manchuism which was combined with an agrarian revolution and with the building of a new government in Nanking that had no special place reserved for them and where the main positions of power were granted only to the Taiping elite—this was much too strong a dose for these gentlemen to take. Thus, having taken the position of opposing the peasant movement, the inexorable logic of historical development pushed them along to take a stand which was the equivalent of acting against the interests of their own country, i.e. into supporting the corrupt and decaying alien Manchu regime.

The Western campaign was thus also basically unsuccessful and ultimately turned into a seesaw struggle between the Taipings and the Hunan army. Under the command of Shih Ta-k'ai, one of their original leaders and best generals, the Taiping forces did succeed finally in capturing Wuhan for the third time in April 1855; they managed to hold on to it until December 1856, when they lost it again and this time forever. In August 1856 the Taipings succeeded, as a result of brilliant manoeuvring, in smashing completely both the Northern and Southern Camps near Nanking which had been threatening their capital. During this entire period, however, they had neglected—for reasons which are not clear—to undertake any large-scale action further to the east, to seek an entry into Kiangsu and Chekiang, the two richest provinces of Central China, which the Ch'ing authorities were utilizing as an essential source of financial support as well as food supplies. Moreover, the victories which the Taipings did gain in this period were overshadowed completely by the terrible crisis which arose within their own camp.

(3) The Inner Crisis of the Taiping Leadership

The roots of the crisis in 1856 can probably be traced to the very beginnings of the movement when the special group of six leaders had been established. Already at that time each of the leaders had his own group of officials and followers and, as the movement increased vastly in size, each of them developed his own very large clique of adherents and hangers-on, as well as his control of a part of the armed forces. As will be remembered, two of the original leaders, Feng Yün-shan and Hsiao Ch'ao-kuei, had died during the march to the North. Of the four that were left, practically all the power was in the hands of the Eastern King who acted more and more as the despotic and dictatorial ruler of the entire state, lording it over and humiliating the other leaders, not excluding the Heavenly King. Yang Hsiu-ch'ing's ability was undoubted, but his ruthlessness and greed for still more power led to ever-greater dissension between him and the remaining three leaders. The rivalry between the cliques of men from Kwangsi and from Kwangtung and the conflict between the "elder brothers" and "new brothers" were also additional factors in bringing about this crisis.

Many contradictory accounts exist of what really happened and who was ultimately responsible for the tragic events of the autumn of 1856 in Nanking. The main facts are these. On September 1 Yang Hsiu-ch'ing was murdered by the troops of the Northern King, Wei Ch'ang-hui, who acted either on his own initiative or on the orders or approval of the Heavenly King who suspected, not without basis in fact, Yang of wanting to usurp his place. It is possible that the original plot called for doing away with the Eastern King himself, but Wei's men did a thorough job; not only was Yang's entire family wiped out but also up to 20,000 of his followers. Upon hearing of this blood-bath Shih Ta-k'ai returned to Nanking only to find that by now Wei Ch'ang-hui had become more arrogant and powerful—and much more dangerous—than the Eastern King had ever been. Shih quickly effected a dramatic escape from the capital and went to rejoin his army. The Northern King followed this up by massacring the Assistant King's entire family, as well as many of his followers in Nanking.

When the news of this reached Shih Ta-k'ai he gathered his troops and marched on the city to take revenge; he rejected, however, the clever offers of the Ch'ing that he should go over to them. The Ch'ing, of course, took full advantage of the situation to attack the Taipings on all fronts. When Shih Ta-k'ai finally reached the capital the head of Wei was presented to him; he and his followers had in the meantime been killed on the order of the Heavenly King who was without doubt—after the unceasing terror carried out by Wei—even more afraid of the Northern King than he had been of Yang Hsiu-ch'ing. Thus, there were now only two of the original leaders left alive.

Shih Ta-k'ai remained in Nanking from November 1856 to June 1857; in this period he took the position of commander-in-chief and head of the government, the post held previously by the Eastern King, for since coming to Nanking the Heavenly King had withdrawn almost entirely from government affairs, or had been relegated from them by Yang, and seldom left the company of the very numerous ladies in his harem. His mental condition, never too good at the best of times, had further deteriorated. However, the members of Hung Hsiu-chüan's family, especially his two elder brothers, had no desire to see the Assistant King establish himself as a new power in Nanking. They intrigued against him constantly with the result that the Heavenly King became evermore distrustful of him. Finally, Shih Ta-k'ai came to the conclusion, more than likely correct, that his life was not safe in the capital; he left it, never to return. He then gathered around himself a vast number of his followers and troops, well over 100,000, and launched his own campaigns against the Ch'ing.

It is just as well to tell the rest of the tragic story of Shih Ta-k'ai at this point, inasmuch as his departure from Nanking was, in effect, tantamount to his separation from the Taiping movement as such, or from what was now left of it. It would seem he had lost hope of restoring the original revolutionary spirit of the movement. His aim was to march his army to Szechuan in order to establish himself there—in the best Chinese historical tradition—as the independent ruler of a new state of Shu; had he succeeded he would have been at least the eighth person to have done so. During the next years he wandered with his troops through most of the provinces of South China, winning many battles, always successfully recruiting new forces, but never establishing himself anywhere permanently. In 1857 he was in Kiangsi, 1858 in Chekiang, 1859 in Hunan. By 1862, still adhering to his original plan, he marched into West Szechuan, with his forces already much depleted. Here he was unsuccessful in his attempted crossing of the Tatu River (which the Red Army, in surprisingly similar circumstances, did succeed in crossing during the Long March in 1935); he was cut off and surrounded by superior Ch'ing forces and, after many futile attempts to break out, he surrendered with the remnants of his troops. Most of his soldiers were then butchered, while he and his son were taken to Ch'engtu to be executed. Throughout the years of his independent campaigning Shih Ta-k'ai steadfastly maintained his anti-Ch'ing stand and refused all the many offers which were made to him to pass over to the Ch'ing. His departure had weakened the Taiping state immeasurably, for it deprived it of its ablest and most popular general, as well as of a great part of its best troops. The effects of this were perhaps even more dire than of the September massacres themselves.

After Shih Ta-k'ai had left Nanking the Taiping government remained during the rest of its existence in the hands of the relatives of the Heavenly King. The two elder brothers, Hung Jen-fa and Hung Jen-ta, were both incompetent and corrupt and the period of their rule brought only new disasters. A certain change did take place later when the government was taken over by Hung Jen-kan. As will be remembered, he was one of the earliest converts of Hung Hsiu-ch'üan and, although he did not join him in going to Kwangsi, he remained his faithful follower. After several attempts to join the Taipings later on had failed, Hung Jen-kan stayed in Hong Kong where he continued his studies and became an active Protestant preacher. Finally, in August 1859, he succeeded in reaching Nanking, where he was greatly welcomed by the Heavenly King who since 1856 trusted no one but the members of his own family and close relatives. Hung Jen-kan was soon promoted to Kan Wang (Shield King) and quickly advanced to become the head of the government. As the only one of the Taiping leaders with any amount of knowledge of the rest of the world he sought to reorganize and strengthen the government and also advocated a programme of modernization which was based on his conception of Western development, as well as a whole series of social reforms. In this Hung Jen-kan hoped, rather naively, for assistance from the foreign powers; this was derived from his previous contacts with the missionaries. He also recommended a departure from the heretofore traditional Chinese approach to other countries, i.e. to cease looking upon all foreigners as complete barbarians.

Due to the conditions within the Taiping state and to the fact that it was too much engaged in warfare to devote any serious effort to social and economic problems, the modernization programme had little chance of realization. Hung Jen-kan's influence lasted only to 1862, when the Heavenly King became distrustful of him in turn, and he was removed from an effective position of power. His status had never been very strong anyhow, as he had little control over the armed forces which in this period were already quite independent and paid little attention to the central Taiping government. The years of his influence do mark, however, the last attempt to reorganize the Taiping administration, to restore some of its original momentum, although in a somewhat different context, especially as regards ideology, where he sought to have the Taiping creed conform somewhat more closely to the accepted Protestant Christian dogma by attempting to tone down some of the more irrational aspects of the Heavenly King's views, as, for example, his divine mission as ruler of the world. However, political problems were now increasingly overshadowed by the question of military struggle and survival. In this sphere the role of the Taiping generals became also more and more important and, inasmuch as the old leaders were now dead or departed, a new generation came to the forefront.

The two most noted new military leaders were Li Hsiu-ch'eng (1824-1864) and Ch'en Yü-ch'eng (1836-1862). Li came from a poor peasant family in Kwangsi; he had been a soldier in the ranks during the march to the Yangtse and later advanced to higher military command. By the end of 1856 he was one of the leading generals and subsequently was to play a vital as well as controversial role throughout the rest of the existence of the Taiping state. Li was primarily a military man who possessed considerable tactical ability and much less a politician, although he was unavoidably involved in the intricate struggle for power of the Taiping leadership, which had by no means ceased after the tragic events of the autumn of 1856. Ch'en came also from poor peasant stock and even from the same village as Li; he had been too young to be a soldier during the advance to the North but joined the army even at that time. He was renowned for his great personal bravery and was also a very capable general. These two military were the mainstay of the Taiping armed forces for most of the last period of its existence (although Ch'en was killed in 1862). What is characteristic, however, of the Taiping movement of this time as a whole was that the co-operation between Li and Ch'en left much to be desired. After the arrival and rapid promotion of Hung Jen-kan in Nanking, both of them were also advanced in rank and were given the title of Wang; Li Hsiu-ch'eng became the Chung Wang—the Loyal King, while Ch'en Yü-ch'eng became the Ying Wang—the Brave King.

CHAPTER 29

The Decline and Fall of the Taiping Kingdom

I. The First Stage: December 1856-September 1861

The Taiping state had been distinctly weakened, first by the terrible bloodbath in the autumn of 1856 in Nanking, then by Shih Ta-k'ai's departure; it thus remained mostly on the defensive throughout 1857 but it was still in control of a very considerable territory in the middle Yangtse area. Simultaneously, the Ch'ing had on their hands the problem of renewed aggression by Britain and France (see Chapter 30). However, in spite of this, in 1858, the first beginnings were already made in the attempt to put into effect the strategic plan of Tseng Kuo-fan and his Hunan army. The main aim here was to deprive the Taipings of all control of the Upper Yangtse, to cut Nanking off from supplies coming from this area and thus to lead to its encirclement and final destruction. Tseng did not regard—correctly enough it must be admitted— the army of Shih Ta-k'ai as anything else than a secondary problem and advocated concentrating the main attention of the Ch'ing forces on Nanking itself, inasmuch as it represented what was left of the principal core of the Taiping movement.

In carrying out the above plan Tseng's forces, having earlier gained full mastery of the Yangtse by completely defeating and destroying most of the Taiping fleet, succeeded in capturing Kiukiang in May 1858. Somewhat earlier in this same year the Great Camp of Kiangnan, which had been smashed in 1856, was once more rebuilt and constituted a direct threat to the capital. Henceforth the main actions of the Taipings were now devoted to an effort of defending their capital at all costs and to breaking the threatening noose which was slowly being drawn up around it by the Ch'ing forces. In these attempts the main role was played by the Loyal King. A see-saw struggle was waged throughout most of 1858 and, in spite of previous successes at breaking the blockade, Nanking was again threatened in 1859.

In the spring of 1860 a new strategic plan was drawn up by the Taiping leadership, although at this time it was already very difficult for them to draft any schemes of overall strategy in view of the ever-greater independence of the individual army leaders, all of whom tended to think primarily in terms of their own interests, i.e. that of their armies and the regions held by them. The main concept of the new plan was to make once more an attempt to regain control of the Upper Yangtse; a new Western Expedition was to be launched—a great pincers movement to the north and south of the Yangtse was to be executed and both of the forces were to meet ultimately around Wuhan, which it was hoped to recapture for the fourth time.

The implementation of the above plan was preceded by a brilliant diversion in which the troops of Li Hsiu-ch'eng marched east to Chekiang and captured its capital, Hangchow, in March 1860, which they held for a few days. This threat to the rich and fertile east and the main supply source of the Ch'ing had the desired effect of bringing about the withdrawal of large numbers of Imperial troops from the Nanking area. The Chung Wang's army then quickly doubled back; in May 1860 the Great Camp of Kiangnan was smashed, for the second time, and the danger to Nanking was thereby relieved. This victory was followed by the rapid advance of the Loyal King's forces east into Kiangsu, leading to the capture, in June, of the very important commercial and manufacturing centre of Soochow, which was to remain his stronghold until December 1863. All of South Kiangsu was then conquered and the Taiping forces finally approached Shanghai itself. They were unable to take this city which had already become the principal base for foreign aggression against China and was also the refuge of all the rich Chinese from Kiangsu and Chekiang. When in August 1860 the Taiping troops neared the city they were attacked directly by British and French forces; this was the first armed intervention on a larger scale in this period (the policy of the foreign powers towards the Taipings in these years will be discussed in the next chapter).

The advance of the Taipings into Kiangsu and Chekiang gave rise to a great panic among the gentry and the merchants of these two provinces, the richest, most fertile and highly developed in every respect in the entire Ch'ing empire. They urgently sought for aid from whomever they could obtain it; considering that the Ch'ing government was hardly in a position to offer much assistance in view of the fact that in September 1860 the British and French Expeditionary Force was marching on Peking, while the Emperor fled in October to Jehol, it was to the foreigners, the same ones who were campaigning in the North, that they now turned for aid.

Later on, in the autumn of 1860, the implementation of the basic strategic Taiping plan, mentioned above, was begun and the second Western Expedition was launched. The armies of the Chung Wang commenced a long campaign; starting from Kiangsu they proceeded in a great semicircle through most of North Kiangsi, then entered South Hupei by the spring of 1861 and reached the Yangtse, east of Wuhan, in May. However, co-ordination between the army of the Chung Wang and that of the Ying Wang, which was active to the north of the river and which had reached the area north of Wuhan a few months earlier, was very defective, among others, for the reason that the overall direction of the campaigns by Nanking was practically non-existent. Thus, the pincers did not meet as planned. Subsequently, Li Hsiu-ch'eng retreated with his forces back to Kiangsu and Chekiang which were to remain his principal base for the rest of the war, and where he successfully expanded Taiping-held territory still further. Various historians have sought to sort out the responsibility for the failure of this great campaign, but this seems rather to be a somewhat futile exercise in armchair generalship a century and more after the events.

The fact remains that the Hunan army was now able to take full advantage of this failure and to pursue the basic strategy of seeking to recover the Upper Yangtse Valley. In this they achieved a considerable success by capturing on September 5, 1861 Anking, one of the three main strategic points on the Great River, which had been besieged since May 1860 by Ch'ing forces under the command of Tseng Kuo-ch'üan (1824-1890), Tseng Kuo-fan's younger brother. This loss of Anking is considered by many historians as the ultimate turning-point of the entire war, inasmuch as after this the Taiping Kingdom remained solely on the defensive. It should be borne in mind that this coincided almost exactly in time with the Anglo-French military operations against the Ch'ing in North China; thus these had in this respect relatively little bearing on the Manchus' war against the Taipings. The victory of the British and French in the North, however, resulted in the acceptance by the Ch'ing government of all their demands and also led to a basic change in the policy of these two countries towards the Taiping movement, to a phase of their now quite unmasked intervention on behalf of the newly subdued and truly meek Manchus. Hence, both the fall of Anking and the events in North China ushered in the last stage in the existence of the T'ai P'ing T'ien Kuo.

II. The Second Stage: September 1861-July 1864

These years witnessed the long-drawn-out agony of the fall of the Taiping movement and with it of all the aspirations and hopes it had first aroused in the country. An interesting question is why this stage lasted as long as it did. A number of reasons can be brought forth to account for this; the Taipings still possessed a number of military leaders of great ability, especially the Chung Wang himself, but, what is more important, they still had the support of the population, especially in the newly acquired areas of Kiangsu and Chekiang. The bulk of the people here much preferred the rule of the Taipings to that of the Ch'ing and feared like the very devil the prospect of being "pacified" by the Imperial army which was notorious for its plundering and indiscriminate massacre of the civilian population in Taiping areas. The policy of Tseng Kuo-fan himself was especially well known; none of the Taipings were to be taken prisoner but were all to be exterminated, in particular the men from Kwangsi, the original core of the movement. His policy was based on the theory that only by means of such mass slaughter could a future repetition of a new peasant uprising be prevented. Thus, all the "long-haired rebels", as the Ch'ing called the Taipings, who at the very outset of the movement, in protest against Manchu rule, had let their hair grow to normal length again and wore no queue, were fundamentally fated to meet, at best, the sword of the executioner.

The Ch'ing commanders were able to follow up their victories of the latter part of 1861, such as the taking of Anking, by defeating the major part of the Taiping army in North Anhwei which had been led by Ch'en Yü-ch'eng; the Ying Wang himself, after having been treacherously betrayed, was killed in May 1862, at the early age of 26. Thus, it was subsequently possible for the Ch'ing to increase their pressure on Nanking from the north, while simultaneously they sought to begin the recovery of the vast territories that had been lost to the Taipings in Kiangsu and Chekiang. These efforts are closely connected with the activity of two Chinese who are notorious for their long-lasting role as the stalwart supporters of the Ch'ing regime and who were to be in the future among the most prominent warlord-politicians—Li Hung-chang (1823-1901) and Tso Tsung-t'ang (1812-1885).

Li Hung-chang came from a rich gentry family in Anhwei and had fought against the Taipings from the moment they had entered the province in 1853. He was a protégé of Tseng Kuo-fan (his father had been Tseng's classmate) and had later served under him in the years 1858-1861. In 1861 he was sent to Anhwei where he organized, on the same principles as Tseng had done in Hunan, the so-called Huai army. With this force he then proceeded on British ships in April 1862 to Shanghai; he had been made governor of Kiangsu, where he was to fight against the Taipings who held practically the entire area of the province. Shanghai itself had been once more attacked unsuccessfully in early 1862 by the Chung Wang. Li Hung-chang was instrumental in developing further co-operation with the foreign powers from whom he obtained both financial and military assistance, as well as being backed by their direct military intervention. He also received considerable financial support from the rich Chinese merchant community of Shanghai. With all this assistance and especially through the employment of the so-called Ever Victorious Army, which served always as a vanguard for his troops, Li embarked on the slow recovery of most of Kiangsu, which culminated in the fall of Soochow in December 1863. The events connected with the taking of this city throw an interesting light on the character of Li Hung-chang. Soochow was strongly held and had already been besieged for more than four months. Eight of the Taiping generals within the city agreed to surrender it, offering also, in order to accomplish this, to kill the main Taiping commander, Mu Wang. Their proposition was accepted, Mu Wang was treacherously assassinated by them, and the city surrendered. They were subsequently invited to a banquet and, on Li's orders, were quickly put to death.

Tso Tsung-t'ang came from a gentry family in Hunan. He had been engaged in a struggle against the Taipings for most of the period from 1853 on and was also a close associate of Tseng Kuo-fan. After having later fought in Kiangsi he was nominated, in December 1861, the commander of all the Ch'ing troops in Chekiang and was later, in January 1862, appointed governor of this province. Here he faced a similar situation to that of Li Hung-chang in Kiangsu, in that practically the entire province was in Taiping hands. Just as Li, Tso relied very heavily on foreign aid, in his case more on the French than on the English, and it was with this assistance that he succeeded in the conquest of Chekiang which culminated in the capture in March 1864 of Hangchow, after a siege of seven months. Subsequently he also participated in the last campaigns against the Taipings after the fall of Nanking by taking his troops into Fukien by 1866. We shall hear more of this man, for his record as the butcher of the national minorities in China, especially the Mohammedans in the North-west—a story which deserves its own narration, is particularly infamous.

Thus, by the end of 1863, in spite of the brave defence of the many isolated Taiping garrisons in the cities of Kiangsu and Chekiang, these two provinces were basically lost to the Taiping movement. The Chung Wang now recommended that the capital be abandoned and that an attempt be made to return to the South, to seek to renew the movement in the coastal provinces, its place of origin. The Heavenly King, as fanatically convinced as ever of his divine mission and still hopeful of divine assistance, refused even to discuss the proposal. A large part of the Taiping forces now permitted itself to be bottled up in Nanking where, by February 1864, the army of Tseng Kuo-ch'üan had successfully completed a total encirclement. The capital was now doomed and its provisions were insufficient to feed both the army and the civilian population, although a large part of the latter had been earlier sent out from the city. The close siege of Nanking started on May 31 and soon starvation ravaged the city, while the Heavenly King still refused to agree to the planned breakout. Hung Hsiu-ch'üan died on June 1: his fifteen-year-old son, Hung Fu, was now proclaimed ruler. On July 19 Tseng's troops succeeded in blowing up a part of the extremely strong walls and drove into the city. Unbelievable carnage followed; the Taipings, unwilling to surrender, fought to the last man and were killed by the thousand. The civilians were also massacred, the whole city pillaged and, when the corpse of the Heavenly King was later found, it was mutilated.

A part of the leaders, including the Chung Wang and Hung Jen-kan, succeeded in escaping, taking with them the young king. Their forces were, however, soon separated; the first to be captured was the Loyal King who had given his better horse to the young king to help the latter escape. The Ch'ing government, at this time, practised the habit of permitting its important prisoners to write an account of their activities before sending them to meet their executioner. Li Hsiu-ch'eng availed himself of this custom; while undergoing tortures and indignities and placed in a bamboo cage he wrote for seven days (July 30-August 7) his account of the T'ai P'ing T'ien Kuo, in over 40,000 characters—the famous work later known as the Autobiography of the Chung Wang. This is still one of the main sources for the history of the Taiping movement and also the subject, as well as the author, of much acrimonious controversy.* Once the writing was finished, the Chung Wang was turned over to the executioner to be quartered.

The young Taiping ruler and Hung Jen-kan were captured in October and met the same fate as the Chung Wang. The Taiping forces which remained in the South and still numbered many thousands were now deprived of practically all their leaders. Nevertheless, they still kept up the struggle in Kiangsi, Chekiang and Fukien against much superior Ch'ing troops. Ultimately, the last of them took refuge in South Kwangtung, where in February 1866 they were surrounded and wiped out. The Taiping forces which were active to the North of the Yangtse were in a somewhat different situation; they had been on their way to aid Nanking when the news of its fall had reached them. Under the leadership of Lai Wen-kuang they joined up with the forces of the Nien in Anhwei and Shantung and together with these they continued a long and bitter struggle against the Ch'ing which lasted until 1868.

The great Taiping Revolution was thus drowned in a sea of blood. Its suppression by the Ch'ing government had led to the devastation of a great part of Central and South China, the ruin of hundreds of cities, the ravaging of some of the most fertile countryside and the death of many millions of Chinese. The most acceptable estimate is that from 15 to 20 million lives had been lost. In its defeat the mistakes of the Taiping leaders themselves—especially their terrible internecine struggle of 1856—as well as their errors of strategy, both military and political, undoubtedly all played a very important part. But the main cause does not lie here, however, but rather in the combined strength of the enemies of this great peasant movement: the despotic Ch'ing regime, the Chinese landlords and the foreign interventionists. Of these three forces the least effective was that of the Manchu aristocracy itself. The whole course of the Taiping war had fully demonstrated the military and political incapacity of the Ch'ing government. If they had been left without support, both domestic and foreign, the

*The main points under debate are whether in his writings Li Hsiu-ch'eng did not go too far in criticizing the movement to which he had devoted his entire existence; whether by trying to save his own life, which he undoubtedly did seek to do—perhaps for the purpose of continuing later the struggle once more, as one of his great admirers, Lo Erh-kang, the great expert on Taiping history, has it—he did not betray the cause he had been fighting for. In recent years this whole controversy has been much too closely connected with current political struggles to have anything in common with a sound historical evaluation. One should note, in passing, that some of the writers who condemn the Chung Wang—from, of course, a super-revolutionary position—are far too young to have ever participated in a revolutionary movement themselves. The above controversy has superseded an earlier one regarding the authenticity of the work itself of which there is now no doubt. However, the first known versions were published on the basis of one which had been appropriately edited by Tseng Kuo-fan himself.

Manchus would have certainly been eliminated from the Chinese arena in the middle of the 19th century, just as thoroughly and effectively as the Mongols had been in the 14th century. But this time the Chinese gentry had not been able to master the peasant insurrection, as they had always been able to do in the past, and as they had done during the beginning of the Ming. The peasants had already their own vision of a new social order and their own ideology, whatever its limitations and crudities. This was perhaps a reflection of the fact that now the crisis of Chinese feudal society was even deeper than ever before, as it assuredly was, among others, due to the "Opening of China", i.e. the aggression of the foreign powers, the ideology of the Taipings being in itself the curious result of Western penetration. Thus now, unable to harness the peasants for their own purposes and eventually to establish a new but traditional Chinese feudal monarchy, which would safeguard all their privileges, political, economic and social, the Chinese gentry took to arms to put down the Taiping movement, thereby not only causing untold miseries to the country but also having the result of preserving the rule of their alien Manchu masters—the very same, but in fact still much more degenerate, whom the best representatives of this same Chinese gentry had considered as uncouth barbarians and whose conquest of China was regarded by them as a national calamity and deepest humiliation. What is more, in availing themselves of foreign assistance in this task—as the actions of the main representatives of the Chinese gentry, Tseng Kuo-fan, Li Hung-chang and Tso Tsung-t'ang demonstrate so well—they ultimately facilitated the further penetration and subjugation of China by the foreign powers and thus helped to place their own country in the pitiable position in which it remained until 1949. All this was the work of well-educated gentlemen who loved to boast of their erudition and to quote the maxims of the Neo-Confucian philosophers.

As for the role of the foreign intervention, to be examined in the next chapter, its scope and significance was perhaps almost as important as that of the Chinese gentry. But then, what was China to them? It was no more a country to be admired from afar as the supposed model of enlightenment and civilization—that fashion had been cast aside quite completely; it was now but another potential India, a country to be colonized, a nation to be despised and treated as coolies by the representatives of a purportedly superior Western civilization.

III. The Social and Political Programme of the Taipings

After the government had been established in Nanking the Taipings issued a document known as the Land Law which was of fundamental importance inasmuch as, in reality, it set forth their entire vision of how society was to be organized. It was foreseen that land would be distributed anew to all the peasants based on nine different categories of its quality. While the peasants would be the holders of this land, all surplus production, above that what would be necessary to sustain them, was to be handed over to the common storehouses and hence to be distributed to those who were not engaged directly in agricultural production. In this theory the elements of an egalitarian primitive communism are quite obvious. Simultaneously, all society was to be organized in a pyramidic and hierarchical structure which, in fact, was identical with the fashion in which the Taiping army had been organized. In this structure the basic unit was to be composed of five families under the supervision of an officer who in his person combined military, administrative and religious functions. At the same time each family was to provide one soldier.

The entire system propounded in the Land Law was once more a utopia and also taken from the *Chou li*; in reality, however, it is extremely doubtful to what degree, if at all, this programme was ever put into practice. There is no documentary evidence of any kind on this point, perhaps due to the large-scale destruction of Taiping records by the Ch'ing. It would also appear that inasmuch as the Taipings were constantly engaged in their military campaigns they did not have sufficient time for a truly effective **organization of a social and administrative system. Simultaneously, the Taiping leaders, while concerned with the maintenance and propagating of their ideological-religious views, showed, on the whole, relatively little concern and interest in the administrative aspect of organizing the government; perhaps in their minds all this was to be tackled after the final downfall of the Ch'ing.**

In the early period, when one can ascertain the existence of an effective central government in Nanking, its main forms were derived from the initial measures dating from the Kwangsi stage when the establishment of a hierarchy of the Kings and the bureaucracy of officials took place. This was further supplemented in Nanking by the establishment of six Boards; it would seem that these existed in the court of each of the Kings and the lines of division separating the powers of each of the Kings are quite unclear. What does emerge, however, is the fact that in all respects the traditional patterns of a feudal monarchy were being followed by the Taipings who were unable to get away, in this domain, from the past. Thus a considerable and obvious contradiction existed between the programme as envisioned in the Land Law and actual practice.

Nevertheless, in the early period, the rule of the Taipings in the areas under their control was easier for the peasants, inasmuch as they were now either paying no rent or less to the landlords (many of whom had anyhow fled from the Taiping areas), while the taxes which they rendered to the Taiping government were, on the whole, considerably lower than those which had been demanded by the Ch'ing. As later on the military position of the Taipings worsened, the policy in this respect probably changed more and more, inasmuch as the prime concern of the Taipings was to obtain the necessary supplies for their armies and therefore less regard was paid to the interests and welfare of the peasants. It should be stated that the Taipings, as shown both from their programme and their practice, never envisioned a programme of land reform in the sense of redistributing the property of the landlords to the peasants. This is also borne out by their attitude to the Chinese gentry; here the principal criterion was not so much whether they were landlords or not, but whether they assisted the main enemy, the Ch'ing government, whether they opposed or supported the Taipings. Those who opposed the Taipings were dealt with sternly. In passing, it should be noted that the severity of the Taipings, especially the ease with which they employed the death penalty on all possible occasions, was quite far-reaching and perhaps, in reality, counter-productive and ultimately self-defeating. The Taipings sought to utilize those of the gentry who were not its obvious opponents and even to include them in their administration, especially in the latter period, in the newly conquered areas of Kiangsu and Chekiang. From the beginning, examinations were regularly held to attract the gentry although the subject matter was changed appropriately so as to represent the Taiping ideology. However, all the commanding positions in the government and the army were always kept in the hands of the remaining original core of the Taiping leadership throughout the entire existence of the Taiping kingdom; thus there was no real possibility for a take-over by the gentry on the pattern of the Ming.

The establishment of a traditional monarchic government, of the hierarchy of kings and of the official bureaucracy which was still expanded in the later period of the Taiping state, even when the area under its control was being seriously curtailed, would seem to be one of the fundamental limitations of the movement. It was, simultaneously, both a reflection and the further cause of the deepening process of demoralization of the leadership after the assumption of power and the conquest of the rich Yangtse area. However, the most important consequences of this process were undoubtedly ultimately derived from the unlimited absolute power of the leaders. The attempts of some historians to demonstrate the so-called democratic and elective nature of the Taiping administration are unfortunately not based on facts; there was no more provision for the participation of the population in the government than there had been in traditional feudal Chinese society and thus no consistent attempt was made to sustain the initial support that the peasants had shown for the Taipings. These consequences were shown up primarily in the rapidity with which the vicious struggle for power between the leaders ensued, culminating in the disaster of autumn 1856. After this, as we have seen, the Taipings were still less able to construct a functioning administration, in spite of the attempts of Hung Jen-kan, while simultaneously, during the last period of Taiping rule, the Nanking central government had less and less power both over the military commanders in the field and the local government which was, in effect, in the hands of the latter. All these weaknesses obviously facilitated the struggle of the enemies of the Taipings against them.

The Taiping ideology, as has been noted, was a most curious blend of Protestant Christian ideas with elements derived from the Chinese traditional culture. The Taipings sought to adjust these latter elements for their own purposes; thus, for example, the Trimetrical Classic, the basic school text, was recast into a version which conformed to the Taiping Christian outlook. It is also known that after the initial period of hostility, the Taipings reissued the Confucian Canon, but in a form appropriately edited to suit their views (one is reminded here of Wang An-shih); unfortunately, none of these works have survived as they were all destroyed by the Ch'ing. What has come down, on the other hand, is a considerable quantity of their religious works, including copies of the Bible, numerous religious tracts, hymns and so on. While their policy towards Confucianism showed this desire to adapt it to their own needs, the hostility of the Taipings towards Buddhism and Taoism was never abated and they were consistent throughout in seeking to destroy all the vestiges of these two creeds. Considering their widespread appeal and the hold of Buddhism and Taoism on the Chinese peasants, this iconoclastic warfare of the Taipings against so-called idolatry must necessarily have had negative results as far as maintaining a support of the peasantry was concerned.

It is not, in fact, easy to define the ideology of the Taiping movement in view of its eclectic nature. The movement has been referred to by some modern Chinese historians (Fan Wen-lan, for example) as subjective peasant socialism. Perhaps utopian would be a better word to use than subjective; there is, of course, no doubt at all regarding the peasant, plebeian nature of the movement. Whether the word socialism should be applied to the unrealized programme or aspirations of the Taipings is, however, debatable. While the Taiping movement was a conscious effort at least to envisage a new society—and this was what differentiated it from preceding peasant insurrections—it was basically a peasant egalitarian movement and its vision was simultaneously still in line with the harking back to the legendary Golden Age. Thus, the Taipings were very much prisoners indeed of the Chinese cultural tradition. Their sinification of Protestant Christianity, on the other hand, was also so far reaching as to make the final product hardly recognizable as the original creed. This is not the last time that such a fate was to meet doctrines imported from abroad; while they may meet current needs of the Chinese domestic situation—and Christianity, in its potential revolutionary and anti-feudal character, did meet them to some degree at this time—they are then transformed quite out of semblance with the original, in order to fit the specific conditions and situation within China itself.

The total defeat of the Taiping state led also to the disappearance of all traces of Taiping ideology, in any organized form whatsoever. However, it seems quite wrong to assume, as some Western historians do, that there was no continuity between the Taiping and future revolutionary movements in China. Not only do the well-known sympathies of Sun Yat-sen for the Taiping cause come to mind; even more, the problem connected with the leading of a peasant revolution, although under the admittedly different historical conditions of the 20th century, endowed the Taiping movement with an unusual degree of topicality. The many striking similarities, as well as, of course, the numerous obvious differences between the T'ai P'ing T'ien Kuo and the history of the Chinese revolutionary movement, both during its struggle for power in the years 1919-1949, and in the period after it had gained victory, assuredly deserve to become the object of careful and serious study. These problems are already outside of our scope; nevertheless, it is also from this point of view that the historical importance of the Taiping movement should be regarded, apart from its very obvious place as the greatest Chinese social movement of the 19th century, and the next to the greatest and next to the last peasant revolution in Chinese history.

CHAPTER 30

The Foreign Powers and China, 1842-1864

I. The General Situation After the First Opium War

Although the gains which the foreign powers had made as a result of the First Opium War, affirmed by the Nanking Treaty and the other pacts, were considerable, these were not regarded by them as sufficient. Only five ports were accessible to the foreigners while the capital and the entire interior were still closed to their activity; the relations with the Ch'ing government remained difficult, inasmuch as the Manchus had not changed their politics to a degree which the foreigners would have found sufficiently satisfactory. Thus, the aim of the foreign powers was now not only to implement in full what had been gained by the initial unequal treaties but also, and this became the main interest, to increase the possibilities of their expansion and penetration into China. The visions which were always prevalent of China becoming an unlimited market for European goods had thus far proved to be illusory; it was felt that this was primarily due to the restrictions which still existed and not to the objective conditions of the Chinese economy and it led, therefore, to strengthening still more the desire to bring about a truly full opening of China. To put it briefly, the Nanking Treaty was but a foot in the door—the task now was to force it wide open.

The main role both in the formulation of policies connected with the above aims and in their implementation was still played by Great Britain. The English continued to be dominant in economic relations with China—two-thirds of the trade was in their hands—and England itself was still in the full swing of mid-Victorian prosperity and expansionism. In the general desire to open up all of China, a particular interest was being displayed by the British, already at this time, in the possibility of exploiting the vast riches of the Yangtse Valley which were considered, correctly, to be a truly tempting prize. This point must be borne in mind in connection with the evolution of British policy towards the Taipings. Politically, the British strove for the establishment of direct diplomatic relations with the Ch'ing government, going on the assumption that this would ultimately result in increasing their political influence over it; once this had been affected, further penetration would be rendered much more feasible. In this the example of Turkey was undoubtedly kept in mind, while the effects of such policies had, of course, been seen to their best advantage in India. It is quite possible that a form of "indirect rule" was also being considered.

The English were also the most active in China in implementing the Nanking agreement; their consulates had been established in all the five ports, while in Hong Kong they possessed an excellent base for continuing their aggression against China—all this made it still easier for them to be the initiators of the policy of the foreign powers towards China. In this a considerable role was played by those on the spot, whose actions would often result in the creation of situations in relations with the Ch'ing government such as would assuredly lead to new conflicts. While divergences undoubtedly existed between the British in China and London itself, the former were, on the whole, always confident that they would receive a full backing for their actions from the British government. It was the local English in the five ports, both the officials and the merchants, who sought to take the fullest advantage of the first unequal treaty and who conceived the need for its rapid revision and modification.

The position of the United States was still second in commercial importance in trade with China. Politically, due to the fact that the Americans were primarily absorbed by their own process of domestic expansion, the United States basically followed the initiative of England, although often quite distrustful of British motives. Occasionally, the Americans did possess ideas of their own, in particular after the beginning of the Taiping movement. In general, they were in favour of employing force in the conduct of relations with China, but much preferred to make use of someone else's force, especially that of the British.

France's trade relations with China in the post-treaty period were still quite insignificant. However, the government of Napoleon III was much interested in continuing the traditional French pose of *Fidei defensor* and adhered to its role as the self-appointed spokesman for the rights of Catholicism in East Asia. It was also in this period that the Napoleonic aspirations of building a colonial empire in Asia were maturing.

The position of Russia differed from that of the other foreign powers in a number of important respects. Practically all Russian trade with China was by land and not by sea; the Russians had so far not drawn any benefits from the Nanking Treaty but were now seeking ways of accomplishing this. What was of much greater importance than this problem was the further consolidation and territorial expansion of Russia in East Siberia which was being steadily pursued. The questions connected with this policy were uppermost in the mind of the Tsarist government as regards their relations with the Ch'ing.

In the overall picture of foreign expansion the role of Shanghai was of considerable importance already in the years immediately following the first treaties. Shanghai quickly became the main commercial base for foreign trade, replacing Canton, and a rapid growth of the foreign merchant community also took place. The exports from Shanghai in 1846 were valued at $7 million and this figure went up to $23 million by 1853. In 1852 already over half of the total of Chinese exports went through Shanghai. Trade, as a whole, increased markedly and this was particularly true of silk; 12,000 bales were exported in 1842 and 80,000 in 1857. The export of tea also increased considerably, reaching the figure of 15 million pounds in 1855, while the average for the years 1858-1860 was 35 million pounds. The foreign merchants paid for this increase by the already-well-tried methods of opium smuggling on an immense scale. The figures are the following:

1852	48,600 chests
1853	54,574 chests
1854	61,523 chests
1855	63,354 chests

The opium trade—still illicit—had now spread to the entire coast and the smuggling proceeded unabashedly in broad daylight. Hong Kong was the principal centre, where the stocks of opium were kept and from which they were distributed to the coastal ports.

Canton was still of importance economically but it was perhaps even more important politically, inasmuch as it continued to be the only place which the Ch'ing government had designated for the conduct of relations with the overseas barbarians; thus, the Governor-general of Liangkwang remained the principal high Ch'ing official entrusted with the responsibility for their management. This position was held until 1848 by Ch'i-ying, who had negotiated all the treaties. He was then replaced, partly because of his failure to keep the British quiet, by Hsü Kuang-chih (1786-1858) who kept this post until 1852, when he was, in turn, replaced by Yeh Ming-ch'en (1807-1859). It is also here that the so-called Canton Entry problem arose which was to become a source of continued friction between the British and the Ch'ing government. Briefly, the question was that the British maintained that the Nanking Treaty had given them the right to enter the walled city of Canton itself (from a legal point they were wrong; the treaty gave them the right to trade at but not in Canton). Such a problem had not arisen in any of the other Treaty Ports; the main reason for its existence in Canton was the hostile attitude of the Canton population to foreigners which was derived, primarily, from their experience of the First Opium War.

The British in 1847 attacked the forts near Canton in pursuance of their so-called right of entry, but then withdrew after an agreement that they would receive this right two years later. This was one of the earliest instances of what was later to become the most frequently employed form of diplomatic relations—the gunboat policy. In 1849 the new Hong Kong governor and commissioner, George Bonham, tried to enter the city; the population of Canton opposed this once more and a threat was made to cut off all trade relations with the English; thus Bonham's attempt ended in failure. The Ch'ing officials were pleased to be able to use this popular opposition as their excuse and even the Emperor "supported" the action of the Cantonese.

The Ch'ing government in this period was still to a great degree smarting from its defeat in the First Opium War and in its policies showed no desire to depart from the principle of isolation, fearing that the consequences of changing this approach would be fatal to the continuation of Manchu rule. It hoped that the Nanking Treaty and its sequels would be the limit of the concessions it had been necessary to grant the foreigners; if these could by any chance be whittled down—so much the better. The Manchus were especially hostile to the attempts made by the foreign powers to establish direct diplomatic relations; this was primarily a question of preserving "face", but its importance should not be underrated. The Manchus regarded the presence of foreigners in Peking as a possible prelude to the end of their rule; they remembered only too well their own arrival in Peking 200 years earlier.

Basically, the line of action followed was that of avoiding, if possible, all contact with the foreigners, which could be defined as a policy of non-communication. There was, however, something very ostrich-like in all this, for the assumption seemed to be "if one doesn't see it, it doesn't exist". Within the Ch'ing ruling group there were at least two schools of thought; one compromised those who were thoroughly hostile to the foreigners—these included Hsien-feng, the Emperor himself, as well as a number of high officials, such as Yeh Ming-ch'en. Others, Ch'i-ying, for example, referred to as "Westernizers" by some Chinese writers, believed in the necessity of a conciliatory policy which, in effect, amounted to capitulation to foreign demands.

II. The T'ai P'ing T'ien Kuo and the Foreign Powers

A completely new situation arose in the relations of the foreign powers and China in connection with the development of the Taiping movement; this became especially true after the taking of Nanking, when it appeared that the days of the Manchus might be numbered. The foreigners almost completely lacked any accurate knowledge regarding the Taipings and the first necessity was to find out who the rebels actually were, and, what was most important, what were their chances of gaining complete victory and what would.be their attitude to the foreign powers—would they honour the agreements which had been imposed on the Ch'ing government, would they be a hindrance to further foreign penetration or could they be utilized to facilitate it? Thus, the reconnoitring missions of the foreigners to Nanking were soon to begin; the first, appropriately enough, were the British, with Bonham sailing to Nanking in April 1853.* The French were to follow suit—A. de Bourboulon arrived in Nanking in December 1853. The American representative, R. M. McLane, made his trip in May 1854 and was then followed by another British mission, that of John Bowring in June 1854.

After having toyed initially with the possibility of immediate intervention in favour of the Ch'ing government, the British, on the basis of Bonham's appreciation of the situation, decided to adopt a "wait and see" policy and to proclaim their neutrality in regard to the conflict between the Taipings and the Manchus. The Christian aspect of the Taiping movement raised the hopes of many that its victory would result in "throwing open China to religious and commercial enterprise". The combination of the interests of religion and commerce is quite characteristic of Western thought in this period. Some of the Americans on the spot, in particular the American commissioner, H. Marshall, suspected the British of scheming to use the Taipings for their own purposes and on this basis, among others, favoured immediate intervention and proposed that "the Chinese government be offered the use of United States military and naval forces to be employed against the Taipings". These suggestions were, however, not approved and acted upon by Washington and the American government followed the British in proclaiming its neutrality.

After the failure of the Northern Expedition of the Taipings, when their victory began to appear less promising, a slow but steady shift of British policy in favour of the Ch'ing government ensued. In the meantime, both the British and American merchants were conducting a thriving business in selling arms—usually almost worthless—to both sides engaged in the conflict.

The policy of the Taipings was touchingly naive. In their religious enthusiasm they believed the foreigners, in particular the Protestant English and Americans, to be "Brothers in Christ" and expected to receive from them sympathy, recognition and aid. Simultaneously, however, they did not display much initiative in seeking to establish relations with the foreigners, to get the expected assistance. There was much also of the Middle Kingdom in their attitude and, in addition, the Divine Rule of the Heavenly King did not provide a particularly easy platform for a *rapprochement* between the Taipings and the foreigners.

The growing political crisis in Europe, with the development of the conflict between

---

*The most interesting contemporary account of this problem is to be found in T.T. Meadows, *The Chinese and Their Rebellions*.

Britain and France on the one hand and Russia on the other hand, which was ultimately to lead to the Crimean War, had a very important bearing on the policy of these countries towards China, inasmuch as it signified an ever-growing, and then complete, absorption with European problems. Thus the "wait and see" policy was well suited to such a situation and it was therefore maintained longer than it otherwise might have been.

At the same time a foretaste of the true intentions of the foreign powers could be noted in their activities in Shanghai. While the Taipings in 1853 had made no attempts to conquer Kiangsu and Chekiang—a policy which they themselves considered later to have been a vital error—an uprising took place in Shanghai on September 7, 1853 which was led by the Hsiao Tao (Small Swords) Society. This was an offshoot of the Triad and its members were mostly Chinese from Kwangtung and Fukien, a very large colony of whom resided in Shanghai; the insurgents had no difficulty in occupying the entire Chinese walled city but did not disturb nor establish their control over the foreign settlements outside of this city. They sought to establish contact with the Taiping leadership in Nanking, but their efforts were unsuccessful, and simultaneously the Taipings paid very little attention to the events in Shanghai.

For a long time the Ch'ing local officials and forces were unable to overcome the insurgents. Then, with the approval of the British and the Americans, the walled city was surrounded and cut off from further supplies. It was, however, the French who were to become the most active in intervening against the insurgents; after negotiations conducted by de Bourboulon with the Ch'ing officials, French troops joined the Ch'ing army in its attacks on Shanghai in December 1854, with the result that finally the town was taken on February 17, 1855, and its capture was accompanied by the customary massacre and plundering of the civilian population by the Ch'ing troops.

In the long run the activities of the British and American representatives in Shanghai were undoubtedly of greater importance. As the result of the existing confusion after the insurgents had taken Shanghai, the British and Americans took over the control of the local Chinese customs and in this way laid the foundation for the creation, later on, of the Imperial Maritime Customs Service, to be run under the control of foreigners. This became a paralysing stranglehold on the finances of the Ch'ing government; all the future indemnities which were to be forced out of China, as well as later loans which were imposed on the Ch'ing government, were to a great degree to be guaranteed by customs receipts. Simultaneously, during the struggle against the Taipings the Shanghai customs became a very important source for the Ch'ing government in financing its military activities and it was made available to them for this purpose by the foreigners in control. This was one of the most important bases for the development of co-operation between the Ch'ing government and the foreign powers, in spite of the conflicts which existed between them during this same period. The Manchus, on the one hand, suspected at this stage that the foreigners might desire to help the Taipings; on the other hand, they sought their aid against them, but wondered what price they would have to pay for such assistance. This latter policy was represented, in particular, by such individuals as Tseng Kuo-fan, as well as by the officials in Shanghai, who were doing business with the foreigners and were well on their way to becoming compradores of the West.

It is also in this period that the foundations were laid in Shanghai for what was to become that curious, cancerous anomaly—the International Settlement and the French

Concession—the part of Shanghai which came under the direct rule of the foreign residents. Here, the foreigners exercised complete control, both political and military, which was also extended to all the Chinese living within the limits of the Settlement and Concession, who, while constituting the overwhelming majority of the population, had no say whatsoever in this peculiar local government.

III. The Immediate Background of the Second Opium War

In order to achieve the basic aims of policy referred to above, the British, taking advantage of the provisions in the Wanghsia Treaty, which dealt with the possibility of reviewing relations after twelve years, began, in 1854, an attempt to start negotiations on the question of the revision of the Anglo-Chinese Treaty. The declared aims of the negotiations could be summed up in four points: (a) the establishment of legations in Peking; (b) the opening of the interior, especially the Yangtse Valley, to foreign trade; (c) freedom for missionary activities in all China; (d) the extension of trade by means of opening further new ports. The negotiations were begun in the spring of 1854 with Yeh Ming-ch'en in Canton; they quickly ran into a stone wall, inasmuch as Yeh was a strict adherent of the policy of non-communication. There was, it is true, some veracity in this argument that he was too busy to talk with the foreigners. since Yeh was one of the worst butchers of the Ch'ing regime. In 1854 most of Kwangtung was in the hands of insurgents from the secret societies, who had contact with the Taipings, and had almost succeeded in capturing Canton itself. Yeh Ming-ch'en was instrumental in putting down this insurrection with the aid of massacres on a vast scale in which well over 100,000 people were killed.

The British then resolved to attempt to conduct the talks elsewhere; J. Bowring was joined in this by R. M. McLane—the position of the United States as far as the basic aims of the foreign powers, especially the question of treaty revisions, was practically identical with that of the British. In September, the two representatives sought to conduct negotiations in Shanghai which produced no results whatsoever. They subsequently proceeded to Tientsin—on warships, always a weighty argument— where talks were held once more. Here, the British attempted to blackmail the Ch'ing with the possibility that they would turn to aid the Taipings if the Manchus failed to agree to the conditions proposed by England. This did not have the desired effect at this time, perhaps because the Ch'ing were aware of the fact that British "neutrality" was already somewhat dubious, as had been proved by their co-operation with the Ch'ing officials in Shanghai.

After returning from Tientsin, both Bowring and McLane reported their failure to their governments and their conclusions that negotiations could be rendered possible only by means of the employment of force. McLane put this as follows: "Diplomatic intercourse can only be had with this government at the cannon's mouth." This conclusion took on a special meaning when the Crimean War was ended, for this freed British and French forces for possible future action in East Asia; the existing alliance between these two countries was considered by both of them to be still useful. Further actions against China were also stimulated by the earlier success in the opening up of Japan in which the United States had played the main role with the Perry expedition of 1854.

IV. The Second Opium War: October 1856-October 1860

(1) Act One: October 1856-March 1858

This conflict between Britain and France on the one hand and China on the other hand can be regarded as a drama in four acts; although the drama had also many aspects of a farce, none of these were comic from the Chinese point of view. The oddity of this conflict lies primarily in the fact that, while they were waging war against the Ch'ing government, the British and the French were by no means anxious or desirous of bringing about its downfall; on the contrary, already during its course, they increased their aid to it in its struggle against the Taipings and after its conclusion they wholeheartedly joined in co-operation with the Manchus by launching a direct military intervention of their own against the Taipings. Simultaneously, the existence of domestic struggle within China was also undoubtedly a factor which rendered a renewed aggression of the foreign powers much easier.

The scene of the first act was Canton and the main incident was the famous case of the lorcha *Arrow*, on which whole seas of ink were poured out at the time. The story, briefly, is as follows. The boat was owned by a Chinese, it had a Chinese crew, but it was registered (though the legality of this whole procedure was dubious) as a British vessel in Hong Kong. On the strength of this it flew the British flag. On October 8, 1856 twelve of the Chinese crew were arrested in Canton on the suspicion of a previous act of piracy; this was more than likely true, as piracy was particularly rife in the Canton area. A violent protest was then made by Harry S. Parkes (1828-1885), the British Consul in Canton; the British flag had supposedly been insulted (it had allegedly been pulled down), British rights had been infringed upon (although it was proved that the registry of the boat had expired earlier), and so forth. After long negotiations, in which Yeh Ming-ch'en finally returned all the twelve sailors, whom now Parkes refused to accept, the incident was properly blown up by Parkes and Bowring, who believed that the Chinese should be taught a lesson, to a *casus belli*. The subsequent war might well deserve the title of Parkes' war but, in fact, it was even more Palmerston's "little war", and as such it was quite in line with his theory that "such half-barbarian countries as China...needed a dressing down every ten years or so".

On October 27 British naval forces opened fire on Canton, part of it aimed at Yeh's residence; they did not have as yet available forces on hand for launching a campaign to capture the city. A number of further local military actions were conducted by the English which included the burning down of a village near Canton on December 5 in reprisal for a supposed killing of an Englishman there. In retaliation, the foreign factories were burned down on December 14 while in January, in turn, the British burned down the Chinese factories. Thus, by means of these "miserable proceedings" (the words are Lord Derby's) of the British, the groundwork was laid for a conflict on a much larger scale, which could be advantageously employed to obtain what the attempted negotiations had failed to secure.

Palmerston's policy of getting into a war with China on the pretext of the *Arrow* incident, described by Elgin as "nothing could be more contemptible", gave rise to considerable opposition in Parliament. On March 3, 1857 his government was defeated on the China issue in the House of Commons by a vote of 263-247; however, he dissolved

Parliament, called for a new election, which he succeeded in winning with a solid majority of 85. Thus Palmerston was now in a position to continue with his war.

Lord Elgin (1811-1863, the son of the scrounger of the Parthenon marbles) was appointed British Commissioner and was dispatched to negotiate with the Ch'ing government, having been furnished with an appropriate armed force. Elgin arrived in Canton in July 1857; however, the outbreak of the Indian Great Revolt in May, 1857 had caused him to divert his troops to India, while still on his way to China, and others which were on their way to China were also sent there. Thus, only a small force was now available for use against the Chinese. In October, Elgin was joined in Canton by the French representative, Baron Gros (1793-1870). The French were eager to join in the action against the Ch'ing government, more so than the British were to have them. The main cause which they employed was the murder by local Ch'ing authorities of a French missionary, A. Chapdelaine, who had been killed in February 1856 in Kwangsi; the French had sought to obtain satisfaction for this from Yeh Ming-ch'en and had failed to do so. The negotiations which had begun with Yeh led to no results and the British and French proceeded to blockade Canton.

On December 12, after the arrival of some still limited reinforcements, the British and French presented a joint ultimatum to Yeh, the main points of which pertained to a demand for entry into Canton and reparations for damages inflicted on foreign property. The answers received were considered to be unsatisfactory and on December 28 Canton, which was quite unprepared for defence, was bombarded for an entire day and extensive damage was inflicted upon it. On the next day, the Allied forces, slightly under 6000, occupied the city and considerable looting took place. Canton was now to remain under an Anglo-French occupation which was to last for three years and ten months. In order to run the city, the Allies re-established the local Ch'ing administration which remained under their complete control. In January, Yeh Ming-ch'en was captured and later sent to Calcutta as a prisoner, where he died the next year.

Having settled the Canton question to their satisfaction, the Allies now proceeded to the north to tackle the accomplishment of their principal aims. After the British and French envoys had landed in Shanghai, they were joined by W. B. Reed (1806-1876), the American representative, and by Admiral Count E. V. Putiatin (1803-1883), the Russian envoy. While Britain and France were on a war footing, although they had never declared war as such, the United States and Russia were in the convenient position of being supposedly neutral. Nevertheless, they were quite willing to join the negotiations and to benefit from the force to be employed by the British and the French. An attempt had been made earlier by the British to persuade the Americans to join in the military campaign but this had met with no success. The Russians had not been approached, for a number of obvious reasons, including the recent Crimean War; both America and Russia were interested in preventing the collapse of the Ch'ing government, while the Russians were bent, among others, on establishing themselves in the role of mediator. Both of the neutrals were also interested in applying the success they had had in opening up Japan to China; earlier, in 1855, Putiatin had negotiated the first Russo-Japanese Treaty.

(2) Act Two: April 1858-July 1858

The talks in Shanghai had been of no avail and all the four envoys now proceeded to the port of Taku, accompanied by the entire Anglo-French fleet. Here, on April 20, an ultimatum was issued to the Ch'ing that negotiations must begin within six days or the Taku forts would be taken. After some very curious discussions, in which the Americans did not participate, relating to the sufficiency of powers granted to the negotiators, the ultimate result was that the Allies occupied the Taku forts on May 20. Thus, the Allies now forced their way up to Tientsin and threatened to march to Peking itself. The Ch'ing court was thoroughly frightened and quickly appointed new negotiators— Kuei-liang (1785-1862), a very highly placed Manchu, and Hua-sha-na, a Mongol. Talks were now held from the beginning of June and their main form was the extensive browbeating and bullying of the Ch'ing representatives by two young British interpreters, H. N. Lay and T. Wade.* These somewhat peculiar diplomatic methods of the British produced the desired effects; the Ch'ing negotiators were forced to concede point after point. Even more important, however, was the fact that the Manchus were frightened by the possibility that the English might turn to support the Taipings, for this underlying threat was always present. The subject of these negotiations gave rise to a great debate at the Ch'ing court, where the faction in favour of capitulation was led by a group of Manchu princes who were concerned with the future fate of the dynasty.

The two "neutrals" were the first to achieve their success, more than likely as the result of Ch'ing policy which sought to split the four foreign powers. The Sino-Russian Treaty was signed by Putiatin on June 13, 1858; in general it pertained to trade, but this was equally important, inasmuch as due to the inclusion of the most-favoured-nation clause Russia only now obtained all the privileges of the earlier Nanking treaties. Putiatin sweetened the pill by offering the Ch'ing government arms and instructors to use against the Taipings; the arms were in fact delivered later in 1862.

However, much more important negotiations were being conducted by the Russians with the Manchus at almost exactly the same time. These were being handled by N. N. Muraviev (1809-1881), who had been the Governor of Eastern Siberia since 1847. The energetic Muraviev had been busy settling and colonizing the Amur Region, while it was still officially a part of the Ch'ing Empire, and now aimed at the obtaining of a favourable revision of the Nerchinsk Treaty in order to acquire additional territory for the Tsar. Thus, the Ch'ing governor of Heilungkiang, I-shan (the same whose behaviour in Canton in 1841 has already been noted), now agreed, *nolens volens*, to negotiate. The conference was held in Aigun on the Amur, beginning on May 11, 1858; it ended by the signing, on May 28, of the Aigun Treaty, in which I-shan gave in to all of Muraviev's demands. Thus, all the territory on the left bank of the Amur (to the north) was recognized as Russian, and that on the right bank to the point where the Ussuri joins the Amur as belonging to the Ch'ing empire; the area between the Ussuri and the Sea of Japan was to belong temporarily to both countries, until its fate was to be

---

*Typical of this behaviour was the famous incident concerning Ch'i-yeng; he now showed up—an old, half-blind man—to take part in the negotiations, after having convinced the Emperor that he was the greatest expert on the management of Western barbarians and seeking to regain thereby his lost position. The British refused to receive him and later during a meeting with all the three Ch'ing envoys, Lay pulled out an old memorandum which had been captured in Canton with Yeh Ming-ch'en's archives, in which Ch'i-ying boasted of the methods he employed in dealing with the English; he made Hua-sha-na read it out loud and thus cause Ch'i-ying to lose face completely. The old man fled from Tientsin in disgrace; he was then sentenced to death for having left it without permission and subsequently the Emperor graciously commuted the death sentence by permitting him to commit suicide.

determined at a later date. Hence, the task of Russian diplomacy was now to assure the ratification of this treaty. I-shan was degraded for signing it; Muraviev was later made Count of the Amur (Amurski). Earlier, in 1851, the Russians had signed the treaty of Kuldja in which they obtained the right to trade in Kuldja (the main city of Ili) and in Tarbagatai, for they were also very interested in penetrating the area of Ch'ing-held Eastern Turkestan.

The Americans signed their treaty on June 18; it contained a provision, which had been included in the Russian treaty, regarding the possibility of establishing direct contact with Peking for the conduct of future relations; inasmuch as it also included the most-favoured-nation clause, all the advantages for which the British were still negotiating would anyhow accrue to both the Russians and the Americans. It is worth noting that the American talks were, in fact, carried out by the two interpreters, S. W. Williams and W. A. P. Martin, both missionaries who were to play a considerable role in future American activities in China.* The role of the American negotiators has been dealt with by the American historian T. Dennett; his description, which is already almost classical, is worth recalling: "The American envoy was dispatched to the other side of the world to stand under a tree with a basket waiting for his associates above to shake down the fruit. He was even instructed to offer mediation in case those in the tree became involved with the owners of the orchard."

The British negotiations were still meeting difficulties and the arm-twisting went on. The main source of the trouble was Elgin's demand that the Ch'ing agree to the residence of foreign envoys in Peking. The strenuous objection of the Manchus to this point was primarily one of "face", but the importance of this fact from the domestic point of view has already been referred to. The second point was the problem of opening the interior, and especially the Yangtse, to trade and the presence of foreigners. These issues were finally won by the British with the threat that otherwise a march to Peking would take place. The treaty was finally signed on June 26, imposed "with a pistol at the throat", in Elgin's own words. Characteristically, Elgin simultaneously claimed: "I am China's friend in all this." The French courteously waited a day to follow the British and signed their treaty on June 27, also taking their indemnity of 4 million taels. A description of the entire Tientsin negotiations by one of the British present goes as follows: "Two powers had China by the throat while the other two stood by to egg them on so that all could share the spoils."

The Tientsin treaties, the next in time and perhaps the most important in the series of unequal pacts imposed on China, achieved one of the principal aims of all the foreign powers—the further opening of China to Western economic penetration. This was primarily accomplished through the addition of eleven more ports (counting all those added in subsequent negotiations) to the list of Treaty Ports which were to be utilized for the above purpose.† A glance at the map will show how far-reaching these new gains

---

*Williams was the editor in Canton of the *Chinese Repository*, an invaluable source of material for the years 1832-1851. He was later also in the American diplomatic service in China and was the author of a well-known large compendium, *The Middle Kingdom*, which was of considerable influence in its time. Martin was later, for a number of years the head of a college established by the Chinese Foreign Office and the author of somewhat curious recollections contained in *A Cycle of Cathay*.

†These ports were: (1) Tamsui (Tanshui), North Taiwan; (2) Taiwan (Tainan), South-west Taiwan; (3) Kiungchow (Haikou), North Hainan Island; (4) Swatow (Shant'ou), East Kwangtung; (5) Chinkiang, Kiangsu, (6) Kiukiang (Chiuchiang), Anhwei, (7) Hankow, Hupei, (8) Nanking—all these four on the Yangtse; (9) Tengchow (later exchanged for Chefoo), Shantung; (10) Tientsin; (11) Newchwang (Yingkow), Liaoning.

were; when taken together with the original five Treaty Ports, they made almost every part of China readily accessible both from the sea and, this is particularly noteworthy, from its jugular vein—the Yangtse, which was now also opened to foreign shipping, both commercial and naval. Simultaneously, the foreign powers were permitted to engage in Chinese coastal trade.

The foreigners now also received the freedom of movement in all the interior of China as well as the freedom for conducting missionary activities; the latter were to be the source of innumerable squabbles and conflicts in the future. For their trouble both the English and the French demanded and received an indemnity of 4 million taels each. One question still remained to be settled; Hsien-feng had to ratify the treaties. This was achieved, with the help of a threat to use the troops in Tientsin, in July, and thus the second act was concluded.

(3) Interlude: Autumn 1858-Spring 1859

The British now pressed their advantage to settle a number of economic questions; these were the subject of talks held in Shanghai in October and can be considered a part of the interlude between the second and third acts. The main results of the talks included the legalization of the opium trade which was still by far the most important item in British import. Thus, the erstwhile smugglers could now convert themselves into properly respectable and honest merchants. Equally important was the establishment of the tariff rate on import and export at 5 per cent (with the exception of opium, tea and silk which were taxed at a slightly different rate). This constituted a vital point, inasmuch as it facilitated the future flooding of the Chinese market by foreign goods and reduced almost to nil the possibility of protection against them, which could stimulate China's own industrial development. A measure which was similar in its nature and effects was the abolition of the *likin* (domestic taxes) on imported foreign goods after the initial payment of a duty of 2.5 per cent.

The terms of the Tientsin Treaties proved extremely hard to swallow for the Ch'ing government; Hsien-feng, in particular, objected vehemently to the point pertaining to the residence of foreign envoys in Peking. Already during the Shanghai talks the Emperor was willing to offer to the foreigners the abandonment of all tariff regulations, if for this economic sacrifice they would consent to relinquish this provision. The Ch'ing negotiators had no success in this respect but did receive from Elgin a promise that this point was not necessarily mandatory. The Ch'ing government now readied itself for the possibility of a renewed conflict and it desired especially to prevent a repetition of the foreign envoys marching with their troops up to Tientsin and hence more than likely to Peking. Orders were now given to the main Ch'ing general, the Mongol Prince, Senggerinchin, to improve the defences of North China and, in particular, to strengthen the Taku forts.

After the conclusion of the Shanghai talks Elgin received permission from the Ch'ing authorities to sail up the Yangtse; he conducted a six-week cruise on the Great River, accompanied by a British naval squadron, during which he inspected the new ports that were to be opened and also reconnoitred the Taiping positions. The latter included the bombardment of Taiping batteries by the superior guns of the British. A characteristic moment in this trip was that the Ch'ing fleet followed right behind the British ships and made use of their presence to attack the Taiping posts.*

(4) Act Three: Summer 1859

The main question now from the British point of view was to accomplish the exchange of ratifications of the Tientsin Treaty in the place and in a fashion of their own choice. As regards the place, they insisted on Peking in order that the lesson which was being taught should sink in properly; as regards the fashion, the decision was to march up with an appropriately impressive military escort. All this was now placed in the hands of F. Bruce, Elgin's younger brother, who was nominated the new British Minister to China. The Ch'ing authorities notified the British that the road through Taku to Tientsin should not be taken; they requested that the British land slightly to the north in Peit'ang and proceed on from here with a modest escort. Bruce refused to listen to this suggestion and accompanied by the French Minister, de Bourboulon, proceeded to Taku with the combined Anglo-French fleet. Here, the Allies sought to enter the Pei River by force, in spite of the fact that it had been obviously barred and the new defences were evident everywhere. On June 25 an Anglo-French landing party of 1000 men attacked the forts only to meet with total defeat; this time, for once, the artillery fire of the Chinese proved to be very effective. Four British ships were sunk and the landing party was forced to retreat with a loss of 434 killed and wounded. The invincibility image of the Westerners was very badly damaged. They retreated rapidly back to Shanghai, where they now settled down to await further reinforcements.

Neither the Russians nor the Americans had been involved in this particular episode. The new Russian Minister, General N.P. Ignatiev (1832-1908), was already ensconced in Peking, where he had successfully carried out the exchange of ratifications; he was now busy conducting negotiations with Su-shun (1815?-1867), the real power at the Ch'ing court, trying to obtain the ratification of the Aigun Treaty and to press further Russian territorial claims, i.e. the question that had been left open by that treaty—the fate of the lands between Ussuri and the Sea of Japan, which the Ch'ing were quite determined not to lose. Ignatiev was to play quite an important role in all the subsequent relations between the Anglo-French Allies and the Manchu government. The new American Minister, J. E. Ward, accompanied by the same two missionary interpreters, undertook a trip to Peking; here the question of the kotow once more cropped up to confuse the issues and the exchanges of ratifications finally took place in Peit'ang on August 16.

In England, although a change of government had taken place earlier—the short-lasting Derby-Disraeli ministry, February 1858-June 1859, which had not resulted in any basic changes in British China policy—Palmerston was back once more as Prime Minister in July to face the problem of what future actions should be pursued after the fiasco of Bruce's mission. In view of his previous position in respect to the *Arrow* incident, it was not difficult to see that a further use of force, another "dressing down" would now be called for. In spite of the fact that the cordiality of relations between England and France was already much strained at this stage, further common action between these two countries in China was agreed upon, probably each side being anxious to keep a watchful eye on the other on the spot. Thus, a new joint ultimatum

---

*An interesting eye-witness account of this, as well as the earlier parts of the Elgin mission, is to be found in the book by his secretary, L. Oliphant. See Bibiography.

was sent to the Ch'ing government in March 1860; its main points were a demand for an apology for the action at Taku of June 1859, for the exchange of ratifications of the **Tientsin Treaty to take place in Peking, and for further increased indemnity.** Simultaneously, a new larger military expedition was being readied and the same envoys who had negotiated the Tientsin treaties were now dispatched once more to China. The stage was thus set for the last act.

(5) Act Four: August 1860-November 1860

In the summer of 1860 the Allies gathered their military forces for a new expedition to the North; the British had over 10,000 troops (a large part of them Indian), the French had over 6000. The joint fleet included over 70 warships and more than 140 transport vessels. The British and French ambassadors, Elgin and Gros, landed on August 1 and, without any attempt whatsoever at initiating talks, they proceeded to order an attack on the Ch'ing positions around Taku. After some stiff fighting the Allied forces succeeded in taking the Taku forts from the rear and marched up to occupy Tientsin. Only then were Elgin and Gros willing to begin negotiations and the Ch'ing again designated Kuei-liang as their main representative. The Allies now demanded that Tientsin be added to the list of Treaty Ports, an indemnity be paid and the entry into Peking of the two ambassadors with a military escort be agreed to. Simultaneously, they refused to hold any further talks except in the town of Tungchow (10 miles east of Peking).

The troops were marched up from Tientsin to a place close to Tungchow and here the terms of the new Peking Convention were settled upon on September 14-18. These arrangements were then upset by the arrest by the Ch'ing of a part of the British and French negotiating group (26 British, 13 French). This played right into the hands of the British and the French; they now proceeded to further military action and on September 21 defeated the troops of Senggerinchin at Palich'iao (a bridge on the approaches to Peking). However, they were unable to push directly towards the capital, inasmuch as they had practically run out of ammunition. Thus, they were forced to wait for further supplies and reinforcements from Tientsin.

In the meantime complete panic ensued in the Ch'ing court; Hsien-feng now decided that a trip of inspection of the provinces was truly vital at this moment, i.e., he fled to Jehol with a part of his court, including his favourite cronies, leaving his younger half-brother, I-hsin, Prince Kung (1833-1898), to face the Anglo-French invaders. Having received their reinforcements the British and French advanced on Peking; on October 6 they reached the Yüan Ming Yüan—the Summer Palace—the favourite residence of the Ch'ing Emperors, on the building of which they had lavished fabulous sums and in which they had gathered untold treasures from the taxes they had ground out during two centuries from the sweat and blood of the Chinese peasants. The Gallic eloquence of the French commander, Montauban, was at a loss to describe all the splendour contained therein.* For three days the Expeditionary Force pillaged the palace, on the whole quite systematically, although a bit wastefully. However, the British complained rather sourly that the French got more than their fair share.

He later received from Napoleon III the title of Comte de Palikao(sic)*for his great victory over the Ch'ing; ten years later he again demonstrated his splendid military talents by being crushingly defeated by the Prussians and fleeing to England.

In Peking itself, almost complete chaos reigned, inasmuch as most of the high officials had fled either with the Emperor or by themselves. The Allies now demanded entry into the capital and threatened to bombard it if this were to be refused. Through the mediation of Ignatiev the entry, as well as willingness to conduct talks, was agreed to by I-hsin. The gates were then opened and the negotiations began. The prisoners who had been previously captured were also released, but only nineteen of them, for twenty had either been killed or had died in the conditions prevailing in Ch'ing prisons. To this act of Manchu barbarity, Elgin now replied with an act which, according to him, was supposedly aimed solely at the Emperor himself, and ordered the complete burning down of more than 200 buildings of the Summer Palace complex; this was carried out by the British troops on October 18-19. Which barbarity was the greater one is rather difficult to judge.

It was now truly no problem any more to get the signature of the Peking Convention accomplished. This was done on October 24; Elgin marched into Peking with an armed escort through the streets lined with British troops for the ceremony which was held in the Hall of Rites in the Imperial Palace. Prince Kung signed for the Ch'ing, his first experience in diplomatic relations with foreign powers, of which he was to have quite a considerable amount during the rest of his future career. The main terms of the Convention were as follows: (1) foreign envoys were to reside in Peking; (2) Tientsin was to become a Treaty Port; (3) the indemnities were increased to 8 million taels each: an additional sum of 500,000 for the British and 200,000 for the French as a special indemnity for the dead prisoners was stipulated; the payment was to be guaranteed by customs receipts; (4) a part of Kowloon peninsula (the territory on the mainland opposite Hong Kong) was ceded in perpetuity to England; (5) all the property of the Catholic Church, which had been confiscated since 1724, was to be restored (the French translator secretly added to the Chinese, but not the French text, a clause regarding the right to buy land and build churches anywhere in China); (6) the Ch'ing government granted permission for the emigration of its nationals abroad; this point concerned the so-called coolie trade.* The French repeated the same performance on the next day in an almost identical fashion. At the same time as the Convention was signed, the exchange ratifications of the Tientsin treaties was accomplished and thus the Allies now obtained everything they had aimed for. Due to the most-favoured-nation clause all the benefits were also acquired by the Americans and the Russians.

The Russians, however, had their own issues to settle. Ignatiev had acted as a mediator between the Manchus and the Allies; he now presented his demands to the Ch'ing government and, after the departure of Elgin and Gros, signed a new treaty with the Ch'ing on November 14. In it Russia obtained not only the ratification of the Aigun Treaty, but also the cession of all the territory between the Ussuri and the Sea of Japan (around 63,000 square miles), the present Primorskaya Region. The foundations of Vladivostok ("Rules the East") were laid in the same year. Simultaneously, the

---

*This was conducted on a large scale by the foreign merchants in Hong Kong and especially in Macao. It was an illicit smuggling out of China of labourers who were then sent to work in the plantations of Cuba, the West Indies, the mines of Peru and Chile, as well as to California and Australia. The "contractual" basis on which they were recruited actually amounted to a semi-slave status. The fundamental motive was the need for cheap labour; over half a million Chinese were shipped out in the years 1840-1880. The conditions prevailing in transport were particularly atrocious, resembling those of the Negro slave trade, and resulting in an extremely high mortality rate.

Russians received permission to establish consulates in Urga (Ulan Bator) and Kashgar (Eastern Turkestan).

The results of the Second Opium War and of the treaties which concluded it constituted a very important step forward in the transformation of China into a semi-colony of the principal foreign powers. The policy of isolation that had been pursued by the Ch'ing government was completely shattered; as a consequence of their defeat the Manchus were now properly chastened and were not only willing to co-operate with the foreign powers but were being turned, more and more, into a useful, subservient instrument of the latter, through which foreign control could be extended over China without the troublesome burden of direct rule. In fact, China was now faced with the distinct possibility of losing its independence altogether, as well as of being partitioned into a number of colonies. Actually, there are two basic reasons why this did not take place. The first is the rivalry of the foreign powers, which increased in time over the problem of the division of such immense loot—and in this the very vastness of China was a complicating factor, which actually goes far to explain its fate. The second was the ever-increasing opposition of the Chinese to what the foreign powers had in store for their country, although the effectiveness of this was to be felt only in the 20th century. In achieving these results, the role of Great Britain was pre-eminent. It is interesting to note the comments of an American eye-witness on the motivations of the wars which the British had waged against China in this period: "The occasion for the unchaining of England's thunder in one instance was to exact payment for the destruction of the prohibited drug, in another to procure satisfaction for an insult implied in the Chinese exercising summary justice on their own people; in the third, in their quibble of words; in the fourth, the assertion of a privilege which the negotiators had forgotten to secure."

At the beginning of November the Allied troops withdrew from Peking to escape the severities of the winter there and were stationed in Tientsin and in Shanghai to await the payment of the indemnities and to prepare for the playing of an entirely new role—that of the supporters of their Manchu erstwhile enemies. The curtain had come down—the play was over; the farcical roles had been divided, on the whole rather evenly, between the Europeans and the Manchus. The tragic roles had been assigned to the Chinese—then, and for a long time yet to come.

V. Foreign Intervention Against the T'ai P'ing T'ien Kuo

A fundamental change of policy of the foreign powers towards the Ch'ing government evolved immediately upon the conclusion of the Peking Convention. But this had been, in fact, long in preparation for, even while they were waging war against the Manchus, the British and the French were by no means anxious to bring about a collapse and fall of the dynasty. To Elgin, for example, the Taipings were "a mischievous convulsion" which ought to be brought to an end. According to him, the British envoy in Peking would serve to sustain the ruling dynasty as a "diplomatic protectorate". It is possible that in the flush of victory in October—when Hsien-feng had already fled to Jehol and the Ch'ing government was practically non-existent—the British on the spot toyed with the idea of replacing it with something else, perhaps even with the Taipings, or so at least the Americans present there suspected. If this were true, this was only a momentary aberration which would have never been acted upon seriously or approved of in London. That this was not the main line of British thinking was shown quite clearly by the fact that British neutrality in the Ch'ing-Taiping conflict was becoming ever more spurious.

The above was illustrated by the curious fact that at the very same time when, in August 1860, the Anglo-French Expeditionary Force was attacking the Taku forts in the north, the British and French troops in Shanghai, which had been left there expressly for that purpose, were equally busy fighting on the exact same day but not against the Ch'ing, perish the thought, but against the Taiping army of the Chung Wang which was advancing for the first time on this main foreign base in China. This was an extremely clear indication of what was to follow. Once the Ch'ing government had signed away all that was demanded, it became the consistent policy of all the foreign powers—in spite of all their rivalries, they all agreed upon this completely—to support it against its domestic enemy to the fullest extent possible, not excluding even direct intervention by foreign military forces. The reason for this was obvious—it was from the Manchus that the fulfilment of all the treaty obligations was to be exacted and the powers had no doubt as to the fact that they would be successful in this. Hence, the legitimacy, the "law and order" aspect of Ch'ing rule was stressed now by the foreigners.

One subsidiary but very crucial factor also entered into these calculations: the Taipings not only were still in possession at this time of most of Kiangsu and Chekiang—a vast and rich area—but also of a large part of the Yangtse, which had now been opened to foreign penetration by the new treaties and where new British Consulates had been quickly established (Hankow, Kiukiang and Chinkiang). Thus, the Taipings were an obstacle to foreign, in particular, British penetration of this area. In Elgin's words: "The opening of the river ports is contingent on the suppression of the rebellion." Therefore, the rebels had to be removed as speedily as possible.

Foreign intervention against the Taipings in 1860 had taken on shape even before the action in August in Shanghai. This was connected with the activity of the American fortune-seeking adventurer, F. T. Ward (1831-1862), who had been previously engaged in filibustering in Central America. In July Ward organized a force from assorted European and Asian riffraff of the Shanghai port, which was to serve the rich merchants of that city in expeditions against the Taipings. For a sum of 30,000 taels he promised to capture the city of Sungkiang, in which he succeeded on the second attempt. This force became the nucleus of what was later to be called, in 1862, by the Ch'ing government, the Ever Victorious Army. The title was not particularly accurate, inasmuch as it was severely defeated a number of times by the Chung Wang's troops. By 1861, the force had become a mixed Ch'ing-foreign outfit, usually around 5000 strong; the soldiers were supplied by the Ch'ing, while all the officers were foreign, mostly American. At first the British authorities in Shanghai looked askance at this outfit, more than likely due to the nationality of the officers, but later on gave it their fullest blessings and, what is much more important, supplied it with all the necessary arms from the large stock of the British Expeditionary Force. Ward's mercenary ruffians were notorious for their plunder of Chinese towns and their outrages on the population. This "army" remained under the command of "General" (for such was his Ch'ing title) Ward until he was killed during a battle against the Taipings in September 1862. The £60,000 fortune which he had amassed in this short time was thus of little avail.

In January 1862 Li Hsiu-ch'eng started his second advance on Shanghai and at this time the intervention of the British and the French was on a much larger scale than in August 1860, in spite of all the assurances of the Taipings of their friendliness towards their "Brothers in Christ" and their declarations that they had no intention to harm the interests of the foreign merchants. British and French forces under the command of Admiral J. Hope (1808-1881) and Admiral A. L. Protet (1808-1861), together with the Ever Victorious Army, now joined Ch'ing troops in attacking Taiping positions in the Shanghai area; they were engaged in this action throughout 1862, acting on the principle that all the territory within a 30-mile radius around Shanghai must be cleared of the insurgents. The British troops employed were obviously a part of the Expeditionary Force that had earlier been used against the Manchus in the north and which had been retained in China for this new purpose. While operating in the flat, canal-criss-crossed area of the great Yangtse delta the foreign interventionists were able to utilize fully their technical superiority; in spite of this they did not have an easy time of it and met frequently with defeats from the Loyal King's army.

The arena of intervention in 1862 was by no means restricted to Kiangsu; the question of regaining Chekiang from the Taipings also had to be faced. In that province the British and French joined once more in common action but, whereas in the Shanghai area the British were dominant, in Chekiang it was the French who played the main role. The Taipings held practically the entire province, including Hangchow and Ningpo—one of the original five Treaty Ports. All accounts agree that they had left the foreign community here quite undisturbed. Nonetheless, the Allies took it upon themselves to drive the Taipings out of the city and in May 1862 naval and army units under A. E. Le Brethon de Caligny attacked the city together with Ch'ing troops and succeeded in occupying it. A unit known as the "French Riflemen", i.e. Ch'ing soldiers commanded by French officers, was established here and remained in action throughout the rest of the campaign to conquer Chekiang, which lasted until the end of 1863 and was always aided by British and French naval forces.

After Ward's death in 1862, the Ever Victorious was then commanded by another American adventurer, a certain H. A. Burgevine. He was a somewhat troublesome man, always demanding that he and the outfit be paid when due. He later left the service of the Manchus and went off to join the Taipings.* Thus, the problem now arose of finding a new commander for the Ever Victorious; this was solved by the British in seconding Captain Charles G. Gordon (1833-1885), who took over the unit in March 1863. This "faintly smiling Englishman", the darling knight-errant of the mid-Victorian empire builders, was lavishly supplied by the British with artillery, ships and money, as well as with other British officers. He then played an important role, leading the Ever Victorious Army as the spearhead of the forces of Li Hung-chang in the offensive against Taiping-held territory in Kiangsu. Gordon was successful in re-taking a number of the walled towns of the Taipings, which he blasted with his superior English guns. The campaign ultimately led to the capture of Soochow in December 1863; then Gordon sulked Achilles-like for a few months, only to rejoin later the further campaign and lead his unit to aid in the capture of Ch'angchou in May 1864, after which the Ever Victorious,

---

*The rest of his career was characteristic; he surrendered to the Ch'ing only to rejoin the Taipings again later in 1864 in Fukien. He was then taken prisoner by the Ch'ing and conveniently quickly died while in their hands.

having been suitably paid off, was almost completely disbanded, its usefulness having come to an end.*

With the loss of their positions in Kiangsu and Chekiang, the situation of the Taipings was rendered well-nigh hopeless; the fall of Nanking in July 1864 followed as a sequel of this, and here the direct assistance of the foreign powers was already superfluous. Thus, the basic aim of the British and French had been achieved—the T'ai P'ing T'ien Kuo was smashed. No truly important hindrances to the further expansion of the penetration of China by the foreign powers existed any more.

*Gordon's pique was due to the fact that he had been made to lose face by Li Hung-chang, inasmuch as he had personally promised safety to the eight Wangs who had betrayed Soochow and were then killed by Li. It was Hart, already then beginning his career in Customs, who brought about the reconciliation between Gordon and Li. Gordon agreed to return and serve the Ch'ing and his own view of his role was as follows: "I do not apprehend the rebellion will last six months longer if I take the field. It may take six years if I leave."

PART X

The Problems of Modernization and Further Foreign Aggression

CHAPTER 31

Internal Development in China, 1864-1894

I. The Ch'ing Government After the Taiping Revolution and the Second Opium War

As a result of both the suppression of the Taiping movement and at the same time of its defeat by the foreign powers during the Second Opium War the Ch'ing regime underwent a number of important changes which were to be reflected in its policy in the subsequent decades. The defeat of the Taipings by the local armies, led by such representatives of the Chinese gentry as Tseng Kuo-fan, Li Hung-chang and Tso Tsung-t'ang, brought about an alteration in the balance of forces within the ruling class of China itself. In the carrying out of their counter-revolution against the Taipings these men had considerably strengthened their own position *vis-à-vis* the Ch'ing court and the Manchu aristocrats. Although they still remained loyal to the Ch'ing dynasty, as the dispenser of top government positions, they became a very important factor which the Ch'ing court had to take full account of. The principal sources of their power were the armies, largely private, which they had created in the course of the war against the Taipings. These were now by far the strongest and also the best-equipped forces with arms which had been obtained from the foreign powers; of these the most important was the Huai army controlled by Li Hung-chang, which constituted the mainstay of his considerable future influence. This army became the early breeding ground for the future Peiyang militarist clique which was to play a vital role in the 20th century. Another source of power was the large degree of financial independence from the central government due to the control of the economic resources of the areas administered by these men, especially Kiangsu, the Yangtse Valley and the metropolitan province of Chihli.

While these men were not quite yet completely independent warlords, they were well on the way to becoming such and the process of political and military decentralization which undermined the authority of Peking was now to continue still further, inasmuch as it became customary for the governors-general to control their own army, to possess their own arsenals, etc. This process was to be subsequently stimulated by the actions of the foreign powers and by the backing which they gave to the individual militarist cliques in the areas of their penetration and influence. Within this group of incipient warlords there existed also much rivalry and struggle for power, as well as for influence in Peking which, in effect, facilitated the maintenance of Manchu rule.

Broadly speaking, there were two main cliques: the first connected with the Huai army, i.e. the group led by Li Hung-chang, of which he was the main and most influential representative for the next thirty years. The second was the Hunan army, composed mainly of followers of Tseng Kuo-fan, but in part also under the influence of Tso Tsung-t'ang, who sometimes was at odds with Tseng's men. A rather intricate pattern of struggle between the various representatives of these groups ensued and one of the results of this process was the much greater role played by Chinese high officials, as against Manchu aristocrats, than was the case previously. Thus, in the period 1861-1890 out of 44 governors-general nominated 34 were Chinese, out of 117 governors 104 were Chinese. Over half of these men came from the anti-Taiping gentry-led armies.

Within the Manchu aristocracy this period also witnessed an involved and embittered struggle for power; it dated already from the years of Hsien-feng's reign and its culmination came shortly after his death in Jehol in August 1861. The story is to a great degree that of the rise of Yehonala (Yehenara, 1835-1908), the concubine of Hsien-feng, which ultimately ended with her assumption of full autocratic powers and with her becoming the *de facto* ruler of the Manchu regime for her entire life, i.e. practically to the end of the reign of the Ch'ing dynasty in China. Energetic, shrewd, completely unscrupulous, avid for wealth and power, Yehonala's position was first strengthened by the fact that in 1856 she became the mother of Hsien-feng's only son and heir; this raised her to the rank of Empress. The principal wife and Empress, Tz'u-an, her cousin, was no match for her in any respect. Upon the death of the Emperor, power in Jehol was taken over by his closest courtier, Su-shun, a high Manchu dignitary, noted for his vast corruption and cruelty. A regency of eight was established to rule in the name of the child Emperor which was headed by two imperial princes, Tsai Yüan and Tuan Hua, though the real leader of it was Su-shun himself. A conspiracy was formed against this regency by the princes and officials who had remained in Peking, where the main role was played by Prince Kung, in contact and co-ordination with the Empresses in Jehol.

In October 1861, when the court was returning with Hsien-feng's coffin from Jehol, the Empresses managed to arrive in Peking a few days earlier. Yehonala had successfully absconded with the Imperial Seal, and the conspiracy was now further advanced. Military support was assured for it, largely due to Jung-lu, the commander of the Imperial Guard, Yehonala's very close friend. The plot succeeded fully, the regents were taken unawares and arrested. Su-shun was decapitated; he died cursing Yehonala and regretting that he had not killed her earlier; the two princes were allowed to commit suicide. Officially, the reign was that of the child Emperor, whose period was called T'ung-chih (1862-1875), but the rule was, in fact, in the hands of the Empresses, of whom only Tz'u-hsi really mattered.* Prince Kung was nominated as Prince-Counsellor and was, at the same time, in charge of relations with the foreign powers.

---

*Tz'u-hsi was Yehonala's honorific title given to her at this time; it meant "Motherly and Auspicious". By the end of her reign she had managed to collect eight pairs of titles similar to the above.

The growing ambitions of Tz'u-hsi led in 1865 to Kung's dismissal. He was soon reinstated in most of his posts, with the exception of that of Prince-Counsellor, but his role was seriously undermined while the power of Tz'u-hsi increased continuously. Politically, she was a thoroughgoing reactionary and the head of the group which still hated the foreigners bitterly, at the same time opposing any innovations in the existing state of affairs. Tz'u-hsi was likewise a clever manipulator, both of the Manchu aristocrats and of the higher Chinese officials, ably playing on their divisions for the purpose of maintaining her own position. Her greed for wealth, as well as her love for ostentation and extravagance, were to have serious consequences for the defensive potential of the country later on. To amass treasures, with the help of her eunuchs, who during her reign were again to play for the first time during the Ch'ing dynasty an important role in the central government, she organized a system of "squeeze" which was levied on all higher officials. Thus, the Peking court itself became the main source of corruption of the entire Ch'ing regime.

Tz'u-hsi's power was threatened after the death of her son in 1874, although it is not impossible that this was hastened by her own actions seeing that, after he had assumed full powers in 1873, he had not shown the expected willingness to continue to submit to her orders.* Now the succession of either of one of the proposed candidates or the possible birth of an heir to the pregnant widow would deprive Tz'u-hsi of any rights to control the government. Riding roughshod over normal Ch'ing practices in regards to the inheritance of the throne, she put through the nomination as successor of her own nephew, the son of I-huan, Prince Ch'un (also a son of Tao-kuang), adopting him as the son of herself and the long-deceased Hsien-feng. Thus, she was now able again to reign undisturbed as the Regent to the baby emperor who was to be the unfortunate Kuang-hsü (1875-1908). A timely "suicide" of T'ung-chih's widow helped to clarify the succession issue.

After this there was no one in the Peking court either strong enough or brave enough to challenge the autocratic rule to Tz'u-hsi and her favourite eunuchs, busily spying on all high officials. The principal leader of these minions was the notorious Li Lien-ying, the chief organizer of imperial "squeeze"; his position in the court became much more important than that of all the Manchu imperial princes. It is true, however, that one man did protest against Tz'u-hsi's high-handed actions. In a thoroughly Confucian style, the censor Wu K'o-tu later on committed suicide at the grave of T'ung-chih, leaving a memorial to account for his action. In 1881 the last possible obstacle to the absolute rule of Tz'u-hsi was removed by the death, probably due to poisoning, of the other Empress, Tz'u-an. Such was the court of the Manchu rulers which was supposed to face all the problems posed before China, among others, by the Opium Wars and all that this implied.

It was not so much among the Manchu aristocrats, but more among the Chinese official-generals, who had suppressed the Taiping movement, that one has to look for the formulation of any policies whatsoever towards the existing situation in China. Generally speaking, the fundamental policy of both the Peking court and the powerful Chinese governors-general such as Tseng Kuo-fan, Li Hung-chang and Tso

---

*T'ung-chih was perhaps even more degenerate and dissipated than his father, Hsien-feng. Supposedly Tz'u-hsi herself, through her eunuchs, encouraged her own son's excesses. His death, while officially claimed as smallpox, was quite possibly the result of venereal disease.

Tsung-t'ang, as far as domestic affairs were concerned, aimed at achieving a complete restoration of the *status quo ante*, i.e. a reversion to the situation which existed before the outbreak of the Taiping Revolution. Having succeeded in carrying out a counter-revolution militarily, these men now wanted to accomplish the same in the no less important political field. Stripped of all the Neo-Confucian verbiage which they employed so copiously and assiduously this meant, in fact, the complete restoration of the political, economic and social position of the gentry and of the Ch'ing autocratic regime. As to the achievement of this aim, almost complete unity of views prevailed between all the segments of the ruling class; it is this which constituted the main content of what is sometimes referred to as the "T'ung-chih Restoration" or "Regeneration".

Divergences did take place, and some of them were very far-reaching, as to whether, after the experience of both the Taiping Revolution and the two Opium Wars, any modernization of China should be undertaken. Broadly speaking, the great majority of the scholar-officials, both Manchu and Chinese, headed by Tz'u-hsi herself, tended to be opposed to all innovations in any field whatsoever. Ignoring, in particular, the effects of the penetration by the foreign powers and its possible future consequences, the fondest hope of this group was to achieve once more, if it were at all possible, the isolation of China.

Different views were represented by the so-called "Westerners"; this group was composed primarily of the Chinese who had led in the struggle against the Taipings, as well as of comprador elements who, from their contact and co-operation with the foreigners, had become convinced of the superiority of Western technology, especially and above all in the military sphere. Their views were expressed by one of their main ideological spokesmen, Feng Kuei-fen, who stressed the necessity of acquiring selected techniques from the West. For the same purposes as mentioned above, i.e. to preserve intact the feudal system, the "Westerners" wished to employ European military techniques, arms and ships, primarily to prevent the repetition of such a threat to their rule as the Taiping Revolution had been, as well as to put down the very extensive other rebellions which were still in existence in North-west and South-west China. In their political influence these two groups were more or less even and the policies which were followed from 1864 on resembled a vector resulting from forces pulling in opposite directions.

II. The Policy of "Self-strengthening"

The policy of the group willing to "learn" from the West, at least in the military sphere, in the sense of not simply purchasing arms abroad but seeking to manufacture modern arms in China itself, has been referred to by their own term as "self-strengthening" (*tzu-ch'iang*). It must be strongly emphasized that this policy did not imply any overall scheme to introduce industrialization, to clear the path for a development of capitalism, to modernize the government and the administration in order to make China capable of meeting effectively the many various problems arising from the aggression of the foreign powers; all of these things were understood and undertaken by the oligarchic leaders of the Meiji Restoration in Japan. The contrast is a stark one, indeed, and the problem why such a great difference in approach existed is one of the most fascinating in the history of East Asia and perhaps of the world. Tentatively, some of the main reasons are as follows:

(1) The Japanese showed much more awareness of the dangers to their national existence which resulted from the unequal treaties and foreign aggression. The samurai seemed to have been much more politically minded in this respect than the Chinese scholar-officials. The existence of a national monarchy in Japan, as contrasted to the alien Manchu dynasty, was undoubtedly a factor. The difference in the size of the country also played a role, inasmuch as vast areas of China were practically not affected at all by foreign penetration and thus many of the gentry ignored the problem altogether.

(2) Economically, although the country was potentially much poorer, there were more elements favouring a quick development of capitalism in Japan; for example, the position of the merchants was much stronger. Simultaneously, the very fact of Japan's poverty caused it to be a less attractive field for Western penetration and the main attempts of the foreign powers were concentrated on China.

(3) While xenophobia was certainly no less evident in Japan, in China this was still in the shape of the Middle Kingdom complex—the belief in the innate superiority of Chinese civilization—which was now continuously less and less valid in relation to the development of the West, whereas in Japan, the civilization, so profoundly Chinese in origin in many respects, was itself a borrowed one; the Chinese had never borrowed, but had been borrowed from. In this respect a special role was played by the Chinese scholar-officials and their defence of Confucianism, of its place as the ruling ideology and the source of their livelihood and careers. The introduction of Western learning signified a challenge to their "rice bowls" — to the very existence of a powerful caste which had a vested interest in the maintenance of the *status quo* in all respects and whose position was still unshaken.

Nonetheless, for vital domestic reasons, i.e. to develop the forces necessary for the further suppression of rebellions, the "Westerners" were able to undertake their programme of "self-strengthening", and this was facilitated by the fact that they were both in charge of the continuing military operations against the various insurrections and also later in control of the key provinces of China. Thus, for example, Tseng Kuo-fan was the Governor-general of Liangkiang (Kiangsu, Anhwei and Kiangsi), residing in Nanking for most of the time until his death in 1872, while Li Hung-chang became the Governor-general in Chihli for twenty-five years (1870-1895), with his seat in Tientsin. It was in the areas under their control that the first significant introduction of Western methods of manufacture was made, but this, it must be remembered, was primarily in the sphere of armaments; in a sense progress had been made from the importation of foreign arms to the manufacture of these in China itself. The best-known example was the construction of the Kiangnan Arsenal in Shanghai which was founded in 1865 by Tseng Kuo-fan and Li Hung-chang; by 1870 it had become quite effective not only in the production of arms but also in shipbuilding. An important feature of the Kiangnan Arsenal was the language school and translation bureau attached to it. The latter was responsible for the publication of a considerable amount, over 200, of Western works pertaining mainly to the sciences.

Another well-known example was the shipyards in Mawei near Foochow, founded by Tso Tsung-t'ang in 1866. This yard produced fifteen ships in the years 1867-1874. Here also a language school was established; both French and English were taught and one of the most famous and important future translators of European literature, Yen Fu (1853-1921), was among the first pupils. While the Kiangnan Arsenal was built mostly with the assistance of British and American engineers and machinery, the Foochow installation was the work of the French. This, in itself, was an interesting reflection of the connections with the foreigners which dated back to the war against the Taipings.

In this early period, the emphasis was on the one-sided development of primarily military production, which was vastly expensive, inasmuch as very high salaries were paid to the foreign experts and much of the materials employed were imported from abroad, although all of them could have been produced in China. Later on, industrialization was extended, especially by Li Hung-chang, into other fields to create something of a necessary but still very limited infra-structure. Thus, in 1872 the China Merchants' Steam Navigation Company was established, which was able to compete successfully for a period of time with British shipping. The first modern coal mine was developed in K'aip'ing in 1878, in connection with the need for coal for the above shipping line. The first telegraph line was installed in 1881, while the first textile mills also dated from the 1880s. The first functioning railway line was built in connection with the K'aip'ing coal mine.

All this development, however, was both very limited in scale and slow in progress; it faced constant opposition of the conservative group of Manchu and Chinese high officials. The group was particularly set against the development of railways, partially because it feared that the railroads would facilitate foreign penetration. This attitude was exemplified by the fate of the first railroad line, a short link between Shanghai and Wusung, which was built by the English in 1876 only to be bought up by the Ch'ing government in 1877 and subsequently torn up. However, it is not only the slow rate of development which should be remarked, but also the fact that almost all the enterprises established in this period, even if subscribed by private capital, remained under bureaucratic government control in accord with the formula "official supervision and merchant operation". This, in the conditions which prevailed under Ch'ing rule, meant that the enterprises were utilized as an additional source of corruption and nepotism and that no real reinvestment of profits for the purpose of further industrialization was made; rather the firms were milked for all they were worth.

Li Hung-chang, a major stockholder in many of them, himself took the lead in the above process. He amassed a vast fortune—he was considered by many to be the richest man in China—and used the firms under his control as a source of profit and graft for his family and his numerous followers. This situation constituted, in particular, a great handicap to an independent private development of capitalist industry, not so much due to the fact that there was insufficient capital, for the Chinese merchants did possess considerable resources resulting, among others, from the growth of foreign trade, but because bureaucratic control discouraged their actions and initiative and foreshadowed the stunted path of bureaucratic capitalist development, which was to be marked also in the 20th century under the rule of the Kuomintang.

Thus, to a considerable degree, this modernization, which was anyhow very limited in its extent, failed to be anything more than a marginal phenomenon, while the bulk

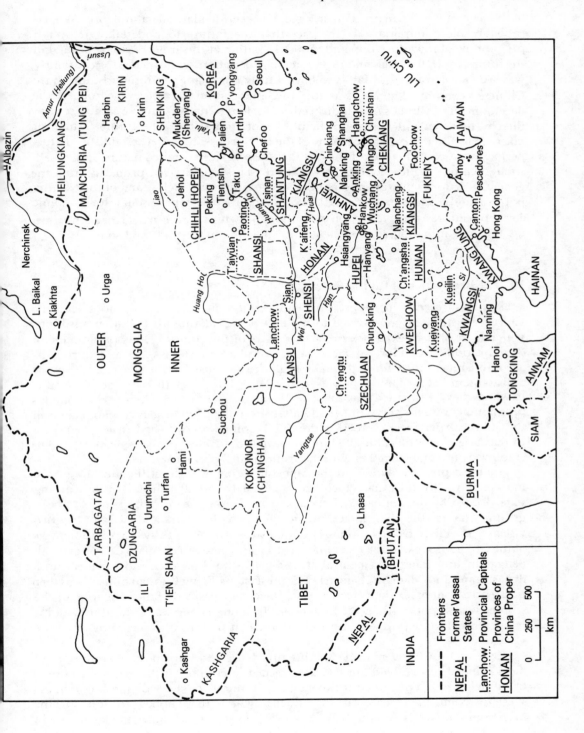

of the economy still remained unchanged in its semi-feudal and natural form. What is probably more important is the fact that the failure to undertake an overall programme of modernization and industrialization at this time was to prove fatal in the future, for in the 1860s and 1870s foreign penetration, while increasing constantly, was still not advanced so far as to have a truly dominant or ruling position in the Chinese economy. Later on, as this foreign position became ever stronger, the development of China's own industrialization and of native Chinese capitalism was thereby rendered much more difficult, if not impossible. The future failure, or takeover by foreign capital, of many of the enterprises which were established in this period was a confirmation of the fact that the one-sided, limited nature of the "self-strengthening" policy doomed it to failure. This was derived primarily from the general reactionary nature and policies of the entire ruling class and of the existing political and economic system in China; the lack of a proper programme for economic development was also a reflection of all the views which had been held for a long time, i.e. the discrimination against merchants, the disdain for trade and so on.

III. The Restoration of Ch'ing Rule

Having succeeded in suppressing with foreign aid the Taiping movement, the Ch'ing government now turned to the task of liquidating all the other rebellions which were still in existence in various parts of the country. This programme of "pacification" extended, in fact, for a period of fourteen years and during its accomplishment the Ch'ing regime was able to avail itself of the benevolent support and assistance of the foreign powers, which helped it for exactly the same reasons due to which they had assisted it against the Taipings. The men who were to carry out this programme were the very same representatives of the Chinese gentry who had saved the Ch'ing earlier; these "heroes" of the anti-Taiping wars, who had earned their spurs in massacring countless hundreds of thousands of Chinese peasants, were now to be employed once more together with the armies which they had created.

The most pressing danger to the Manchu regime was the still continuing Nien movement in North China, which had not abated at all after the fall of the Taiping state. Joined by the remnants of the northern Taiping army, who proved to be of great assistance, the Nien forces, due to their mobile tactics and bases in fortified villages, as well as their continuous popular support, successfully beat off the attacks of the Ch'ing troops. In 1865 they managed to defeat and kill the main Ch'ing general, Senggerinchin. The movement at this stage assumed an even more evident anti-dynastic and anti-Manchu character. The prestigious Tseng Kuo-fan himself was then ordered to command the forces against them, but basically failed, in spite of the scorched-earth policy he applied. Later on, Li Hung-chang was ordered in with his Huai army, fully equipped with foreign arms; at first, he also met with very little success.

However, the Ch'ing generals finally employed a laborious and costly technique of blockading the Nien-held areas and succeeded in cutting off the main Nien forces from their bases. These then became separated into two—Eastern and Western; the Western Nien then marched into Shensi where they hoped to join in the Mohammedan uprising—in 1867 they even constituted a threat to Peking itself.

Nevertheless, they were ultimately surrounded and wiped out by government forces commanded by Tso Tsung-t'ang in 1868, and later, in the same year, an identical fate met the Eastern Nien.

A revolt of equally long standing was still continuing in Yunnan; this was a rebellion of the Moslem population, which was always a large minority in this province, perhaps as much as 30 per cent. It had risen at least three times earlier in the 19th century against the oppression of the Ch'ing officials, as well as other various forms of discrimination. The Mohammedans had risen once more in 1855 and had become masters of most of the province, being particularly strong in the west, where under the leadership of Tu Wen-hsiu they established their own state which was known as P'ing-nan Kuo, with its capital in Tali. The rising also had serious repercussions in the neighbouring provinces of Kweichow and Szechuan.

The long-lasting and indecisive campaigns of the Ch'ing generals resulted in the devastation of most of Yunnan. Tu Wen-hsiu defended himself brilliantly with his forces in possession of fifty-three walled towns. However, the Manchus succeeded in splitting the movement and in bringing about the desertion of a part of the Moslem gentry to the Ch'ing side. Finally, all the area was reconquered with the exception of Tali; this fell in January 1873 and here, with characteristic Ch'ing treachery, the entire population of many thousands was later put to the sword. But this was only one of the many episodes, inasmuch as the overall results of Ch'ing "pacification" were such that only 3 million out of 8 million of the previous population of the province survived by the end of the war.

The fate of the Miao in neighbouring Kweichow was no better than that of the Moslems in Yunnan. They had also risen once more in revolt against Ch'ing rule in 1854 and their movement was undoubtedly closely connected with that of the Yunnanese. Here, however, an additional problem existed: the progressing colonization of the province by Chinese landlords which resulted in the fact that the Miao were being continuously robbed of their best lands in the low-lying areas. In a short time the tribesmen held almost the entire province, with the exception of the capital, and the rising was further stimulated in the years 1860-1862 by the presence of the forces of Shih Ta-k'ai. Only after the fall of the Taiping state were the Ch'ing able to concentrate sufficient troops in this province; the same applied, of course, also to Yunnan. The campaigns dragged on to 1873 and here, as well, similar methods of "stabilization" were employed. At least one million Miao were killed, while some sources claim that only one-tenth of the population survived. The Miao lost all their lands and were forced either to flee to the hills or, if they chose to remain in the lowlands, they had to become tenants of Chinese landlords.

An even greater threat, perhaps, to Ch'ing rule was posed by the great rising of the Moslems in the North-west which began in 1862. During this entire period the greatest nightmare for the Manchu court was the possibility that the rebellions in the various parts of China would link up together. Some attempts were made by the Taipings and later by the Nien to join forces with the Moslems; unfortunately, these efforts were made too late and were insufficiently effective. The rising under the main leadership of Ma Hua-lung spread to practically all of Kansu and most of North Shensi. The problem was complicated in this area by the animosity which existed between the Moslem (partially of non-Chinese origin) and the Chinese, which was incited by the Ch'ing authorities and resulted in much struggle between these two groups of the population. It was only after the total suppression of the Nien movement that the Ch'ing armies advanced into Shensi in 1869. These were troops from Hunan under the command of Tso Tsung-t'ang.

After the clearing of Shensi, in which Tso's usual methods of massacring nearly the entire civilian population were employed, the main event was the long, almost three-year siege of Suchou in Kansu. Finally, with the help of foreign artillery, i.e. guns manufactured by Krupp which Tso Tsung-t'ang had imported, the city was taken in 1873; the entire family of Ma Hua-lung was subjected to execution by the slicing process and the whole garrison was treacherously massacred. The same performance was repeated later on further to the west in Hami. Even the Russian general Kaufmann, whose own record and methods in Western Turkestan (and probably also in Lithuania) were not of the gentlest, was horrified by the conduct of Tso Tsung-t'ang. Tso's policy was "first pacify and then punish", but his concept of punishment was extermination. As a result nine-tenths of the Mohammedan population in Shensi and two-thirds of it in Kansu were wiped out. The North-west did not recover for many decades from his methods of "stabilization". At the same time Tso, who was always accompanied by his Chief Executioner, advocated the complete sinification of the Moslems and some success had been attained in this area as well in inducing a part of the Moslem gentry to pass over to the side of the Ch'ing.

Almost at the same time as the Mohammedan population revolted in the North-west the rising spread to Kashgaria and Dzungaria. In Kashgaria the main population group, the Uighurs, also Mohammedan, suffered from the oppression of Ch'ing officials and, undoubtedly under the influence of the events in the North-west, a revolt was launched here in 1864. Its leader was Yakub Beg, who came originally from Khokand, where he had been fighting against the Russian penetration of Western Turkestan. By 1873 Yakub Beg was the master of all the Tarim Basin and also of Urumchi, north of the T'ien Shan. He probably would have gained control of all of Dzungaria had it not been for the Russian intervention and occupation of its western part, i.e. the Ili region, in 1871.

The problem of the Uighur revolt and the rule of Yakub Beg in this area was further complicated by the policies of both Great Britain and Russia. These two powers eyed each other suspiciously and both were planning to utilize the situation for their own benefit. Both countries recognized the state created by Yakub Beg; the British sent the Forsyth mission to his capital in 1870 and 1873 and were obviously interested in having Kashgaria become a buffer state to protect their possessions in India. They were also instrumental in having the Turkish Sultan grant Yakub the title of Amir of Kashgaria as well as sending him Turkish officers.

In the areas to both the north and south of the T'ien Shan there was very little Chinese population and the Ch'ing garrisons had been mostly wiped out during the revolt. The majority of Mohammedans of Chinese origin—the Dungans in Dzungaria—had joined in the rising; after all, the entire territory had only been conquered during the reign of Ch'ien-lung. The problem which now faced the Manchu government was whether it should try to recover this vast region; this subject became one which was hotly debated at the Ch'ing court. Until the suppression of the Mohammedan revolt in the North-west such a conquest was not feasible, inasmuch as all the routes leading thither were occupied by the rebels.

The main proponent of putting down the Uighur rebellion was Tso Tsung-t'ang, who maintained that "Turkestan is needed to protect Mongolia, while Mongolia is needed to protect Peking"; he put forth the above view against Li Hung-chang, who advocated concentrating on China proper, especially on the maritime provinces. Ultimately, the party in favour of the reconquest won the upper hand. In 1875 Tso Tsung-t'ang began his campaign which led quickly to the overrunning of all the territory north of the T'ien Shan with the exception of Ili, held by the Russians. For the purpose of this campaign Tso negotiated in 1876 the first foreign loan by the Ch'ing government from the foreign banks of Shanghaï for a sum of 10 million taels.

The British made continuous diplomatic efforts to save Yakub Beg; the British Minister in Peking, T. Wade (the same one who had been the interpreter during the Tientsin Treaty), proposed that he be left as the king of the territory south of the T'ien Shan, to rule the eight cities there. However, in 1877 the forces of Tso Tsung-t'ang took Turfan which opened the road to the south; this led to the rapid collapse of Yakub Beg's kingdom and to his death in 1878, which was followed by the subsequent conquest of all the territories south of the T'ien Shan. Tso Tsung-t'ang now proposed that the entire area, both Kashgaria and Dzungaria, be reorganized as a Chinese province; this was done in 1884 when Sinkiang ("New Dominion") was established.

The conquest of Sinkiang marked the completion of the re-establishment of the Ch'ing regime's rule over the entire present territory of China; the cost of this, especially in human lives and suffering, was immense, particularly if it is added to the vast losses which resulted from the putting down of the Taiping movement. This was the primary and principal accomplishment of the leaders of the T'ung-chih Restoration, so often uncritically praised by many Western historians as great statesmen.

At the same time as the military measures outlined above were employed, the Ch'ing regime also rebuilt its government apparatus and paid some attention to the rehabilitation of the economy. All the actions in this field were in line completely with the general policy of restoring the *status quo ante*. Thus, the examination system was continued and much attention was paid to the further propagation of Neo-Confucian ideology, while its use for indoctrination purposes was stressed more and more. This was intimately bound up with the previously mentioned prevailing reactionary viewpoint of the great majority of the ruling class. But even the so-called "Westerners", who adopted European military techniques, were just as adamant in their beliefs that the basic political, social and ideological foundation of the feudal order should remain intact. This was expressed in their well-known formula which stated that "Chinese learning is the basis; Western learning is for practical use".

The ruined economy, especially agriculture, was ultimately restored, as so many times in the past, by the arduous toil of the customarily hard-working Chinese peasants. However, the Ch'ing officials did everything in their policies applied in the areas which were rehabilitated to favour the landlords; thus a further growth of great estates followed, the number of tenant farmers increased still more and the social crisis, which had characterized the countryside before the Taiping revolution, was not really alleviated, in spite of all the bloodletting. The incapacity of the Ch'ing regime was further demonstrated by its inability to cope with natural disasters such as those, for example, which caused a terrible famine in Shansi in 1878, where over 10 million died. Thus, the leaders of the T'ung-chih Restoration were sterile in their thinking in all respects and were absolutely incapable of extricating the country from its critical situation; their only achievement was keeping the peasants "in their place" and this, among others, by means of the full reintroduction of the notorious *pao-chia* system of collective responsibility.*

It should be noted, however, that already in the 1860s and 1870s there were some Chinese who were aware of the problems which faced their country and thought in terms of a programme of overall modernization which, in fact, would have made the development of capitalism in China possible. Such, for example, was Jung Hung (Yung Wing, 1828-1912), a truly serious advocate of modernization. He was the first Chinese to graduate from a Western university (Yale, 1854) and possessed a good knowledge of the West; he favoured the methods which would have been indispensable for the transformation of the country. In 1859 he sought to present his programme to the Taiping leaders but he did not meet with any success. Later on, he became connected with the "Westerners" and was entrusted with the mission of buying machinery abroad for the Kiangnan Arsenal. However, his basic programme also found no response among them, inasmuch as they were disinterested in and basically opposed to the road of capitalist development. Yung Wing also encouraged the sending of Chinese youth for education abroad; he was in partial charge of the first group of students sent to the United States (120, of whom 80 were from Kwangtung; all of them Chinese). The programme was sabotaged by reactionary Ch'ing officials and was never developed properly on any overall basis. The exodus of Chinese students abroad on a large scale to seek modern education, especially in Japan, was a later phenomenon dating from the turn of the century.

There were also a few among the high Ch'ing officials who were likewise aware of the need to modernize; such, for instance, was Kuo Sung-tao (1818-1891), the first Ch'ing Minister to England in 1876. He was particularly struck by the contrast **between England and China (he phrased this: "Confucius and Mencius have misled** us"), as well as by the systematic, well-planned fashion in which the Japanese were proceeding to acquire Western learning and technology. His advocacy of such measures as the introduction of railways, machinery, etc., made him the object of virulent hatred of most of the scholar-officials. After his short tenure in London, he retired from public life completely, in spite of the fact that he had previously had very good connections with the Hunan clique.

IV. The Foreign Policy of the Ch'ing Government

The basic attitude of the ruling groups within the Ch'ing government towards the foreign powers was one of continuing profound distrust and, in many cases, of still thorough hatred and contempt. However, this was more than somewhat modified by the discovery that the foreigners were not aiming at the overthrow of the dynasty but,

---

*The attitude towards and the appraisal of the leaders and the programme of the T'ung-chih Restoration became an extremely topical subject in the future political development of China up to 1949. It is not at all surprising that the Kuomintang, after its betrayal of the 1925-1927 Revolution, turned to the T'ung-chih Restoration for its political model, that the favourite hero of Chiang Kai-shek was Tseng Kuo-fan. This also accounts for the strong polemical vein with which progressive Chinese historians from the 1920s onward, especially the Marxists or those under Marxist influence, castigated all the activities of the "heroes" of the Restoration, seeing in their reactionary programme one of the principal causes for the maintenance of China's backwardness and subsequent political tragic fate.

on the contrary, were interested in its preservation for the reasons mentioned earlier. On this basis there arose a curious sort of *modus vivendi*, in particular between the "Westerners" and the foreign powers, which was especially strengthened by their co-operation in putting down the Taiping movement; this led to a peculiar relationship, almost a "comradeship-in-arms". While both the conservative and the "Western" groups were well aware of the fact that the appetites of the foreign powers were basically insatiable, both felt that, by means of putting into effect appropriately conciliatory policies towards them, the future scope of new demands on China could perhaps be restricted, while simultaneously the Ch'ing government would be able to continue to obtain the necessary support from the foreign powers for maintaining its own rule over the Chinese people. This was the essence, among others, of the policy of Li Hung-chang, whose tenure for twenty-five years in Tientsin made him also the most influential individual in dealing with the foreigners; his yamen there was in fact much more the real foreign office of the Ch'ing government than the bureau which was set up for this purpose in Peking.

The latter was the well-known Tsungli Yamen (an abbreviation of *Tsungli ko-kuo shih-wu yamen,* General Office for Affairs of Other States) which was established in 1861 and headed at first by three Manchu dignitaries, Prince Kung, Wen-hsiang (1816-1876) and Kuei-liang. The policies of the Tsungli Yamen coincided on the whole with those of Li Hung-chang, especially in their generally conciliatory approach which often verged on capitulation. However, it is an oversimplification to maintain that this group did not attempt at the same time to defend the interests of the Ch'ing government as it saw them; for this purpose they relied on the hoary Chinese adage of "Using barbarians to fight barbarians", i.e. they sought to utilize the rivalries of the foreign powers as well as to "halter" the barbarians by means of negotiations. The fact that they had precious little success in these proceedings is quite a different matter.

The Tsungli Yamen was still not a true foreign office in the European meaning of the word (for that matter the Six Boards were not real ministries either). The heads of the Tsungli Yamen all held at the same time other posts in the Ch'ing administration and were delegated to it *ad hoc* to handle relations with the foreign envoys. In time, however, a permanent staff of officials was built up and also a certain amount of expertise gained — for instance, a knowledge of international law acquired so as to be able to use the arguments of the Westerners against them; a beginning was made to follow world affairs in the respect to which they affected the fate of China. A foreign language school (the *T'ung-wen Kuan*) was also established attached to the Tsungli Yamen. At first, all its pupils were only Manchus; the school was to supply the necessary interpreters and future foreign service employees. It was headed by the American missionary, W. A. P. Martin, previously mentioned, and later on its curriculum was also extended to include modern scientific subjects. The Ch'ing government was quite unwilling, in line with its overall approach to things foreign, to establish its own diplomatic posts abroad. This was finally begun in 1876 and then a gradual expansion of its diplomatic service followed.

Two other offices were of no smaller importance for the conduct of relations with foreigners than the Tsungli Yamen; these were the Office of the Superintendent of Trade in the North (three ports under its jurisdiction with headquarters in Tientsin— this position was also held by Li Hung-chang, together with the governor-generalship of Chihli, hence precisely one of the sources of his influence in foreign affairs) and the Superintendent for Trade in the South (five ports, headquarters in Shanghai; this position was usually held simultaneously by the Governor-general of Liangkiang). Inasmuch as the Liangkiang Governor-general was customarily a representative of the Hunan clique, while the northern post was in the hands of the Huai clique, this was one of the most important sources of rivalry between these two groups.

One aspect of Li Hung-chang's "self-strengthening" policy, which was closely bound up with the problem of foreign affairs, was the question of the building of a modern fleet. Both he, and even more Tso Tsung-t'ang, attached great importance to this and saw in the creation of a navy a great prestige factor and a possible bargaining counter in the relations with foreigners, for it is difficult to believe that any of them seriously thought of the fleet as being a really adequate means of defence in case of renewed foreign aggression. Thus, very much effort and considerable means were concentrated on this phase of modernization. However, and this was most typical of the thinking of the "Westerners", the fleet did not arise as the result of an overall programme of industrialization, which would have made it possible to create the necessary economic background for the building of China's own navy, assuming that the finances for this would have been adequate, but came mostly from extremely costly purchases of foreign-built vessels from abroad. The shipyards that had been constructed in China with foreign aid, such as those in Foochow, for example, were incapable of producing the ever more complex modern warships of the steam age.

Going somewhat ahead in time, the rest of the story can be told at this stage. The main point here is that the naval forces, which were organized by Li Hung-chang, were as prone to corruption and inefficiency as the industrial enterprises which had been started by him and for much the same reasons. The situation became still worse later on when, after the sad experiences of the Sino-French War, the decision was made to unite all the naval forces (heretofore there were three, one in the North under Li Hung-chang, one in the South controlled by Nanking, and one based in Foochow); this was accomplished by the establishment of the Naval Yamen. Prince Ch'un, the Emperor's father, was its nominal head, but the real power there rested with Li Hung-chang, who saw to it that the best ships, twenty-eight all told, were placed under his control in the famous Peiyang (North Ocean) Fleet.

The yearly budget of the Naval Yamen was quite sizeable—4 million taels. What happened, however, was quite typical of the conditions in the Ch'ing government and court. The bulk of the funds were not devoted to the further extension of the fleet or to the improving of its equipment; after 1888 no more ships were bought, instead over 33 million taels were diverted by Tz'u-hsi for her extravagant and lavish reconstruction of the I Ho Yüan—the present Summer Palace. The results of this were to come to light in a most tragic fashion during the Sino-Japanese War of 1894-1895; the famous marble boat in the artificial lake in the Summer Palace, atrociously ugly and vastly expensive, which was built with this money, proved to be of little use in resisting the attack of the Japanese cruisers.

CHAPTER 32

The Foreign Powers and China, 1864-1894

I. The Policy of "Co-operation"

From the point of view of the foreign powers the basic requirement of the situation in China, after the Second Opium War and the fall of the Taiping state, was the achievement of a necessary degree of stabilization which would make possible the full utilization of the benefits newly acquired in the Tientsin treaties. It is for this purpose, primarily, that the policy of support for the Ch'ing government was followed by all the powers; in this, as well as in the general field of action in China during these years, the lead continued to be given by Great Britain which still occupied the predominant economic and political position. The policy pursued by the powers in this period is sometimes referred to as the "policy of co-operation"; this could be interpreted in a double meaning—as co-operation between the powers, as well as that of the powers and the Manchus.

In the first sense, it is true that while rivalries between the powers were certainly present, although by no means as acute as they were to become later in the following decades, it was still possible to follow a more or less common policy in China which could prove to be of benefit to all the powers. In the second sense, it was also undoubtedly true that the existence of the Ch'ing government and its relative strengthening was now in the interests of the foreigners, for it was already sufficiently subservient to carry out most, if not all, of the wishes and commands of the powers and it was the instrument which was to execute the fulfilment of the concessions that had been imposed earlier. In this respect the policy of co-operation of the powers had the added advantage of creating a situation in which joint pressure could be exerted and a degree of joint control could be maintained over the Manchu regime. Thus, all the principal aims of the foreigners *vis-à-vis* China could now be accomplished without a renewed direct resort to military measures on a large scale which were always costly, somewhat risky and likely as well to be unpopular with the populace at home.

The question arises whether the concessions which had been obtained as a result of the Second Opium War were considered in the 1860s and 1870s to be sufficiently far-reaching by the foreign powers. In fact, they were regarded as both sufficient and insufficient. Sufficient, in the sense that a given period of time was considered necessary to make truly effective use of what had been gained, to digest properly all that had been swallowed, to oversee the effective implementation by the Ch'ing regime of all the newly acquired rights. Insufficient, in the sense that the initial emphasis of the powers on the opening up of China as a market for trade was now being gradually changed into something of much greater significance for the

Map 19.   The foreign powers and China (up to 1906)

Canton   Treaty Ports (not all)

Hong Kong   Colonies

Talien   Leaseholds

0   150   300

km

CHIHLI

Tientsin

Newchwang

Talien

Port Arthur
(Russ. 1895-1905)

Weihaiwei
(Brit)

Chefoo

SHANSI

KANSU

Huang Ho

SHANTUNG

Tsingtao
Kiaochow Bay
(Germ. 1898-1914)

Wei

SHENSI

HONAN

Huai

KIANGSU

ANHWEI

Chinkiang

Nanking

Han

Wuhu

Shanghai

SZECHUAN

HUPEI

Yangtse

Ichang

Shasi

Hankow

Kiukiang

Ningpo

CHEKIANG

Wenchow

HUNAN

KIANGSI

KWEICHOW

Foochow

FUKIEN

Tamsui

KWANGSI

KWANGTUNG

Hsi

Swatow

Amoy   TAIWAN
(Jap. 1895-1945)

Canton

Taiwan

Kwangchow(Fr.)

Hong Kong (Brit.)

Macao (Port.)

Pakhoi

foreigners, into regarding China as a vital location for the export of capital and as a source of invaluable raw materials.

In connection with this new approach, the aims now were to acquire rights to build railways (of special importance in view of the fact that the basic construction in Europe and America had been completed and that the prospects for railway building in China seemed immense), to engage in mining operations, to establish foreign-owned and operated factories, etc. In this respect the foreigners felt that the concessions heretofore obtained were not sufficiently far-reaching, although they undoubtedly constituted an excellent basis for the extortion of new ones. To this programme the Ch'ing government was steadfastly opposed, although, in the final analysis, this was of no avail because it feared, among others, the social consequences of such a development of elements of a capitalist economy.

The interest in economic expansion in this new direction was also, more than probably, bound up with a considerable degree of disappointment with the results obtained thus far in the development of trade with China. This great El Dorado had turned out to be much less promising than the eager visions of the Western merchants had forecast. This was so in spite of the fact that the opening of the Suez Canal (1869) brought China closer to Europe by one-half the distance and facilitated an increase of European pressure. The self-sufficient nature of the Chinese economy on an overall scale and, in particular, the semi-natural economic conditions of the countryside, in spite of the inroads of foreign products, still did not constitute a really sizeable market, especially for those manufactured foreign goods which it had been hoped to place there. This problem can be best illustrated by the trade figures in millions of taels for the 1864-1894 period (Table 1).

Table 1

	Import	Export
1864	51.3*	54.0
1870	69.3	61.6
1876	70.2	80.8
1887	102.2	85.8
1891	134.0	100.9
1894	162.1	128.9

*The import figures do not include the value of opium which, for example, in 1870 amounted to 70,000 chests, worth 35 million taels. The problem of the actual increase of imports and exports shown by these figures is further complicated by the fact that in this period the tael was steadily losing its value. Thus, in U.S. dollars it was worth: 1872, $1.60, 1882, $1.38, 1892, $1.07, 1897, $0.72.

What the figures in Table 1 do show, however, is a gradual but nevertheless steady worsening of China's position in respect to the balance of trade. This was partially derived from the restrictions which had been imposed on its economic development by the unequal treaties and, in particular, by its loss of tariff autonomy. This became more and more painful, among other things, in connection with the fall in the value of silver (reflected in the above-mentioned fall in the value of the tael). Thus, the 5 per cent *ad valorem* customs rate of the 1860s was down to between 2 and 3 per cent by the end of the century.

The question of the opening up of China to further economic penetration in line with the new needs of the powers could be handled either by the revision of the existing treaties within ten years of their conclusion or by the exertion of sufficient pressure on the central as well as the provincial governments to obtain whatever new concessions would seem desirable. While the first method was employed only partially, and not always successfully, as we shall see subsequently, the second was pursued consistently and successfully throughout the entire period, being particularly useful when applied in relation to the powerful provincial governors-general, such as Li Hung-chang, for example, who had already a well-established reputation for co-operating with the foreigners. Although further trade development had not lived up to expectations, this period did see a subsequent great growth of the foreign community in the Treaty Ports, an extension in size, especially in Shanghai, of the foreign enclaves on Chinese soil. These became more and more privileged communities which were in a strategic position to dominate the Chinese economy.

Simultaneously the period of the two decades after the Second Opium War was one in which preparations were made and the first steps taken in the very significant process of nibbling away at the edges of the vast Ch'ing realm, especially in the areas which were considered as the vassal states of the Manchus and which constituted very attractive, juicy morsels for the appetites of the colonizing powers. This was particularly the case of South-east Asia, but it was also true of an area which was even more vital to the defence of China proper, such as Korea. The main steps in this process were the British conquest of Burma and the French expansion in Indo-china, as well as the Japanese annexation of the Liuch'iu Islands and the first penetration into Korea.

In this policy towards the Ch'ing government the powers pressed insistently for normalization of diplomatic relations between China and the rest of the world, which they envisaged as ultimately benefiting the extension of foreign influence and control. Thus, the Manchus were to be taught the proper observance of international law which, bearing in mind the position which had been imposed on China by the unequal treaties, would be of advantage primarily to the powers. In this process a very important role was played by the foreign control of the Ch'ing customs service and by Robert Hart, the Inspector-general of this service, who, after the transfer of the head office of the customs service to Peking, began to assume the function of the principal adviser to the Manchus on foreign affairs. This was exemplified, for instance, by the elaborate memorial submitted by him in 1866 to the Ch'ing government, in which he sought to instruct them on the methods of proper conduct and procedures in international affairs. It was on Hart's advice that the first Manchu mission was sent abroad in the same year; this, however, produced no results. The somewhat unusual concept of nominating subsequently the former U.S. Minister to China, A. Burlingame, after the end of his term of office in Peking, as a representative of the Ch'ing regime and entrusting him with a mission to the foreign powers was also Hart's brainchild.

The Burlingame mission set out in February 1868; it included, in addition to Burlingame as its head, two high Ch'ing officials, as well as a British and French secretary. The first country visited was the United States; here Burlingame, carried away by his oratorical powers, painted a roseate picture, depicting China as willing and able to absorb all the blessings which Western civilization could bestow on it. He then signed an agreement with the American government (eight supplementary articles to the Tientsin Treaty), which he had not been authorized by the Manchus to do, the most important provision actually being one which facilitated unlimited Chinese immigration into the United States, in which the Americans were interested at this period, only to turn against it completely somewhat later on.*

The mission then proceeded to London where the British government issued a typically vague policy statement that "unfriendly pressure" would not be applied to China *if* that country would faithfully observe the treaty obligations. After passing through France and a number of other European countries, the mission travelled on to Russia where Burlingame died of pneumonia in February 1870. The rest of the mission continued on its odd voyage, returning to China in October 1870. Its results were actually minimal.

A further chapter in the "policy of co-operation" phase was an attempt by the British to arrange for a treaty revision in 1868. This was primarily the work of R. Alcock, the British Minister in Peking. The terms which were arrived at, while extending British privileges, were not too onerous from the point of view of the Ch'ing government and the Tsungli Yamen was proud of the advances it had made in its learning of the methods of modern diplomacy. However, the Alcock Convention, as the agreement was called, was considered to be quite insufficient by the British merchant community in China and, as a result of the pressure exerted by it, the British government refused to ratify the agreement, causing the Ch'ing officials to lose much face, inasmuch as they had firmly believed that the negotiations had been completed. The failure of the British to ratify this Convention actually showed up the shallowness of the "policy of co-operation", as well as the pretences to "fairness" of British policy towards China. This policy, in fact, was aimed at retaining the predominant position of England and for this purpose the "integrity" of the Ch'ing regime was favoured. There are some grounds, however, for the belief that the British would have envisaged converting China into another India had not their forces been engaged in expansion at this period in other parts of the world, especially Africa and South-east Asia.

II. The Tientsin Incident, 1870

The concessions which had been obtained in the Tientsin Treaty had made possible not only the further economic penetration of China but also the extension on a considerable scale of missionary activities by the Westerners, both Catholic and Protestant. From the viewpoint of the Ch'ing government this phase of foreign activity was perhaps the most troublesome, inasmuch as the missionaries were quite aggressive in their demands that their alleged rights to proselytize the Christian faith be recognized and their behaviour was the source of constant conflict with the local and central Ch'ing authorities. The missionaries were only too willing to avail

*The story of the Chinese immigration into America is a dismal and tragic episode. By 1868 there were between 90,000 and 100,000 Chinese in America, mostly in California. The American capitalists had been quite interested in exploiting this cheap labour force, especially in railway construction; thus, in the building of the Central Pacific nine-tenths of the 10,000 labour force were Chinese. After the 1873 depression, when railroad construction had been completed, their labour was deemed to be unnecessary and the Chinese community became the object of brutal treatment and racial discrimination, many Chinese being lynched and murdered. In 1882 the American government "suspended" Chinese immigration and further unilateral action in this field then followed.

themselves of the armed protection of the gunboats from their home countries. The attitude of even the most conciliatory of the Manchus was succinctly summed up in the well-known statement of Prince Kung to Alcock in 1869: "Take away your opium and your missionaries and you will be welcomed."

The activities of the missionaries were viewed with great and growing hostility by practically all strata of Chinese society. For the scholar-officials and the gentry they were, above all, the propagators of unorthodox, subversive views which were considered inimical to Confucian doctrines; the peasants regarded them as representatives of the aggressive foreign powers, while the creed preached by them was on the whole difficult to comprehend. Many, if not most, of the missionaries were completely intolerant of various age-old Chinese customs and beliefs and arrogant in their proselytizing zeal. The Catholics were especially insistent on being recognized as the equivalent in standing of the Ch'ing officials, the bishops as the equal of a provincial governor, etc. All this made it easy for the enemies of the missionaries to spread the most fanciful stories regarding their behaviour, which found easy acceptance and belief among the broad masses of the populace. Thus, anti-Christian views—which were basically anti-foreign—became more and more widespread in those parts of China where the foreigners had penetrated. Hostility towards the missionaries was also stimulated quite often by the behaviour of some of the Christian converts who would take advantage of the privileged position of the missionaries and Christian churches—all the product of the unequal treaties and the rights of extraterritoriality—to further their own interests. An additional source of irritation, and this is particularly true of the actions of the Catholic Church, was the restoration of property which had been earlier confiscated, as well as the acquiring of considerable quantities of new land. The strong and unconcealed rivalry between the Protestant and Catholic missionaries was a factor which did not help to raise the prestige of the missionary movement.

As a result of the above causes, innumerable conflicts ensued in the 1860s in various parts of China, which culminated in what was undoubtedly the most serious of them—the Tientsin Incident of June 1870. Among the various factors in the background of this incident, mention should be made of the following. In general, the policy of the French government continued, in view of its still limited economic interests, to emphasize its role as the self-chosen protector of Catholic missionary efforts, with the aim of increasing its political influence. In particular, the French had made themselves especially distasteful to the population of Tientsin by their behaviour during the Allied occupation of that city in 1860-1863. They had not helped matters by their further actions, among others, the building of the Catholic Cathedral on a site of a former Confucian temple, etc. The activity of the French Catholic missionaries here was much resented and the unfortunate practices of the French sisters in their running of an orphanage (paying money for children delivered to it, often accepting infants on the verge of death in order to baptize them *in articulo mortis*) gave rise to widespread rumours regarding the orphanage, that it was engaged in kidnapping and various abominable crimes.

The matters reached a fevered pitch on June 20, when the worried Ch'ing officials proposed to the French Consul that the only solution would be an inspection of the premises to discredit the rumours. After this had been agreed to, the further incredibly hazardous behaviour of the French Consul, H. Fontanier (he stormed into the Ch'ing official yamen, then into the crowd outside of it, shooting and killing a Chinese), triggered off a riot in which the consul and his secretary were killed and later two French priests, ten sisters, four other Frenchmen, three Russians (mistaken for French), as well as thirty to forty Chinese working for the French were all murdered. The cathedral, mission and other buildings were destroyed.

The incident aroused the ire of all the foreign powers; a demand was made that proper protection be given by the Ch'ing authorities to all the foreigners in China, and that those responsible for the killings in Tientsin should be appropriately punished. The Ch'ing government sent Tseng Kuo-fan himself, then Governor-general of Chihli, to investigate the matter, while foreign naval vessels began to arrive in Taku. The outbreak of the Franco-Prussian War had considerable bearing on the situation, inasmuch as it made it impossible for the French to proceed on what otherwise would have undoubtedly been done—the sending of a military expeditionary force. The Ch'ing authorities cynically agreed to pacify the foreigners by proceeding to execute sixteen Chinese, allegedly participants of the riots, and this, together with an indemnity of 250,000 taels, was finally accepted as the solution. In addition, a high Manchu official, Ch'ung-hou (the same one who had sought to work out the compromise solution preceding the riot), was sent to France with a mission of formal apology.

III. Early Relations with Japan

Although the opening of Japan had placed that country in almost as unfavourable a position as that to which China had been subjected as a result of the two Opium Wars, the Meiji Restoration of 1868 marked the beginning of the rapid process of modernization of Japan which was to result in that country soon becoming one of the most dangerous, aggressive capitalist powers with marked expansionist tendencies aimed in the first place at its two closest neighbours, Korea and China. The economic basis of this policy lay, among others, in the quite inadequate domestic market, due to the semi-feudal conditions still prevailing in the Japanese countryside, which made the search for an outlet for Japanese manufactured goods seem imperative. An additional factor was the relative poverty of Japan in necessary raw materials. Initially, however, the problem was that of regulating relations between China and Japan in a fashion which would correspond both to the changes which had taken place in Japan's position and to those in the world. It was the Japanese who took the initiative, and a mission was sent from Japan which resulted in the signing by Li Hung-chang of the Treaty of Tientsin in September 1871. The agreement was more or less on the basis of two equal powers and the Japanese were given the possibility to conduct economic activities in China. However, the rights of the Japanese were not as extensive as those which had been granted to the Westerners in the unequal treaties; there was no most-favoured-nation clause and no specific guarantee of unilateral extraterritoriality.

From the very outset of establishing these new diplomatic relations the territorial appetites of Japan were evident and this was particularly true, at this stage, of two areas—the Liuch'iu (Ryukyu in Japanese) Islands and Taiwan. The first mention of the problem of the Liuch'iu Islands was made during the visit to China in 1873 of the Japanese Foreign Minister, Soyejima Taneomi; the islands had, in fact, been a vassal of

China since the times of the Ming dynasty, but they became later on simultaneously also a vassal of Japan. The Japanese were now aiming clearly at the annexation of this territory. The issue became likewise connected with the problem of Taiwan, inasmuch as earlier, in 1871, some sailors from the Liuch'ius had been shipwrecked off Taiwan and killed there by the aborigines who inhabited the eastern half of the island. The inept Ch'ing officials disclaimed any responsibility for this action, thus putting the rights of the Ch'ing government to Taiwan under question; simultaneously, they did not rebut the Japanese claim to seek redress for the Liuch'iu sailors, thus partially admitting the Japanese pretence to sovereignty over these islands.

It was on the basis of this issue that the Japanese government proceeded to launch a military expedition against Taiwan in April 1874; a force of over 3000 Japanese landed there. The Ch'ing government responded to this by shipping their own troops to Taiwan without, however, engaging in any military action against the Japanese. Ultimately, through the mediation of Wade, the British Minister in Peking, a solution of the conflict was reached by the signing of a Sino-Japanese Protocol in Peking in October 1874. The Ch'ing government agreed to pay the Japanese an indemnity of 500,000 taels (100,000 taels for the sailors, 400,000 for the roads built in Taiwan, etc., by the Japanese). The Japanese forces then withdrew from Taiwan but this agreement was also, in effect, a tacit recognition of the Japanese claims to the Liuch'ius, which were annexed in 1879 and declared to be the Prefecture of Okinawa. After some ineffective protest the Ch'ing government recognized this state of affairs in 1881. The importance of this whole affair lay in the fact that it provided the first indication that all the efforts of the "self-strengthening" of the T'ung-chih restoration had been, in fact, in vain. Even the Japanese could not be resisted effectively and the unpreparedness of the Ch'ing regime was thus fully revealed. The buying off of the Japanese served only to stimulate their appetite for the future.

IV. The Margary Affair and the Chefoo Convention

Both the subservient nature of the Ch'ing government and the essence of the policies of the foreign powers, in this case Great Britain, were also revealed by the most notable event in the relations between China and the West during the 1870s—the Margary Affair. In this period the British were also interested in extending their sphere of influence to South-west China; this was connected with the extension of British rule in Burma—Lower Burma having been conquered in 1862. The British were now busy searching for overland communications between Burma and Yunnan with the view of increasing the economic penetration of Western China, including the development of the opium trade in this area. This was the main purpose of a special mission which was sent in the autumn of 1874 from Bhamo to the Burma-Yunnan border; a young British Chinese-speaking consular official, A. R. Margary, was dispatched from Shanghai to join this mission. After having reached it in Burma he proceeded towards China and was killed somewhere in the border area on February 21, 1875; by whom and under what circumstances is still far from clear. It is not unfair to quote Margary's own words on the methods of behaviour to be applied to the Chinese, as these well might have a bearing on his fate: "A kick and a few words telling him he is an ignorant boor will make a common Chinaman worship you...."

When the news of his death finally reach Peking on March 13, Thomas Wade, the British Minister, demanded an investigation of the incident and then utilized the delay of the Ch'ing government, which was awaiting a report, to press for the settlement of all the issues outstanding that the British had wanted to have solved. These included economic privileges—as, for example, the exemption of foreign goods from the payment of the *likin* taxes—the general aim being the extension of British trade. Wade had been waiting for some such opportunity for two years and the Margary affair was a godsend to him. His methods of diplomacy were somewhat curious; not only did he spread rumours regarding the alleged possibility of a joint action by the British and the Russians (with the Russians to act in the Ili region and the British in Yunnan), but he also threatened the Manchus with a break of diplomatic relations between England and China, as well as with war. His bullying manners and speech were already well known to the Ch'ing officials. At this moment he proclaimed to an acquaintance, "They will have to accept this or there will be a war; and I, Thomas Francis Wade will make it, as sure as there is a God in Heaven!"

To emphasize his threats Wade left Peking and went to Shanghai; the Ch'ing government, properly frightened by Wade's antics and at the same time still engaged in a reconquest of Turkestan and faced with the problem of the Ili region under Russian occupation, was ready to conciliate the British and grant further new concessions. Ultimately, Li Hung-chang was entrusted with the task of negotiations with Wade; these took place in the seacoast resort town of Chefoo in Shantung, where the agreement known as the Chefoo Convention was signed on September 13, 1876. The British obtained a settlement of the Margary affair (including 200,000 taels indemnity), which made their further penetration of Yunnan as well as the development of trade between Burma and Yunnan possible. China's recognition of the conquest of Burma by Great Britain was implicit in the agreement. Further economic benefits were also obtained by the British (and, in effect, by all the powers due to the most-favoured-nation clause). **Four new ports were opened to trade—Ichang (Hupei), Wuhu (Anhwei), Wenchow (Chekiang), Pakhoi (Peihai, Kwangtung)**, while six other towns on the Yangtse were opened as ports of call. Thus, the further penetration of Szechuan was rendered feasible, while an arrangement for the "exploration" of Tibet was also made. Likewise a further advantageous interpretation of the extraterritorial rights of the foreign settlements in the Treaty Ports was obtained. In effect, the Chefoo Convention constituted a continuation of the process of unequal treaties which had been initiated by the treaties of Nanking and Tientsin. Simultaneously, it marked basically the end of the policy of "co-operation", as the mutual rivalries of the powers became obvious already in connection with it, and were to increase to a considerable extent in the future.

V. The Ili Question

As will be recalled, Russia had taken advantage of the anti-Ch'ing revolt of the population of Eastern Turkestan to occupy the Ili part of Dzungaria in 1871, promising to return it once peace and order had been restored in the area. The region was of importance for the Russian plans of economic penetration into China and could also serve as a buffer to **protect the newly conquered areas of Western Turkestan. More** than likely the Tsarist government thought that this promise would never have to be carried out. However, the Ch'ing government was successful in suppressing the uprisings in all of Eastern Turkestan and all possible schemes for dividing this region into areas under either the influence or direct rule of Russia and England were thus frustrated.

In July 1878 the Ch'ing government raised the problem of the restoration of the Ili region to its rule. For this purpose a Ch'ing envoy, Ch'ung-hou (the same who had been sent to France to apologize for the Tientsin incident), was dispatched to St. Petersburg. His mission there was not as simple as might appear; the Russians were not at all anxious to relinquish Ili and it was only after nine months of negotiations that the Treaty of Livadia was signed on September 15, 1879. Its terms provided for the cession to Russia of the richer and larger part of Western Ili, including the Tekes Valley, as well as vital passes in the western part of the T'ien Shan; greater trade privileges were granted to the Russians as well, and a 5 million roubles (2.8 million taels) indemnity for the Russian costs of occupation was demanded.

When the news of the treaty reached Peking an uproar ensued. Ch'ung-hou was recalled in disgrace and threatened with the death penalty. The conservative faction in the court clamoured for a war against Russia and this view was held, in particular, by Tso Tsung-t'ang, who considered Russia to be the greatest threat to Ch'ing rule due to its policy of "gradual encroachment, inch by inch, foot by foot on the frontier". It was in the debate on the Ili question that Chang Chih-tung (1837-1909) first made his appearance as a spokesman of the war party. He was later to become one of the most prominent high Ch'ing officials. Ultimately, the views of Li Hung-chang prevailed— he hoped to be able to use the help of Russia against the increasing expansion of the Japanese in Korea—and the war fever abated, especially in view of the movements of Russian army and naval forces. Li Hung-chang also brought Gordon to China where the latter expressed the view, as was to be expected, that the Ch'ing government had no chance of resisting the Russians, who would be in Peking in sixty days in case of a war. The attempts of the Ch'ing government to obtain support of the other European powers against Russia also failed despite Anglo-Russian rivalry. However, the British were worried that a war might "upset the dynasty which there is nothing to replace" in the words of Wade. This view expressed the essence of British policy during the entire period of 1864-1911.

Ch'ung-hou was now reprieved and a new envoy—Tseng Chi-tse (1839-1890), Tseng Kuo-fan's son, the Ch'ing minister in London—was sent to Russia. New negotiations were begun after his arrival in St. Petersburg in July 1880, the Ch'ing government having in the meantime renounced the Livadia Treaty. Ultimately, on February 24, 1881 a new Treaty of St. Petersburg was signed. According to it Russia returned the Tekes Valley and the passes in the T'ien Shan, while retaining a smaller part of Western Ili; for this the indemnity to be paid by China was increased to 9 million roubles. The Russians were also granted the right to extend their trading operations in Sinkiang and Mongolia, as well as to open new consulates in these areas. On the whole, the Ch'ing government had done better than it had itself expected on the Ili question; the time for the next stage of intensive Tsarist expansion in East Asia was to come a decade later. A large part, however, of the population of this area was by no means anxious to await the return of its Manchu masters and fled for shelter to neighbouring Russian-ruled regions.

VI. The Sino-French War, 1884-1885

In the process of nibbling away at the vassal territories of the Ch'ing Empire the gradual French conquest of Indo-china played an important role; it also resulted in the first major clash between China and one of the powers in the post-Tientsin Treaty period. The initial crucial steps of the French colonizers were taken already in the 1860s. As a result of the war against Vietnam, which it had begun with the aid of Spain in 1858, France gained control by the Treaty of Saigon, in September 1862, of a part of South Vietnam (the three eastern provinces of Cochinchina, including Saigon itself). In the next year the French imposed on Cambodia a treaty which transformed that country into a French protectorate. In 1867 they seized the rest of South Vietnam, the three western provinces of Cochinchina, and the attention of France was now concentrated on the conquest of the remaining parts of Vietnam, the central (referred to as Annam in the literature of that period, with Hué as its capital) and the northern, Tongking, with Hanoi as its main city.

The French showed particularly strong interest in extending their rule to North Vietnam, inasmuch as this area provided direct contact and the possibility of entry up the Red River into Yunnan. Earlier, the French had discovered that the Mekong failed to furnish such an entry because it was unsuitable for navigation. There is little doubt that one of the principal aims of French aggression in Indo-china, apart from the conversion of this country into a colony, was precisely the desire to create a base for the future penetration of South-west China. Admiral Dupré, the Governor of Cochinchina, wrote in 1873: "To establish ourselves in the rich country bordering on China is a question of life and death for the future of our rule in the Far East." In passing, it should be pointed out that there was an ever-present growing rivalry in this area between Great Britain and France, inasmuch as both were progressing in the same direction, towards Yunnan, the British from Burma and the French from Vietnam.

After the Franco-Prussian War, French policy aimed at recouping its losses by the building of a colonial empire. This was reflected in Indo-china and the first attempt to seize the Tongking area was made in 1873, when two French adventurers, the smuggler-merchant J. Dupuis and the naval officer and writer F. Garnier, captured Hanoi in November 1873. This resulted in the Vietnamese government turning for aid to the Black Flags, who proved to be successful in overcoming the French; Garnier was killed and the French force was later withdrawn.* However, in the next year the French were successful in forcing the weak Vietnamese government in Hué into signing a new Treaty of Saigon (March 15, 1874) in which France recognized the complete independence of Vietnam, offered its protection, while simultaneously its possession of South Vietnam was confirmed. This was aimed both at eliminating Chinese suzerainty and at transforming Vietnam into a French protectorate on the Cambodian model. The Vietnamese government sought the help of Peking to escape from the clutches of its new master, sending the customary tribute mission in 1874 and 1880, but the Ch'ing government was both unable and unwilling at this moment to assert its traditional role as the overlord of Vietnam, although later, in 1881 and 1882, some feeble diplomatic protests were made to the French on this issue.

*The Black Flags were one of the fairly sizeable forces of remnants of the Taiping army which had taken refuge after the suppression of the Taiping movement in the border areas between Yunnan and North Vietnam. They formed semi-independent states here and continued to maintain their military organization. Their principal commander was Liu Yung-fu.

Having extended their influence over central Vietnam and the Vietnamese government, the French were now ready to expand their aggression once more to the north to the Tongking area. In 1881 the French demanded of the Vietnamese government that it expel the Black Flags from North Vietnam; this the Vietnamese were unwilling to do, and the French determined to do it themselves. Thus, in March 1882 a French expeditionary force under H. L. Rivière occupied Hanoi but it was, in fact, soon surrounded by Black Flag and Vietnamese units and unable to proceed as yet to the conquest of Tongking. However, this presence of the French in North Vietnam marked already the beginning of the struggle between the French on one side and the Vietnamese and Chinese on the other, the outcome of which was ultimately to decide the fate of Vietnam for many decades.

Although at the end of 1882 France had declared in its negotiations with the Ch'ing government a willingness to withdraw troops from Tongking in exchange for an opening up of Yunnan to French trade, the new French government of J. Ferry, the renowned protagonist of imperialist expansion, decided on an out-and-out war policy and credits were voted for a new military expedition to Tongking on May 15, 1883; this was the beginning of twelve years of slaughter of the Vietnamese known as the "pacification" of Tongking. At the same time fighting in Tongking increased and the Black Flags were successful in their operations against the French, Riviere being killed in battle against them. In this situation of undeclared war the Ch'ing government finally resolved to take some action and ordered its troops from Yunnan and Kwangsi to proceed to the Vietnam border, where they were to serve as secret reinforcements for the Black Flags and to start slowly also participating themselves in the military campaign against the French.

However, as usual, the policy of the Ch'ing government was vacillating and contradictory. Li Hung-chang, the main spokesman in foreign affairs and now definitely the strongest individual political force in China, was adamantly opposed to any policy which might lead to a war with France. It is true that at the same time the Ch'ing government faced the problem of the aggressive actions of the Japanese in Korea (see p. 337). Likewise, it had hoped for assistance from the British, against the background of Anglo-French rivalry in South-east Asia, but this proved to be of no avail. As always, China faced too many enemies at once and the government had to compromise with one in order to turn against the next. The Ch'ing court itself was also frightened of the consequences, although some of the anti-foreign conservative party were in favour of a strong policy against French aggression.

In the meantime, the French continued their military campaign in Tongking and also succeeded, after a bombardment of the Vietnamese capital, in imposing a new treaty on the Vietnamese government, which was signed in Hué on August 23, 1883. According to it, Vietnam was now officially recognized as a protectorate of France with the latter to control its foreign relations, including those with China. This was an open challenge to the Manchus and in making it the French banked on the conciliatory, in effect capitulationist, policies of Li Hung-chang. The treaty also sanctioned the French military occupation of Tongking and thus created a situation in which a further conflict between the French and the Black Flags and other Chinese troops would be inevitable, unless these were to desert the Vietnamese and withdraw from Vietnam completely.

The French followed their political success by further military operations in the Red

River Delta. By the spring of 1884 the French troops were on the offensive and were driving both the Vietnamese and the Chinese units northwards towards the Chinese border, taking no prisoners, while units of the French navy under Admiral A. Courbet blockaded the Vietnamese coast and were threatening to do the same to the ports of South China. This was an important factor in bringing about still greater alarm of the Ch'ing court, and especially of Tz'u-hsi herself. She utilized the defeat of the Ch'ing troops in Vietnam and the generally perilous situation to bring about the dismissal of Prince Kung from all his offices, including the Tsungli Yamen, thus repaying all her old grudges.

Against this background Li Hung-chang had an excellent possibility to pursue his chosen policy and to seek to negotiate a settlement with France at the expense, obviously, of Vietnam, as well as of China's own interests. Li conducted negotiations with a French representative, F.E. Fournier, a navel officer; the result known as the Li-Fournier Convention was signed on May 11, 1884. In it the Ch'ing government agreed to withdraw all its troops from Vietnam in exchange for a French promise not to invade South China; simultaneously, it was to recognize all the treaties between France and Vietnam, i.e. acquiesce in the transformation of Vietnam into a French colony. The Ch'ing government also promised to open Yunnan and Kwangsi to French trade; the French magnanimously offered not to demand an indemnity. Negotiations for a permanent treaty on the basis of these terms were to be commenced within three months. The announcement of this agreement gave rise to considerable opposition in China, especially by the rival Hunan clique, of which Tseng Chi-tse was a representative. It was so strong that Li Hung-chang was even unable to announce that he had agreed to a troop withdrawal by June.

The settlement proposed above was upset by the action of French troops, who were pressing forward towards the Kwangsi border, where they attacked at Baclé (Peili) on June 23 some Chinese units which had not yet received orders to withdraw; the French attack was repulsed with fair losses (22 killed, 68 wounded). This was now seized upon by France as an excellent pretext for obtaining further concessions from the Ch'ing government; on July 12 a demand was made for the immediate implementation of the terms of the Li-Fournier Convention, as well as for an indemnity of 200 million francs. If this were not to be accepted within a week, the French threatened "to seize material guarantees", i.e. to attack Chinese ports, ships and so on. Simultaneously, France ordered its fleet into action against China and occupied the Pescadore Islands. The French threat was successful; the Ch'ing government was now more frightened than ever—it agreed to order the withdrawal of all its troops on July 16 and began new negotiations with the French in Shanghai, haggling over the size of the indemnity.

In the meantime, the French increased their military pressure on the Ch'ing. On August 4 the French fleet attacked the forts of Keelung in North Taiwan but failed in the attempt to take the port. Thus, in fact, France was waging war against China without bothering to declare it. At the same time, another part of the French fleet under Admiral Courbet had earlier, on July 13, sailed into Foochow harbour where they had been received in a friendly fashion by the local authorities. Here, ten French ships, much superior in armament, anchored for over a month close to the Chinese vessels of the Southern fleet, which had been built in Foochow. On August 23 a treacherous attack was launched by the French navy which started to fire on the Chinese ships. The result was such as could be expected; eleven of the Chinese ships were sunk within one hour—

the overall loss of Chinese lives was around 3000. At the same time the French destroyed the arsenal and the dockyard which had been built with the help of French engineers.

This massacre was more than even the Manchus could tolerate; the Ch'ing government now finally declared that a state of war existed between China and France. It is worth noting, in passing, that no action was taken against the hundreds of French missionaries throughout China and the many French merchants who continued their trade. The declaration of war did not mean, however, that the Ch'ing court was determined to pursue any serious military action against the French, although its position was by no means unfavourable, inasmuch as the French forces in Asia were far from adequate. Typically, Li-Hung-chang refused the use of his pride and joy, the Northern fleet, which then included ten modern warships, against the French in the south. As a result the French were able to blockade all the South China ports and to prevent the shipment of food supplies to the north—a curious employment of international law. They also resumed operations against Taiwan in September, but here, in spite of their attacks on Tamsui, they were again driven off. They were unable to utilize Hong Kong for supplies, as here all the Chinese workers refused to handle or service French ships. At the same time France sought to find allies in the struggle against China, primarily by seeking to persuade Japan to declare war on the basis of her conflict with China over Korea. This did not lead to any success and, on the whole, the international situation was not favourable to France, especially in view of sharp Anglo-French rivalry over the problem of Egypt.

The ubiquitous and ever more influential Robert Hart now took a hand in the situation and, through his intermediary, J.D. Campbell, began his own negotiations with the French in Paris in January 1885.* During the course of these secret talks, the French continued their advance in Tongking and while attacking Chinese positions in Chennankuan met on March 23 with a sharp defeat by Chinese troops, commanded by Feng Tzu-ts'ai (1818-1903), a rare phenomenon of a brave Ch'ing general, who, despite his age, personally led his troops in a counterattack. As a result of this, the French were driven back, losing the border town of Langson (Liangshan) on March 28, 1885.

The news of this fiasco brought about the downfall of the Ferry government (March 30), and increased the inclinations of the French to put an end to the war. The Ch'ing government was neither able nor willing to follow up its advantage and quickly ordered its troops to withdraw once more to China. The Paris talks were concluded by a protocol, signed on April 4, which provided for the cessation of military activities by both sides and for the negotiation of a peace treaty on the basis of the terms of the Li-Fournier Convention. The peace treaty was signed in Tientsin on June 9 by Li Hung-chang and the French Minister J. Patenôtre. Basically, it followed the terms previously conceded by the Ch'ing, but it also surrendered the border towns of Langson and Laokai to the French. Thus, now the Ch'ing government renounced all its rights of suzerainty over all Vietnam and left the Vietnamese people to the tender mercy of the new French masters. The Vietnamese continued a brave struggle up to 1895, until they were finally crushed by the terroristic campaigns of the French army. At the same time possibilities

---

*The Customs Service had by now expanded; 600 European (half of them British) and 2000 Chinese officials were employed in 1885 and its control of a vital sector of the Chinese economy was much strengthened. In the same year Hart declined the British government's offer to become its Minister to Peking in order to continue at his post as Inspector-general, which was of undoubtedly greater importance.

were created for future economic and political penetration by the French of China's South-west.

The process of the subjection of South-east Asia to foreign rule was speedily advanced. In 1886 the British conquered Upper Burma and this was almost immediately recognized by the Ch'ing government. In 1893 the French annexed Laos and thus, with the exception of Siam, all of South-east Asia was in the hands of the colonial powers. The entire extent of China's southern border was now contiguous with these two colonial empires, while its position in the north and east, facing Russia and Japan, was no better. The ineptitude and vacillating nature of Ch'ing policy and especially the capitulationist tendencies of Li Hung-chang, which were shown up during the course of the Sino-French War, demonstrated the complete unfitness of this regime to defend the country it was pretending to rule. All this, however, was to be exposed fully, for all the world to see, only during the course of the next great conflict—the Sino-Japanese War.

CHAPTER 33

The Sino-Japanese War, 1894-1895

I. The Situation in the Ch'ing Regime

Although China was at peace during the decade between the struggle against France and the beginning of the war with Japan there was little change on the domestic scene; the prevalence of corruption, the ineptness of the Manchu court and government with the concomitant struggle of cliques for power remained much as before. The real ruler of the Ch'ing Empire was still Tz'u-hsi; when Kuang-hsü reached his seventeenth birthday in 1886 and should have been allowed to assume full powers, the high dignitaries and Manchu aristocrats petitioned the Empress to provide him with necessary "political guidance", and thus she officially remained the Regent until 1889. In that year Tz'u-hsi finally retired formally to the Summer Palace but, in effect, she still busily watched all the moves of the Emperor, among others, with the help of her niece whom she had married to Kuang-hsü, read all the important state papers, approved all vital decrees, nominated all higher officials, while her eunuch henchmen were still grafting and spying as lustily as ever.

At the same time, however, two basic groupings were being formed within the top ruling body in Peking, a party gathered around the Emperor, which was composed almost entirely of high Chinese officials, headed by Weng T'ung-ho (1830-1904), the Emperor's tutor, who remained faithful to his pupil and now held the position of President of the Board of Revenue. The aim of this party was to enhance the Emperor's authority and, ultimately, to eliminate the influence and rule of Tz'u-hsi and her minions. Partially, the struggle of this party reflected a strong rivalry between the southern and northern provinces, inasmuch as the majority of the Emperor's party came from the provinces on the Yangtse.

Another factor in the above conflict was the bitter antagonism between Weng T'ung-ho and Li Hung-chang, who was now the most powerful, by far, of all the Ch'ing officials and, on the whole, a supporter of the party of the Empress, which was composed of practically all the Manchu princes and aristocrats, as well as the majority of court officials. Simultaneously, in the provinces new powerful governors-general, also Chinese, had arisen, who likewise constituted a rival source of power to Li Hung-chang; the most important of these was Chang Chih-tung, Governor-general of Hukwang in 1889-1894 and in 1896-1907. In the area under his control Chang also pursued a programme of limited modernization, similar to that of Li Hung-chang, building up his own industrial base, as well as armed forces. Another was Liu K'un-i (1830-1901), the Governor-general of Liangkiang, who was to play an important role both during the Sino-Japanese War and in the years following.

On the whole, regardless of the differences between the groups, the Ch'ing regime continued its basic policy of disregarding the need to reform the existing conditions and to proceed with an indispensable minimum of modernization; the contrast with the development of post-Meiji Japan became ever sharper. On the eve of the Sino-Japanese War the main concern of the court in Peking was to prepare the celebrations of Tz'u-hsi's coming sixtieth birthday; all the high officials were being dunned 25 per cent of their salaries for this purpose and vastly expensive and elaborate ceremonies were being planned.

II. Japanese Development

Japan in the years following the Meiji Restoration continued to make rapid strides in the modernization of practically all fields, especially in the development of industry and the building up of a military potential. The specific nature of the development of Japanese capitalism, which resulted from a revolution imposed from above, also implied the existence of many vestiges of early relations, particularly in agriculture and the countryside.

A considerable role was played by the government itself in the development of the economy while the political supremacy of the great landowners and the newly formed capitalist class, mostly of samurai origin, was rigidly maintained, and the government apparatus remained in their hands with a particularly prominent role being played by the military.

The opening of Japan by the foreign powers had been only slightly less brutal than that of China. However, the conclusions drawn from this by the Japanese ruling class were quite different from those of the Ch'ing regime. The emphasis which they placed on modernization had as its aim, among others, the emancipation of the country as rapidly as possible from the inferior status which had been imposed upon it by the powers. The goal here was to get rid of the unequal treaties which, as in the case of China, signified extraterritorial rights for the foreigners, the loss of tariff autonomy (the same 5 per cent) and so forth. From 1883 on the Japanese conducted negotiations with the powers to regain the status of a country equal to that of the Western nations; in this they were successful and thus, for example, the first new treaty on an equal basis was signed with England in July 1894, on the eve of the Sino-Japanese War.

At the same time, however, the Japanese were aiming at imposing on their neighbours, Korea and China, exactly the same type of unequal status which they themselves were struggling against. Here, the expansionist plans of Japan had, of course, also an historical background, dating back to the 16th century, to the Japanese aggression of the time of Hideyoshi. The first moves of the Japanese government of the 1870s in respect to Taiwan and the Liu-ch'iu Islands have already been noted. Korea was now to become the main area for Japanese penetration and also the principal scene of conflict between Japan and China.

III. The Situation in Korea

The conditions in the Hermit Kingdom had remained practically unchanged up to the 1870s. Korea had a petrified, economically stagnant feudal society with a particularly oppressive, corrupt and faction-ridden court and parasitic nobility. Its predominantly agrarian and undeveloped economy was little affected by foreign trade and the Korean peasantry lived in conditions of dire poverty and semi-serfdom. Korea had remained for 200 years a vassal of the Ch'ing dynasty and in a way it was a reflection on a smaller scale of Chinese civilization in its decaying stage, where, in this miniature form, the Confucian ideology was perhaps even more stultifying, because it was foreign in origin, than in its native habitat. The conscious policy of isolation from the rest of the world had been continued for centuries; what experiences it had had with contacts had been truly bitter, especially that of the Japanese invasion at the end of the 16th century.

The unfortunate geographical position of the country, as the gateway to North China, made of Korea in this period a new focal point of interest and intrigue of all the powers active in increasing their influences in East Asia. Thus, the question of the Opening of Korea was now placed on the agenda. The earliest attempts to solve this problem by force were made by the French and the Americans; the most important role, however, in the process was undoubtedly played by the Japanese. Already in 1873 the Japanese government had seriously considered the advisability of proceeding with a war against Korea and plans for this were quite far advanced. However, a majority ultimately opposed open aggression, going on the assumption that the strength of Japan was still inadequate for this purpose; nevertheless, the first steps towards penetration were taken quite soon thereafter.

In 1875 Japanese ships attacked Kanghwa Island, close to Seoul, destroying the forts there. This was followed up by a military expedition, which led to the signing of the Treaty of Kanghwa (February 1876) and signified the opening up of Korea to Japanese penetration. Three ports—Pusan, Inchon (Chemulpo) and Wonsan—were declared open to Japanese trade (Pusan was, in fact, already open to Japan since the end of the 17th century). In the treaty Korea was referred to as "independent and sovereign state" (however, this interpretation of the text is debatable), which was intended as a challenge by the Japanese of Chinese suzerainty, although both the Ch'ing government and the Koreans considered this relationship to be still extant. On the whole, the treaty had been patterned on the one which the French had imposed on Vietnam in 1874.

The Ch'ing government did not react immediately to the above challenge. Subsequently, however, Li Hung-chang advised the Korean government to apply the antidote of "meeting poison with poison", i.e. to establish relations with other powers. This advice was but a reflection of Li Hung-chang's well-beloved policy of using "barbarians against barbarians", i.e. playing on the rivalries of the powers, which constituted the quintessence of his entire approach to foreign affairs, the complete futility of which was to be demonstrated precisely in the ensuing conflict between China and Japan.

As a result of this Ch'ing policy and the further pressure from the powers, Korea did, in fact, establish relations with a number of countries (United States—1882; Great Britain and Germany—1883; Russia and Italy—1884; France—1886). All this had the effect of weakening considerably Ch'ing suzerainty over its vassal. While some of the powers gave a semblance of recognition to this suzerainty by accrediting to Korea their ministers in Peking, both the Japanese and the Americans insisted on establishing their missions in Seoul.

The traditional conflicts for power between the factions of the Korean nobility and court were now further complicated by the influence and intrigues of the foreign powers. The strongest had been the extremely conservative faction headed by the Taewongun (Lord of the Great Court), the father of the Korean king (he had ascended the throne in 1864 at the age of 12), who had been Regent in the years 1864-1873. This faction was usually pro-Ch'ing and it was now opposed by the faction of the Queen (who came from the Min clan, the most powerful in all Korea), as well as by a group of so-called Progressives led by Kim Ok-kyun. The latter were much impressed by the development of Japan and were supported by the Japanese.

It was against the background of these complicated conflicts that the riots of Korean soldiers took place in Seoul in July 1882, which were almost certainly inspired by the Taewongun, who had been removed from power by the Min faction in 1874. These led also to the attack against the Min group, as well as against the Japanese, the Japanese Minister being forced to flee for safety to the coast. As a result, both the Japanese and the Ch'ing governments sent in their troops to restore order; the Ch'ing commanders kidnapped the Taewongun and exiled him to China, where he was kept for the next three years. The Koreans agreed to pay an indemnity to the Japanese, while the Japanese now stationed troops to guard their legation in Seoul; the Ch'ing also left their soldiers in Korea. One of the commanders of these was Yüan Shih-k'ai (1859-1916), who was subsequently to play a most prominent role in the future events in Korea and still more in Chinese history itself. The intervention of the Ch'ing government in these events brought about a realignment in Korean politics; the Min faction now assumed a pro-Chinese position, while the Progressive group continued its collaboration with the Japanese, who were busily engaged in extending their political and economic penetration of Korea.

In December 1884 the Kim Ok-kyun group attempted a *coup détat* in the traditional Korean feudal fashion. The king was captured and a number of ministers of the Min faction assassinated; all this was done in close co-ordination with the Japanese Minister in Seoul, who probably masterminded the whole plot. The more numerous Ch'ing troops, led by Yüan Shih-k'ai, reacted to this by attacking, together with Korean units, the Japanese who were holding the king prisoner. The king managed to escape, and the Japanese, facing defeat, withdrew to the coast together with the main leaders of the Kim group, only to return in the following month when Inoue Kaoru, the Japanese Foreign Minister, landed with a strong military force. The Koreans were again forced to pay an indemnity and to apologize to the Japanese.

The above conflict, however, had almost brought about a war between Japan and China; it failed to materialize probably only because the Japanese government did not feel itself adequately prepared for a war at this stage. Nonetheless the entire affair had been concocted by the Japanese, more than likely due to the absorption of the Ch'ing regime in the conflict with France over Vietnam. Negotiations then followed between the Ch'ing and the Japanese governments which were held in Tientsin. The main representatives were Li Hung-chang and Ito Hirobumi, one of the main political leaders of the post-Meiji Restoration period, and the talks ended with the conclusion on April 18, 1885 of the so-called Li-Ito Convention. According to this, both Japan and China were to withdraw all their troops in Korea within four months. In the case that either side should consider it necessary to send their troops there in the future, advance notice of such a move was to be given. This treaty was a considerable success for Japan and it, in effect, converted Korea into a co-protectorate of both Japan and China. In view, moreover, of the expansionist policy of Japan, which aimed at the conquest and subjugation of Korea, in spite of all the verbiage then employed regarding the concern of the Japanese for Korean "independence", the 1885 Treaty actually constituted a time bomb for the future conflict.

IV. The Immediate Background of the Sino-Japanese War

The next nine years witnessed a constant jockeying for power and influence in Korea between the Japanese and the Ch'ing government. The basic aim of Ch'ing policy now was to exert true suzerainty, to a much greater degree than earlier, and to make Korea really dependent on China. In the implementation of this policy a major role was played by Yüan Shih-k'ai, who was designated by Li Hung-chang as the Ch'ing Commissioner for Trade in Seoul and was, in effect, the Ch'ing Resident for Korea during the 1885-1895 period. The arrogant behaviour of Yüan Shih-k'ai, his constant intrigues and meddling in Korean domestic affairs, undoubtedly gave rise to much irritation and anti-Ch'ing sentiment among the Korean ruling group, pushing even the anti-Japanese Min faction into seeking either Russian or American support.

However, Ch'ing policy was, on the whole, successful in extending China's political influence and this by means of supporting the most conservative elements in Korea; the consequences of this were to exacerbate the Korean domestic crisis and to make it possible for the Japanese to assume the role of the protagonists of progress. The Ch'ing also increased their control over the Korean government, of the Korean customs service, as well as of its Office for Foreign Affairs. At the same time the Chinese were surprisingly successful in engaging in economic rivalry with the Japanese; Chinese trade increased steadily and by 1892 almost equalled that of Japan, although the Chinese were middlemen for European products while the Japanese were exporting their own goods. However, the Japanese pressed on also with their economic penetration and over 10,000 Japanese recent immigrants in the country played a significant role in this respect.

Simultaneously, the Japanese increased their efforts at political penetration, primarily by backing the Progressive group; they were unable, however, to weaken Chinese influence appreciably, largely due to the fact that the distrust of the great majority of the Koreans towards the Japanese was too great. As a result of the above, the situation in Korea and Sino-Japanese relations had become unusually tense by 1894. The Japanese government was now only waiting for an opportunity to settle the so-called Korean question by force of arms, by a war against China; it had been pressing towards this goal throughout the entire period, primarily for the purpose of imperialist expansion, but also due to a number of domestic reasons. The oligarchic government was in considerable political trouble and saw in the launching of a war an excellent remedy to its problems.

The assassination in Shanghai of the main pro-Japanese Progressive leader, Kim Ok-kyun, under dramatic circumstances, aroused the fury of the Japanese, who also—with good reason—suspected the Ch'ing authorities of complicity in this affair. The later barbarous dismembering of Kim's body, after its return to Korea, did nothing to assuage their feelings. Of much greater importance, however, for the future course of events was the beginning in March 1894 of the Tonghak Uprising in Korea. The

Tonghak ("Eastern Learning") movement was a religious sect which had arisen in the 1860s; its ideas were a compound of Confucianism, Buddhism and Taoism, while the circumstances of its formation and development showed some striking similarity to that of the Taiping movement, the influence of the latter even being possible. The Tonghak creed was basically anti-foreign, especially anti-Japanese, as well as anti-feudal, i.e. opposed to the corrupt Korean officialdom and landlord class. In the 1890s the movement spread rapidly throughout a large part of the country, especially the main agricultural areas of the South, where it acquired mass peasant support and took on politically the character of an agrarian peasant revolution. The Korean government was at first quite incapable of dealing with the uprising in the South, its troops having met with defeat. It has been suggested (though this is dubious) that the Japanese themselves instigated the movement, since it could provide them with an excellent pretext for future intervention in Korea. It is quite clear that the Japanese were now anxious to avail themselves of the opportunities offered by this crisis and were also interested in having the Ch'ing government become involved in it, so as to be able to force a showdown. In view of its helplessness against the Tonghak insurrection, the Seoul government did call the Ch'ing court for assistance; however, Peking was very hesitant in coming to the rescue of its vassal. Li Hung-chang himself insisted that a formal appeal by the Korean king be made. When this was done, 1500 Ch'ing troops were finally sent in and, in accord with the Li-Ito Convention, the Japanese were notified. The Japanese, who had already decided on intervention anyhow in the meantime, immediately followed this up by sending in 7000 of their soldiers, directed straight to the capital. The ostensible reason they offered was their desire to protect their own nationals and property.

However, even before the arrival of the Ch'ing and Japanese troops, the leaders of the Tonghak had agreed to an armistice and temporarily suspended the uprising. Hence, the pretext for the presence of both the Ch'ing and the Japanese troops ceased to exist. Under these circumstances the Ch'ing government now turned to the Japanese with the proposal that both sides should carry out a simultaneous withdrawal of all their troops. The Japanese first delayed their answer to this request and then raised instead the completely extraneous issue of the alleged necessity to carry out "reforms" of the Korean government and administration, proposing that both Japan and China join together for this purpose. The idea was rejected immediately by the Ch'ing government as constituting unauthorized meddling in Korean domestic affairs. During these negotiations the Japanese utilized the time for the sending in of additional forces, all to the Seoul area. Thus, by the end of June, while there were only around 3000 Ch'ing troops in Korea, the Japanese force had risen already to 18,000.

The policy of Li Hung-chang—and he was definitely the main foreign policy-maker of the Ch'ing government at this time—was to avoid a war with Japan at all costs, probably largely due to the fact that he himself was aware of the fact that all the forces he had built up during his twenty-five years as the Governor-general of Chihli were not truly a match for the Japanese, inasmuch as the former were shot through with graft and corruption from top to bottom. Therefore, he placed his main hopes throughout the entire period preceding the war, as well as during its course, on the help and intervention of the foreign powers, especially Great Britain and Russia, feeling that their interests would be threatened by Japanese aggression to a sufficient degree to have them react as he hoped. In this respect, in spite of his feverish diplomatic activity in

June and July 1894, all his plans went astray. While Great Britain was also anxious to avoid a war, her interests were primarily in the Yangtse Valley and thus the advance of the Japanese in Korea was not considered a sufficient menace, especially in view of the fact that the Japanese had assured the British, as requested, that the Shanghai area would not become the scene of military operations. In addition, the British were not interested in opposing the Japanese by themselves and the complicated rivalries of the powers, both in Europe and in other parts of the world, especially Africa as well as East Asia itself, made a concerted opposition against Japan of all the interested parties practically impossible.

The United States essentially held throughout the entire period to a pro-Japanese position and rebuffed all British proposals for possible joint action. Russia was perhaps most threatened by Japanese aggression, inasmuch as she was very much interested in future penetration in both Manchuria and Korea. However, the Japanese succeeded in assuring the Russians that they intended to honour the independence and integrity of Korea. The profound distrust and mutual rivalry of Great Britain and Russia was probably the most important single factor which rendered joint action ineffective and excluded the possibility of foreign intervention at this stage.

The Ch'ing court itself was divided, vacillating and frightened. The group around the Emperor was in favour of a policy of resistance to Japan, hoping that by means of achieving success in this it could strengthen the position of the Emperor and weaken that of Tz'u-hsi and Li Hung-chang. On the whole, it was inclined to hope, in the first place, for British aid. While up to this point Li Hung-chang himself had also tended to rely on co-operation with the British, he now placed more hope on obtaining Russian support. Both the parties were to be completely disappointed in their calculations, inasmuch as the powers were not particularly concerned, at this stage, with the plight of the Ch'ing court and still less with the fate of Korea or China.

By July the Japanese had acquired a completely dominant position in Seoul and were able to start launching by themselves the "reform" programme. After having failed to win over the Korean government, in spite of immense pressure, to acquiesce in their plans, the Japanese, on July 23, surrounded the palace of the Korean king, imprisoned him and his family, placed his father, the Taewongun, at the head of the government and concluded an alliance with the newly established regime, thus obtaining "official" Korean blessing for the policy of expelling the Ch'ing officials and troops from the country.

Yüan Shih-k'ai had already fled Seoul, escorted from the coast by a guard of British sailors. Although in the same month Li Hung-chang sent in more reinforcements, 8000 soldiers to P'yongyang, he still maintained his policy of avoiding war at any price, wishing that if a conflict were to follow the responsibility for it should be placed entirely on the Japanese. This, he hoped, would have proper international repercussions and would facilitate foreign intervention on behalf of the Manchus.

On July 25 a British-owned transport ship, the *Kowshing*, chartered by Li Hung-chang and carrying a further reinforcement of 1200 troops to Korea, was stopped by Japanese naval units and then sunk with a great loss of life—over 1000—the losses being augmented by the Japanese shooting of the drowning Chinese soldiers. On July 29 the Japanese attacked the Ch'ing troops stationed in Asan (Yashan, 80 miles south of Seoul) and routed them completely. Thus, the Japanese started war activities without a declaration of war, which was by no means the last time that they were to do so.

V. The Sino-Japanese War, August 1894-March 1895

After the initial Japanese attacks mentioned above, war was finally declared by both Japan and China on August 1. The military operations proved very quickly to be a one-sided affair, inasmuch as the complete incapacity of the Ch'ing military establishment, itself the result of the very nature of the social and political order in China, was quite soon revealed and the war was actually an almost unending string of relatively easy Japanese victories. There is also little doubt that the entire Ch'ing policy of constantly relying and expecting foreign aid and intervention had a debilitating effect on the conduct of the war itself.

The Japanese took full advantage of the tactical superiority of their position in Korea and, having driven out the Ch'ing troops from the Asan area, prepared methodically for an advance from Seoul to the north. The main forces, over 20,000, of the Ch'ing army were now concentrated in P'yongyang. Although it was quite adequately supplied with arms and ammunition, it was a typical disorganized Ch'ing outfit, inasmuch as each general refused to heed the other and was only concerned with his own welfare and graft. While initially the Ch'ing troops had been welcomed enthusiastically by the Korean population, their atrocious behaviour—the pillaging, looting, etc.—was such as to change these sentiments very quickly.

When the Japanese army advanced in September in three columns on P'yongyang it soon gained a rapid victory, although the position there was both strong and easily defensible. The Ch'ing generals took the lead in fleeing to the Yalu, the troops followed the example of their leaders. On September 15 the Japanese occupied P'yongyang and the retreat of the Ch'ing army turned into a panic, vast quantities of equipment being lost.

At almost exactly the same time as the Japanese conquered P'yongyang, the most important naval engagement of the war was being fought near the mouth of the Yalu on September 17; here the famous Peiyang fleet, after escorting a transport of Ch'ing troops to Korea (reinforcements for P'yongyang, of course too late), encountered a Japanese squadron. The size of the two fleets was almost the same: thirteen ships on the Ch'ing side, including the pride of the navy—two German-built battleships—commanded by the chief admiral, Ting Ju-ch'ang, against twelve ships on the Japanese side. It can be noted in passing that all the ships on both sides were foreign built. In the four-hour battle which ensued four of the Chinese vessels were lost as against the loss of only one Japanese ship; this was the result both of inadequate leadership on most of the Ch'ing ships and the lack of sufficient supply of ammunition due to graft (the battleships had only three shells each for their Krupp guns).

Although the defeat was not decisive, it frightened the patron of the fleet, Li Hung-chang, to such a degree that hence, under his orders, the fleet avoided any future meeting with the Japanese. After repairs in Port Arthur it remained bottled up until the last month of the war in the harbour of Weihaiwei in Shantung, passively awaiting its final doom. Thus, the many millions that had been spent abroad on the purchasing of this main object of Li Hung-chang's "self-strengthening" proved to be of no avail and the Japanese navy was now in complete control of the seas. Li Hung-chang became the object of a campaign against him by the party of the Emperor and was deprived of some of his honours; however, he was still left in charge of the war, both of its military and its diplomatic aspects. More than ever he had no faith in the outcome of the fighting and continued only to hope for foreign intervention.

After the victory in P'yongyang, the Japanese easily forced out all the remnants of the Ch'ing forces from Korea and proceeded to the border on the Yalu; here, on the other side of the river, new Ch'ing forces were concentrated in large numbers—over 40,000— which were again quite amply supplied with all the necessary war material. On October 24 the Japanese crossed over on the ice of the frozen Yalu without meeting any opposition and put the entire Ch'ing army to complete rout—the story of P'yongyang being basically repeated once more.

The Ch'ing court was now even more panic-stricken since the war was now on Chinese soil. Li Hung-chang continued his fruitless efforts to obtain foreign intervention. At the beginning of November, Prince Kung, old, ill and disgruntled, was now restored once again to office in the Tsungli Yamen; he tried his hand and appealed to the representatives of the powers in Peking for mediation in the conflict, offering the recognition of Korean independence and the payment of the Japanese war costs. His efforts also were of no avail.

The Japanese army continued its offensive into South Manchuria. A special force landed on the Liaotung Peninsula and proceeded to attack the very strong Chinese position of the two ports, the commercial, Talien, and the naval, Lushun (Port Arthur). Much time and effort and prodigious sums of money had been spent on fortifying these ports. Talien had six forts with twenty-four brand-new Krupp guns, while Port Arthur was guarded by twenty-one forts, in which over seventy large Krupp guns had been placed. Due to the defection of the Ch'ing generals and panic of the troops, the Japanese succeeded, after the initial advance, in occupying Talien on November 7 without the loss of a single soldier and captured undamaged vast supplies of equipment. They subsequently surrounded Port Arthur, beat off attempts to rescue it, and captured the great naval base from the land, while its massive defences which faced seaward proved to be quite useless (November 21). The Japanese followed up their success with an indiscriminate massacre of the civilian population, over 2000 people being killed.

After the above débâcle, the Ch'ing government had given up practically all hope and Tz'u-hsi and Li Hung-chang, in particular, were doing their utmost to have the war concluded. At the end of November Li Hung-chang sent a special emissary to Japan; this was G. Detring, the German Customs Commissioner in Tientsin, who had been Li's adviser on foreign affairs for the past twenty years. However, his mission was a complete failure, inasmuch as the Japanese refused to recognize him as a properly accredited negotiator. The main reason, of course, was that the Japanese wanted to deliver still further knockout blows at the Ch'ing regime so as to make their victory truly complete.

The above aim of the Japanese government was accomplished in January and February. On January 20 a force of 20,000 Japanese landed unopposed in Yungcheng in Shangtung, 30 miles east of Weihaiwei, the shelter of the remnants of the Peiyang fleet. The strong fortifications defending Weihaiwei were quickly taken from the rear and the port was surrounded. Soon the Japanese were in a position to shell the Chinese ships in the harbour, damaging and sinking four of them. In this situation the commander of the fleet, Ting Ju-ch'ang, proposed that the remaining force of eleven ships make an attempt to break the blockade of the port, sail out and try to save itself in this fashion. His proposals were rejected by the majority of the officers, who were afraid of the dangers involved. Ting and his deputy committed suicide, while the other officers then proceeded to surrender on February 12 all the ships and equipment, without any effort to damage or scuttle them. In this way the Peiyang fleet, the mainstay of Li Hung-chang's military position and prestige, met its inglorious end.

The loss of the navy now made the position of the Ch'ing regime, given its inherent limitations, almost completely hopeless from the military point of view. It is true that the Emperor's party still wished to continue resistance and in this it was supported by some of the most influential Chinese governors-general, such as Chang Chih-tung and Liu K'un-i. It was equally true that only a small part of the potential capabilities of China had been employed in the war and that the southern provinces had not even been involved in it. However, since the best-equipped and most modern troops of the Ch'ing army had been already completely shattered there seemed little chance of improving the situation. This was, in fact, soon proved by the fate of the next army, mostly units of the Hunan army, the rival to Li Hung-chang's Huai army. Its forces were sent against the Japanese in Manchuria, and although they were sizeable, over 60,000, they were as defective in leadership and training and as graft-ridden as the army of Li Hung-chang. They soon suffered a series of defeats in March at the hands of the Japanese, who were approaching the borders of Chihli and thus posing a threat to Peking itself. In this way the Japanese aim of gaining a quick military victory in order to avoid the possibility of an intervention by the powers had been fully realized.

Further attempts by the Ch'ing regime to negotiate with Japan took place in January when two Ch'ing envoys were dispatched to Japan. However, they were turned away ignominiously by the Japanese under the pretext that their powers for negotiating were insufficient. Apart from the aim of humiliating the Ch'ing government still further, this move was also connected with the desire to continue the Manchurian offensive and to finish off the Peiyang fleet. Once both these tasks had been accomplished, the Japanese government was now willing to receive the Ch'ing peace mission, especially as it was to be headed by Li Hung-chang himself, whom they themselves had suggested. His powers were obviously not open to questioning due to his position, but to make certain the Ch'ing government cabled his plenipotentiary powers to Tokyo for approval.

VI. The Peace Settlement

Li Hung-chang arrived at Shimonoseki on March 19, 1895 accompanied by a large suite—135 people; the negotiations began on March 21. One of the first issues raised was the question of an armistice, inasmuch as military operations were still being continued in Manchuria. The Japanese demands in connection with this were so outrageously high (the occupation of Tientsin, Taku, etc.) that even Li Hung-chang was unable to accept them. However, the attempted assassination on March 24 of the 73-year-old Li by a Japanese member of an ultra-chauvinistic Black Dragon Society compelled the Japanese, for the sake of prestige, to agree to a partial armistice; this was restricted to Manchuria and North China, and did not apply to the South, where the Japanese now occupied the Pescadore Islands. They agreed to the armistice also because they were now becoming apprehensive of the possibility of foreign intervention, especially by Russia. The wounded Li Hung-chang was still able to hold the talks, while the Japanese side was represented by Prime Minister Ito and the Foreign Minister Mutsu Munemitsu. It is really difficult to speak of any true negotiations, inasmuch as the Japanese were in a position to impose their peace conditions and took full advantage of the situation to do so; apart from a few secondary concessions made by the Japanese in comparison with the first version of their conditions, the Ch'ing delegation was forced to accept all the Japanese peace proposals.

The treaty was signed on April 17 and its main points were as follows: (1) the recognition by China, but not by Japan, of the full independence and autonomy of Korea; (2) the cession by China to Japan of the Pescadore Islands, Taiwan and the Liaotung Peninsula in South Manchuria; (3) the payment by China of a 200 million tael indemnity; (4) the annulment of all earlier Sino-Japanese treaties; a new treaty to be drawn up on a basis identical with the treaties between China and the Western powers; (5) the opening up of four new Treaty Ports—Shasi (Shashih, Hupei), Soochow (Kiangsu), Chungking and Hangchow, as well as the right to navigation of the Upper Yangtse and a number of other rivers; (6) a provision that the future trade treaty (which was signed on July 21, 1896) would give the Japanese the freedom to engage in trade, manufacturing and industry in the Treaty Ports where this activity would be exempt from Chinese taxation.

Thus, the terms were extremely far-reaching—the question of Liaotung, especially, meant that now not only the loss of vassal states was involved, but that the territory of China proper was at stake. The economic consequences of the right to develop industry by foreigners was also of basic importance as this proved to be, in effect, a fatal blow to the Chinese economy since it favoured foreign development at the expense of native Chinese industry and thus truly emphasized the semi-colonial nature of relations. All these economic advantages would and did accrue to all the powers on the basis of the most-favoured-nation clause; this coincided also with the plans of the Japanese to purchase support for their expansionist policy from the powers by sharing the new benefits with them. In this respect the calculations of the Japanese government were well founded, inasmuch as it had been able to conduct the entire war without meeting with any attempt at intervention by the powers, which had not counted on the possibility of such a rapid, crushing Japanese victory or, for that matter, with any victory at all. The principal reason for this state of affairs, as mentioned earlier, was the rivalries between the powers, both in the Far East and on a world scale, which made unity of action impossible. It is also true that Japanese expansion, at this stage, had not yet come to be considered a basic challenge to the interests of any of the powers most active in China.

Great Britain was still dominant in respect to both its economic stake and its political influence in Peking; the main concern of the British was rivalry with Russia, which extended to all of Asia, from the Pacific to the Caspian Sea. In this context China had been regarded by them as a buffer to protect India and also as a possible ally against Russia. During the course of the Sino-Japanese War a distinct shift in British policy took place towards the winning side, to viewing Japan as potentially a much more effective ally against Russia than the inept Ch'ing regime, and thus the benevolent neutrality of Britain towards the Japanese aggression in China was assured. The first steps were now being taken which were to lead to the Anglo-Japanese alliance of 1902. One of the main consequences of this change in British policy was that the Ch'ing regime embarked on its policy of seeking an alliance with Tsarist Russia.

While Russia and her new ally France had also regarded Japanese expansion with, on the whole, a fair degree of equanimity during the course of the war, the Japanese demand for the cession of Liaotung gave rise to fears, especially on the part of Russia, that here the ambitions of the new contender for power in the Far East were too far-going, particularly in view of Russia's own plans for expansion in this area. These were connected, amongst others, with the construction that was under way of the Trans-Siberian Railway, which by now had reached the area of Lake Baikal. Russia's aims for future penetration in the direction of Manchuria and Korea and its search for an open-water port on the Pacific were now imperilled by the Japanese claim to Liaotung. Thus, the Tsarist government took the lead in organizing an intervention of the powers against this provision of the Shimonoseki Treaty; it was ready to press this issue to the point of war, if necessary, in line with the concepts formulated by S. Witte, the Minister of Finance and the main policy-maker of Russian expansion in the Far East.*

Russia was joined in her effort by her ally, France, which, while primarily interested in expansion in another area, South-west China, was more than willing to co-operate with Russia on this issue for the political purpose of cementing the newly formed Franco-Russian alliance. The third European power which was willing to join in this intervention was Germany; while a relative newcomer to this part of the world, Germany had already developed considerable economic interests here, as well as great ambitions for future expansion in East Asia at China's expense. One of the principal general aims of German foreign policy, which had already been formulated earlier by Bismarck, was to encourage Russia's drive to the East in the hope of having her become more and more engaged there, thus lessening Russia's influence in Europe and undermining the value of the Franco-Russian alliance. Simultaneously, the Germans were already planning to acquire a base in China for purposes of further expansion and saw the possibility of achieving this by receiving "compensation" for their action on the Liaotung problem.

The British refused to participate in the proposed intervention, more than likely in order not to antagonize Japan unduly, and also because Liaotung in Japanese hands was not a great threat to their own interests, which were centred still primarily in the Yangtse Valley. At the same time, however, they were also afraid that the Japanese might be going too far and were especially apprehensive of the possibility of a Japanese protectorate over all of China. Thus, they were not unwilling to see the Japanese cut down to size by somebody else's efforts and therefore did not actively oppose the proposed intervention. It should be added that the actions of Russia, France and Germany were stimulated from February on by the Ch'ing government, especially Li Hung-chang himself, who revealed the suspected territorial demands and appealed for aid to resist them.

Having quickly co-ordinated their policies, Russia, France and Germany submitted identical notes in Tokyo on April 23—only six days after the signing of the Shimonoseki Treaty. In this *démarche* they "recommended" that Liaotung be retroceded to China, inasmuch as in foreign hands "it would be a constant menace to Peking and at the same time render illusory the independence of Korea and would henceforth be a perpetual obstacle to the peace of the Far East". This assessment of the strategic importance of Liaotung happened to be quite correct; the "friendly advice"

---

*Witte's memoirs contain much interesting material on this point, as well as on later dealings of the Russian government with China and Japan. However, this material must be checked against other sources, as Witte is not too reliable, especially in view of his attempts to whitewash Russian policy and, in particular, his own role.

was accompanied by an obvious implication that force would be employed if the Japanese were not to accept this recommendation. The Japanese government had no alternative but to acquiesce, inasmuch as its military forces were already exhausted by the operations against China, while its financial position was also not much better. Prolonged haggling followed, in which the Japanese demanded a vast increase in the indemnity if they were to give back Liaotung; this issue almost broke up the temporary Triple Alliance, but, ultimately, the increase was set at 30 million taels and all the Japanese schemes to hold on to Liaotung as a security for the payment of the indemnity were frustrated.

It is characteristic that the exchange of ratifications of the Shimonoseki Treaty, which took place in Chefoo on May 8 as scheduled—the Ch'ing government had debated the issue but had come to the conclusion, in spite of great domestic opposition, that it had no choice but to ratify—was witnessed by many foreign naval vessels, including a Russian fleet of seventeen ships. Within the very near future the bill for the services rendered in connection with Liaotung was to be presented to the Ch'ing government by all the three powers engaged in this intervention. The Japanese government, on the other hand, hid its anger and humiliation, to prepare for revenge which was to take place ten years later—in the shape of the Russo-Japanese War.

All the other gains of the Japanese remained unchallenged and, having earlier occupied the Pescadore Islands, the Japanese proceeded in June to take possession of Taiwan; one of the sons of Li Hung-chang accompanied the Japanese for this ceremony. However, here the Japanese met with considerable resistance from the Chinese population of Taiwan. First, an attempt had been made to set up an independent republic of Taiwan in May, but this was soon doomed to fail, partially because the people placed at its head were the top Ch'ing officials, including the governor who was made president; they were only interested in fleeing back to China with all their possessions. Here, once more, Liu Yung-fu and his Black Flag Army were present. This force, although numbering only two battalions, had been sent to the island in 1895; it increased in size considerably and became the main force in resisting Japanese occupation. However, during its brave but forlorn struggle, it received no assistance whatsoever from the Ch'ing government and the Japanese were finally successful in overrunning the entire island which was to remain their colony for fifty years.

The defeat of the Ch'ing regime in the Sino-Japanese War was an event of very far-reaching significance for the future development of China in all respects. It revealed the complete bankruptcy of the policies of partial modernization, restricted primarily to the military field, such as had been pursued for thirty years by the Manchus and their main Chinese supporters, Li Hung-chang and the others. These policies, which were also bound up with subservience to the powers, had failed dismally in the efforts to safeguard China against foreign aggression, while the collaboration with the powers, based on the assumption that they would be always vitally interested in the maintenance of the Ch'ing government, also did not produce the desired results, inasmuch as they proved to be ready to leave their protégé to his fate, as long as their own basic interests in China were not threatened too seriously. The fiasco of the Ch'ing armed forces showed how deeply the rot had set in in the entire structure of the Ch'ing administration, how corruption and graft on all levels had made the carrying out of an adequate defence of the country impossible. From a domestic point of view the débâcle signified a crisis of the Ch'ing regime and raised the question of its very existence. It was against this background that the first serious attempt to initiate a programme of reform was to take place, which culminated in the famous Hundred Days Reform episode of 1898.

From an international point of view the outcome of the war resulted in a great enhancement of the position and prestige of Japan. It was now able to eliminate the rest of the effects of the unequal treaties and to take its place as one of the main contenders in the struggle of the imperialist powers for the division of the world, with its sphere of principal interests being clearly marked to lie in Korea and North China. The powers were also surprised by the rapidity and thoroughness of the Japanese victory and the scope of the ineptitude of the Ch'ing regime. While still willing to prop up the Manchus, especially in order to avoid the possibility of a Japanese protectorate over all of China, they now also envisaged the prospect of a breakup of China, a partitioning in which each of the powers was interested in staking out, as quickly as possible, an area which should be reserved for its exclusive penetration and eventual annexation. Thus now the existence of the Chinese Question—similar in many respects to the problem of Turkey in the Near East—was to be of prime importance in the international relations of the period preceding the First World War and was to bring about a marked increase in the rivalries of the powers in the Far East. The consequences of this for China, as we shall see, were very far-reaching; as a result of this process she was to lose most of what had remained of her sovereignty and to become transformed into a joint colony of all the Great Powers present in East Asia.

PART XI

Imperialism and China: the Hundred Days Reform and the I Ho T'uan

CHAPTER 34

Slicing the Melon, 1895-1899

I. The General Situation After the Sino-Japanese War

All the weaknesses of China and of the Ch'ing regime were revealed fully as a result of the disastrous defeat in the war against Japan; this gave rise, in turn, in international affairs to a wild scramble of the powers for obtaining new economic and political concessions in China. The intensity of this pressure was unprecedented in comparison with any other period during the 19th century and it was intimately bound up with the general nature of world development, with the transition from early capitalism to imperialism. Perhaps nowhere else were all the basic features of imperialism and of its methods shown as clearly and nakedly as in the case of China which, now more than ever before, became in the last years of the 19th century one of the most important focal points of international rivalry. As a result of this, the events in China and the policies of the powers towards China were now also closely connected with general world politics, with the entire gamut and interlocking complex of international relations.

All this was of vital significance for the future development of China in all respects. It is only from this period on that the growth of the capitalist forms of economy, resulting mainly from increased foreign penetration, takes on really important proportions, which affected both the economic and the social structure of the country. Politically, the heightened aggression of the imperialist powers was of no lesser importance, inasmuch as the very existence of the Middle Kingdom as a political and territorial entity was now at stake.

The Chinese were faced, therefore, in these years with the vital problem—how to preserve their country from the fate of so many others in Asia and Africa, how to save their independence which was already much circumscribed, how to oppose the mounting offensive of imperialism. The search for the answers to these problems is the main essence of the domestic political history of China during this period; it is reflected both in the growth of the reformist and revolutionary movements, as well as in the anti-foreign strivings of the I Ho T'uan (see p. 374). The urgency of the struggle against imperialism was to remain one of the paramount features of Chinese political life for the next half-century, and its bearing on the ideological and intellectual development in this period was of crucial importance. It is quite impossible to grasp the essential factors which shaped life in 20th-century China without keeping the above feature constantly in mind.

The complete bankruptcy and total sterility of thought and concept of the Ch'ing regime, which was exposed during the Sino-Japanese War, was to be brought to light still more in the years 1895-1899. It became ever more obvious to the best minds of China that the Manchus were totally incapable of defending China against the threat of increased imperialist aggression, that their only concern was the preservation of their own rule, for the sake of which they were willing to continue their policy of capitulation to the powers, if only the latter would persist in their efforts to maintain the Ch'ing regime in power. Thus, the need to replace the Manchu government by one capable of defending China—and simultaneously of carrying out the necessary transformation of the country which would make such a defence feasible—was becoming slowly but surely apparent already in this period. The road to the Revolution of 1911 was first entered upon precisely during these last years of the 19th century.

II. Financial Penetration

One of the results of the aftermath of the Sino-Japanese War was a decisive change for the worse in the financial position of the Ch'ing government. Up to the war the foreign indebtedness of Peking was relatively insignificant; during the period 1864-1894 only 40 million taels of foreign loans had been negotiated. The huge indemnity imposed by the Shimonoseki Treaty created, however, a completely new situation; 230 million taels (£30 million) were to be paid in three years and this could not possibly be met from normal revenues, inasmuch as the yearly income of the Ch'ing government was only between 75 and 80 million taels. Thus, inevitably the Manchus now turned to the foreigners for loans and this, in turn, led to an extremely sharp struggle between the powers as to who was to provide the necessary funds, inasmuch as the benefits, both economic and political, which would accrue from granting loans were quite obvious. In the years 1895-1899 the Ch'ing government borrowed a sum total of 370 million taels and thus reached a state in which practically the entire normal revenue was consumed by the need to cover the interest on these loans. In this process of financial dependence three transactions were most important and deserve separate mention.

Two members of the Triple Alliance, which had brought about the retrocession of Liaotung, Russia and France, took the initiative in providing the funds for the first loan, closely bound up with their plans, especially those of Russia, for the future penetration of China. The loan, granted in July 1895, was for the sum of 400 million francs (almost 100 million taels; £15.8 million), the term was thirty-six years and the interest rate 4 per cent. The Russian Ministry of Finance was the organizer of the loan, i.e. Witte himself was the prime mover, but six French banks subscribed 250 million francs and four Russian banks 150 million francs. The repayment of the loan was to be guaranteed by the customs revenue of the Ch'ing government and the specific feature of this transaction was that the Russian government itself was the guarantor. For future transactions with China, Witte founded in December of the same year the Russo-Chinese Bank, in which five-eighths of the capital was French but majority control of the management was Russian. In this first Russo-French venture the nature of the Franco-Russian alliance—the combination of Russian political influence and power and French financial resources—was already clearly demonstrated.

Both Great Britain and Germany had been left out in the cold in the making of the arrangements for the above loan; this was much resented, especially by Germany, who also had hoped to obtain reward for her participation in the Liaotung intervention. These two powers then engaged in intense diplomatic activity which resulted in their success; they were able to grant the next loan to the Manchus. This was signed on March 25, 1896 and financed by the Hong Kong and Shanghai Bank (the largest British financial institution in the Far East) and the Deutsch-Asiatische Bank. The sum was 100 million taels—£16 million for thirty-six years at 5 per cent interest. The terms were 94 for 100 (i.e. the Ch'ing received 94 million, the rest was taken as the commission by the banks). This loan was also guaranteed by the customs revenue of the Ch'ing government. In connection with this, an important question was now raised which led to much wrangling between the powers—whether the British control of the Customs Service was to be preserved. In spite of all the Franco-Russian efforts, the British were successful in maintaining this vital service in their own hands and Hart remained the Inspector-general until his retirement in 1908.

Although the competition of the French and the Russians was intense, the same British-German banking consortium was successful, probably with the assistance of huge bribes to the appropriate Ch'ing officials, in negotiating the third large loan to the Ch'ing government on March 1, 1898. This was for the same sum as the previous loan, but the terms were much worse. The loan was for forty-five years at 4.5 per cent interest, but it was at 83 for 100. It was guaranteed this time not only by the customs revenue but also by receipts from the salt monopoly and *likin* taxes from a number of areas in the Yangtse Valley. It was in connection with this loan that the British assured themselves of their further control of the Customs Service. But now these customs revenues, in spite of their constant increase (although this was still limited by the lack of tariff autonomy), were only sufficient to service the loans. The financial exploitation involved in these three loans was such that their full repayment would have involved a sum more than double the money that had been effectively obtained by the Ch'ing government.

III. The Expansion of Tsarist Russia

Russia, the initiator of the Liaotung intervention, was also the most successful power in pursuing its new plans for expansion and penetration of the Ch'ing realm. The Russian schemes were intimately bound up with the construction of the Trans-Siberian Railway and the question of its continuation. Already in 1895 Witte, the main driving force in the creation of the Trans-Siberian and the advocate of "peaceful" economic penetration of China, put forth the concept and examined all the possibilities of extending the line further through North Manchuria—a course which would provide a much easier route to Vladivostok, shorter (by 350 miles) than the one following the Amur in Russian territory. The advantages to Russian imperialism from such a plan would be great indeed; its position would be vastly strengthened thereby, and Russia would be prepared for all future alternatives, including a possible partition of China. The railway across Manchuria was also to be one element of "compensation" for the actions of Russia on the Liaotung problem. This issue was now closely bound up with the general question of arranging Sino-Russian relations in the wake of the Sino-Japanese War, when a majority of top Ch'ing leaders, especially Tz'u-hsi and Li Hung-chang, were veering to the idea of forming an alliance with Tsarist Russia.

The negotiations for the Sino-Russian alliance and the building of the extension of the Trans-Siberian across Manchuria were conducted in April-June 1896, during Li Hung-chang's stay in Russia. The question of his trip there is in itself interesting; although his position had been greatly weakened by the outcome of the Sino-Japanese War (he had ceased to be, among others, the Governor-general of Chihli), Li was still a power to be reckoned with in the Ch'ing regime. The Russians made a point of seeing to it that he should be invited to the coronation of the Tsar which was to take place in Moscow in May 1896. Tz'u-hsi agreed to send him, and Li Hung-chang departed with his usual vast suite to Europe by boat. When he reached Suez the Russians were afraid that the other powers would be anxious to be the first to negotiate with him, and thus Witte sent a special ship and an emissary, Prince E. E. Ukhtomsky, the President of the Russo-Chinese Bank and the propagator of Russo-Asian "affinity", to make sure that Li Hung-chang would be brought straight to Russia. There he was met with great pomp and ceremony; what was perhaps more important, he was offered a bribe of 3 million roubles to help achieve an agreement on the question of the extension of the Trans-Siberian Railway.*

In order to take advantage of the current political situation and also to make the Trans-Siberian Railway question more attractive, the Tsarist government offered the Manchus a secret fifteen-year treaty of alliance against aggression by Japan; however, the treaty was drawn up in such a fashion that the alliance would become operative only when the arrangements regarding the railway extension had been approved by Peking, i.e. the contract for the construction of the line concluded. The treaty was signed on June 3, 1896; Witte tells the story vividly, including the amazing contretemps whereby the words "by Japan", which had inadvertently been dropped out of the text, were added literally at the last moment. The agreement regarding the railway—which was to be the famous Chinese Eastern—was signed on September 8, 1896 by the Russo-Chinese Bank and the Ch'ing minister.

In order to keep up the fiction, as requested by Li Hung-chang, that the railway was not to be owned and run by the Russian government, the Russo-Chinese Bank (itself completely under the control of the Russian Ministry of Finance) established, for the purpose of building the railway, a special "private" corporation, the Chinese-Eastern Railway Company, whose shares were all held by the Russian Treasury. The Chinese-Eastern Railway Company was formally the owner of the railroad; after eighty years it was to revert to China, although it could be bought out at the end of thirty-six years;

*Witte denies this in his memoirs by stating that Li Hung-chang did not receive a bribe while in Russia at this time. Formally, this is true since he was paid off later in China. However, Witte also maintained that he bribed Li only once, in 1898—this is quite untrue. In fact, for his services in 1896 Li received, according to the Protocol to the Treaty which was approved by Witte, one million of the promised three—this was paid to him in Peking in May 1897. His death in 1901 saved the Russians from paying the rest of the sum. A special fund of 10 million roubles had been established for the specific purpose of bribing Ch'ing officials. See commentary to Witte's *Memoirs*, Vol. II, p. 588. For the next bribe in 1898, connected with the Port Arthur question, see p. 357.

however, the costs would have been so high, around 700 million roubles, as to have made this impossible. The Company was granted extensive additional rights, among others, the exploitation of minerals in territory adjacent to the line, as well as the maintenance of its own railway guards in this territory, which was completely under its administration. The building of the line, which was in the broad gauge used only by the Russians, was begun in 1897 and finished in 1903. It resulted in a great influx of Russians (along with also a sizeable number of Poles) into Manchuria. The basic line ran from Manchuli through Harbin to Suifenho; it was 970 miles long. Later on, after the Russians had "leased" Port Arthur in March 1898, the second line linking Harbin with Port Arthur was built; this was the South Manchurian Railway, 440 miles long. From the strategic, economic and political point of view the value of the Chinese-Eastern was immense; it made possible the penetration by Russia on a vast scale not only of Manchuria itself, but ultimately of all North China. The railway itself was to appear time and again for over half a century as the object of rivalry and strife in the Far East.

Li Hung-chang's stay in Russia had thus been most profitable for the Russians and for him personally. Before leaving the country he visited the fair at Nizhni Novgorod; there a marvellous scene took place, graphically described by Gorky—Li Hung-chang, openly and unabashedly, tucked away into his silken sleeve a huge emerald, the prize exhibit in one of the pavilions. The Russians did not even murmur. The Chinese-Eastern was worth much more. Later, Li Huang-chang proceeded to Germany, France and England where he was fêted everywhere, but here his successes were rather limited. He failed completely in the official object of the talks held in these three countries—the obtaining of an agreement on raising the customs rate.

Russia's success in the penetration of Manchuria was accompanied at the same time by an almost equal advance in Korea; here, due to the crudity of Japanese methods, the political situation had turned greatly in Russia's favour, after the Korean king took refuge from the Japanese in the Russian mission. The Russians were now able to send in military instructors and financial advisers; this gave them a dominant place in Seoul, which they managed to maintain for the next two years. This strengthened their position *vis-à-vis* Peking still further.

Moreover, the general Russian advance was more than likely co-ordinated with the actions of her ally France, who was also pursuing during the same period intensive diplomatic activity in Peking and was equally busy in extorting new concessions and rights from the Ch'ing government. Some authors even maintain that the plans of Russia and France aimed at eventually joining together their spheres of influence which were now being created—the Russians in the North and North-east, the French in the South-west—by pressing their advance into Central China, i.e. into the Yangtse Valley, which the British had considered up to this moment as their own exclusive preserve. Whatever the case, Russo-French co-operation, both political and financial, was an undoubted factor and the competition of this alliance was taken as a serious threat by the British.

IV. French Expansion

France continued on her campaign to extend her influence in South-west China which had been made feasible in the first place by her conquest and colonization of

Vietnam. The French were, in fact, the first to raise new demands after the Sino-Japanese War and were successful in forcing the Ch'ing government to sign two new conventions in June 1895. One of these provided for a delimitation of the Sino-Vietnamese border in France's favour; the second granted the French, among others, priority in the receiving of mining rights in Yunnan and Liangkwang as well as a general agreement that railroads which were to be built in Vietnam could be extended into Chinese territories in the three provinces. By these moves the French initiated the process of marking out special spheres of influence and the obtaining of exclusive rights of future economic penetration which was to be characteristic of the entire 1895-1899 period and to stimulate intensive competition between the powers in this respect.*

It is characteristic that the French blackmailed the Ch'ing into accepting the above conventions by threatening that otherwise the 400 million franc loan, which had already been arranged, would not be forthcoming. It was also the French who were successful in obtaining, in March 1896, the first concession for the building of a railroad on Chinese territory. This pertained to a small line running from Langson in Vietnam to Lungchow in Kwangsi; its significance obviously cannot be compared at all with that of the Chinese-Eastern, gained a few months later by the Russians. The French followed up this move by obtaining, in June 1897, a further concession for the building of a railroad to Nanning in Kwangsi. This move was accompanied by the French extorting a promise of non-alienation, i.e. equivalent to the recognition of belonging to a sphere of influence, of the island of Hainan. This was also the first move of its kind and was promptly acted upon by the other powers.

In general, the French plans in this period were quite ambitious and far-reaching and aimed at the conversion of Yunnan as well as Liangkwang into a French sphere of influence while, simultaneously, a further advance in the direction of Szechuan was being planned. If this had been accomplished, it would have created a barrier between the British possessions in Burma and their position in the Yangtse Valley. For this reason, the activity of the French met with very strong British opposition, especially as the British were interested in this same area of the South-west to no less a degree. In February 1897 the British demanded and received, as compensation for the concessions that had been made to the French, new rights of their own, among others, the opening of the West River in Kwangtung to foreign trade. While both these countries were successful in extending their penetration of the South-west, their rivalry in this area prevented any clear demarcation of it into British and French spheres. It could be maintained, however, that the influence of the British was stronger in West Yunnan and East Kwangtung while that of the French was stronger in East Yunnan, West Kwangtung and Kwangsi.

Obtaining concessions for the construction of railroads was one of the most significant and certainly one of the most profitable forms of imperialist penetration of China in this period; not only were loans made to the Ch'ing government for this purpose, but the bulk of the equipment to be employed was also imported from abroad. In this field France and Russia were to gain one more significant success, where again

---

*Some authors distinguish the terms "sphere of interest" and "sphere of influence", the former being supposedly less far-reaching in its implication. There seems to be, however, little justification for this distinction. The sphere, whatever it was called, was intended to be but a half-way house on the road to outright annexation.

French money and Russian political pressure were effectively combined. This was the concession for the building of the vital Peking-Hankow line which was of crucial strategic importance. The struggle between all the powers for this right was very bitter; the concession was gained ultimately, after the rejection of an American bid, by a Belgian company. This, however, was only a dummy, inasmuch as 80 per cent of the capital was, in effect, French, while the Russo-Chinese Bank also played a role in this transaction. The first agreement was signed in May 1897 and completed, in spite of determined British opposition, in June 1898. Provision was made for a loan of £4.5 million for the building of the road, and to achieve this agreement the Belgian company also made judicious use of bribes. Now the main recipient was Sheng Hsüan-huai (1844-1916), a prominent Ch'ing official, the principal collaborator of Li Hung-chang in the economic field and the Director-general of the Chinese Railways. His "fee" was 1 million taels; another million went to other officials.

The British, however, were successful in obtaining a number of other important railroad concessions, among others, for the Shanghai-Nanking line, as well as for the extension of the Peking-Shanhaikuan-Newchwang line, the latter being in turn bitterly opposed by the Russians. By November 1898 the total concessions granted by the Ch'ing government (but by no means all of these were to be implemented in the future) were as follows: 2800 miles to the British, 1530 miles to the Russians, 720 miles to the Germans, 650 miles to the Belgians (but see above), 420 miles to the French, 300 miles to the Americans. Anglo-Russian rivalry in this field was also partially settled by an agreement reached on April 28, 1899, in which the two spheres of activity were delimited. The area north of the Great Wall was to be reserved for the Russians and all of China to the south of it for the British. This was, in fact, not only a regulation of the railway problem but also a tacit recognition of their spheres of influence by both the powers.

V. The German Annexation of Kiaochow

In the process of imperialist aggression against China a significant role was played in this period by Germany, a newcomer to this area. After its participation in the Liaotung intervention the German government was also seeking to receive proper "compensation" for its actions. Already by 1895 its stated aim was that of gaining a *point d'appui* in the Far East, by which was meant the acquisition of a proper naval base in China. The Germans were going on the assumption, in Bülow's words, that a "gradual but progressive dissolution of the Chinese Empire" was taking place and they had every intention of making certain that they should get their share of the booty. With their usual thoroughness of organization, all possible alternatives were examined and the subject was also discussed, but without any results, with Li Hung-chang during his visit to Germany in 1896. Finally, the previously mentioned G. Detring advised that the best choice would be Kiaochow (Chiaochou) Bay, inasmuch as it possessed a rich hinterland in Shantung province and a good strategic position which could command all of North China. The German government took the decision to acquire Kiaochow as "suitable as a starting point for the establishment of a German Colonial Territory" already, *nota bene*, on November 29, 1896. Many diplomatic manoeuvres and much pressure was exerted on Peking to obtain this end, but all of it of no avail.

However, fate smiled upon the German government; on November 1, 1897, two

German Catholic missionaries were killed in Shantung by a group of bandits which had plundered the entire village where they lived. The German fleet, which had been ordered into Chinese waters already in September, now swiftly went into action; the Kaiser instructed it to proceed "if necessary, with the most brutal ruthlessness". On November 14 the port and forts of Tsingtao were seized by the Germans; the Ch'ing troops were ordered not to resist this new act of imperialist aggression. By November 20 the German government had made known its first demands to Peking; these included the granting to Germany of priority in mining rights and railway construction in all of Shantung, as well as indemnity and the punishment of those responsible for the death of the missionaries. However, the principal aim of the Germans was to be revealed only in December during the course of the negotiations with the Ch'ing government when the demand for a leasing of Kiaochow was made.

During the period which preceded a final capitulation by Peking on the issue in March 1898, the Ch'ing regime once more based its hopes on the fact that it would be able to utilize the rivalry of the powers to reject Germany's demands; in particular, it counted on obtaining Russian assistance in view of the secret treaty of alliance of 1896. However, once again these hopes proved to be in vain, inasmuch as both the successful diplomacy of the Germans and the stimulation of the appetites of the other powers were such that the Germans were able to obtain, after prolonged diplomatic haggling, the acquiescence in their new conquests of all the powers concerned. The agreement of Russia was obtained by the recognition by Germany of the Russian sphere of influence which was to extend to Manchuria and North China, as well as to Korea. The English, who were by no means particularly alarmed by the German move, inasmuch as they considered it to be directed primarily against Russia, were assured that the Germans had no intentions of threatening the British interests in the Yangtse Valley. Japan was mollified by the German promise that she would not oppose future Japanese expansion in China. Germany herself now claimed all of Shantung as her sphere of influence, while her ambition was to penetrate further inland into the basin of the Yellow River.

The final treaty with Peking was signed on March 6, 1898; Germany was granted a ninety-nine-year lease on Tsingtao and both the capes at the entry of Kiaochow Bay (an area of 200 square miles). A 30-mile neutral zone around this area was established (2740 square miles). The Germans were granted the right to railway construction in Shantung which was utilized by them to build the line from Tsingtao to Tsinan (246 + 38 miles). The case of the two missionaries had been already settled earlier in January, and by now had been quite forgotten by everyone, except their families. The particularly rapacious nature of German imperialism was revealed in the entire affair but especially in the notorious "mailed fist" speech of Kaiser Wilhelm II on December 18, 1897 upon the occasion of the departure of German reinforcements for China; this also reflected his well-known views on the "Yellow Peril".

VI. Further Russian and British Expansion

One of the principal reasons why the Tsarist government had agreed to the German occupation of Kiaochow was that it provided Russia with a convenient pretext for proceeding with her own further imperialist expansion. This was foreseen in the plan presented by M. N. Muraviev (1845-1901), the new Minister of Foreign Affairs since 1897 (grandson of N. N. Muraviev, the Hangman); it was supported by the Tsar and other ministers and presented the aims of the most adventurist Russian imperialist political group. The goal was the total annexation of Manchuria and its conversion into "Yellow Russia" as an integral part of the Russian Empire. With this ultimate purpose in mind it was now decided to occupy Port Arthur amd Talien—both ice-free, unlike Vladivostok which is ice-bound for four to five months—and to obtain a lease on this area similar to that of the Germans in Kiaochow.

The Russian fleet then sailed into Port Arthur in December 1897 with troops aboard, but pending negotiations with the Ch'ing it did not yet occupy the port. At first, Russian diplomats pretended that the presence of the fleet was to protect China and to assist in bringing about a German withdrawal from Kiaochow. The move of the Tsarist government was bitterly opposed by Witte, who considered it a piece of folly, a betrayal of the recently concluded secret alliance with China and a provocation to Japan, which had only two years earlier been deprived of this same territory by the Triple Alliance led by Russia. But being a faithful Tsarist minister, Witte swallowed his objections and his pride and played an instrumental role in the negotiations with Peking, reverting to methods previously employed. He offered and paid Li Hung-chang 500,000 taels (609,000 roubles) and offered the same sum to another important Tsungli Yamen official—Chang Yin-huan (1837-1900); this man, however, was too frightened and received less than one-tenth of the bribe.

The effect was quickly achieved and the lease of Port Arthur and Talien (later called Dalny by Witte) for a period of twenty-five years, renewable if necessary, was signed on March 27, 1898. To the north of the leased area a much larger territory (1350 square miles) was also declared a neutral zone where Chinese troops could enter only with Russian permission (the entire area is also referred to at times as the Kwantung Peninsula). Port Arthur was declared to be a naval base open only to Russian and Chinese ships; Dalny was declared an open port, to avert the complaints of other powers, as had been Tsingtsao. An arrangement also provided for the extension of railway communication from Harbin to Port Arthur. The congratulations of the Kaiser to the Tsar on this occasion were characteristic: "We two will make a good pair of sentinels at the entrance of the Gulf of Peichihli (P'ohai) . . . you are now, morally speaking, the Master of Peking." The German agreement to the Russian move was assured by the previous Russian approval of the occupation of Kiaochow. Japanese acquiescence was obtained by ceding in its favour Russia's position in Korea, by withdrawing Russian financial and military advisers. The British were opposed to this Russian move and had attempted to inveigle the Germans into preventing it, but were unsuccessful.

Both the German and the Russian acquisition of Chinese territory constituted a direct challenge to the predominant position of Great Britain, and the British quickly reacted in attempting to safeguard their stake in China. Already from 1897 onwards the British government had made its first tentative steps to work out a general settlement of the rivalry with Russia, not only in China but on a larger scale. At the same time the English were probing the possibility of reaching an understanding with Germany. They failed in both cases; Russia and Germany exchanged information on the English moves and this did not, by any means, increase confidence in British diplomacy. In respect to China, the policy was to recognize all of China north of the Yellow River as lying within the Russian sphere of influence, in exchange for a Russian recognition of the Yangtse Valley as a British sphere. It was, however, too early to succeed as yet in reaching an agreement and the British proceeded to a simpler solution, to force the Ch'ing regime to issue a declaration of non-alienation of the entire Yangtse Valley area in February 1898, even before the final agreement on Kiaochow and Port Arthur had been reached.

Having thus obtained this recognition by Peking of their own sphere of influence, the British at the same time conducted a policy aimed at the obtaining of "equal opportunities" in the spheres claimed by the other powers, in order to maintain in this way its previous paramount position. They would have preferred, of course, not to have to recognize the spheres of the other powers but had to adjust their policy to suit the changed circumstances. Simultaneously, they followed the same path of "leasing", i.e. the annexation of Chinese territory in two areas. In the North, Great Britain acquired a "lease" on the naval base of Weihaiwei, with a neutral zone around the area (230 square miles). This involved negotiations with Germany, inasmuch as Weihaiwei lay in Shantung, which was now regarded by the Germans as their sphere; the problem was intertwined with that of railway construction and British-German rivalry in this field. Talks were likewise held with Japan which was still occupying Weihaiwei as security for the last payments of indemnity.

The above powers were consulted, but the Ch'ing regime was simply faced, in March 1898, with the demands, which were backed up by the presence of British naval units, and it was thus forced once more to capitulate and to sign on July 1 the lease for Weihaiwei "for as long as Port Arthur should be occupied by Russia". It should be noted in passing that the Russians lost Port Arthur to the Japanese in 1905, but the British stayed in Weihaiwei until 1930. In the South the British considerably enlarged the area of the Hong Kong colony by "leasing" now, for a period of ninety-nine years, the rest of the Kowloon Peninsula (376 square miles as against the originally held 29 square miles).

Other powers rushed into the fray as well. In April 1898 France obtained a ninety-nine-year lease on the area of Kwangchow Bay in West Kwangtung, a non-alienation declaration in respect to Yunnan and Liangkwang, and a railroad concession to Kunming in Yunnan. In the same month Japan forced the Ch'ing regime to issue a declaration of non-alienation for Fukien province, opposite recently conquered Taiwan. Further concessions were also obtained by the powers in the Treaty Ports. The favourite gambit during this period was the demand for "compensation" in respect to concessions offered to another power, allegedly to preserve a balance of benefits gained.

Only one European power, Italy—the weakest of the European imperialists—failed in its attempt in March 1899 to obtain a lease of Sanmen Bay in Chekiang and the recognition of that province as lying within its sphere of influence. The Ch'ing government by this time had had more than enough of the entire business and could afford to reject the Italian claim, for it knew that that country was in no position to enforce its bluster by the use of arms. However, up to this moment the capitulationist policy of the Manchus had gone to the extreme; simultaneously, all its calculations, based on utilizing the rivalries between the powers, had turned out to be a complete fiasco. The Peking regime and its diplomacy were considered by the powers as a negligible quantity, but this did not mean that the powers wished to see it disappear; they were still willing to provide it with the minimum support necessary for maintaining itself in power. The capitulationism of the Ch'ing was not simply the result of the pressure of the powers, but also reflected the desire of the Manchus to retain the support of the latter by proper subservience and by an intertwining of interests.

VII. The United States and the Open Door Policy

Only one major power—the United States—did not participate directly in the "Battle of the Concessions" which raged in the 1895-1899 period. The years 1860-1895 had witnessed a relative decline in American activity and interest in China; this was true of both the economic and political fields. The basic reason for this lay in the absorption of America in her own domestic development, which was marked by the rapid growth of the economy in the post-Civil War decades. This led in turn to the assumption by the United States of its place as the strongest industrial power in the world. These changes were likewise reflected in renewed activity on the Chinese scene and thus a distinct upturn in American trade with China can be noted from 1895 on, after decades of stagnation and even decline. Although the Americans were late-comers in the field, they joined eagerly in the pursuit of railway concessions and competed strongly with the European powers. However, in spite of all their exertions, they were rather unsuccessful and, as noted earlier, ranked lowest in the list of acquired railway rights.

The Spanish-American War with the resulting annexation of the Philippines, as well as the earlier acquisition of Hawaii, marked the new stage in American policy towards China; the United States was rapidly becoming a major power in the Pacific and now possessed bases which could make further expansion in the Far East, especially in China, much more feasible. The attraction of the Chinese market and resources, both natural and human, was no less for the American capitalists than for their European and Japanese rivals, while the process of subjugation of China by the other powers faced the United States government with the problem of formulating a policy which could meet the requirements of facilitating American expansion in China in the circumstances existing at the end of the century.

The above need was partially expressed by the so-called Open Door policy, which was first set forth in the notes sent by John Hay, the Secretary of State, to all the major powers on September 6, 1899. In view of the considerable subsequent myth-making regarding the nature of this policy, it is worth while to examine it more closely. Hay's notes dealt with three points: the desire that the powers should not infringe on the interests of other countries in their spheres of influence, that customs rates should be equal for all, and that no trade discrimination should be practised. There are no political issues, such as the integrity of China, raised in these notes at all. Most of the powers agreed to accept the American viewpoint with the reservation, however, that such an approval must be unanimous; the Russian answer was sufficiently equivocal to have enabled the other powers to consider their acceptance not binding, had they wished to do so. However, Hay chose to regard all the answers, including the Russian, as a full approval of his views and no one particularly bothered to challenge his interpretation as, in fact, very little attention was paid by the powers at the time to this whole American diplomatic manoeuvre.

In many respects the policy enunciated by the United States corresponded closely to that of Great Britain. Its basic assumption was the fullest acceptance of the unequal treaties, which were considered to be binding for China, and the extension of the most-favoured-nation principle to the new situation, created by the spheres of influence and the prospect of the partition of China. In these circumstances, the Americans wished, like the British, to assure for themselves equal opportunities for unhindered economic expansion into the spheres, the existence of which the American government, in fact, recognized. According to some authors the resemblance between the American and British positions was by no means fortuitous; it was the result both of British diplomatic influence and of the developing co-operation of American and British finance in joint enterprises in China. The main significance of the proclamation of the Open Door policy was to mark clearly the arrival on the scene of one more contender in the struggle for the control of China—one whose economic might presaged the fact that her role would be of ever-growing importance in the future.

VIII. General Appraisal

Although many historians show a tendency to depict the actions of one given power as more aggressive and injurious to China than that of other given powers, the choice of the principal villain is, sadly enough, almost always determined in inverse relation to the nationality of the writer. There is, however, no basis in the facts for this type of discrimination; the dismemberment of China seemed to have begun and all the beasts of prey were now drawing in for the final kill (with the only exception of one still too far away, the United States, who, however, made known her demands not to be left out). But, to use Lenin's description made in 1900, the powers had started the partition of China "stealthily like thieves robbing a corpse". However, as events were soon to prove, China was far from dead; it was only the Manchu monarchy that was moribund. The gigantic Chinese nation was beginning to awaken, very slowly it is true, from its deep slumber; the Lilliputians were not going to be able to prance about with their ropes for too long a time.

The envisaged partition of the Middle Kingdom failed to materialize. It should be noted that in all the contemporary writing doubts are never expressed about this fate. Anticipating the narrative to a certain degree, it is worthwhile at this stage to examine the reasons for its survival. One of the major causes was the progressing opposition of the Chinese people to the fate which was being prepared for it by the imperialist powers. It is, of course, true that this opposition at the turn of the century was still largely only latent and its first outward manifestations—such as the anti-foreign movement of the 1890s which culminated in the I Ho T'uan—were to a great degree spontaneous and quite lacking in a clearly formulated programme or conscious leadership. This, in itself, was but a reflection of the nature of Chinese society of the period, although the degree of national consciousness that was present, and especially the feeling of cultural identity and uniqueness, should not be underestimated. A concomitant cause, closely bound up with the first, lay in the very size of the country and the vastness of its population—both these factors rendered the implementation of the partition schemes very difficult indeed. The second major cause was to be found in the ever sharper rivalries of the powers, which for all practical purposes nullified the possibility of arriving at an agreement on this issue. This did not preclude the achievement of a certain unity of views in regards to the continued usefulness of maintaining the Manchu regime in power. Thus, the powers, unable to take the next step in the progress of subjugation of China, i.e. her dismemberment, satisfied themselves basically by preserving the specific status of the country as a semi-colony of all the powers.

CHAPTER 35

The Reform Movement, 1895-1898

I. General Background

The disastrous outcome of the Sino-Japanese War affected not only the position of China in relation to the powers; its consequences in the field of domestic development were of equal or, in the long run, of even greater importance. The threat to the very existence of China, the prospect of imminent partition, now made the question of what policies should be adopted and followed to avoid such a fate one not of academic interest but of vital concern and burning urgency. It became clear to the group of those educated Chinese who reflected on this problem that all the attempts of self-strengthening, of partial and superficial modernization, such as had been carried out in the country by the Li Hung-chang type of official, had proved themselves to be a complete and utter failure.

The series of defeats inflicted upon China by the European powers since the First Opium War was galling enough; it gave rise to the increasingly noticeable stirring of national consciousness already during the war with France. However, the easy victory of the Japanese seemed to be particularly humiliating; here, a neighbouring, small Asian people, somewhat contemptuously regarded as a former pupil of China in acquiring the arts of civilization, had managed to transform itself in an astoundingly brief period of one generation and to become as great a threat to China's integrity as, perhaps even greater than, any of the Western imperialist powers. It is thus against this background of political crisis and demonstrated total incapacity of the Ch'ing regime that the movement which was to culminate in the famous Hundred Days of Reform took shape.

In the half-century which had passed since the First Opium War the isolation of China from the rest of the world had been shattered almost completely; the state of total ignorance of the outside world had also given way, although to a still limited degree, under the pressure of the West. The problems which faced Lin Tse-hsü, of starting almost from scratch to gather information on the enemy he was facing, had been partially solved. By the 1890s a certain amount of knowledge regarding the West and modern Japan was available to those who would wish to make use of it. The crux of the problem, however, lay in whether any use should be made of this knowledge; herein rested one of the basic issues.

The great majority of the ruling class in China, almost the entire Manchu aristocracy and the bulk of the Chinese scholar-officials of gentry origin, still adhered to a completely reactionary position and saw no need to adopt anything that the West had to offer in any field (with the possible exception of military technology), and thus continued to oppose any programme of consistent modernization of the country, the implementation of which would, of necessity, entail a reform of the entire structure, beginning with its political system. Intellectually, this refusal to contemplate change and reform was defended by them as being in harmony with their belief in the superiority of the Chinese way of life in all its aspects. Under the smokescreen of Neo-Confucian platitudes, however, lay the much more basic desire to preserve intact the entire feudal system, with all its corruption, graft and ineptitude, which was, after all, the source of all their wealth and power. The constantly worsening position of China in the face of the growing aggression of the powers did not shake these beliefs to any appreciable degree.

Mention has been made earlier of the advocates of a consistent overall modernization of China and of the reforms which this would necessitate. One of these, Yung Wing, was to reappear again on the scene during the 1890s. Another, whose role is of interest, was Wang T'ao (1828-1897), one of the founders of modern Chinese journalism. Wang had spent over ten years in Hong Kong, among others, working with Legge on the latter's famous translation of the Chinese Classics. He had also stayed in England (1867-1869) and afterwards returned to Hong Kong and Shanghai, where he became active in publishing. Wang T'ao was a prolific writer on many subjects and his articles on things Western are of considerable interest. For China, he advocated a gradual programme of extensive reform which included industrialization. Politically, Wang favoured a transition to a constitutional monarchy of the British type.

It is, however, the activities of the foreign missionaries which undoubtedly contributed the most to the aforementioned increase in the available fund of knowledge relating to the outside world. A number of Chinese newspapers were founded by them during the last two decades of the 19th century and a sizeable number of translations into Chinese of Western works—by no means only religious tracts—was published. The best known perhaps of the missionaries of this period was the Welshman, Timothy Richard (1845-1919), whose contacts with Ch'ing officials were quite extensive and whose influence on the formation and the ideas of the reform movement was considerable. It has been pointed out by some authors, however, that, on the whole, the proselytizing zeal of the missionaries obstructed the effect that they could have had in the dissemination of Western Learning; the great majority of the Chinese scholar-officials distrusted them for this reason, inasmuch as they saw in them a form of competition in the ideological sphere.

It is in this setting that a small group of young intellectuals, almost all of gentry origin, established itself in opposition to the overwhelming majority of their own class and came forth as the advocates of reform and modernization, the programme of which was based, precisely, on the knowledge of the West that had been now made available. The most prominent spokesman of this group was K'ang Yu-wei (1858-1927); his pupil Liang Ch'i-ch'ao (1873-1929) and T'an Ssu-t'ung (1865-1898) were among its most important members. It was by no means fortuitous that most of the group came from Kwangtung and that Canton later became one of the centres of the movement. This was a reflection of the fact that in this area the penetration of Western influence was the strongest. In the case of Kwangtung there was an added factor—it was from this province that the great majority of the Chinese emigration, especially to South-east Asia, originated; its views were more progressive and close contact was always maintained by the emigrants with China.

Kwangtung was always traditionally more anti-Ch'ing than any other part of China. It was also in the Canton area (apart from Shanghai) that it is possible to speak of the beginning of the formation of national Chinese capitalism, as against both the type of government-run enterprises of the past and the activities of the foreign capitalists. The presence of these beginnings was also to make its mark on the programme of the Reform Movement. It is, however, an oversimplification to regard the leaders of this movement as only the spokesmen of the newly arising national bourgeoisie. Their connections with this new phase of economic development were, in reality, non-existent.

While the group referred to above played the most significant and creative role in the Reform Movement, it is also true that a part, although very small, of high Ch'ing court officials was also inclined, after the experiences of 1894-1895, towards a search for means to escape the existing critical situation. The most noted of these was Weng T'ung-ho himself. His position and that of his few followers was intertwined with the continuing struggles between the factions at the court, i.e. between the Northerners (most of whom belonged to the Party of the Empress Dowager) and the Southerners (most of whom supported the Emperor's party). In this conflict foreign policy also played a role; Tz'u-hsi's party was completely pro-Russian, while the Emperor's group was inclined to seek the support of Great Britain and later of Japan. Weng T'ung-ho's principal aim was to strengthen the position of the Emperor and the state and, being basically conservative by nature, he favoured only a gradual, very careful programme of reforms.

II. The Nature of the Reform Programme

K'ang Yu-wei—the intellectual leader and inspirer of the Reform Movement—occupies a place of considerable importance, both in Chinese political development and in the history of Chinese thought. He was born in Kwangtung and came from a well-known family of scholar-gentry. A precocious, brilliant youngster, K'ang received a very thorough traditional Classical education the most important part of which was the six years which he spent with his teacher, Chu Tz'u-ch'i (1807-1882), an eminent eclectic scholar, who inspired K'ang with a passion for the Classics which was never to leave him. Later on, K'ang also acquired a broad knowledge of Buddhist philosophy. In spite of his initial objections, he followed the traditional pattern of taking all the official examinations; by 1895 he had received the highest *chin-shih* degree and had gained a considerable reputation as an outstanding Classical scholar whose views, however, seemed to depart drastically from the accepted orthodoxy. These views were expressed both in his writings and his teaching, for he taught in Canton from 1891 on, gaining fame for his broad and progressive teaching methods, and gathered around him pupils, many of whom, like Liang Ch'i-ch'ao, were to become his followers in the Reform Movement.

The innovatory nature of K'ang Yu-wei's views was expressed in a work published in 1891 entitled "The Forgery of the Classics by the Hsin School". Declaring himself an advocate to the "New Text" School and utilizing his undoubtedly vast erudition, K'ang sought to prove that all the Classics on which Neo-Confucianism was based were, in fact, nothing but forgeries produced for political reasons by Liu Hsin during the Wang Mang period. This theory, which incidentally is incorrect and of which

K'ang Yu-wei was not really the inventor—he employed most of the arguments which had been put forth earlier by "New Text" scholars—was to serve not only the purpose of discrediting and undermining the influence of Neo-Confucian orthodoxy, but also as the basis for the further development of his views, of reinterpreting the role and place of Confucius in Chinese history and ideology.

This first work, which became widely known, already scandalized the great majority of Ch'ing scholar-officials; it was the object of fierce denunciation and persecution, and its printing blocks were ordered to be burned in 1894. K'ang Yu-wei's second work was "Confucius as a Reformer", written in 1892 and widely known before its publication in 1897, which created an even greater furore. In it he developed further the ideas mentioned above and gave a fuller exposition of his philosophical views. K'ang presented Confucius as a "God-like Sage-king", the actual creator of all the Classics; one of his purposes in this was to establish Confucianism, as interpreted by him, as a national cult which could be a rival to Christianity.

More important, however, is K'ang's concept of Confucius himself envisioning an evolutionary progress of human society through the Three Sequences and Three Ages. This, as well as the claim that Confucius invented the myth of the Golden Age to justify the innovations he himself introduced, all served K'ang Yu-wei for his basic aim—to show the inevitability of change and to use the authority of Confucius for the propagation of a reform programme, thus, to have on hand a seemingly unimpeachable orthodox argument for repelling attacks on such a programme by reactionary scholar-officials. K'ang Yu-wei's reinterpretation of Confucianism was undoubtedly a brilliant *tour de force*; it demonstrated at the same time that the hold of Confucian ideology was still sufficiently strong so as to necessitate such an approach, even if only for tactical purposes.

Some authors place K'ang Yu-wei as the last in the line of important Confucian philosophers. There is little doubt that he was himself inclined to this view for, not being overly afflicted with modesty, he regarded himself as a Great Modern Sage, as the new Confucius. However, how much there was really left of traditional Confucianism in K'ang Yu-wei's outlook is an interesting question. Already early in his life he came into contact with Western learning, which he approached with an eager and open mind, reading everything that he could get his hands on in Chinese translations. As a result, his views became something of a synthesis, or perhaps more an eclectic mixture, of both Chinese and European ideas; the former were undoubtedly dominant, while his grasp of the latter was probably somewhat superficial due to the relatively meagre material available to him.

All this is especially true of what is his most interesting and valuable work, the *Ta-t'ung shu* ("The Book of the Great Unity"). While it did not have perhaps as direct a bearing on the Reform Movement as the other works previously mentioned, it nevertheless reveals his ideas most fully, inasmuch as he started working on it already in 1884 and had most of it written by 1887; the final version was not finished until 1902 and it was published in its entirety only after his death. It was well known, however, to his closest pupils and followers. The *Ta-t'ung shu*,* although unfortunately little known, should rank as one of the boldest and most imaginative utopias in world literature. It is a

---

*There are many ways in which the word *ta-t'ung* can be translated—"The Great Commonwealth", "Grand Harmony", "Cosmopolitan Society", "One World", "The Great Togetherness", etc. The words themselves come from the famous passage of the *Li chi*.

truly noble book and K'ang Yu-wei's vision of the future is splendid in its optimism. His One World is a free, classless, democratic society with full public ownership of the means of production and complete equality of the sexes. All the nations have disappeared, all the races have melted together and a universal language is employed. Everything is arranged in much detail in neat symmetrical patterns, very much in the well-field vein. K'ang's concepts are basically original, as the ideas of the European utopians were practically unknown to him. Thus, the great Golden Age, perhaps the best fruit of all Chinese thought, is now placed not so much in the past as in the future.*

So much for the future. It was the present to which K'ang Yu-wei and his followers primarily devoted their attention, with a feeling of intense urgency and mission. The principal *leitmotif* of their thought was "If we cannot change we shall perish". K'ang maintained that: "Those states which undertook reforms became strong while those that clung to the past perished . . . China's present trouble lies in our clinging to old institutions without knowing how to change." One of his basic aims was to gain the ear of the young Kuang-hsü in a way reminiscent of Wang An-shih; K'ang believed that under the conditions of an absolute monarchy this was the only way to put into effect a reform programme. He persisted in presenting his views to the court and wrote at various times seven separate memorials to the Emperor, the first in 1888. However, all the earlier ones were kept back from the ruler by the court officials who were aghast at K'ang Yu-wei's views.

The terms proposed by the Japanese in the Shimonoseki Treaty dismayed most Chinese intellectuals and aroused their patriotic fervour. K'ang Yu-wei was in Peking in May 1895 to take his *chin-shih* examinations; with his pupil Liang Ch'i-ch'ao he wrote the famous "Ten Thousand Word Petition" to the Emperor, which was supported by around 1200 other scholars and signed by over 600 of them, who were present in Peking for this examination. In it, it was proposed not to ratify the treaty (this would have meant, in effect, a continuation of the war), to move the capital to Sian and to initiate a programme of basic reforms. In fact, all the reforms to be promulgated in 1898 were already referred to in this petition, which was a basic document of the Reform Movement.

In view of the prevailing usage the above was in itself a step of completely unprecedented nature. However, this petition was also kept from the Emperor and only a few months later did K'ang Yü-wei succeed, for the first time, in presenting his views to Kuang-hsü in a memorial, which was a recasting of the ideas expressed in the petition. Nevertheless, the reactionary forces in the court, i.e. Tz'u-hsi and her entire entourage, were still too strong for the Emperor to attempt to follow any policy of his own at this time. Kuang-hsü was a man of some intelligence and learning, perhaps somewhat too vacillating in nature, although undoubtedly potentially a much better ruler than any of his immediate predecessors. However, in spite of the fact that he had been allegedly reigning since 1889, all the levers of power were still completely in the hands of the Empress Dowager.

The May petition can be regarded as the actual beginning of the Reform Movement and its influence on the Chinese intellectuals was very far-reaching. It was against this background that the first attempts to organize the Reform Movement began; the most

---

*The generally progressive and humanitarian nature of K'ang Yu-wei's views can be seen also in the fact that he was one of the pioneers in opposing the barbarous custom of foot-binding, which had made cripples of untold millions of Chinese women since the Sung period.

important of these was the establishment in August 1895 in Peking of the *Ch'iang Hsüeh Hui* with several scores of members, of which K'ang Yu-wei and Liang Ch'i-ch'ao were the leaders.* A Shanghai branch of the Society was also founded. The Peking Society, which was supported by a number of high officials, among others, by Yüan Shih-k'ai and Chang Chih-tung, published its own periodical of which Liang Ch'i-ch'ao was the editor.†

Liang Ch'i-ch'ao was also a Kwangtung man of gentry origin. He too had received a thorough Classical education and had shown great capabilities at a very early age. He became K'ang Yu-wei's pupil in the years 1891-1893. Liang demonstrated immense gifts as a writer, especially as a publicist, and was to become perhaps the most influential man in this field in the entire period up to 1911. In the years up to 1898 his views, on the whole, corresponded to those of his teacher K'ang Yu-wei; however, Liang probably advanced faster and further to reach ultimately an abandonment of Confucianism. Just as K'ang, he was also much under the influence of Western Learning, as transmitted by the translations and commentaries of Yen Fu.

The Peking branch of the Society was fairly quickly suppressed by the reactionary court of officials. The Shanghai branch managed, however, to continue its activity in a different form and to begin the publication of the periodical *Shih Wu Pao* ("Current Affairs"), which existed until 1898 and exerted a very considerable influence. It was this form of enterprise—the establishing of Reform Clubs and publications—which formed the main content of the Reform Movement up to June 1898. In the three years, twenty-four such societies, eighteen schools and eight publishing houses were founded and by these means reformist ideas were spread to ever-wider circles of intellectuals. One of the most important was the periodical published in Tientsin, in which Yen Fu participated. In 1897 he published in it his famous translation of Huxley's *Evolution and Ethics*, a work which made an immense impact on its readers. Yen Fu, who was an admirer of Spencer, embellished his translations, which were in the Classical style, with extensive commentaries, in which he expounded his own views on Western Learning, especially his leanings to Social Darwinism. Yen Fu's translations (he later also rendered works of Montesquieu, Adam Smith, J. S. Mill) opened the window of China to European thought, and his influence in these years was as great as that of the talented propagandist work of Liang Ch'i-ch'ao. Yen Fu, while sympathetic to the general ideas of reform, remained, nevertheless, on the sidelines and never became an active participant of the movement.

One of the most rapidly developing reformist groups in this period was in Hunan and its activity was to a large degree connected with that of T'an Ssu-t'ung, certainly one of the ablest and most progressive, as well as perhaps the most attractive of the reformist leaders. T'an was a native of this province, the son of a high official. He also had received the customary Classical education, but his independent spirit and intellectual curiosity

---

*A literal translation is Strengthening Study Society; the actual meaning would be National Rejuvenation—while the Study Society could be rendered as the Reform Club.

†Chang Chih-tung also posed as being in favour of reform; in 1898 he published under his name the very well-known work "Exhortation to Study" which was widely distributed. While stressing the need for more education and favouring economic development Chang, in fact, opposed the reform ideas put forward by the K'ang Yu-wei group, upheld Ch'ing absolutism and favoured a revival of Confucianism. His early support of the reformers turned to virulent opposition. When Tz'u-hsi suppressed the Reform Movement, Chang, always a trimmer, was one of the first to congratulate her and urge her to severe measures. As to the true nature of Yüan Shih-k'ai's "progressiveness", see p. 370.

did not incline him to follow the usual path of an official career. His reading was broad and his interest in Western Learning dated from his early youth. T'an was also of a speculative turn of mind, a talented writer with a taste for philosophical inquiry. His work *Jen hsüeh* ("The Study of Humanity", perhaps "On Humanitarianism"), written in 1896, also entitles him to a place in the history of Chinese thought. It is likewise, in its own way, an attempt at a synthesis of Buddhism, Confucianism, Christianity and Western science, a curious mixture in which the most modern ideas are to be found side by side with a belief in the validity and profundity of the Book of Changes. But T'an Ssu-t'ung did reject a large part of the Confucian ballast, particularly everything pertaining to its sanctioning of existing feudal relations, especially as applied to the family.

T'an Ssu-t'ung came under the influence of K'ang Yu-wei's views in 1895 and thereafter considered himself his follower. He was instrumental in propagating the views of the reformers in Hunan; here, with the help of a number of relatively progressive high officials, including the governor, Ch'en Pao-chen (1831-1900), the *Nan Hsüeh Hui* (Southern Study Society) was established in 1897. It was to gather all those favouring reform in South China and by 1898 had around 1000 members. In Ch'angsha the reformers also set up a school—the Academy of Current Affairs—where Liang Ch'i-ch'ao became the principal lecturer; a newspaper was published as well, the first in Hunan, to disseminate their views. In his political outlook T'an Ssu-t'ung was also influenced by Wang Fu-chih, and this was reflected in his strong anti-Manchu views, as distinct from both K'ang Yu-wei and Liang Ch'i-ch'ao, who favoured Manchu-Chinese co-operation. In general, T'an was definitely more inclined to democratic ideas than the other reform leaders and even contemplated doing away with the monarchy. It is characteristic that he sympathized with the anti-Ch'ing aims of the Taipings. Likewise, he was more far-reaching in his advocacy of a really thorough-going programme of reforms, of a complete modernization, i.e. "Westernization", of China in all fields, especially the political. The Hunan reform movement became the object of particularly strong hatred on the part of the majority of the gentry of that province, as was to be demonstrated by its later fate.

The political platform of the reformers was relatively limited; their vision of modernization in this field did not go beyond the limits of a constitutional monarchy. In this respect, just as in many others, the basic model for the K'ang Yu-wei group was post-Meiji Japan and the reforms of Peter I. K'ang had written books on both of these subjects; in 1898 he presented them to Kuang-hsü, who read them attentively. In his January 29, 1898 Memorial to the Emperor, K'ang wrote: "I beg Your Majesty to adopt the purpose of Peter the Great of Russia as our purpose and to take the Meiji Reform of Japan as the model for our reform. The time and place of her reforms are not remote and her religion and customs are somewhat similar to ours. Her success is manifest; her example can be easily followed."

In the conditions of the Ch'ing absolute monarchy, however, even such a programme was a great step forward and presented a profound challenge to the ruling class and its vested interests. The limitation of the reformist programme extended also to the mode of action; basically, the aim, as shown by the model of Japan, was that all the changes were to be introduced by the ruler himself. Thus, it was conceived of strictly as a revolution from above; within this concept the idea of a Palace *coup d'état*, bearing in mind the relation of forces at the Peking court, was perhaps also not far from the minds of the reformers. There was little place in the plans of the reformers for a mass action or large-scale participation of the people, certainly none for a peasant revolt on the Taiping model. This was not fortuitous, for K'ang Yu-wei himself came from a family that had been prominent in helping to put down the Taiping movement. Nor, consequently, did the programme envisage any fundamental changes in agrarian relations, i.e. in the very basis of Chinese feudal society. In its economic proposals, however, much attention was paid to measures which would have facilitated the development of Chinese national capitalism and would have enabled it to compete with imperialist penetration and influence.

One of the principal aims of the reformers was to prevent the imminent dismemberment and the disappearance of China as an organized political entity. In this respect K'ang Yu-wei often pointed to the fate of other countries, such as India. He also referred a number of times, as did Liang Ch'i-ch'ao, to the fate of Poland who had failed to reform herself at the proper time. K'ang Yu-wei wrote a special work entitled "Notes on the Partition and Fall of Poland", which he submitted to the Emperor in July 1898. In the preface to it he wrote: "I cannot read the history of Poland quietly and am impelled from time to time to cease reading, inasmuch as tears pour down from my eyes. I lived through the tragic fate of the Polish nation and king, and thought of the future of China."

The reformers thus opposed the aggression of the powers. Nevertheless, they felt that China was still too weak to be able to meet this threat solely by her own forces. Therefore they sought to find allies amongst the powers, i.e. to utilize the support of those whom they considered less dangerous at the moment—England and Japan—against the power they regarded as the greatest danger—Tsarist Russia. Simultaneously, they were very critical of the previous Ch'ing foreign policy of seeking to play on the rivalries of the powers. The alliance which Tz'u-hsi and her entourage had concluded with the Russians and the support of the latter for the Ch'ing regime was of course the main reason why the K'ang Yu-wei group, as well as the Emperor's party, took an anti-Russian position. Their naive hopes for support from the British and the Japanese, in spite of expressions of some interest and even sympathy on the part of the latter, proved—at the time when such help could have been useful—to have been in vain. However, the reformers had made a great step forward in overcoming the Middle Kingdom complex and in realizing that China was now but one of many countries in the world and surrounded, to boot, by states much stronger than herself.

III. The Hundred Days of Reform

It was the next phase of imperialist aggression against China—the German seizure of Kiaochow and the Russian annexation of Port Arthur—which, by emphasizing the threat to the country's very existence, gave rise to a new upsurge of the Reform Movement. K'ang Yu-wei proceeded to Peking in December 1897 and submitted another extensive memorial, his fifth, to the Emperor, in which he called for the immediate launching of a Reform programme. This was still too bold for the officials to dare even to transmit it. However, his next, the sixth, was somewhat toned down and some high court officials of the Emperor's party now saw to it that the memorial finally reached the Emperor.

The most active of the Reformers gathered in Peking; here, in April, they organized the *Pao Kuo Hui* (Save the Country Society), the activity of which rapidly spread to other principal cities. Although its membership was relatively limited and it soon found itself the object of attacks by reactionary officials, this Society had all the hallmarks of a political party. A number of the leading Reformers, including K'ang Yu-wei, were now given posts as junior officials in the government and were thus in a somewhat better position to attempt to present their views to the Emperor. On June 11 Kuang-hsü issued his first famous edict proclaiming the necessity of initiating a series of reforms. This edict marked a beginning of the Hundred Days of Reform—one of the most dramatic and significant episodes in modern Chinese history.

On June 16 K'ang Yu-wei was received for the first time by the Emperor; the audience lasted an unprecedented two and a half hours. The result, among others, was that now the influence of the Reformers became paramount with the 27-year-old ruler. An entire series of over sixty edicts, prepared by them and proclaimed by Kuang-hsü, now issued forth in an unceasing stream; in them almost the entire programme found its expression. The edicts dealt with practically all the aspects of the Ch'ing government and administration. They called for the change of the existing examination system—the abolition of the "eight-legged" essay, and for the establishment of new schools and of a new system of education, including the founding of a university in the capital, to be based on Western Learning along with the Chinese Classics. The central administration was to be reorganized, a multitude of sinecure posts was to be abolished, the worthless Banner Armies were to be reduced in size, while the parasitic Manchu Bannermen were to be given permission to work for a living. Simultaneously, the economic development of the country was to be stimulated, among others, by the establishment of a Board for Mining and Railways, as well as a Board for Agriculture, Industry and Trade. A Government Translation Bureau was founded to make Western Learning available, Government finances were to be subjected to strict control and auditing. A National Militia was to be formed and the entire defence system reorganized. Freedom of association and publishing was to be assured, while the right of appeal and direct petition to the Emperor was to be guaranteed.

However, although many political matters were dealt with in the edicts, there was insufficient time to formulate the main political aim of the Reform—the declaration by the Emperor of a constitution and the calling of a parliament which would inaugurate the new constitutional monarchy. Generally speaking, it was the extension of democratic freedoms—against the background of Ch'ing autocracy—which formed the most outstanding characteristic of the Reform edicts.

The Emperor and his group of reformist advisers could issue the edicts; their implementation was another matter. With the exception of Hunan, all the high officials of the other provinces paid only lip service to them, if that, and did nothing to carry them into effect, waiting for the outcome of the struggle for power in Peking, which they were quite certain would take place. The Emperor was well aware of this, and over twenty edicts were issued against the officials who were sabotaging the Reform programme.

In fact, the reactionary party, headed by Tz'u-hsi, began to prepare its countermoves from the very outset of the reform period. Already on June 15 the Empress Dowager forced the Emperor to acquiesce in the dismissal of his most trusted supporter among the high officials—Weng T'ung-ho. At the same time she placed her longtime favourite, Jung-lu, in the position of Governor-general of Chihli and commander of the three

Peiyang armies in that province. These were the Kansu army under the command of Tung Fu-hsiang (1839-1908), the Wu I army under Nieh Shih-ch'eng (d. 1900) and the New Army of Yüan Shih-k'ai. The last of these was the most important, inasmuch as it was the only one which was relatively well equipped with modern arms and trained according to the European model. Simultaneously Tz'u-hsi still retained complete control of the main government organ, the Grand Council, where the majority of members were her reactionary henchmen, such as the Manchus Kang-i and Yü-lu.

In an attempt to circumvent these officials, Kuang-hsü appointed four young Reformers as secretaries to the Grand Council—Yang Jui (1857-1898), Lin Hsü (1875-1898), Liu Kuang-ti (1859-1898) and T'an Ssu-t'ung—to take the work of the Council into their hands. The moving spirit of this group, and the boldest of all the Reformers, was T'an Ssu-t'ung. It should be noted that all the Reformers—with the sole exception of Kuang-hsü himself—were Chinese, while the mainstay of Tz'u-hsi's faction were mostly Manchu high officials.

Kuang-hsü and the Reformers were not unaware of the dangers facing them and of the schemings of the reactionaries. The thought was broached of moving the capital to an area close to Shanghai, in order to escape from the reactionary milieu of Peking; this, assuredly, would have strengthened the position of the Reformers and of their "sinicized" Emperor. They saw, correctly enough, that one of their basic weaknesses lay in their lack of military strength. To remedy this a plan was conceived at first to organize a special Imperial Guard; then it was thought advisable to seek the aid of Yüan Shih-k'ai, whose alleged progressive views, as well as his strategic position as the Commander of the New Army, seemed to augur well for the Reformers' hopes. The urgency of the situation was clearly emphasized by a memorandum of one of the censors, presented on September 11 at the instigation of the reactionaries, calling for the arrest and execution of the main Reformers—K'ang Yu-wei and Liang Ch'i-ch'ao.

In reality plans had already been well advanced to carry out a dethronement of Kuang-hsü in October during a trip to Tientsin. The Emperor also learned of this and on September 14 he turned to his Reformer advisers to devise a way out of the emergency. The plan to utilize Yüan Shih-k'ai was set into motion. On September 16 Yüan Shih-kai was received in audience by the Emperor; he promised his full, loyal support to the ruler and was promoted to Board Vice-President in charge of military training. However, the wise and sound appraisal of this man made earlier by Weng T'ung-ho, who had found him to be "vain and insincere", went unheeded.

On September 18 T'an Ssu-t'ung held a secret meeting on instructions of the Emperor with Yüan and requested him to use his armed forces for assisting the Emperor against the plots of the reactionaries, among others, by killing Jung-lu and bringing his own army to Peking to render Tz'u-hsi powerless.* Yüan Shih-k'ai pretended to agree and promised his obedient assistance. Then he quickly scurried off to Tientsin where he revealed the entire plan to Jung-lu. The latter immediately telegraphed Tz'u-hsi and then hurried by train to Peking with picked troops. The whole reactionary coterie was gathered by Tz'u-hsi at her residence in the Summer Palace and now "requested" her to assume once more control of the government.

In the early dawn of September 21, Tz'u-hsi, accompanied by Li Lien-ying and Manchu guardsmen, proceeded to the Imperial City in Peking, which had already been

---

*There are two quite different accounts of this meeting: one by Yüan Shih-k'ai, another from the pen of Liang Ch'i-ch'ao, the latter being undoubtedly much closer to the truth.

surrounded by troops faithful to Jung-lu. Kuang-hsu, not suspecting that he had been betrayed, was arrested, as were those of his entourage who had remained faithful to him. He was then imprisoned for the rest of his life in a small pavilion on a lake within the palace grounds. The order was also issued immediately for the arrest and execution of all the Reform leaders. K'ang Yu-wei, who had left Peking one day earlier at the Emperor's urging, managed to escape with the help of the British; Liang Ch'i-ch'ao also succeeded in evading capture with the assistance of the Japanese. The others, however, were soon caught; T'an Ssu-t'ung refused to seek flight, although he had the opportunity. He first sought unsuccessfully to rescue the Emperor from captivity and then calmly awaited arrest and certain death, declaring that: "No one has yet shed his blood for the Reforms— without this there is no hope for a new China; I shall be the first to do so."

In the early morning hours of September 28, T'an and five others—Yang Jui, Lin Hsü, Liu Kuang-ti, Yang Shen-hsiu (1849-1898, one of the Reformist censors) and K'ang Kuang-jen (1867-1898, Yu-wei's younger brother)—were executed by the Manchus, to take their place in Chinese history as the six *Chün-tzu* or six Martyrs of the 1898 Reform. All the other participants who did not manage to escape were also arrested and sentenced to long terms of imprisonment or exile. Within the next month all the Reforms which had been postulated in the edicts were abolished. The full sway of the reactionaries was again re-established; Jung-lu, Yüan Shih-k'ai and the other conspirators in the plot were suitably rewarded.

IV. The Aftermath of the Hundred Days

The Reform Movement failed due to a number of causes; one of the principal reasons was the great opposition to its programme which it aroused among the vast majority of the scholar-official class, whose vested interests in the maintenance of the existing *status quo* were directly endangered by its proposals. Liang Ch'i-ch'ao summarized this as follows: "The Reforms hurt the feelings of several hundred members of the Hanlin Academy, several thousand *chin-shih*, several scores of thousands of *chü-jen*, and several millions of *hsiu-ts'ai* and licentiates. Those people joined together to attack the Reforms." But it was not so much the hurt feelings as the threat to their "rice bowls" which determined the opposition of this powerful group—the existing and future bureaucracy, i.e. the whole Establishment of the Ch'ing absolutist monarchy. The Manchu aristocracy and high officials were clearly no less alarmed at the challenge to their rule implied by the Reform programme, which they regarded as a plot of the Chinese to put an end to Manchu dominance, in spite of the fact that the Reformers—as distinct from the revolutionary movement—did not advocate this, and rather called for a union of Chinese and Manchu in line with their confused ideas of acting in defence of the "yellow" race.

The weaknesses of the Reformers were derived primarily from the consciously restricted nature of their programme, from the unwillingness of the Reformers to base themselves on any broad popular support, which would entail the possibility of setting into motion an agrarian movement. Such a prospect was far from the minds of K'ang Yu-wei and his followers. Having sought to carry out a revolution from above, the Reformers also proved unsuccessful in their attempts to gain support of any significant part of the Establishment and of the ruling class and thus found themselves isolated and open to counter-attack by the reactionary party and to a crushing defeat.

The attitude of the powers to the Reform Movement during the Hundred Days was, to say the least, ambivalent. On the whole, they inclined to prefer the maintenance of the *status quo*, to have to do with such "statesmen" as Li Hung-chang, who were willing to play, as has been well said, the role of a Porfirio Diaz, i.e. to keep order internally while assuring and facilitating the continuous political and economic penetration of the country by foreign interests. The Russians were particularly concerned in preserving the maintenance in power of Tz'u-hsi's party which they considered, correctly, to be their subservient client. While the British and the Japanese did have some contacts with the Reform Movement, which they would have utilized for their own benefit had the K'ang Yu-wei group managed to gain real power, they gave it little real support, criticized rather sarcastically the rapidity of the Reformers' actions, and then gave their blessings to Tz'u-hsi's coup, after is success. The effective implementation of a general programme of modernization which would have resulted in a real strengthening of China was the farthest thing possible from the minds of the foreign statesmen and one which they would have joined in opposing.

After their escape, both K'ang Yu-wei and Liang Ch'i-ch'ao took refuge in Japan, where for a time they continued their political activities; their defeat had not caused them to change their position. K'ang Yu'wei, with a price of 100,000 taels on his head offered by Tz'u-hsi, remained, in particular, adamant in his advocacy of a constitutional monarchy and opposed the revolutionary programme calling for an overthrow of the Ch'ing autocracy and the establishment of a Chinese Republic, put forth by Sun Yat-sen. He opposed likewise all plans for co-operation with Sun and his followers and proceeded to establish the *Pao Huang Hui* (Protect the Emperor Society) which became very active among the Chinese living abroad, competing, at first quite successfully, with Sun's organization.

The aim of K'ang Yu-wei's organization was, among others, literally to protect the life of the Emperor, which was in imminent danger inasmuch as Tz'u-hsi's party was ready to do away with him at any moment had it not been afraid of the political consequences, as well as to plan a restoration of Kuang-hsü to power. The last action of any great significance in this period of the *Pao Huang Hui* was the plan conceived and led by T'ang Ts'ai-ch'ang (1867-1900), a friend of T'an Ssu-t'ung for a rising in support of the Emperor in the Yangtse Valley provinces. This was preceded by a meeting in Shanghai, in July 1900, of the main Reform leaders present in China, where a parliament was nominated with Yung Wing elected as president, Yen Fu as vice-president and T'ang as general secretary. An armed force for the rising, the Army of Independence, was prepared and co-operation established with the secret societies, especially the Ko Lao Hui.

Inadequate precautions led to a discovery of the plan and the main leaders of the movement were arrested in August 1900; T'ang Ts'ai-ch'ang and nineteen of his followers were secretly executed on the orders of Chang Chih-tung, who was now busy currying favour with Tz'u-hsi. A large number of other Reformers in Hupei, around a hundred, as well as the most prominent members of the movement in Hunan, also close to a hundred, were likewise put to death. All of them were progressive intellectuals, the first, after the Six Martyrs, of the long line of those who during the next half-century were to give their lives for the emancipation of their country.

The Reform Movement had met with complete defeat. Nevertheless, its place in modern Chinese history is of vital significance, due to its bold criticism of the Ch'ing feudal autocracy and its struggle against the further subjugation of China by the imperialist powers. The fate of the movement provided much food for thought for the best minds of China who learned from its mistakes and limitations; they were to gather around Sun Yat-sen and his revolutionary, republican programme. The bravery and idealism of such of the Reformer leaders as T'an Ssu-t'ung became a prime source of inspiration to future generations of Chinese revolutionaries.

CHAPTER 36

The I Ho T'uan Movement

I. General Background

At the end of the 19th century China under Ch'ing rule faced an ever-growing crisis resulting from a number of factors. The suppression of the Reform Movement had meant the restoration of the completely reactionary rule of the Empress' Party and had led the Ch'ing regime into a domestic political impasse. Simultaneously, the constant and increasing pressure of the powers in the years following the Sino-Japanese War had a two-fold effect—of further undermining the prestige of Manchu rule and of arousing an ever-greater opposition of the Chinese population, especially in those areas where foreign penetration was now most active. This opposition, in turn, was further stimulated by numerous economic difficulties, many of them precisely the result of foreign penetration. Thus, for example, the burden of the indemnitites had been shifted to the populace by means of increased taxation, while the government itself, in fact, faced total bankruptcy. At the same time, during the last three years of the century, North China was visited by a series of natural disasters, such as the very severe flooding of the Yellow River in 1898, which created famine conditions. All this tended to bring about disaffection on a vast scale among the peasantry of this area—this was especially marked in Shantung, known for its rebellious past—giving rise to increased activity of the secret societies, the traditional form of peasant revolt.

What was characteristic of this period, however, is that while in the past such activity was always directed primarily against the government and the gentry in the countryside, this time, due to the increase in the aggressive acts of the powers, the popular movement of discontent was directed also against the foreigners. In the last decade there had been many examples of this, such as the widespread anti-missionary riots in the Yangtse area in 1891, similar ones in Szechuan in 1895 and in a number of other provinces in 1898 and 1899. Basically, the movement against the foreigners was a spontaneous reaction against the depredations of the powers, a patriotic form of defending the country, faced with the prospect of partition, a reflection of a growing feeling of national consciousness.

The anti-foreign aspect of the peasant movement also assumed an anti-Christian hue and this too was a new phenomenon. There is little doubt that to the vast bulk of the North China peasants the activities of the missionaries was the main, probably the only, type of foreign penetration with which they came into direct contact; thus, the general resentment against the imperialist intrusion could not but assume, at the same time, an anti-Christian character. In the minds of most Chinese Christianity and its advocates were discredited by their intimate association with the foreign powers and their aggression. All the negative aspects of missionary activity mentioned earlier, which had led to the Tientsin Incident of 1870, were still present but on a much greater scale, inasmuch as their scope, as well as the number of Christian converts, had considerably increased in the last three decades of the 19th century. By 1898 there were 4600 missionaries in China—almost 3900 Protestant, the rest Roman Catholic; the number of Chinese Christians was estimated at 700,000, half a million of whom were Catholics. Thus, now considerably greater grounds existed for conflict between the missionaries and their converts and the overwhelming non-Christian majority of the population.

II. The Origins and Nature of the I Ho T'uan

The activity of the peasant secret societies had been, as we had seen, a marked feature of conditions under Ch'ing rule from the end of the 18th century. While the Manchus had been successful in suppressing the revolts led by these societies, they had never been able to exterminate them entirely, in particular, because the social conditions which had brought about their existence never changed. Thus, both the type of organization and ideology which was prevalent in these societies continued to exist, although deeply underground, ready to rise again to the surface when the situation became once more sufficiently critical, and such was definitely the case in the years 1897-1899.

The society which was now to play a prominent role was the I Ho Ch'üan whose origins dated back to the 18th century.* The I Ho Ch'üan, according to most authorities, was itself an offshoot of the famous White Lotus and its activity spread to exactly the same areas in which the White Lotus had been present in earlier periods, also to the territory that had been the main stronghold of the Nien Movement, of which the I Ho Ch'üan considered itself the heir. The ideology of I Ho Ch'üan was fairly typical of the older peasant secret societies—a curious blend of popular beliefs, mostly of Taoist and Buddhist origin, with a considerable presence of superstitious and magical practices, including charms and incantations, as well as physical and spiritual exercises which were supposed to result in invulnerability and immortality for its practitioners. It was the physical exercises which also included the practice of callisthenics (of which judo is, in fact, a descendant), as well as the word *ch'üan*—"fist"—in their title which gave rise to the name applied by the Europeans to this movement—the Boxers.

In its initial stages the I Ho Ch'üan, which became particularly widespread in Shantung, remained, on the whole, close to the pattern of previous peasant movements of this type in being both anti-dynastic and anti-feudal. However, as noted above, from its very beginnings it took on also the character of being both anti-foreign and anti-Christian. In time, it was this new feature which was to become the dominating trait of the movement, but this change did not, by any means, occur spontaneously; it was rather the result of the policies of a number of Ch'ing officials who wanted to utilize the anti-foreign aspect of the movement to divert it from attacks on the dynasty to action against the foreigners.

In its social composition the I Ho Ch'üan remained basically a peasant movement, although there was undoubtedly also some participation of other elements, such as ex-soldiers, urban poor and even some gentry. Its fighting units were composed almost

---

*The usual literal translation, not particularly fortunate, is Righteous and Harmonious Fists; it would be better to say "Harmonious Brotherhood or Society". In Russian, it is rendered as "Fists in the Name of Peace and Justice".

entirely of young peasant lads, well under 20, sometimes as young as 12 and 13. A unique characteristic was the existence of separate units of young girls. The military organization of the I Ho Ch'üan in its early stages, for that matter throughout much of its history, was on the whole quite primitive, while its equipment, mostly pikes and swords, was totally inadequate.

When first faced with the presence of the I Ho Ch'üan, the Ch'ing officials, on the whole, tended to regard it as but one more peasant revolt to be suppressed by the usual methods, i.e. military force. This was especially true of the initial period, when the movement under its original leaders adhered to a programme of struggle against both the Manchu dynasty and the foreigners. The anti-foreign aspect of the movement became especially strong in Shantung, the main area of I Ho Ch'üan activities, because this province was the scene of new aggression by the German imperialists, whose arrogant and brutal behaviour added fuel to anti-foreign sentiments. A considerable number of Ch'ing officials in this area were little less anti-foreign than the I Ho Ch'üan and this was particularly true of the Manchu imperial clansman, Yü-hsien, the Governor of Shantung from March 1899.

As the I Ho Ch'üan spread throughout the province, burning churches, attacking and killing Chinese Christians, some attempts were made by Ch'ing officials to suppress the movement. However, by October 1899, when a clash between the I Ho Ch'üan and Ch'ing troops took place in the town of P'ingyüan, there were already signs of a significant shift of policy towards the I Ho Ch'üan on the part of the Ch'ing authorities to one of toleration and even support. Such change was undoubtedly not undertaken without the knowledge and approval of Peking itself. The results of this shift were to be of crucial importance, especially after the arrest and execution of the original anti-dynastic leaders of the movement. The bulk of the remaining I Ho Ch'üan was now willing, undoubtedly under the inspiration of Ch'ing officials, to alter their slogans from anti-dynastic ones to the famous *Fu Ch'ing, mieh yang* ("Support the Ch'ing Exterminate the Foreigners"). However, a part of the I Ho Ch'üan, as well as the still extant original White Lotus, remained opposed to the Ch'ing and persisted in their attempts to overthrow Manchu rule.

It was also at this time that the name of the movement was changed, probably by Yü-hsien himself, from I Ho Ch'üan to I Ho T'uan; the word *t'uan,* meaning unit or band, implied in this case that the organization had semi-official status, similar to a local militia (almost always gentry-led), which was occasionally authorized by Ch'ing authorities and whose existence was once more sanctioned in 1898. Nevertheless, this change in policy was by no means a simple matter inasmuch as, on the one hand, there was no unity of views regarding the policies to be pursued towards the I Ho T'uan among the ruling group in Peking and, on the other hand, the question of the I Ho T'uan and the attitude towards them became a prime issue in the relations between the Ch'ing government and the powers.*

III. The Ch'ing Government, the Powers and the I Ho T'uan

The situation at the court was further complicated after the suppression of the

*It is worth noting that during the so-called Cultural Revolution of 1966-1968, the Red Guards were told to consider the I Ho T'uan as their spiritual ancestors—Tientsin, for example, was plastered with coloured posters to this effect.

Reform Movement by Tz'u-hsi's new schemes aimed againt the Emperor. Having abandoned her original idea of disposing of him altogether by a convenient illness, Tz'u-hsi now adopted a plan, probably that of Jung-lu, of nominating an heir-apparent to the throne—one P'u-chün, the son of Tsai-i, Prince Tuan. This was accomplished in January 1900, and the dethronement of Kuang-hsü was planned for February of the same year. However, the plan was upset by strong protests of the Chinese both within China and abroad (these organized by K'ang Yu-wei's "Protect the Emperor Society") and the negative attitude of the powers who were not in favour of overly strengthening the power of Tz'u-hsi. This increased the bitter anti-foreign sentiments of the Empress' Party—always present, in spite of subservience, and resembling the resentment of a servant towards a demanding master—especially of its most reactionary members, in particular of Tsai-i, now disappointed in his hopes of having his son ascend the Imperial Throne. It was against this background that the idea of utilizing the I Ho T'uan against the foreigners gained ground in Peking; nonetheless, a considerable part of the Ch'ing officials maintained that the I Ho T'uan were basically rebels and ultimately a danger to the dynasty and should, therefore, be suppressed. Others, such as Jung-lu, then commander in chief of the Northern army, vacillated and were afraid to take any stand. As a result of these different tendencies, the policy of Peking became contradictory and undecided throughout most of this crucial period.

A very important factor in bringing about an aggravation of the situation, which ultimately was to result in open warfare between the powers and China, was the constant pressure exerted on the Manchu government by the diplomatic corps in Peking. From November 1899 on, the representatives of the powers continued to demand that the Ch'ing government suppress the I Ho T'uan because of its anti-foreign activities, as well as punish officials for the failure to put down the movement. As a result of this pressure, for example, Yü-hsien was recalled from Shantung on December 7, and Yüan Shih-k'ai was sent to replace him as acting governor with orders to put down the I Ho T'uan. Yüan, always the scheming seeker for power, utilized the occasion both to ingratiate himself with the foreigners and to increase his own strength. Having transferred his own army to Shantung—the only really well-equipped and trained unit in all of China—he proceeded to smash the I Ho T'uan by means of wholesale massacres, a task not too difficult considering the discrepancy of arms. This done, Yüan then increased the size of his own armed forces, as well as his personal fortune.

The defeated remnants of the I Ho T'uan now fled to the north to enter the metropolitan province of Chihli, where they rapidly increased in strength in spite of the initial opposition of Ch'ing officials. Thus, the problem of what policy should be employed towards them was posed before the Peking government still more sharply. To show her resentment of increasing foreign pressure Tz'u-hsi found a new post for Yü-hsien; he was sent to be the governor of Shansi, where he was later directly responsible for the murder of a large number of defenceless foreigners, almost half of all those who lost their lives in the ensuing holocaust. However, it should be noted that, in spite of the spread of I Ho T'uan anti-foreign and anti-Christian activity, first in Shantung and then in Chihli, only one foreigner was killed up to the end of May 1900; this was the Anglican missionary, S. M. Brooks, murdered in Shantung at the end of December 1899 and, at that, not by the I Ho T'uan, but by members of another secret society. On the other hand, the burning of churches, pillaging and killing of Chinese Christians was carried out wherever the I Ho T'uan came.

After the death of Brooks and the entry of the I Ho T'uan into Chihli the demands of the diplomatic corps in Peking for action against the I Ho T'uan by the Manchu government constantly increased. On January 26 notes were sent to the Ch'ing government by the powers insisting that membership in the I Ho T'uan be declared a criminal offence and that steps be taken immediately to suppress the movement. Further *démarches* followed in February and March and already by March 7 the diplomats in Peking were suggesting to their governments that a proper demonstration of strength—the bringing of naval forces to Taku—was imperative to exert the necessary pressure on the Manchus.

Against the background of these incessant demands of the powers, the policy of the Ch'ing government was still vacillating and contradictory; the reactionary group headed by Tsai-i, Kang-i—Jung-lu's bitter rival and the most vehement of the members of the Grand Council opposing the reform movement—the notorious chief eunuch, Li Lien-ying, and the fierce xenophobic octogenarian Hsü T'ung, openly called for a policy of supporting the I Ho T'uan, employing them to drive out the foreigners and then eliminating the Emperor. However, no clear decision had been reached by May, when the first conflicts between the I Ho T'uan and Ch'ing troops ensued on a large scale. These took place between them and the army of Nieh Shih-ch'eng, the only other, apart from that of Yüan Shih-k'ai, which was equipped adequately with modern weapons, although it was much inferior to it in training. These conflicts led to a considerable loss of life, especially among the I Ho T'uan, but did not by any means dampen their activity, which was particularly marked in the area of Tientsin, Paoting and around Peking itself. Their attacks on the Chinese Christians and on missionary property were now launched on a larger scale.

On May 21 the diplomatic corps reverted to its demands that the I Ho T'uan be suppressed without fail; however, the Ch'ing government was more wavering than ever, among others, in view of the increased strength and spread of the I Ho T'uan in Chihli. The I Ho T'uan now also attacked one of the objects of its displeasure, the Peking-Tientsin Railway, cutting it for the first time on May 27. This led the diplomatic corps in Peking to call for guards to be sent from Tientsin to protect the legations (May 28) and to demand that railway communication between the two cities be maintained. It has been well stated that this particular move was probably more responsible than any other for the consequent development of the conflict, inasmuch as it was the first of a chain of events which led to this most peculiar war. The threat of the foreign representatives had no effect on the I Ho T'uan; they attacked the railway again and now also a number of foreigners fell victim, as some European engineers (four to nine) were killed in the struggle against them.

IV. The Warfare in North China

By the beginning of June 1900 the stage was set for warfare on a large scale in North China of a quite complex nature. The I Ho T'uan, although it was already using its "Support the Ch'ing, Exterminate the Foreigners" slogan, was still the object of attacks by Ch'ing troops, in spite of the fact that its main aim was to fight foreigners. The foreigners were now getting ready to put down the I Ho T'uan themselves—this aim, however, would lead them inevitably to an armed invasion of the country and ultimately also to a struggle against the Ch'ing army. In such a situation it could be expected that a complete unity of action between the Ch'ing troops and the I Ho T'uan against a common foreign enemy would be forged. However, in most cases, nothing of the sort happened; the Ch'ing generals continued to fight against the I Ho T'uan at the same time as they opposed the invading foreign armies which were advancing on China's soil. This reflected primarily the deep and persistent distrust which the Ch'ing officials felt for the peasant I Ho T'uan and which, for that matter, was fully reciprocated.

In the first days of June the fighting between the I Ho T'uan, which had already supposedly a semi-legal status in Chihli, and the army of Nieh Shih-ch'eng increased in intensity; for this, however, Nieh was then reprimanded by Tz'u-hsi. The contradictory position of the Ch'ing government at this time was well illustrated by the edict of June 6 which, on the one hand, took the I Ho T'uan under the government's protection and, on the other hand, called for their extermination, if they were to continue to rebel against the dynasty. In the meantime, the powers progressed from demands and threats by word of mouth to armed intervention; sixteen foreign naval vessels from seven countries arrived off Taku on June 4 and the first landing parties disembarked two days later. After having received the guard force which had been requested for the legations (around 450 men), the diplomats in Peking now demanded additional aid from their armed forces in the Taku area.

The above request led to the dispatching of the ill-fated expedition under the command of the British Vice-Admiral E. H. Seymour. Seymour left Tientsin on June 11, following the railway line from Tientsin to Peking with a force of around 2000 men (900 British, over 200 Germans, 200 Russians, 200 French, 200 Japanese, 120 Americans, 100 Italians). However, the progress of this force was slowed down very soon by attacks of large units of the I Ho T'uan, who simultaneously tore up the railway tracks both ahead and behind the expeditionary force, which became bogged down on the half-way mark of the road to Peking. After the Allied forces captured the Taku forts, the Ch'ing troops were also given orders to oppose Seymour's advance and thus joined in the attack. Seymour was forced to retreat on June 18; on his way back he captured a vast arsenal close to Tientsin in Hsi-ku, then his force managed to fight its way out of encirclement with the help of a relief column, and to regain Tientsin by June 26, having suffered relatively heavy casualties (62 killed, 238 wounded). As he himself stated later on, had the I Ho T'uan possessed adequate arms, his force would have been wiped out completely. The peasant boys' courage was great indeed; they charged the position of Seymour's troops time and again, with their spears and swords against machine guns and artillery. Their losses were immense.

Meanwhile, the situation in Peking itself was becoming ever more tense; on June 11 the Counsellor of the Japanese Mission, Sugiyama, was murdered by a Ch'ing soldier; on June 13 large units of the I Ho T'uan entered the capital. Attacks on churches and Chinese Christians, as well as on Ch'ing officials, took place immediately on a large scale with much plunder and killing, as well as burning of foreign shops. Some Chinese historians maintain that the I Ho T'uan was joined now by all type of riffraff and see in this the main reason why the previously supposedly strict discipline of the I Ho T'uan disintegrated after the entry into Peking.

The Ch'ing court, which acquiesced in the coming of the I Ho T'uan, was still undecided on what policy to follow ultimately. On June 16 the first of a series of dramatic debates was held in the court in the presence of Tz'u-hsi and the Emperor and attended by all the highest dignitaries. All the previously mentioned divergent positions were represented, some calling for action against the I Ho T'uan, some for supporting it and for preparing war against the powers in view of the aggression of which the Seymour expedition was considered to be an example. Tz'u-hsi herself was at a complete loss to take a stand; finally, the next day, swayed by a report that the foreigners had presented a four-point demand which included the call for her removal from power and the restoration of the Emperor, she came out in full support of the pro-I Ho T'uan faction. The report was a forgery, probably concocted on the orders of Tsai-i, the most vehement of the I Ho T'uan supporters among the Manchu reactionaries.

The decision to act against the powers was further strengthened by the action of the foreign naval forces (not including the Americans), which on June 16 delivered an ultimatum demanding the surrender of the Taku forts; these, which fired back in defence an hour before the expiry of the ultimatum, were then attacked and taken. Immediately thereafter the foreigners started their advance on Tientsin. All this was definitely considered by Peking to be an open declaration of war by the powers against China, and there is little doubt that this incident was of crucial importance in precipitating the war. The Taku action also caused, as seen above, the attack on the Seymour expedition by the Ch'ing troops. Another factor affection Tz'u-hsi's decision was the growing force of the I Ho T'uan in Peking itself; they now numbered well over 30,000 and constituted a serious potential threat to the court.

By June 19, when the news about Taku reached Peking, the die was cast, the decision to break diplomatic relations and to declare war was made and the diplomatic corps was requested to leave for Tientsin. The diplomats demanded that the question be discussed and negotiations on the subject were to be conducted the following day. For this purpose the German minister, Baron K. von Ketteler, proceeded on June 20 to the Tsungli Yamen; on his way there he was killed by a Ch'ing sergeant from Tung Fu-hsiang's army. This outfit was composed mostly of Mohammedans from Kansu, noted for their lack of discipline and tendency to plunder; Tung himself had made his career by betraying his Mohammedan fellow rebels in the North-west and going over to the side of the Manchus. This same day the siege of the Legations began and on the subsequent day the official declaration of war was announced by the Ch'ing government against all the eight powers participating in the intervention (Great Britain, France, Russia, Germany, the United States, Japan, Italy and Austria). A tariff for heads of foreigners, as well as an edict to provincial governors calling for the extermination of all foreigners, was issued (June 24).*

The siege of the Legations lasted 55 days; while being one of the most profusely described events in modern history it was, in effect, as Purcell puts it, but "a small incident in the vast history of China". It was also a somewhat curious affair. The Legations were defended by a force of 409 officers and men of the guard, aided by 125 volunteers; their

*It has been maintained that some Ch'ing officials changed the key word in this edict, when it was being cabled to the provinces, from "kill" to "protect". The question of the authenticity of this edict is still controversial. It is a fact that the overwhelming majority of attacks on foreigners took place only after June 17, i.e. after the taking of the Taku forts.

losses were 66 killed and 150 wounded. Considering the forces at the disposal of the Ch'ing government in Peking (without even counting the I Ho T'uan), the Legations, as well as the Roman Catholic Cathedral which was the object of a separate siege, could have been taken, as Hart put it, in a week or a day. In fact, only some of the I Ho T'uan **and part of Tung Fu-hsiang's Kansu Army participated in the attack. The entire** inconsistent and contradictory nature of Manchu policies was revealed here once more. The Legations were shelled up to July 14, then a truce ensued which lasted to July 29; attacks were then resumed and kept up unevenly until Peking was taken by the new Allied Expeditionary Force. During the siege most of the artillery available in Peking, including excellent new Krupp guns, which was in the hands of the crafty Jung-lu, was not used against the Legations.*

All this proved that many of the Manchus, especially Tz'u-hsi herself, were not at all anxious to fight the foreigners and were seeking means to extricate themselves from the predicament into which their own policy, as well as the pressure of the powers on the one hand, and of the I Ho T'uan on the other hand, had placed them. On July 1 Tz'u-hsi cabled an appeal to the rulers of Great Britain, Russia and Japan to help her out of the impasse. Each of the telegrams was appropriately composed to bring about a sympathetic response, while simultaneously the old trick of playing on the rivalry of the powers was being obviously employed once more. All this, however, was to produce no effect. These constant fluctuations also reflected both the situation in the country as a whole, as well as the struggle of factions at the court; the latter led to the execution on July 28 of Yüan Ch'ang and Hsü Ching-ch'eng, the most prominent opponents of the I Ho T'uan among the higher officials. A most characteristic incident was Tz'u-hsi's sending of food supplies to the besieged foreigners on at least two occasions (July 20 and 26).

The policy which the great majority of Ch'ing officials really wanted to follow was exemplified by the situation in other parts of the country, where they were not under the pressure of the I Ho T'uan anti-foreign movement. Thus, the warfare was, in fact, restricted primarily to Chihli, although the I Ho T'uan also took some action in the North-east, which was later utilized by Russia as an excellent pretext for the occupation of all of Manchuria. Co-ordinating their policies, and more than likely inspired by directives from Jung-lu himself, the governors-general of Central and South China (Li Hung-chang in Liangkwang, Liu K'un-i in Liangkiang, Chang Chih-tung in Hukwang, as well as Yüan Shih-k'ai in Shantung) declared that the I Ho T'uan was, in fact, a local anti-dynastic rebellion, quickly suppressed all attempts at anti-foreign action in the areas under their control, came to an understanding with the representatives of the foreign powers in their territory, collaborated with them and promised protection of foreigners and their property in exchange for the non-intervention of foreign armies. They also completely ignored the "declaration of war" issued by the Peking government, as well as its calls for military assistance against the Allied Expeditionary Force. They had similarly refused to listen to Tz'u-hsi's earlier appeal for aid against the I Ho T'uan in Peking (June 15 and 18). A master in all this was Yüan Shih-k'ai who answered the Peking appeals with fulsome obedience, while his **troops simply stayed on in Shantung; by the end of the war Yüan had achieved the**

*The role of Jung-lu in this period is still the subject of some controversy, among others, due to the question of validity of a document pertaining to his activity—the famous diary of Ching-shan. Some authorities maintain that this is a clever forgery, while its translator, J. Edmund Backhouse, defended its authenticity.

strongest position, especially militarily, of all the governors. In the case of Chang Chih-tung he was more concerned, as has been mentioned, in dealing with the planned uprising of the "Army of Independence" and executing its leaders (see p. 372).

In passing, it should be noted that the above group of followers of the Reform Movement, as well as its leaders, K'ang Yu-wei and Liang Ch'i-ch'ao, took a negative view of the I Ho T'uan, considering them to be a reactionary force. The same was true of the adherents of Sun Yat-sen; Sun himself, in particular, felt that the I Ho T'uan were being used entirely as a tool by the Manchu dynasty whose overthrow he was already advocating. However, the intellectuals had proved themselves ineffectual in 1898, and now the leaderless peasants were, in turn, to go down in defeat. Another quarter of a century was necessary before these two groups were to form an effective fusion in the struggle for their country's freedom—half a century before they were to gain victory.

The defeat of the Seymour expedition caused a serious alteration in the plans of the powers for a quick and easy victorious march to Peking. The legend dating back from the 1860s that a few companies of European soldiers could march at will through the length and breadth of China now faded away. It was at first thought necessary to build up a vast new expeditionary force—the figure 60,000 and more was even suggested—to launch a new attack. The question of who was to participate, and in what strength, gave rise to much feverish diplomatic activity between the main capitals which revealed a vast amount of mutual distrust. The aim officially was to rescue the Legations in Peking but, while this was undoubtedly true, it was believed at the time that the effort would come too late and this goal was only subsidiary. The principal purpose was both to smash the I Ho T'uan and to bring the Ch'ing government quickly back to the previous role of a subservient and docile client of the foreigners; the powers had, in fact, little doubt that this could be easily accomplished as they did not take—and correctly—the new "anti-foreignism" of Tz'u-hsi and her henchmen seriously.

All the rivalries inherent in the actions of the powers in China revealed themselves even in the process of undertaking the joint military operation; had their opponents been capable of taking advantage of this, the road to Peking would have been very much more difficult to traverse. However, the ineptness of the graft-ridden Ch'ing army remained unchanged; the Ch'ing generals still preferred to fight the I Ho T'uan or to sacrifice them by sending them ahead in suicidal attacks on the lines of the foreigners. They were unable to defend Tientsin, where the European concessions had been under the attack of the I Ho T'uan since June 14. The city fell into the hands of the powers on July 14; a large part of the I Ho T'uan there was wiped out, while the remaining Ch'ing troops, having lost their commander, Nieh Shih-ch'eng, in battle, fled. Other large Ch'ing units in the area did not even participate in the struggle. Tientsin already at this time had over half a million population and was of great economic importance; over a third of it now lay in total ruin and all of it was completely plundered and looted by the Allies.

Using Tientsin as its base the new Allied Expeditionary Force began its march to Peking on August 4. Its strength amounted to around 19,000 men and the breakdown according to nationality was as follows; 8000 Japanese, 4500 Russians, 3000 British (practically all Indian), 2500 Americans, 800 French (almost all Vietnamese) and 50 each Italians and Austrians. It should be noted that the Japanese took the occasion to furnish by far the largest contingent for the entire operation; by the end of the war they **had over 25,000 troops in China. This was due not only to geographical proximity, but** also to the plans of the Japanese government for future expansion and the desire to take the fullest advantage possible of the opportunity now offered to strengthen its position in North China. The same can be said for the actions and plans of Tsarist Russia, whose troops in occupying Manchuria and suppressing the I Ho T'uan in that area committed countless atrocities. The dominant tendency in the Tsarist government was that represented by the Minister of War, A. N. Kuropatkin (1848-1925), who wished to utilize the occasion for the permanent acquisition of the North-east in the form of a protectorate, in his own words, "something like Bukhara".

By August 14 the resistance of the Ch'ing troops and the I Ho T'uan was broken without difficulty and the Allied Forces were dashing ahead in competition to be the first to enter Peking. Some fighting still occurred in the capital itself, to be then followed by many days of looting and murder, plunder and rape, which made the burning of the Summer Palace in 1860 pale in comparison. It was in this fashion that the bearers of "Western Civilization" proved their great cultural superiority over the savage heathen of the Middle Kingdom. It is difficult to say whose behaviour was the worst (all accounts agree that the Japanese were careful this time not to repeat their Port Arthur **performance, and were the most disciplined and least inclined to rapine, plundering** systematically, but not brutally).

But after the sack of Peking itself was over, the Germans arrived. They were latecomers and had not participated in the march on Peking, most of their 19,000 troops arriving in September and October under the command of Field Marshal A. von Waldersee (1832-1904), appointed at this time, due to the Kaiser's pressure, Commander-in-Chief of all the Allied Forces. The Germans now made certain that the Kaiser's order of instilling a fear of the German name and of giving no quarter and taking no prisoners (all this in his notorious Hunnic speech) were followed to the letter. In the numerous punitive expeditions (45 of them, in which 35 were manned exclusively by the Germans), which continued until April 1901 in various parts of North China, they more than rivalled the atrocities of the Tsarist troops in Manchuria and became the most hated by the Chinese of all the foreign interventionists.

Of the many contemporary eye-witness accounts dealing with the behaviour of the Allied troops in North China the most exact is, oddly enough, that of Robert Hart. He wrote:

> The men of one flag showed their detestation of the most ancient of civilizations by the wanton destruction of whatever they could not carry off; those of another preached the gospel of cleanliness by shooting down anybody who committed a nuisance in public; while those of the third spread their ideas on the sanctity of family life by breaking into private houses and ravishing the women and girls they found there ....
>
> The population of Peking regarded the Allied troops as "a band of brigands who kill, burn, ravish and loot and who will one of these days disappear as brigands disappeared before and leave the Chinese to themselves again.*

*The personality and role of Hart is somewhat more complex than some modern Chinese historians imagine. They castigate him fiercely, and justly, for his role in reducing the Ch'ing government to subservience of the powers, and for advancing the interests of his own country—Great Britain. However, this undeniably able Ulsterman developed throughout the decade of his stay in China something of a split personality; he acquired a great admiration for the country and the people. His book, *These From the Land of Sinam* written right after the I Ho T'uan, is a fascinating document. Hart considered the I Ho T'uan a fundamentally patriotic movement and clearly forecast with prophetic insight the day, fifty years hence, when their spirit would bring about the complete downfall of imperialist domination. His profound knowledge of the country and the people (and his description of the Chinese is perhaps the most favourable of any contemporary Western writer) made the presumptuous arrogance and smug superiority to things Chinese of other Westerners especially insufferable to him.

It was only the Marxists in Europe, especially the Russian and German Social Democrats, who upheld the honour of true European culture, speaking out in defence of the Chinese and castigating the greed and brutality of their own imperialist governments. A fine example of this was Lenin's article "The Chinese War", published in the *Iskra* in December 1900, in which, analysing the anti-foreign actions of the I Ho T'uan, he wrote:

> It is true that the Chinese hate the Europeans. But what kind of Europeans do they hate and why? The Chinese do not hate the European peoples with whom they have no conflict. They hate the European capitalists and the European governments which are subservient to the capitalists. How could the Chinese not hate those persons who have come to China only to make money, those who make use of their so-called civilization to cheat, rob and commit violence, those who have made wars upon China only to gain rights to sell opium which poisons the people and those who hypocritically preach Christianity to camouflage their policy of robbery?

V. The Settlement

In the early dawn of August 15, a day after the entry of the Allied troops into Peking, Tz'u-hsi, disguised as a peasant woman, accompanied by the few of her henchmen who had not already escaped, fled the city to the north-west. She took along with her the Emperor, her prisoner, being afraid to leave him behind. A suggestion that this be done so that he could negotiate the peace with the foreigners cost his only friend, the faithful Pearl Consort, her life, for Tz'u-hsi in a rage ordered her thrown down one of the palace wells. The Ch'ing government, in effect, disintegrated; Jung-lu took flight to Paoting, other high Manchu officials—especially those who had supported the I Ho T'uan—all scurried in various directions. A number of them committed suicide, many with their entire families. Chaos reigned.

However, one man whose personality was well known to all the foreigners was soon to return to Peking, to salvage what could be saved for the mistress he had served for so many decades—the cleverest and most corrupt of them all—old Li Hung-chang himself. Already on August 11 he had been appointed the principal Ch'ing negotiator with the powers; for that matter, Tz'u-hsi had in vain sought to have him come to Peking from Canton in July, when she nominated him once more Governor-general of Chihli. Li Hung-chang was in no hurry; he dallied in Shanghai on his way north, waiting for the Allies to enter Peking. Only then did he continue his journey to the capital and for the last part of the trip he was given an escort of Cossacks by the Russians who welcomed their well-known friend. His presence as the negotiator was interpreted by the powers, correctly, to mean that the Ch'ing government had recovered its senses and was ready to revert to its previous role, for no one had ever made more concessions to the foreigners than Li himself. His appearance at the negotiating table implied that the Manchus were now more willing to pay any price, if only the powers would agree to leave the dynasty on the throne, even if its rights were to be reduced still further and the sovereignty of the country they ruled brought to practically nil.

It took almost a year before the negotiations were ended. In the meantime, the Ch'ing government had accomplished a complete *volte-face* and the Ch'ing troops joined in with the foreign forces in common campaigns against the I Ho T'uan; the latter, deceived and betrayed, and now reverting, too late, to anti-dynastic aims, continued their resistance in various parts of North China throughout most of the following year.

These pacification campaigns resulted in the devastation of much of the North and North-east—Chihli itself was turned into a "foodless waste"—and the death of thousands of Chinese, also from starvation, during the terrible winter of 1900-1901, many times more than the number of foreigners killed during the summer months of 1900, totalling 242.

With complete cynicism characteristic of her Tz'u-hsi now turned against those of her faithful followers, who were compromised in the eyes of the powers by their support for the I Ho T'uan, and to appease the foreigners either ordered them to commit suicide or had them executed. Such was, for example, the fate of Yü-hsien, but some of the others, like Prince Tuan, escaped the executioner's axe or the foreign firing squad.

After their entry into Peking and the beginning of negotiations with Li Hung-chang in December, the powers, in imposing their settlement on the now once more thoroughly cowed Manchus, faced a number of problems regarding the policy to follow. The main ones were whether the country should be partitioned between the victors, whether the Ch'ing dynasty should be maintained or replaced by another and, if kept on the throne, whether the ruler should be Tz'u-hsi or the Emperor. The first of these choices, although it was seriously debated throughout the year, was, in fact, not feasible at all, and this for two principal reasons. While the resistance of the I Ho T'uan was ultimately broken, the movement had revealed the great latent power of the Chinese to resist foreign aggression and made the prospect of partition unthinkable, as it would entail an endless struggle against the vast population. In this too lay the fundamental significance of the I Ho T'uan. Secondly, the rivalries of the powers, already marked during the expedition to Peking and much more obvious during the year in which the negotiations were being conducted, also made any agreement on the division of China almost impossible.

The main rivalry between the imperialists was that of Great Britain and Russia. The Russians, having already occupied Manchuria, now reverted to their policy of supporting Tz'u-hsi and counted on becoming the dominant influence in Peking. In line with this they advocated a rapid withdrawal of foreign troops from North China (but not of their own from the North-east), even before the beginning of the negotiations. This was followed up by the withdrawal of the Russian force from Peking at the end of September; then an attempt was made, lasting throughout most of the spring of 1901, to arrange a treaty with the Ch'ing government which would convert Manchuria into a Russian protectorate. In spite of all the efforts, and the assistance of Li Hung-chang, the Russian plans were ultimately frustrated by the other powers.

The British, who had been toying during the summer of 1900 with the idea of setting up "independent" Chinese governments in South and Central China (they had entered into negotiations for this purpose with anti-Peking Chinese groups, both with the followers of K'ang Yu-wei and Sun Yat-sen, as well as even with Li Hung-chang), now, once Peking had been taken, changed their approach and took up the position of opposing partition and favouring the restoration of the Manchus. One of the principal motives in this was to seek to counter the plans of the Russians. In their actions, the British could count on the assistance of the Japanese, who were bitterly opposed to the growing power of Russia in the North-east, and thus the road to an official Anglo-Japanese alliance, which was to be concluded in 1902, was being prepared.

The Japanese were simultaneously seeking to gain influence with Ch'ing officials and working towards a Sino-Japanese entente against all the European powers. France, on the whole, supported her Russian ally and concentrated primarily on her rivalry with England in South-west China, while Germany tried to take advantage of the Anglo-Russian rivalry to obtain as great as possible benefits for herself. By concluding an agreement in October 1900 with Great Britain, Germany seemingly sided with her; in reality, the support of the Germans for the Open Door policy of the British was interpreted in such a way as not to cover Manchuria, thus it had more the effect of blocking British plans in the Yangtse Valley. The Germans, who were the most vindictive of all the powers, were also responsible for delaying the beginning of the negotiations in order to gain time for their army to show its prowess—once the war was already over.

The United States continued its previously announced Open Door policy, which was now extended by Hay in his note of July 3, 1900, to favour the maintenance of China's "territorial integrity". The basic reasons for this policy were still the same as those which had formed the motive for the first proclamation. This declaration did not prevent the Americans from seeking to obtain territorial concessions from the Manchus for themselves; in November 1900 they tried to acquire a naval base in Fukien. This, however, was frustrated by the opposition of the Japanese. On one point all the powers saw eye-to-eye; this was to take revenge on the Chinese for having dared to oppose them, to impose as heavy an indemnity on the country as possible, and to prevent a recurrence of an anti-foreign movement. The decision was also quickly reached that the Ch'ing dynasty and Tz'u-hsi would be permitted to retain "power", inasmuch as precisely such a corrupt and decadent regime corresponded most closely to the interests of the powers.

The negotiations dragged out till September 1901, not due to Ch'ing resistance, for the Manchus, once they had been assured of being left in power, surrendered without a whimper to all the demands of the imperialists, but due to the wrangling between the powers themselves. Finally, the so-called Boxer Protocol was signed on September 7 between the Ch'ing government and eleven states (the eight interventionist powers plus Spain, Holland and Belgium). Its twelve points provided for the payment by China of a huge indemnity of 450 million taels in gold ($334 million) which, with interest (4 per cent) during a period of thirty-nine years, would in reality have amounted to 980 million taels. The payment of this crippling sum was to be guaranteed by the receipts of the maritime customs, the *likin* taxes and the salt gabelle—all now under foreign control. The powers thoughtfully permitted the raising of the customs rates to an effective 5 per cent—they had fallen to a level of 2 to 3 per cent—so as to assure adequate revenue for the payment of the indemnity. The right to station foreign troops, both in the Peking Legation Quarter (now a completely exclusive and extraterritorial area, a stone's throw from the Imperial City) and along the Peking-Tientsin railway, was provided for.* The Taku forts were to be razed forever. The Ch'ing government was also obliged to put down immediately any anti-foreign movement. Punishment of those high officials who had supported the I Ho T'uan was stipulated, official apology for the killing of von Ketteler and Sugiyama demanded.

The overall effect of this settlement was to complete the process of the transformation of China into a joint semi-colony of all the imperialist powers and to turn the Manchu government even more completely into a puppet of the powers, little more, as has been

---

*It is small wonder that after 1949 the Chinese government saw to it that practically all the foreign embassies were to be relocated in new areas, far from the centre of the city.

well said, than a debt-collecting agency for the powers. But it now continued to benefit from foreign support in order to be able to carry out this function, as well as that of further oppressing the Chinese people. This support enabled the Manchus, especially Tz'u-hsi herself, to regain their badly shaken confidence.

After her flight from Peking Tz'u-hsi had proceeded to T'aiyüan, the capital of Shansi, where she inspected with evident satisfaction the yamen in which Yü-hsien had carried out the murder of a large number of missionaries. By the end of October 1900 Tz'u-hsi and her entourage, now considerably enlarged since she was joined by many other high officials who had also escaped from Peking, established themselves in Sian, in Shensi. Here, her court again became the centre of the Ch'ing government and her emissaries travelled to all the provinces, busily fleecing the local officials and population, imposing new taxes and donations for her benefit. It was in Sian that Tz'u-hsi issued in November her first edict on the punishment of those responsible for supporting the I Ho T'uan. As for her own role, she maintained that she had been misled—the only mistake in her whole political career—and shifted all the blame on to Prince Tuan and his followers, as well as on to the I Ho T'uan. This was followed, in turn, in January 1901 by the so-called conversion of the Empress Dowager to the ideas of reform, which she now expounded in an edict (January 28). The purpose of this manoeuvre was to render her more respectable in the eyes of the foreigners, as well as to mislead those of the Chinese who could be taken in by her schemes.

After the signing of the Protocol, Tz'u-hsi thought that it was finally safe to return to Peking and, taking along with her all the newly acquired plunder from the provinces, she proceeded leisurely on her way, reaching the capital on January 7, 1902, showing her new progressive nature by travelling the last part of the trip by train. Upon arrival she smiled graciously on the foreigners who gathered to witness the spectacle and hurried quickly to the palace to dig up her buried treasure, which the Germans who had been occupying the palace had been unable to find, though not for want of trying. All had been forgotten—complete concord between the Manchus and the powers reigned once more, with everyone playing the role allotted. But—as history was soon to show—not for very long.

PART XII

China on the Eve of and During the 1911 Revolution

CHAPTER 37

China After the I Ho T'uan

I. The Powers in China

The defeat of the I Ho T'uan and the settlement as determined by the Boxer Protocol rendered still stronger, for the time being, the position of the powers in relation to the Ch'ing government. While the plans for a partition of the country had to be abandoned due to the reasons mentioned previously, still greater possibilities for the economic penetration of China now offered themselves; these were provided for, among others, by the revision of the commercial treaties undertaken in 1902-1903. As a result, a further growth of foreign investments in the Chinese economy took place in the 1902-1914 period, which is illustrated by the following figures:

	1902	1914
Great Britain	US$260.3 m. (35%)	US$ 607.5 m. (38%)
Japan	1 m. (0.1%)	219.6 m. (13.6%)
United States	19.7 m. (2.5%)	49.3 m. (3.1%)
Russia	246 m. (31%)	269 m. (16.7%)
Total including all other countries	788 m.	1610 m.

The control of external trade fell to a still greater degree into foreign hands, especially as this was, in effect, financed mostly by the foreign-owned banks active in China, in spite of the existence and development during the same period of China's own banking institutions. The dominant position of foreign finance was particularly obvious in connection with the Ch'ing government, which was completely at the mercy of foreign financiers. In spite of the unceasing rivalry between the imperialist powers there was an ever more marked tendency for united action in the conduct of financial dealings with the Manchus, which was reflected in the establishment of an international consortium, finally agreed upon by 1911, to be composed of four major powers—Great Britain, France, Germany and the United States, which possessed a monopoly position for the granting of further loans to the Ch'ing government, an example of which was the £10 million "Currency Reform and Economic Development" loan made by this consortium in April 1911.

The main field of interest and penetration, however, lay in the further attempts to obtain new railway and mining concessions and in the granting of loans for this purpose to the Peking government, as exemplified by the $10 million railway loan made by the Japanese in April 1911 and the £6 million railway loan of the Four Power Consortium made in May 1911. All the financial arrangements of this period between the powers and the Manchu government constituted a source of still-deepening corruption and graft of the Ch'ing administration; this was particularly true of the venal Sheng Hsüan-huai, who was most active in this field. The overall effect was to place more and more of the country's economy directly under the control of the foreigners.

II. Imperialist Rivalry in the Far East

While all the imperialist powers had succeeded in presenting a common front against China during the I Ho T'uan uprising, already during the subsequent period of negotiating the Boxer Protocol all the inherent rivalries, centring primarily on China herself, rapidly came once more to the surface. Of these, the principal ones were the continuing struggle between Japan and Russia for the mastery of North-east China and Korea and the overall conflict between Great Britain and Russia in Asia, in which the question of China was also of crucial importance. The Russian occupation of Manchuria during the I Ho T'uan movement and the obvious attempts to transform this area into a new Tsarist protectorate became one of the prime objects of dispute in Russo-Japanese relations, inasmuch as the Russian plans were regarded by the Japanese as a most serious threat to their own plans of expansion both in North and North-east China, as well as in Korea, where the position of the Japanese was already predominant after the Sino-Japanese War of 1894-1895.

It is against the background of the Russo-Japanese rivalry that a realignment of the relations between the powers in the Far East took place, the most important feature of which was the conclusion of the Anglo-Japanese Alliance (signed January 30, 1902). The policy of seeking this rapprochement with England had been preceded by considerable debate within the Japanese government, but the views of the militarist group, aiming at a war with Russia, prevailed, and an alliance with Great Britain was regarded as an essential step in enabling Japan to envisage an armed struggle with her potentially much stronger northern neighbour. In signing this treaty—an unprecedented act on their part signifying the end of "Splendid Isolation"—the British, in effect, gave the Japanese *carte blanche* for the strengthening of their position in Korea, recognizing the "peculiar degree" of the Japanese interests in that country, as well as assuring them of the fact that Russia would have to face a struggle against Japan singlehanded.

The policy of the Tsarist government in Manchuria also facilitated the aggressive plans of the Japanese imperialists. Under the pressure of the other powers, Russia finally concluded an agreement with the Ch'ing government relating to Manchuria (April 8, 1902). In it the Russians promised to evacuate the North-east by three six-month stages—the entire process to be completed in eighteen months. However, although a part of the territory was evacuated, the basic promise was not adhered to; this provided the Japanese government with an excellent pretext for the implementation of its own well-laid war plans. The Tsarist government was not particularly concerned with the possibility of drifting into a war, inasmuch as it felt certain of victory, and it was considered by Plehve that "in order to repress the revolution, a little victorious war is necessary".

The long-drawn-out Russo-Japanese negotiations, which involved the problem both of Manchuria and Korea, were broken off on February 6, 1904. War was declared by Japan on February 10 but, characteristically enough, this was preceded already on February 8 by a successful Japanese attack on Port Arthur, which damaged and bottled up the Russian fleet there. The Russo-Japanese War turned into a series of heavy and humiliating defeats for the Tsarist autocracy. The débâcle on the Yalu in April was followed by the loss of Talien (Dalnyi) on May 30; Port Arthur's long and bitter siege ended with its surrender on January 1, 1905, while the ill-prepared and badly led Russian armies were forced northward and defeated, first at Liaoyang (August 29-September 3, 1904) and then in the great battle of Mukden (February 20-March 6, 1905). The final blow came with Tsushima—there, on May 27-28, the Russian Baltic Fleet, which had sailed around half of the world, met its doom almost in its entirety.

The Tsarist government had suffered a complete disaster. More important, however, were the internal repercussions. The war, detested by the peoples of Russia from the outset, greatly stimulated the revolutionary movement within the country, which rose with ever-greater force from the summer of 1905 onwards. It was against this background that Russia willingly sought to put an end quickly to the conflict in the Far East. The Japanese were no less anxious inasmuch as their victories had almost completely exhausted the country's resources, both human and economic. Witte, who had been ignominiously dismissed from his post as Minister of Finances in 1903 for his opposition to the Tsarist government's policy in the Far East, was now dispatched to conduct—on the whole quite successfully—the negotiations, which ended with the signing of the Portsmouth Treaty (September 5, 1905). According to its terms Russia turned over its entire Liaotung concession (Port Arthur and Talien) to the Japanese, as well as the part of the Russian-built railway system in South Manchuria from Changchun to Port Arthur. This railway was then reorganized by the Japanese as the South Manchurian Railway Company and later transformed by them into a vast industrial-military complex, which was to be the basic core of Japanese imperialist expansion and aggression against China for the next forty years.

Nothing could portray more vividly the utterly degraded position of the Ch'ing government and the true nature of China's semi-colonial existence than the fact that the Russo-Japanese War had been waged almost entirely on Chinese soil—a struggle between two imperialist powers for the mastery over a part of China herself. At stake, among others, were the three North-east provinces with their vast economic potential and a population which already then had reached the figure of around 15 million Chinese. The Manchu government sought to maintain a policy of "neutrality" during the conflict which had raged in its own original homeland. In this, it met with considerable difficulties, especially due to the rapacious activities of the Japanese. It was the Chinese civilian population of the North-east who suffered from the war operations and bore the brunt of the devastation of the country.

The settlement of the war provided for the evacuation of the North-east by both the Japanese and Russian military forces (but not the railway guards) and for a recognition of Chinese "sovereignty" over the entire area. In effect, the Ch'ing government was now required to recognize all the changes which had taken place there, i.e. the transfer of Liaotung, etc. This it promptly did, signing a new treaty with the Japanese on December 22, 1905. In a purportedly secret arrangement the Manchus simultaneously also agreed not to build any more railway lines in the North-east which could compete with the South Manchurian Railway.

In a relatively short time after the war, Russia and Japan regulated their relations in Manchuria by signing a treaty on July 30, 1907; the secret clauses of this agreement, in reality, provided for a partition of the North-east into two spheres of influence and this arrangement was subsequently confirmed by further secret treaties in 1910 and 1916. Simultaneously, Russia recognized once more Japan's complete control of Korea. This unfortunate country was, in effect, already a Japanese colony from the moment of Russia's defeat; it now became the defenceless victim of Japanese imperialism, abandoned to its fate by all the powers, including those who had talked so glibly of their friendship for it and had guaranteed its "territorial integrity". The process of its subjection to the Japanese yoke—a story of almost unparalleled brutality—ended with its annexation in 1910. However, the resistance of the Koreans to the loss of their independence, particularly strong and marked in the decade up to 1919, continued undaunted throughout the entire forty-year period of the Japanese colonial regime.

The British government, well satisfied with the results of the Russo-Japanese War, hurried to renew the Anglo-Japanese alliance even before the Portsmouth Treaty was signed. The new treaty was concluded on August 12, 1905 and was still directed, like the original one, primarily against Russia. It also explicitly recognized the right of Japan to transform Korea into her colony. The alliance was further renewed on July 13, 1911. However, by this time it had lost most of its anti-Russian aspect and this owing to the fact that, due to the continuous worsening of Anglo-German relations, a general settlement of Anglo-Russian rivalry in Asia had been achieved by the agreement reached on August 31, 1907. While this pertained primarily to Persia and Afghanistan, it also affected China, especially as it ended—officially at least—the conflict between Russia and Great Britain over Tibet, by recognizing Chinese suzerainty in this land.

Both Great Britain and Russia were interested in infiltrating this territory, but the British, obsessed—especially Curzon himself—by the alleged Russian threat to India, were much more active. One of the results was the British invasion of Tibet, the Younghusband expedition of 1903-1904. Accompanied by much slaughter of defenceless Tibetans, it ended in the conclusion of the Lhasa Convention, which made British influence in Tibet paramount.

The Anglo-Russian agreement included the by now ritual phrase to be found in all the treaties of this period—respect for the "territorial integrity" of China, i.e. the preservation of her *status quo* as a semi-colony of all the powers. A similar "respect" was expressed also in the treaty between Japan and France signed on June 10, 1907; this was, in effect, a reciprocal recognition of the spheres of interest in China of these two powers, with the subsidiary aim of improving Russo-Japanese relations, in which France was interested from general motives of foreign policy.

The decade after the I Ho T'uan also witnessed a notable increase in American activity in the Far East in general, and in China in particular, derived partially from the newly acquired position of the United States, after the annexation of Hawaii and the Philippines, as one of the major powers in the Pacific. While the degree of economic penetration in China was still relatively insignificant, the hopes and aspirations of American capital for increasing its stake in the Middle Kingdom were quite far-reaching and ambitious, especially in respect to railway construction. In its foreign policy the American government had pursued a line favouring Japanese expansion; this was particularly true in the period of the Russo-Japanese War but was also, in the main, followed in the subsequent years. Thus, like Great Britain, the United States acquiesced with complete equanimity in the Japanese subjugation of Korea (the Taft-Katsura Agreement, July 29, 1905), subscribed to the ideas of the Anglo-Japanese alliance, being in fact a "silent partner" to it, and supported Japan both financially and diplomatically.

American relations with Japan, in spite of their rivalry in Manchuria, were further regulated by the signing of the Root-Takahira Agreement (November 30, 1908), in which the formula regarding respect for the Open Door and Chinese territorial integrity was repeated once more. This, in reality, was a recognition of the Japanese position in Manchuria and it simultaneously frustrated the current hopes of the Ch'ing government of obtaining United States support against the Japanese. However, at the same time, American attempts at economic penetration, precisely in this very same area, were not abandoned by any means, especially in the period of so-called Dollar Diplomacy. This was particularly true of the well-known plans of E. H. Harriman, the railroad magnate, for acquiring control of the railway system in the North-east, either through the purchase of the Japanese and Russian property or the building of competing lines.

When the above schemes failed, the United States government put forth its plan for the international control of all the railways in Manchuria—the famous Knox "Neutralization Memorandum" (November 6, 1909). This clumsy move did not gain the support of any of the powers; it met with particularly stiff opposition from Russia and Japan and also ended in a fiasco, having as its only result a further strengthening of Russo-Japanese co-operation. Nevertheless, American capital persisted in its attempts and finally, with the help of the United States government, it was successful in 1911 in forcing its admittance to the financial consortium, when a number of the leading American banks participated in the transactions with the Ch'ing government mentioned earlier.

The treaties and arrangements outlined above did undoubtedly lead to a certain relative stabilization of the situation in the Far East, to an outward toning down of the rivalries of the powers in this area by means of some clarification of their "rights and interests". They did not and could not eliminate the real sources of the rivalries—the seeking of each imperialist power to obtain the greatest advantages for itself—but assuaged the sharpness of the struggle to a certain degree. The Far East—and within it primarily China herself—continued to remain one of the main focal points of imperialist contradictions in the years preceding the First World War. However, it became still more closely intertwined, through the mechanism of alliances which now embraced almost all the powers, with conflicts in other areas, which were to prove to be of greater importance than the rivalries in the Far East themselves in the bringing about of the terrible holocaust of the first imperialist world war.

III. The Economic and Social Development of China

While the increase in foreign economic penetration in the first decade of the 20th century, as well as the disadvantages inherent in the country's semi-colonial status, constituted an extremely great handicap for the development of Chinese national capitalism itself—as distinguished from the development of foreign-owned capitalist enterprises in China—the same period witnessed, nevertheless, considerable progress in this field as well. An increasing number of Chinese gentry and merchants were becoming interested in investing their capital in industrial enterprises of various types, as well as in trade—instead of the traditional land—and continued to do this in spite of foreign competition and the above-mentioned disadvantageous conditions. This was particularly true of light industry, in itself a typical phenomenon for an undeveloped country. Thus, there was a marked growth in Chinese-owned modern textile industry in these years, while a number of other branches, such as flour mills, tobacco and match factories, etc., were also developed. Perhaps the most prominent in these endeavours at industrialization was the well-known Chang Chien (1853-1926), himself a scholar of gentry origin, who was successful in building up an entire industrial complex in his native region in Kiangsu.

However, it should be stressed that this new economic development was both limited in scope and uneven in character. In particular, its geographical location was very restricted, primarily to the Treaty Ports and the coastal provinces. This was partially due to the problem of communication; although the railroad network had increased to over 5000 miles by 1910, it was still completely inadequate. Vast parts of the country, particularly most of the interior, were little, if at all, involved in capitalist development. Its predominant agrarian economy still persisted in semi-natural and semi-feudal conditions, in spite of being to a degree affected—rather marginally—by the export of some of its products to a world market. On the whole, it preserved its self-contained character. It is difficult to speak of the existence of a truly nation-wide market as well; the overwhelming poverty of the countryside was a factor which retarded such a development, as well as that of the economy as a whole. It is true that the imports of such foreign goods as textiles, as well as the growth of light industry in China itself, led to a certain decline of the rural handicraft industries;. the scale of this had been often exaggerated, inasmuch as these industries put up a stubborn defence, and while a worsening of the position of peasant families did undoubtedly ensue, the general character of the rural economy was not basically altered as a result of all the above-mentioned processes.

Therefore, while the growth of capitalist industry resulted in the introduction of a new type of production—as well as of new social relations—this did not by any means signify that the country, as a whole, had entered the capitalist stage of development; on the contrary, the old economic forms were still dominant and the economy as a whole could be best described as a mixed one, which, indeed, was typical of its semi-colonial status. One could even venture to pose the question whether and to what degree did China ever develop into a capitalist country, in the full meaning of the word, during **the 20th century. The answer to this seems to be definitely in the negative and herein lies** one of the basic keys to its characteristic development.

Although restricted in scope, the development of capitalist forms in the economy did have a number of significant social consequences, the most obvious of which were the formation of new social classes—an industrial working class, as well as a Chinese national bourgeoisie, as distinguished from those Chinese groups connected with foreign economic penetration, usually referred to as comprador elements. What was characteristic of the growth of these two new classes was the fact that the Chinese working class increased in size and importance more rapidly than the national bourgeoisie, for the obvious reasons, among others, that a large part of it was employed in foreign-owned enterprises. This factor, however, was to prove to be of importance only in a later period—in the 1920s. The changes in the class structure of Chinese society were to be reflected also in the country's political development and in the nature of the political struggle to be waged during the first two decades of the 20th century. This reflection was not, however, anywhere as direct and seemingly simple as some modern Chinese historians would wish to have it. Of equal, if not perhaps greater, importance for the political development of this period was the further penetration of Western ideology—extremely varied in its scope and nature—and its effect on the outlook of the Chinese intellectuals, still the most important social group in the country and the one which was also destined to play the leading role in the struggle against the Ch'ing dynasty.

The penetration of Western ideology—relatively limited in the last decades of the 19th century—now increased vastly in this period as a result also of the complete breakdown of Confucianism, itself a reflection of the crisis of Ch'ing rule and China's fate. Among the immediate factors facilitating this flood of Western Learning were the educational reforms, finally enacted by the Ch'ing government, which led to the establishment of a rather unbalanced government system of schools with a more or less modern curriculum (by 1910—around 57,000 schools, 89,000 teachers, 1,600,000 pupils, but 65 million children of school age), the considerable increase in the number of foreign schools and even universities in China and, perhaps the most important, the vast migration from 1900 onward of Chinese students seeking education abroad. While a fair number of these found their way to Europe (400) and the United States (800), the overwhelming majority of the Chinese students made their way to Japan. The reasons for this are fairly obvious—Japan being the closest and least expensive country, and the language and customs presenting less difficulties. A more indirect, but very cogent, reason was Japan's success in modernization—it was thus an example to be studied and followed.

While in 1898 there were perhaps around 100 Chinese students in Japan, this number grew rapidly, reaching the figure of 13,000 to 15,000 by 1905-1907. A large part of these students were recipients of government or provincial scholarships; by no means all of them completed their studies in Japan and the level of education to be obtained there varied considerably. The students, who were mostly of gentry and merchant origin, came from almost all the provinces of China and quickly organized themselves into provincial clubs and associations; just as rapidly they became engaged in political, primarily anti-Manchu, activity. It is almost impossible to exaggerate the importance for the future political history of China of this hegira to Japan of the Chinese students— practically all the leading figures of the next two decades had studied abroad—most of them in Japan. It was there that Western ideology was acquired, that the great initial debates on the future of China were held, that the struggle for influence among and support of the students was waged by the principal exiled Chinese political leaders, and that the first effective Chinese revolutionary organizations were formed.

IV. The Ch'ing Government, 1901-1911

Having been left in power in Peking by the victorious powers in its role of caretaker and debt collector, the Ch'ing government changed very little, if at all, in its general nature. It was now still more discredited in the eyes of the nation it purported to rule, while its oppressiveness and corruption grew even more acute. Nonetheless, the Manchus sought to extend the agony of their rule as long as humanly possible, and this was the principal cause of the "Reform" programme initiated, as mentioned earlier, under the auspices of Tz'u-hsi herself. This programme was based, among others, on the proposals submitted in 1902-1903 by two of the most powerful of the Chinese governors-general, Chang Chih-tung and Liu K'un-i. The first measures undertaken pertained to the educational system; the eight-legged essay was abolished in 1901, the beginnings of a government school network was introduced shortly thereafter, the examination system finally abolished in 1906, and the sending of students abroad permitted. These changes did not imply by any means the establishment of universal education, as noted earlier. The aim rather was to assure the government of an inflow of future bureaucratic cadres, which would be educated in a way that would make them somewhat more capable of dealing with the problems facing the government and the country.

The mounting political ferment in the country—particularly the increasing discontent of the intellectuals and the rapid growth of revolutionary activities, especially after 1905, which itself was the result of expanded education and the further penetration of Western education—also forced the Manchus to consider the necessity of administrative reforms and political concessions aimed at the preserving of their rule. Of these measures probably the most important, as far as their effect on the country's future was concerned, were the efforts of the Ch'ing government to reorganize its military establishment, which had been completely shattered and proved totally ineffective during the I Ho T'uan period.

There can be little doubt that the main aim here was not to provide the country with proper means of defence against future foreign aggression, but to forge an armed force capable of propping up the tottering Manchu throne. Very considerable means, in view of the pitiable resources of the Manchu government, were devoted to this purpose of training, with the assistance of foreigners, a large standing army, equipped with modern arms. The task was placed primarily, though not solely, in the hands of Yüan Shih-k'ai. At the death of Li Hung-chang in November 1901, Yüan had been chosen, in accord with Li's deathbed recommendation, to replace him as Governor-general of

Chihli; with Jung-lu, Yuan now ranked as the most powerful official in the Empire. After Jung-lu's death in 1903, Yüan joined forces with perhaps the most corrupt of all the Manchu princes, I-k'uang, Prince Ch'ing, to continue to sway the realm. He utilized the building up of the New Army (by 1905, six new divisions were formed, from 60,000 to 70,000 men) to the fullest extent for the enhancement of his own power, in particular, by assuring the promotion and proper placement of all his military and civilian protégés, thus leading to the creation of the notorious Peiyang military clique which was later to assist him in his further rise to power.

It was the Peiyang clique which was also to provide the bulk of the militarists, who were to terrorize the torn and divided country in the fifteen years following the 1911 Revolution. Most of Yüan's officers were graduates of Chinese military academies, such as the ones in Paoting and Tientsin, but a number of them had also studied abroad, again mostly in Japan. The majority of them were of gentry origin and retained close links with their families in the countryside, later investing their ill-gotten gains in land. They have been well described as landlords with machine guns and this social role of theirs was to be demonstrated fully in subsequent developments.

Yüan Shih-k'ai's growing power gave rise to much disquiet and bitter resentment among the leading Manchu aristocrats, as well as that of his main Chinese rival, Chang Chih-tung, who had also built up his own modern armed forces. For this reason both Yüan Shih-k'ai and Chang Chih-tung were transferred in 1907 to high posts in Peking, in order to deprive them of their direct control of these military forces. However, the Peiyang clique remained, on the whole, loyal to its chief and creator.

Towards the end of 1905, the first promise to introduce a constitutional form of government was made by Tz'u-hsi and an appropriate mission was sent abroad to study this question. In the following year further promises—to establish a National and Provincial Assemblies, both purely consultative in nature—were also made. In November of the same year, a reorganization of the administration of the central government was announced; this, in effect, amounted to little more than an alteration of the names of the already existing ministries. In all this Tz'u-hsi and her entourage were only playing for time and had no intention whatsoever to relinquish anything of the real political power of the Manchus. That this was so was borne out fully by the outlines of the future constitution, which were announced in September 1908. It was copied almost in its entirety from the Japanese constitution, with the difference that the powers of the Manchu Emperor were to be even more extensive than those of the Japanese ruler, while the eternal hold of the Great Ch'ing Dynasty on the Chinese throne was also stipulated. This great gift to the Chinese nation was to come into effect after a nine-year preparatory period, i.e. in 1918.

Shortly thereafter the death of both Tz'u-hsi and Kuang-hsü took place. According to the official version the Emperor was said to have died on November 14, the Empress Dowager on the next day. The circumstances of Kuang-hsü's death were very suspicious and have given rise to much speculation. More than likely—and it is to this view that his successor was himself inclined—Tz'u-hsi, being quite ill and already 74 years old, did not wish to have the Emperor survive her. Her henchmen—both Li Lien-ying and Yüan Shih-k'ai, particularly the latter, whose chances of keeping his head, if Kuang-hsü were to regain power, were nil—were equally interested in such a solution. Kuang-hsü was thus more than likely appropriately done away with, probably poisoned, on the orders of one or all of this trio.

Tz'u-hsi's illness did not prevent her from asserting her will once more in the matter of the succession; a day before Kuang-hsü's death she arranged that the throne be given to his 2½-year-old nephew, P'u-i, son of the Emperor's younger brother, Tsai-feng, Prince Ch'un, and grandson of her favourite Jung-lu. The boy was to reign under the title of Hsüan-t'ung for the last three years of the Ch'ing dynasty, while his father was the Regent and the real ruler of the Empire.*

This turn of events meant the end of the power of Yüan Shih-k'ai; he had earlier tried to propose another candidate to the throne in order to save himself. Tsai-feng was, after all, Kuang-hsü's brother, and while he did not fulfil the Emperor's deathbed wish that Yüan be executed immediately for his treachery during the 1898 Reform Movement, it was soon discovered that Yüan supposedly suffered from a foot ailment, which made the carrying out of his duties impossible and he was therefore graciously permitted to retire to his estate to treat the said complaint.

The new Regent proved to be a singularly ineffective ruler, quite incapable of coping with the growing struggle of factions at the court, both between the Manchus themselves and between the Manchus and Chinese. The latter struggle had become already quite sharp in the first years of the century; its acuteness was now further increased against the background of the deteriorating position of the Ch'ing government. However, at first, the coming to power of the Regency was welcomed by the relatively strong group of upper class, mostly gentry, supporters of a constitutional monarchy, whose hopes for further progress in this direction were raised by the establishment of the Provincial Assemblies in October 1909 and of the National Assembly in October 1910. In both these bodies—the Provincial Assemblies chosen indirectly on an extremely restricted property (5000 taels) and educational (secondary school) basis and the National Assembly, composed of 100 delegates elected by the Provincial Assemblies and 100 appointed by the government—the constitutional monarchists were in great majority and used the Assemblies as an arena for putting forth new political demands.

As a result of this pressure the government now promised that the new Constitution would be enacted and the new Parliament called in 1913—five years earlier than planned. The strong demands for the introduction of a system of responsible cabinet government was finally met in April 1911—but the choice of ministers was typical of the true intentions of the Manchu court. Of the thirteen cabinet ministers—eight were Manchus (five of them imperial princes), one Mongol and only four Chinese. Even the most faithful Chinese supporters of the dynasty found this hard to swallow. Simultaneously, Tsai-feng sought to strengthen the power of the Ch'ing by placing his brothers—even less capable than himself—in key command positions in the armed forces, a move made easier by the earlier removal of Yüan Shih-k'ai. However, all these measures were soon shown to be of no avail. The Mandate of Heaven of the Ch'ing Dynasty had run out; for that matter it had really come to an end already sixty years earlier during the Taiping Revolution. The Manchus had remained on the throne in Peking primarily due to their usefulness to their foreign masters. But even these were

---

*P'u-i was then briefly restored to the throne in 1917. From 1924 he lived in retirement in Tientsin and after the 1931 conquest of Manchuria became the puppet of the Japanese there—first as the Chief Executive of Manchukuo, later as Emperor. Taken prisoner by the Soviet Army he was repatriated to China in 1949. He spent the next ten years in re-education in a prison for war criminals and was released in 1959 to resume work as a botanist. He was the author of an extremely interesting autobiography. He died in 1968.

now unable and, what is more important, unwilling to try once more to prop up this completely decadent and hopelessly incapable ruling caste.

V. Reform and Revolution

After the tragic downfall of the 1898 Reform Movement, the two principal surviving leaders escaped, as we have seen, to continue their political activity abroad. K'ang Yu-wei's views, as shaped in the earlier period, remained basically unaffected by future developments; he continued to maintain his allegiance to Kuang-hsü, and his entire programme to 1908 was based on the hopes that the Emperor would ultimately outlive Tz'u-hsi, regain power and then revert to the platform of the Reform Movement. Thus, K'ang Yu-wei remained a follower of the Ch'ing dynasty, a monarchist in a period when political development was sharply advancing to more progressive ideas. His philosophical views also remained quite unchanged; his partial orientation towards modernization made no further progress, while he still adhered to his own version of Confucianism. History was soon to leave him completely behind and his political role sank relatively quickly into an insignificant obscurity, from which he was to emerge only once more, pathetically and even ludicrously, during the farcical Ch'ing restoration of 1917.

The path of his younger follower, Liang Ch'i-ch'ao, proved to be quite different. Liang relatively quickly shed most of his attachment to Confucianism, became an outstanding spokesman for modernization and undoubtedly the most influential propagandist of Western Learning among the intellectuals during the first decade of the 20th century. However, his views were a curious, shifting and eclectic hodgepodge derived from an omnivorous reading of Western and Japanese literature, all of which he communicated to his audience in his books and the many articles contained in the periodicals he published in Japan. Politically, Liang remained a conservative; while not an outright supporter of the Ch'ing government, he favoured the introduction of a constitutional monarchy and was bitterly opposed to the growing revolutionary movement and the ideas of republicanism and democracy advanced by Sun Yat-sen.

At first, attempts were made under the auspices of the Japanese hosts to bring about co-operation between all the exiled Chinese groups working against Tz'u-hsi's regime. Due to the arrogant attitude of K'ang Yu-wei, who refused to consider the Western-educated Sun Yat-sen as his equal, these attempts met with complete failure and a sharp competition was waged between the Reformists and the followers of Sun Yat-sen for the support of and influence among the Chinese immigrants in Japan and other countries, which resulted temporarily, among others, due to the unscrupulous tactics of Liang Ch'i-ch'ao, in the victory of the reformist Protect the Emperor Society.

It should be noted, in passing, that the influence of the Japanese on the development of Chinese politics, including the revolutionary movement, was quite considerable. It was of a rather complex nature; on the one hand, Japanese progressive and early socialist groups sincerely supported the Chinese, Sun Yat-sen in particular. On the other hand, the Japanese government also pursued a policy of interesting itself in the Chinese revolutionary movement, but for quite different purposes—for utilizing it for the realization of ultimate plans of imperialist expansion.

Undoubtedly the outstanding representative, principal leader and ideologist of the revolutionary trend among the Chinese intellectuals abroad was Sun Yat-sen himself.* Sun was born on November 12, 1866 in a village in Hsiangshan (Chungshan) district in South-west Kwangtung, 35 miles from Canton. His family were poor tenant farmers. In the region he came from the traditions of revolutionary peasant struggles, particularly that of the Taiping movement, in which many of the inhabitants, including members of Sun's family, had participated, were quite strong. These traditions had a considerable influence on the shaping of the views of the young Sun Yat-sen, who already in his early teens saw himself as a second Hung Hsiu-ch'tian. His family sent Sun at the age of 12 to Hawaii to be cared for by his brother, Sun Te-chang (older by 15 years), a prosperous cattle raiser. For three years the boy attended a Church of England Mission school, acquiring the first rudiments of a Western education. Upon returning to China, he spent the years 1886-1892 completing his studies in medicine in Hong Kong, where he graduated with honours; thus, he had become a completely Western-educated intellectual.

Sun Yat-sen's political views developed already during his years as a medical student, when he became an advocate first of the need to modernize and liberate China and then later—in order to achieve this aim—of overthrowing the rule of the Ch'ing dynasty. However, up to the Sino-Japanese War, Sun did not exclude the possibility of effecting some indispensable reforms by means of the existing regime; his plans in this respect were outlined in a memorandum which he submitted to Li Hung-chang in the summer of 1894. There was no proper response to Sun's initiative, and the humiliating defeat of the Ch'ing regime in the conflict with Japan convinced him now of the necessity of revolutionary political action against the Manchu dynasty. Giving up his medical practice, he was to devote himself to this task completely. His first attempt in this direction was the organization, at the end of 1894, in Hawaii, of the *Hsing Chung Hui* (literally, "Revive China Society"—Sun's English version—"Association for the Regeneration of China". Its membership, which included no representatives of the gentry, as well as its influence, was at first quite limited, while its main aim was to organize from its base in Hong Kong an anti-Ch'ing rising in Kwangtung with the assistance of the traditionally anti-Manchu secret societies.

The first attempt at an uprising was made in Canton in October 1895; it ended in total failure and the death of some of Sun's closest followers. He himself managed to escape to Hong Kong and was now to spend the next sixteen years abroad as a political exile with a price on his head; only once, in 1907, was he able to set foot on his native soil for a few days. But it was precisely during this long period of exile that, having become a professional revolutionary, Sun Yat-sen devoted himself to intensive political activities, developed his views still further and ultimately emerged as the undisputed leader of the Chinese revolutionary movement.

Unable to return to his homeland, Sun concentrated his activities on the large groups of Chinese immigrants scattered throughout much of South-east Asia, Hawaii and the United States; these communities by 1910 numbered probably close to two and a half million. It was in this milieu that he was later to find most of his basic support and the role of the overseas Chinese communities was of inestimable importance in the development of the revolutionary movement. It was they who provided a part of the

*His original name was Sun Wen, one of his given names was I-hsien, which in Cantonese is pronounced Yat-sen. He is also referred to by a pseudonym he employed—Chung-shan.

early leaders of the movement, as well as the funds which made its activity possible. Their life abroad inclined them to become more prone to the acceptance of Western views and thus they were more progressive than their kinsmen in China. Simultaneously, the humiliating conditions of their native country, with which they always maintained the closest and most intimate contact and which was also unable to defend them against the discrimination from which they suffered (especially, although not only, in the United States), increased greatly both their feeling of national consciousness, as well as their anti-Manchu sentiments. The great bulk of the immigrants came from the southern coastal provinces, most of them from Kwangtung itself, which had anyhow been among the most advanced, politically and economically, areas of China, with the longest contacts with the West.

Sun travelled for years assiduously from one Chinese community to another, organizing, lecturing, raising funds, instilling among the immigrants a still greater awareness of China's fundamental needs. It was in 1896, during one of his early trips, that the Manchus, who considered him already then one of their greatest enemies, kidnapped him while in London and imprisoned him in the Chinese Legation in Portland Place, planning to ship him back to China to meet his death. He was rescued from his fate by the intervention of the English, in particular by that of his former medical teacher in Hong Kong, James Cantlie, to whom, through the intermediary of an English servant in the Legation, Sun had managed to smuggle a plea for aid. The incident, described by himself in a lengthy pamphlet, helped to make Sun a well-known figure on a world scale.

While Sun Yat-sen pursued his activities abroad, the anti-Ch'ing movement in China also continued to spread in the period after the I Ho T'uan in spite of constant and severe Manchu repression. Its main centre was Shanghai, where a group of young intellectuals connected with the newspaper *Su Pao* engaged in considerable revolutionary agitation and propaganda. The paper was suppressed and its editors arrested, but the movement continued nevertheless with new papers appearing in turn. One of those arrested was the young Tsou Jung (1885-1905), author of a famous and influential anti-Ch'ing pamphlet called "The Revolutionary Army". Revolutionary activity was also being conducted in a number of provinces such as that, for example, of the *Hua Hsing Hui* ("Society for the Revival of China"), founded in December 1903 by Huang Hsing (1874-1916), a school teacher's son from Hunan, who was later to become one of the most important leaders of the revolutionary movement. Another such organization was the *Kuang Fu Hui* ("Restoration Society") in Chekiang, which was led by the eminent scholar Chang Ping-lin (1868-1936). Huang Hsing's society in Hunan planned an anti-Ch'ing uprising to take place in November 1904; the conspiracy misfired but its leaders, all young intellectuals, managed to escape.

The increasing political awareness and rise of national consciousness was also well illustrated by the large-scale boycott of American goods which was organized in 1905 to protest at the discrimination against the Chinese in the United States. This campaign, which lasted from May to September, centred in Shanghai and extended to practically all the other major cities of the country. It was ultimately suppressed by the Ch'ing authorities.

However, as remarked earlier, it was among the Chinese students in Japan that the most considerable political activity of this period was being conducted. Sun Yat-sen, who between his travels among the Chinese diaspora resided mostly in Yokohama in

1901-1903, now drew closer to the Chinese student community in Japan, which was falling more and more under the influence of revolutionary ideas. It was in Japan that in 1905 a successful attempt was made by the representatives of the various revolutionary political associations mentioned above to unite into one organization. This was to be the well-known *Chung-kuo T'ung Meng Hui* ("United League of China"), which was established under Sun Yat-sen's auspices in August-September in Tokyo, with the enthusiastic approval and attendance of many hundreds of Chinese students.*

From the very outset, Sun Yat-sen, as the eldest and most experienced revolutionary, respected for his zeal and devotion, was recognized as the principal leader of the T'ung Meng Hui, and it was his views which were reflected in the organization's programme. Sun formulated his outlook, which was to be a considerable degree the result of his studies of and contact with Western civilization, in his famous *San Min Chu I* ("Three People's Principles") which he continued to elaborate until the end of his life. Briefly speaking, the doctrine was as follows: the First Principle was Nationalism, which in this period implied primarily a struggle against the Manchu domination of China. It was only in a later period—the 1920s—that this principle began to be interpreted in an anti-imperialist sense. The Second Principle was Democracy, understood by Sun to mean the introduction of a republican and constitutional form of government on the French or American model in place of the Ch'ing autocratic monarchy. The Third Principle was People's Livelihood—a concept which Sun himself referred to as Socialism. This was actually a somewhat nebulous promise to deal with social problems in the future, among others, by means of land equalization. It was derived from Sun's awareness of the existence of such problems, both in China and, in particular, in the West, where the inability of the capitalist system to resolve them had become obvious to him. It was also bound up with the idea that the specific nature of China's society and economy might make possible the avoidance of the arising of the problems plaguing the West, by passing over the capitalist stage of development.

Of the three principles, it was more than likely that the first had the greatest appeal to the members of the T'ung Meng Hui, and the main efforts of the organization were aimed at bringing about the downfall of the Ch'ing regime. But it was the programme as a whole, very much imbued with the spirit of the French Revolution, and especially the emphasis on the imperative need for revolutionary action, which served as the basis for extensive propaganda aimed, among others, against the constitutional monarchist views of Liang Ch'i-ch'ao and his followers. This ideological battle was conducted primarily by the T'ung Meng Hui press, the most important of which was the monthly periodical *Min Pao* ("People's Tribune"), published in Japan in 1905-1910, with the collaboration of some of the ablest of Sun's young followers who were to play a very important and varied role in the political life of China. As a result of this campaign the views of the T'ung Meng Hui gained ever-greater support among the students—and through them ultimately in China as well—and among the overseas Chinese communities.

The organization of the T'ung Meng Hui and its future activities reflected primarily

*The word "revolutionary" was dropped from the title for conspiratorial purposes. Sun's own translation was "The Chinese Federal Association". Characteristically, the foundation meeting of the T'ung Meng Hui was held in a hall belonging to a member of the Japanese Black Dragon (Amur River) Society—a notorious chauvinist and expansionist organization.

the further growth of the political and national consciousness of the Chinese intellectuals, as well as the growing ferment within China itself. This revolutionary upswing was, however, a more general phenomenon, true not only of China, but also of colonial and semi-colonial Asia—a part of the process referred to by Lenin as "The Awakening of Asia". In the case of China, two events were of considerable significance in stimulating this growth of political activeness—the Russo-Japanese War and the 1905 Russian Revolution. The defeat of the outwardly mighty Tsarist autocracy by a newly modernized, supposedly constitutional, small Asian power, which only half a century earlier had itself been the victim of Western aggression, made a powerful impression on all politically minded Chinese. It also emphasized more sharply the differences between the position of China and Japan, and brought into still clearer relief the urgency of the need for China's modernization. As to how this was to be accomplished—here the roads between the reformist and the revolutionary trends diverged even more sharply. The 1905 Russian Revolution, although ultimately unsuccessful, pointed to the necessity of waging a revolutionary political struggle against autocracy and, in this sense, influenced the thinking and also to some degree the strategy and tactics of the T'ung Meng Hui and its leaders.

The T'ung Meng Hui, while it was larger than the Hsing Chung Hui and the other earlier groups, was still, nevertheless, a small organization; its membership in the years 1905-1907 was little more than 1000, although it spread to most of the overseas Chinese communities where it gained much support, and through the returned students became also a political force in China herself. The tactics of the T'ung Meng Hui inclined to the concept of organizing armed military coups, aimed rather at serving as a signal and stimulus for a general nationwide anti-Manchu rising. Sun Yat-sen and his followers did not seek to organize a movement on a mass scale, which would set into motion the peasantry on the Taiping pattern. They concentrated instead on infiltration into the Ch'ing armed forces and on utilizing the powerful anti-Manchu secret societies. In his autobiography Sun refers to his "ten unsuccessful revolutionary attempts" which preceded the 1911 Revolution. The first two of these were the 1895 Canton conspiracy already mentioned, and an attempt at a rising in Huichou in Kwangtung in October 1900. The last eight were all coups organized by the T'ung Meng Hui in the years 1907 to 1911. The third—Ch'aochou (Kwangtung), May 27, 1907; the fourth—Huichou, June 2, 1907; the fifth—Ch'inchou and Lienchou (Kwangtung), September 1907; the sixth—Chennankuan (Southern Kwangsi), December 1907, in which Sun himself participated; the seventh—Ch'inchou and Lienchou again, March-April, 1908; the eighth—Houkou (Yunnan), April 1908; the ninth—the rising of the New Army in Canton, February 12, 1910; the tenth—the Huang Hua Kang rising in Canton, April 27, 1911.

As can be seen, all these attempts took place in the South and South-west border provinces and not only because this region was the most anti-Manchu and revolutionary by tradition, but also because it was the most accessible for the shipment from abroad of arms, supplies, money and men by the T'ung Meng Hui. Almost all of these actions, especially the most important April 1911 rising, were led by Huang Hsing. Although all these coups ended in failure and were followed by severe repressions by the Ch'ing authorities, they did lead to a further increase in revolutionary and anti-Manchu feelings and showed up the utter rottenness of the Ch'ing regime, as well as the relative ease with which it could be toppled if only one more, still better organized, attempt were to be made.

A number of other actions against the Ch'ing government in the same period, which were not organized by the T'ung Meng Hui, should also be mentioned. Among these was the rising in December 1906 of the miners in P'inghsiang, Kiangsi, perhaps the first large action of this class. Another was the Anking revolt led by Hsü Hsi-lin (1873-1907), who assassinated the governor of Anhwei (July 1907). It was in connection with this attempt that one of the earliest women revolutionaries, Ch'iu Chin (1877-1907), a member of the T'ung Meng Hui and a leader of the revolutionary underground in Chekiang, met her death at the hands of the Manchu executioners, the first of many women to give their lives for the revolution. In this and a number of other actions a fairly strong trend of anarchist influence can be noted (derived in part from the Russian Narodniks) and it was to lead to further attempts at assassination of Ch'ing officials, including an unsuccessful attack against the Regent in 1910.

All these actions constituted a remarkable chapter in Chinese history, a saga of great bravery and devotion. This was particularly true of the 1911 Canton rising, the largest of all and the one which came closest to success. Much effort had been devoted to the organization of this uprising; funds had been collected among the Overseas Chinese, a special picked "Dare to Die" corps of 800 men organized. However, a lack of proper co-ordination ruined the chances for success and the uprising was suppressed with great losses. A monument now graces the Huang Hua Kang (Yellow Flower Mound) in memory of the "Seventy-two Martyrs" buried there (more had died in fact), who had given their lives for their country's freedom. They were truly the elite of the T'ung Meng Hui. Within six months of their deaths, the cause for which they had fallen was to triumph in the Wuchang rising.

CHAPTER 38

The 1911 Revolution

I. Immediate Background

The complex struggles which were being waged in China on the eve of the 1911 Revolution, both within the Ch'ing court and among the Manchus and their Chinese opponents of different political persuasions, were further sharpened by an issue which had both economic and political implications and raised the bitterness of the conflict to a new pitch.* This was the question of railroad construction which became inextricably intertwined with all the already extant political problems facing the country. The basic issue was whether the future building of railroads was to be carried out by the central government which, in effect, meant by the foreign powers, inasmuch as the Ch'ing had no financial means at their disposal for this purpose and could proceed only with the help of foreign loans, or by Chinese national capital, i.e. that of the Chinese gentry and merchants, who were willing to invest in such projects. The latter had organized themselves for this purpose, especially in those provinces where the issue was most topical (Kwangtung, Hunan, Hupei and Szechuan), into associations and companies which claimed the right to proceed with railroad ventures and to collect funds for this aim.

The Provincial Assemblies became involved in the dispute, representing the interests of their local railway associations; this led, in turn, to attacks by the Assemblies on the central government over this issue and served to stimulate still further the trend towards provincial autonomy and a decentralization of political power. The pressure exerted by these provincial actions was quite considerable and, in some cases, successful, leading, for example, to buying back by the Peking government of the concession which had been granted earlier to the Americans for the building of the Hankow-Canton line. This was one of the two most important lines whose future was at stake—the other being the projected Hankow-Szechuan line.

It was against this background of intense provincial agitation that the Ch'ing government came forward with its so-called railway nationalization plan in May 1911. The scheme had little in common with a true programme of railway construction by the central government on a national scale; it was primarily the brain-child of the newly appointed Minister of Communications, the notoriously corrupt Sheng Hsüan-huai, and its main object was the obtaining of a new loan from the aforementioned Four

---

*In Chinese literature the 1911 Revolution is usually referred to as the Hsin Hai; this is the name of the cyclical year of the old Chinese Calendar which covered the period from January 30, 1911 to February 17, 1912, i.e. the months during which the main events of the revolution including the Manchu abdication occurred.

Power Consortium, which in itself constituted a prime source of graft for Sheng and the Manchu court. The contract for this loan (the Hukwang Loan) and for the building of the Hankow-Canton and Hankow-Szechuan lines was signed on May 20—eleven days after the issuing of the nationalization edict. Both events created a furore in the entire country, but especially in the provinces affected. The Ch'ing government was denounced for selling out the country to the foreign powers, inasmuch as the conditions attached to the loan meant, in fact, the further subjection of the country's economy to foreign control, while Sheng Hsüan-huai's immediate dismissal and impeachment was demanded.

The reaction was especially strong in the vast, rich and traditionally independent minded province of Szechuan; here the movement for the local building of the railroad had been quite advanced and the government's move meant a considerable financial loss to those who had invested in the railway project. By the beginning of August the entire province was set into motion against the government; the merchants and the students organized strikes and protests, while the disturbances spread everywhere with the population beginning to refuse to pay taxes. In September demonstrations took place in the capital, Ch'engtu, which were brutally suppressed by the Ch'ing governor; the only result of his actions was to spark uprisings in almost all of Szechuan. The Manchu government now faced a massive political crisis and troops were mobilized in the neighbouring province of Hupei to be sent to Szechuan to quell what was developing into a full-scale rebellion.

II. The Wuchang Uprising

After the failure of the April 1911 uprising in Canton, a part of the T'ung Meng Hui leaders, led by one of the ablest, Sung Chiao-jen (1882-1913), had decided to put an end to the policy of organizing uprisings in the frontier provinces of the South and South-west and to concentrate their efforts instead on the region of the Yangtse Valley. A special T'ung Meng Hui committee was established in Shanghai for this purpose in July 1911. Considerable work had already been undertaken in this area in infiltrating the army units stationed here; this had been accomplished by two revolutionary organizations under T'ung Meng Hui influence—the "Literary Society" and the "Common Advancement Society", in which returned students from Japan played an important role. In particular, much success had been obtained in influencing the soldiers stationed in the triple-city of Wuhan, where perhaps as many as a third of the Wuchang garrison were already members of the "Literary Society" in 1911. It was under these circumstances that the T'ung Meng Hui now set its plans for a new rising against the Manchus in this region, which was scheduled for the late autumn of 1911. The considerable degree of large-scale popular discontent and unrest, as evidenced by widespread rice riots, particularly the famous one in Ch'angsha in April 1910, also argued in favour of initiating revolutionary action against the Ch'ing in this region.

Under the influence of the events in Szechuan the plans for a rising in Wuhan were set for October 6, but, due to the lack of sufficient preparation, the date was postponed to October 16. However, all the plans miscarried, inasmuch as on October 9 the accidental explosion of a bomb being manufactured by the conspirators in Hankow led to the discovery of their headquarters and arms cache, to the arrest and execution of a number of the revolutionary leaders and, still worse, to the seizure by the Ch'ing authorities of a list of names of all those in the army involved in the plot. It was against this background that a small group of soldiers, members of the "Literary Society", led by a sergeant who, though deprived of their leaders, decided themselves to launch the uprising before it would be too late. They were soon joined in this venture by other troops and thanks, among others, to the cowardice of the Manchu commander, were successful in taking possession of all of Wuchang on October 10. Hanyang, with its important arsenal and great military stores, and the large and prosperous city of Hankow—both north of the river—were taken by the revolutionary troops on October 12. The leaderless soldiers had been faced at the outset with the problem of finding a commander; they solved this by dragging out of hiding a terrified Ch'ing brigade commander, Li-Yüan-hung (1864-1928), forced him to take command, to become the military governor of Hupei and to support the revolution, with which he had nothing in common, thus launching him on a varied political career, which was later to include the presidency of China.

The success of the Wuchang uprising served as the proverbial spark setting off a prairie fire; within the next two months Ch'ing authority disappeared in most of Central and South China. By the end of November fifteen provinces had declared their independence of Peking—all of these changes occurred with very little fighting and almost no bloodshed. Only the North-east, Chihli, Honan and Shantung remained under the control of the Manchus or, to put it more precisely, under the sway of the Peiyang army's divisions stationed in these areas. In November the Ch'ing navy also declared itself for the revolution. South of the Yangtse, practically the entire Ch'ing army, especially the New Army units, joined the revolutionary cause. Only some of the troops of General Chang Hsün (1854-1923), a fervent supporter of the Manchus, held out in Nanking; they were soon attacked by revolutionary troops from Shanghai and Chekiang and Nanking was taken on December 2.

However, from a military point of view the situation was far from simple, inasmuch as the Peiyang divisions—undoubtedly the best equipped and trained in the entire country—still remained loyal to Peking, and even more so to their creator, Yüan Shih-k'ai. They now began to move down south to attack the revolutionary centre in Wuhan. Politically, the situation was also confused. While the T'ung Meng Hui had been the initiator and inspirer of revolutionary actions for the past six years, it was not this organization which was to emerge as the main ruling force in the revolutionary South. The newly established provincial governments were quickly taken over, in most cases, by erstwhile supporters of a constitutional monarchy, including many former Ch'ing officials and generals, now climbing on the bandwagon as newly fledged advocates of a Chinese Republic. Simultaneously, the provincial authorities were jealous of their own rights and slow in joining together in common action against the Ch'ing government.

The T'ung Meng Hui itself was too weak, heterogenous and disorganized to be able to offer sufficient resistance to this flood of careerists searching for profitable posts in a new administration. Its principal leader was still absent from China, for the Wuchang uprising had caught Sun Yat-sen unawares in Denver, Colorado, while on still another of his tours among the overseas Chinese. Sun quickly left the States but he did not proceed to China across the Pacific; instead he made his way back through England. His aim in this was at least threefold: to obtain financial assistance for the new revolutionary government, to prevent any such aid from being given to the Manchus, and to assure the neutrality of the powers, of which Great Britain was still the most important, towards the conflict in China, i.e. to prevent the kind of foreign intervention that had proved fatal to the Taipings. In this, while he failed in his first aim, he was—as we shall see later on—on the whole, temporarily and partially successful in his other two aims.

The collapse of Ch'ing rule south of the Yangtse had brought the Peking government to a state of complete panic and chaos. The Regent and his followers now turned for help to the one man whose prestige and following in the Peiyang army could possibly bolster up the tottering Manchu throne—Yüan Shih-k'ai who, while in exile, had kept fully in touch with all the developments. On October 14 Tsai-feng announced the appointment of Yüan as the Governor-general of Hukwang to be in command of the army for suppressing the Wuhan "bandits", a move warmly welcomed by the Peking diplomatic corps, which had always held Yüan in high esteem for his previous record. However, Yüan found that he had not recovered sufficiently from his foot ailment. He waited calmly for the position of the Ch'ing government to deteriorate still further, putting forth demands the acceptance of which would place all power, especially military, in his hands and would enable him to have the Manchus completely at his mercy. His cunning scheme quickly met with total success. On November 2 the Regent accepted all of Yüan's demands and appointed him Premier of a newly formed constitutional cabinet, for the Ch'ing had converted their government with lightning speed into a new constitutional monarchy; the appointment was confirmed on November 8 by the National Assembly.

In the circumstances Yüan was now willing to leave his estate and to take command of the army in the South, where two of his closest military protégés—Feng Kuo-chang (1859-1919) and Tuan Ch'i-jui (1865-1936)—both future "Heads of State", were in charge of the operations against the revolutionary forces in Wuhan. He arrived with great pomp in Peking on November 16 and all the authority of the Ch'ing government was rapidly gathered in his hands. Within a very brief time he asserted his total control of all the military forces in the North, among others, by the assassination and purging of all officers suspected of revolutionary sympathies or actions. The dominance of the Peiyang clique in the North was thus completely assured.

Yüan's forces now began their offensive against the positions of the revolutionaries in Wuhan; the disunited and disorganized Military Government there, although strengthened by the arrival of Huang Hsing who became the Commander-in-Chief, proved unable ultimately to withstand the attacks of the superior Peiyang divisions. Hankow fell on November 1, an attempt to retake it in mid-November failed and then, after a bitter struggle, the revolutionary forces lost Hanyang as well on November 27. The Peiyang artillery was now freely able to shell their opponents' positions in Wuchang.

However, it was not a part of Yüan's plans at this stage to bring about a victory over the revolutionary armed forces—a long-drawn-out civil war would probably have been necessary to achieve this, inasmuch as the revolutionary army had been increased considerably in size by a mass influx of volunteers; while its training was poor, its morale was still relatively quite high in the first months of the revolution. Yüan preferred to reach a truce quickly and to begin negotiations with the revolutionaries, all with the aim of strengthening his own position with respect to both sides—the Manchus and the revolutionaries. In fact, from the beginning of December on, practically all military action between the opposing armies had come to an end.

Long and tortuous negotiations were begun in the middle of December in Shanghai; the revolutionaries had been all along offering Yüan the presidency of the future republic, if he would only agree to betray his Manchu masters and bring about their downfall. Yüan was quite willing to do this, but he demanded the time required to persuade the Ch'ing court of the hopelessness of its position, as well as wishing to ascertain whether the presidency would give him at least as much power as he already possessed in Peking.

III. The Establishment of the Republic

On December 25, 1911 Sun Yat-sen arrived in Shanghai. On his way he had stopped at Hong Kong; here one of his closest followers, Hu Han-min (1886-1936), then military governor of Kwangtung (later on a prominent leader of the right-wing Kuomintang), sought to persuade him to establish a revolutionary government in the South, revealing in this proposal the profound distrust of Yüan Shih-k'ai felt by many of the T'ung Meng Hui leaders. However, Sun disregarded this advice. His return to Shanghai, where he was welcomed with great acclaim, brought an important new factor into the extremely complicated political situation. The representatives of the fifteen provinces which had declared their independence of the Ch'ing government had, after much squabbling between the leaders in Wuchang and Shanghai, transferred their main headquarters to Nanking. On December 29 they elected Sun Yat-sen as Provisional President of the Chinese Republic, which was proclaimed in Nanking on January 1, 1912 (the first day of the first year of the Republic, which now shifted to the Gregorian Calendar). Li Yüan-hung was chosen as Vice-President and a provisional government was likewise established in which, characteristically, the majority of ministers were not T'ung Meng Hui members but constitutionalists and former Ch'ing officials; on the other hand, all the vice-ministers were T'ung Meng Hui men. Actually, the government was quite weak as it had little, if any, control over the provinces. The new republican government now called for the immediate abdication of the Ch'ing dynasty as the indispensable precondition for the reunification of the divided country.

Already earlier—during the drawing up of the T'ung Meng Hui programme—Sun Yat-sen had formulated his ideas regarding the future shape that the government of the Republic should assume once the anti-Ch'ing revolution had been victorious. His plans provided for three stages of government: the first was to be a military government lasting for three years. This was then to be succeeded by a provisional government for a period of six years, during which a permanent constitution was to be drafted. The provisional and military rule were to come to an end after these nine years and a fully democratic constitutional government, based on Western parliamentary models, was to follow.

For the implementation of the scheme—especially of the first stage—a unified central control of the military forces of the country was obviously imperative. But this was precisely what the Nanking government never had; its control over the armies of the provinces, which acknowledged its rule, was extremely vague due to the lack of unity and the growing ambitions of both the newly fledged revolutionary leaders and the former Ch'ing army officers. What was still more important, the strongest single military forces of the country were not in its hands but in those of Yüan Shih-k'ai. Sun's plans were thus doomed from the outset, especially by the eagerness of most of the Nanking government's politicians to come to an agreement with Yüan as quickly as possible for the purpose of preventing a civil war, extending the Republic to the entire country and avoiding foreign intervention. It was with these aims that his colleagues persuaded Sun to announce that he would immediately resign the presidency to Yüan, once the latter was ready to bring about the downfall of the Manchus, who were practically at his mercy.

The negotiations between Nanking and Peking now continued in these new circumstances with, needless to say, profound mutual mistrust of each other's intentions. Both parties were also in desperate financial straits, as the country was bankrupt and the foreign financiers were unwilling to come forth with new loans until the political situation had become clarified. The provincial governments turned to the easy but ruinous method of issuing vast quantities of paper money, with the inevitable result of a galloping inflation and a further deterioration of general conditions; the Nanking government, on the other hand, sought to obtain loans from the Japanese capitalists on usurious terms. Yüan was somewhat more successful in this field; he assured the Ch'ing of his loyalty—which they had every reason to distrust—by having his Peiyang generals send in telegrams voicing their support for the Ch'ing monarchy (this device of politics by circular telegram was to become a great favourite during the entire ensuing period of militarist rule). On this basis Yüan was able to extract some of the hoarded Ch'ing treasures which he utilized primarily for the upkeep of his armies.

In spite of their desperate position the Manchu princes were still quite unwilling to abandon the remnants of their power and were, in particular, fearful of what fate might have in store for them if the dynasty were to be overthrown in a revolutionary fashion. Against the background of disunity and wrangling between the Manchus, Tsai-feng resigned as Regent already on December 6, and the Empress Dowager Lung-yü (Kuang-hsü's widow) became formally the head of the Ch'ing court. On January 16 an attempt was made in Peking to assassinate Yüan Shih-k'ai; although some of his bodyguards were killed, he himself emerged unscathed. This raised the trust of the Manchus in him and enabled Yüan to exert still more pressure in the direction he was aiming—the abdication of the Ch'ing emperor from his throne.

A number of Imperial Conferences attended by the main Manchu princes were held to debate the future. The assassination on January 26 of Liang-pi, the outstanding Manchu opponent of abdication, greatly frightened the court. At this moment the very same Peiyang generals who had declared at the beginning of January their complete loyalty and full support for the monarchy now sent in a new telegram on January 28, this time proclaiming the need for a Ch'ing abdication and their devotion to the ideals of republican government. The final blow, prepared by Yüan, was thus delivered. The comedy had been well acted out—the Peiyang military clique now entered the Chinese political arena as the most formidable, if not the most decisive, force.

IV. The Fall of the Ch'ing Dynasty

The stage was now set for the last act—the end of the 267-year-long rule of the Manchus over the Chinese people. The Ch'ing government, deceived and betrayed by Yüan Shih-k'ai, the man in whom they had placed their last hope of survival, surrendered without any further resistance. On February 12 the Empress Dowager, in the presence of the Manchu princes, high court officials and the members of Yüan's cabinet read out, crying bitterly, in her name and that of P'u-i, his abdication from the throne. The Abdication Edict was in itself an extremely curious document; in it the Emperor, acknowledging the desire of the majority of the Chinese people for a republic, designated Yüan Shih-k'ai as the official who was fully empowered, with the approval of the retiring monarch, to carry out the organization of a provisional Republican government (this point is not surprising considering that the edict was written by Liang Shih-i (1869-1933), one of the cleverest of Yüan's followers). The Emperor, his family and court were to be left in full possession of the Imperial Palace, as well as of all their wealth and property, and to become pensioners of the Republican government. These terms—the so-called Articles of Favourable Treatment—had been the subject of earlier secret negotiations between Yüan and the Nanking government.

Sun Yat-sen celebrated the abdication of the Manchus with great ceremony; he delivered an oration at the mausoleum near Nanking of Chu Yüan-chang, the founder of the Ming dynasty, in which he informed Chu's spirit of the victory which had been finally gained in the driving out of the Manchus.*

Yüan Shih-k'ai had kept, for once, his part of an agreement—he had engineered the fall of the Ch'ing dynasty, emerging as its supposedly legitimate heir; he now demanded that the Republican government keep its part of the compact. This followed without delay; on February 13 Sun Yat-sen resigned his post as Provisional President, in the hope that in this way the Republic would be extended to the entire country and would quickly obtain international recognition. On February 15 the Senate of the Provisional Republican Government (a body composed of representatives from the provinces) elected Yüan in his place as Provisional President. However, well aware of at least a part of Yüan's schemes, Sun had stipulated three conditions, which he considered indispensable before the transfer of all power to Yüan should take place: that the seat of the Republican government be situated permanently in Nanking (thus Yüan should proceed for his inauguration to this city), that Yüan should promise to observe the Provisional Constitution which was then being drafted in Nanking, and that Sun should continue in his post until Yüan had been duly sworn in.

The aim of the above conditions was obvious—to establish the new Republican government away from the centre of Yüan's military power, of former Ch'ing officialdom, still a powerful force, as well as from the direct pressure of the Peking diplomatic corps. But it was a relatively easy matter for Yüan to see through the ideas behind these conditions and to frustrate them completely. On February 18 a special delegation composed of some of the most prominent Republican leaders was dispatched from Nanking to Peking to negotiate these matters with the new Provisional President, who had declared that he saw considerable difficulties in agreeing with these conditions and could not see his way clear to leave Peking.

By a curious coincidence, a few days after the arrival of this delegation one of the Peiyang divisions stationed in Peking—the Third, known as the most disciplined and devoted to Yüan of all the Peiyang units and commanded by one of his most trusted

*The great bulk of the Manchu people, already almost completely sinified, quietly melted into the Chinese population after the revolution. They were to reclaim their national identity only over 40 years later when the conditions in People's China made such an action possible.

generals, Ts'ao K'un (1862-1938), yet another future "Head of State"—staged an excellently organized mutiny, looting and burning, in a most orderly fashion, a considerable part of the centre of Peking, including the residence of the Nanking delegation, which had to flee for safety to the Legation Quarter. After this incident Yüan declared that he could not possibly leave the Northern capital in such circumstances of unrest and lack of stability, which might even bring about a foreign intervention. The Nanking delegates had nothing more to say.

On March 10, 1912 the inauguration of Yüan took place in Peking; on the same day the Nanking government passed its draft of the Provisional Constitution—its last political act. The seat of the government was now firmly established in Peking, the official transfer being made on April 4, while Sun's official resignation had taken place on April 1. This was an act which he himself was to criticize bitterly in the future. A new government was established with one of Yüan's closest and ablest protégés, T'ang Shao-i (1860-1938)—a member of the first group of Chinese who had studied abroad with Yung Wing—as Premier. T'ang had earlier been Yüan's main representative in the negotiations with the South and had now joined the T'ung Meng Hui. In the new cabinet T'ung Meng Hui members held four out of ten portfolios; thus, seemingly, unity between the revolutionaries and the militarist and bureaucratic forces represented by Yüan Shih-k'ai had been established. But, characteristically, Yüan placed his own closest henchmen in the three key posts—the Ministry of Interior, the Army and Finance. The struggle for power in the Republic was now to enter a new stage.

In reality, the taking over of the Presidency by Yüan Shih-k'ai meant already at this moment the defeat and failure of the 1911 Revolution, although this was still by no means obvious to the contemporary witnesses of these events, even to Sun Yat-sen himself. The reasons for this defeat rested primarily in the weakness of the revolutionary movement, especially of the T'ung Meng Hui itself. While its programme had been sufficient for bringing about the downfall of the Ch'ing dynasty, it was inadequate for facing the problem of constructing a new, republican and democratic society. Such a reconstruction would have of necessity entailed dealing with the vast social and economic tasks involved in the transformation of the semi-feudal and semi-colonial country (and the directions in which such a transformation should be made were quite unclear at the time), as well as the political measures indispensable for their implementation. There was little awareness of these enormously difficult tasks in the thinking of the T'ung Meng Hui and even in the ideology of Sun Yat-sen himself. The young and politically inexperienced revolutionaries soon found themselves out-manoeuvred by the constitutionalist careerist office-seekers on the one hand, and the militarist-bureaucratic hangers-on of Yüan's Peiyang clique on the other. Another basic reason—itself a reflection of the weakness of the T'ung Meng Hui—was the relatively limited amount of support for the Republic on the part of the vast masses of the population, especially the peasantry. While there had been much peasant discontent in the period preceding the Revolution and much initial popular support for it, this was neither taken advantage of, nor organized for future political purposes by the T'ung Meng Hui. As a result, the new provincial republican authorities, which were mostly taken over by gentry elements, quickly put down all attempts of peasant revolt; some of the T'ung Meng Hui leaders supported such actions as well.

Nevertheless, in spite of all the above, the 1911 Revolution did have a great accomplishment to its credit—the downfall of the absolute monarchy, a political institution with over 2000 years of tradition and prestige behind it, buttressed, until now, by the all-pervasive influence of Confucian ideology. This was a truly historical landmark. At least one extremely important encumbrance and handicap on the road to China's modernization and her emergence once again in the future as a powerful country had been swept away into the dustbin of the past.

V. The Powers and the Revolution

While the growing weakness and ineptitude of the Ch'ing government had been becoming ever more obvious to the powers and their representatives in Peking, the outbreak of the Revolution caught them to a great degree unawares, especially as they had tended always to belittle, if not malign, the activities of the T'ung Meng Hui and of Sun Yat-sen, whom they portrayed as, at best, a utopian visionary. When the Wuchang uprising had proved successful, most of the powers felt quite sure that the Ch'ing government would have relatively little trouble in suppressing the growing revolutionary movement, especially if it utilized for this purpose Yüan Shih-k'ai and his Peiyang forces. However, as the panic and utter helplessness of the Manchus became apparent, the powers, interested primarily in the maintenance of the *status quo*, i.e. in preserving intact all their political and economic privileges, cast about quickly for the men and forces who could prove capable of accomplishing this aim. Without any hesitation—and the unanimity of the Peking diplomatic corps was quite far-going in this respect—the imperialists saw only one choice for their "Strong Man", the very same Yüan Shih-k'ai.

It seems quite clear that the establishment of a constitutional monarchy, in which the real power would have rested in the hands of Yüan, rather than in those of the discredited Manchus, was the preferred choice of all the powers, including the United States and France. In spite of the attempts of the Provisional Government in Nanking to obtain recognition of the Republic after its proclamation in January 1912, not a single foreign country welcomed the newly established government.

The powers did not, however, intervene directly, i.e. militarily, into Chinese affairs at this time for a number of reasons. Most important, the rivalries between the powers militated against the organization of such an intervention, which could have resulted in an open conflict between the imperialists themselves. This does not mean, however, that some of the imperialist governments, especially the Japanese, did not give serious thought to the possibility of a military intervention on behalf of the Ch'ing government. The relatively limited scale of the armed conflict between the revolutionaries and the Ch'ing government, ending with the December truce, also did not give rise to fears that foreign interests would be imperilled by a large-scale civil war, which would have necessitated rapid armed intervention. At the very outset of the Revolution, the consuls of the powers in Hankow had declared their neutrality in the conflict and had played an instrumental role, to be continued later on by the Peking legations, in helping to bring about the negotiations between the two sides. The aim was, needless to say, not altruism but self-interest, based on a realistic assessment of the relative strength of the two parties in the conflict. The powers banked from the very beginning on the ultimate victory of the forces of "law and order", as represented by Yüan, regardless of what the ultimate shape of the government would be.

Nevertheless, from the very outset of the Revolution, and for that matter, even during the stage of its preparation, Sun Yat-sen and the T'ung Meng Hui had been quite apprehensive that the powers might intervene to save their Manchu clients from annihilation. For this reason, both in its programme as well as in its activities, the T'ung Meng Hui went to great lengths to persuade the powers that a victorious revolutionary government would not infringe the foreign interests in the slightest, would not raise the issue of the unequal treaties. The only point made was the demand that, once the Revolution had been successfully begun, the powers should refrain from offering the Ch'ing government any assistance, particularly financial.

The rapid unfolding of events in the spring of 1912, the abject abdication of the Manchus and the assumption of the Presidency by Yüan Shih-k'ai all assured the powers that the control of the government was passing into hands which could be considered as quite safe from their point of view. Thus, while they had refused to deal with or recognize the Republican Provisional Government in Nanking, all the necessary steps to grant such recognition to Yüan and, what was still more important, to furnish him with sufficient aid to consolidate his rule were now being taken, while the weakness of the T'ung Meng Hui and its surrender to Yüan was greeted with evident satisfaction. Thus, the neutrality had in reality proved to be definitely weighted and one-sided. However, to a certain degree, the developments in China were not followed by the powers with the concern and interest which might have been the case even a few years earlier; this was largely due to the continuously growing deterioration of international relations, to imperialist conflict and tension on a world scale and to the absorption of all the major powers, with the exception of Japan and to a certain degree the United States, in the crises in other parts of the globe, particularly in Europe, which were to lead to the First World War. As against these, the drama in China seemed relegated to a secondary role in world politics, although this did not diminish its importance from the point of view of the history of China itself.

PART XIII

China Under the Rule of the Militarists (1912-1919)

CHAPTER 39

The Dictatorship of Yüan Shih-k'ai

I. The Political Situation After Yüan's Assumption of the Presidency

Due to the weakness of the revolutionary forces led by the T'ung Meng Hui, Yüan Shih-k'ai had been successful in assuming supreme power on his own terms. The political situation, however, still remained fluctuating and confused; its main features now were a further struggle for power between the forces represented by Yüan Shih-k'ai—the gentry, officials and militarists, primarily of North China—and the advocates of the Republic, consisting mostly of intellectuals and bourgeois groups mainly from South and Central China. The basic content of this struggle revolved around the nature of the future government which was to rule the new Republic. It was against this background that the formation of political parties took place rapidly, with each of the above sides organizing its adherents.

After various shifts and changes in alignment the main political groupings which emerged from this jostling were the Progressive Party (*Chinputang*), formed in May 1913 from the coalescing of the three smaller groups, which served as the principal support of Yüan Shih-k'ai, and the newly organized *Kuomintang*. The Progressive Party was mostly a coterie of former Ch'ing officials and military, as well as conservative intellectuals, among whom the most prominent role was played by Liang Ch'i-ch'ao. Its programme—if it had anything deserving the name—was primarily that of buttressing the power of the new president and engaging in rivalry for the perquisites of office with its main opponents, the Kuomintang.

The Kuomintang, on the other hand, organized in August 1912 and composed of the T'ung Meng Hui, already much adulterated with post-revolutionary careerists, and four other smaller political groups, had a somewhat clearer conception of the future government structure. Its main aim was the development of a constitutional and parliamentary form of rule which would serve, among others, as a check on the obvious tendencies of the central government, especially of Yüan Shih-k'ai himself, to assume autocratic power. However, the Kuomintang had deliberately restricted the scope of its activities to purely conventional political forms, organizing itself for the purpose of parliamentary elections, and had abandoned any attempt at setting into motion a mass movement which could have given it a broad, popular support, especially among the peasantry. The land equalization proposal, in particular, which had been mentioned in the original T'ung Meng Hui programme and could have served as the basis for a land reform was now consigned to oblivion. This abandonment of any attempt to conduct a policy of social and economic reform and transformation was to cost the Kuomintang very dear, inasmuch as its forces turned out to be much weaker than those of Yüan Shih-k'ai's Peiyang clique, which had the bulk of the country's military forces at its disposal. This was especially so in the case of the provincial governments, for already in 1912 Yüan Shih-k'ai had placed all the power in the provinces in the hands of the military commanders who, as the military governors, were now the only real rulers of the provinces. With the exception of some southern provinces, the great majority of the new military governors were Yüan's henchmen from the Peiyang clique. The strength of the Kuomintang was further weakened by the fact that most of the revolutionary army—which had grown considerably in size during the 1911 revolution—was now disbanded by Huang Hsing, primarily owing to the lack of funds for its maintenance.

From the outset of the political struggle and at this early stage it was also quite obvious that Yüan Shih-k'ai was definitely benefiting from full support of all the powers, which had all along favoured his rise to the presidency as the "Strong Man" who should prove able to maintain the type of "law and order" necessary for safeguarding all the interests of foreign imperialism in China. This factor of foreign support proved to be of the utmost value for the realization of Yüan Shih-k'ai's plans aimed at the achieving of complete dictatorial rule.

Within only a few months it became clear that the plans of the Kuomintang for the creation of a parliamentary government on the basis of the Provisional Constitution which, following largely the French model, provided for a strong cabinet government and a relatively weak executive, were considered to be a serious obstacle by Yüan Shih-k'ai, and that all means would be employed by him to rid himself of such encumbrances. There was no particular finesse in the means to be used by Yüan for this purpose. He was the advocate of basically only two methods—either gold or bullets; he sought either to bribe the politicians into complete subservience to him, or to do away with his opponents by means of physical annihilation.

The attempts of the first cabinet during Yüan Shih-k'ai's presidency to establish some respect for the principles of constitutional government quickly came to a sorry end due to Yüan's obstructive tactics, although it had been headed by T'ang Shao-i, himself a long-time protégé of Yüan. By mid-June 1912 T'ang, who had taken his post and tasks seriously, resigned in disgust. While his place was formally taken for a while by Lu Cheng-hsiang (1871-1949), a professional diplomat, the Minister of the Interior, Chao Ping-chün, one of Yüan's most reliable and unscrupulous henchmen, was made Premier in September. Thus, the facade of constitutional government began to wear very thin already within half a year of Yüan's assumption of the presidency; real power rested obviously in the hands of the military and the police.

Nonetheless, the leaders of the Kuomintang still had some illusions as to Yüan Shih-k'ai's real intentions. This was shown, for example, by the acceptance in August 1912, by both Sun Yat-sen and Huang Hsing, of the invitation to come to Peking to discuss the political future of the country. The crafty Yüan successfully pulled wool over their eyes; Sun accepted a post from him in September—he was placed in charge of railway construction. This was one of Sun's favourites—a grandiose scheme for the building of a vast network of 200,000 miles of railways, which he considered to be indispensable for China's economic development and modernization. Where the funds were supposed to come from for this was quite a different problem. Sun also took in good faith Yüan's assurance that he too was in favour of a land reform programme. Huang Hsing was even more naive politically, believing that Yüan and his minions should be persuaded to join the Kuomintang; he actually succeeded in convincing Chao Ping-chün, Yüan's chief policeman, to become a Kuomintang member, together with the majority of the ministers of his cabinet.

In effect, the eight-point agreement, which was reached by Sun Yat-sen and Huang Hsing with Yüan Shih-k'ai at this time, was a further step of political surrender, perhaps even a greater mistake than the earlier relinquishment of the presidency by Sun. This temporary political settlement, however, made it possible for the Kuomintang to obtain Yüan's agreement, much against his inclinations, to the holding of the promised scheduled elections to the new bi-cameral parliament. These took place from the middle of December 1912 to February 1913 and were conducted once more on the basis of a restricted property and education franchise (10 per cent of the population), thus without the participation of the overwhelming majority of the nation. In these elections the Kuomintang, ably led by the brilliant and devoted Sung Chiao-jen, who had been instrumental in its organization, did extremely well and emerged as the strongest single party, with complete control of the parliament and the claim to form the future government—all much to Yüan's chagrin.

Yüan's reaction to this Kuomintang victory and the potential threat to his plans for achieving quickly full dictatorial powers was simplicity itself. On March 20, 1913, the 31-year-old Sung Chiao-jen, the Kuomintang's obvious choice for Premier of the future government, was murdered by a hired thug at the Shanghai railway station. It was relatively quickly revealed that the murder had been committed by assassins hired by Chao Ping-chün, and therefore on the orders of Yüan himself. But to cover up the traces of the crime, the assassin was quickly murdered while in jail, the organizer of the plot in Shanghai was also killed by the police and very shortly thereafter Chao himself died under mysterious circumstances. This affair made it obvious to all what Yüan Shih-k'ai's true intentions and methods were; after this, no possible illusions could still be held by any politically aware Chinese. The problem now had to be faced by the Kuomintang—whether to commence a struggle aimed at Yüan's overthrow, or to await passively its own complete annihilation and the suppression of all vestiges of constitutional government.

It was precisely at this time that the powers hastened to the aid of their chosen "Strong Man", and this in the field where he required assistance the most—the financial. Negotiations for a loan to Yüan's government had been going on between it and the Six-Power Consortium since the previous year (Russia and Japan had forced their way into the Consortium in June 1912; the Americans, however, left it in March 1913). Now, in April, 1913, the arrangements were rapidly concluded and on April 27 the so-called £25 million Reorganization Loan was signed. Its principal political aim was to buttress Yüan's regime; simultaneously, it served to strengthen the hold of the powers on China's economy, especially as far-reaching rights of supervision and the control of the Salt Gabelle were provided for. The terms were exceptionally usurious (the loan was issued at 84 with 5 per cent interest) and the bulk of the sum was allocated to cover outstanding Chinese debts to the powers. The Consortium had made full use of its monopoly position which it had successfully defended against all attempts, Chinese and foreign, to break. Thus, of the effective sum of £21 million, Yüan's government received only £8.5 million for its own use; this, however, proved sufficient to tide it over for a whole year and served primarily to cover the expenses of the armed forces. Yüan was enabled thereby to carry out successfully his campaign aimed at the crushing, once and for ever, of all domestic opposition to his tyranny.

The opposition of the parliament to the loan was of no avail; its objections to the loan being signed directly by Yüan, by-passing parliamentary approval as provided for in the Provisional Constitution, were contemptuously ignored by the Peking diplomatic corps, in spite of the abject pleas of the members of parliament.

This had also the effect of increasing still further the already spreading demoralization of political life in Peking, which affected a considerable part of the Kuomintang parliamentarians as well; some of these were still hopeful, in spite of all the evidence to the contrary, that parliament might play a role in the curbing of Yüan's schemes. However, at this time, the most prominent Kuomintang leaders, including Sun Yat-sen and Huang Hsing, saw the necessity for waging an armed struggle against Yüan Shih-k'ai. But the disunited Kuomintang was in a disadvantageous position for such an undertaking, inasmuch as the military forces in those provinces where Kuomintang members were still governors were much weaker than Yüan's Peiyang army. What is more, only three of these governors, Li Lieh-chün (1883-1946) in Kiangsi, Po Wen-wei in Anhwei and Hu Han-min in Kwangtung, were willing to prepare for armed combat. The initiative lay anyhow in the hands of Yüan. In June he ordered the dismissal from office of the above-mentioned three Kuomintang governors, while Peiyang units advanced to attack Kiangsi, where the strongest Kuomintang forces were stationed.

II. The "Second Revolution" and Its Aftermath

It was in these circumstances that the ill-fated resistance of the Kuomintang to Yüan's aggressive schemes, which bore the name of the "Second Revolution", was launched. While the anti-Yüan movement was joined by seven provinces (Kiangsi, Hunan, Kwangtung, Fukien, Szechuan, Anhwei, Kiangsu), it was marked from the outset by a lack of co-ordination, bad planning and half-heartedness among many of the participants. Due to the restricted nature of the Kuomintang programme and activities since the 1911 Revolution, at this moment, when in a critical position, it failed to obtain any appreciable mass support for its struggle against Yüan Shih-k'ai. Its financial situation was hopeless from the outset and it could not count, this time, on any support from the gentry or the merchants.

The military actions started on July 12 with operations being waged by Yüan's troops against the units of Li Lieh-chün. The Peiyang armies had very little trouble in achieving a quick victory—much applauded by the powers—over their disorganized and disunited opponents. Nanchang fell into their hands on August 18; Nanking was taken and looted by the troops of Chang Hsün, still wearing their queues, on September 1, while the Vice-President, Li Yüan-hung, also actively supported Yüan by suppressing all Kuomintang resistance in Hupei. By mid-September, the Kuomintang forces were completely crushed and the principal leaders had fled into exile once more, Sun Yat-sen and Huang Hsing going to Japan. As a result, the power of the Peiyang clique was now extended fully not only to the vital Yangtse Valley region, but also to a number of the southern provinces, such as Kwangtung, which had always been one of the main bases of Kuomintang support.

After achieving his victory over the Kuomintang in the "Second Revolution", Yüan Shih-k'ai still retained his parliamentary facade for a few months more, inasmuch as he desired to carry out a "legal" assumption of full powers, to be elected to the permanent presidency. In these plans Yüan was still aided by the Progressive Party, which agreed to form a new government in September, under the premiership of Hsiung Hsi-ling (1870-1942), erstwhile member of the 1898 Reform Movement in Hunan. This government served as a pliable tool for the approving of all of Yüan's moves. Even so, the question of the presidential elections, held in October, proved to be more troublesome than Yüan had foreseen. Parliament had to be surrounded by his police agents, the members either bribed or intimidated until finally, on the third ballot, Yüan Shih-k'ai was elected as the President of the Republic.

Lenin, who had followed the fate of the Chinese Revolution with considerable interest and sympathy, had noted earlier with biting irony that "progressive and civilized" Europe was not interested in China's rebirth and had not recognized the Republic. But now that their "Strong Man" had assumed full "legal" status, the formal recognition of the Republic by the powers followed. (Only the United States had extended an earlier recognition to Yüan's government in May 1913.) There was still a price to be paid even for this act. The 1911 Revolution had resulted in the crumbling of Chinese authority in both Tibet and Outer Mongolia. The situation in Tibet was taken advantage of by the British, who were seeking to transform this land into their own buffer state. In Outer Mongolia, Tsarist Russia had moved just as quickly to utilize the Mongolian autonomy movement in order to convert this region into a Russian protectorate. In exchange for the recognition of his presidency by these two powers, Yüan Shih-k'ai now agreed to recognize the "autonomy" of both these lands.

Having "legalized" his position as the ruler of China, Yüan now felt that he could dispense with all pretences of constitutional rule and he proceeded to crush what little there remained of organized opposition within the country. Parliament was not permitted to finish its work on the drafting of the Permanent Constitution, on which it had been engaged. On November 4, 1913 the Kuomintang was outlawed; its 438 members (132 Senators, 306 Representatives) were stripped of their parliamentary seats. By this simple move Parliament was deprived of a quorum and thus of the possibility of continuing to function. Its formal dissolution took place on January 10, 1914, and at the same time all the Provincial Assemblies were likewise disbanded. Thus, all the handicaps were removed; the elected President became the effective dictator of the country with no constitutional checks on his rule left in existence.

However, Yüan still felt, perhaps partially for the purposes of international respectability, that further pseudo-legal moves were still necessary to buttress his dictatorship. Thus, a Political Council appointed by him was established, on January

26, 1914, in place of the disbanded Parliament with the task of concocting a new constitution. On May 1, 1914, a new "Constitutional Compact" was announced, which bestowed on Yüan all the *de facto* and *de jure* powers of a supreme dictator. Subsequently, on December 28, 1914, new rules for the election of the President were promulgated; the term was now set for ten years with no restriction on the number of terms which could be served. Thereby Yüan's presidency was established, in effect, as a lifetime dictatorship. Provisions were also made at the same time which would enable him to name his successor. Only the title of Emperor was still lacking to add more lustre to this splendid achievement. The essence and the mechanism of Yüan's power did not, however, rest in these pieces of paper, but in his control of the armed forces, in his omnipotent, all-pervasive secret police which, masquerading under the name of the Military Court Department, spied on everyone and busily annihilated all the opponents of his regime it could lay its hands on. Simultaneously, Yüan still continued to receive substantial support from all the powers.

Having achieved this pinnacle of supreme authority one could have assumed that Yüan's lust for power—which had been so obvious a characteristic of the past two decades—would have been fully satisfied. However, there seem to be no limits to the megalomania of "Strong Men", "Outstanding Individuals" and "Great Leaders". Yüan hankered after one more accolade—the title of Emperor itself—undoubtedly abetted in this by his family and his sycophantic henchmen, who saw in this a possibility for still further advancement and material gains. Thus, already in the autumn of 1914, the first indications that a restoration of the monarchy was afoot became apparent. In September the restoration of Confucian worship was proclaimed, while on December 23 the Republican President, dressed in imperial-style robes, carried out at the Temple of Heaven in Peking the rites which had been the exclusive privilege and duty of the Chinese Emperor for over 2000 years.

III. The Outbreak of the World War and Its Effect on China

From the very outset the situation created by the beginning of the First World War had considerable bearing on the development of events in China. Its most readily apparent aspect was the change in the relative influence of the powers in China; the absorption of the Europeans in the conflict was of great advantage to the Japanese, who were now able to exercise overwhelming pressure in the entire Far East and in China in particular. Although the Chinese government had made a pathetic and unavailing plea that war activities be not extended to its territory and had declared its neutrality on August 6, the Japanese disregarded this completely and seized the opportunity to attack and conquer for themselves the German possessions in Shantung. By their swift action they anticipated both a German move to return these to China, as well as the possibility that the Chinese government itself would proceed to occupy them.

On August 14 the Japanese government presented an ultimatum to Germany, demanding the withdrawal of all German naval forces from the Far East and the surrender to the Japanese of the entire leased territory of Kiaochow "with a view to the eventual restoration of the same to China", a point which the Japanese took good care not to observe. A declaration of war against Germany followed on August 23, and a short Japanese military campaign, with some token British participation, ended with the surrender of the main German base, Tsingtao, on November 7, 1914. Throughout the entire campaign, Chinese neutrality was flagrantly violated by the Japanese, while the population of Shantung had to endure much suffering due to the barbarous behaviour of the Japanese soldiery. The entire German concession, including the Tsingtao-Tsinan railway line, was now taken over by the Japanese who, thus practically in control of all Shantung, gained an additional important base and could proceed to what was a still more important aim—the further extension of Japanese influence or, more precisely, domination over all China.

The plans of Japanese imperialism in regard to China were already by this time of long standing; their latest reflection was contained in a memorandum of the expansionist Black Dragon Society, which was presented to the Japanese government in the autumn of 1914. In it, a clear plan for the subjugation of China was outlined, calling for, among others, the conclusion of a defensive alliance with China, the secret clauses of which would assure full Japanese economic, military and political control of the entire country. The war in Europe was considered to have created an unusually fortunate opportunity, such as would not occur again for hundreds of years to come, and it was therefore, in the opinion of the authors of the memorandum, the divine duty of the Japanese government to act immediately. It was against this background that the presentation of the notorious Twenty-one Demands, reflecting the ideas of the above memorandum, was made.

The delivery of the note containing the Twenty-one Demands was made by the Japanese Minister on the night of January 18, 1915, directly to Yüan Shih-k'ai himself. The note was written on paper which had been water-marked—a touch of appropriate subtlety—with machine guns and dreadnoughts. The Demands were set forth in five groups. The first dealt with Shantung; in effect, it called for the recognition by China of the Japanese acquisition of Germany's rights there, as well as for further concessions to the Japanese in this region. The second was concerned with South Manchuria and East Inner Mongolia; here the Japanese demanded an extension to ninety years of the validity of their concessions, as well as a further expansion of Japanese rights, especially economic, in this entire area. The third dealt with the vital Hanyehp'ing iron, steel and coal complex in the Yangtse Valley, which the Japanese now desired to convert into a joint Sino-Japanese concern. In the fourth group the Japanese demanded that, in order to preserve the country's "territorial integrity", the Chinese government should not grant in the future any leases on territory along the Chinese coastline.

The above four groups, however, paled into nothingness in comparison with the fifth. Here the true intentions of Japanese imperialism—as followed consistently for half a century, from 1895 to 1945—were outlined with unabashed arrogance and cupidity. In it, the Japanese demanded that the Chinese government agree to employ influential Japanese as advisers in political, financial and military affairs, that the police in "important places" be under joint Sino-Japanese control, that arms should be purchased primarily from Japan and a jointly owned arms industry be built, that Japan be given priority for any future concessions in Fukien and so forth. The acceptance of this group would have meant, quite simply, the transformation of China into a Japanese protectorate on the Korean pattern—to be followed, in line with this same model, by its rapid annexation and full colonization.

Moreover, the perfidy of the Japanese imperialists was not limited to putting forth the above demands. Having a first-rate knowledge of the Chinese domestic scene—and the Japanese intelligence service always excelled in this respect—they were well aware of Yüan's monarchical ambitions. It seems fairly certain that at this juncture they promised him aid in attaining this aim as the price for acceding to all Japanese demands, while they simultaneously threatened to support the Kuomintang exiles if he refused to co-operate. Nonetheless, there was very little trust on both sides due to the mutual experience with each other, which dated back to the period when Yüan had been the Ch'ing Resident in Korea, and to the fact that the Japanese were inclined to regard him as a tool of the British.

While the Japanese Minister had insisted on absolute secrecy when presenting the demands to Yüan Shih-k'ai, within a few days, as could have been well expected, all Peking knew what had taken place. Thus, the Japanese plans for obtaining a quick Chinese surrender were now frustrated by an intense opposition to their demands on the part of Chinese public opinion, which was on a completely unprecedented and unexpected scale. A great press campaign was initiated and a very successful boycott of Japanese goods was launched. This movement against Japanese aggression was to be of great importance in the further stimulation of Chinese national consciousness and in the country's future political development.

The Japanese, at first, denied that any demands had been made. Then they published an expurgated, new "official" version, in which the fifth group was not included. Negotiations between the Japanese and Yüan Shih-k'ai followed. Yüan had not welcomed the popular anti-Japanese movement and, in fact, did everything to suppress it. The Sino-Japanese talks lasted for four months and finally the Japanese increased pressure, by sending additional troops to Manchuria and Shantung, and presented an ultimatum on May 7 with a 48-hour deadline. The Japanese terms were accepted by Yüan on May 9—a day which was immediately designated by patriotic Chinese as a "Day of National Humiliation".

The only power which could have effectively aided China in resisting Japan was the United States; many Chinese had placed their hopes on obtaining American assistance against Japanese aggression. However, the basic American position had been already outlined in the autumn of 1914 in connection with the Shantung problem, when the Acting Secretary of State, R. Lansing, had put the matter in a nutshell, stating that: "It would be quixotic in the extreme to allow the question of China's territorial integrity to entangle the United States in international difficulties." Having rejected the Chinese request for assistance at this time, the Americans followed basically the same procedure during the period of the Twenty-one Demands, backing away from the possibility of conflict with Japan. While repeating the well-worn phrases about the Open Door and territorial integrity, the Secretary of State, W. J. Bryan, in his note of March 13, 1915, had thought it necessary to state that, in regard to Shantung, South Manchuria and East Inner Mongolia, "Territorial contiguity created special relations between Japan and these districts", in effect, withdrawing all objections to Japanese expansion.

The new concessions, which had been extorted by the Japanese, were now embodied in a series of treaties concluded in May and June 1915, while the fifth group was left in abeyance, like the sword of Damocles, as the "subject of future discussion".

IV. Yüan Shih-k'ai's Restoration of the Monarchy

After his surrender to the Japanese demands Yüan Shih-k'ai, seemingly assured of Japanese support, proceeded now to the realization of his domestic ambition—the restoration of the monarchy. A most elaborate farce, lasting from August to December, was enacted, the main purpose of which was to present the restoration as emanating entirely from the deep-felt desires of the Chinese people. In August, the puppet show began with the organization of the so-called Peace Planning Society (*Ch'ou An Hui*), purportedly a private group of scholars concerned with the discussion of the merits of monarchism versus republicanism. The activity of this Society was preceded, however, by an even stranger move. An American professor, Frank J. Goodnow (1859-1930, Professor of Law at Columbia and President of Johns Hopkins, 1914-1918), had been present in China in 1913-1914, when he served as Yüan's constitutional adviser and played an important role in the drafting of the Constitutional Compact. When he revisited the country in the summer of 1915, he was requested to produce a memorandum on the advisability of a monarchical restoration. The professor obligingly performed this task, composing on the cuff a sententious collection of platitudes. Demonstrating a properly cavalier and contemptuous attitude towards the political level and intelligence of the Chinese, he buttressed his thesis with the statement that "it is of course not susceptible of doubt that a monarchy is better suited than a republic to China". It was this bit of "foreign expertise" which now served as the theoretical basis for the Peace Planning Society. Its main organizer was an opportunist turncoat and hanger-on of Yüan's, Yang Tu, the author of a curious pamphlet advocating monarchist views. The respectability of the Society was supposedly assured by the presence among its founders of six prominent scholars, three of them previously active in the 1911 Revolution. These were now ironically referred to by the Chinese public as the Six Gentlemen of the Society, in contrast to the Six Martyrs of the 1898 Reform.

The restoration scheme progressed quickly in the autumn of 1915; it was taken in hand also by one of the most astute of Yüan's adherents, Liang Shih-i, now Minister of Communications. His control of that ministry dated back for a number of years and had assisted the growth of his personal fortune quite phenomenally. Liang now organized a so-called Union of Petitioners for the Restoration; this demanded that a special meeting of representatives from the entire country be elected to voice their opinion on the political future of the state. With amazing rapidity the elections were held in October and all the results were in by November 20. Astoundingly enough, all the 1933 representatives had cast an identical vote in favour of the monarchy and, even stranger, in an identical forty-five-character petition they all proposed that the new Emperor should be the Great President of the Republic—Yüan Shih-k'ai.

On this basis of popular will the Political Council, on December 11, humbly requested that Yüan agree to accept the throne. Naturally, he refused. The request was repeated a second time in the same terms—then the Great Man acceded. The organizers of this farce had felt that it would be wiser if no records were to be left in existence of the mechanism of this unique plebiscite. Therefore, proper instructions were dispatched from Peking to all the provincial capitals that all the incriminating documents be sorted out and burned. Unfortunately, either bureaucratic inefficiency— or perhaps Chinese respect for the written word—resulted in failure to carry out this prudent injunction. When the anti-Yüan movement started in the South, the revolutionaries found the files intact and with great glee published all the telegraphic instructions which had emanated from Peking during the course of this entire comedy.

Although he had shown himself to be an agile and unscrupulous politician all his life, this time Yüan miscalculated the situation in China. Whereas in 1913 he had been able to crush the attempt to overthrow him with relative ease, the conditions had in the meantime altered considerably. Yüan's rule, i.e. that of his brutal soldiery and police and his extortionate officials and tax collectors, most of them taken over from the Ch'ing administration, had proved within these few years to be even more oppressive and hateful to the people than the Manchu regime. While in 1913 the population had been to a great extent indifferent to the political struggle between Yüan and the Kuomintang, now, in conditions of growing political awareness, resistance to him would find more popular backing.

What is more, in his striving for supreme personal power, Yüan had alienated the support of most of his closest followers. The conservative politicians of the Progressive Party, who had aided him in his rise to power, had been cast away as unnecessary; they were now willing to join forces with their erstwhile rivals of the Kuomintang in bitter opposition to the restoration of the monarchy. Paradoxically, an important role in this respect was played by Liang Ch'i-ch'ao, who had been an opponent of the Republic and the Revolution before 1911 and a faithful supporter of Yüan up until 1915. Liang now wrote, from the safety of the foreign concession in Tientsin, a sarcastic and influential denunciation of the monarchist movement, having reputedly rejected an offered bribe of 200,000 yuan not to publish it. From this refuge he began his conspiracy against Yüan, with his followers among the Progressive Party officials and military.

Of still greater importance was the fact that, with a few exceptions, most of Yüan's military henchmen from the Peiyang clique were also dissatisfied with his restoration plans, as these would have eliminated their chance of succeeding him eventually as the head of state. Some of Yüan's policies, such as the building up of new army units as his own pretorian guard, had also given rise to much mutual distrust. Thus, his heretofore most faithful and important lieutenants, Tüan Ch'i-jui and Feng Kuo-chang, showed much reserve towards Yüan's plans. This loss of the loyal support of the Peiyang militarists was quite shortly to have fatal consequences for Yüan.

Another very vital element weakening Yüan's position was the policy of the powers towards his restoration scheme, more precisely, the blow dealt him by the Japanese, whose influence in shaping the actions of the other powers, especially Great Britain and Russia, was of crucial importance in this period. Having at first encouraged Yüan in his endeavours, the Japanese by October began to turn against the monarchist movement and were instrumental in bringing about the first *démarche* on the subject of three powers on October 28 (Japan, Great Britain and Russia, joined later by France and Italy) in which the advisability of the restoration was seriously questioned. The deviousness and duplicity characteristic of Japanese diplomacy make an analysis of this *volte-face* rather difficult, especially in view of the fact that there were probably differences in approach among the Japanese ruling circles themselves. It seems more than likely that the Japanese, foreseeing Yüan's ultimate failure due to mounting domestic opposition, wished to bank on the winning side, i.e. the forces favouring the maintenance of the Republic, hoping thereby to increase their political influence. Such tactics were already outlined in the Black Dragon Memorandum referred to earlier. The considerable aid which the Japanese subsequently gave to the anti-Yüan forces in the organization of the struggle against him would seem to support this view. The position of the other powers was perhaps somewhat simpler; they were apprehensive of the possible damage to their interests if a new revolution were to be the consequence of Yüan's restoration schemes. A second *démarche* of the same five powers followed on December 15, already after Yüan's acceptance of the proposed throne.

The warnings of the powers did not impede Yüan from proceeding with his plan. The ease of his victory in 1913, the thoroughness with which he had crushed all domestic opposition and the confidence—misplaced though it soon proved to be—in the loyalty of the Peiyang militarists, made him feel certain that his restoration scheme would meet with full success and would be accepted as an accomplished fact by all the powers, including Japan. Events were soon to show that the ruthless and cunning fox had miscalculated completely. On December 25 the first rumble of an anti-Yüan revolt was heard from remote Yunnan; within six months the monarchy and the entire regime built up by Yüan crumbled into nothingness, resulting in the death of the man himself.

V. The Fall of Yüan Shih-k'ai

While Yüan had been careful to place his Peiyang generals in charge of the armed forces of practically all the provinces of China, he had not thought it necessary to extend his control to the two distant and impoverished provinces of Yunnan and Kweichow. In this south-western part of the country the Progressive Party politicians and military had managed to preserve a certain degree of independence; the most prominent of these had been Ts'ai Ao (1882-1916), a very talented commander, a participant in the 1911 Revolution. Yüan had distrusted him sufficiently to have him brought to Peking and kept under strict surveillance—a precaution which he had exercised towards a number of prominent personalities, not excluding Li Yüan-hung. When the opposition to the restoration began, Ts'ai Ao, by means of a clever deception—well-simulated dissipation—managed to escape from his captivity in Peking to Tientsin from where, in contact with his teacher Liang Ch'i-ch'ao and other anti-Yüan plotters, he made his way back to Yunnan.

Ts'ai Ao's arrival in Yunnan was a signal for the beginning of the anti-Yüan revolt, referred to also sometimes as the "Third Revolution". The initial scheme was a bold one; the Yunnanese demanded an immediate abandonment of the monarchy and the execution of the main organizers of the restoration movement. Simultaneously, they planned an invasion of Szechuan, hoping to occupy it and initiate thereby a revolt against Yüan by all the provinces of South and Central China. While the initial plan to occupy Szechuan by surprise failed, and the Yunnan forces led by Ts'ai Ao, to be called the National Protection Army, met with considerable difficulties as they faced much stronger Peiyang forces, soon strengthened on Yüan's orders, the revolt spread to other parts of South China with fair speed. In January, Kweichow declared its "independence" of Peking and Kwangsi followed suit in March. An extremely involved struggle for drawing Kwangtung into the anti-Yüan movement then ensued, ending in April with the victory of the rebellious forces.

Yüan's accession to the throne had been planned for January 1, 1916, and elaborate preparations in connection with this had been already made. In view of the Yunnan revolt, it was then postponed until March. As the anti-Yüan movement spread, the powers intervened once more with a third *démarche* in March in which they posed the question of how Yüan thought he could suppress the rebellion; it was clear that the Japanese, in particular, were already writing Yüan off as a lost cause. It was against this background that the revocation of the monarchical restoration took place on March 22. This was followed by a truce on the front in Szechuan and an attempt on the part of Yüan to reach a compromise with his opponents in the South. These efforts, however, were of no avail; the Southern provinces, now joined in April by Chekiang, organized in a Military Council of the South, pressed for Yüan's immediate resignation from all power, including the presidency, which he had had the audacity to reassume. In the meantime the key provinces of the Yangtse Valley, which under the leadership of Feng Kuo-chang had maintained an uneasy neutrality in the conflict, showed by their actions that Yüan could not count on support also from this region. In this area, as well as in Kwangtung, the Kuomintang became active once more, playing its part in the anti-Yüan movement; some of the exiled leaders, including Sun Yat-sen, returned from Japan in the late spring of 1916 to Shanghai, which served once more as the main base for their activities.

Deserted by more and more of his followers, Yüan's days as the ruler of China were numbered. The decisive blow came in May; on the 22nd, Szechuan, ruled by one of his most trusted adherents, declared its "independence", followed a few days later by Hunan. Yüan Shih-k'ai was by now already mortally ill; his death—supposedly due to uraemia induced by nervous prostration—came on June 6, at the age of 56. With this the struggle against his rule automatically came to an end. Li Yüan-hung succeeded him to the presidency; the Provisional Constitution of 1912 was restored, after some initial haggling, and the Military Council of the South dissolved itself.

However, the disappearance from the historical arena of the main actor, in itself, did not mean that it would be possible to make a fresh and easy new start in the building up of the Republic. The results of over four years of Yüan's rule were to weigh heavily on the country's future. His reign had resulted in a far-reaching corruption of Chinese political life, and in the spread of warlordism on an immense scale throughout the entire country. Not only was each province now controlled by the militarists but also, within almost every province, smaller warlords competed and fought with each other for the privilege of exploiting the population and benefiting from the support of the foreign powers. The plague of warlordism had become endemic and the political history of China for the next decades was to be a sorry chronicle of the struggles for power between the militarist cliques. In these circumstances, the chances for China's effective resistance to foreign aggression, especially that of Japanese imperialism, were reduced to practically nil. This was to be borne out fully by the developments of the next few years—a period in which it became clear to all politically minded, patriotic Chinese that the country's salvation would prove impossible without a struggle to rid the country of the two closely intertwined evils—militarist rule and imperialist control.

CHAPTER 40

China Under Warlord Rule, 1916-1919

I. Political Development After the Fall of Yüan Shih-k'ai

The heritage of Yüan's reign was, as noted, most unfortunate in its consequences for future Chinese development. The country was, in effect, in the hands of the warlords, either of the Peiyang clique or of the Southern militarists. With the exception of six provinces—Kwangtung, Kwangsi, Yunnan, Kweichow, Szechuan and Hunan—all the rest of China was controlled by the Peiyang warlords and the central government in Peking was likewise basically in their hands, specifically in those of Tuan Ch'i-jui. Tuan had already manoeuvred himself into a position of power during the last weeks of Yüan's rule and now, having been nominated Premier by the new President Li Yüan-hung, he proceeded with the help of his hangers-on, such as the brutal and greedy Hsü Shu-cheng, to strengthen his control of the Peking government and, still more important, of the armed forces.

While the Provisional Constitution of 1912 had been restored and the Parliament, which had been dissolved by Yüan in 1914, also reassembled on August 1, 1916, the militarists were in a much stronger position than the political parties. This was so not only due to the nature of these parties, but also because one of the main political groupings, the Progressive Party, which had been an ardent supporter of Yüan Shih-k'ai up until the moment of his monarchical restoration, was now just as eagerly seeking crumbs from the table of Tuan Ch'i-jui. The main political leader of this party, Liang Ch'i-ch'ao, busily ingratiating himself with Tuan, accepted a ministerial post in the latter's cabinet. Liang thought of Tuan as a pillar for unifying and strengthening the country; the pillar proved, however, to be quite rotten. After a while, by 1918, when Tuan and his militarist entourage had consolidated their hold on the government, they dispensed with the services of the Progressive Party politicians in favour of their own group of followers. On the other hand, the Kuomintang, still the largest party in the Parliament, while opposed in theory to warlord rule, was badly disorganized and disunited. A large faction was willing to co-operate with the Peking government, in spite of the obvious autocratic tendencies of Tuan and his cohorts. A somewhat more progressive wing of the Kuomintang, which remained under Sun Yat-sen's influence, showed a greater degree of distrust of the Peking regime and demanded a full restoration of parliamentary forms of government. This wing was partly composed of those who had been members of the *Komingtang*—the small conspiratorial and not particularly effective Revolutionary Party which Sun Yat-sen had established in 1914 as a weapon to fight Yüan's dictatorship. There was little hope of success for these views in the light of the systematic campaign began by Tuan against both the Parliament and the weak President; this led to an increased political struggle in Peking and a rapid deterioration of the political situation in the autumn and winter of 1916.

However, while Tuan's Peiyang clique was in control of the Peking government, as well as of most of North and Central China, already the process of disintegration within it had begun, which ultimately was to lead to its division into two warring factions. What was basically at stake was a power struggle for offices and the benefits thereof. Simultaneously, a still greater decentralization of power in the country ensued due, among others, to the marked rise of almost completely independent warlords; two outstanding examples of this phenomenon were Yen Hsi-shan (1883-1960) and Chang Tso-lin (1876-1928). Yen, a clever and opportunistic military officer, had been a T'ung Meng Hui member and a participant in the 1911 Revolution. Having been made military governor of his native province, Shansi, he succeeded in gaining complete control of it after Yüan's fall; taking advantage of its geographical position, he successfully eliminated all interference of the Peking government in his satrapy. Chang, an ex-bandit and later Ch'ing officer, who had been in Japanese service during the Russo-Japanese War, managed to establish mastery by 1916 over the most important province of the North-east, Fengtien (Liaoning), and within the next two years had extended his sway to all of Manchuria.

II. China and the World War

The question of China's breaking off relations with Germany and entering into the war on the side of the Entente had been the subject of much political intrigue and pressure ever since its start. The Allies had been anxious to drag China into the conflict for a number of reasons, among others, to avail themselves of all China's potential power, especially her labour force, as well as possible future cannon fodder, and to eliminate German interests in the Far East. However, all the Allied attempts in this respect had been frustrated up to 1917 by Japanese opposition, inasmuch as the Japanese government feared that China becoming an Ally would make it impossible for Japan to maintain her hold on the former German concessions in China, which had been annexed in 1914. The conclusion of secret agreements between Japan and Great Britain, France, Russia and Italy, in February 1917, by which they recognized Japan's "rights" to the former German property, brought about a change in the Japanese government's attitude, especially as in the meantime it perceived additional advantages for itself in China's entry.

It was, however, the United States which brought the most pressure to bear to make China break diplomatic relations with Germany over the issue of unrestricted submarine warfare. The break came on March 14, 1917, and had been manoeuvred through the Peking government and Parliament without too much trouble. The question now was whether the next consequence of this step should be a declaration of war. This, in reality, was quite a different issue and the move for entry into the war met with very considerable opposition on the part of Chinese opinion of various political hues—extending from Sun Yat-sen to K'ang Yu-wei. In Sun's case, he saw no reason whatsoever why China should participate in the holocaust in Europe and no basic differences between the powers engaged in the conflict. The Tuan militarist clique, on the other hand, pressed—with the full support of the Allies and the unabashed pressure of their diplomatic representatives in Peking—for China's immediate entry into the war, in spite of public opinion and the opposition of the majority of Parliament. The warlords saw in this move an opportunity for increasing further their power and wealth by an expansion of armed forces, which they intended to use primarily for domestic purposes, and by the obtaining of foreign loans which would serve, in the first place, to line their own pockets. In pursuing this aim, the Peking regime was now fully abetted by the Japanese. Liang Ch'i-ch'ao was also a strong advocate of war; in his inordinate ambitions and visions of grandeur he saw himself in the role of a Cavour, allegedly obtaining favours for China from the victorious Allies.

The opposition of Parliament and of President Li Yüan-hung was not easy to overcome, in spite of all the means employed by Tuan, including a blustering conference in Peking of most of the country's military governors in April 1917, which demanded that war be declared. The conflict led, in May, to Parliament's definite refusal to declare war, to the dismissal of Tuan from his post as Premier by Li, and to Tuan's withdrawal with his followers to Tientsin, where they set themselves up as an independent power—therefore, to a complete stalemate, political crisis and breakdown of the central government.

III. The Manchu Restoration

Although Li Yüan-hung had shown enough determination to bring about Tuan's dismissal, he himself lacked any armed forces on which he could base himself. In these circumstances, he turned for assistance and mediation to—of all people—Chang Hsün, the notoriously reactionary commander of an independent army of around 30,000 bandit-like troops. In June, Chang Hsün's men occupied Peking; under the pressure of this "mediator", Li was now forced to agree to dissolve Parliament (June 13). The way was thus made clear for the next step—the ludicrous Manchu restoration, engineered primarily by Chang Hsün himself. The farce lasted but a short time.

In the early morning hours of July 1, the 11-year-old P'u-i was dragged away from his toys and books and, to his own considerable anxiety but to the joy of some of the former Ch'ing court members, placed once more on the throne. The police now ordered that the old Dragon Flag be hoisted all over the city; the seamstresses had a busy time sewing them, the tailors equally engaged in making up new or restoring old Ch'ing court robes, but the busiest of all were the barbers concocting new false queues. K'ang Yu-wei, whose role in the conspiracy was quite considerable, now happily composed new edicts in beautiful classical Chinese, thinking that a constitutional monarchy would result from this *coup d'état*. Li Yüan-hung, rejecting high office, fled to the Japanese legation, sending his seals of office to his Vice-President, Feng Kuo-chang, and calling for help from the recently dismissed Tuan Ch'i-jui.

However, Chang Hsün had not taken the precaution of assuring the other militarists that he would share—fairly and squarely—power and loot with them. Cleverly outmanoeuvred by Tuan's clique, he found that all the *tuchuns* were opposed to his coup, although undoubtedly a large number of them, as former Ch'ing generals, were monarchist sympathizers. Tuan proclaimed himself the head of the Army to Save the Republic and his troops marched on Peking from all sides. There was some fighting, much shooting and even a few casualties.

By July 12, the bubble had burst; Chang Hsün fled to the safety of the Dutch Legation, while K'ang Yu-wei took refuge with the Americans—his political activity, this time, was over for ever. Chang's troops surrendered their arms amicably for a given sum of money per head and marched back, minus their queues, to their villages in Shantung. The boy P'u-i went back to his palace, while his court entourage quickly washed its hands of the whole affair. The indisputable victor in this whole comedy—which had at least the one merit of discrediting monarchism still further—was Tuan, back again in the saddle as Premier, having rid himself in the process of all his political enemies in Peking—both the parliamentarians and President Li. The latter's office was now taken over by Feng Kuo-chang; he was, however, an old rival of Tuan, and thus the seeds were sown for further conflict within the Peiyang clique.

IV. The Rule of the Anfu Clique

The success of the Peiyang clique facilitated a decision on the war-entry problem. On August 14, 1917, the Peking regime declared war on the Central Powers and thus China became officially a belligerent and an associate of the Allies. There was to be no active military participation in the conflict in Europe. China was utilized, however, primarily as a source of labour power; around 200,000 Chinese workers had been shipped off to Europe by the end of the war to be engaged there either in transport and other types of work behind the front lines or in mines and factories. This group included also a considerable number of students and intellectuals. The consequences, incidentally, of this were to be quite significant; a large number of the participants, both the workers and the students, were to play a prominent role in the Chinese labour movement. Some of them founded, together with students who arrived after the war, the first Chinese Marxist groups in France, and a number of them were later to become leading figures in the Chinese Communist Party, in some cases, up to the present day.

The domestic results of Tuan Ch'i-jui's victory brought about, however, a further disintegration of the central government. A majority of the members of Parliament, especially most of the Kuomintang, had fled Peking after its dissolution and made their way south to Shanghai and Canton. In July 1917 Sun Yat-sen, taking with him most of the Chinese navy—which always sided with the Kuomintang—left Shanghai for Canton. Here, in the beginning of September, a separate military government was established, which claimed to be the only legal one with the purpose of upholding and protecting the 1912 Provisional Constitution. On September 3, Sun was elected Grand Marshal (Generalissimo) and head of the government. However, real power in Canton did not rest in the hands either of Sun Yat-sen or of the Parliament, always disunited, but in those of the Southern militarists. These were mainly the so-called Kwangsi clique which had been in control of Kwangtung and Kwangsi since 1916. The creation of the government in Canton now meant the division of China into two separate parts; the influence of the Southern government extended to the entire South and South-west, while the Peking regime officially controlled the rest of the country, but its effective rule was seriously reduced by the aforementioned rise in power of the provincial warlords.

The Tuan clique aimed at liquidating the state of division by force of arms, hoping to employ for this purpose the larger and stronger army which it had at its disposal. From

October 1917 to the spring of 1918, armed conflict was waged with shifting success between the North and the South for the control of the key province of Hunan. At the same time, the struggle was extended to Szechuan, where it was further aggravated and complicated by a series of local wars among individual warlords and armies from other provinces stationed in Szechuan. On the whole, Tuan's attempt to resolve the conflict by force was a complete failure, and the country was fated to remain divided. Moreover, the situation in the South was little better, if at all, than that in the North; the Southern government also could not provide a proper solution to the country's problems, inasmuch as the Southern militarists were basically no different from their Peiyang counterparts in the North. Thus, by May 1918, Sun Yat-sen had been forced out of his post as Grand Marshal, and he soon left Canton in disgust to settle down in Shanghai, where he devoted himself to studying and writing about the basic problems of the country's reconstruction.

The war of the Peking regime against the South actually helped to hasten the disintegration of the old Peiyang clique as well. It now split into two separate groups—the Anfu clique headed by Tuan and his henchmen and the Chihli faction, whose main leaders were the President Feng Kuo-chang, Ts'ao K'un, military governor of Chihli, and the rising new militarist, Wu P'ei-fu (1878-1939). The main base of the Chihli clique were the provinces Kiangsu, Kiangsi and Hupei.* Both Ts'ao and Wu were in charge of the troops fighting the South and Wu's role was especially prominent and successfully utilized by him for his own political purposes. While the struggle between the Anfu and Chihli cliques was basically aimed at controlling the Central Government in Peking and its revenues, it was simultaneously a reflection of the rivalry of the powers in China. As time went on, especially after the end of the World War, the Chihli clique became closely bound up with British and American interests and benefited from their financial and political support. The Anfu faction, on the other hand, already during the years of the war had become the out-and-out tool of the Japanese imperialists.

The Japanese government, in the period from the fall of Yüan Shih-k'ai to the end of the World War, continued to take the fullest advantage possible of the international situation to become the master of China. The successes achieved in the extortion of the Twenty-one Demands were now followed up systematically and consistently, although with the use of somewhat different, less obvious and thus even more effective tactics. Basing themselves on the corruption of the Anfu-controlled regime, the Japanese proceeded to entangle the Peking government with a series of loans and secret agreements, the overall effect of which was still more far-reaching than the Twenty-one Demands. The loans, usually referred to as the Nishihara (the name of the main negotiator), amounted to vast sums, differently estimated as ranging from 250 to 500 million yen. In exchange for these sums, the Anfu clique bartered away China's natural resources and industries, granting the Japanese extensive new economic rights, not only in the North-east but in other parts of the country as well. Thus, the Japanese capitalists were converting China successfully into an exclusive market for Japanese

---

*There are two versions regarding the origin of the name "Anfu". According to one, it came from the name of a street in Peking where the members of the so-called Anfu club formed by Tuan's followers met; according to the second, it was derived from the names of the two provinces which were the main stronghold of Tuan's men— *A*nhwei and *Fu*kien.

manufactured goods, as well as the source of indispensable raw materials such as, for example, iron ore. While the offensive of Japanese imperialism in China of this period suffered something of a setback after the war, due both to Chinese resistance and the rivalry of other powers, the experience of these years was undoubtedly of crucial importance, as it constituted a great incentive for the future resumption of Japanese expansion in the 1930s and the launching of the attempt to subjugate the entire country.

Tuan's regime utilized this stream of Japanese gold not only for personal enrichment—although its members did very well indeed in this respect—but also for the building up of its armed forces, the main purpose of which was to extend the rule of this clique to the entire country. The entry of China into the war provided a convenient pretext for this and Tuan had himself nominated Commander-in-Chief of a so-called War Participation Army, which was supposedly being trained for future use in Europe. On the basis of secret agreements the Japanese assisted Tuan in the building up of this army by providing him not only with the necessary arms but also with officers for training purposes. In effect, they were well on their way to implementing a major part of the programme outlined in the fifth group of the Twenty-one Demands.

The confused and unstable situation in Siberia and the Russian Far East, where the White armies aided by the Entente had obtained some temporary successes, also served as an excellent excuse for the Japanese to strengthen their hold on the Peking regime by concluding, in May 1918, special secret military agreements for "joint action" in a future anti-Soviet intervention, in which the Japanese were to play the leading role. However, the subservience of the Anfu clique to the Japanese was becoming ever more obvious; the news regarding the above-mentioned military agreement also leaked out and the indignation of Chinese public opinion increased, leading to the first organized protest by Chinese students, in both Peking and Tokyo. These protests were but a harbinger of what was to come a year later during the famous May Fourth Movement.

The Tuan clique sought to bolster its position in Peking by political measures as well. In March 1918, Tuan Ch'i-jui's followers had organized themselves in the notorious Anfu Club—a precious collection of corrupt politicians, office-holders and generals. In August of the same year, the regime thought it necessary to give itself a semblance of constitutional respectability and a new, properly selected Parliament was called into being. This was the so-called Anfu Parliament which, needless to say, was completely in the hands of Tuan's faction. Advantage was also taken of the fact that Feng Kuo-chang's tenure of office expired in October 1918, to replace him with a "neutral", elder member of the Peiyang warlords, Hsü Shih-ch'ang (1858-1937), who now became President.

The war between the North and the South had ground to a halt by the summer of 1918, with the conquest of Hunan by the armies of the Chihli faction. Once the World War had come to an end, there was increased domestic pressure to bring about a unification of the country and both sides finally agreed to the holding of a Peace Conference which took place in Shanghai from February to May 1919 without, however, achieving any results whatsoever. In the meantime, the conflict between the Anfu and Chihli cliques during 1919 increased in intensity, and the first steps were being taken which were ultimately to lead to the Anfu-Chihli War of 1920, to the further ruination and degradation of the country and extension of warlord rule.

V. China and Versailles

The end of the World War was greeted with relief in China and also with great hopes that the country, which was to participate in the peace negotiations, would be able to gain some important benefits and improve its international position. These hopes were based, primarily, on the considerable attention which Chinese public opinion had paid to the well-advertised Wilsonian programme for meeting and solving the problems of a post-war world, particularly his Fourteen Points. Chinese opinion, especially of the great majority of intellectuals (and by no means only those who had been educated in the States), firmly believed that Wilsonian diplomacy was about to inaugurate a new era in international relations, which could only prove to be a blessing to countries such as China.

Thus, the Chinese hoped—and their delegation to the Paris Peace Conference had prepared itself with appropriate briefs for the purpose—to raise the issues most closely affecting the country's situation, i.e. to obtain an equal status for China, by bringing to an end extraterritoriality, recovering full customs autonomy, declaring void other provisions of the unequal treaties, doing away with spheres of influence and the presence of foreign troops and, in particular, eliminating the menace of the agreements signed with Japan in connection with the Twenty-one Demands. At the same time, the most burning current issue was the Shantung question. Here, the Chinese demanded the full reversion to China of all the German rights and concessions which had been taken over by the Japanese.

It was to the United States that the Chinese looked for sympathy and support for their position. This was due not only to the Wilsonian programme, but also to the fact that they still tended to regard America in a different light from the other imperialist powers. After all, the United States had never been a direct participant in the Opium Wars—only an indirect beneficiary; after all, the Americans had no sphere of interest of their own like the British, Russians, Japanese and so on. All these somewhat naive illusions could have been at least partially dispelled had the Chinese paid closer attention to the course which American foreign policy in the Far East had been following. The position taken in 1915 had been indicative enough; it was to be reflected even more in the Japanese-American negotiations in the autumn of 1917, which resulted in the signing of the Lansing-Ishii notes on November 2.

This agreement confirmed once more that, in spite of all the elements of undoubted American-Japanese rivalry in the Far East, the United States was at no time willing to risk a serious entanglement with Japan, especially for the sake only, or primarily, of China's benefit. Thus, while the clichés regarding the Open Door and China's "territorial integrity" were repeated, the curious doctrine of territorial propinquity was now formulated even more precisely, to the effect that this factor "creates special relations between countries and, consequently, the government of the United States recognizes that Japan has interests in China, particularly in that part to which her possessions are contiguous". The Japanese considered, and rightly, this agreement to be a great victory for them, signifying a free hand for further expansion in China.*

The policy revealed by the Lansing-Ishii Agreement thus demonstrated a further tendency to appease Japan and a complete indifference to Chinese claims and interests

---

*The Japanese minister took great satisfaction in revealing it to Reinsch, the American Minister in Peking, whom the State Department had not informed about either the negotiations or their results.

shown also by the fact that the Chinese had not even been consulted beforehand. The Lansing-Ishii Agreement, however, was not aimed against Soviet Russia, as one modern, quite talented Chinese historian would have it. Carried away by polemical fervour, he fails to note that it was signed five days earlier than the October Revolution which took place on November 7. Neither the Americans nor the Japanese were that prescient.

At Versailles the Japanese revealed the secret treaties with Great Britain, France and Italy regarding Shantung and demanded that the Allies adhere to these earlier agreements. Much to the embarrassment of the Chinese delegation—which was composed of representatives of both the Peking and the Canton governments but headed by the Northern Foreign Minister—they also disclosed the secret agreements which Japan had concluded with the Tuan regime in September 1918, in which the latter "gladly accepted" the retention by the Japanese of German rights in Shantung. Both these factors facilitated the decision of the Big Three on April 30, 1919, to rule in favour of Japan on the issue, and this was later incorporated in Articles 156, 157 and 158 of the Versailles Treaty. All the other problems raised by the Chinese delegation, pertaining to the equal status of China, had been earlier swept aside contemptuously as not being within the terms of reference of the Conference. The Chinese government now faced the problem whether, under such circumstances, it should sign the Peace Treaty or not; the government itself was inclined to do so, while the delegation, always badly divided due to its composition, hesitated as to the course of action it should follow. But the fate of these decisions was to be determined, above all, by the vast storm of indignant protest that was to sweep China and constituted one of the principal component factors in the political crisis of which the May Fourth Movement was the most eloquent expression.

CHAPTER 41

The May Fourth Movement—the Road to China's Rebirth

I. General Background

The years of the First World War had a significant bearing on the further economic and social development of China. The total involvement of the European powers in their conflict appreciably reduced their economic activity in China for over four years, leaving the field open thereby to their Japanese and Chinese competitors. Availing themselves of this opportunity, the new Chinese capitalists, as well as merchants and gentry, invested in modern industry to a greater scale than ever before. As a result, during the four years of the war period Chinese-owned light industry grew markedly (textile production, for example, doubled), while Chinese financial institutions also increased their strength and scope of operations. However, this development was restricted almost entirely to light industry, the manufacture of a limited number of goods, primarily for China's own market. It was not accompanied by any significant growth of heavy industry or mining—a field where Japanese economic penetration was particularly active.

A concomitant result of this economic development was the considerable growth of a new working class, which in this same period increased from around one million to well over two million, including workers in transport. As noted earlier, the working class grew at a faster rate than the Chinese national bourgeoisie itself. This newly formed proletariat faced conditions of completely unbridled exploitation—whether in foreign or Chinese-owned factories—and was still almost completely unorganized for its own defence, even on a modern trade union basis. It was easily replaceable and constantly replenished by the unceasing flow of village poor from the countryside, where the conditions of warlord rule and extortion had worsened the position of the peasantry to a still greater degree.

Alongside of the above economic and social changes which were of considerable importance, there was another factor present—perhaps of even more immediate bearing on the political scene—which was the effect produced by the process of modern education. This had been a relatively new phenomenon, dating back in the main for only a decade, but its result was the creation of a potent social group of new intellectuals who were now to play a vital role in determining China's political future. It was this group, above all, which bore witness to the rapid increase in national consciousness and which took on the role of spokesman for the entire nation in protesting against the injustices which had been committed and in raising all the current issues in 1918-

1919—Japanese imperialist aggression and the trampling of Chinese rights by the powers in Versailles.

II. The Cultural Revolution

It was against this background of economic, social and intellectual development that one of the most inspiring and stirring movements in Chinese history took place, truly deserving the name of the Cultural Revolution. This revolution covered a period roughly from 1915 to 1920 and coincided in time to a great extent with the May Fourth Movement, which can be considered to be its political manifestation. The ideological and political content is basically the same—the still more urgent, topical question of seeking the roads which would lead to the country's salvation. In this sense the Cultural Revolution can be actually considered an integral part of the May Fourth Movement. It reflected at the same time an unusually intense, creative intellectual ferment, an eagerness to grasp at whatever seemed to be new, promising and progressive, while rejecting the old, stale and backward.

One of the fundamental problems involved was the question of the Chinese language and literature itself, i.e. whether the future development of Chinese culture was possible if it were to remain in the fetters of a dead classical language (as remote from the vernacular as Latin is from Italian, or perhaps even more so) and of literary conventions, equally antiquated, obstruse and incomprehensible to the overwhelming majority of the people. This problem was posed in all its sharpness by a group of brilliant intellectuals in the years 1916-1918, among whom the leading role was played by Ch'en Tu-hsiu (1879-1942), an eminent scholar and writer, later one of the two most important co-founders of the Chinese Communist Party, and Hu Shih (1891-1962), an able student of philosophy and literature, and a follower of John Dewey's pragmatism.

It was basically the ideas put forth by these two men—in this Hu was the originator and Ch'en the real driving force—which initiated a radical transformation in Chinese cultural life, the substitution of the vernacular *pai hua* for the classical language *wen yen*, as the approved means of expression in all fields of literary endeavour. These ideas could bear such fruit so quickly and successfully because they corresponded completely to the country's needs and their implementation was a vital and indispensable step in making a future modernization possible. The ideas were welcomed with enthusiasm by the overwhelming majority of the students and the new intellectuals, and within the short space of a few years from its beginning the movement succeeded completely in overcoming all opposition of traditional scholars; the vernacular step by step replaced the classical language in general education as well as in all other fields.

It was this breakthrough in language reform which made possible the development of a new Chinese living literature, beginning precisely in these same years and employing the vernacular, as had been the case earlier of at least one previous genre— the novel. Many talented writers were to take part in the shaping of new modes of expression and the new literature was, as a whole, eminently progressive in nature. There was little doubt that the most gifted of them was Lu Hsün (real name—Chou Shou-jen, 1881-1936), whose short stories were to become world famous. Lu Hsün's bitter, sardonic irony was employed as a sharp weapon against everything that was decadent, obscure and backward in Chinese culture and customs, everything that constituted a handicap to the country's progress.

The employment of the vernacular not only facilitated the expression of new ideas in the new literary forms, but also led to a vast increase in the number of publications of various types, both newspapers and periodicals, in a marked increase of translations from foreign languages and thus to a still greater opening up of windows to the world, to the inflow of challenging, invigorating, fresh new ideas. All of these were eagerly grasped by the students and new intellectuals and were examined mostly through the prism of their adaptability to meet the crucial needs of the country, to solve its overwhelming problems. But the most influential single periodical in China in this era dated back to the very beginning of the Cultural Revolution; this was the famous *New Youth* (first called "Youth"), of which Ch'en Tu-hsiu was the chief editor. It is often referred to by its sub-title "La Jeunesse"; the choice of this sub-title was by no means fortuitous, it was in itself a reflection of the profound influence of French culture and of French revolutionary and democratic ideals not only on Ch'en himself but also on many of his generation, older by two decades than the students, who were to participate in the May Fourth Movement.

It was in this periodical that the ideas regarding language reform were first broached—characteristically it was first written in the classical language itself and then went over to the vernacular in the beginning of 1918. But what was still more important, it was here—although by no means exclusively—that the principal ideological arguments of the Cultural Revolution were put forth to reach out and influence profoundly the thinking of the new intellectuals. Above all, the writers in the *New Youth* called for a complete casting away of Confucianism with all its many and varied connotations of a moribund and decadent culture. If China were to achieve a true modernization, then this ideology must of necessity be replaced and in its stead the two twin concepts—in Ch'en Tu-hsiu's words—"Mr. Science" and "Mr. Democracy" should be established as guiding principles. It was felt that only in this way—by a completely sceptical and iconoclastic approach to the past and to the entire cultural heritage—could the path be cleared for progress.

What, in reality, was the content of the New Learning and the new ideas which permeated the entire intellectual community in these years? Up until the beginning of the First World War, the New Learning implied an acceptance, to a certain degree uncritical, of most of the ideas of the West in all spheres—ideological, cultural and political. In this last respect, in particular, it meant the taking of Western parliamentary democracy as a model for carrying out the political transformation of China. However, from the very outset, there were a number of difficulties connected with this process which arose from certain inherent contradictions; these, in turn, were to become evermore apparent during the period of the May Fourth Movement. For one, it became more and more obvious that the Western powers regarded their form of democracy as suitable only for themselves, and not as a thing to be exported to the benighted peoples of Asia and Africa. Furthermore, the actions of the Westerners in China had been—taken as a whole—in glaring contrast to the ideals which their own ideology purportedly represented. There was precious little of fraternity, equality and liberty in the relations between the powers and semi-colonial China. Now that the New Learning had made the ideas of the West available to the Chinese intellectuals on an ever greater scale, this contrast between the proclaimed ideals and actual performance—especially the constant support given by the powers to backward and reactionary forces in China—could not but give rise to much searching doubt and criticism among thinking Chinese. All these problems were further aggravated by the World War itself; this terrible holocaust could not be regarded by the Chinese intellectuals as anything else but a total bankruptcy of everything that the West had supposedly stood for. If Science and Democracy were to lead but to such an end, did they really constitute principles on which a new China should be rebuilt? Many Chinese regarded the World War with bitter disillusionment and saw in it a collapse of Western civilization. Numerous advocates of the traditional Chinese world outlook, and even adherents of partial modernization, took this moment as an opportunity to belabour the West for its "materialism" and to laud the alleged superiority of the "spirituality" of the East—a dichotomy which was obviously and palpably false.

It was in this setting of ideological confusion and intellectual ferment that the ideas of Marxian socialism, as represented by the victorious October Revolution, were to enter the Chinese scene and make a vital—and ultimately decisive—impact on the thinking of the Chinese intellectuals. Here was the answer to the many questions which had been raised in their minds. What was at fault was not Western civilization as such, but the forms and nature of its capitalist stage of development; the solution, therefore, to the problems of the world, hence of China as well, lay in the direction of socialism. These novel ideas entered into what was, for all practical purposes, a virgin field, inasmuch as Marxism had been almost completely unknown in China before the Russian Revolution. Even the name of Marx himself could have been known to hardly more than a handful of intellectuals, while Marxism as such had made thus far no impression whatsoever on the Chinese intellectual scene, owing to the simple fact that none of the works of its founders—except for a few excerpts from the Communist Manifesto—had so far been translated into Chinese. It is true that a nodding acquaintance with some socialist ideas had been obtained by some of the Chinese who had studied in Japan, where socialism, as a movement and an ideology, had developed earlier. Nevertheless, the socialist ideas which were current in China before 1918 lacked both in precision and clarity, and this was reflected also in the eclectic thinking of the intellectuals, both of the older generation, such as Ch'en Tu-hsiu, as well as the students. One of the participants of the May Fourth Movement described his own outlook at the time as "a curious mixture of ideas of liberalism, democratic reformism and Utopian Socialism". This description can be accepted as an accurate appraisal of the Chinese intellectual scene as a whole.

The entry of Marxism-Leninism on this scene was now buttressed not only by the victory of the Bolsheviks, but also by the policy which they were soon to apply in respect to China. Already in 1918, the Soviet government announced its denunciation of all the unequal treaties which had been imposed by the Tsarist government on China, resigned from all the privileges and concessions that had been obtained on their basis, and later called for the establishment of relations between the two countries on the new foundation of complete equality. All this was in glaring contrast to the policies which the Western powers continued to follow towards China, especially as manifested at Versailles. This contrast was, indeed, a most revealing one. The Russians were seen to represent a completely new and different Western ideology—one which was not inimical to China, but, on the contrary, which seemed to provide a key to the solution of the country's fundamental problems. The first sign that this was to be so understood by a number of leading Chinese intellectuals was shown by the article written for the *New Youth*, already in 1918, by Li Ta-chao (1888-1927), in which he welcomed the victory of the Bolshevik Revolution. Li, a gifted professor of political science and writer, was to become one of the two co-founders of the Communist movement along with Ch'en Tu-hsiu.*

In the formative stage of the Cultural Revolution it was still Peking itself—and not Shanghai—which was the true cultural centre of the country and which was to play a leading role in the development of the May Fourth Movement. This was due, among others, to the fact that Peking possessed the largest number of institutions of higher learning and thus the biggest single student community in the entire country. Still another important factor was the presence in Peking of most of the prominent figures of the Cultural Revolution; many of them were connected with the principal and oldest university of the city, Peita—the famous Peking University. Under the guidance of Ts'ai Yüan-p'ei (1876-1940), who became the Chancellor of Peita at the beginning of 1918, the university became the fountainhead of the entire intellectual movement, not only of Peking but of the country as a whole. Ts'ai—a profound and brilliant humanitarian—was one of the outstanding progressive educators in China. He had been an early T'ung Meng Hui member and Minister of Education in the first Republican government in 1912; his own outlook tended towards philosophical anarchism. It was he who attracted the best minds of the country to Peita; thus Li Ta-chao became the Chief Librarian, Ch'en Tu-hsiu Dean of the School of Letters, and Hu Shih a professor of philosophy. It was this intellectual elite, which included also a large number of other extremely gifted people, that served as the inspirers of the May Fourth Movement.

III. The May Fourth Movement

While the term, May Fourth Movement, has come to be used as a generic term to embrace all the intellectual and political development of the years 1915-1920, it was the events of the months May-June 1919 which gave it its name and themselves constituted a crucial historical landmark. Basically, the May Fourth Movement was an organized campaign of protest against China's humiliating position—against the Japanese annexation of Shantung, against the actions of the powers at Versailles, and against the reactionary, militarist Peking regime which acquiesced in and assisted the imperialist subjugation of China. Thus, objectively, this was to be the first indisputably anti-imperialist and anti-militarist movement in modern Chinese history; herein precisely lay its fundamental importance for the shaping of the country's future. This nature of the movement was clearly reflected in its two principal slogans: "Internally, throw out the traitors" and "Externally, struggle for sovereignty, resist the Great Powers".

It was the students at Peking who were the principal leading force of the Movement. They had planned to hold a demonstration on May 7, National Humiliation Day, the third anniversary of the Twenty-one Demands. However, the demonstration had to be scheduled for an earlier date in view of threatening government repressions. On May 4, 3000 students from thirteen Peking universities and colleges, two-thirds of them from Peita, gathered with their banners at the T'ien An Men, whence they sought to gain

---

*Li Ta-chao remained engaged in Communist activity until 1927, when he was arrested and murdered in Peking on the orders of Chang Tso-lin. Ch'en Tu-hsiu left the Chinese Communist Party in 1927, after having been its first Secretary-General. He was arrested in 1933 by the Kuomintang government and died in 1942.

admittance to some of the Missions in the Legation Quarter to present their protests regarding the Versailles decisions. They were prevented from accomplishing anything.

The demonstrators then sought out the house of one of the leaders of the Anfu clique, the notoriously corrupt T'sao Ju-lin, then Minister of Communications, regarded by the students as one of the principal three pro-Japanese traitors in the Peking regime, the other two being Chang Tsung-hsiang, the Chinese Minister to Tokyo, and Lu Tsung-yü, former Minister to Tokyo, and the director of a Japanese-financed bank. T'sao managed to escape the students' wrath but his house was burned down. Chang was found by them and thoroughly beaten up. Lu had made himself scarce. The Peking police then went into action and thirty-two of the students were arrested. This, in turn, only aroused still greater indignation in the entire Peking student community while, when the news of events in Peking rapidly spread to the rest of the country, it gave rise to a vast movement of support and sympathy in all the other main cities, especially in all the other universities and colleges. A struggle now developed against the Peking government, connected with the demand for the immediate freeing of the arrested students; this, in effect, became a political struggle of the population against the Tuan militarist clique. All the opposition political groups participated in the countrywide support of the students—Sun Yat-sen, for example, quickly declared his sympathy for them—and thus the government was forced to release the arrested thirty-two on bail.

However, the government soon attempted to suppress the movement; this resulted in Ts'ai Yüan-p'ei's resignation in protest from his post and added still more fuel to the fire. The Peking students, who had now successfully organized themselves into a student union—an example which was followed in other cities—prepared to meet the government's repressive policy with a general strike, aimed at gaining still more popular support. Simultaneously, the students launched a very well-organized campaign of public meetings and propaganda to explain to the population the aim of their struggle, to which the slogan of an anti-Japanese boycott was now added. The general strike of the university students began in Peking on May 19; it was almost immediately joined by all the students of the secondary schools as well. This was soon followed by identical actions in Tientsin and Shanghai; in the latter city the strike was particularly effective.

The Peking government continued its policy of seeking to put down the movement by force and was also prompted in this by Japanese intervention and demands for the suppression of the students. In the days June 2 to June 4, mass arrests of the leading student activists were undertaken in Peking and over 1100 of them were placed in improvised prisons, i.e. converted university buildings. This savage action, which was accompanied by much brutality, now caused a storm of indignation in the entire country, and especially in Shanghai. In this city the students had managed to obtain broad support from the entire population—the workers as well as the merchants. The answer to the government's repression was the famous Shanghai strike, in which both the workers and the merchants participated. The Shanghai general strike began on June 5 and was soon extended to the entire vast city; all commercial activity came to a complete halt, while around 60,000 to 70,000 workers, from over 100 Chinese and foreign-owned factories, went out on the streets to hold mass demonstrations in what was the first political strike in Chinese history. Characteristically, this action of the Shanghai workers met with an extremely hostile reception by the foreign, mainly British, community in Shanghai.

The Shanghai general strike and the distinct possibility that similar actions would now be repeated in a number of other cities forced the Peking regime to beat a fast retreat. Orders were quickly given that the arrested students be set free. However, the students refused to leave their prisons until they had received the proper apologies; when this had been done—which of course made the government completely lose face—the students marched out on June 8 from their prisons in a triumphant procession to hold a mass meeting celebrating their victory. Further demands were raised immediately—the dismissal of the three traitor ministers, which had been called for all along, was emphasized again. Simultaneously, the students demanded that the government should refuse to sign the Versailles Treaty and that Ts'ai Yüan-p'ei should be reinstated in his post.

Inasmuch as the strike actions had, in fact, spread to other cities, as feared by the government, it was forced to give in on these points as well. The three ministers were made to resign on June 9. By June 12, all the strike actions had come to an end; the student-led movement had ended in a great—although of course only temporary— victory over the Peking regime. Ts'ai Yüan-p'ei returned to his post in September, while the Chinese delegation in Paris, well aware of what was happening in the country, refused to sign the Peace Treaty with Germany. Even the government sent an instruction to this effect although, characteristically, it was dispatched at a later moment, when it had no meaning whatsoever.

IV. The Aftermath

Although the victory gained in June 1919 led to great joy and elation among the students and intellectuals, events were soon to show that the successes gained were but ephemeral, that the enemies of progress, the combined forces of foreign imperialism and Chinese reaction, were still extremely powerful and could not be swept aside by means of youthful enthusiasm and demonstrations alone. What is more, while during the events of 1919 a great deal of unity had prevailed among the intellectuals and the students, this was soon proved to be but a temporary phenomenon. The intellectual ferment of the Cultural Revolution, while stimulating greatly the influx of new concepts and ideas, did not signify by any means that clear-cut decisions and choices, either of ideology or political means to be employed in the moulding of China's future, had already been made. A battle of "isms" soon followed, in which the temporary allies of the May Fourth Movement were to take sharply divergent roads in the future.

The main trends began to become apparent in the years 1919-1921. The first was represented by that group of revolutionary intellectuals who now chose Marxism-Leninism as their ideology. In it, they saw a world outlook which provided them—in their opinion—with all the necessary guiding principles for the carrying out of what they conceived to be the primary tasks facing them—the modernization of China and her re-emergence as a great and powerful country—a status to which, they ardently believed, China was fully entitled to on the basis of her splendid former civilization and thousands of years of culture. It was Marxism-Leninism which offered them a programme for a consistent struggle against imperialism and warlord rule, based on the carrying out of a social revolution, on the full utilization of the vast potential strength of the Chinese masses—both the workers and the peasantry. In following the precepts of this ideology, these young intellectuals—many of gentry origin themselves—broke with all the traditions of their class and of Chinese scholardom and went out among the people to be the first to organize the workers and later peasants. It was with the aid of these forces—and in the later period primarily with the help of the peasants—that they succeeded ultimately in achieving the aims which they had set for themselves and their country in the days of the May Fourth Movement. However, it was to prove to be a long, difficult and tortuous road; most of them were to sacrifice their lives in the process.

But the attraction of Marxism went still further. It provided an intellectually satisfying, monolithic world outlook which seemed capable, if used creatively, of answering a large number of nagging and worrisome problems, relating both to China's past and to her present position. It could furnish replies to these questions in a way which would remove any feeling of inferiority and backwardness and provide a proper solution to them by placing Chinese historical development in a world perspective in which the ultimate balance sheet would certainly not be in China's disfavour.* It was this complex of ideas that led the revolutionary intellectuals into the small Marxist study groups in the principal cities of China which were ultimately to take the organized shape of the Communist Party of China in July 1921.

A second trend was represented by a number of intellectuals who, like Hu Shih, after playing a most prominent role in the Cultural Revolution and in the May Fourth events themselves, refused to devote their lives to political activity and to the cause of the Chinese Revolution. They retired instead, mostly to the comfortable ivory towers of academic life, often dealing with obstruse subjects which were quite remote from the country's urgent problems. A third group, while not eschewing politics, chose a different road from the revolutionary, and later followed the Kuomintang on its weird path to reaction, ultimately fascism and then complete bankruptcy. In this they were perhaps remaining true, after a fashion, to the traditional role of the scholar-gentry in its double function of both member and spokesman of the ruling class. Having made this choice, they were to enjoy—for a time at least—the spoils of office and the privilege of being supported by the powers, until the renewed aggression of Japanese imperialism brought their regime crashing down around their heads.

The problems of this later period of Chinese history—the years of the domestic revolutionary struggles of the 1920s and the 1930s, the years of the anti-Japanese War and, still more, the final *dénouement* of the years following the Second World War, which culminated in the victory of the Chinese Revolution and in the establishment of People's China—are of such vast scope, interest and importance as to deserve, each individually, a separate treatment of at least the same size as the present volume. Whether the time is ripe to undertake such a task is, however, a different question and one which it is very difficult to answer with complete clarity and honesty. The May Fourth Movement—in its broad sense—was clearly but a harbinger, although of crucial importance, of a stormy period in which the future of one-fourth of humanity was ultimately to be decided.

*Whether and to what degree Chinese Marxist historiography, both before 1949 and in the decades since, has succeeded in presenting a true and accurate account of China's past is a separate and most interesting problem, deserving a study all of its own, and cannot be dealt with just in passing.

Selected Bibliography

The Polish edition of this book contained an annotated bibliography; this has been replaced in the present English edition by a completely revised Selected Bibliography consisting of the most important books consulted at the time of writing. It has also been brought up to date to the beginning of 1977.

The works listed include only those which appeared in book form in English, French, German and Russian and thus no mention is made of the very rich literature of the subject which is to be found in specialized periodicals, such as, for example: *Bulletin of the Museum of Far Eastern Antiquities* (Stockholm), *Bulletin of the School of Oriental and African Studies* (London), *Harvard Journal of Asiatic Studies* (Cambridge, Mass.) and *T'oung Pao* (Leiden).

Apart from general works contained in Section I, all other sections are listed in chronological order of their coverage. However, in the case of an overlap, a book is usually listed under the earliest time span to which it is most pertinent.

I. GENERAL WORKS

(a) **Bibliographical References**

Cordier, H. *Bibliotheca Sinica*, 5 vols. Paris, 1904-1924.
Hucker, C. O. *China: a Critical Bibliography*. Tucson, 1962.
Lust, J. *Index Sinicus*. Cambridge, 1964.
Skachkov, P. Ie. *Bibliografiia Kitaia*. Moscow, 1960.
Yuan Tung-li. *China in Western Literature, A Continuation of Cordier's Bibliotheca Sinica*. New Haven, 1958.
Journal of Asian Studies (Annual bibliography). Ann Arbor.

(b) **General Histories, Special Surveys**

An Outline History of China. Peking, 1958.
Chi Ch'ao-ting. *Key Economic Areas in Chinese History*. London, 1936; New York, 1963.
Cordier, H. *Histoire générale de la Chine et de ses relations avec les pays étrangers*, 4 vols. Paris, 1920-1921.
Dawson, R. *Imperial China*. London, 1972.
Eberhard, W. *A History of China*. London, 1950; 4th ed., 1977.
Eichorn, W. *Chinese Civilization: an Introduction* (tr. J. Seligman). New York, 1969. (German ed., Stuttgart, 1964.)
Elvin, M. *The Pattern of the Chinese Past*. London, 1973.
Fairbank, J. K. *The United States and China*. Cambridge, Mass., 1948; 3rd ed., 1971.
Fairbank, J. K., Reischauer, E. O. and Craig, A. M. *East Asia: The Modern Transformation*. Boston, 1965.
Fan Wen-lan. *Drevnaia istoriia Kitaia*. Moscow, 1956. (Chinese ed., Peking, 1949.)
Fan Wen-lan. *Novaia istoriia Kitaia*. Moscow, 1955. (Chinese ed., Peking, 1955.)
FitzGerald, C. P. *China: a Short Cultural History*. London, 1935; 4th ed., 1976.
Franke, H. and Trauzettel, R. *Das chinesische Kaiserreich*. Frankfurt, 1968.
Franke, O. *Geschichte des chinesischen Reiches*, 5 vols. Berlin, 1930-1952; 1965.
Gernet, J. *Le Monde chinois*. Paris, 1972.
Goodrich, L. C. *A Short History of the Chinese People*. New York, 1943; 3rd ed., 1959, 1969.
Grousset, R. *Histoire de la Chine*. Paris, 1947.
Grousset, R. *The Empire of the Steppes: A History of Central Asia* (tr. N. Walford). New Brunswick, 1970. (French ed., Paris, 1939.)
Hookham, H. *A Short History of China*. London, 1969.
Hucker, C. O. *China's Imperial Past*. Stanford, 1975.
Latourette, K. S. *The Chinese: their History and Culture*. New York, 1934; 4th ed., 1964.
Lattimore, O. *Inner Asian Frontiers of China*. New York, 1940; Boston, 1962.
Li, D. J. *The Ageless Chinese*. New York, 1965, 1971.
Loewe, M. *Imperial China: the Historical Background to the Modern Age*. London, 1966.
Maspero, H. and Balázs, É. *Histoire et institutions de la Chine ancienne*. Paris, 1967.
Maspero, H. and Escarra, J. *Les Institutions de la Chine*. Paris, 1952.
Meskill, J., ed. *An Introduction to Chinese Civilization*. New York, 1972.
Reischauer, E. O. and Fairbank, J. K. *East Asia: the Great Tradition*. Boston, 1958.
Rossabi, M. *China and Inner Asia, from 1368 to the Present Day*. London, 1975.
Tikhvinskii, S. L., ed. *Novaia istoriia Kitaia*. Moscow, 1972.
Wiethoff, B. *Introduction to Chinese History* (tr. M. Whittall). London, 1975.

(c) **Historiography, Philosophy, Religion, Science**
de Bary, W. T. *et al.*, comp. *Sources of Chinese Tradition*. New York, 1960.
Beasley, W. G. and Pulleybank, E. G., eds. *Historians of China and Japan*. London, 1961.
Carter, T. F. and Goodrich, L. C. *The Invention of Printing in China and its Spread Westwards*. New York, 1925; rev. ed., 1955.
Chan Wing-tsit, tr. and comp. *A Source Book in Chinese Philosophy*. Princeton, 1963.
Ch'en, K. K. S. *Buddhism in China*. Princeton, 1964.
Fung Yu-lan. *A History of Chinese Philosophy* (tr. D. Bodde), 2 vols. Princeton, 1952, 1953.
Fung Yu-lan. *A Short History of Chinese Philosophy* (ed. D. Bodde). New York, 1948, 1960.
Gardner, C. S. *Chinese Traditional Historiography*. Cambridge, Mass., 1937, 1961.
Granet, M. *The Religion of the Chinese People* (tr. M. Freedman). Oxford, 1975. (French ed., Paris, 1951.)
Hou Wai-lu. *A Short History of Chinese Philosophy*. Peking, 1959.
Leslie, D. D. *et al.*, eds. *Essays on the Sources for Chinese History*. Canberra, 1973.
Meskill, J., ed. *The Pattern of Chinese History: Cycles, Development, or Stagnation?* Boston, 1965.
Needham, J. *Science and Civilisation in China*, Vols. I, II, III, IV, parts 1-3, V parts 2, 3. Cambridge, 1954-1976.
Nikiforov, V. N. *Sovetskie istoriki o problemakh Kitaia*. Moscow, 1970.
Shryock, J. K. *The Origin and Development of the State Cult of Confucius*. New York, 1932, 1966.
Weber, M. *The Religion of China: Confucianism and Taoism* (tr. H. H. Gerth). Glencoe, 1951; New York, 1968.
Welch, H. *The Practice of Chinese Buddhism, 1900-1950*. Cambridge, Mass., 1967, 1973.
Wright, A. F. *Buddhism in Chinese History*. Stanford, 1959.
Yang, C. K. *Religion in Chinese Society*. Berkeley, 1961.

(d) **Sociology, Institutions, Economics**

Balázs, É. *Chinese Civilization and Bureaucracy, Variations on a Theme* (tr. H. M. Wright). New Haven, 1964.
Balázs, É. *Political Theory and Administrative Reality in Traditional China*. London, 1965.
Bodde, D. and Morris, C. *Law in Imperial China*. Cambridge, Mass., 1970.
Chang Chung-li. *The Chinese Gentry: Studies on their Role in Nineteenth Century China*. Seattle, 1955.
Chang Chung-li. *The Income of the Chinese Gentry*. Seattle, 1963.
Cheng Yu-kwei. *Foreign Trade and the Industrial Development of China*. Washington, D.C., 1956.
Ch'ü T'ung-tsu. *Law and Society in Traditional China*. Paris and The Hague, 1961.
Ch ü T'ung-tsu. *Local Government in China under the Ch'ing*. Cambridge, Mass., 1962.
Fei Hsiao-t'ung. *China's Gentry: Essays in Rural-Urban Relations*. Chicago, 1953, 1968.
Fei Hsiao-t'ung. *Peasant Life in China*. London, 1939.
Fei Hsiao-t'ung and Chang Chih-i. *Earthbound China*. Chicago, 1945, 1975.
Ho Ping-ti. *Studies on the Population of China, 1368-1953*. Cambridge, Mass., 1959.
Ho Ping-ti. *The Ladder of Success in Imperial China: Aspects of Social Mobility, 1368-1911*. New York, 1962.
Hou Chi-ming. *Foreign Investment and Economic Development in China, 1840-1937*. Cambridge, Mass., 1965.
Hsiao Kung-ch'üan. *Rural China: Imperial Control in the Nineteenth Century*. Seattle, 1960, 1967.
Lang, O. *Chinese Family and Society*. New Haven, 1946, 1968.
Levenson, J. R. *Confucian China and its Modern Fate*, 3 vols. Berkeley, 1958-1965.
Menzel, J. M., ed. *The Chinese Civil Service: Career Open to Talent?* Boston, 1963.
Metzger, T. A. *The Internal Organization of the Ch'ing Bureaucracy*. Cambridge, Mass., 1973.
Perkins, D. H. *Agricultural Development in China, 1368-1938*. Chicago, 1969.
Remer, C. F. *Foreign Investments in China*. New York, 1933, 1968.
Sprenkel, S. van der. *Legal Institutions in Manchu China. A Sociological Analysis*. London, 1962.
Wang Yeh-chien. *Land Taxation in Imperial China, 1750-1911*. Cambridge, Mass., 1974.
Watt, J. B. *The District Magistrate in Late Imperial China*. New York, 1972.
Yang Lien-sheng. *Money and Credit in China: a Short History*. Cambridge, Mass., 1952.
Yang Lien-sheng. *Studies in Chinese Institutional History*. Cambridge, Mass., 1961.

(e) **Literature, Language**

Birch, C., ed. *Anthology of Chinese Literature from Early Times to the Fourteenth Century*. New York, 1965.
Birch, C., ed. *Anthology of Chinese Literature from the Fourteenth Century to the Present Day*. New York, 1972.
Ch'en Shou-yi. *Chinese Literature: A Historical Introduction*. New York, 1961.
Demiéville, P., ed. *Anthologie de la Poèsie chinoise classique*. Paris, 1962.
Feng Yüan-chün. *A Short History of Chinese Litrature*. Peking, 1959.
Fiodorenko, N. T. and Kuo Mo-jo, eds. *Antologiia kitaiskoi poezii*, 4 vols. Moscow, 1957.
Forrest, R. A. D. *The Chinese Language*. London, 1948.
Hightower, J. R. *Topics in Chinese Literature: Outlines and Bibliographies*. Cambridge, Mass., 1950, 1967.

Hsia, C. T. *The Classic Chinese Novel*. New York, 1968.
Karlgren, B. *The Chinese Language*. New York, 1949.
Liu, J. J. Y. *The Art of Chinese Poetry*. London, 1962.
Liu Wu-chi. *An Introduction to Chinese Literature*. Bloomington, 1966.
Liu Wu-chi and Lo Yu-cheng, eds. *Sunflower Splendor: Three Thousand Years of Chinese Poetry*. New York, 1975.
Lu Hsün. *A Brief History of Chinese Fiction* (tr. Yang Hsien-yi and G. Yang). Peking, 1959.
Margouliès, G. *Histoire de la littérature chinoise*, 2 vols. Paris, 1949, 1951.
Prušek, J. *Chinese History and Literature*. Prague, 1970.
Waley, A., tr. *Chinese Poems*. London, 1946, 1976.

(f) **Art**

Bush, S. *The Chinese Literati on Painting*. Cambridge, Mass., 1971.
Cahill, J. *Chinese Painting*. Cleveland, 1960.
Chiang Yee. *Chinese Calligraphy: An Introduction to its Aesthetic and Technique*. London, 1954; Cambridge, Mass., 1973.
Chiang Yee. *The Chinese Eye: an Interpretation of Chinese Painting*. London, 1936; Bloomington, 1971.
Cohn, W. *Chinese Painting*. New York, 1952.
Jenyns, S. *A Background to Chinese Painting*. London, 1935; New York, 1966.
Rowley, G. *Principles of Chinese Painting*. Princeton, 1947; 2nd ed., 1959.
Sickman, L. and Soper, A. *The Art and Architecture of China*. Harmondsworth, 1956.
Siren, O. *Chinese Painting: Leading Masters and Principles*, 7 vols. London, 1956-1958.
Sullivan, M. *The Arts of China*. London, 1973.
Sze Mai-mai. *The Tao of Painting*, 2 vols. New York, 1956.
Waley, A. *An Introduction to the Study of Chinese Painting*. London, 1923, 1958.
Watson, W. *Style in the Arts of China*. Harmondsworth, 1974.
Willetts, W. *Chinese Art*, 2 vols. Harmondsworth, 1958.
Willetts, W. *Foundations of Chinese Art*. London, 1965.

(g) **Archaeology**

Andersson, J.G. *Children of the Yellow Earth*. London, 1935; Cambridge, Mass., 1972.
Chang Kwang-chih. *The Archaeology of Ancient China*. New Haven, 1963; 2nd rev. ed., 1968.
Chang Kwang-chih. *Early Chinese Civilization*. Cambridge, Mass., 1976.
Cheng Te-k'un. *Archaeology of Ancient China*, 3 vols. Cambridge, 1959, 1960, 1963.
Creel, H. G. *The Birth of China*. New York, 1937, 1970.
Ho Ping-ti. *Cradle of the East*. Chicago, 1975.
Watson, W. *Early Civilisation in China*. London, 1966.
Watson, W. *Cultural Frontiers in Ancient East Asia*. Edinburgh, 1971.

(h) **Geography**

Cressey, G. B. *Land of the 500 Million*. New York, 1955.
Geelan, P. J. M. and Twichett, D. C., eds. *The Times Atlas of China*. London, 1974.
Herrman, A. *An Historical Atlas of China*. Cambridge, Mass., 1935; Edinburgh, 1966.
Tregear, T. R. *A Geography of China*. London, 1965.

(i) **Collections of Essays on Above and Related Topics**

Dawson, R., ed. *The Legacy of China*. Oxford, 1964.
Fairbank, J. K., ed. *Chinese Thought and Institutions*. Chicago, 1957.
Fairbank, J. K., ed. *The Chinese World Order; Traditional China's Foreign Relations*. Cambridge, Mass., 1968.
Fairbank, J. K. and Kierman, E. A., eds. *Chinese Ways in Warfare*. Cambridge, Mass., 1974.
Konrad, N. I. *Zapad i Vostok*. Moscow, 1972.
Lattimore, O. *Studies in Frontier History*. Oxford, 1962.
MacNair, H. F., ed. *China*. Berkeley, 1946.
Maspero, H. *Mélanges posthumes sur les religions et l'histoire de la Chine*, 3 vols. Paris, 1950.
Wright, A. F., ed. *Studies in Chinese Thought*. Chicago, 1953.
Wright, A. F., ed. *The Confucian Persuasion*. Stanford, 1960.
Wright, A. F. and Nivison, D. S., eds. *Confucianism in Action*. Stanford, 1959.
Wright, A. F. and Twitchett, D. C., eds. *Confucian Personalities*. Stanford, 1962.

II. THE FORMATIVE PERIOD, SHANG, CHOU (Chaps. 1-3)

Bykov, F. S. *Zarozhdenie politicheskoi i filosofskoi mysli v Kitae.* Moscow, 1966.
Courvreur, S., tr. *Tch'ouen ts'iou et Tso tchouan. La Chronique de la Principauté de Lou,* 3 vols. Hien hien, 1914; Paris, 1951.
Couvreur, S., tr. *Chou King: les Annales de la Chine.* Hien hien, 1927; Paris, 1950.
Creel, H. G. *Confucius, the Man and the Myth.* New York, 1949.
Creel, H. G. *The Origins of Statecraft in China:* vol. I—*The Western Chou Empire.* Chicago, 1970.
Creel, H. G. *What is Taoism? and Other Studies in Chinese Cultural History.* Chicago, 1970.
Crump, J. I., tr. *Chan-kuo Ts'e.* Oxford, 1970.
Dubs, H. H., tr. *The Works of Hsüntze.* London, 1928.
Duyvendak, J. J. I., tr. *The Book of Lord Shang.* London, 1928; Chicago, 1963.
Feoktistov, V. F. *Filosofskie i obshchestvenno-politicheskie vzgliady Siun Tszy.* Moscow, 1976.
Gernet, J. *Ancient China* (tr. R. Rudorff). London, 1968. (French ed., Paris, 1964.)
Granet, M. *Chinese Civilisation* (tr. K. E. Innes and M. R. Brailsford.) London, 1950. (French ed., Paris, 1929.)
Griffith, S. B., tr. *Sun Tzu, The Art of War.* Oxford, 1963, 1976.
Hawkes, D., tr. *Ch'u Tz'u, the Songs of the South.* Oxford, 1959.
Hsü Cho-yun. *Ancient China in Transition: an Analysis of Social Mobility, 722-222 B.C.* Stanford, 1965.
Hughes, E. R., tr. and ed. *Chinese Philosophy in Classical Times.* London, 1932.
Kaltenmark, M. *Lao Tzu and Taoism* (tr. R. Greaves). Stanford, 1969. (French ed., Paris, 1965.)
Karlgren, B., tr. *The Book of Odes.* Stockholm, 1950, 1974.
Karlgren, B., tr. *The Book of Documents.* Stockholm, 1950.
Konrad, N. I., tr. *Sun Tszy: Traktat o voiennom iskusstve.* Moscow, 1950.
Kriukov, M. V. *Formy sotsial'noi organizatsii drevnykh kitaitsev.* Moscow, 1967.
Lau, D. C., tr. *Lao Tzu.* Harmondsworth, 1963, 1976.
Lau, D. C., tr. *Mencius.* Harmondsworth, 1970, 1976.
Legge, J., tr. *The Chinese Classics,* 5 vols. London, 1893-5; Hong Kong, 1962.
Liao, W. K., tr. *Han Fei-tzu,* 2 vols. London, 1939, 1959.
Maspero, H. *La Chine antique.* Paris, 1927; rev. ed., 1955, 1965.
Mei Yi-pao, tr. *The Ethical and Political Works of Motse.* London, 1939.
Pozdneeva, L. D., tr. and ed. *Ateisty, materialisty, dialektiki drevnego Kitaia.* Moscow, 1967.
Prušek, J. *Chinese Statelets and the Northern Barbarians.* Dordrecht, 1971.
Rubin, V. A. *Individual and State in Ancient China* (tr. S. I. Levine). New York, 1976. (Russian ed., Moscow, 1970.)
Vandermeersch, L. *La Formation du légisme.* Paris, 1965.
Vandier-Nicolas, M. *Le Taoisme.* Paris, 1965.
Vasil'ev, K. V. *Plany srazhaiushchikhsia tsarstv.* Moscow, 1968.
Vasil'ev, L. S. *Kul'ty, religii, traditsii v Kitae.* Moscow, 1970.
Waley, A., tr. *The Way and its Power.* London, 1934, 1977.
Waley, A., tr. *The Book of Songs.* London, 1937, 1969.
Waley, A., tr. *The Analects of Confucius.* London, 1938, 1971.
Waley, A. *Three Ways of Thought in Ancient China.* London, 1939, 1974.
Watson, B. *Early Chinese Literature.* New York, 1962.
Watson, B., tr. *Mo Tzu: Basic Writings.* New York, 1963.
Watson, B., tr. *The Complete Works of Chuang Tzu.* New York, 1968.
Watson, B., tr. *Hsün Tzu: Basic Writings.* New York, 1970.
Welch, H. *The Parting of the Way: Lao Tzu and the Taoist Movement.* Boston, 1957.
Yang Hsing-shun. *Drevnekitaiskii filosof Lao-tszy i ego uchenie.* Moscow, 1950.
Yang Yung-kuo. *Istoriia drevnekitaiskoi ideologii.* Moscow, 1957. (Chinese ed., Peking, 1954.)

III. CH'IN, HAN, PERIOD OF DIVISION (Chaps. 4-11)

Bielenstein, H. *The Restoration of the Han Dynasty,* 3 vols. Stockholm, 1954-1959.
Bodde, D. *China's First Unifier: A Study of the Ch'in Dynasty as seen in the Life of Li Ssu (280?-208 B.C.).* Leiden, 1938; Hong Kong, 1967.
Bodde, D., tr. *Statesman, Patriot and General in Ancient China.* New Haven, 1940.
Bodde, D. *Festivals in Classical China.* Princeton, 1975.
Chavannes, E., tr. *Les Mémoires historiques de Se-ma Ts'ien,* 5 vols. Paris, 1895-1905; 6 vols., 1967-1969.
Ch'ü T'ung-tsu. *Han Social Structure.* Seattle, 1972.
de Crespigny, R., tr. *The Last of the Han.* Canberra, 1969.
Dubs, H. H., tr. *The History of the Former Han Dynasty,* 3 vols. Baltimore, 1938, 1944, 1955.
Eidlin, L. Z. *Tao Yuan'-min i ego stikhotvoreniia.* Moscow, 1967.
Fang, A., tr. *The Chronicle of the Three Kingdoms,* 2 vols. Cambridge, Mass., 1952, 1965.

Forke, A., tr. *Lun Heng: Philosophical Essays of Wang Ch'ung*, 2 vols. London, 1907; New York, 1962.
Gale, E. M., tr. *Discourses on Salt and Iron*. Leiden, 1931.
Hightower, J. R. *The Poetry of T'ao Ch'ien*. Oxford, 1970.
Krol', Iu. L. *Syma Tsian'—istorik*. Moscow, 1970.
Loewe, M. *Everyday Life in Early Imperial China during the Han Period*. London, 1968.
Loewe, M. *Crisis and Conflict in Han China*. London, 1974.
Petrov, A. A. *Wan Chun: drevnekitaiskii materialist i prosvetitel'*. Moscow, 1954.
Shih, V. Y. C., tr. *The Literary Mind and the Carving of Dragons*. New York, 1959.
Swann, N. L., tr. *Food and Money in Ancient China*. Princeton, 1950.
Viatkin, R. V. and Taskin, V. S., trs. *Syma Tsian'—Istoricheskie zapiski ("Szi tszi")*, Vols. 1, 2. Moscow, 1972, 1975.
Watson, B., tr. *Ssu-ma Ch'ien—Records of the Grand Historian*, 2 vols. New York, 1961.
Watson, B. *Ssu-ma Ch'ien: Grand Historian of China*. New York, 1958.
Wilbur, C. M. *Slavery in China during the Former Han Dynasty (206 B.C.-A.D. 25)*. Chicago, 1943; New York, 1967.
Yü Ying-shih. *Trade and Expansion in Han China*. Berkeley, 1967.
Zürcher, E. *The Buddhist Conquest of China: The Spread and Adaptation of Buddhism in Early Medieval China*, 2 vols. Leiden, 1959.

IV. SUI, T'ANG (Chaps. 12-15)

Bingham, W. *The Founding of the T'ang Dynasty: the Fall of the Sui and the Rise of T'ang*. Baltimore, 1941; New York, 1970.
Bynner, W. and Kiang Kang-hu, trs. *The Jade Mountain*. New York, 1929, 1972.
Cooper, A., tr. *Li Po and Tu Fu*. Harmondsworth, 1973.
Edwards, E. D., tr. *Chinese Prose Literature of the T'ang Period*, 2 vols. London, 1937, 1974.
Gernet, J. *Les Aspects économiques du bouddhisme dans la société chinoise au V-e—X-e siècles*. Saigon, 1956; Paris, 1973.
Graham, B.C., tr. *Poems of the Late T'ang*. Harmondsworth, 1965.
Hung, W. *Tu Fu; China's Greatest Poet*, 2 vols. Cambridge, Mass., 1952; New York, 1969.
Pulleyblank, E. G. *The Background of the Rebellion of An Lu-shan*. Oxford, 1955.
Reischauer, E. O. *Ennin's Travels in T'ang China*. New York, 1955.
Reischauer, E. O., tr. *Ennin's Diary*. New York, 1955.
Robinson, G. W., tr. *The Poems of Wang Wei*. Harmondsworth, 1973.
des Rotours, R., tr. *Histoire de Ngan Lou-chan*. Paris, 1962.
Schafer, E. H. *The Golden Peaches of Samarkand: a Study of T'ang Exotics*. Berkeley, 1963.
Schafer, E. H. *The Vermilion Bird: T'ang Images of the South*. Berkeley, 1967.
Twitchett, D. C. *Financial Administration under the T'ang Dynasty*. Cambridge, 1963; 2nd ed., 1970.
Waley, A. *The Life and Times of Po Chü-i*. London, 1949.
Waley, A. *The Poetry and Career of Li Po*. London, 1950.
Wechsler, H. J. *Mirror to the Son of Heaven: Wei Cheng at the Court of T'ang T'ai-tsung*. New Haven, 1974.
Wright, A. F. and Twitchett, D. C., eds. *Perspectives on the T'ang*. New Haven, 1973.

V. FIVE DYNASTIES, NORTHERN AND SOUTHERN SUNG (Chaps. 16-18)

Chang, C. *The Development of Neo-Confucian Thought in China*, 2 vols. New York, 1957, 1962.
Franke, H., ed. *Sung Biographies*, 3 vols. Wiesbaden, 1976.
Gernet, J. *Daily Life in China on the Eve of the Mongol Invasion* (tr. H. M. Wright). London, 1962. (French ed., Paris, 1959.)
Haeger, J. W., ed. *Crisis and Prosperity in Sung China*. Tucson, 1975.
Kracke, E. A. *Civil Service in Early Sung China, 960-1067*. Cambridge, Mass., 1953.
Kychanov, Ie. I. *Ocherk istorii tangutskogo gosudarstva*. Moscow, 1968.
Lapina, Z. G. *Politicheskaia bor'ba v srednevekovym Kitae*. Moscow, 1970.
Lewin, G. *Die ersten fünfzig Jahre der Song Dynastie*. Berlin, 1973.
Liu, J. T. C. *Reform in Sung China: Wang An-shih (1021-1086) and his New Policies*. Cambridge, Mass., 1959.
Liu, J. T. C. *Ou-yang Hsiu: an Eleventh Century Neo-Confucianist*. Stanford, 1967.
Liu, J. T. C. and Golas, P. J., eds. *Change in Sung China: Innovation or Renovation?* Lexington, Mass., 1969.
McKnight, B. E. *Village and Bureaucracy in Southern Sung China*. Chicago, 1971.
Meskill, J., ed. *Wang An-shih: Practical Reformer?* Boston, 1963.

Shiba Yoshinobu. *Commerce and Society in Sung China* (tr. M. Elvin). Ann Arbor, 1970.
Smolin, G. Ia. *Antifeodal'nye vosstaniia v Kitae v X-XII vekakh*. Moscow, 1974.
Vorob'ev, M. V. *Chzhurchzheny i gosudarstvo Chin'*. Moscow, 1975.
Wang Gung-wu. *The Structure of Power in North China during the Five Dynasties*. Kuala Lumpur, 1963;
    Stanford, 1967.
Williamson, H. R. *Wang An-shih*, 2 vols. London, 1935-1937.

VI. YÜAN, MING (Chaps. 19-22)

de Bary, W. T., ed. *Self and Society in Ming Thought*. New York, 1970.
de Bary, W. T., ed. *The Unfolding of Neo-Confucianism*. New York, 1975.
Bokshchanin, A. A. *Kitai i strany iuzhnykh morei v XIV-XVI vekakh*. Moscow, 1968.
Borovkova, L. A. *Vosstanie "krasnykh voisk" v Kitae*. Moscow, 1971.
Brewitt-Taylor, C. H., tr. *San Kuo: or the Romance of the Three Kingdoms*, 2 vols. Shanghai, 1925;
    Rutland, 1959.
Buck, P., tr. *All Men are Brothers*, 2 vols. New York, 1933, 1957.
Dardess, J.W. *Conquerors and Confucians: Aspects of Political Change in Late Yüan China*. New York,
    1973.
Egerton, F. C., tr. *Chin P'ing Mei*, 4 vols. London, 1939, 1972.
Goodrich, L. C. and Fang Chao-ying, eds. *Dictionary of Ming Biography, 1368-1644*, 2 vols. New York, 1976.
Huang, R. *Taxation and Governmental Finance in Sixteenth Century Ming China*. Cambridge, 1974.
Hucker, C.O. *The Traditional Chinese State in Ming Times (1368-1644)*. Tucson. 1961.
Hucker, C.O. *The Censorial System of Ming China*. Stanford, 1966.
Hucker C.O. ed. *Chinese Government in Ming Times: Seven Studies*. New York, 1969.
Parsons J.B. *Peasant Rebellions in the Late Ming Dynasty*. Tucson, 1970.
Rowbotham, A.H. *Missionary and Mandarin: The Jesuits at the Court of China*. Berkeley, 1942; New York, ,
    1966.
Schurmann, H. F., tr. *The Economic Structure of the Yüan Dynasty*. Cambridge, Mass., 1956.
Simonovskaia, I.V. *Antifeodal 'naia bor'ba kitaiskikh krest'ian v XVII veke*. Moscow, 1966.
Svistunova, N. P., *Agrarnaia politika dinastii Ming XIV veka*. Moscow, 1974.
Waley, A., tr. *Monkey*. London, 1942; New York, 1958.
Waley, A., tr. *The Secret History of the Mongols*. London, 1963.

VII. CH'ING, 1644-1840 (Chaps. 23-25)

Bland, J. O. P. and Backhouse, E. *Annals and Memoirs of the Court of Peking*. London, 1914; New York, 1973.
Cranmer-Byng, J. L., ed. *An Embassy to China*. London, 1962.
Dawson, R. *The Chinese Chameleon: An Analysis of European Conceptions of Chinese Civilization*.
    London, 1967.
Dermigny, L. *La Chine et l'Occident: le Commerce à Canton au XVIII-e siècle, 1719-1833*, 3 vols. and album.
    Paris, 1964.
Feuerwerker, A. *The State and Society in Eighteenth Century China: The Ch'ing Empire in its Glory*. Ann
    Arbor, 1976.
Fu Lo-shu. *A Documentary Chronicle of Sino-Western Relations, 1644-1820*, 2 vols. Tucson, 1966.
Goodrich, L. C. *The Literary Inquisition of Ch'ien-lung*. Baltimore, 1935; New York, 1966.
Greenberg, M. *British Trade and the Opening of China, 1800-1842*. Cambridge, 1951, 1969.
Hawkes, D., tr. *Cao Xueqin, The Story of the Stone*, Vols. I-II. Harmondsworth, 1973, 1977.
Hsü, I. C. Y., ed. *Readings in Modern Chinese History*. Oxford, 1971.
Huang Pei. *Autocracy at Work: a Study of the Yung-cheng Period, 1723-1735*. Bloomington, 1975.
Hughes, E. R. *The Invasion of China by the Western World*. London, 1937; 2nd ed., 1968.
Hummel, A. W., ed. *Eminent Chinese of the Ch'ing Period, 1644-1912*. 2 vols. Washington, D.C., 1943-1944.
Kahn, H. L. *Monarchy in the Emperor's Eyes: Image and Reality in the Ch'ien-lung Reign*. Cambridge, Mass.,
    1971.
Kessler, L. D. *K'ang-hsi and the Consolidation of Ch'ing Rule, 1661-1684*. Chicago, 1976.
Kuhn, F., tr. *The Dream of the Red Chamber* (Engl. tr. F. and I. McHugh). New York, 1958.
Lee, R. H. G. *The Manchurian Frontier in Ch'ing History*. Cambridge, Mass., 1970.
Liang Ch'i-ch'ao. *Intellectual Trends in the Ch'ing Period* (tr. I. C. Y. Hsü). Cambridge, Mass., 1960.
Michael, F. *The Origin of Manchu Rule in China*. Baltimore, 1942; New York, 1972.
Naquin, S. *Millenarian Rebellion in China: the Eight Trigrams Uprising of 1813*. New Haven, 1976.
Nivison, D. S. *The Life and Thought of Chang Hsüeh-ch'eng (1738-1801)*. Stanford, 1966.

Oxnam, R. B. *Ruling from Horseback: Manchu Politics in the Oboi Regency, 1661-1669*. Chicago, 1976.
Reichwein, A. *China and Europe: Intellectual and Artistic Contacts in the Eighteenth Century*. New York, 1925, 1968.
Spence, J. *Ts'ao Yin and the K'ang-hsi Emperor: Bondservant and Master*. New Haven, 1966.
Spence, J. *The Emperor's World: A Self-portrait of K'ang-hsi*. New York, 1974.
Waley, A. *Yuan Mei: Eighteenth Century Chinese Poet*. London, 1956.
Wu Ching-tzu. *The Scholars* (tr. Yang Hsien-yi and G. Yang). Peking, 1957.
Wu, S.H.L. *Communication and Imperial Control in China: Evolution of the Palace Memorial System, 1693-1735*. Cambridge, Mass., 1970.

VIII. MODERN HISTORY, 1840-1864 (Chaps. 26-29)

Banno, M. *China and the West, 1858-1861: The Origins of the Tsungli Yamen*. Cambridge, Mass., 1964.
Brine, L. *The Taeping Rebellion in China*. London, 1862.
Callery, J. M. and Yvan, M. *History of the Insurrection in China*. London, 1853; New York, 1969.
Chang Hsin-pao. *Commissioner Lin and the Opium War*. Cambridge, Mass., 1964.
Cheng, J. C. *Chinese Sources for the Taiping Rebellion, 1850-1864*. Hong Kong, 1963.
Chesneaux, J. *Secret Societies in China in the 19th and 20th Centuries* (tr. G. Nettle). London, 1971.
Chesneaux, J., ed. *Popular Movements and Secret Societies in China, 1840-1950*. Stanford, 1972. (French ed., Paris, 1970.)
Chesneaux, J. and Bastid, M. *La Chine: Des guerres de l'opium à la guerre franco-chinoise, 1840-1885*. Paris, 1969.
Clyde, P. H. and Beers, B. F. *The Far East*. New York, 1966.
Cohen, P. A. *China and Christianity: The Missionary Movement and the Growth of Chinese Antiforeignism*. Cambridge, Mass., 1963.
Costin, W. C. *Great Britain and China, 1833-1860*. Oxford, 1937, 1969.
Curwen, C. A. *Taiping Rebel: The Deposition of Li Hsiu-ch'eng*. Cambridge, 1977.
Dennett, T. *Americans in Eastern Asia*. New York, 1922, 1963.
Dulles, F. R. *China and America*. Princeton, 1946, 1967.
Eckel, P. E. *The Far East since 1500*. New York, 1948.
Fairbank, J. K. *Trade and Diplomacy on the China Coast: the Opening of the Treaty Ports, 1842-1854*, 2 vols. Cambridge, Mass., 1953.
Fay, P. W. *The Opium War, 1840-1842*. Chapel Hill, 1975.
Franke, W. *China and the West* (tr. R. A. Wilson). New York, 1967.
Franke, W. *A Century of the Chinese Revolution* (tr. S. Rudman). New York, 1971.
Gregory, J. S. *Great Britain and the Taipings*. London, 1969.
Hail, W. J. *Tseng Kuo-fan and the Taiping Rebellion*. New Haven, 1927, 1964.
Hao Yeh-p'ing. *The Comprador in Nineteenth Century China: Bridge between East and West*. Cambridge, Mass., 1970.
Hsü, I. C. Y. *China's Entry into the Family of Nations: the Diplomatic Phase, 1858-1880*. Cambridge, Mass., 1960.
Hsü, I. C. Y. *The Rise of Modern China*. Oxford, 1970; 2nd ed., 1975.
Hu Sheng. *Imperialism and Chinese Politics, 1840-1925*. Peking, 1955.
Iliushechkin, V. P. *Krest'ianskaia voina taipinov*. Moscow, 1967.
Jen Yu-wen. *The Taiping Revolutionary Movement*. New Haven, 1973.
Kuhn, P. A. *Rebellion and its Enemies in Late Imperial China: Militarism and Social Structure, 1796-1864*. Cambridge, Mass., 1970.
Kuo, P. C. *A Critical Study of the First Anglo-Chinese War*. Shanghai, 1935.
Li Chien-nung. *The Political History of China, 1840-1928* (tr. and ed. Teng Ssu-yü and J. Ingalls). Princeton, 1956.
Lin Yi. *A Short History of China, 1840-1911*. Peking, 1965.
MacNair, H. F., ed. *Modern Chinese History: Selected Readings*. Shanghai, 1923.
Meadows, T. T. *The Chinese and their Rebellions*. London, 1856; Stanford, 1953.
Michael, F. and Chang Chung-li. *The Taiping Rebellion: History and Documents*. 3 vols. Seattle, 1965-1970.
Michael, F. and Taylor, G. E. *The Far East in the Modern World*. New York, 1964; 3rd ed., 1975.
Morse, H. B. *The International Relations of the Chinese Empire*, 3 vols. London, 1910-1918.
Oliphant, L. *Narrative of the Earl of Elgin's Mission to China and Japan*, 2 vols. London, 1860, 1970.
Pellisier, R., ed. *The Awakening of China, 1793-1949* (tr. M. Kieffer). London, 1967. (French ed., Paris, 1963.)
Reclus, J. *La Révolte des Tai-ping (1851-1864): Prologue de la Révolution chinoise*. Paris, 1972.
Shen Wen-tai. *China's Foreign Policy, 1839-1860*. New York, 1932.
Shih, V. Y. C. *The Taiping Ideology: Its Sources, Interpretations and Influences*. Seattle, 1967.

Spector, S. *Li Hung-chang and the Huai Army: A Study in Nineteenth Century Chinese Regionalism.* Seattle, 1964.

Teng Ssu-yü. *The Historiography of the Taiping Rebellion.* Cambridge, Mass., 1952.

Teng Ssu-yü. *The Taiping Rebellion and the Western Powers.* Oxford, 1970.

Teng Ssu-yü and Fairbank, J. K., eds. *China's Response to the West: a Documentary Survey, 1839-1923,* 2 vols. Cambridge, Mass., 1954.

Torr, D., ed. *Marx on China, Articles from the New York Daily Tribune, 1853-1860.* London, 1951.

Vinacke, H. M. *A History of the Far East in Modern Times.* New York, 1950, 1961.

Wakeman, F. *Strangers at the Gate: Social Disorder in South China, 1839-1861.* Berkeley, 1966.

Waley, A. *The Opium War Through Chinese Eyes.* London, 1958; Stanford, 1968.

Williams, S. W. *The Middle Kingdom,* 2 vols. New York, 1883, 1966.

Wong, J. Y. *Yeh Ming-ch'en.* Cambridge, 1976.

Zaretskaia, S. I. *Vneshnaia politika Kitaia, 1856-1860.* Moscow, 1976.

Zhukov, Ie. M., ed. *Mezhdunarodnyie otnosheniia na Dal'nem Vostoke, 1840-1949,* 2 vols. Moscow, 1973.

IX. 1864-1901 (Chaps. 30-35)

Ayers, W. *Chang Chih-tung and Educational Reform in China.* Cambridge, Mass., 1971.

Bau, M. J. *The Open Door Doctrine in Relation to China.* New York, 1923.

Bland, J. O. P. and Blackhouse, E. *China under the Empress Dowager.* London, 1910; Peking, 1939.

Chang Hao. *Liang Ch'i-ch'ao and Intellectual Transition in Modern China, 1890-1907.* Cambridge, Mass., 1971.

Chesneaux, J., Bastid, M. and Bergère, M.C. *Histoire de la Chine comtemporaire, 1885-1921.* Paris, 1972.

Chu, S. C. *Reformer in Modern China: Chang Chien, 1853-1926.* New York, 1965.

Chu Wen-djang. *The Moslem Rebellion in Northwest China 1862-1878.* Seattle, 1966.

Cohen, P. A. *Between Tradition and Modernity: Wang T'ao and Reform in Late Ch'ing China* Cambridge, Mass., 1974.

Cordier, H. *Historie des relations de la Chine avec les puissances occidentales, 1860-1890,* 3 vols. Paris, 1901-2, 1966.

Eastman, L. E. *Throne and Mandarins: China's Search for a Policy during the Sino-French Controversy, 1880-1885.* Cambridge, Mass., 1967.

Feuerwerker, A. *China's Early Industrialization: Sheng Hsüan-huai (1884-1916) and Mandarin Enterprise.* Cambridge, Mass., 1958.

Feuerwerker, A. *The Chinese Economy, ca. 1870-1911.* Ann Arbor, 1969.

Feuerwerker, A. *et al.,* eds. *Approaches to Modern Chinese History.* Berkeley, 1967.

Griswold, A. W. *The Far Eastern Policy of the United States.* New Haven, 1938, 1964.

Hart, R. *These from the Land of Sinim: Essays on the Chinese Question.* London, 1901.

Hsiao Kung-ch'üan. *A Modern China and a New World: K'ang Yu-wei, Reformer and Utopian.* Seattle, 1975.

Hsü, I. C. Y. *The Ili Crisis: A Study of Sino-Russian Diplomacy, 1871-1881.* Oxford, 1965.

Iefimov, G. V. *Vneshnaia politika Kitaia, 1894-1899.* Moscow, 1958.

Joseph, P. *Foreign Diplomacy in China, 1894-1900.* London, 1928.

Kaliuzhnaia, N. M. *Vosstanie Ikhetuanei.* Moscow, 1973.

Kiernan, E. V. G. *British Diplomacy in China, 1880-1885.* Cambridge, 1939.

Lo Jung-pang. *K'ang Yu-wei: A Biography and Symposium.* Tucson, 1967.

Martin, W. A. P. *A Cycle of Cathay.* New York, 1900, 1966.

Pelcovits, N. A. *Old China Hands and the Foreign Office.* New York, 1948, 1967.

Purcell, V. *The Boxer Uprising: a Background Study.* Cambridge, 1963.

Rawlinson, J. L. *China's Struggle for Naval Development, 1839-1895.* Cambridge, Mass., 1967.

Schrecker, J. E. *Imperialism and Chinese Nationalism: Germany in Shantung.* Cambridge, Mass., 1971.

Schwartz, B. *In Search of Wealth and Power: Yen Fu and the West.* Cambridge, Mass., 1964.

Smith, A. H. *China in Convulsion,* 2 vols. New York, 1901; Shannon, 1972.

Stoecker, H. *Deutschland und China im 19-n Jahrhundert.* Berlin, 1958.

Thompson, L. G., tr. *Ta T'ung Shu: The One-World Philosophy of K'ang Yu-wei.* London, 1958.

Thomson, H. C. *China and the Powers.* London, 1902; Ann Arbor, 1969.

Tikhvinskii, S. L. *Dvizhenie za reformy v Kitae v kontse XIX veka i Kan Iu-vei.* Moscow, 1959.

Witte, S. I. *Vospominaniia,* 3 vols. Moscow, 1960.

Wright, M. C. *The Last Stand of Chinese Conservatism: The T'ung-chih Restoration, 1862-1874.* Stanford, 1957.

Young, L. K. *British Policy in China, 1895-1902.* Oxford, 1970.

X. 1901-1919 (Chaps. 36-41)

Aisin Gioro Pu-yi. *From Emperor to Citizen,* 2 vols. Peking, 1964-5.

Belov, Ie. A. *Uchanskoie vosstanie v Kitae.* Moscow, 1971.
Bergère, M. C. *La Bourgeoisie chinoise et la révolution de 1911.* Paris, 1968.
Bernal, M. *Chinese Socialism to 1907.* Ithaca, 1976.
Boorman, H. L. and Howard, R. C., eds. *Biographical Dictionary of Republican China,* 4 vols. New York, 1967-1971.
Cameron, M. E. *The Reform Movement in China, 1898-1912.* Stanford, 1931; New York, 1963.
Ch'en, J. *Yuan Shih-k'ai.* London, 1961, 2nd ed., Stanford, 1972.
Chow Ts'e-tung. *The May Fourth Movement: Intellectual Revolution in Modern China.* Cambridge, Mass., 1960.
Clubb, O. E. *Twentieth Century China.* New York, 1965.
Esherick, J. W. *Reform and Revolution in China: the 1911 Revolution in Hunan and Hubei.* Berkeley, 1976.
Friedman, E. *Backward to Revolution: The Chinese Revolutionary Party.* Berkeley, 1974.
Gasster, M. *Chinese Intellectuals and the Revolution of 1911.* Seattle, 1969.
Hsieh, W. *Chinese Historiography on the Revolution of 1911.* Stanford, 1975.
Hsüeh Chün-tu. *Huang Hsing and the Chinese Revolution.* Stanford, 1961.
Jansen, M. B. *The Japanese and Sun Yat-sen.* Cambridge, Mass., 1954.
Kostiaieva, A. S. *Narodnyie dvizheniia v Kitae, 1901-1911.* Moscow, 1970.
Krymov, A. G. *Obshchestvennaia mysl' i ideologicheskaia bor'ba v Kitae, 1900-1917.* Moscow, 1972.
Levenson, J. R. *Liang Ch'i-ch'ao and the Mind of Modern China.* Cambridge, Mass., 1953; Berkeley, 1967.
Liew, J. S. *Struggle for Democracy: Sung Chiao-jen and the 1911 Revolution.* Berkeley, 1971.
Meissner, M. *Li Ta-chao and the Origins of Chinese Marxism.* Cambridge, Mass., 1967.
Powell, R. L. *The Rise of Chinese Military Power, 1895-1912.* Princeton, 1955; London, 1972.
Rankin, M. B. *Early Chinese Revolutionaries: Radical Intellectuals in Shanghai and Chekiang, 1902-1911.* Cambridge, Mass., 1971.
Reinsch, P. S. *An American Diplomat in China.* Garden City, 1922.
Rhoads, E. J. M. *China's Republican Revolution: The Case of Kwangtung, 1895-1913.* Cambridge, Mass., 1975.
Schiffrin, H. Z. *Sun Yat-sen and the Origins of the 1911 Revolution.* Berkeley, 1969.
Sharman, L. *Sun Yat-sen: His Life and its Meaning.* New York, 1934; Stanford, 1968.
Tikhvinskii, S. L., ed. *Sin'khaiskaia revoliutsiia v Kitae.* Moscow, 1966.
Wang, Y. C. *Chinese Intellectuals and the West, 1872-1949.* Chapel Hill, 1966.
Wright, M. C., ed. *China in Revolution: The First Phase, 1900-1913.* New Haven, 1968.
Wu Yü-chang. *The Revolution of 1911.* Peking, 1962.
Yu, G. T. *Party Politics in Republican China: The Kuomintang, 1912-1924.* Berkeley, 1966.

Chronological Table of Dynasties

Hsia Era	2000 (?)-1766 (?) B.C.	
Shang	1766 (?)-1122 (?)	
Chou	1122 (?)-256	
1. Western Chou	1122 (?)-771	
2. Eastern Chou	771-256	
(a) Spring and Autumn period	722-481	
(b) Warring States period	403-221	
Ch'in	221-207	
Han (Western)	202 B.C.-A.D. 9	
Hsin (Wang Mang)	9-23	
Han (Eastern)	25-220	
Three Kingdoms Era	220-280	
1. Wei	220-226	
2. Shu-Han	221-263	
3. Wu	222-280	
Chin (Western)	266-316	
Chin (Eastern)	317-420	
Northern and Southern Dynasties period	420-589	
Southern Dynasties		
Liu Sung	420-479	
Southern Ch'i	479-502	
Liang	502-557	
Ch'en	557-589	
Northern Dynasties		
Wei (Northern)	386-534	
Eastern Wei	534-550	Western Wei 534-557
Northern Ch'i	550-577	Northern Chou 557-581
Sui	581-618	
T'ang	618-907	
Five Dynasties Era	907-960	
1. Later Liang	907-923	Nomad dynasties in
2. Later T'ang	923-936	North China
3. Later Chin	936-947	Liao 916-1125
4. Later Han	947-950	Hsi Hsia 990-1227
5. Later Chou	951-960	Chin 1125-1234
Sung (Northern)	960-1226	
Sung (Southern)	1127-1279	
Yüan	1279-1368	
Ming	1368-1644	
Ch'ing	1644-1912	

Index